HAMITO-SEMITIC ETYMOLOGICAL DICTIONARY

MATERIALS FOR A RECONSTRUCTION

HANDBUCH DER ORIENTALISTIK
HANDBOOK OF ORIENTAL STUDIES

ERSTE ABTEILUNG
DER NAHE UND MITTLERE OSTEN
THE NEAR AND MIDDLE EAST

ACHTZEHNTER BAND

HAMITO-SEMITIC ETYMOLOGICAL DICTIONARY

MATERIALS FOR A RECONSTRUCTION

TUTA SUB AEGIDE PALLAS · 1683 ·

HAMITO-SEMITIC ETYMOLOGICAL DICTIONARY

MATERIALS FOR A RECONSTRUCTION

BY

VLADIMIR E. OREL AND OLGA V. STOLBOVA

E.J. BRILL
LEIDEN · NEW YORK · KÖLN
1995

The paper in this book meets the guidelines for permanence and durability of the Committee on Production Guidelines for Book Longevity of the Council on Library Resources.

Library of Congress Cataloging-in-Publication Data

Orel, Vladimir E.
Hamito-Semitic etymological dictionary : materials for a reconstruction / by Vladimir E. Orel and Olga V. Stolbova.
p. cm. — (Handbuch der Orientalistik. Erste Abteilung, Nahe und Mittlere Osten, 0169–9423 ; 18. Bd.)
Includes bibliographical references and index.
ISBN 9004100512
1. Proto-Afroasiatic language—Etymology—Dictionaries.
2. Afroasiatic languages—Etymology—Dictionaries. I. Stolbova. Olga V. II. Title. III. Series: Handbuch der Orientalistik. Erste Abteilung, Nahe und der Mittlere Osten ; 18. Bd.
PJ994.073 1994
492—dc20 94-32911
CIP

Die Deutsche Bibliothek – CIP-Einheitsaufnahme

Handbuch der Orientalistik / hrsg. von B. Spuler unter Mitarb. von C. van Dijk ... – Leiden ; New York ; Köln : Brill.
Teilw. hrsg. von H. Altenmüller. – Teilw. mit Parallelt.: Handbook of oriental studies
Abt. 1, Der Nahe und Mittlere Osten – The Near and Middle East / hrsg. von H. Altenmüller ...
NE: Spuler, Bertold [Hrsg.]; Altenmüller, Hartwig [Hrsg.]; Handbook of oriental studies
Bd. 18. Orel, Vladimir E.: Hamito-Semitic etymological dictionary. – 1994

Orel, Vladimir E.:
Hamito-Semitic etymological dictionary : materials for a reconstruction / by Vladimir E. Orel and Olga V. Stolbova. – Leiden ; New York ; Köln : Brill, 1994
(Handbook of oriental studies : Abt. 1, The Near and Middle East ; Bd. 18)
ISBN 90-04-10051-2
NE: Stolbova, Ol'ga V.:; HST

ISSN 0169-9423
ISBN 90 04 10051 2

PRINTED IN THE NETHERLANDS

And the whole earth was of one language, and of one speech . . . And the Lord said, Behold, the people is one, and they have all one language; and this they begin to do: and now nothing will be withheld from them, which they have schemed to do. Come, let us go down, and there confound their language, that they may not understand one another's speech. So the Lord scattered them abroad from there upon the face of all earth: and they ceased to build the city.

Genesis 11: 1, 6–8

CONTENTS

INTRODUCTION

The present Dictionary comprises the reconstruction of the main lexical stock of Hamito-Semitic (Afro-Asiatic).[1] It is based on previous studies in the field (including such works as COHEN 1947 and DJAKONOV 1981–1986) as well as on the results of our joint research in 1987–1993. The authors were and are quite aware of the challenge presented by the present project as well as of numerous shortcomings and potential fallacies of the resulting work. However, we are certain that the absolutely clear necessity of such a work in the Hamito-Semitic field overweighs eventual drawbacks and imperfections in what we are presently suggesting to the reader. Moreover, we consider it an inevitable fate of our Dictionary to be in constant use and, therefore, to be constantly verified and corrected in the course of time. We will be grateful to all our prospective readers for their amendments, notes and marginalia as well as for more general constructive discussion.

The term Hamito-Semitic is used as a name of a protolanguage and of a linguistic phylum whose limits are explicitly shown below, in the classification of Hamito-Semitic languages. Proto-Hamito-Semitic was spoken not later than 10,000–9,000 B.C.E.[2] in the areas of Levant and/or North Africa (see OREL 1995). The present Dictionary may be used as a source of lexical data reflecting the Proto-Hamito-Semitic culture and homeland.

Main families belonging to the Hamito-Semitic phylum are traditionally described as Semitic, Berber, Egyptian, Chadic and Cushitic. Indeed, some of these families (Egyptian) are characterized by more or less definite boundaries and inner structure, or at least, by well-determined outer contours (Semitic, Berber, Chadic).

---

[1] We use here a triad of terms *phylum—family—branch* in order to facilitate the description technically and not to use the same term in a confusing way for different time depths and different positions in the taxonomy. There is no theoretical difference between the three. As to the term *Hamito-Semitic* itself, it is used as an absolute synonym of *Semito-Hamitic* and *Afro-Asiatic*. Our choice of this particular variant reflects a long tradition which, from our point of view, is the only relevant factor in terminology.

[2] Approximate time of divergence according to the glotto-chronological evaluation based on the *Star* programme. See also MILITAREV 1984.

In the case of Cushitic even the limits of the family are not exactly known and have to be established on a certain level of approximation, cf. the famous case of Mbugu ~ Mao (see COPLAND 1933–1934; GOODMAN 1971) which we do not include in the Dictionary.[3]

It seemed practically justified to present Chadic and Cushitic data without recurring to Common Chadic and Common Cushitic resonstructions. Even though Common Chadic reconstructions are possible, both theoretically and practically, and may correspond to a certain historical reality, a Proto-Chadic language, it seemed much more convenient to group Chadic material under three headings: West, Central and East Chadic. These (sub)families also seem to be a linguo-historical reality. At the same time, using them allows us to group Chadic data into more compact and manageable clusters. Thus, our presentation of Chadic as separate West, Central and East Chadic is purely conventional. We deal similarly with Cushitic but for different reasons. Cushitic material appears in the Dictionary not as an integral whole but as a number of separate (sub)families (e.g. Werizoid or Omotic), some of them consisting of one language (Beja, Mogogodo, Dahalo).

In contrast to Chadic, our reasons, as far as Cushitic is concerned, are less technical. Although all Cushitic (sub)families belong to the Hamito-Semitic phylum, we cannot be absolutely sure whether their prehistory included a stage that might be called "Cushitic" (see OREL, STOLBOVA 1992d). It is quite possible that grammatical and lexical features which are similar in Cushitic languages but differ from other Hamito-Semitic idioms are, in fact, nothing more than a result of a series of secondary interactions. If so, Cushitic is an areal but not a genetic union, a Sprachbund of certain Hamito-Semitic dialects. But even if Proto-Cushitic existed, the relations between its branches are so vague that is, obviously, rational to present the material of different branches separately as it is, in fact, done in our Dictionary. Thus, the presentation of Cushitic data on the level of subfamilies and without a Proto-Cushitic reconstruction may be treated either as a pure technicality or as a meaningful solution depending upon the view of the reader.

---

[3] This is a technical decision having no immediate connection with our opinion on the actual position of Mbugu ~ Mao.

Within the individual families, their classification (whenever it is well established and defendable) is reflected by the order in which data are presented in the Dictionary.

Unfortunately, numerous elements of the Hamito-Semitic linguistic taxonomy are known to have more than one name. In such cases, our practical solutions are usually traditional and have no theoretical or extralinguistic implications.

The resulting classification of Hamito-Semitic languages is as follows:[4]

(A) *SEMITIC*

- Akkadian;
- Ugaritic, Phoenician, Punic, Amoraic, Moabite, Hebrew, Aramaic (Syriac, Palestinian etc.);
- Arabic;
- South Arabian (Sabaic, Minaean etc.);
- Ge^{c}ez, Tigre, Tigray, Amharic, Argobba, Gafat, Harari, Gurage (Selti, Gogot etc.);
- Mehri, Jibbali, Shheri, Harsusi, Soqotri.

(B) *BERBER*

- Shilh (Semlal, Ntifa, Baamrani, Aksimen), Tamazight (Izdeg, Izayan, Segrushen);
- Rif, Iznasen, Snus, Menaser, Shenua, Senhaja, Kabyle, Shauya, Figig, Mzab, Wargla, Sened, Jerba;
- Awjila, Nefusa, Ghadames, Siwa, Sokna;
- Ghat, Ayr, Ahaggar, Tawlemet, Taneslemt;
- Zenaga;
- Guanche;
- Libyan.

(C) *EGYPTIAN*

- Egyptian, Demotic, Coptic (Old Coptic, Fayumian etc.).

(D) *CHADIC*

(D^{1}) *WEST CHADIC*

- Hausa, Gwandara;
- Sura, Angas, Ankwe, Mupun, Chip, Montol, Gerka;

---

[4] See the *List of Abbreviations*.

- Bolewa, Karekare, Dera, Tangale, Pero, Ngamo, Maha, Bele, Kirfi, Gera, Galambu, Geruma;
- Warji, Kariya, Diri, Miya, Paa, Cagu, Siri, Mburku, Jimbin, Jimi;
- Boghom, Kir, Mangas, Geji, Tala, Burma, Guruntum, Buu, Zul, Buli, Polchi, Zem, Tule, Dokshi, Dwot, Zakshi, Zaar, Sayanchi;
- Fyer, Bokkos, Sha, Kulere, Dafo-Butura;
- Ngizim, Bade.

(D²) *CENTRAL CHADIC*

- Tera, Jara, Gaanda, Gabin, Boga, Hwona;
- Bura, Chibak, Kilba, Ngwahi, Margi, Wamdiu, Heba, Hildi;
- Higi Futu, Higi Nkafạ, Higi Ghye, Fali Kiri, Fali Gili, Kapiski;
- Dghwede, Mandara, Padokwo, Glavda, Guduf, Zeghwana, Gvoko, Gava, Nakaci, Lamang;
- Matakam, Mofu, Mafa, Gisiga, Balda, Muktele;
- Sukur;
- Daba, Musgoy;
- Musgum, Mbara, Munjuk;
- Bata, Bachama, Gude, Gudu, Nzangi, Fali Jilvu, Fali Mubi, Fali Muchela, Fali Bwagira, Mwulyen;
- Logone, Buduma, Gulfey, Kuseri, Afade;
- Gidar;
- Lame, Lame Pewe, Zime, Zime Bata;
- Masa, Mesme, Banana.

(D³) *EAST CHADIC*

- Somray, Sibine, Tumak, Ndam;
- Nanchere, Tobanga, Lele, Gabri, Kabalay, Dorma;
- Kera, Kwan, Mobu, Ngam;
- Dangla, Migama, Jankor, Jegu, Bidiya;
- Mubi, Birgit;
- Mokilko;
- Sokoro, Barayn.

(E) *BEJA*

(G) *AGAW*

- Bilin;

- Xamir, Xamta;
- Kwara, Dembea, Kemant;
- Aungi, Damot.

(H) *"EAST CUSHITIC"*

(H[1]) *SAHO – AFAR*

- Saho, Afar.

(H[2]) *LOWLAND EAST CUSHITIC*

- Somali, Oromo, Boni, Rendille, Bayso;
- Arbore, Dume, Geleba, Konso, Gato, Bussa, Gidole.

(H[3]) *WERIZOID*

- Warazi, Gawwada, Dullay, Gobeze, Camay, Harso, Dobeze, Gollango, Gorrose, Gaba.

(H[4]) *HIGHLAND EAST CUSHITIC*

- Sidamo, Darasa, Hadiya, Alaba, Kabenna, Bambala, Kambata, Tambaro.

(I) *DAHALO*

(J) *MOGOGODO*

(K) *OMOTIC*

- Ometo (Gidicho, Basketo etc.);
- Yamma, Kaficho, Mocha, Bworo, Anfila;
- Hozo, Sezo, Gim, Nao, Sheko, Maji;
- Dime, Ari, Banna, Hamer, Karo, Basada.

(L) *RIFT ("SOUTH CUSHITIC")*

- Iraqw (dial.: Gorowa), Alagwa, Burunge;
- Asa, Kwadza.

Within the framework of the present Dictionary, several types of lexical items appear. Some of the reconstructed roots are not only

Proto-Hamito-Semitic; they may be also called Common Hamito-Semitic. In other words, they are present in all or nearly all families and branches of the Hamito-Semitic phylum. Proto-Hamito-Semitic **les-* "tongue" is also a part of Common Hamito-Semitic heritage as it is found in Semitic (**lišan-* id., derivative with a suffix **-ān-*), Berber (**lVs-* id.), Egyptian (Eg *ns* id., Copt **les*), Chadic (WCh **ḥa-lis-um-* id., CCh **ʾV-lyas-* id., ECh **lyas-* id.) and Cushitic (Omot **mi-las-* id., with a prefix **mi-*). A similar case is represented by Proto-Hamito-Semitic **ḫab-/*ḫabiʔ-* "vessel" which is also Common Hamito-Semitic registered in Semitic (Sem **ḫabiʔ-/ḫabiy-* "jug, bowl"), Berber (**ḫVb-* "big wooden plate"), Egyptian (*ḫbb* "vessel"), Chadic (WCh **ḫabi(ʔ)-* "pot, gourd") and Cushitic (LEC **ḥabub-* "kind of gourd"). Cf. other roots attested in numerous branches of Hamito-Semitic: **sim-* (Sem **šVmVw-/*šVmVy-* "call, give name", Berb **sVm-* "call, name" (v.), Eg *smy* "tell" (n), CCh **syam-sim-* "whisper", LEC **sim-* "welcome (v.)"), **kün-* (Sem **kann-/*kinn-* "co-wife, female in-law", Berb **kVn-* "co-wife", WCh **kin-* "co-wife, sister", Agaw **kwin-* "woman").

However, Common Hamito-Semitic words and roots form only a modest part of the reconstructed Proto-Hamito-Semitic vocabulary. Common Hamito-Semitic status is not a *conditio sine qua non* for a root to be unequivocally reconstructed as a Proto-Hamito-Semitic element. According to the theories accepted in modern historical linguistics and, particularly, in Indo-European linguistics, weaker requirements are acceptable (see SZEMERÉNYI 1962; PORZIG 1954). The reconstructed word may be attested in three or even in two branches if they are known not to be in direct contact. Thus, fairly acceptable are such Hamito-Semitic reconstructions as, e.g., **bür-* (Sem **birr-* "grill, lettice (of doors, windows)", Berb **bur-* "door", LEC **bor-* "back (of a house)"), **ṭin-* (Sem **ṭin-* "clay, earth, dirt", Eg *ỉtn, ỉwtn* "earth", CCh **ṭVn-* id.), **gaʔ-* (Sem **gVʔVy-* "rise, be high", ECh **gaʔay-* "increase", Agaw **gwiʔ-* "be high"), or even **kün-* (Eg *ṯny* "raise high", WCh **kunwa-*), **ʕeb-* (Eg *ʕbw* "kind of bird", WCh **Hyabi-* "hen, chicken"), **ŝab-* (ECh **ŝVb-* "rib", Rift **ŝab-* "diaphragm, rib"), **mabar-* (WCh **mabar-* "mouth", Bed *ambar* id.), **pasuq-* (Sem **pašḫ-* "spear", WCh **pasuq-* "arrow"). Exclusive isoglosses linking peripheral branches are of particular value since they are believed to reflect lexical archaisms, cf., e.g., isoglosses between Semitic and Rift that may be compared to Indo-Celtic isoglosses of Indo-European.

In some cases, morphological and/or phonological peculiarities lead us to a reconstruction of a Hamito-Semitic root based on the data of *one* branch. Such a reconstruction may be justified as an archaic relic of a root, better preserved in derivatives as in the case of **ʾab-* "stone" registered in several Cushitic languages (Agaw **ʾab-* "mountain", Bed *awe* "stone", LEC **ʾeb-* id.). This root is reconstructed as Hamito-Semitic because its derivative **ʾabun-* "stone, millstone" is a well-attested Hamito-Semitic lexical element. Another example of a similar approach is our reconstruction of HS **bay-* "build" based exclusively on CCh **bV-* id. and ECh **bay-* id. Such a reconstruction, as we believe, is justified by the archaic status of this verb whose derivative **bayit-* "house" is attested in Semitic as well as in Chadic.

Unfortunately, our knowledge of the Hamito-Semitic languages is extremely limited and most of the languages belonging to the Hamito-Semitic phylum have a very short written tradition or have no such tradition at all. Naturally, many of our reconstructions are based on scarce lexical material which is often excerpted from recently published sources. This may diminish or deteriorate the credibility of certain reconstructions for lack of additional data. However, we prefer to adduce this kind of material as well, hoping that in future it will be partly supported by new discoveries and partly discarded. At the present stage, it is obviously preferable to create an extensive data base open to a profound critical study. Thus, we tend to adduce even comparisons based on a very limited number of facts as, e.g., in **kaber-* (CCh **kabyar-* "bull": Bud *kāber* ~ HEC **ko-bir-* "buffalo": Had *kobira*), **nawaĉ-* (Sem **na[w]aŝ-* "kind of beer": Akk *nāsu* ~ Eg *wnš.t* "wine"), **roʾ-* (Eg *rꜣ* "snake" ~ WCh **rwaʾ-* "cobra": DB *rwa*). As in other cases, we treat peripheral isoglosses as more reliable. A study of the Hamito-Semitic isoglosses may be an objective *per se* that in future will constitute a special subdiscipline similar to the linguistic geography of Indo-European (see OREL, STOLBOVA 1989; 1992a; 1992c).

Historical and comparative phonology of Hamito-Semitic is *terra incognita* no more. As a whole, it was adequately summarized in a number of recent publications, see, e.g., an outline of the reconstruction suggested in DJAKONOV ET AL. 1987; cf. also DJAKONOV 1988. As far as the phonological inventory of Hamito-Semitic is concerned, only a few corrections must be made in Djakonov's phonological inventory. Thus, we do not accept his reconstruction of labialized consonants (*k^w, *$ḳ^w$, *g^w etc.) because, in individual families and branches of the phylum, they may be explained as secondary reflexes of velars and laryngeals before rounded vowels (see below). We also abstain from accepting highly hypothetical reconstruction of sonants and laryngeals in *syllabic* function. As far as stops are concerned, the reader will notice that **ṗ*, even though it is present in our reconstructions of West Chadic, is missing in Hamito-Semitic. Despite a number of tentative etymologies suggested by GREENBERG 1958 and DJAKONOV 1965, we do not have sufficient evidence to corroborate the existence of this Hamito-Semitic phoneme and prefer to interpret a few cases where it was reconstructed as a result of various individual irregularities in the development of **b* and **p*.

The inventory of Hamito-Semitic consonants is shown in table 1.

Table 1. Hamito-Semitic consonants.

	Stops			Fricatives		Affricates					
Labial	*p*		*b*	*f*							
Dental	*t*	*ṭ*	*d*	*s*		*c*	*c̣*	*č*			
						č	*č̣*	*ǯ*			
Lateral				*ŝ*		*ĉ*	*ĉ̣*				
Velar	*k*	*ḳ*	*g*								
Postvelar	*q*	*q̇*		*ḫ*	*ġ*			Sonants			
Pharyngeal				*ḥ*	ʿ						
Laryngeal			ʾ	*h*			*m*	*n*	*l*	*r*	*y*

Some of the roots included in the present Dictionary reflect various alternations of consonants on the level of reconstructed Proto-Hamito-Semitic. The most important cases show us alternations of **w*, **y* and *ʾ. We tend to register them in the notes, hoping that the phenomenon will be further studied and analyzed on the basis of our material.

On the level of individual branches and families, some elementary notes are necessary as far as their consonantal systems (and their transliterations) are concerned. The presentation of Semitic material is fairly traditional (see, for example, DJAKONOV 1967); note only **ś* vs. **ŝ* as Semitic correspondences of Hamito-Semitic **ŝ* vs. **ĉ*. Thus, we reconstruct Semitic **śib-* "wind" (Akk *šub-tu*, Soq *šiboh*) and also **śVb-* "burn, be hot, set fire" (Akk *šabābu*, Arab *šbb*, Soq *šbb*) but **ŝaʿr-* "hair, wool" (Akk *šārtu*, Ug *šʿrt*, Hbr *ŝēʿār*, *ŝaʿarā*, Aram (Syr) *šaʿrō*, Arab *šaʿr-*, Gz *ŝeʿert*, Soq *ṣaʿihor*). It is also worth notice that we follow certain conventions as far as the consonantal skeleton of the root is concerned. Namely, Semitic verbal roots $C^1VC^2VC^2$- as well as most of the roots with C^2 or C^3 = **w, *y, *ʾ* are usually reconstructed as *C^1VC^2- if the third consonant or the "weak" consonant is not supported etymologically in other branches of Hamito-Semitic.[5] Thus, we reconstruct Semitic **ḥVŝ-* "cut" (Arab *ḥšš*), **ḥVr-* "be dry, be dried up" (Akk *erēru*, Gz *ḥrr*), **ḳVd-* "cut, tear" (Hbr *qdd*, Aram *qdd*, Arab *qdd*, Gz *qdd*, Tgr *qdd*, Amh *qdd*, Arg *qdd*, Hrr *qdd*, Gur *qdd*), **rVm-* "be high" (Hbr *rwm*). In Semitic nouns where an alternation of $C^1aC^2C^2$- and C^1aC^2- is possible, we always reconstruct $C^1aC^2C^2$- as, for example, in **dabb-/*dubb-* "bear".

The reconstruction of the Proto-Berber consonantism is comparatively much less definite. The system accepted in our Dictionary has one important peculiarity to be noted here: reflexes of Hamito-Semitic unvoiced consonants are believed to remain *unvoiced* in Proto-Berber. Thus, the overall change of unvoiced phonemes to voiced ones is projected on a later chronological level while Proto-Berber lexical units appear as, for example, **cVlaɣ-* "goat" (Siwa *zalaq*, Ayr *ə-zolaġ*, Ahg *a-hulaġ*, Twl *e-zolaġ*, Sha *zalaġ*) or **çVp-* "marry" (Ayr *əṭṭəf*). The problem of the initial Hamito-Semitic **b-* in Berber still remains to be solved. In the Dictionary, we prefer to abstain from reconstructing two different reflexes, **b-* and **β-*, and use the symbol **b-* in all cases including the words where the merger **b-* > *h-* is observed. Thus, we reconstruct **bVy-* "drive, bring, come" (Ghd *əbbi*, Siwa *əbba*, Ayr *huii-ət*, Twl *huii-ət*, Ahg *əhi*, Tsl *ihai*), **bag-/*bagag-* "calf, lamb, kid, ram" (Nfs *bɣu*, Ayr *a-bagag*, Ahg *a-baɣuɣ*, Twl *a-bagag*), **baḳ-* "hair disease" (Ahg *ta-haɣa*), **bVḳ-* "soak, contain (liquid)" (Kby *əbbəɣ*, Ahg *a-həɣ*), **b(V)war-* "lion" (Nfs *wär*, Ght *ä-ḅər*, Ayr *a-har*, Twl *a-har*, Zng *war*), **ʾubay-* "camel's hump" (Ghat *t-uhi*, Ayr *t-uhəy*, Ahg *t-uhə*, Twl *t-uhəy*, Sml *ta-yyu*).

Egyptian data appear in a usual transliteration, but, in contrast to ERMAN, GRAPOW 1957, *s* stands for the unvoiced sibilant and *z*—for the voiced one. Coptic material is adduced in Common Coptic (supradialectic) reconstruction together with dialectal forms (for a detailed description see OREL, STOLBOVA 1990).

---

[5] Sometimes in our notes we use the obsolete terms *bi-* and *triliteral*. The reader is expected to understand them as a poetic licence used instead of *bi-* and *triconsonantal*.

Reconstructions of Chadic consonantism, both at the Common Chadic level and at the level of West, Central and East branches, are presented in STOLBOVA 1987 (West Chadic) and STOLBOVA 1995. In our Dictionary, however, we chose not to operate on the Common Chadic level. As far as our orthographic conventions for Chadic are concerned, the situation is rather complicated. In most cases, when our data come from old sources, we have to follow the outdated transcriptions of the original texts. At the same time, we try to unify our transliteration wherever it seems possible (thus, various signs for *ṭ* and *t'* are reflected as *ṭ* in the Dictionary while numerous ways of expressing pre- or postnasalization are uniformly replaced with superscript ^{n}). The same is true of Cushitic orthographies where similar problems arise and similar "half-measures" are taken. As to the phonological reconstructions of Cushitic branches, they are tentative and highly hypothetical. Although the general picture seems to be more or less understandable, a number of minor phonological questions remain unsolved. To some extent, our reconstructions are based on the unpublished materials on several branches prepared by OREL (a few publications are forthcoming), partly, on HEINE 1978 (Lowland East Cushitic), SASSE 1979, 1982 and HUDSON 1989 (Highland East Cushitic), EHRET 1980 (Rift). However, the basic work of reference on Cushitic comparative phonology and etymology remains DOLGOPOLSKIJ 1973.

Basic correspondences of consonants are demonstrated in tables 2–4 (double reflexes of a phoneme either are in a complementary distribution to each other or remain unclear).

Table 2. Hamito-Semitic occlusives.

HS	Sem	Berb	Eg	WCh	CCh	ECh	Agaw	Bed
**p*	**p*	**f*	*p*	**p*, **p* [1]	**p*	**p*	**p*, **f*	*f*
**f*	**p*	**f*	*f*	**f*	**f*	**p*	**f*	*f*
**b*	**b*	**b*	*b*	**b*	**b*	**b*	**b*	*b*
**t*	**t*	**t*	*t*	**t*	**t*	**t*	**t*	*t*
**ṭ*	**ṭ*	**ṭ*	*ṭ*, *d* [2]	**ṭ*	**ṭ*	**t*	**ṭ*	*ḍ*
**d*	**d*	**d*	*d*	**d*	**d*	**d*	**d*	*d*
**k*	**k*	**k*	*k* [3]	**k*	**k*	**k*	**k*	*k*
**ḳ*	**ḳ*	**ḳ*	*ḳ* [3]	**ḳ*	**k*	**k*, **g* [4]	**ḳ*	*k*, *ḳ*
**g*	**g*	**g*	*g* [3]	**g*	**g*	**g*	**g*	*g*

Notes. 1. **ṗ* is a WCh innovation. 2. The distribution is unknown. 3. In certain conditions, after and before palatal and rounded vowels, > *ṯ*, *ḏ*. 4. **-g-*, mainly in the intervocalic position.

Table 2. Continued.

HS	SA	LEC	Wrz	HEC	Dhl	Mgg	Omot	Rift
*p	*f, *p	*f, *p	*p	*f, *p [1]	p		*p, *f	*p
*f	*f	*f	*f	*f	f		*f, *p	*f
*b	*b	*b	*p	*b	b, β/ḅ		*b	*b
*t	*t	*t	*t	*t	ṯ, t'	t	*t	*t
*ṭ	*ḍ	*ḍ		*ṭ	ṯ		*ṭ	
*d	*d	*d		*d	ḏ	d	*d	*d
*k	*k	*k	*k, *χ	*k	k	k(h)	*k	*k
*ḳ	*ḳ	*ḳ	*ḳ, *k	*ḳ	k'		*ḳ	*ḳ
*g	*g	*g	*k	*g	g	k	*g	*g

Note. 1. *p in the intervocalic position.

Table 3. Hamito-Semitic affricates and sibilants

HS	Sem	Berb	Eg	WCh	CCh	ECh	Agaw	Bed
*s	*š	*s	s	*s	*s	*s	*s, *š	s, š
*c	*s	*c	s	*c	*c	*s	*c	*s
*c̣	*ṣ	*c̣	ḏ	*c̣	*c	*s	*c̣ [1]	
*ʒ	*z	*ʒ	z	*ʒ	*ʒ	*ʒ	*ʒ	s
*č	*ṯ	*s, *č	s, šs	*č	*č	*č		
*č̣	*c̣	s, ḏ	*č̣	*č̣	*č̣ [2]	č̣		
*ǯ	ḏ	*ʒ	ḏ	*ǯ	*ǯ	*ǯ	*ǯ	d, ǯ
*ŝ	*ś	*s	š	*ŝ	*ẑ	*ŝ [3]		š
*ĉ	*ŝ	*c	š	*ĉ	*ŝ	*ĉ [4]	*š, *s	s
*ĉ̣	*ṣ̂	*c̣	ḏ	*ĉ̣	*ŝ/*ẑ	*ĉ̣ [5]	*š	

Notes. 1. Orthographically, also č̣. 2. Reconstructed on the basis of the inlaut continuants *-č-* ~ *-ḍ-*. 3. Yielding in most languages to *l* but appearing as *s* in Lele. 4. Generally, reflected as *s* but preserved as *č* in Bid. 5. Note Bid *ḍy* ~ *ʾǯ* as a regular reflex. Our reconstruction of ECh *ĉ ~ *ĉ̣ is purely conventional as far as their real phonological value is concerned. However, the opposition between these two elements, separating them from *c ~ *c̣ and *č ~ *č̣, is beyond any doubt.

HS	SA	LEC	Wrz	HEC	Dhl	Mgg	Omot	Rift
*s	*s	*s, *š	*š	*s, *š	s		*s, *š	*s
*c	*s	*s, *č	*s	*c̣, *s	ṯ		*c̣ [1]	*c
*c̣	*s	*c̣	*č	*c̣ [1]	ts, ṯ		*c̣ [1]	*c
*ʒ	*ʒ, *s	*ʒ					*ʒ	*ǯ, *s
*č	*š	*s, *š		*č, *c̣	ṯ, ts		*č	*s
*č̣	*c̣	*c̣		*c̣ [1]	ṯ		*c̣ [1]	*č̣
*ǯ	*ǯ, *ʒ	*ǯ, *ʒ	*t	*ǯ	dz, ḏ		*ǯ	*ǯ, *d
*ŝ	*s	*s		*s	hl, ṯ' [2]			*ŝ
*ĉ	*s	*s	*s	*s, *š	hl, ṯ' [2]		*š	*ĉ
*ĉ̣		*c̣		*c̣	l, ṯ' [2]		*c̣	*ĉ

Note. 1. Orthographically, also č̣. 2. *-ṯ'-* between vowels.

Table 4. Hamito-Semitic laryngeals

HS	Sem	Berb	Eg	WCh	CCh	ECh	Agaw	Bed
*ʾ	*ʾ	*ʾ	ȝ, ỉ [1]	*ʾ	*ʾ	*ʾ	*ʾ	0
*ʿ	*ʿ	*ʾ, *h	ʿ	*ʿ	*ʾ	*ʾ [2]	*ʿ, *ʾ	ʾ
*h	*h	*h	h	*h	*h	*h	*ʾ	h
*ḥ	*ḥ	*ḥ	ḥ	*ḥ	*χ	*ʾ, *h		h, 0
*ḫ	*ḫ	*ḫ	ḫ, ẖ [3]	*ḫ	*γ	*γ	*χ	h
*ġ	*ġ	*γ	ʿ	*ġ	*γ	*g	*χ	
*q	*ḫ	*k, *g	ḫ, ẖ	*q	*q	*k	*χ	
*q̇	*ḫ	*γ	ḫ, ẖ	*q̇	*q̇	*k, *g	*ḳ	k

Notes. 1. The distribution is regulated by a set of not fully known rules. 2. Occasional -*h*- in Kera and Birgit seems to reflect ECh *-ʿ- different from *-ʾ- < HS *-ʾ- 3. Rules of distribution unknown.

HS	SA	LEC	Wrz	HEC	Dhl	Mgg	Omot	Rift
*ʾ	*ʾ, *ʿ	*ʾ	*ʾ	*ʾ	0	0	*ʾ	*ʾ
*ʿ	*ʿ, *ʾ	*ʿ, *ʾ	*ʿ	*ʿ, *h	ʾ	0	*ʾ	*ʿ, *ʾ
*h	*h	*h		*h	h		*h	*h
*ḥ	*ḥ	*ḥ		*h	h, ḥ		*h	*h, *ḥ
*ḫ	*h, *ḥ	*h, *ḥ		*h	h, ḥ			*ḥ, *ḫ
*ġ	*ʿ	*ʿ, *ġ		*g	k'		*ḳ	
*q					k			*ḫ
*q̇		*ḳ	*χ		k'		*ḳ	*ḫ

Table 5. Hamito-Semitic sonants

HS	Sem	Berb	Eg	WCh	CCh	ECh	Agaw	Bed
*m	*m	*m	m	*m	*m	*m	*m	m
*n	*n	*n	n	*n	*n	*n	*n	
*r	*r	*r	ỉ, n, r [1]	*r	*r	*r	*r	r
*l	*l	*l	ỉ, n, r [1]	*l	*l	*l	*l	l, n
*w	*w	*w	w	*w	*w	*w	*w	
*y	*y	*y	ỉ, y	*y	*y	*y	*y	y

Note. 1. Distribution of variants remains unknown.

HS	SA	LEC	Wrz	HEC	Dhl	Mgg	Omot	Rift
*m	*m	*m	*m	*m	m	m	*m	*m
*n	*n	*n	*n	*n	n		*n	*n
*r	*r	*r	*r	*r	r		*r	*r
*l	*l	*l	*l	*l	λ, l		*l	*l
*w	*w	*w	*w	*w			*w	*ʿ
*y	*y	*y	*y		*y		*y	*y

The Hamito-Semitic system of vowels as an important part of the phonological structure has been traditionally neglected. Deep changes of vocalism and vocalic alternations in individual branches of Hamito-Semitic, primarily in Semitic, prevented scholars from reconstructing a consistent system of vowels. In DJAKONOV ET AL. 1987 a binomial pattern was suggested in the form of an opposition *a vs. *ə (the latter suggested as a further source of much later *i and *u). A new attempt of reconstruction has been recently undertaken in OREL, STOLBOVA 1989–1990 and 1992. Our tentative results are used in the present Dictionary and, therefore, Hamito-Semitic roots are correspondingly vocalized, thus allowing other scholars to proceed in the studies of the vowel structure of Hamito-Semitic. Our potential opponents are welcome to replace vowel signs with generalized *V* or *Λ* symbols, thus arriving at a more usual variant of the Hamito-Semitic reconstruction.

The system of Hamito-Semitic vowels is represented in Table 5. Its reconstruction is based on Semitic, Chadic, Egyptian (Ancient and Coptic) and Cushitic data.

Table 6. Hamito-Semitic vowels.

i	*ü*				*u*
		e		*o*	
			a		

It may be shown that in Hamito-Semitic there existed certain distributional rules which were applied to the vocalism and which were similar to the rules that may be established for reconstructed Proto-Chadic, namely, two middle vowels (**e* and **o*) could not appear within one $C^1VC^2VC^3$-root. Some of the vocalic alternations observed in Hamito-Semitic seem to have no immediate phonetic explanation, a factor caused by certain morphological factors (e.g., grammatical number) and thus similar to the ablaut (*alias* apophony) of Indo-European and Kartvelian languages (see BRUGMANN 1904; KURYLOWICZ 1956; GAMKRELIDZE, MACHAVARIANI 1965). Such alternations may be described as Hamito-Semitic ablaut (cf. OREL 1994; an early and extremely contradictory sketch of the ablaut in Semitic is represented in KURYLOWICZ 1961). Within the Dictionary we prefer not to use this term, leaving morphonological alternations of vowels to be studied later, on the basis of the present collection of material.

On the level of separate branches, some clarifications are necessary. In Semitic, a "usual" inventory of vowels is traditionally limited to the reconstruction of nouns. It is generally believed that, in the verbal system, all traces of the ancient vocalism were completely destroyed due to a process of total rebuilding of verbal morphology. As we tried to demonstrate in OREL, STOLBOVA 1990, certain forms of the Semitic (actually, of Arabic) verb display reasonable correspondences with Chadic verbs. Such forms, including the vowel of the second syllable in the imperfect, are regularly shown in the Dictionary and used as a basis for the corresponding Proto-Semitic reconstruction. Thus, along with vocalized nominal forms such as **ʾiš̃š̃-* "fire", **dam-* "blood", **dimm-* "cheetah, cat", **gabr-* "man", **ḫūṣ-* "leaf", **ŝahr-* "new moon", **ṭāḥin-* "molar", the Dictionary presents vocalized reconstructions of Semitic biconsonantal and triconsonantal verbs, e.g. **gad-* "be considerable, be respectable (of men)" (Arab *gdd* [-*a*-]), **gVlaʾ-* "throw, overturn" (Arab *glʾ* [-*a*-]), **ḥuŝ-* "cut" (Arab *ḥš̃š̃* [-*u*-]), **ḫVyal-* "imagine" (Arab *ḫyl* [-*a*-]), **nVpaḥ-* "strike (with a sabre)" (Arab *nfḥ* [-*a*-]), **nVŝaḳ-* "smell" (Arab *nšq* [-*a*-]), **pid-* "shout, call" (Arab *fdd* [-*i*-). It is also possible that some Arabic *masdars* preserve the original vocalism of the verbal root. At the same time, both on Semitic and Hamito-Semitic levels there exists a certain correlation between the grammatical meaning of a verbal root and its vocalism. While it is relatively well described on the Semitic level, this phenomenon still remains practically unknown as far as its Hamito-Semitic manifestations are concerned. We hope that the present Dictionary will be useful to those who will study the vocalism of the Hamito-Semitic verb in the future.

It is worth noticing that Hamito-Semitic vowels in verbs are also sporadically reflected by the "weak" consonants of Semitic roots. Thus, in a number of cases, Hamito-Semitic verbs with **o*, **u* may have Semitic continuants of *CūC-* structure while some of the Hamito-Semitic verbs with front vowels correspond to Proto-Semitic *CīC-*.

A similar phenomenon may be hypothetically presumed for Berber. In verbal roots, structures *CVwVC-* and *CVyVC-* seem to form correspondences to Hamito-Semitic roots with front and rounded vowels, correspondingly. In nouns, the reflexes of the ancient vocalism also seem to be close to Semitic.

In Egyptian, ancient vowels are graphically reflected as *matres lectionis*, namely as *ꜣ*, *w*, *y*, that are optionally used when positioned between two consonants or in the beginning, or in the end of a word, to denote root vowels, cf., e.g.: *ḳꜣb.t* "knee" (BD) < HS **ḳab-*, *hꜣy* "capture" (MK) < HS **hay-*, *ẖꜣb* "hyppopotamus" (OK) < HS **ẖab-*, *sḥꜣ.t* "herd of donkeys" (OK) < HS **caḥ-*, *ꜣsb* "burn" (BD) < HS **sab-*; *syꜣ.w* "kite" (gr) < HS **ciʾ-*, *ỉmny* "Sun-god" (reg) < HS **ʾ[i]men-*; *rwhꜣ* "evening" (n) < **ruh-*, *swḥ* "wind" (XXII) < HS **suḥ-*. Sometimes, the original vocalism may be also reconstructed on the basis of Egyptian palatalizations of velars (yielding to *ḏ* and *ṯ* in contact with front and rounded vowels) in such cases as *ḏs* "person" (pyr), *ḏr* "calf" (MK), *ḏwy* "call, say" (pyr), *ḏbꜣ* "palace" (OK), *ṯb.t*, *ṯbw* "sandal" (pyr), *ṯꜣy* "man" (pyr), *ỉṯy* "take, catch, seize" (pyr). Coptic material is also of certain value since Coptic vowels seem to result from the ancient Egyptian vocalism, in its turn going back to the original Hamito-Semitic system (see OREL, STOLBOVA 1990), cf. such correspondences as Copt **kas* "bone" (Boh *kas*, Shd *kas*) < HS **ḳas-*, Copt **halme* "source" (Lyc *halme*) < HS **haram-*, Copt **[ṯ]ōw* "mountain" (Boh *tōou*, Shd *toou*) < HS **go(ʾ)-*, Copt **sēh* "young of an ass" (Boh *sēh*, Shd *sēh*) < HS **sek-*, Copt **rē* "sun, Sun-god" (Akh *ri*, Boh *rē*, Shd *rē*) < HS **riʿ-*.

Chadic vocalism is one of the most important sources for the reconstruction of Hamito-Semitic vowels. On the level of Chadic subfamilies, historical vocalism was reconstructed, including hypothetically accepted vowels of the second syllable (see OREL, STOLBOVA 1990; STOLBOVA 1995). We prefer to reconstruct middle vowels in Chadic as **ya* < **e* and **wa* < **o* since individual Chadic languages tend to use both *ya* and *e*, *wa* and *o* indiscriminately. At the same time, in contact with velars, they are normally reflected as diphthongs or even as combinations of labiovelars with a vowel. Hence a natural assumption that, on the Proto-Chadic level Hamito-Semitic middle vowels were represented by **ya* and **wa*. As far as Cushitic vocalism is concerned, preliminary notes on the reconstruction and basic correspondences may be found in OREL, STOLBOVA 1992. Cushitic vowels still represent an interesting field of future research.

Basic correspondences of Hamito-Semitic vowels are demonstrated in Table 7.

Table 7. Hamito-Semitic vowels

HS	Sem	Berb	Eg	WCh	CCh	ECh	Agaw	Bed
*a	*a		ꜣ	*a	*a	*a	*a	a, e
*e	*i, *y	*i, *y	ꜣ, y	*ya	*ya	*ya, *i	*a, *i	e, a
*i	*i, *y	*i, *y	y, ỉ	*i	*i	*i, *ya	*i	i
*o	*u, *w [1]	*u, *w	ꜣ, w	*wa	*wa	*wa, *u	*wa, *a	o, u
*u	*u, *w [1]	*u, *w	w	*u	*u	*u, *wa	*u	u
*ü	*i	*i, *y	y, w	*u, *wi	*u	*u	*(w)i	i, wi

Note. 1. Also *a in contact with labials.

Within the framework of the phonological reconstruction certain conventions are observed. The alphabetical order of the transliteration and transcription signs is as follows:

ɔ a b c ç č ç̌ ĉ ç̂ d e f g ġ ᶜ h ḥ ḫ H i k ḳ
l m n o p q q̇ r s š ŝ t ṭ u ü V w y ʒ ǯ

We also use certain additional symbols: _V_ and _C_ stand for any or unknown vowel and consonant, _R_ stands for any sonant. A symbol in _( )_ means that it is optional: *duḫ(ḫ)- may be read as *duḫḫ- or *duḫ-. A symbol in _[ ]_ means that its reconstruction is probable but not certain: *da[p]- implies that the reconstruction *dap- is more probable than any other (eventually, than *daf-). / stands for "and" whenever variants of the same root or phoneme are reconstructed: *daɔ-/*daw- indicates that both *daɔ- and *daw- existed in Hamito-Semitic. Alternations are denoted by ~. Different meanings of a word within one linguistic branch are tagged with superscript numbers.

In a number of our comparisons we have to accept metathesis in order to reconstruct Hamito-Semitic prototypes. Quite often, the phonological phenomenon described as a metathesis may be more exactly defined as a shift of a laryngeal, i.e., of a phoneme especially unstable and liable to morphonologically irrelevant movements within the root. Thus, we have to deal with metathesis in such cases as Sem *ɔadam- "earth" ~ ECh *dVHVm- "field"; Sem *ɔVlVṭ- "drive, press close" ~ WCh *laɔaç̌- "press"; Sem *bVɔuš- "be strong" ~ ECh *basuɔ- id.; CCh *baraw- "arrow, bow" ~ ECh *ɔa-bawar- id.; Sem *dūr- "turn" ~ ECh *wVdVr- id.; Sem *ᶜVbal-/*ᶜVbul- "be thick" ~ WCh *baHal- "big, be abundant" ~ ECh *bVHVl- "big"; Eg ḥsr "arm" ~ WCh *saHar- "hand, arm"; Eg ḫzd "rot" (n.) ~ ECh *ʒaHwad- "rotten". Another typical case in which we are ready to accept a comparison implying a metathesis is that of a "long" word, i.e., of a composite or of an otherwise abnormally long structure exceeding the bounds of a standard triliteral pattern. Such structures are expected to be unstable, in particular, as far as order of phonemes is concerned, cf., for example: Sem *ʔ*argāb-* "intestines" ~ CCh **bVrwag-* "intestines" ~ ECh **burwag-* "stomach"; Sem **binVṭur-* "vulva" ~ CCh **pičurin-* "testicles"; Sem **ḫanzab-* "kind of pot" ~ Eg *ḥnbȝs* "vessel". In some cases, we also deal with metathesis in usual triliteral roots: Sem **bVṭun-* "be pregnant, have a big belly" ~ Eg *bnd* "difficult delivery"; Sem **sVlVḳ-* "gather" ~ CCh **caḳal-* "gather, collect"; Sem **diman-* "insect" ~ Eg *dnm* "worms" ~ WCh **dyaman-* "spider". It is worth noticing, that under the same name *metathesis* we also deal with some regular correspondences that have not been sufficiently studied, e.g. such cases as Sem **ŝakīn-* "knife" ~ WCh **ĉank-* id. and Sem **dagan-* "corn" ~ WCh **dang-* id.

Within the Dictionary, words with derivational peculiarities that may be projected on the Hamito-Semitic level are, normally, placed under separate entries. Thus, words going back to *ʔ*i-nas-* "man" and **nüs-* id. form separate articles although there is no doubt that they belong to one and the same Hamito-Semitic *root*. In other words, the Dictionary is organized according to the *lexical* and not the *radical* principle. Correspondingly, we prefer to separate nouns from verbs and, whenever it is possible, to put them under different headings. If, for some reason, a noun and a verb are brought together, under the same reconstruction, their corresponding meanings in the heading are separated with a semi-colon. Some of the words in Hamito-Semitic, as in any other linguistic family, have a dubious status of onomatopoeia. As we cannot guarantee their antiquity or disprove it, we mark such words as *descriptive stems*. As to loanwords and elements of old cultural vocabulary, they are also marked correspondingly in the notes.

While phonologically, all lexical comparisons adduced in the present Dictionary were checked and corrected in accordance with established phonetic correspondences, the problem of semantic verification turned out to be much more complicated. In order to minimize the arbitrariness in our lexical comparisons, we followed certain heuristic rules. Within the framework of the present Dictionary, preference is always given to comparisons based on complete semantic identity, cf., for example:

> *ʾiben- "sleep": Eg *ibʒn* id. (pyr) ~ CCh *HVbyan- id.
> *calaḳ- "gather": Sem *sVlVḳ- id. ~ Eg *sʒḳ* id. (pyr) ~ CCh *caḳal- id.
> *dibür-/*dubür- "back": Sem *dubr- "back" ~ CCh *di(m)bur- "back".
> *gač- "spear": WCh *gač- id. ~ CCh *gač- id. ~ SA *gaš- id.
> *ḥak- "stone": Eg *ḥṯ* id. (n) ~ WCh *ḥVk- id. ~ CCh *χakwa- id.
> *mag- "be bad": WCh *mug- id. ~ Bed *maag* id. ~ LEC *mag- id.
> *taʾ- "eat": Sem *tVʾ-/*tVw- id. ~ WCh *taʾ-/*tiʾ- id. ~ CCh *ti- id. ~ ECh *ta(y)-/*ti(y)- id.
> *war- "throw": Sem *wur- id. ~ ECh *war- id. ~ Agaw *wa-wVr- id.
> *ʒaḥaf- "drag (oneself)": Sem *zVḥVp- id. ~ LEC *ʒaHaf- id.

If the meanings of compared words are not identical, the comparison is still treated as valid if the "semantic distance" between two meanings may be covered *in one derivational step* (whatever the concrete meaning of this vague term may be). Thus, we accept the following comparisons:

> *ʾigan- "vessel": Sem *ʾigān- "cup, bowl" ~ LEC *ʾagan-/*gaHan- "jar".
> *ʾoraẖ- "way, road": Sem *ʾur(a)ẖ- "way" ~ WCh *ʾwara- "road" ~ ECh *ʾwar- "road" ~ HEC *ʾor- "road" ~ Rift *ʾuruw- "path, way".
> *baʾ- "bush, tree": Eg *bʒ.t* "bush" (a) ~ WCh *baʾ- "tree" ~ CCh *bwaH- "bush" ~ SA *bah- "wood".
> *baʿ- "dirt, mud": CCh *ba- "dirt" ~ Rift *baʿ- "mud".
> *baẖ-/*biẖ- "burn, be hot": Eg *bẖẖ* "burn" (reg) ~ WCh *baH- "hot" ~ CCh *bVH-bVH- "hot" ~ ECh *biHwa- "roast".
> *gab- "weapon": Sem *gabāb- "sling" ~ HEC *gab- "bow and arrow".
> *yaraʾ-/*yaraw- "reed": Sem *yaraʾ- "reed not used for writing" ~ Eg *iʒrw* "reed, rush" (pyr) ~ WCh *yVraw- "reed".

If the semantic distance between the words seems to be critically big, then we consider it a compulsory measure to confirm the possibility of such a comparison with typological parallels. Thus, we accept the reconstruction of *ʾadid- "female relative" based on ECh *ʾadid-

"daughter-in-law" ~ LEC *ʾ*adad-* /*ʾ*aded-* "aunt" ~ HEC *ʾ*adad-* "maternal aunt" ~ Wrz *ʾ*atit-* "elder sister" because similar types of semantic development are attested outside Hamito-Semitic, cf. Alb *motër* "sister" ~ Eng *mother*, Lith *moša* "sister-in-law" ~ OPrus *moazo* "aunt". We also feel free to reconstruct **tibin-* "brain, marrow" on the basis of Eg *tbn* "marrow" (med) and CCh **tiḇin-* "brain" since in a number of languages the same word is used for "brain" and"marrow", cf. Russ *mozg* and NPers *maγz*. We also accept the reconstruction of **daʾ-*/**daw-* "man, chief" including such forms as CCh **daʾi-* "man, people" and Rift **daH-* "stranger" because of the corresponding typological data (see BENVENISTE 1970, 92 f.).

The present Dictionary covers all categories of lexical units with the exception of numerals, pronouns, prepositions and particles. These grammatical and semi-grammatical elements will be analyzed and etymologized elsewhere. Basically, the words within the Dictionary are either nouns or predicates. The latter group includes verbs, adjectives (usually translated as verbs, i.e., not *red* but *be red* etc.) and some adverbs.

* * *

The present project was started in 1986 in Moscow and, after August 1990, continued simultaneously in Israel and Russia. Three main types of work were carried out:

(a) processing of the previously published comparative material;
(b) search for phonologically predictable counterparts of already known forms;
(c) semantic screening.

While (a) and (b) are traditionally used methods of data processing in comparative linguistics, (c) was an innovation. To carry it out, semantic card indices (databases) of individual linguistic branches were created. In such a database, words were grouped under generalized semantic headings, e.g., in the West Chadic card index, a card with a heading *WALK* contained various words for "go", "come","enter","run" and so on, in various West Chadic languages. A card with a heading *HOUSE* contained words for "house","town","compound","hut","fence","roof" and the like. In some cases, when a certain language was of particular importance for the study of vocabulary, we created card indices of individual languages (e.g. of Akkadian). At the next stage, databases were used for semantic screening, i.e. for a cross-comparison of semantic units within the limits of semantically and phonologically acceptable parallels (see above).

Although the work of lexicographers is devoid of many simple human joys, many friends and colleagues helped us during all these years.

The authors appreciate the helpful criticism and/or assistance of the following colleagues:

Dr. Anna Belova (Moscow)
Prof. Igor' M. Djakonov (St.Petersburg)
Prof. Aaron Dolgopolski (Haifa)
Prof. Vladimir A. Dybo (Moscow)
Dr. Sergej Nikolaev (Moscow)
Dr. Baruch Podolski (Tel-Aviv)
Prof. Andrzej Zaborski (Krakow)

Some of the material used in the Dictionary was kindly provided by:

Dr. Alexander Militarëv (Moscow)
Dr. Baruch Podolski (Tel-Aviv)
Mrs. Rachel Torpusman (Jerusalem).

We are also grateful to *Mrs. Natalia Orel* and *Mr. Alexander Kulik* for their technical assistance.

At the preliminary stage, the authors used the computer data base editor *Star* kindly submitted by its author *Prof. Sergej Starostin* (Moscow).

Vladimir Orel
Olga Stolbova

LIST OF ABBREVIATIONS

a(ncient)
adj. – adjective
Afd – Afade
Ahg – Ahaggar
Akh(mimian)
Akk(adian)
Aks(imen)
Ala(ba)
Alb(anian)
Alg – Alagwa
Amh(aric)
Amor(aic)
Anf(illa)
Ang(as)
Ank(we)
Arab(ic)
Aram(aic)
Arb(ore)
Arg(oba)
Aun(gi)
Av(estan)
Awj(ila)

Ban(na)
Bay(so)
Bch – Bachama
BD – Book of the Dead
Berb(er)
Bgh – Boghom
Bid(iya)
Bil(in)
Bks – Bokkos
Bld – Balda
Bmb – Bambala
Bmr – Baamrani
Bnn – Banana
Boh(airian)
Bol(ewa)
Bret(on)
Brg – Birgit
Brm – Burma
Brw – Barawa
Bry – Barayn
Bsd – Basada
Bud(uma)
Bur(unge)
Bus(so)
Bwo(ro)

Cam(ay)
CCh – Central Chadic
Ch(adic)
Chb – Chibak
Copt(ic)
Cush(itic)

DB – Dafo-Butura
Dar(asa)
Dem(otic)
Dgh(wede)
Dhl – Dahalo
Dmb – Dembea
Dmt – Damot
Dng – Dangla
Dok(shi)
Dor(ma)
Dul(lay)

ECh – East Chadic
Eg(yptian)
Eng(lish)

FBw – Fali Bwagira
Fgg – Figig
FGl – Fali Gili
FJl – Fali Jilvu
FKi – Fali Kiria
FMb – Fali Mubi
FMch – Fali Mucella
Fym – Fayumian

Gaa(nda)
Gaf(at)
Gaw(wata)
Gbn – Gabin
Gbr – Gabri
Gdf – Guduf
Gdl – Gidole
Gel(eba)
Ghd – Ghadames
Gid(ar)
Gis(iga)
Gk – Greek
Gll – Gollango

Gob(eze)
Gog(ot)
Gor(owa)
Goth(ic)
gr – Greek papyri
Grm – Geruma
Grn – Geruntum
Gul(fey)
Gur(age)
Gvo(ko)
Gwn – Gwandara
Gz – Geez

Had(iya)
Hbr – Hebrew
HEC – Highland East Cushitic
HF – Higi Futu
HGh – Higi Ghye
Hil(di)
Hmr – Hamar
HNk – Higi Nkafa
Hrr – Harari
Hrs – Harso
Hs – Hausa
HS – Hamito-Semitic
Hss – Harsusi
Hwn – Hwona

IE – Indo-European
Irq – Iraqw
Izd(eg)
Izn(asen)
Izy – Izayan

Jib(bali)
Jmb – Jimbin
Jnk – Jonkor

Kab(enna)
Kaf(fa)
Kap(iski)
Kbl – Kabalay
Kby – Kabyle
Kem(ant)
Klb – Kilba
Klr – Kulere
Kmb – Kambatta
Kon(so)
Kr – Karekare
Krf – Kirfi
Kry – Kariya
Kus(eri)
Kwn – Kwang
Kwr – Kwara
Kwz – Kwadza

l(ate)
Lat(in)
LEC – Lowland East Cushitic
Lib(yan)
Lith(uanian)
Lmn – Lamang
Log(one)
LPe – Lame Pewe
Lyc(opolitan)

math(ematical papyri)
Mba(ra)
Mbu(rku)
Mch – Mocha
med(ical papyri)
Mgg – Mogogodo
MHG – Middle High German
Mhr – Mehri
Mig(ama)
MK – Middle Kingdom
Mkk – Mokilko
Mnd – Mandara
Mng – Mangas
Mnj – Munjuk
Mns – Menaser
Mnt – Montol
Moab(ite)
Mpn – Mupun
Mrg – Margi
Msg – Musgum
Msm – Mesme
Mtk – Matakam
Muk(tele)
Mus(goy)
Mwu(lyen)

n(ew)
n. – noun
Nak(aci)
Nch – Nanchere
Nfs – Nefusa
Ngm – Ngamo
Ngw(ahi)
Ngz – Ngizim
NIr – New Irish
NK – New Kingdom
NPers – New Persian
Ntf – Ntifa
Nz(angi)

OCopt – Old Coptic
OEng – Old English
OIr – Old Irish
OK – Old Kingdom
Ome(to)
Omot(ic)
ON – Old Norse
OPers – Old Persian
OPrus – Old Prussian
Or – Oromo
Ox(yrinhian)

Pad(uko)
Phn – Phoenician
PIE – Proto-Indo-European
pl. – plural
Pol(chi)
Pun(ic)
pyr(amids)

reg – royal tombs
Rnd – Rendille
Russ(ian)

SA – Saho-Afar
SAr – South Arabian
sarc(ophagi)
Say(anchi)
Sbn – Sibine
Sbn – Sibine
Sem(itic)
sg. – singular
Sgr – Segrushen
Shd – Sahidic
Shh – Šḥeri
Shk – Sheko
Shn – Shenua
Sid(amo)
Skt – Sanskrit
Slav(ic)
Slt – Selti
Sml – Semlal
Smr – Sumray
Snh – Senhaja
Sok(oro)
Som(ali)
Soq(otri)
Sp(anish)
Suk(ur)
Syr(ian)

Tgr – Tigre
Tgy – Tigray
Tmb – Tambaro
Tng – Tangale
Tob(anga)
Tsl – Taneslemmet
Tum(ak)
Twl – Tawlemmet

Ug(aritic)

v. – verb

W(elsh)
War(azi)
WCh – West Chadic
Westc(art)
Wmd – Wamdiu
Wrg – Wargla
Wrj – Warji
Wrz – Werizoid

Xmr – Xamir
Xmt – Xamta

Yam(ma)

Zak(shi)
ZBt – Zime Batua
Zgh – Zeghwana
Zng – Zenaga

MAIN WORKS OF REFERENCE

ABRAHAM, R.C. 1962 *Dictionary of the Hausa Language* London.

ABRAHAM, R.C. 1964 *Somali-English Dictionary* London.

AISTLEITNER, J. 1963 *Wörterbuch der ugaritischen Sprache* Berlin.

ALBRIGHT, W.F. "Notes on Egypto-Semitic etymology" *Journal of the American Oriental Society* v. 47 # 1–4.

ALIYO, KH., JUNGRAITHMAYR, H. 1989 *Lexique bidiya: une langue centre-africaine (Republique du Tchad)* Frankfurt a/M.

ALOJALY, GH. 1980 *Lexique touareg-français* Copenhague.

AMBORN, H., MINKER, G., SASSE, H.-J. 1980 ,,Das Dullay:Materialien zu einer ostkuschitischen Sprache" *Beiträge zur Afrikanistik* 6, 228–282.

ANDRZEJEWSKI, B.W. 1975 "Verbs with Vocalic Mutation in Somali and Their Significance for Hamito-Semitic Comparative Studies" *Hamito-Semitica* The Hague 361–374.

APPLEYARD, D.L. 1975 "A descriptive outline of Kemant" *Bulletin of the School of Oriental and African Studies* 38/2 316–350.

APPLEYARD, D.L. *A Word List of Kemant* [typescript].

APPLEYARD, D.L. 1977 "A Comparative Approach to the Amharic Lexicon" *Afroasiatic Linguistics* 5: 2.

BALDI, PH. (ed.) 1990 *Linguistic Change and Reconstruction Methodology* Berlin–New York (= *Trends in Linguistics: Studies and Monographs 45*).

BARGERY, G.P. 1934 *Hausa-English Dictionary and English-Hausa Vocabulary* London.

BARRETEAU, D. 1992 *Lexique Mafa* Paris.

BARTH, H. 1971 *Collection of Vocabularies of Central-African Languages I–II* [2nd ed.] London.

BARTH, J. 1893 *Etymologische Studien zum Semitischen inbesondere zum hebräischen Lexicon* Leipzig.

BELOT, J.B. 1898 *Vocabulaire arabe-français* Beyrouth.

BENDER, M.L. 1975 *Omotic: A New Afroasiatic Language Family* Carbondale.

BENDER, M.L. *The Non-Semitic Languages of Ethiopia* East Lansing.

BENDER, M.L. 1988 "Proto-Omotic Phonology and Lexicon" *Proceedings of the First Symposium on Cushitic and OmoticLanguages* Hamburg 121–162.

BENTON, P.A. 1968 *The Languages and Peoples of Bornu I* [2nd ed.] London.

BENVENISTE, E. 1970 *Le vocabulaire des institutions indo-européennes* I Paris.

BIBERSTEIN-KAZIMIRSKI, A. DE 1860 *Dictionnaire arabe-française* I–II.

BIEBER, F. 1920 *Kaffa: Ein altkuschitisches Volkstum in Inner-Afrika* Münster.

BLACK, P. 1972 "Cushitic and Omotic Classification" *Language Sciences* [December] 27–28.

BLACK, P. 1974 *Lowland East Cushitic: Subgrouping and Reconstruction* Ann Arbor Microfilms, Ann Arbor.

BOULIFA, S.A. 1913 *Lexique kabyle-français* Alger.

BROCKELMANN, C. 1908–191 *Grundriss der vergleichenden Grammatik der semitischen Sprache I–II* Berlin.

BROCKELMANN, C. 1928 *Lexicon syriacum* Halis Saxonum.

BRUGMANN, K. 1904 *Kurze vergleichende Grammatik der indo-germanischen Sprachen* Strassburg.

CALICE, E. 1936 *Grundlagen der ägyptisch-semitischen Wortvergleichung* Wien.

CAPRILE, J.-P. 1975 *Lexique tumak-français* Berlin.
CERNY, J. 1976 *Coptic Etymological Dictionary* Cambridge.
CERULLI, E. 1936–1951 *Studi etiopici I–IV* Roma.
COHEN, D. 1970 *Dictionnaire des racines sémitiques* Paris–La Haye.
COHEN, D. 1974 "Alternances vocaliques dans le système verbal couchitique et chamito-sémitique" *Actes du Prémier Congrès International de linguistique sémitique et chamito-sémitique* The Hague 40–48.
COHEN, D. (ed.) 1988 *Langues chamito-sémitiques* Paris.
COHEN, D. 1991 "Berbère et couchitique. Notes comparatives sur des noms de parties du corps" *Semitic Studies. In Honor of Wolf Leslau.* Wiesbaden 225–233.
COHEN, M. 1947 *Essai comparatif sur le vocabulaire et la phonétique du chamito-sémitique* Paris.
COHEN, M. 1953 "Sémitique, égyptien, libyco-berbère, couchitique et méthode comparative" *Bibliotheca Orientalis* v. 10.
CONTI ROSSINI, C. 1912 *La langue des Kemant en Abyssinie* Wien.
CONTI ROSSINI, C. 1940 *Lingua tigrina* Milano.
COPLAND, B.D. 1933–1934 "A Note on the Origin of the Mbugu, with a Text" *Zeitschrift für eingeborenen Sprachen* v. 24 241–244.
DALLET, J.-M. 1982 *Dictionnaire kabyle-français* Paris.
DELHEURE, J. 1984 *Aġraw n giwalen tumẓabt t-tfransist* Paris.
DESTAING, E. 1920 *Etude sur le Tachelhit de Sous* Paris.
DJAKONOV, I.M. 1965 *Semitoxamitskie jazyki* Moscow.
DJAKONOV, I.M. [DIAKONOFF, I.M.] 1965 *Semito-Hamitic Languages* Moscow.
DJAKONOV, I.M. 1967 *Jazyki drevnej Perednej Azii* Moscow.
DJAKONOV, I.M. [DIAKONOFF, I.M.] 1970 "Problems of Root Structure in Proto-Semitic" *Archiv Orientalni 8* # 4.
DJAKONOV, I.M. (ed.) 1981–1986 *Sravnitel'noistoricheskij slovar' afrazijskix jazykov* I–III Moscow.
DJAKONOV, I.M. 1988 *Afrasian Languages* Moscow.
DJAKONOV, I.M. ET AL. 1987 "Obshcheafrazijskaja fonologicheskaja sistema" *Afrikanskoe istoricheskoe jazykoznanie* Moscow 9–29.
DJAKONOV, I.M., PORXOMOVSKIJ V.JA. 1979 "O prinicpax afrazijskoj rekonstrukcii" *Balcanica* Moscow
DOLGOPOLSKIJ, A.B. 1966 "Materialy po sravnitel'no-istoricheskoj fonetike kushitskix jazykov:gubnye i dental'nye smychnye v nachal'nom polozhenii" *Jazyki Afriki* Moscow 35–88.
DOLGOPOLSKIJ, A.B. 1972 "Materialy po sravnitel'no-istoricheskoj fonetike kushitskix jazykov:vel'arnyj zvonkij v anlaute" *Problemy afrikanskogo jazykoznanija* Moscow, 197–216.
DOLGOPOLSKIJ, A.B. 1973 *Sravnitel'no-istoricheskaja fonetika kushitskix jazykov* Moscow.
DOLGOPOLSKIJ, A.B. 1983 "Semitic and East Cushitic: Sound Correspondences and Cognate Sets" *Ethiopian Studies* Wiesbaden, 123–142.
DOLGOPOLSKIJ, A.B. 1987 "South Cushitic Lateral Consonants As Compared to Semitic and East Cushitic" *Proceedings of the IVth International Hamito-Semitic Congress* Amsterdam 195–214.
DROWER, E.S., MACUCH, R. 1963 *A Mandaic Dictionary* Oxford.
EBERT, K.H. 1975–1976 *Sprache und Tradition der Kera (Tschad)* Berlin.
EHRET, CHR. 1980 *The Historical Reconstruction of Southern Cushitic Phonology and Vocabulary* Berlin.
EHRET, CHR. 1987 "Proto-Cushitic Reconstruction" *Sprache und Geschichte in Afrika* 8 7–180.

EHRET, CHR., ELDERKIN, E.D., NURSE, D. 1989 "Daxalo lexis and its sources" *Afrikanistische Arbeitspapiere* # 18 1–49.
EMBER, A. 1930 *Egypto-Semitic Studies* Leipzig.
ERMAN, A. 1928 *Ägyptische Grammatik* Berlin.
ERMAN, A., GRAPOW, H. 1957 *Wörterbuch der ägyptischen Sprache I–VI* Berlin.
FAULKNER, R. 1962 *A Concise Dictionary of Middle Egyptian* Oxford.
FLEMING, H.C. 1964 "Bayso and Rendille, Somali outliers" *Rassegna di studi etiopici* 20 35–96.
FLEMING, H.C. 1969 "Asa and Aramanic. Cushitic Hunters in Masai-Land" *Ethnology* 8: 1, 1–36.
FLEMING, H.C. 1969a "Classification of West Cushitic within Hamito-Semitic" *Eastern African History* New York 3–27.
FLEMING, H.C. 1988 "Reconstruction of Proto-South Omotic" *Proceedings of the First Symposium on Cushitic and OmoticLanguages* Hamburg 163–178.
FOOT, E.C. 1913 *A Galla-English, English-Galla Dictionary* Cambridge.
FOUCAULD, CH. DE 1951–1952 *Dictionnaire touareg-français* Paris.
FOULKS, S. 1915 *Angass Manual* London.
FRAJZYNGIER, Z. (ed.) 1989 *Current Progress in Chadic Linguistics* Amsterdam–Philadelphia.
FRIEDRICH, J. 1952 "Semitisch und Hamitisch" *Bibliotheca Orientalis* 9.
FRONZAROLLI, P. 1964–1968 "Studi sul lessico comune semitico" *Rendiconti dell'Accademia Nazionale dei Lincei, Classe di Scienze morali, storiche e filologiche* 19, 155–172, 20, 135–150, 246–269, 23, 267–303, 24, 285–321.
GAMKRELIDZE, T.V., MACHAVARIANI, G.I. 1965 *The system of sonants and the ablaut in Kartvelian languages* [in Georgian] Tbilisi.
GARDINER, A. 1957 *Egyptian Grammar* Oxford.
GASPARINI, A. 1983 *Sidamo-English Dictionary* Bologna.
GELB, I.J. 1957 *Glossary of Old Akkadian* Chicago.
GESENIUS, W. 1954 *Hebräisches und aramäisches Wörterbuch über das Alte Testament* [bearb. von F. BUHL] Berlin.
GOLDENBERG, G. 1977 "The Semitic languages of Ethiopia and their classification" *Bulletin of the School of Oriental and African Studies* 15/# 3 461–507.
GOODMAN, M. 1971 "The Strange Case of Mbugu" *Pidginization and Creolization of Languages* Camridge 243–354.
GRAGG, G.B. 1982 *Oromo Dictionary* East Lansing.
GRAGG, G.B. 1988 "An Etymological Cushitic Database" *Proceedings of the First Symposium on Cushitic and OmoticLanguages* Hamburg.
GREENBERG, J.H. 1947 "Arabic Loanwords in Hausa" *Word* 3 85–97.
GREENBERG, J.H. 1954 "The Labial Consonants of Proto-Afro-asiatic" *Word* v. 14.
GREENBERG, J.H. 1955 *Studies in African Linguistic Classification* New Haven.
GREENBERG, J.H. 1958 "The Labial Consonants in Proto-Afroasiatic" *Word* v. 14 # 2–3.
GREENBERG, J.H. 1963 "Mogogodo, A Forgotten Cushitic Language" *Journal of African Languages* 2: 1, 29–43.
GREENBERG, J.H. 1965 "The Evidence for */mb/ as a Proto-Afroasiatic Phoneme" *Symbolae Linguisticae in Honorem G. Kurylowicz* Krakow 88–92.
GREENBERG, J.H. 1966 *The Languages of Africa* The Hague.
HAYWARD, R.J. 1978–1979 "Bayso Revisited: Some Preliminary Linguistic Observations" *Bulletin of the School of Africanand Oriental Studies* 41 (1978) 539–570; 42 (1979) 101–132.
HAYWARD, R.J. 1984 *The Arbore Language: A First Investigation* Hamburg.
HAYWARD, R.J. (ed.) 1990 *Omotic Language Studies* London.

HEINE, B. 1978 "The Sam Languages. A History of Rendille, Boni and Somali" *Afroasiatic Linguistics* 6/2 23–115.
HEINE, B. 1981 "Some Cultural Evidence on the Early Sam-Speaking People of Eastern Africa" *Sprache und Geschichte in Afrika* 3, 169–200.
HEINE, B. 1982 *Boni Dialects* Berlin.
HETZRON, R. 1969 *The Verbal System of Southern Agaw* Berkeley–Los Angeles.
HETZRON, R. 1976 "The Agaw Languages" *Afroasiatic Linguistics* 3/# 3.
HINTZE, F. 1951 "Zu hamito-semitischen Wortgleichungen" *Zeitschrift für Phonetik und allgemeine Sprachwissenschaft* 5 65–87.
HODGE, C.T. 1970 "Afroasiatic: An Overview" *Current Trends in Linguistics VI* The Hague–Paris.
HODGE, C.T. (ed.) 1971 *Afroasiatic: A Survey* The Hague.
HODGE, C.T. 1989 "Hausa and the Prothetic Alif" *Current Progress in Chadic Linguistics* Amsterdam–Philadelphia 219–232.
HUDSON, G. 1989 *Highland East Cushitic Dictionary* Hamburg.
HUYGUE, G. 1906 *Dictionnaire français-chaouia* Alger.
IBRISZIMOW, D. 1989 *Towards a Common Chadic Lexicon* Cracow 1989.
ILLICH-SVITYCH, V.M. 1966 "Iz istorii chadskogo konsonantizma: labial'nye smychnye" *Jazyki Afriki* Moscow, 9–34.
ILLICH-SVITYCH, V.M. 1971 *Opyt sravnenija nostraticheskix jazykov. Vvedenie. Sravnitel'nyj slovar' (b–k)* Moscow.
ILLICH-SVITYCH, V.M. 1976 *Opyt sravnenija nostraticheskix jazykov. Sravnitel'nyj slovar' (l–ǯ)* Moscow.
ILLICH-SVITYCH, V.M. 1984 *Opyt sravenija nostraticheskix jazykov. Sravnitel'nyj slovar' (p–q)* Moscow.
JAHN, A. 1912 *Die Mehri-Sprache in Südarabien* Wien.
JOHNSTONE, T.M. 1977 *Ḥarsūsi Lexicon and English-Ḥarsūsi Word-List* Oxford–London.
JOHNSTONE, T.M. 1981 *Jibbāli Lexicon* Oxford.
JOHNSTONE, T.M. 1987 *Mehri Lexicon and Mehri-English Word-List* London.
JONES, P.M.E. 1988 *Glossary of Ancient Egyptian Nautical Titles and Terms* London.
JUNGRAITHMAYR, H. 1963–1964 "Die Sprache der Sura (Maghavul) in Nordnigerien" *Afrika und Übersee* 47, 8–89, 204–220.
JUNGRAITHMAYR, H. 1964–1965 "Materialien zur Kenntnis des Chip, Montol, Gerka und Burrum" *Afrika und Übersee* 48, 161–182.
JUNGRAITHMAYR, H. 1970 *Die Ron-Sprachen* Glückstadt.
JUNGRAITHMAYR, H. 1983 "On Mono- and Triradicality in Early and Present-Day Chadic" *Studies in Chadic and Afroasiatic Linguistics* Hamburg 139–156.
JUNGRAITHMAYR, H. 1989 "Hausa–An Early or Late Stage Chadic Language?" *Current Progress in Chadic Linguistics* Amsterdam–Philadelphia 251–266.
JUNGRAITHMAYR, H. 1990 *Lexique mokilko: mokilko-français et français-mokilko* Berlin.
JUNGRAITHMAYR, H. 1991 *A Dictionary of the Tangale Language* Berlin.
JUNGRAITHMAYR, H., ABAKAR ADAMS 1991 *Lexique migama* Berlin.
JUNGAITHMAYR, H., ALIO, K. 1989 *Lexique bidiya* Frankfurtam-Main.
JUNGRAITHMAYR, H., SHIMIZU, K. 1981 *Chadic Lexical Roots* Berlin.
KOEHLER, L., BAUMGARTNER, W. 1967–1968 *Hebräisches und aramäisches Lexikon zum Alten Testament* I–III Leiden.
KRAFT, C. 1981 "Chadic Wordlists" *Marburger Studien zur Asien- und Afrikakunde* Marburg.
KURYLOWICZ, J. 1956 *L'apophonie en indo-européen* Wrocław.
KURYLOWICZ, J. 1961 *L'apophonie en sémitique* Wrocław–Warszawa–Krakow.

LANE, E.W. 1955 *Arabic-English Lexicon I–VIII* New York.
LANFRY, J. 1973 *Ghadames. II. Glossaire* Fort-Nationale.
LAOUST, E. 1932 *Siwa. I. Son parler* Paris.
LESLAU, W. 1938 *Lexique soqotri* Paris.
LESLAU, W. 1956 *Etude comparative et descriptive du gafat* Paris.
LESLAU, W. *Ethiopic and South Arabic Contributions to the Hebrew Lexicon* Berkeley–Los Angeles.
LESLAU, W. 1959 *A Dictionary of Moca (Southern Ethiopia)* Berkeley–Los Angeles.
LESLAU, W. 1962 "Semitic and Egyptian Comparisons" *Journal of Near Eastern Studies* v. 21.
LESLAU, W. 1963 *Etymological Dictionary of Harari* Berkeley–Los Angeles.
LESLAU, W. 1962 "The Prefix *h* in Egyptian, Modern S. Arabian and Hausa" *Africa* 32 65–68.
LESLAU, W. 1979 *Etymological Dictionary of Gurage I–III* Wiesbaden.
LITTMANN, E, HOFNER, M. 1962 *Wörterbuch der Tigre-Sprache* Wiesbaden.
LOUBIGNAC, V. *Etude sur le dialecte berbère des Zaian* Angers.
LUKAS, J. 1936 *Die Logone-Sprache im zentralen Sudan* Leipzig.
LUKAS, J. 1937 *Zentralsudanische Studien* Hamburg.
LUKAS, J. 1939 *Die Sprache der Buduma im Zentralen Sudan* Leipzig.
LUKAS, J. 1941 *Deutsche Quellen zur Sprache der Musgu* Berlin.
LUKAS, J. 1970 *Studien zur Sprache der Gisiga (Nordkamerun)* Glückstadt–Hamburg.
MEINHOF, C. 1912 *Die Sprachen der Hamiten* Hamburg.
MILITAREV, A.JU. 1983 [Addenda in:] MAJZEL', S.S. *Puti razvitija kornevogo fonda semitskix jazykov* Moscow.
MILITAREV, A.JU. 1984 "Sovremennoe sravnitel'no-istoricheskoe afrazijskoe jazykoznanie: chto ono mozhet dat' istoricheskoj nauke?" *Lingvisticheskaja rekonstrukcija i drevnejshaja istorija Vostoka* (Part 3) Moscow 3–26, 44–50.
MILITAREV, A.JU., OREL, V.E., STOLBOVA, O.V. 1989 "Hamito-Semitic Word-Stock: 1. Dwelling" *Lingvisticheskaja rekonstrukcija i drevnejshaja istorija Vostoka* Moscow, 137–158.
MORENO, M.M. 1938 *Introduzione alla lingua ometo* Milano.
MOSCATI, S. ET AL. 1964 *An Introduction to the ComparativeGrammar of the Semitic Languages: Phonology and Morphology* Wiesbaden.
MUKAROVSKY, H.G. 1987 *Mande-Chadic Common Stock* Wien.
NEWMAN, P., MA R. 1966 "Comparative Chadic: Phonology and Lexicon" *Journal of African Linguistics 5.*
NEWMAN, P. 1977 "Chadic classification and reconstructions" *Afroasiatic Linguistics* 5/# 1 1–42.
NEWMAN, P. 1980 *The Classification of Chadic within Afroasiatic* Leiden.
NEWMAN, P. 1984 "Methodological Pitfalls in Chadic-Afroasiatic Comparisons" *Current Progress in Afro-Asiatic Linguistics. Papers of the Third International Hamito-Semitic Congress* Amsterdam 161–163.
OREL, V.E. 1994 "Studies in the Hamito-Semitic Morphonology" *Orbis* [forthcoming].
OREL. V.E. 1995 "The World of Hamito-Semites" *Orbis* [forthcoming].
OREL, V.E., STOLBOVA, O.V. 1989 "Chadsko-egipetskie izoglossy v oblasti kul'turnoj leksiki" *Lingvisticheskaja rekonstrukcija i drevnejshaja istorija Vostoka* Moscow 131–136.
OREL, V.E., STOLBOVA, O.V. 1989–1990 "K rekonstrukcii praafrazijskogo vokalizma" *Voprosy jazykoznanija* 5 (1989) 66–84, 2 (1990) 75–90.
OREL, V.E., STOLBOVA, O.V. 1992 "Reconstruction of the Afrasian Vocalism: Cushitic and Chadic" *Nostratic, Dene-Caucasian, Austric and Amerind* Bochum 225–236.

OREL, V.E., STOLBOVA, O.V. 1992a "On Chadic-Egyptian Lexical Relations" *Nostratic, Dene-Caucasian, Austric and Amerind* Bochum 181–203.
OREL, V.E., STOLBOVA, O.V. 1992b "Cushitic, Chadic and Egyptian: Lexical Relations" *Nostratic, Dene-Caucasian, Austric and Amerind* Bochum 167–179.
OREL, V.E., STOLBOVA, O.V. 1992c "Position of Cushitic (Preliminary Report)" *Nostratic, Dene-Caucasian, Austric and Amerind* Bochum 205–223.
PALMER, F.R. 1971 "Cushitic" *Linguistics in South West Asia and North Africa* The Hague (= *Current Trends in Linguistics* 6).
PARKER, E.M., HAYWARD, R.J. 1985 *An Afar-English Dictionary* London.
PENCHOEN, TH.G. 1973 *Tamazight of the Ayt Ndhir* Los Angeles.
PICARD, A. 1958 *Textes berbères dans le parler des Irjen* Alger.
PILSZCZIKOWA, N. 1960 "Le haoussa et le chamitosémitique a la lumière de l'"Essai comparatif" de Marcel Cohen" *Rocznik Orientalistyczny* v. 24 # 1.
PLAZIKOWSKY-BRAUNER, H. 1964 "Wörterbuch der Hadiya-Sprache" *Rassegna di Studi Etiopici* v. 20 133–182.
POKORNY, J. 1959 *Indogermanisches etymologisches Wörterbuch* Bern.
PORXOMOVSKIJ V.JA. 1982 "Problemy geneticheskoj klassifikacii jazykov Afriki" *Teoreticheskie osnovy klassifikacii jazykov mira* Moscow 195–257.
PORZIG, W. 1954 *Die Gliederung des indogermanischen Sprachgebiets* Heidelberg.
PRAETORIUS, F. 1894 "Über die hamitischen Sprachen Ostafrikas" *Beiträge zur Assyriologie und vergleichenden Sprachwissenschaft* 2 312–341.
PRASSE, K.-G. 1969 *A propos de l'origine de H touareg (Ta-haggart)* Copenhagen.
PRASSE, K.-G. 1972–1974 *Manuel de grammaire touareg* I–VII Copenhagen.
RAPP, E.L., BENZING, B. 1968 *Dictionary of the Glavda Language.* I. *Glavda-English* Frankfurt a/Main.
REINISCH, L. 1882 *Die Bilin-Sprache in Nordost-Afrika* Wien.
REINISCH, L. 1883–1884 *Die Chamir-Sprache in Abessinien I–II* Wien.
REINISCH, L. 1885 *Die ʿAfar-Sprache I* Wien.
REINISCH, L. 1885–1887 *Die Quara-Sprache in Abessinien I–III* Wien.
REINISCH, L. 1887 *Wörterbuch der Bilin-Sprache* Wien.
REINISCH, L. 1888 *Die Kafa-Sprache in Nordost-Afrika* Wien.
REINISCH, L. 1890 *Wörterbuch der Saho-Sprache* Wien.
REINISCH, L. 1893 *ʿAfar-Deutsches Wörterbuch* Wien.
REINISCH, L. 1895 *Wörterbuch der Beḍaue-Sprache* Wien.
REINISCH, L. 1900–1903 *Die Somali-Sprache* Wien.
RENISIO, A. 1932 *Etude sur les dialectes berbères* Paris.
ROESSLER, O. 1964 "Libysch–Hamitisch–Semitisch" *Oriens* v. 17.
SACHNINE, M. 1982 *Lame, un parler zime du Nord Camerun* Paris.
SASSE, H.-J. 1979 "The Consonant Phonemes of Proto-East-Cushitic: A First Approximation" *Afroasiatic Linguistics* 7: 1, 1–66.
SASSE, H.-J. 1981 "Afroasiatisch" *Die Sprachen Afrikas* Hamburg 129–148.
SASSE, H.-J. 1982 *An Etymological Dictionary of Burji* Hamburg.
SCHLEE, G. 1978 *Sprachliche Studien zum Rendille* Hamburg.
SCHUH, R. 1981 *A Dictionary of Ngizim* London.
SEIGNOBOS, CH., TOURNEUX, H. 1984 "Note sur les Baldamu etleur langue (Nord Camerun)" *Africana Marburgensia* 17.
SKINNER, A.N. 1984 *Afroasiatic Vocabulary. Evidence for Some Culturally Important Items* Marburg = *Africana Marburgensia* Sorgenheft 7.
SKINNER, A.N. 1987 "'Eye' and 'Tongue' in Afroasiatic", *Proceedings of the IVth International Hamito-Semitic Congress* Amsterdam, 73–83.
SKINNER, A.N. 1994 *Hausa Lexicon. Comparative data* [manuscript].
SODEN, W. VON (bearb.) 1965 *Akkadisches Handwörterbuch* Wiesbaden.

STOLBOVA, O.V. 1987 "Sravnitel'no-istoricheskaja fonetika i slovar' zapadnochadskix jazykov" *Afrikanskoe istoricheskoe jazykoznanie* Moscow 30–268.
STOLBOVA, O.V. 1995 *Sravnitel'no-istoricheskaja fonetika chadskix jazykov* Moscow [forthcoming].
SZEMERENYI, O. 1962 "Principles of Etymological Research in the Indo-European Languages" *II. Fachtagung für indogermanische und allgemeine Sprachwissenschaft* Innsbruck 175–212.
TAIFI, M. 1988 *Le lexique berbère* Paris.
TOMBACK, R. S. 1978 *A Comparative Semitic Lexicon of the Phoenician and Punic Languages* Missoula.
TOSCO, M. 1991 *A Grammatical Sketch of Dahalo: IncludingTexts and Glossary* Hamburg.
TOURNEUX, H., SEIGNOBOS, CH., LAFARGE, FR. 1986 *Les Mbara et leur langue (Tchad)* Paris.
TUCKER, A.N., BRYAN, M.A. 1956 *The Non-Bantu Languages of North-Eastern Africa* London.
VERGOTE, J. 1945 *Phonétique historique de l'égyptien* Louvain.
VERGOTE, J. 1960 *De oplossing van een gewichtig probleem: de vocalisatie van de Egyptische werkwoordvormen* Brussel.
VYCICHL, W. 1949 "Histoire de la langue berbère" *Actes du XXI-e Congrès Internationale des Orientalistes.*
VYCICHL, W. 1958 ,,Grundlagen der ägyptisch-semitischen Wortvergleichung" *Mitteilungen des Deutschen Archäologischen Instituts (Kairo)* Wien 67–405.
VYCICHL, W. 1963 ,,Die zweiradikalige Verben im ägyptischen und berberischen" *Zeitschrift für Aegyptische Sprache* v. 88 148–150.
VYCICHL, W. 1983 *Dictionnaire étymologique de la langue copte* Leuven–Paris.
WADA, SH. 1973 *Iraqw Basic Vocabulary* Tokyo.
WALDE, A., POKORNY, J. (Hrsg.) 1926–1932 *Vergleichendes Wörterbuch der indogermanischen Sprachen* I–III Berlin–Leipzig.
WARD, W. 1962 "Some Egyptian-Semitic Roots" *Orientalia* v. *1* # 4.
WHITELEY, W.H. 1953 *Studies in Iraqw* Kampala.
ZABORSKI, A. 1967 "Arabic Loan-Words in Somali: Preliminary Survey" *Folia Orientalia* 8 125–174.
ZABORSKI, A. 1975 *The Verb in Cushitic* Kraków.
ZABORSKI, A. 1989 ,,Der Wortschatz der Bedscha-Sprache. Eine Vergleichende Analyse" *XXIII. Deutscher Orientalistentag* Stuttgart 573–591.

*ʾ

1 *ʾa- ''walk, go''

Eg *ꜣ* ''walk'' (Westc.).
WCh *ʾ*a*- ''come'': Diri ʾ*a*-.
ECh *ʾ*a*- ''go'': Tum *a*-, Mkk ʾ*aa*ʾ-.
Partial reduplication in Mkk?

Cf. a possible derivative in *ʾ*ay*- ''come, run''.

2 *ʾab- ''father''

Sem *ʾ*ab*- ''father'': Akk *abu*, Ug ʾ*ab*, Phn ʾ*b*, Pun ʾ*b*, Hbr ʾ*āb*, Aram ʾ*ab*, Syr ʾ*abbā*, Arab ʾ*ab*-, SAr ʾ*b*, Gz ʾ*ab*, Tgy ʾ*abbo*, Amh *abbat*, Har *āw*, Soq ʾ*eb*, Mhr *ḥayb*, Hss *ḥayb*, Shh ʾ*iy*.
Berb *ʾ*ab(b)*- ''father'': Twl *abba*, Izy *ibba*, Izn *ebb*^{w}*a*.
Eg *ꜣb.t* ''family'' (OK), ''parents'' (n).
Since the semantic relationship between ''family'' and ''father'' is quite obvious, Eg *ꜣb.t* may well be a derivative of an initial word for ''father''.
CCh *ʾ*ab*- ''father'': Bud *aba*.
Hardly an Arabic loanword.
Agaw *ʾ*ab*- ''father'': Bil *abba*, Kem *abaa*.
SA *ʾ*ab*- ''father'': Saho *abba*.
LEC *ʾ*ab*- ''father'': Som *aba*, *aaba*, Or *abbaa*.
HEC *ʾ*ab*- ''father, uncle'': Sid *aabbo*, Dar *aabbo*, Bmb *aabboo*.
Rift *ʾ*ab*- ''father'': Asa *aba*.

Doubtlessly, an onomatopoeia similar to numerous forms outside Hamito-Semitic. Cf. a similar stem in WCh *ʾ*ub*- ''father'': Hs *ubā*. Cush forms may be borrowed from Sem.

3 *ʾab- ''stone''

Agaw *ʾ*ab*- ''mountain'': Xmr *abaa*, Xmt *aaba*, Kwr *abaa*.
Bed *awe* ''stone''.
Note *-*b*- > -*w*- in the intervocalic position.

LEC *ʾ*eb-* ''stone'': Bay *eʾebo*.
Secondary **e*?

Present only in Cush. Probably, an archaism from which a widely attested derivative *ʾ*abun-* ''stone, millstone'' was formed.

4 *ʾab-/*ʾub- ''fall, descend''

ECh *ʾ*ab-* ''fall'': Tum *ab*, Mubi *ebī*.
SA *ʾ*ob-* ''descend'': Saho *ob-*, Afar *oob-*.
**o* < **a* before a labial.
HEC *ʾ*ub-* ''fall'': Sid *ub-*, Had *ub-*.

Alternation **a* ~ **u*.

5 *ʾabac- ''house, manger''

Sem *ʾ*abūs-* ''warehouse'' [1], ''manger'' [2]: Akk *abūsu* [1], *Hbr ʾēbūs* [2].
Secondary labialization of HS **a* > Sem **u* after a labial. Related to Arab *ʾbš* ''collect, gather''?
WCh **ḅac-* < **HVbac-* ''compound, farm'': DB *ḅas*, Bks *ḅas*.
An earlier laryngeal indicated by the emphatic occlusive.

6 *ʾabaw- ''plant''

Sem *ʾ*ab-/*ʾabaw-* ''water-lily'': Akk *abu*, Hbr *ʾēbe*, Arab *ʾabā-*.
Eg *ꜣbw* ''plant used in medicine'' (med).

7 *ʾa-biḳ- ''run (back)''

Sem *ʾ*Vbiḳ-* ''run away (of slaves)'': Arab *ʾbq* [*-i-*].
WCh **HVbaḳ-* ''return'': Ank *bak*.
The prefix is manifested by initial voiced *b-*. Note the irregular root vowel.
Omot **biḳ-* ''run away'': Ome *biḳ-ič-*.

Derived from HS **baḳ-/*buḳ-* ''run''.

8 *ʾabol- ''genitals''

Sem *ʾ*abal-* ''genitals'' [1], ''body'' [2]: Gz *ʾabāl* [1], Tgr *ḥabəl* [1], Tgy *abal* [2], Amh *abal* [1 2], Gur *abal* [1 2].

WCh *ḅwal- < *HVbwal- "penis": Bks ḅwel.
CCh *bwal- "penis": Bata *bolle*.

9 *ʾabun- "stone, millstone"

Sem *ʾabn- "stone": Akk *abn-*, Ug *ʾabn*, Hbr *ʾeben*, Pun *ʾbn*, Aram (Emp) *ʾbn*, (Syr) *ʾabnā*, (Mand) *abna*, Src *ʾabnaʾ*, SAr *ʾbn*, Soq *ʾoben*, Sha *ḥōbin*, Mhr *ḥaubīn*, Gz *ʾəbn*, Tgr *ʾəbn*, Tgy *ʾəmni*, Har *un*.
Eg *bnw.t* "stone, millstone" (MK).
No traces of the initial *ȝ-*.
WCh *ʾabun(i)- "millstone": Bol *buni*, Krk *buni*, Dera *buni*, Ngm *buni*, Krf *bini*, Ger *bini*, Glm *biin*, Grm *biŋni*, Wrj *vən-ay*, Paa *van-ka*, Mbu *avəna*.
Forms with *-i-* seem to have appeared under the influence of *-i-* in the last syllable. Otherwise WCh *ʾabun- /*ʾabin- should be reconstructed.
CCh *bun- < *ʾVbun- "millstone": Dgh *vra*, Mnd *uvra*, Log *funi*, Gid *buna*, ZBt *vəna*.
Rhotacism *-n- > -r- in Dgh and Mnd. Initial *v-* in individual languages reflects *ʾ-.

Status of *ʾa- is not quite clear. Presumably, it is a prefix not preserved in Eg. On the other hand, cf. HS *ʾab- suggesting a segmentation *ʾab-un-.

10 *ʾabVnan- "bird"

Sem *ʾabun(n)- "kind of bird": Akk *abbunnu*.
Eg *ȝbnn* "kind of bird" (NK).
ECh *bVnan- "duck": Ndm *bənan*.

Looks like a derivative of unattested *ʾabVn-. Sem *-u- may go back to HS *-a- after a labial.

11 *ʾa-cin-H- "leg, foot"

WCh *ʾacin-H- "leg": Gej *ašən*, Brw *asən*, Say *yasən*, Grn *ʾasaŋ*, Dwot *ʾazuŋ*, Buli *asin*, Wnd *ʾasən*, Tala *asən*.
The final cluster *-nH- or *-nVH- is normally reflected as *-ŋ-*.
CCh *Hasin- "knee": Hnk *šini*, FKi *šini*, Kap *γašine*.

Morpheme *-*H*- shifted to the beginning of the word and appearing as a prefix.

ECh *ʾ*[a]sin-H*- "leg":Mig ʾ*asin*, Jeg ʾ*isin-to*, Bid ʾ*eseeno*, Mubi *sin*, Brg ʾ*isiŋ*, Mkk *zina*.

Bid may go back to *ʾ*asiHVn*- with *-ee-* < *-*iHV*-.

Agaw **sin-H*- "calf": Bil *siŋ*.

HS *ʾ*a*- seems to be a prefix not preserved in Agaw. Note a potential Sem reflex in Arab ʾ*sn* "kick with a foot". Cf. **cin-*/**cun-* "leg"

12 *ʾacir- "bind, tie"

Sem *ʾ*Vsir*- "bind, join" ^{1}, "hobble" ^{2}: Akk *esêru* ^{1}, Ug ʾ*sr* ^{1}, Hbr ʾ*sr* ^{1}, Arab ʾ*sr* [-*i*-] ^{1}, Jib ʾ*esɔr* ^{2}, Hss *wesōr*, Mhr *wesōr*, Shh ʾ*ɛsor*.

CCh **ca-car*- "plait, weave" ^{1}, "tie" ^{2}: Mofu - *sasər*- ^{1}, Mafa *cacar* ^{2}.

Partial reduplication.

ECh **saʾir*- "tie": Tum *hīr*, Kbl *sa:rr*, Lele *saar*.

Metathesis.

HEC *ʾ*usur*- "tie": Sid *usur*-, Kmb *usur*-.

Unexpected *-*s*- and irregular vocalism.

13 *ʾač-/*ʾič- "meat"

CCh *ʾ*ič*- "flesh": Gis ʾ*iše*.

An isolated form. A Cush loanword?

Agaw *ʾ*Vč*- "meat": Aun *əšši*.

Omot *ʾ*ač*- "meat, body": Ome *ačo*, Mch ʾ*ačco*, Yam *ašaa*, Gim *ač*, Nao *aš-ku*, Shk *aš-ko*, Maji *ač-ku*.

Alternation **a* ~ **i*.

14 *ʾaĉVw-/*ʾaĉVy- "illness"

Sem *ʾ*aŝVy*- "kind of illness": Akk *ašû*.

Eg *ȝšy.t* "kind of illness" (med).

ECh *ʾ*VsVw*- "fever": Sok *osso*.

Assimilation of vowels.

The vowel of the second syllable may be **a*. The root displays an alternation of sonants **w* ~ **y*.

15 *ʾad- "skin, hide"

Bed *ada* "skin, hide".
SA **ʾad(d)-* "hide": Afar *adday*.
Mgg *ata* "bull hide".

The word is preserved only in Cush branches. However, cf. a possible derivative in HS **ʾadam-* attesting the HS status of the present root.

16 *ʾadam- "earth, field"

Sem **ʾadam-* "earth": Pun *ʾdmt* "country", Hbr *ʾ^a^dāmā*, Aram *ʾ^a^damtā*.
WCh **dam-* "place": Tng *tɔm*.
No traces of the initial laryngeal.
CCh **dam-* "field" [1], "place" [2]: Tera *dam* [1], Ngw *dama* [2].
May reflect an earlier **ʾadam-*. However, considering ECh data, we could reconstruct **daʾam* > **dam-*.
ECh **dVHVm-* "field": Mkk *doome*.
Mkk *-oo-* does not necessarily imply ECh **-wa-*. It may also go back to **-aHa-* or **-awa-*. Metathesis of the original **ʾadam-*.
HEC **ʾud(V)m-* "desert": Kmb *udmaʾa*.
A derivational and semantic variant of the original HS stem?

The alternative HS reconstruction is **daʾam-*.

17 *ʾadam- "skin"

Sem **ʾadam-/*ʾadīm-* "skin": Arab *ʾadam-*, *ʾadīm-*.
Probably related to Arab *ʾdm* "be brown".
WCh **ʾadam-* "skin": Tng *hadam*.
If not borrowed from Arab.

Derived from HS **ʾad-* "skin, hide". Cf. also LEC **ʾidim-* "tanned hide": Som *idin* (pl. *idmo*). It may continue **ʾadim-* with a regular change of Som *-m* > *-n* in the auslaut.

18 *ʾadar- "vessel"

Sem **ʾadar-* "metal vessel": Akk *adaru*.

WCh *ḍyar- < *dVHVr- ''pot'': Brm ḍer.
LEC *ʾadar- ''pot'': Som adar.

Cf. Eg ỉdꜣ ''expression related to the polishing of vessels'' (OK) < *ʾidVr-.

19 *ʾader- ''master, lord''

Sem *ʾadīr- ''majestic, powerful'': Ug ʾdr, Phn ʾdr, Pun ʾdr, Hbr ʾaddīr.
Agaw *ʾadir- ''master, lord'' [1], ''God'' [2]: Bil adäraa [1], Xmr iederaa, adäraa [2], Xmt adaraa [2], Kwr adarte [1], Kem adaraa [1 2].
LEC *ʾader- ''uncle'': Som adeer, Or adeeraa.
Rift *daʾar- ''chief'': Gor daari.
Metathesis.

Semantically, the HS word may go back to an adjective with a meaning similar to Sem.

20 *ʾadid- ''female relative''

ECh *ʾadid- ''daughter-in-law'': Kera adīdə.
LEC *ʾadad-/*ʾaded- ''aunt'': Som eddo, Or adada.
Presumably, Som eddo < ededo < adedo.
HEC *ʾadad- ''maternal aunt'': Sid adaada, Dar adaada.
Assimilation of vowels.
Wrz *ʾatit- ''elder sister'': Gaw ta-atite.

Cf. Sem *ʾad- ''lady'': Ug ʾdt, Phn ʾdt, Aram (Palm) ʾdt. A descriptive stem.

21 *ʾadil- ''dress''

Sem *ʾadīl- ''attire, garment'': Akk adīlu, Gz ʾadl.
*ʾa- may be a prefix.
Eg dꜣy ''coat'' (pyr).
Reflects an earlier *dil- (with *l > ꜣ).

An alternative reconstruction may be *dil-. A cultural (loan)word?

22 *ᵓadus- ''wall''

Sem *ᵓaduš- ''wall'': Akk *aduššu*.
CCh *ᵓadus- ''fence'' [1], ''town'' [2]: Gude *ēdsa* [1], LPe *duso* [2], Lame *mba-dušo* [2].

The anlaut in Gude reflects an intermediary stage of **yadus-* < **ᵓadus-*.

Cf. a corresponding verb in LEC **HVdis-* ''build'' (Boni *ḍis*)?

23 *ᵓaḫ- ''brother''

Sem *ᵓaḫ- ''brother'': Akk *aḫu*, Ug *ᵓaḫ*, Phn *ᵓḥ*, Pun *ᵓḥ*, Hbr *ᵓāḥ*, Aram (Epigr) *ᵓḥ*, (Syr) *ᵓaḥā*, (Mand) *aha*, Arab *ᵓaḫ-*, SAr *ᵓḫ*, Soq *ᵓaεḫa*, Mhr *ga*, Shr *(e)ga*, Gz *ᵓəḫəw*, Tgr *ḥu*, Har *əḥ*.
WCh *ᵓah(ya)- ''uncle'' [1], ''brother'' [2]: Klr *ahy-* [1], Wrj *yahə-* [2].
Initial *ya-* in Wrj reflects the influence of the second syllable.
CCh *ᵓaγ- ''son'': Msg *aḫī*.
Msg auslaut *-ī* may go back to **-ya*.

24 *ᵓaḫ- ''fire''

Eg *ꜣḫ.t* ''fire'' (BD).
CCH *ᵓaγ(u)- ''fire'': Bura *ᵓuᵓu*, Klb *huᵓu*, FKi *uγu*, Kus *ahu*, Gul *u*, Bud *au*, Mba *hū*.
Assimilation of vowels in several languages. In Gul, *u* goes back to **ᵓuγu-* with the consequent loss of the second syllable. Reduplication in Bura and Klb.

25 *ᵓaḫuƷ- ''take''

Sem *ᵓVḫuḏ- ''take'': Akk *aḫāzu*, Ug *ᵓḫd*, Hbr *ᵓḥz*, Moab *ᵓḥz*, Aram (Epigr) *ᵓḥd*, (Palest) *ᵓᵃḥad*, (Syr) *ᵓeḥad*, (Mand) *ahad*, Arab *ᵓḫḏ* [-*u*-], SAr *ᵓḫḏ*, Gz *ᵓḫz*, Amh *yazä*.
Agaw *ᵓaʒ- ''take'': Bil *ad-*, Kwr *az-*, Aun *as-*.
Reflexes of intervocalic **-ʒ-* in Agaw are extremely unstable. The intervocalic laryngeal is completely lost.
HEC *ᵓaḍ- < *ᵓaHVʒ- ''take'': Sid *aḍ-*.
Emphatic *-ḍ-* seems to reflect the lost laryngeal.

26 *ʾakür- ‘‘till’’

Sem *ʾ*Vkir-* ‘‘till’’: Aram (Syr) ʾ*akar*, (Mand) ʾ*kr*, Arab ʾ*kr* [-*i*-].
Sem *-*i*- indicates HS **e*, **i* or **ü*.
CCh **kur-* ‘‘hoe, prepare field for sewing’’: Mofu *kərw*, Lame *kura*.
Cf. Hwn *kūra* ‘‘hoe’’ (n.), Bnn *kawira* id., Zime *kura*.
ECh **kur-* ‘‘hoe’’: Jegu *kur-gees*.
The laryngeal left no traces.

Connected with HS *ʾ*ekar-* ‘‘farmer’’.

27 *ʾal- ‘‘fat’’

Sem **aly-* ‘‘fat tail (of sheep)’’ [1], ‘‘fat (of leg)’’: Hbr ʾ*alyā* [1], Aram (Palest) ʾ*alyᵉtā* [1], Arab ʾ*aly-at-* [2].
Cf. Akk *ellu* ‘‘sesame oil’’.
LEC *ʾ*al-*ʾ*al-* ‘‘fat’’ (n.): Or *alala*.
Reduplication.
Dhl ʾ*ahli* ‘‘fat, oil’’.
Note lateral -*hl*- reflecting HS *-*l*-!

Note the Rift form reflecting *-*ŝ*- (Kwz *aŝ-ito*) as Dhl.

28 *ʾal-/*ʾil- ‘‘be’’

Berb *ʾ*il-* ‘‘be, become’’: Izn *ili*, Snh *ili*, Tua *ili*.
LEC *ʾ*al-*/*ʾ*il-* ‘‘be’’: Som -*aal*, -*iil*.
CCh *ʾ*al-* ‘‘be’’: Mofu *ala*, Log *āli*, *li*.

Alternation **a* ~ **i*.

29 *ʾal-/*ʾul- ‘‘stick’’

Sem *ʾ*al-* ‘‘stick, club’’: Hbr ʾ*alā*.
WCh *ʾ*al-* ‘‘stick’’: Tng *ala*, *wala*, Bks *yal*.
Tng *w*- and Bks *y*- are occasional reflections of *ʾ- in the initial position.
LEC *ʾ*ul-* ‘‘stick’’: Som *ul*, Or *ulle*.
Wrz *ʾ*ul-* ‘‘stick’’: Gaw *ul-itte*.

Cf. SA *ʿ*il-* ‘‘stick’’ (Saho ʿ*iloo*, Afar ʿ*iloo*) with initial *ʿ-.

30 *ʾalač̣- "press"

Sem *ʾ*VlVṭ*- "drive" [1], "press close" [2]: Hbr ʾ*lṣ* [1], Aram (Syr) ʾ*elaṣ* [2].
WCh **laʾač̣*- "press": Hs *lāç̣a*, Tng *laḍ*-.
Metathesis.

Another possible reconstruction is **laʾač̣*-.

31 *ʾalan-/*ʾalun- "tree"

Sem *ʾ*alān*- "oak": Akk *allānu*, Hbr ʾ*allōn*.
WCh **lan*- "bush": DB *lan*.
The first syllable completely lost.
CCh **luʾan*- "tree": Mba *luŋ*, Msg *lūŋ*, pl. *lūaŋai*.
Metathesis. Cf. also a partial reduplication in **lalan-H*- "kind of tree": Mofu *lalaŋ*.

Related to *ʾ*al*-/*ʾ*ul*- "stick"?

32 *ʾalVk- "bite, chew"

Sem *ʾ*VlVk*- "bite, champ (the bit)": Arab ʾ*lk*.
Bed ʾ*ayəkʷ*- "chew".
Note intervocalic *-*l*- > -*y*-. The labiovelar may reflect a back vowel in the second syllable.

Related to *ʾ*ilik*- "tooth".

33 *ʾam- "arm"

Sem *ʾ*am(m)*- "elbow": Akk *ammatu*, Ug ʾ*amt*, Hbr ʾ*ammā*, Aram (Epigr) ʾ*mh*, (Syr) ʾ*ama*, ʾ*amta*, (Mand) *ama*, SAr ʾ*mt*, Gz ʾ*əmmat*, Tgr ʾ*ammat*.
WCh *ʾ*am*- "arm": Bgh *am-ŝi*, Kir *wam*, Pol *am*, Geji *wom-ẑi*, Ngz *amai*.
Kir *wa*- indicated a rounded vowel of the second syllable.

Related to *ʾ*am*- "catch, seize" (for the semantic development cf., for example, Lith *ranka* "hand" ~ *rinkti* "grasp, seize").

34 *ʾam- ''woman''

Sem **ʾam-* ''maid, girl'': Akk *amtu*, Ug *ʾamt*, Phn *ʾmt*, Pun *ʾmt*, Hbr *ʾāmā*, Aram (Emp) *ʾmh*, (Syr, Palest) *ʾamtā*, (Mand) *amta*, *amuta*, Arab *ʾam-at-*, Gz *ʾamat*, Tgr *ʾamät*.

WCh **ʾam-* ''woman'': Wrj *amai*, Kry *am*, Diri *am*, Cagu *omey*, Jmb *ama*, Sha *ʾamuy*, Ngz *ama*.

Cagu *o-* < **a-* before a labial.

HEC **ʾam-* ''mother, wife, woman'': Sid *ama*, Had *ama*, Dar *ama*, Bmb *aama*, Kmb *ama-ta*.

Rift **ʾam-* ''grandmother'' [1], ''sister'' [2], ''mother'' [3], ''girl'' [4]: Irq *ama* [1], Bur *ama* [2], Kwz *ama* [3], Asa *ʾama-ʾeto* [4], *ʾamama* [1].

Onomatopoeia.

35 *ʾam- ''catch, seize''

Eg *ꜣmm* ''catch, seize'' (pyr).

Partial reduplication.

CCh **ʾam-/*ʾim-* ''catch, seize'': Tera *ōom*, Msg *ima*, *ime*.

Tera indicates **Hwa-ʾam-*. The original form must have been **ʾam-*.

ECh **ʾam-* ''catch'': Lele *ōm*, Kbl *am*.

Lele *ō-* either reflects **-a-* before a labial or goes back to **Hwa-ʾa-* as in Tera, see CCh.

Related to **ʾam-* ''hand, arm''.

36 *ʾamam- ''honey''

Sem **ʾamūm-* ''kind of spice'': Akk *amūmu*.

Secondary **-ū-* influenced by surrounding labials.

Berb **ʾamVm-* ''honey'': Izn *ṭammemṭ*.

CCh **ʾamam-* ''honey'': Bld *ʾamam*, Mofu *amam*, Glv *məma*, Gvo *mama*, Mnd *nama*, Mrg *mumu*.

Root vowel in Mrg assimilated to the auslaut.

Probably, a reduplication of a root preserved in ECh **ʾim-/*ʾum-* ''bee, honey'': Mubi *ūm*, Jegu *ʾimo*, Brg *imiyu*.

37 *ʾaman- ''believe, know''

Sem **ʾVman-* ''be certain, believe'': Hbr *ʾmn*, Aram (Palest) *hēmīn*,

Arab *ʾmn* [*-a-*], Shr *ōmen*, Mhr *hāmōn*, Hss *ʾāmōn*.
Related are SAr *hʾmn* "confide", Sab *ʾmn* "belief", Jib *ʾun*.
WCh **ʾaman-* "know": Sura *man*, Ang *man*, Ank *man*, Tal *āman*, Mnt *man*, Maha *monayo*, Bol *mon-*.
The first syllable is preserved only in Tal.
Agaw **ʾamVn-* "believe": Aun *amn-əŋ*.
Borrowed from Sem?
Wrz **ʾemen-* "see": Cam *emena*.
Secondary vocalism.

38 *ʾamas- "darkness, evening"

Sem **ʾamš-* "night" [1], "evening" [2]: Akk *mūšu* [1], Hbr *ʾemeš* [2], Arab *ʾams-* [2].
Cf. also Akk *amšali* "yesterday", Hss *yemši* id., Mhr *yemši* id.
CCh **mVs-* "shadow": Gudu *məšü*.
From **ʾVmVs-*.
Bed *amas* "late evening".
Borrowing from Sem?
Rift **ʾamas-* "middle of the night" [1], "tomorrow" [2]: Irq *əmsi* [1], Gor *amsi* [1], Alg *amasi* [1], Bur *amasi* [1], Kwz *amasiya* [2].
Borrowing from Sem?

39 *ʾambür- "termite"

CCh **mVbur-* "termite": Gude *mubəra*, Bch *mburey*, Mwu *muburu*, FG *mbur-tə*, FJb *mubəle*.
-u- in Gude and Mwu may be influenced by the initial *m-*.
Bed *embira* "termite".
In the anlaut, *e-* is due to the influence of the following vowel.
LEC **ʾabor-* "termites": Som *aboor*.
HS **-mb-* > LEC **-b-*, cf. LEC in HS **ʾanbab-/*ʾanbib-* "plant, flower". LEC **-o-* is a regular reflex of HS **- ü-*.

As in a few other cases initial **ʾam-* in Cush corresponds to Chadic **mV-*, **ma-*. There are serious reasons to believe that both Cush **ʾam-* and Chadic **ma-* are prefixes going back to the same HS source. The alternative HS reconstruction is **mabür-*.

40 *ʾan- "speak"

Berb *ʾVn- "say, tell": Izn *ini*, Snh *ini*.
WCh *ʾan- "speak": Ngm *aŋ*.
In fact, the WCh prototype must be reconstructed as *ʾan-H- with a non-etymological laryngeal suffix.
ECh *ʾan- "speak": Ndm *ane*, Kwn *ane*, Dng *ane*.
Related to Kwn *ə:ne* "argue"?
Bed *an-* "say".

Related to Sem *ʾVn- "moan" (Arab *ʾnn* and the like)?

41 *ʾan- "go, walk"

WCh *ʾanwa- "go": Bol *ʾon-*, DB *wan-*.
CCh *ʾan- "return": Heba *anu*.
ECh *ʾVnwa- "come, enter": Mkk *ʾinn-*, Jeg *ʾony-*, *ʾəny-*, Mig *ʾunyo-*.
Mig and Jegu reflect initial *ʾwa-.
LEC *ʾan- "walk": Kns *anna*.
Omot *ʾan-H-"go": Ome *aŋ-*.
No external justification for the laryngeal in the auslaut.

42 *ʾan-/*ʾayin- "sheep"

Berb *ʾan- "sheep": Gua *ana*, *haña*.
WCh *yān- < *ʾyayVn- "she-goat": Siri *yāni*.
Contraction.
ECh *ʾayin- "goat": Mig *ʾīnu*, Brg *ʾayney*, Jegu *ʾēn* (pl.).
Bed *ano* "sheep".

Berb and Bed seem to reflect HS *ʾan-. Note the root-variant with an inlaut sonant.

43 *ʾanbab- "plant, flower"

Sem *ʾanbūb- "reed": Akk *embūbu*, NHbr *ʾabbūb*, *ʾibbūb*, Aram (Syr) *ʾabbūbā*, Arab *ʾanbūb-*.
Tgr *ʿəmbobā* and the like are borrowed from Cush. In the second syllable, *-ū- is explained by the influence of surrounding labials.
WCh *ʾanbVb- "flower": Pero *anbibi*.

Secondary vocalism of the second syllable influenced by final *-i*.
Agaw **ʾambab-* "flower": Bil *amboobaa*, Kem *ambaab*.
Bil *-oo-* < **-a-* in the contact with labials.
LEC **abab-* "kind of flower": Som *ababo*.
Lack of nasalization may be a result of later change **-nb-* > **-b-* or, on the contrary, an archaic feature.

Unusual root structure with a prenasalized *-C²-*.

44 *ʾankol- "liver, kidneys"

ECh **ʾakwal-* "liver": Brg *ʾokolo*.
Note **-nk-* > ECh **-k-*. Assimilation of vowels.
Bed *ʾənkʷelʾa* "kidneys".

Prefix **ʾa-/*ʾan-*. Related to **kul-* "kidney".

45 *ʾantuʾ-/*ʾantaw- "mouse, rat"

CCh **manduwa-* < **ma-ʾanduwa-* "rat": Gis *monduwa-ŋ*, Mtk *muduwa*, Mkt *madawa*.
Prefix **ma-*.
SA **ʾandaw-* "mouse, rat": Saho *andɔwa*, Afar *andawaa*.
LEC **ʾantu-* "mouse": Or *antu-ta*.

Voiced *d* of CCh and SA are not regular correspondences of LEC *t*. However, **-nt-* seems to be a more probable reconstruction. The variants of the auslaut are reminiscent of usual alternations of ʾ ~ *w* ~ *y*. A cultural term with an irregular phonology.

46 *ʾap- "mouth"

Sem **ʾanp-* "nose": Hbr *ʾāp*, Aram (Syr) *ʾa(n)pā*, Arab *ʾanf-*.
Consonantal assimilation in Hbr. Secondary assimilation and change of meaning on the Semitic level.
Bed *yaaf* "mouth".
Prothetic *y-*.Cf. HS **ʾap-/*wap-* "yawn, open mouth"?
Agaw **ʾaff-* "mouth": Bil *ʾäb*, Kwr *af*.
Bil *-b-* is believed to reflect an unvoiced geminate.
SA **ʾaf-* "mouth": Saho *af*, Afar *af*.

LEC *ʾ*af-* "mouth": Som *af*, Or *af-an*, Rnd *af*, Arb *oho*, Gel *aaf*, Kns *afa*.
HEC *ʾ*af-* "mouth": Sid *afo*, Dar *afaʾo*, Had *afoʾo*, Ala *afo*, Bmb *afay*, Kmb *afo*.
Dhl *afo* "mouth".
Omot *ʾ*af-*/*ʾ*ap-* "mouth": Dime *ʾappo*, Gll *afa*, Ari *aaffa*, Ban *aapo*, Hmr *a(a)fo*.
Rift *ʾ*af-* "mouth": Irq *afa*, Alg *aafa*, Bur *aafa*, Asa *ʾaf-ok*, Kwz *ʾafu-ko*.

Related to *ʾ*ap-*/**wap-* "yawn, open mouth".

47 *ʾap-/*wap- "yawn, open mouth"

Eg *wp*, *wpy* "open (mouth)".
WCh *ʾ*ap-* "throw into the mouth" [1], "yawn" [2]: Hs *afa* [1], Sura *ap* [2], Ang *ep* [2].

Note a consonantal alternation in the anlaut. If the present stem is *not* related to the HS word for "mouth", it may be compared with HEC *ʾ*af-*/*ʾ*if-* "spread (in the sun)": Bmb *af-*, Kmb *if-is-*.

48 *ʾaq- "field"

Sem *ʾ*aḫ-* "meadow": Ug *ʾaḫ*.
Eg *ꜣḫ.t* "fertile land" (NK).
ECh *ʾ*ak-* "field": Kera *aka*.
ECh *-*k*- is a regular reflex of HS *-*q*-.

49 *ʾar- "husband"

Sem *ʾ*aray-* "family member, relative": Ug *ʾary*, Arab *ʾarā-*.
Agaw *ʾ*ar-* "husband": Aun *ŋ-ära*.
Prefix ŋ-.
HEC *ʾ*ar-* "husband": Sid *aroo*, Had *aroʾo*, Dar *aroʾo*.
Omot *ʾ*ar-* "husband": Anf *aroo*.
Borrowing from Sid?

50 *ʾar- "ram, goat"

Berb **ʾar-* "she-goat": Gua *ara*.
LEC **ʾar-* "sheep": Boni *eriya*, Rnd *ari*.
Cf. Arb *ʾaar* "bull".
HEC **ʾaray-* "sheep" (pl.): Bmb *araay*.
Rift **ʾar-* "goat": Irq *ari*, Alg *ara* (pl.), Bur *ara* (pl.), Kwz *ali-to*.
Note Kwz *-l-* < **-r-*.

Cf. also WCh **ʾar-* "meat": Dera *ara*.

51 *ʾar- "vegetable"

Sem **ʾār-* "greens, vegetables": Ug *ʾar-t*, Hbr *ʾōrā*.
WCh **ʾar-* "vegetable": Pero *ara*.

52 *ʾar-/*war- "eagle"

Sem **ʾarVw-* "eagle": Akk *arû*.
WCh **war-* "sea-eagle": Hs *wāra*.
CCh **war-* "kite": HNk *wəri*, HGh *wəri*, HF *wari*, Kap *wəri*.

A consonantal alternation **ʾ-* ~ **w-* in the anlaut.

53 *ʾaram- "enclosed dwelling"

Sem **ʾaramm-* "dam" ¹, "road" ²: Akk *ʾarammu* ¹, Hss *wōrem* ².
Cf. a derivative in Hbr *ʾarmōn* "fortress, palace".
Berb **rVm-* "town, village": Ahg *a-rrem*.
Complete loss of the first syllable.
WCh **ram-* "land, place" ¹, "town, village" ²: Bks *ram* ¹, Sha *ram* ², Klr *ram* ².
No traces of the initial laryngeal.
CCh **ʾVrVm-* "house": Ngw *ərəma*.

54 *ʾariĉ- "earth"

Sem **ʾarŝ-* "earth": Akk *erṣetu*, Ug *ʾarṣ*, Phn *ʾrṣ*, Pun *ʾrṣ*, Moab *ʾrṣ*, Hbr *ʾereṣ*, Aram (Emp) *ʾrq*, (Nab, Palm) *ʾrʿ*, (Bibl) *ʾᵃraʿ*, (Palest, Syr) *ʾarʿō*, (Mand) *arqa*, *arda*, Arab *ʾarḍ-*, SAr *ʾrḍ*, Jib *ʾɛrḍ*.
WCh **HVriĉ-* "earth": Paa *riŝa*, Cagu *hīŝe*, Siri *rəŝu*, Mbu *riŝi*.
ECh **ʾiraĉ-* "valley": Bid *ʾiraaḍya*.

Metathesis of vowels.

May be connected with HEC *ʾirVš- "farm" (Sid irša) and Agaw *ʾaris- "till, plough" (Aun ares-əŋ).

55 *ʾariw- "metal"

Sem *ʾVrVw- "copper": Akk werû, erû.
CCh *ʾariy- "iron": Bld ʾariya, Mnd ʾire.
CCh *-iwa- > -iya-.
ECh *ʾaraw- "iron": Jegu ʾarro.
Assimilation of vowels.

56 *ʾa-ruw-/*ʾa-ruy- "lion"

Sem *ʾarway-/*ʾarwiy- "lion" 1, "ferocious animal, beast" 2: Hbr ʾᵃrī, ʾaryē 1, Aram (Palm) ʾryʾ 1, (Bibl, Syr) ʾaryō 1, (Mand) arya 1, Gz ʾarwē 2.
Derived from *ʾarw-. Cf. Arab ʾarwīy-at- "wild sheep"?
Eg rw "lion" (pyr).
Probably, a form without prefix reflecting *ruw-.
CCh *ʾVruw- "hyaena" 1, "lion" 2:FKi řu 1, Mwu řu 1, Mnd ʾuruw-vəri 2, FJl luwi 1.
In Mnd -u- of the 1st syllable was influenced by the next vowel. FKi and Mwu may go back directly to *ruw- < HS *ruw- and correspond exactly to Eg rw.
ECh *ʾaruw- "leopard" 1, "lion" 2: Tum ərəw 1, Mubi orūwa 2.
Mubi o- is influenced by the following vowel.
LEC *ʾar- "lion": Som ar.
Cf. also Som awr "he-camel", Rnd or id. < *ʾawr-?

*ʾa- seems to be a prefix that is not reflected (or not preserved?) in Eg and, partially, in CCh.

57 *ʾarVḫ̮- "cattle"

Sem *ʾarḫ̮- "kind of cattle": Akk arḫ̮u, Ug ʾarḫ̮, Tgr ʾarḥi, Tgy ʾarḥi.
HEC *ʾar(H)- "calf": Bmb aʾre.
The function of inlaut -ʾ- is not clear.

Related to HS *raḫ̮il- "sheep, ram"? Cf. Eg ȝḫ̮.t "divine cow, priestess" (gr).

58 *ᵓas- "seize, grasp"

Sem *ᵓ*Všš*- "grasp": Akk *ašāšu*.
WCh *ᵓ*as*- "take away": Kr ᵓ*as*.
CCh **sVy*- "seize": Klb *asiya*.
Derivative of **si*-?

59 *ᵓas- "come"

Berb *ᵓ*Vs*- "arrive": Tua *as*, Kby *as*.
WCh *ᵓ*as*-/*ᵓ*is*- "come": Gwn *iso*, Bks *yes*, DB *yes*.
Bks and DB *y*- may go back to *ᵓ-.
ECh *ᵓ*as*- "come": Dng *ase*, Jnk ᵓ*asso*, Jegu ᵓ*as*, Brg ᵓ*asi*, Bid ᵓ*aseŋ*.
Wrz *ᵓ*as*- "go": Gaw *ašš*-.

60 *ᵓaseᵓ- "iron"

Sem *ᵓ*ašiᵓ*- "iron": Akk *ašiu*.
CCh **siᵓ*- "iron": Glf *siu*, Bud *hyu*.
The initial laryngeal lost.
ECh **syay*- < **syaᵓ*- "iron": Lele *sayu*, Mubi *ma-siyo*.
Prefix **ma*- in Mubi.

61 *ᵓaŝ- "send"

Sem *ᵓ*VŝVy*- "send": SAr ᵓ*śy*.
HEC *ᵓ*as(s)*- "send": Had *ass-eᵓ*-.
Derivative in -ᵓ*e*-.

62 *ᵓaŝaf- "burning"

Eg *išf* "burn" (XX), "be painful" (n).
Unexpected *i*- before a non-palatal vowel as in some other cases.
WCh **ŝaᵓaf*- "heat, pain": Hs *zāfī*.
Metathesis.

Reconstruction **ŝaᵓaf*- is also possible.

63 *ʾat- "walk, come"

Sem **ʾVt-* "come" ^{1}, "pass" ^{2}, "come back" ^{3}: Ug *ʾatw* ^{1}, Hbr *ʾty* ^{1}, Aram (Emp) *ʾty* ^{1}, (Nab) *yʾtʾ* ^{1}, (Palm) *ʾtʾ* ^{1}, (Palest) *ʾ^{a}tā* ^{1}, (Syr) *ʾeta* ^{1}, (Mand) *ata* ^{1}, Arab *ʾty* ^{1}, SAr *ʾtw*, *ʾty* ^{1}, Soq *ʾete* ^{2}, Gz *ʾatawa* ^{3}, Tgy *ʾatawa* ^{3}, Tgr *ʾata* ^{3}.

Various derivations of the original **ʾVt-* using *w*, *y* and ʾ as C^3.

WCh **ʾat-* "ride": Bks *ʾat*.

Bed *ʾat-* "tread".

SA **ʿat-* "tread": Afar *ʿat-*.

Irregular ʿ-.

Omot **ʾat-* "come": Gim *at-*.

64 *ʾawan-/*ʾawin- "time"

Sem **ʾawān-* "time, moment, season": Arab *ʾawān-* .

Cf. also secondary morphonological variants *ʾān-* id., *ʾiwān-* id.

WCh **win-* "evening time" ^{1}, "day" ^{2}: Tng *wini* ^{1}, Ngz *wəna* ^{2}.

The initial laryngeal lost.

CCh **wan-* "year": Nza *wane*, Mwl *wan-ti*, Bch *wan-to*.

No traces of the initial laryngeal.

HEC **ʾawin-* "month, moon": Bmb *awin-co*.

Wrz **ʾawVn-* "evening": Gaw *awne*.

Since CCh might have lost **ʾa-* for phonetic reasons, it is not clear if it is a prefix or a part of the root. Is their any connection with Agaw **ʾiman-* "time" (Bil *emaanaa*), SA **ʾaman-* id. (Saho *amaana*) and LEC **ʾamin-* id. (Som *amin*)?

65 *ʾay- "come, run"

Sem **ʾīʾ-* "go and stay": Arab *ʾyʾ*.

Based on **ʾVy-*.

Berb **ʾVy-* "come": Tua *ayu*.

ECh **ʾaw-/*ʾay-* "go" ^{1}, "gallop" ^{2}: Ndm *ao* ^{1}, Sbn *ʾaya* ^{2}.

An ancient morphonological variant **ʾaw-* preserved only in ECh?

Bed *ee-* "come".

From **ʾay-*.

HEC **ʾe-* "enter": Sid *ʾe-*.

From **ʾay-*.

Omot *ʾ*ay*- ''come'': Omet *ai*.

In Bed and HEC development *-ay- > *-e- seems to be possible. Is there any connection between *ʾ*ay*- and *ʾ*a*- ''walk, go''?

66 *ʾayal- ''deer''

Sem *ʾ*ayal*- ''deer, ibex'': Ug *ʾayl*, Pun *ʾyl*, Hbr *ʾayyāl*, Aram (Emp) *ʾylʾ*, (Palest) *ʾayyālā*, (Syr) *ʾaylā*, (Mand) *ayala*, *ayla*, SAr *ʾyl*, Arab *ʾayyil-*, *ʾiyyal-*, Gz *hayyal*.

Eg *ỉyr* ''deer'' (l), Dem *ʾywr* id., Copt *ʾ*eyul*: Boh *eoul*, Shd *(e)eioul*. Borrowed from Sem?

LEC *ʾ*ēl*- < *ʾ*ayVl*- ''gazelle'': Som *eelo*.

Dhl *ʾeele* ''hartebeest''.

From *ʾ*ayal*-.

Cf. HEC *ʾ*ayan*- ''gazelle'' (Bmb *ayaane*) and SA *ʾ*al*- ''goats (coll.), she-goat'' (Saho *ala*, Afar *alaa*).

67 *ʾa-yil- ''ram, sheep''

Sem *ʾ*ayil*- ''mythological bull'' 1, ''ram'' 2: Akk *ʾâlu* 1, Ug *ʾil* 2, Phn (pl.) *ʾlm* 2, Hbr *ʾayil* 2.

Berb **yil-*/*ʾ*il*- ''sheep'': Nfs *t-ili*, Sml *t-ili*.

SA **yil-*/*ʾ*il*- ''sheep'': Saho *ille*, *illi*, Afar *ille*, *illi*.

Though a phonetic process leading to the loss of *ʾ*a*- is not excluded, *ʾ*a*- is, more probably, a prefix. The connection with *ʾ*ayal*- ''deer'' is problematic.

68 *ʾayVm- ''snake''

Sem *ʾ*aym*- ''snake'': Arab *ʾaym-*.

WCh *ʾ*am*- ''python'': Klr *ʾamo*.

WCh *ʾ*am*- < *ʾ*aym*- as *ʾ*ac*- ''dog'' < *ʾ*awc*- (see WCh *ʾ*aw[a]c*- ''dog, wolf''). This type of development may reflect a specific variety of roots with no vowel between C^2 and C^3.

69 *ʾekam- ''mountain''

Sem *ʾ*akam*- ''hill'': Arab *ʾakam-at-*.

Assimilation of vowels *ᵓakam- < *ᵓikam-.
WCh *kyaᵓam- "mountain": Bgh kyaam.
  Metathesis.

The alternative HS reconstruction is *keᵓam-.

70 *ᵓekar- "farmer"

Sem *ᵓikkar- "farmer, plougher": Akk ᵓikkar-, Hbr ᵓikkār, Aram
(Syr) ᵓakārā, Arab ᵓakkar-.
  Assimilation of vowels in Aram and Arab. An alleged Sum
  loanword in Sem.
Eg ꜣkr "Earth-god" (a).
  Initial ꜣ- makes the reconstruction of *e more probable.
  Semantically, "Earth-god" ← "plougher". Semitic loan-
  word?

The root is etymologically connected with HS *ᵓakür- "till".

71 *ᵓel- "leather sack"

Sem *ᵓil- "leather sack": Akk īlu.
WCh *ᵓal-ay- < *ᵓyal-ay- "skin bottle used as an oil container": Hs
ālāya.

72 *ᵓem- "be hot, burn"

Eg ꜣm, iꜣm "burn" (pyr).
  No palatalization of ꜣ-.
WCh *ᵓyam- "hot": Ngm yam.

73 *ᵓen- "child"

WCh *ᵓyan- "boy": Grk a-yan.
  Prefix a- in Grk.
LEC *ᵓin- "child": Kon ina.

74 *ᵓer- "tongue"

LEC *ᵓer- "tongue": Gel ɛre.
Mgg erei "tongue".

Omo *ʾ*er-* "tongue": Anf *ɛrii-co*.

Although this stem is present only in Cush, its derivatives are found elsewhere and, therefore, it is treated as a HS archaism.

75 *ʾer- "see, know"

ECh *ʾ*yar-* "see": Smr *yēro*, Sbn *yara*.
Bed *iray-*, *iree* "see".
Agaw *ʾ*ar(V)ʾ-* "know": Bil *arʾ-*.
The source of -ʾ- is not clear. Note *-*a*- in the root.
Wrz *ʾ*ar-* "know": War *aʾaari*, Gaw *ara*, Gob *ʾaar*, Cam *ara*, Hss *ar-*, Dob *ar-*, Gll *ar-*.
Secondary *-*a*-.
Omot *ʾ*er-* "know": Ome *ʾer-*, *ɛrɛ*, Mch *ari(hä)*, Anf *ɛrri*, Gim *ɛrr-*, *era*.
Rift *ʾ*ar-* "see": Irq *ara*, Alg *ar-*, Bur *ar-im-*.
Secondary *-*a*-.

Related to HS *ʾ*ir-* "eye"? Some of the above forms may reflect HS *ʾ*ar-*.

76 *ʾer- "woman"

Eg *ỉrw.t* "women" (pyr).
ECh *ʾ*yar-* "woman": Mkk *ʾere*, *ʾerowo*.

Probably related to LEC *ʾ*or-* "wife": Som *oori*. If Mkk *ʾerowo* goes back to ECh *ʾ*yaraw-*, one could think of HS *ʾ*eraw-* as a prototype of both Eg and ECh.

77 *ʾer- "tremble"

Sem *ʾ*Vr-* "tremble": Akk *arāru*, *ḫarāru*.
ECh *ʾ*yar-* "tremble": Tob *yore*.

78 *ʾerar- "container"

Eg *ỉrr* "vessel" (n).
ỉ- reflects a front vowel.
LEC *ʾ*arar-* "basket": Arb *ʾarar*.
Assimilation of vowels.

79 *ᵓeray- "word, speech"

WCh **ᵓyaray-* "language": Hs *yārē*.
LEC **ᵓeray-* "word, speech": Som *ᵓeeray*, *ᶜeeray*.

Derived from **ᵓer-* "tongue".

80 *ᵓerib- "sew, tie"

Sem **ᵓVrib-* "tie (a knot)": Arab *ᵓrb* [-*i*-].
WCh **rVHib-* > **riḅ-* "sew": Wnd *rip*, Zaar *ri:p*, Pol *reḅ-in*, Dwot *rip*.
ECh **ᵓVrVb-* "sew" [1], "untie" [2]: Brg *ᵓorbi* [1], Tum *ərəb* [2].
Brg *-o-* is secondary.
SA **rib-* "sew": Saho *rib*, Afar *rib*.
LEC **ᵓerVb-* "sew": Or *erba*.

81 *ᵓerin- "tongue"

CCh **ᵓirVn-* "tongue": Gis *ᵓirne*, Mtk *ᵓərne*, Mofu *ᵓərne*.
Probably, from an earlier **ᵓyarin-*?
Omot **ᵓeren-* "tongue": Ome *eren-šaa*.
Assimilation of vowels, from **ᵓerin-*.

Derived from HS **ᵓer-* "tongue".

82 *ᵓes- "fire"

Sem **ᵓiš-* "fire": Akk *ᵓišat-*, Ug *ᵓišt*, Hbr *ᵓeš*, Phn *ᵓš*, Aram (Emp) *ᵓšh*, (Bibl) *ᵓeššā*, (Palest) *ᵓiššātā*, (Mand) *ᶜšᵓtᵓ*, Gz *ᵓəsat*, Tgr *ᵓəsat*, Amh *əsat*.
Berb **HVs-* "big fire": Ahg *a-həs*.
WCh **ᵓyas-* "fire": Ang *wus*, Chip *wus*, Ank *wuss*, Grk *wus*, Bol *osi*, Krk *yasi*, Ngm *yasi*, Maha *woši*, Bele *ihi*, Krf *wūšī*, Gera *wusi*, Glm *wuši*, Grm *uši*, Gej *iši*, Klr *waše*.
Forms in **w-* are not clear. Contamination with **wuŝ-* "roast"?
ECh **ᵓis-* "fire": Brg *ᵓissi*.
Probably, from an earlier **ᵓyasi-*.

Cf. Rift **ᵓaŝ-* "fire" (Irq *aŝa*, Gor *aŝa*, Alg *aŝa*, Bur *aŝa*) with a lateral **-ŝ-*. An alternative reconstruction of the HS word for "fire" may be based on the fact of *wi-* pattern forbidden in Sem. If initial HS **wi-* (or **we-*) yielded to Sem *ʾ*i-*, it could also explain dubious WCh forms in **w-* .

83 *ʾet- "eat"

WCh *ʾ*yat-* "eat": Fyer ʾ*et*.
HEC *ʾ*it-* "eat": Sid *it-*, Bmb *it-*.

84 *ʾew- "be old"

Eg *iꜣwy* "be old" (OK).
-ꜣ- and *-y* are a joint reflection of **e*.
ECh *ʾ*yaw-* "be old": Sbn *yə*, Kera *hiwi*, Mobu *yewe*.

Another possibility should be considered if Eg *-ꜣ-* goes back to HS **r*. In this case, comparison with CCh *ʾ*ir-* "old" (Mw *i*ʾ*iri*, Bch ʾ*iyrey* and the like) leads to the reconstruction of HS *ʾ*ir-* "be old".

85 *ʾi- "time, period of time"

Eg *ꜣ.t* "time" (MK).
Cf. *iꜣ.t* "moment of time" reflecting a front vowel.
WCh **yi-* < *ʾ*i-* "year" [1], "time" [2]: Ang *yi-* [1], Mnt *yi* [2], Grk *yi* [1].

Any relation to HS *ʾ*i(w)-* "be, become"?

86 *ʾib- "thirst"

Eg *ib.t* "thirst" (pyr), Copt *ʾ*ibi* id.: Fym *ibi*, Ahm *eibe*, Bhm *ibi*, Shd *eibe*.
WCh **yib-* < *ʾ*ib-* "thirst": Bgh *yip*, Kir *yip*.
Secondary *y-* reflecting *ʾ- before a front vowel.

Cf. Arab ʾ*bb* [*-u-*] "desire"?

87 *ʾibad- "lose, be lost"

Sem *ʾ*VbVd-* "lose, be lost": Ug ʾ*bd*, Phn *y*ʾ*bd*, Hbr ʾ*bd*, Aram (Epigr) ʾ*bd*, (Palest) ʾ*ᵃbad*, (Mand) *abad*.
CCh **bidVH-* "lose": Zime *viḍi*.

SA **bad-* "perish, be extinguished": Saho *bad-*, Afar *baad-*.
No traces of the initial syllable.
LEC **bad-* "be lost": Or *bad-*, Gel *bad-*.
No traces of the initial syllable.
Wrz **pat-* "get lost, disappear": Gaw *pat-*, Hss *pat-*, Gol *pat-*.
No traces of the initial syllable.

88 *ʾibaq- "insect"

Sem **ʾibẖ-* "kind of bug": Akk *ibẖu*.
Berb **baγ-* "insect": Izy *aβaẖẖu*.
Irregular reflex of **-q-*.
ECh **bag-* "locust" [1], "cricket" [2], "spider" [3]: Jegu *bago* [1], Bid *bago* [2], Kbl *bagəbagə* [3].

89 *ʾiben- "sleep"

Eg *ỉbꜣn* "sleep" (pyr).
Eg *ỉ-* indicates HS **ʾe-* or **ʾi-*. Note intervocalic *-ꜣ-* reflecting a middle vowel.
CCh **HVbyan-* "sleep": Boka *ḅweni*, Hwn *ḅena*.
In Boka *-we-* < *-ya-* after a labial.

Since HS **ʾeben-* is hardly possible from the point of view of the vowel pattern, **ʾiben-* remains the only tenable reconstruction.

90 *ʾi-bil- "camel, donkey"

Sem **ʾib(i)l-* "camel": Arab *ʾibil-*, *ʾibl-*, SAr *ʾbl*, Hss *ḥe-ybīt*, Mhr *ḥe-ybīt*, Shh *yit*.
ECh **bil-* "donkey": Lele *bila-he*.
The first syllable left no traces.

The initial **ʾi-* is either a prefix (preserved only in Sem), or a part of the root (lost in ECh for phonetic reasons). In the anlaut HS **ʾe-* is also possible.

91 *ʾic- "tooth"

WCh **ḥa-ʾic-* "tooth": Ang *ās*, Chip *ʾaγas*, Mnt *γəəs*, Ank *hag-has*, Grk *γas*, Bol *udo*, Krk *wudo*, Tng *wudo*, Dera *wuro*, Ngm *udo*,

Maha *udo*, Krf *iččo*, Gera *waša*, Glm *yiizu*, Grm *očoŋ*, Mpn *ōs*.
Prefix **ḥa-*. Note some difficult forms with initial *w-*, cf. our notes to **ʾes-* "fire".
HEC **ʾis-* "tooth": Dar *isso*.
Omot **ʾic-* "tooth": Dime *iicu*.

92 *ʾicay- "be sad, be angry"

Sem **ʾVsay-* "be sad": Arab *ʾsy* [*-a-*].
For Sem **-s-* cf. a derivative in Hbr *ʾās-ōn* "misfortune".
ECh **ʾisVy-* "bad": Lele *isiya*.
-iya may be a Lele suffix.

93 *ʾid- "eye"

WCh **ʾid-* "eye": Hs *ido*, Sura *yit*, Ang *yit*, *yid*, Mnt *yit*, Ank *has-yid*, Grk *yit*, Bol *ʾido*, Krk *ʾido*, Dera *yero*, Tng *idu*, Ngm *ido*, Maha *ida*, Bele *ido*, Krf *iro*, Gera *iiḍi*, Glm *iirya*, Grm *ida*, Diri *adō*, Jmb *ida*, Ngz *da*.
Some forms with *-r-* may go back to HS **ʾir-* "eye" as well.
CCh **ʾid-* "eye": Tera *idi*, Nza *di*.
ECh **ʾid-/*ʾud-* "eye": Dng *udā*, Mig *ʾiḍe*, Jeg *ʾude*, Sok *id-*.
ECh **ʾud-* < **ʾidu-* or a trace of an apophony?

Although this root is preserved only in Chadic, its derivatives also occur in Cush, see HS **ʾind-* "eye" and we may, therefore, consider it as a HS archaism.

94 *ʾigan- "vessel"

Sem **ʾigān-* "cup, bowl": Akk *agannu*, Hbr *ʾaggān*, Arab *ʾiggān-at-*.
Assimilation of vowels in Akk and Hbr?
LEC **ʾagan-/*gaHan-* "jar": Som *agaan*, Or *gaanii*.
Assimilation of vowels.

95 *ʾiʿal- "snake"

Eg *iʿr.t* "snake" (pyr).
ECh **ʾiʾal-* "snake": Dng *aalo*, Bid *ʾaalo*, Jegu *ʾillo*, Brg *ʾeli*.
Assimilation of vowels in Dng and Bid.

An unusual combination of -ʾ- and -ʿ- in one root.

96 *ʾikoy- "hold, seize"

Eg *i̓ṯy* "take, catch, seize" (pyr), Copt **ṯ'i*: Boh *ṯ'i*, Sd *ṯi*.
Initial *i̓*- indicates **ʾi*- or **ʾe*-. -*ṯ*- is palatalized before **-o-*.
WCh **kway*- < **HVkway*- "hold" [1], "seize,grasp" [2]: Dera *kway* [1], Miya *kwi* [1], Bgh *kye* [1], Bks *k'ay* [2], DB *kay* [2].
The first syllable lost without traces.

Since **e* and **o* seem to be incompatible within one root, the reconstruction **ʾekoy*- is less probable.

97 *ʾiküĉ- "relative"

Sem **ʾikīŝ*- "family member": Akk *ikīŝu*.
WCh **kiʾuĉ*- "child": Ang *keus*, Ngz *kuŝai* (pl.).
Metathesis.

An alternative reconstruction is **kiʾüĉ*-.

98 *ʾil- "swear; oath"

Sem **ʾVl*- "swear": Hbr *ʾly*, Arab *ʾly* [-*i*-], SAr *ʾlh*.
Dhl *ʾilo* "oath".

Cf. Rift **loʾ*- "oath" (Irq *loʾi*)?

99 *ʾil- "bring"

Eg *i̓ny* "bring" (pyr), Copt **ʾini*: Fym *ini*, Ahm *eine*, Boh *ini*, Sd *eine*.
HS **-l-* > Eg -*n*-. -*y* in the auslaut as well as initial *i̓*- suggest a front vowel in the root.
WCh **ʾal-/*ʾil*- "bring": Bol *ʾal*-, Krk *ʾil*-.
Traces of old alternation **a* ~ **i*?

100 *ʾilab- "wall"

Eg *i̓nb* "wall" (OK).
ECh **labiʾ*- "fence": Kera *laḇi*.
Metathesis.

Another possible reconstruction is HS *labiʾ-.

101 *ʾilam- "skin"

Eg *inm* "skin" (pyr), Copt *ʾ*anom* id.: Boh *anom*.
Seems to have no connection with HS *ʾ*adam-*/*ʾ*adim-* "skin".
WCh *ʾ*Vlam-* "hide": Bade *alm-ən*.
Cf. a denominative verb: Bks *lamoʾ*, DB *lamoʾ*, Sha *lamoʾ* "skin" (v.).

102 *ʾilaw-/*ʾilay "saliva"

Sem *ʾ*ilaw-*/*ʾ*ilay-* "saliva": Akk *illâtu*.
ECh *ʾ*Vlaw-*/*ʾ*Vlay-* "saliva": Mkk *lee*, Mubi *lawe*, Mig *ʾolo*.
Consonantal alternation *-*w*- ~ *-*y*-.

103 *ʾilik- "tooth"

Agaw *ʾ*ilVk-* "tooth": Bil *ʾəlkʷi*, *eruk*, Xmr *erəkʷ*, Xmt *erəkʷ*, Kwr *yerkʷ*, Kem *yərko*, Aw *ərkʷi*.
LEC *ʾ*ilik-* "tooth": Som *ilig*, pl. *ilko*, Bay *ilko*, Rnd *ilko*, Or *ilka*, Kon *ilga*, Bus *iliča*, Gid *ilit*, Arb *ilkʷa*, Arb *ʾilig*.
Wrz *ʾ*ilVg-* "tooth": Gaw *əlge*, Gob *ələgo*, War *ilge*.
HEC *ʾ*ilVk-* "tooth": Had *inḳe*, Bmb *ilkaa*, *irḳa*, Kmb *inḳu-ta*.
Other HEC forms reflect *ʾ*in(V)k-*.

Related to *ʾ*alVk-* "bite, chew". Even though exact correspondences between **l* and other laterals in Cush remain uncertain, cf. Rift *ʾ*iŝik-* "tooth" (Kwz *iŝikuko*). The word for tooth looks like a Cush deverbative innovation and is preserved here because of the HS status of the corresponding verb.

104 *ʾi-maʾ- "(be) good"

Eg *imꜣ* "good" (pyr).
ECh **maʾi-* "good": Sok *maia*.

*ʾ*i-* may be a prefix or a part of the root (phonetically lost in ECh).

105 *ˀimen- "sun, day"

Eg *imny* "Sun-god" (reg).
Initial *i-* stands for HS *ˀi-.
WCh *myan- "day": Mnt *mene*.
CCh *myan- "day": Dng *mena*, Mig *me:ne*.

HS *ˀi- may be a prefix.

106 *ˀin- "cord, tie"

Eg *iny* "cord" (MK).
Ancient deverbative?
WCh *ˀin- "tie": Diri *in*.
CCh *ˀin- "tie": Gude *ˀyin-*, FB *ˀyiŋ-*, FM *ˀin-* , FJ *ˀin-*.
Secondary *-yi-* < *-i- in Gude and FB. Note *-ŋ-* < *-nˀ- reflecting a former shift of the laryngeal.
ECh *ˀVn-/*ˀVwVn- "tie": Kera *ən-tiⁿ*, Kwn *en-tē*, Mig *ˀonno*, Sok *una*, Mubi *ewen*, Brg *ˀunaayi*.
The vowel in Kwn could point out to ECh *-ya-. Other forms are explained by contraction.

107 *ˀin- "flow, be wet"

Sem *ˀin- "spread (of water)": Arab *ˀnn* [-i-].
Imperfect may reflect an original *ˀin-.
WCh *ˀVn- "be wet": Jim *nu*, Tala *ˀunu*.

108 *ˀi-nas- "man"

Sem *ˀin(a)š- "man": Hbr *ˀᵉnōš*, Aram (Syr) *(ˀ)naš*, Arab *ˀins-*, SAr *ˀns*, Jib *ˀɛnsi*.
Berb *ˀinVs- "young man": Ahg *a-ynəs*.
Agaw *ˀanVš- "in-law": Kem *anš-ən*.
By assimilation, from *ˀinaš-.

Derived from HS *nüs- "man".

109 *ˀinawal-/*ˀinayal- "plant"

Eg *inwn* "kind of plant" (med).
ECh *ˀinayal- "grass": Mig *nyālu*, Mubi *inālo*.

Both Mig *-yā-* and Mubi *-ā-* reflect a contraction of **-aya-*.

An ancient composite or a structure with a prefix **ʾi-*?

110 *ʾind- "eye"

CCh **ʾVnd-* "eye": Dgh *nde*.
No traces of the original first syllable.
SA **ʾint-* "eyes" (pl.): Saho *intit*, Afar *intit*.
Unvoiced **-t-* <HS **-d-* is not clear.
LEC **ʾind-* "eye": Som *inḍo-* (pl.), Rnd *indo*, Arb *iynḍa*, Gdl *iinda*.
Secondary *-ḍ-* in Som and Arb?

Derived from **ʾid-* "eye" with a nasal infix.

111 *ʾi(n)t- "louse"

ECh **ʾint-* "louse": Dng *itta-*, Jegu *ʾint-aato*, Mig *itata*.
Assimilation **-nt-* > *-tt-* in Dng and > *-t-* in Mig.
Agaw **ʾant-/*ʾint-* "louse": Aun *inti*, *antii*.
The vowel is fluctuating.
Dhl *ʾiṯṯoni*, *ita* "louse".
Rift **ʾit-* "louse": Irq *itna* (pl.), Bur *ita*, Alg *ita*, Asa *ita*.

Dhl and Rift either display a specific morphonological variant of the root without infix (**ʾit-*) or are explained from assimilations of **-nt-*.

112 *ʾir- "eye"

Eg *ỉr.t* "eye" (pyr), Dem *yr.t* id., Copt **yiri* id.: Lyc *ieire*.
WCh **ʾir-/*yir-* "eye": Pol *yir*, Say *yir*, Grn *yerr*, Kir *yir*, Tala *ge-ir*, Fyr *yeer*.
**yir-* is a result of further development of **ʾir-*. Note a prefix in Tala.
CCh **ʾir-* "eye": Lame *iri*, Msm *ir*, Bnn *ira*.
Related to **ʾir-* is a CCh derivative **ʾaray-* "eye" (< **ʾiray-?*): Bld *ʾaray*, Mnj *aray*, Masa *arai*.
ECh **ʾir-* "eye": Mubi *ir-in*.

113 *ʾiruʾ- "caviar, fish roe"

Sem **ʾiru[ʾ]-* "caviar": Akk *erūtu*.
Eg *iȝr.t* "part of fish" (med).
Metathesis.

Derived from **ʾur-* "fish".

114 *ʾirVy- "stick"

Sem **ʾiry-* "twig, stick" 1, "stake" 2: Akk *urû* 1, Arab *ʾiry-* 2.
Cf. also Akk *aru*, *ḫaru* id.
Eg *ȝry.t* "kind of stick" (MK).

Cf. ECh **ʾwar-* "stick": Jegu *ʾorra*. Related to **ʾariw-* "tree"?

115 *ʾisVʾ-/*ʾisVw- "piece of wood"

Sem **ʾVš̃š̃Vʾ-* "fir-tree splinter": Akk *eš̃š̃eʾu*.
Eg *isw.t* "thick wooden bar" (n).

A cultural *Wanderwort*? Note the consonantal alternation **w* ~ **ʾ*.

116 *ʾitah- "pull"

Eg *itḥ* "pull" (pyr).
Eg *i-* stands for **ʾi-*.
CCh **taH-* "pull": LPe *taʾ*, Msm *ta*.
The initial syllable completely lost.

HS **ʾi-* may be a prefix.

117 *ʾi(w)- "be, become"

Eg *iw* "be" (pyr).
WCh **ʾi-* "become" 1, "be" 2: Ang *g'yi* 1, Bol *i-* 1 2.
CCh **ʾya-* "become": Gis *ye-*.

Related to **ʾiw-/*ʾiy-* "come", cf. Eng *become* ~ *come*? Note that the original root seems to have a structure *CV-*, i.e. **ʾi-*.

118 *ʾiw-/*ʾiy- "come"

Eg *ỉy*, *ỉw* "come", Copt **ʾey* id.: Bhr *i*, Shd *ey*.
CCh **ʾiy-* "go, come": Masa *iy*.
Bed *ʾi-* "come".
LEC **ʾi-* "go": Arb *ʾiʔit-*.

Consonantal alternation of **w* ~ **y*. Cush data may indicate an earlier form of the root, namely, **ʾi-*.

119 *ʾiw-/*ʾiy- "jackal, dog"

Sem **ʾiy-* "jackal": Hbr *ʾī*.
Eg *ỉw* "dog" (MK).
WCh **ʾiy-* "dog": Wrj *iye-na*.
Suffix in Wrj.
LEC **ʾiy-* "wild cat": Or *iyyaa*.

Consonantal alternation of **w* ~ **y*.

120 *ʾor- "vomit"

Sem **ʾVrVw-* "vomit": Akk *arû*.
Based on an earlier biconsonantal **ʾVr-*.
ECh **ʾwar-* "vomit": Mig *werro*, Mobu *wəre*.
Cf. also Smr *hūrə* reflecting the same root with a prefix.

121 *ʾor- "curse, insult" (v.)

Sem **ʾur-* "curse": Akk *arāru*, Hbr *ʾrr*, Soq *ʾerer*.
Eg *wȝr* "curse" (XXII).
Vocalic *w-*.
WCh **ʾar-* < **ʾwar-* "insult, scold": Wrj *ār-*, Kry *ār-*, Ngz *aru*.
CCh **ʾir-* "insult": Zime *ir*.
Unexpected vocalism.
ECh **war-* "insult": Dng *ware*.
HEC **ʾar-* "be angry, be annoyed": Sid *aar-*, Dar *aar-* , Bmb *aar-*.
Vocalism of a stative.

122 *ʾoraḫ- "road, way"

Sem **ʾur(a)ḫ-* "way": Akk *ʾurḫu*, *ʾarḫu*, Hbr *ʾōraḥ*, Aram (Emp,

Palm) *ʾrḥ*, (Syr) *ʾūrḥā*, (Mand) *ʿwḥrʾ*, (NAram) *ʾurḥ*.

WCh **ʾwara-* < **ʾwaraH-* "road": Sura *ar*, Ang *ar*, Ank *war*, Klr *ʾaraw*.

**-H-* is, probably, preserved as *-w-* in Klr but lost elsewhere.

ECh **ʾwar-* "road": Bid *ʾoora*.

An alternative reconstruction could be **ʾwaHar-* with a metathesis and a regular contraction of **-waHa-* > Bid *-oo-* .

HEC **ʾor-* "road": Dar *ora*.

No traces of the laryngeal.

Rift **ʾuruw-* "path, way": Gor *uruwa*.

Secondary formation in *-uwa*. The loss of the laryngeal in Rift is irregular.

123 *ʾow-/*ʾoy- "river, tide"

Eg *wꜣw* "tide" (a).

Initial *w-* is a vowel sign.

ECh **ʾway-* "water, river": Mkk *ʾooye*.

Certainly connected with WCh **(ʾ)waw-* "pour" (Glm *waaw-*). Note the consonantal alternation **-w-* ~ **-y-*.

124 *ʾubun- "vessel"

Sem **ʾubun-* "vessel": Akk *ubbunu*.

CCh **bun-H-* "water pot": Wmd *buŋ*.

Metathesis of the laryngeal forming a cluster with **-n-*: **-nʾ-* > *-ŋ*.

Note LEC **ʾub-* "vessel": Som *ubbo*.

125 *ʾucok- "temple" (anat.)

Sem **ʾusuk-* "temple": Akk *usukku*.

Eg *sskꜣ* "temple" (BD).

Initial *ss-* may reflect **c*. *-ꜣ* probably indicates **o*, or may be a result of the metathesis.

126 *ʾudun-/*ʾuǯun- "ear"

Sem **ʾuḏn-* "ear": Akk *ʾuzn-*, Ug *ʾudn*, Hbr *ʾozen*, Aram *ʾudnā*, (Syr)

ʾednō, (Emp) *ʾdn*, Arab *ʾuḏn-*, SAr *ʾḏn*, Soq *ʾidihen*, Shr *iḏen*, Mhr *heyḏēn*, Gz *ʾəzn*, Tgr *ʾəzn*, Tgy *ʾəzni*, Har *uzun*.
Eg *i͗dn* "ear" (a).
i͗- palatalized from *ȝ- under the influence of *-u-.
ECh *ʾudun-H- "ear": Jegu *ʾuduŋe*, Brg *uduŋi*.
-*ŋ*- may be explained by the shift of the laryngeal.

An unexpected *d ~ *ǯ variation in the root.

127 *ʾudur- "heart"

Eg *i͗dr* "heart" (l).
i͗- palatalized from *ȝ- under the influence of *-u-.
WCh *ʾudur- "chest" [1], "heart" [2]: Sura *tugur* [1], Ang *dur* [1 2].
Sura inlaut -*g*- is regular. The first syllable is reconstructed on the basis of the anlaut in Sura and Ang.
ECh *dur- "middle": Lele *duro ni*.
Dhl *ḏuura* "gut".

128 *ʾuf- "body, meat"

Eg *i͗wf*, *i͗f* "flesh" (pyr), "body (med).
Eg -*w*- indicates HS *u palatalizing the preceding aleph *ȝ- > *i͗*-.
CCh *ʾ[u]fwa- "body": Bud *fu*, Gis *vaa*, Mofu *vaw*, Tera *və-də*, Gbn *fə-tə*, Gudu *fwā-si*.
The initial syllable is lost. Cf. also Kap *guva* id., Glv *vuγa* id., Zgh *vuγa* id., Mnd *vuwa* id. If these forms belong to the CCh root, they may continue *γV-ʾufwa- with a prefix *γV-.

129 *ʾug- "burn"

Sem *ʾug- "burn": Arab *ʾgg* [-*u*-].
ECh *ʾig-/*ʾug- "burn" [1], "fry" [2]: Ndm *yuga* [1], Mig *ʾiggo*.
Ndm *yu*- < *ʾu-.

Related to LEC *ʾeg- "fire": Arb *ʾeeg*.

130 *ʾukok- "jump, run"

Eg *i͗ṯṯ* "fly" (pyr).

Palatalization of *k > ṯ after labials.
WCh **kwak-* "jump, gallop": Ang *kwok*.
The first syllable completely lost.
ECh *ʾ*ukVk-* "run": Mig ʾ*ukk-*, Mkk ʾ*ukke*.

*-*o*- reconstructed on the basis of reflexes in WCh. Cf. Dhl ʾ*uk'*- "rise" with emphatic *-k'-*.

131 *ʾum- "people"

Sem *ʾ*umm-* "people, clan": Ug ʾ*um-t*, Hbr ʾ*ummā*, Arab ʾ*umm-at-*.
Rift *ʾ*im-* "people" [1], "crowd" [2]: Irq *imi* [1], Alg *imi* [2], Bur *im-et* [1].
Assimilation of vowels.

132 *ʾun- "today"

Eg *ỉn* "today" (BD).
CCh *ʾ*unya-* "today": Klb ʾ*unya*.

133 *ʾunay- "meat"

Sem *ʾ*unVy-* "kind of meat": Akk *unû*.
CCh **nay-* "meat": Bld *ne*.
No trace of the first syllable.

134 *ʾup- "goat, sheep"

Eg *wȝp* "sheep" (pyr).
w- reflects a labialized vowel after *ȝ*. However, cf. *ʾ*up-* "strike".
WCh *ʾ*up-* "she-goat": Cagu *ufe*.

135 *ʾup- "strike"

Eg *ỉp* "blow" (n.) (MK).
ỉ- < **ȝ-* before *-*u*-.
WCh *ʾ*up-* "strike": Mnt *wup*.
Secondary initial *w-* in Mnt.
ECh *ʾ*up-* "strike": Mig ʾ*uppo*.

136 *ʾur- "day"

Sem *ʾurr- "day" [1], "light" [2]: Akk *urru* [1], *ūru* [2], Ug *ʾar-* [2], Hbr *ʾōr* [2].
CCh *ʾur- "morning": Gudu *wüř*.
HEC *ʾor- "midday": Bmb *orra*.

Related to *ʾur- "burn, be hot".

137 *ʾur- "burn, be hot"

Sem *ʾur- "set fire": Arab *ʾrr* [-*u*-], *ʾry* [-*i*-].
Cf. also Arab *ʾirr-at-* "fire".
ECh *ʾur- "be hot" [1], "burn" [2]: Smr *ʾura*, Bid *ʾoor*, Dng *ʾere*.
Assimilation of vowels in Dng.
SA *ʾur- "burn": Afar *ur-*.

138 *ʾur- "fish"

WCh *ʾur- "kind of fish": Hs *ūrī*.
ECh *ʾyar- "fish": Ndam *ere*.
Assimilation of vowels.
Omot *ʾor- "fish": Shk *or-us*, Gim *oru*, Dime *or-χo*.

139 *ʾuril-/*ʾurul- "reed"

Sem *ʾurul- "reed": Akk *urullu*.
LEC *ʾulul- "flute": Or *ulullee*.
Assimilation of liquids.
Omot *ʾuril- "flute": Mch *urillo*.

An alternative reconstruction is *ʾulul- (reduplication?). Assimilation of vowels in Sem and LEC?

140 *ʾurüd- "vessel"

Sem *ʾurīd- "vessel": Akk *urīdu*.
WCh *ruʾud- "beer-gourd": Hs *rūdū*.
Metathesis.

An alternative reconstruction is *ruʾüd-.

141 *ʾus- "woman"

CCh **ʾus-* "woman": Glv *ʾusa*.
Agaw **ʾus-* "female" (adj.): Bil *us-äri*, Xmr *oos- räy*.
Cf. also Kem *iyusee* "woman" < **ʾi-ʾus-*.
Omot **ʾus-* "woman having a child": Ome *uso*.

142 *ʾutal-/*ʾutil- "jump"

Sem **ʾVtil-* "take short steps": Arab *ʾtl* [-*i*-].
LEC **ʾutal-* "jump": Or *utaala*.

143 *ʾün- "cut"

Eg *ỉnỉn* "cut" (pyr).
Reduplication of the original **ỉn*.
ECh **ʾVn-* "cut": Mubi *iwin*.
An alternative (and less probable) reconstruction is **ʾi-ʾin-*.

Since there us a possibility that **-w-* in ECh is a secondary development of **ʾ-*, the original HS root may be **ʾin-* .

144 *ʾür- "belly, stomach"

Sem **ʾir-* "breast": Akk *irtu*, Ug *ʾirt*.
CCh **ʾur-* "stomach": Msg *ur-ni*.
Cf. also **war-* < **ura-* "belly": Mba *war*, Msg *wara*. Reduplication in Log *werwer* "lungs".
ECh **ʾur-* "navel": Jegu *ʾurre*.
LEC **ʾur-* "belly": Som *uur-*.

145 *ʾüs- "man"

Sem **ʾiš-* "man": Phn *ʾš*, Hbr *ʾīš*, Aram *ʾyš*, SAr *ʾys*.
If not from **ʾin(a)š-*.
WCh **wus-* < **ʾus-* "brother": Siri *wuši*, Jmb *wuša*.
CCh **ʾus-* "man": Mba *wus*, Msg *us*, *wus*.
HEC **ʾos-* "child, boy": Sid *osoo*, Dar *ose* (pl.), Had *oos-ičo*, Kmb *osoo*.

Cf. Agaw **ʾas-* "man" (Xmr *aasaw*) and Omot **ʾas-* "man" (Ome *asa*, Mch *ʾašo*) with a different root vowel. It is possible that these forms belong to a different root including also WCh *ʾ*as*- "grandfather": Fyer ʾ*ās*.

146 *ʾVcup- "gather, harvest"

Sem *ʾ*VsVp*- "gather, collect" [1], "harvest" (v.) [2]: Akk *esēpu* [1 2], Ug ʾ*asp* [1], Hbr ʾ*sp* [1 2], Aram (Palest) ʾ*asap* [2].
ECh *ʾ*Vsup*- "harvest" (v.): Tum *sub*.
Tum vocied *-b* is regular.

147 *ʾVgor- "chew"

Sem *ʾ*VgVr*- "chew": Arab ʾ*gr*.
ECh **gwar*- "chew": Sbn *gwərə*, Tob *gure*.
No traces of the first syllable.

Initial *ʾ*V*- may be a prefix.

148 *ʾVkul- "eat"

Sem *ʾ*Vkul*- "eat": Akk *akālu*, Ug ʾ*akl*, Phn ʾ*kl*, Hbr ʾ*kl*, Aram (Emp) ʾ*kl*, (Syr) ʾ*ekal*, (Mand) *akal*, Arab ʾ*kl* [*-u-*].
Derived from this root are Gz ʾ*əkl* "food", Tgr ʾ*əkəl* "grain", Amh ʾ*əhəl* id.
WCh **kal*- < **ka*ʾ*Vl*- "food": Hs *kālāčī*.
Secondary derivative in *-či* in Hs. Metathesis.

149 *ʾVl- "be exhausted"

Sem *ʾ*VlVw*- "be unable, be incapable": Arab ʾ*lw* [*-u-*].
Based on *ʾ*Vl*-.
LEC *ʾ*el*- "exhaustion": Or *eelaa*.
Nominal derivative.

150 *ʾVles- "deceive"

Sem *ʾ*Vliš*- "deceive": Arab ʾ*ls* [*-i-*].
CCh **lyas*- "deceive, lie": Msg *leš*.
ECh **las*- < **lyasa*- "deceive, lie": Mobu *lase*, Ngam *lase*.

HS *ʾ*V*- may be a prefix or a part of the root lost in CCh and ECh for phonological reasons.

151 *ʾVniḥ- "breath; breathe"

Sem *ʾVniḥ- "sigh" [1], "moan" [2]: Akk *anāḫu* [1 2], Ug *ʾanḫ* [1], Hbr *ʾnḥ* [2], Aram (Syr) *ʾenaḥ* [2], *Arab ʾnḥ* [*-i-*] [1].
Eg *nḥw.t* "soul" (n).
A deverbative formation reflecting *nuḥ-. Related to Eg *ỉnḥ* "live"?

Initial *ʾV- may be a prefix.

152 *ʾVrVg- "plait, weave; mat"

Sem *ʾVrVg- "plait, weave": Hbr *ʾrg*.
Cf. Pun *ʾrg* "weaver".
WCh *rag- "net" [1], "thread" [2]: Hs *rāgā* [1], Krf *rogho* [2].
Secondary *-o-* in the first syllable in Krf. No traces of the initial laryngeal.

153 *ʾVsuk- "dwell"

Eg *ỉsk* "linger" (XVIII), Copt *ʾōsk id.: Ahm *ōsk*, Boh *ōsk*, Sd *ōsk*.
WCh *suki- "sit" [1], "rest" [2]: Bol *siki* [1], Paa *siki* [1], Pol *šək* [1], Gej *šuki* [2], Brw *suk* [1], Dwot *suk* [1].

Initial *ʾV- may be a prefix.

*b

154 *baʾ- "father"

Berb *baʾ- "father, owner, master": Kby *βa*.
CCh *baʾ- "father": Log *bā*.

An onomatopoeia.

155 *baʾ- "bush, tree"

Eg *bꜣ.t* "bush" (a), Copt *bu id.: Akh *bou*, Boh *bō*.
WCh *baʾ- "tree": Ang *bau*, Krk *ḅa*, Tng *ḅau*.
ḅ- in Krk and Tng reflects a lost laryngeal.

CCh *bwaH- < *baH- "bush": Gis *ḅoh*.
*-wa- < *-a- after a labial. Note an unexpected laryngeal. Initial emphatic is caused by a laryngeal.
SA *bah- "wood": Afar *bahoo*.
Note an irregular laryngeal.

CCh and SA may belong to a specific variant or a different word *bah- id.

156 *baʾ-/*baw- "(gourd) vessel"

CCh *baʾ- "pot" [1], "calabash" [2]: Tera *ḅo* [1], Gudu *ḅa* [2].
ḅ- in Tera and Gudu reflects a lost laryngeal.
Agaw *baw- "gourd bottle": Xmr *baw*, *bawa*.

Note a consonantal alternation *-ʾ- ~ *-w-.

157 *baʾ-/*baw-/*bay "walk, go"

Sem *būʾ- "go, come" [1], "enter" [2], "return" [3]: Akk *bâʾu* [1], Ug *baʾ* [3], Phn *bʾ* [2], Hbr *b(w)ʾ* [3], Arab *bwʾ* [-u-] [3], SAr *bwʾ* [3], Gz *boʾa* [2], Tgr *bäʾa* [2], Tgy *boʾe* [2], Hrr *bōʾa* [2].
Based on biliteral *bVw- or *bVʾ-.
Berb *bVy- "drive, bring" [1], "come" [2]: Ghd *əbbi* [1], Siwa *əbba* [1], Ayr *huii-ət* [1], Twl *huii-ət* [1], Ahg *əhi* [1], Tsl *ihai* [2].
Berb *b- > *β- yielding to *h*- under not quite certain conditions.
Eg *byꜣ* "go away" (pyr).
Vocalic *-ꜣ*.
WCh *baʾ-/*baw- "return" [1], "go" [2], "come" [3]: Sura *bā* [1], Mnt *ba* [1], Ang *be* [1], Dera *bə* [2], Wrj *buw* [3], Kry *ba-* [2], Diri *mbu* [3], Miya *ba-* [2], Cagu *ba-* [2], Mbu *ba-* [2], Jmb *bo-* [3], Klr *bo* [3].
Wrj, Diri and Jmb seem to reflect *baw-. Note prefix *mV- in Diri.
CCh *baʾ-/*baw-/*bay "go" [1], "come" [2], "go away" [3], "follow" [4]: Tera *ḅa* [2], Gaa *aḅi* [2], Gbn *bei* [1], Hwn *bai* [1], Mrg *ḅu* [1], Wmd *ba* [2], Gis *be* [3], Daba *va* [1], Bch *bəy* [4], Masa *ba* [2], Bana *bəwə* [2], Boka *ḅe-ḍi* [3].
Cf. also Chb *bi-ti* "return" that may go back to *bay-.
ECh *baʾ-/*baw-/*bay- "accompany" [1], "come" [2], "enter" [3], "go" [4]: Tob *be* [1], Kera *bi* [2], Mobu *baye* [3], Mubi *ḅa*, *ḅow* [4], Sok *bā*, *bē* [4].

Bed *bay-* "go".
SA **baʾ-* "go away": Afar *baʾ-*.
LEC **baʾ-* "go out": Or *baʾ-*.
Related to Som *baḥ-* id. with a different laryngeal?
HEC **baʾ-* "go away, go out": Sid *ba-*, Had *baʾe*, Bmb *baʾ-*.
Dhl *be-* "go".
From **bay-*?
Omot **baʾ-* "go": Om *baa-*.
Rift **baw-* "follow": Asa *bow-at-*.
Secondary *-o-* in Asa.

Consonantal alternation **-ʾ-* ~ **-w-* ~ **-y-*. Forms in **-y* and **-w* may reflect earlier **baʾi-* and **baʾu-*.

158 *baʾ-/*biʾ- "hole, pit"

Sem **bīʾ-* "hole": Akk *bīʾu*.
Berb **bV-* "irrigation ditch": Siwa *ta-ba*.
Eg *bꜣbꜣ* "hole" (pyr), *bꜣꜣ* "snake's hole" (pyr), *bꜣy.w* "hole" (n).
Reduplication. The form *bꜣy.w* seems to display a front vowel in the root.
WCh **baʾ-* "hole": Krf *boɣo*, Tng *ba*.
LEC **boʾ-* "furrow": Or *boʾoo*.
Secondary rounded vowel after a labial.
Dhl *ḅoowi* "nostril, small hole".
From **baʾaw-*?
Rift **baʾ-* "pit": Irq *baʾi*, Bur *baʾa*.

Alternation **a* ~ **i*.

159 *baʾ-/*buʾ- "dig, hoe"

Eg *bꜣ* "hoe" (v.) (OK).
WCh **buʾ-* "dig, bury": Klr *buy*, Sha *bu*.
Final *-y* in Klr is not very clear. Probably, Klr *buy* < **bui* < **buʾi*.
CCh **baʾ-* "dig": Log *ba*.

Alternation **a* ~ **u*. Related to **baʾ-/*biʾ-* "hole, pit".

160 *baʾas- "be rotten, be bad"

Sem *bVʾaš- "be rotten" [1], "be poor" [2]: Hbr *bʾš* [1], Arab *bʾs* [-*a*-] [2].
WCh *baʾas- "stink" (n.) [1], "bad" [2]: Hs *bāšī* [1], Diri *ḅāsā* [2], Paa *basa-n* [2], Cagu *baši-n* [2].
The intervocalic laryngeal is reflected in the Hs lengthening and, in particular, in the Diri initial emphatic.
Agaw *bas- "be bad": Aun *bas-ən*.
LEC *baʾas- "spoiled, rotten": Som *baas*.
HEC *buš- "bad": Sid *buša*.
Secondary vocalism?

161 *baʾuc- "fill"

WCh *baʾVc- "fill to the brim": Hs *bāçe*.
*-c- > Hs -ç- is regular.
LEC *bVʾus- "fill up": Or *buusa*.

162 *baʾuc- "vessel"

Eg *bꜣs* "wine vessel" (sarc).
ECh *baʾus- "pot": Sbn *ḅəsa*, Smr *busa*, Ndm *ḅəs*, Gbr *basa*, Kbl *besā*.
Smr and Ndm *ḅ*- reflect the inlaut laryngeal.

Derived from *baʾuc- "fill".

163 *baʾus- "be strong"

Sem *bVʾuš- "be strong": Arab *bʾs* [-*u*-].
ECh *basuʾ- "be strong": Gbr *basua*.
Metathesis. Or from *ba-sua*?

164 *baʾVr-/*buʾVr- "well, pit"

Sem *buʾr- "pit, well, hole": Akk *būr*-, Phn *bʾr*, Moab *br*, Hbr *bōr*, Arab *buʾr-at*-, SAr *bʾr*, Gur *bʷər*.
*-u- < HS *-u- before -ʾ-.
LEC *boHVr- "pit": Som *boor*.

Secondary vowel after a labial?

Related to **buˀar-* "dig". Cf. **bar-* "ditch".

165 *bab- "father"

Sem **bāb-* "father" [1], "grandfather" [2]: Aram (Syr) *bābā* [1], Arg *bāba* [2], Hrr *bāb*, *bābā* [2], Soq *bāba* [1].
Berb **bab-* "father" [1], "owner, master" [2]: Nfs *bābā* [1], Ghat *bab* [1], Zng *baba* [1], Sml *baba* [1], Rif *βaβa* [1], Izn *bab* [2], Snh *băba* [1], Kby *βaβa* [1 2].
At least partly borrowed from Sem.
WCh **bab-* "father": Hs *bāba*, Ang *baba*, Krk *babo*, Ngz *baba*.
CCh **bab-*"father": Tera *baba*, Gbn *babu*, Gis *baba*, Bud *băbei*.
ECh **bab-* "father": Mubi *bāba*.
Bed *baaba* "father".
LEC **ˀa-bab-* "father": Or *ababo*.
May be also treated as a reduplication of HS **ˀab-*: **ˀab-ˀab-*.
Omot **bab-* "father": Gim *babe*.
Rift **bab-*"father": Irq *baba*.

An onomatopoeia. Probably, a reduplication of **baˀ-* "father". Some of the above forms may be borrowed from one branch into another.

166 *bab- "child"

Sem **bāb-* "infant": Akk *bāb-*.
ECh **bab-* "son": Mubi *bobu*.
LEC **bab-* "child": Or *baabuu*.

An onomatopoeia. Sem and LEC may indicate an inlaut laryngeal. Cf. **bab-* "father".

167 *bab-/*bib- "shoulder"

Eg *bb.wy* "collar-bones" (dual.) (med).
WCh **bi-bi-* "back": Krf *bībi*.
CCh **bi-bi-* "shoulder": Bud *bibi*.
Bed *baba* "shoulder, armpit".
LEC **bob-* < **b[a]-ba-* "armpit": Or *boba*.
HEC **bob-* < **b[a]-ba-* "armpit": Dar *boba*, Bmb *boba*, *bobaa*.

Omot **bV-b[i]-* ''armpit'': Mch *bəbbiiho*.

Descriptive stem with a reduplication and irregular vocalism. Cf. **bay-* ''back, hump''.

168 *baç- ''coal''

Sem **baṣṣ-* ''coal'': Arab *baṣṣ-at-*.
WCh **ḅic- < *baçi-* ''coal'': Ank *ḅis*.
WCh may also reflect an original **ḅic-*.

169 *baçaḳ-/*baçuḳ- ''expectorate''

Sem **bVṣuḳ-* ''expectorate'': Arab *bṣq* [-*u*-].
Agaw **baçaḳ-* ''expectorate'': Bil *bač̣aḳ-*.

170 *baĉaᶜ- ''tear off, break off''

Sem **bVŝVᶜ-* ''tear off'' 1, ''pierce'' 2: Tgr *bŝᶜ* 1, Tgy *bŝᶜ* 2, Amh *bässa* 2.
WCh **baHaĉ-* ''break off'': Hs *ḅāsā*.
Metathesis.

Note Rift **baŝ-* ''field cleared and dug up for cultivation'': Irq *baŝa*.

171 *bad- ''separate''

Sem **bud-* ''take away'' 1, ''separate'' 2, ''disperse'' 3: Ug *bd* 1, Hbr *bdd* 2, Aram (Emp) *bdd* 3, Arab *bdd* [-*u*-] 2, Hss *abdōd*, Mhr *abdēd*, Shh *ɛbded*.
Secondary **-u-*.
HEC **bad-* ''separate'': Sid *bad-*.
Omot **bad-* ''split, cut (wood)'': Kaf *bad*, Mch *badda-*.

172 *badaͻ- ''begin''

Sem **bVdaͻ-* ''begin, create'': Arab *bdͻ* [-*a*-], Jib *bedeͻ*, Soq *bedeͻ*, Shr *bdeͻ*, Hss *bedō*.
Berb **bVd-* ''begin'': Kby *əβδu*.
WCh **badVͻ-* ''begin'': Ngz *badii-tu*.

ECh *badaʾ- "begin": Mubi *badā*.
May be borrowed from Sem.

173 *bag- "goat, sheep"

Berb **bag-/*bagag* "calf" [1], "lamb" [2], "ram" [3]: Nfs *bɣu* [1], Ayr *a-bagag* [3], Ahg *a-baɣuɣ* [2], Twl *a-bagag* [3].
Partial reduplication in most languages.
CCh **bag-* "sheep": Gude *baga*, FJ *bəga*, FBw *bəgə-n*, Bch *m-baga-te*, FM *bəgə*.
ECh **bag-* "goats" (pl.): Sbn *bage*.
Agaw **bag-/*big-* "sheep": Bil *bägga*, Xmr *bega*, Xmt *biga*, Kwr *baga*, Kem *bäga*.
The variant in **-i-* may be of no morphonological significance.
Omot **bag-* "sheep": Kaf *bagee*, Bwo *baggoo*.

174 *bag- "tiredness"

Eg *bꜣgy* "be tired" (pyr), *bgʿ* "weariness" (l).
-ʿ in the late form is of no importance for the historical phonology of the word. *-y* in the anlaut may reflect a suffix (**-ay-*).
WCh **bag-* "fatigue, sickness": Tng *bog-*.
Tng *-o-* is a regular continuant of **-a-*.

Connected with **bag-* "be angry".

175 *bag- "be angry"

Eg *nbḏ* "angry" (OK).
Palatalization of **g* > *ḏ* may be explained by preceding HS **e* or **o*. Note prefix **nV-*.
ECh **bag-ay-* "be angry": Mobu *bagay*, Ngm *bagaye*.

176 *bag- "pierce"

Sem **bag-* "pierce": Arab *bgg* [*-a-*, *-u-*].
Berb **bVg-* "pierce": Twl *a-beg*, Sml *ī-bgu*.

177 *bag-/*bagVy- "(gourd) vessel"

Berb **bagVy-* "plate": Snh *ta-bagi-t*.

Eg *bḏ*, *bḏꜣ* "pot" (OK).
Vocalic *-ꜣ*. Note the palatalization of **-g-*.
CCh **bayVg-* "gourd": Log *m-boigo*, Afd *beiga*.
Metathesis from **bagVy-*.

An alternative reconstruction is **bayVg-*.

178 *baġ- "fear" (n.)

ECh **ḇag-* "fear": Mubi *ḇaga*.
From **baġ-*. Emphatic *ḇ-* in Mubi is due to the influence of HS **-ġ-*.
Agaw **baḳ-* "horror, fright": Bil *baġaaġaa*.
LEC **baġ-* "fear": Som *baġa*.
A normal reflex of HS **-ġ-* is LEC **-ˁ-*. In the present case, *-ġ-* may indicate a loanword.

179 *baˁ- "dirt, mud"

CCh **ba-* "dirt": Tera *ba*, Daba *buba*, Mus *bəba*.
Reduplication in Daba and Mus.
Rift **baˁ-* "mud": Irq *baˁa*.

An ancient deverbative form? Cf. Dhl *baaˁ-* "defecate".

180 *baˁ- "pour"

Sem **bVˁ-* "rain" (v.): Arab *bˁˁ*.
Eg *bˁḥy* "pour" (pyr).
Cf. *bˁˁ* "drink (blood)" (gr). The stem seems to be based on Proto-Eg **bˁ*.
WCh **baˁ-* "pour": Cagu *va-*, *vo-*, Mbu *vaɣ*, *vaw*.
ECh **bwa(y)-* "pour": Smr *bo*, Kbl *bəyi*, Mkk *buuye* (perf.), Lele *boy*.
**bwa(y)-* < **bwaH(i)-*. Secondary labialization of HS **a* > **wa* after **b*.

Cf. Dhl *buʔ-* id. and Rift **buʔ-* id. (Alg *buʔ-*) with a different laryngeal.

181 *baᶜar "catch"

Sem *bVᶜVr- "catch (fish, birds)", [1], "fish" (v.) [2]: Akk *baʾaru* [1], Soq *bᶜr* [2].
WCh *baHar- "catch, take": Sura *ḅeer*.

182 *baᶜil- "man"

Sem *baᶜl- "husband, master": Akk *bēlu*, Ug *bᶜl*, Phn *bᶜl*, Pun *bᶜl*, Hbr *baᶜal*, Aram (Epigr) *bᶜl*, Arab *baᶜl-*, SAr *bᶜl*, Shr *baᶜl*, Soq *baᶜl*, Mhr *bâl*, Gz *baᶜal*, Tgr *baᶜl*, Amh *bal*.
CCh *bVl- "man": Log *bəlo*, Gul *bel-ewe*.
Derivative in *-aw- in Gul.
SA *bal- "father-in-law": Saho *ballaa*, Afar *ballaa*.
LEC *Hobol- "relative": Or *obbolaa*.
Metathesis and secondary labialization of vowels under the influence of *-b-.
HEC *beHil- "master" [1], "friend" [2]: Sid *biilo* [1], Bmb *beeli* [2].
Vocalism may be archaic and reflecting *baHil-.

183 *baᶜür- "bull"

Sem *baᶜīr- "bull" [1], "young bull" [2], "camel" [3], "ox" [4]: Akk *bīru* [1 2], Hbr *beᶜīr* [1], Aram *beᶜīrā* [1], Arab *baᶜīr-* [3], SAr *bᶜr* [3], Gz *bəᶜr-awi* [4], Tgr *bəᶜər-ay* [4], Tgy *bəᶜəray* [4], Amh *bäre* [4], Arg *bara* [4], Hrr *baʾara* [4], Gur *bawra* [4], Soq *beᶜer* [3], Mhr *beyr* [3].
WCh *bar- "ram" [1], "bull" [2]: Cagu *barē-n* [1], Gera *bara* [2].
CCh *bar- "bull": Bud *baru*.
ECh *bur- < *bVHur- "bull": Mkk *buru*.
Bed *beʾraay* "bull".
Derivative in *-ay-.
Agaw *bir- < *bVHir- "bull": Bil *biiraa*, Xmr *biiraa*, Xmt *biraa*, Kwr *biira*, Aun *birii*, Dam *berii*.
SA *baʾer- "bull": Saho *beʾer*, Afar *baʾeraa*.
HEC *baʾor- "oryx, bull": Had *baara*, Kmb *bora*.
Omot *bVʾor- "bull": Ome *booraa*.
Omot *o < HS *ü.
Dhl *ḅiʾira* "water-buck".

Maybe related to Berb *barar- "she-camel" (Zng *ta-barār-t*).

184 *ba^{c}Vl- "be able"

Sem *$bV^{c}Vl$- "rule, sway": Hbr *b^{c}l*.
ECh *baHVl- "can": Lele *ḅal*, Kbl *ḅal*.

Cf. Rift *bel- "be, become" (Kwz *bel-*)? Related to *ba^{c}il- "man". Sem may be a denominative.

185 *bah[ü]l- "pit, well"

Berb *baw[i]l- "pit (made in search of a well)": Twl *bawel*.
From *baH(w)il-??
ECh *bal- "well": Smr *bəla*, Tum *bal*, Ndam *bal*, Sok *bal*.
LEC *bahol- "hole, pit, well": Som *bahol*, *bahul*, Or *booll*.
HEC *baHVl- "hole" [1], "ravine" [2], "precipice" [3]: Sid *baallee* [1], Had *balle*, *ballee* [2], Kmb *balliyaa* [3].
Wrz *ṗVHol- "well": Dob *ṗoolle*.

186 *baḥal- "wild animal"

Sem *bVḥVl- "fierce animal": Aram (Pehl) *bḥl*.
LEC *baḥal- "wild animal" [1], "lion" [2]: Som *bahal* [1], Rnd *baḥaši* [2].
Rnd goes back to *baḥal-ti* with *-š-* < *-lt-.

Cf. in CCh: Mnd *ʾuḅula*, Glv *ʾuḅula* "leopard" from *ʾu-bVHVl-*.

187 *baḥar- "choose"

Sem *bVḥVr- "choose": Akk *bêru*, *beḫēru*, Hbr *bḥr*, Aram (Palest) *b^{e}ḥar*, SAr *bḥr*.
ECh *baHar- "choose": Sbn *ḅər*, Lele *bāar*, Kera *vere*, Kwn *ṗari*.

188 *baḥar-/*baḥir- "cut, tear"

Sem *bVḥar- "cultivate, cut (camel's ear)": Arab *bḥr* [-*a*-].
Berb *bVHVr- "pinch and turn": Kby *βe^{cc}eř*.
From Arab?
WCh *baHar- "cut": Tng *bεr*, Glm *ḅar-*.
Dhl *ḅiir-* "cut grass, mow".
Assimilation of vowels from *baḥir-.

189 *baḫ-/*biḫ- "burn, be hot"

Eg *bḫḫ* "burn" (reg).
Partial reduplication.
WCh **baH-* "hot": Paa *bubau*, Grn *baʾa*.
Partial reduplication in Paa. The root vowel may be secondary.
CCh **bVH-bVH-* "hot": Gbn *ḅeḅe*, Boka *ḅweḅwe*, Hwn *ḅiḅa-t*.
Reduplication with modified vocalism.
ECh **biHwa-* "roast": Mig *biyyu*, Sbn *ḅwə*.

Alternation **a* ~ **i*.

190 *baḫül- "leg"

Berb **baḫil-* "camel's leg": Izy *aβaḫil*.
CCh **baHul-* "thigh": Tera *boli*, Bnn *ḅala*, Masa *ḅala-mo*, Msg *bul*.

191 *baḫuy- "be good"

Sem **bVḫuy-* "be beautiful": Arab *bḫy* [-*u*-].
CCh **bayVH-* "good": Zime *ḅayʾ*.
Metathesis.

An alternative reconstruction is **bayuḫ-*. Note Rift **boᶜ-* "better, superior" (Alg *boᶜ*) with a different laryngeal.

192 *baHal- "horn"

WCh **baHal-um-* "horn": Mnt *bulu*, Grk *ḅəl*, Bol *ḅoolu-m*, Krk *ḅeelə-m*, Dera *ḅili*, Tng *ḅɔl*, Ngm *ḅalu-m*, Maha *bele-m*, Glm *balu*.
ḅ- in several languages reflects a lost intervocalic laryngeal. Note a suffix of body parts **-um-*.
Omot **baHal-* "horn": Dime *bal-tu*, Gll *baali*.

193 *baHur- "thread, band"

CCh **mV-bar-* "thread": Masa *mbaro*.
Prefix **mV-*. Note that in forms with prefixes, traces of laryngeals and contraction of *-VHV-* patterns are usually lost.
ECh **baHur-* "thread": Kwn *ba:ru*, Jegu *burre*.
SA **bōr-* < **bVHor-* "loin-cloth" [1], "band" [2]: Saho *bor* [1], Afar *booruu* [1], *boor* [2].

Omot *būr- < *bVHur- ‘‘belt’’: Kaf *buuroo*, Mch *buro*.

194 *bak- ‘‘squeeze, strike’’

Sem **buk-* ‘‘squeeze’’ [1], ‘‘tear’’ [2]: Hbr *b(w)k* [1], Arab *bkk* [-*u*-] [1 2]. Secondary *-u-.
Berb **bVk-* ‘‘strike, pound’’: Tua *bakkat*.
Eg *bk* ‘‘kill (with a sword)’’ (gr).
CCh **bak-* ‘‘strike, beat’’: Mnd *bak*.
SA **bak-* ‘‘destroy’’: Afar *bak*.

ECh **ɓak- < *HV-bak-* ‘‘push’’ (Bid *ɓak*) may be related to this root. Note also Dhl *ɓakk-eeδ-* ‘‘kindle (fire)’’ ← * ‘‘strike’’.

195 *bakaʾ- ‘‘be pregnant’’

Sem **bVkaʾ-* ‘‘have little milk’’: Arab *bkʾ* [-*a*-].
Note an interesting semantic shift * ‘‘be pregnant’’ → ‘‘be unable to suckle a child’’.
Eg *bkꜣ* ‘‘become pregnant’’ (MK).
SA **bak-* ‘‘be born’’: Saho *bak*, Afar *bak*.
A resultative derived from the main root.
LEC **baʾak-* ‘‘not giving much milk’’: Or *baakkuu*.

196 *bakVr- ‘‘young animal’’

Sem **bakr-* ‘‘young camel’’: Akk *bakru*, Hbr *beker*, Arab *bakr-*, SAr *bkr*, Mhr *bōker*, Shr *okrit*, Hss *bōker*.
Berb **bVkVr-* ‘‘lamb’’ [1], ‘‘kid’’ [2]: Ayr *e-bakar* [1], Ahg *e-bəkər* [1], Twl *e-bakar* [1], Sml *a-bukir* [2].

197 *baḳ- ‘‘insect’’

Sem **baḳḳ-* ‘‘midget’’ [1], ‘‘bug’’ [2]: Akk *baqqu* [1], Aram (Palest) *baqqā* [2], Arab *baqq-* [2], Hss *beḳḳet* [2].
WCh **baḳwa-/*baḳya* ‘‘cockroach’’ [1], ‘‘scorpion’’ [2]: Bks *buko* [1], Fyer *ɓakya-n* [2].
Note the shift of emphatization in Fyer: **baḳya- > ɓakya-*.

198 *baḳ- ‘‘baldness’’

Berb *baḳ- ‘‘hair disease’’: Ahg *ta-haɣa*.
Agaw *baḳ(u)- ‘‘baldness’’ [1], ‘‘bald’’ [2]: Bil *bakʷ* [1], Aun *boχu* [2].
SA *bak- ‘‘bald spot’’: Saho *bɔka*, Afar *bɔka*.
-ɔ- < *-a- after a labial.

This root is probably reflected in Sem *bahaḳ- ‘‘herpes; white patches on the skin’’ (Aram *buhq-*, Arab *bahaq-*, Gz *bōq*, Jib *bhɔḳ*) with a secondary inlaut laryngeal.

199 *baḳ- ‘‘pour, flow’’

Sem *buḳ- ‘‘pour out’’ [1], ‘‘rain’’ (v.) [2]: Hbr *bqq* [1], Arab *bqq* [-u-] [2].
Secondary *-u-.
Berb *bVḳ- ‘‘soak’’ [1], ‘‘contain (liquid)’’ [2]: Kby *əbbəɣ* [1], Ahg *a-həɣ* [2].
ECh *ḅwak- < *baḳ- ‘‘rain (v.)’’ [1], ‘‘ooze’’ [2]: Mubi *ḅok* [1], Bid *ḅok* [2].
Note the shift of emphatization.
Agaw *baḳw- ‘‘flow’’: Kwr *boɣʷ-*, *bov-*.
Cf. derivatives in Kem *bukʷ-ana* ‘‘rain’’ (v.), Bil *bəkʷ-ana* ‘‘cloud’’.
LEC *baḳ- ‘‘flow’’: Or *baq-*.

200 *baḳ- ‘‘cut, split’’

Sem *bVḳ- ‘‘split’’: Arab *bqq*, Gz *bqq*.
WCh *ḅak- < *ba(Ha)ḳ- ‘‘cut’’ [1], ‘‘split’’ [2], ‘‘divide’’ [3]: Sura *ḅak* [3], Ang *bak* [1], Fyr *bak* [2], Bks *ḅak* [2].
Shift of emphatization.
CCh *ḅak- < *ba(Ha)ḳ- ‘‘cut’’: Dgh *ḅaka*.
Shift of emphatization.
LEC *baḳaḳ- ‘‘tear’’: Or *baqaqa*.
Partial reduplication.
Wrz *paḳ- ‘‘chop’’: Gaw *paqq-as-*.

201 *baḳ- ‘‘look, see’’

Sem *bVḳ- ‘‘examine’’ [1], ‘‘look’’ [2]: Aram *bᵉqā* [1], Arab *bqw* [-u-].
Various triliteral structures built on the basis of *bVḳ- .
Eg *bȝḳ* ‘‘see, notice’’ (l).
Here, -ȝ- is a sign for a vowel.

WCh **baḳ-* "look for": Bgh *bak.*
LEC **beḳ-* "observe" [1], "know" [2]: Som *beeq-* [1], Or *beeka* [2].
HEC **be[ḳ]-* "know": Bmb *beeh-, beek-.*
Omot **baḳ-/*beḳ-* "see" [1], "know" [2]: Ome *biḳ-* [1], Kaf *beḳḳ-* [2], Mch *baḳḳi-* [1], Anf *beḳ-* [1], Bwo *beḳ-* [1], Gim *beḳ-, bek-* [1].

Vocalism *-*e*- is a Cush innovation.

202 *baḳ-/*buḳ- "run"

CCh **baḳ-* "drive": Dgh *baka*, Mnd *ʾabaka.*
Berb **bVḳVy-* "hurry, hasten": Kby *bbuqqi.*
Based on **bVḳ-.*
Eg *bḳ* "run" (pyr).
Agaw **buḳ-* "run away": Aun *buḳ-, buk-.*
SA **buk-* "running away": Saho *buka, bukaa.*
LEC **baḳ-* "run away": Som *baqa-d-*, Or *baqa*, Arb *baqa-ḍ-.*
HEC **baḳ-* "flee": Dar *baḳ-at-*, Bmb *baḳa-ḍ-.*

Alternation **a* ~ **u*. Probably, connected with Sem **bVḳaʿ-* "go away" (Arab *bqʿ* [-*a*-]).

203 *baḳ-/*buḳ- "gourd bottle"

Sem **baḳ-būḳ-* "bottle": Hbr *baqbūq*, Aram (Syr) *bagbūgā.*
Reduplication.
WCh **ku-bak-* "clay gourd": Gera *kubaako.*
Prefix **ku-.*
Agaw **baḳw-* "gourd bottle": Xmr *baw, bawa*, Kem *bəɣwa.*
LEC **buḳ-* "gourd": Or *buqe.*
HEC **bukk-* "gourd": Dar *bukke.*
Irregular *-*kk*-.
Omot **buḳḳ-* "gourd": Kaf *buḳḳoo*, Mch *buḳḳo.*

Alternation **a* ~ **u*.

204 *bal- "eye, eyelid; blind"

Berb **bVl-* "eyelash" [1], "eyelid" [2]: Sgr *a-blu* [1], Mzab *a- bil* [1], Snus *a-bəl* [2], *Snh abel* [2].
Eg *br* "both eyes" (gr), Copt **belle* "blind": Bhr *belle*, Shd *bolle.*

LEC *ball- ''one-eyed'': Or *ballaa*.
HEC *ball- ''blind'': Sid *ball-icca*, Dar *balla*ʔ*a*, Bmb *balla*ʔ*a*.

205 *bal- ''wing, feather''

Sem *nu-ball- ''eagle's feather'': Akk *nuballu*.
Prefix *nu- (probably, from *mu-, see below).
SA *bal- ''feather'': Afar *bal*.
LEC *bal- ''wing'': Som *baal*, Or *baala*, Bay *baale*, Kon *balla*.
HEC *ball- ''feather'': Sid *balle*, Had *balla*ʔ*e*, Bmb *baalle*.
Omot *bal- ''feather'': Kaf *baaloo*.

Probably, related to CCh *mV-bal- ''arm, shoulder'' (Log *m-phala*, Gul *m-bala*) and WCh *bV-bal- id. (Sura *bāl*, Ang *bēl*, Krk *bebalia*, Bks *bāl*). If this connection is valid, a form with a prefix *mV- (dissimilated in Sem and assimilated in WCh) should be reconstructed.

206 *bal- ''cloud, sky''

CCh *bal- ''sky'' 1, ''cloud'' 2: Glv *balabala* 1, Log *bəlukʷi* 2.
Suffix -*kʷi* in Log. Reduplication in Glv.
Bed *bal* ''cloud''.

For the semantic development cf. Skt *nabhas*- ''cloud'' ~ Av *nabah*- ''sky''.

207 *balag-/*balug- ''shine''

Sem *bVlug- ''shine'' 1, ''dawn'' (v.) 2: Hbr *blg* 1, Arab *blg* [-*u*-] 2.
LEC *balag- ''shine, sparkle'': Or *balag*.
Cf. a deverbative in Som *bilig* ''sparkling''.

208 *balaʕ- ''eat, swallow''

Sem *bVlaʕ- ''swallow'' 1, ''eat'' 2: Hbr *blʕ* 1, Aram (Mand) *bla* 1, Arab *blʕ* [-*a*-] 1, Gz *balʕa* 2, Tgr *bälʕa* 2, Tgy *bälʕe* 2, Amh *bälla* 2, Hss *bōla*, Mhr *bōla*, Shh *belaʕ*.
Agaw *balVʕ- ''eat'': Bil *bəlʕ*.
Agaw may be borrowed from Sem. Bil -*ə*- may reflect *-*a*- .

209 *balaḳ- "stone"

Sem *balaḳ- "marble" [1], "limestone" [2]: Arab *balaq-* [1], SAr *blq* [2], Gz *balaq-* [1].
WCh *bVlak- "stone": Hs *ta-blaka*.
Unexpected non-emphatic *k. Prefix *ta-.
CCh *palaḳ- "stone": Lmn *palak*.
Irregular development of HS *b- > CCh *p-.

210 *ban- "field"

Eg *bn.t* "field" (n).
WCh *ḅun- < *Hu-ban- "field": Hs *ḅunā*, Sura *bon*.
Prefix *Hu-. Cf. a partial reduplication in Bks *bibin* "garden".
LEC *ban- "open space, plain": Som *ban*.

211 *ban- "hand, arm"

Sem *bann- "finger": Arab *bann-*, *bunn-*.
WCh *ban-H- "arm": Brm *baŋ-li*, Fyr *beŋ*.
A laryngeal suffix.
CCh *bin- "arm": Tera *bən*, Jara *binna*.
Vocalism is not clear.

212 *ban- "open"

WCh *ban- "open, uncover": Hs *banye*.
CCh *ban-H-/*byan-H- "open": Mofu *baŋ*, *beŋ*.
ECh *bVn-H- "open": Kera *biŋi*.
LEC *ban- "open": Or *bana*.

Alternation *a ~ *i. A laryngeal suffix in CCh and ECh.

213 *bar- "child"

Sem *bar- "son": Aram *bar*, SAr *brw*, Shh *ber*, Mhr *ber*, Soq *bar*, Hss *ber*.
Berb *barar- "son": Ayr *a-barar*, Ahg *a-burir*, Twl *barar*.
Partial reduplication. Irregular vocalism in Ahg.
WCh *bar-/*byar- "young girl" [1], "child" [2]: Hs *bēra* [1], Ang *par* [2], Glm *baryawa* [1].
Hs indicates *e in the 1st syllable.

214 *bar- "man"

WCh **(mV-)bar-* "person": Glm *mbər* (pl.), Gera *bar-mi*, Zul *mbar-me*, Geji *mbali-ŋ*, Paa m-*barə-ŋ*, Mbu *bar-gi*.
Cf. Hs *bārē* "stranger", Paa *mbarə-ŋ* id.
CCh **-bwar-* "man, person": Gis *mburo*, Bch *ɓwara*.
Secondary labialization of the root vowel. Individual forms contain prefixes **mV-* and **HV-*.
ECh **bar-* "man, person": Gbr *barua*, Dor *bara*, Ndam *bər*.
SA **bar-* "man": Afar *barra*.

Related to **bar-* "child" (cf. "human being" = "human child" in early Near and Middle Eastern traditions)?

215 *bar- "take"

Berb **bVr-* "take (in handfuls)": Tua *a-bər*.
CCh **mV-bwar-* "seize, grasp": Suk *mbwɔř*.
**-wa-* may be explained by the influence of the preceding labial consonant.
Bed *bari* "get, collect, have".
SA **bar-* "grasp, hold": Saho *bar-*.

216 *bar- "clean, wash"

Sem **bVr-* "(be) clean": Ug *brr*, Hbr *brr*, Aram (Palest) *bᵉrar*, Gz *brr*.
CCh **bar-* "wash": Glv *bar-*, Mnd *bara-*.
Cf. also **mV-bar-*, **ʔa-bar-* "cleanliness": Tera *m-bari*, Mnd *ʔabbara*.

217 *bar- "antelope"

Berb **bVrVy-* "young antelope": Ahg *e-bərəy*.
Formation in **-ay-*.
WCh **bar-* "gazelle": Hs *barēwā*.
Cf. partial reduplication **ba-bar-* "gazelle": Paa *babar*, Siri *babari*.

Probably related to LEC **baʔir-* "antelope" (Som *bair*) and Rift **baʔur-* id. (Bur *baʔuru*).

218 *bar- "ditch"

Berb **bar-* "ditch": Ghd *a-βar*.
Cf. reduplicated Mzab *burbur* "underground irrigation channel".
HEC **bar-* "ditch": Had *bare*.

219 *bar- "fly" (v.)

Eg *bhꜣ* "fly" (MK).
Goes back to **bahar-*, a triliteral stem built upon original **bar-*.
CCh **bar-* "fly, jump": Msg *bara*.
ECh **bVr-* "fly": Kwn *bre*.
Agaw **birir-* "fly": Aun *berer-əŋ*.
Partial reduplication. Note the modified vocalism.
LEC **bar-* "fly": Or *barr-isa*, *barara*.
Partial reduplication in *barara*.

220 *bar- "wind"

Sem **bāriḥ-* "hot wind": Arab *bāriḥ-*.
Based on **bar-*?
CCh **baraw-* "wind": Mba *baraw-ay*.
Cf. partial reduplication in Msg *bebēr*.
ECh **ka-bar-* "wind": Kera *ka-bar*.
Prefix **ka-*.

221 *bar- "beast of prey"

Sem **bar-bar-* "wolf": Akk *barbaru*.
Reduplication.
Eg *bꜣ* "panther" (MK).
WCh **bar-* "hyaena": Hs *bārū*.

222 *bar- "see"

Sem **bVr-* "see, examine": Akk *barû*, Arab *bry* [*-i-*]. Jib *ebrer*.
Various triliteral derivatives of the original root.
Eg *br* "see" (gr).
CCh **bur-* "remember": Bch *bur-ina*.
The root vowel is irregular.

SA **bar-* "learn": Afar *bar*.
LEC **bar-* "learn": Som *baro*.
Dhl *ḅar-* "know".

223 *bar-/*bur- "morning"

ECh **bur-* "morning": Ndm *buri*, Mubi *burburu*.
SA **ber-* "morning": Saho *beeraa*, Afar *beeraa*.
The root vowel is irregular. Cf. also SA **bar-* "night": Saho *baar*, Afar *baar*.
LEC **bar-* "dawn, morning": Som *bärii*, Or *barii*, Arb *barri*.
HEC **bar-* "day": Bmb *barra*, Kmb *barra*.
Dhl *ḅurra* "morning".

Alternation **a* ~ **u*.

224 *bar-/*bur- "grain, cereal"

Sem **barr-/*burr-* "cereal" [1], "wheat" [2]: Akk *burru* [1], Hbr *bar*, *bār* [1], Arab *burr-* [2], SAr *br* [2], Soq *bor* [2], Mhr *barr* [2], Shr *barr* [2].
Berb **bVr-* "flour" [1], "sorghum" [2], "bread" [3]: Ghd *a-βar-ən* [1], Awj *əβr-ūn* [2], Ayr *a-bora* [2], Ahg *a-bōra* [2], Twl *a-bōra* [2], Zng *būru* [3].
WCh **bar-/*bur-* "kind of flour" [1], "gruel" [2]: Hs *buri*, *biri* [1], Ngz *barbari* [2].
Hs *biri* < *buri* with assimilation of vowels. Reduplication in Ngz.
ECh **bar-/*bur-* "flour" [1], "kind of millet" [2]: Smr *bura* [1], Tum *bař* [1], Kbl *ku-bəra* [1], Lele *ku-bra* [2].
A derivative in **ku-* in Kbl and Lele.
Agaw **bur-* "groats": Xmr *bura*.
LEC **bur-* "wheat": Som *bur*.
Dhl *ḅuru* "maize".
Rift **bar-* "grain": Bur *baru*.

Alternation **a* ~ **u*.

225 *baraʾ- "recover"

Sem **bVraʾ-* "recover": Hbr *brʾ*, Arab *brʾ* [*-a-*].
Cf. also SAr *bry* "health".
WCh **ʾVbar-* "recover": Sura *bar*, Ang *bār*, Chip *bar*.

Metathesis. The voiced anlaut corroborates the loss of the prefix.

An alternative reconstruction is HS *ʾ*abar-*.

226 *baraḳ- "lightning"

Sem **barḳ-* "lightning": Akk *berq-*, *birq-*, Ug *brq*, Hbr *bārāq*, Aram (Syr) *barqō*, Arab *barq-*, SAr *brq*, Shr *berq*, Mhr *bōreq*, Tgr *bärq*, Tgy *bärqi*.
CCh **baraḳ-* "lightning": Log *barak*.
HEC **baraḳ-* "lightning": Sid *banḳo*, *biraḳo*, Dar *balaḳa*, Kmb *banḳu-ta*.
Irregular changes of *-*r*- in the cluster *-*rḳ*-.

Related to **bariḳ-* "shine". A parallel formation **biriḳ-* "lightning" seems to be preserved in Dhl *birik'ina* id., Agaw **birVḳ-* id. (Xmr *birqa*).

227 *baraḳ- "ram, goat, calf"

Sem **baraḳ-* "ram": Arab *baraq-*.
Berb **barak-* "calf" [1], "cattle" [2]: Ahg *a-bərk-aw* [1], Gua *a-barak-i* [2].
Irregular *-*k*-.
WCh **barVḳ-* "goat": Bol *barke*.
ECh **birVk-* "bull": Bid *birki*.
Unexpected front vowel.

228 *baraw-/*baray- "stick, arrow"

Berb **buray-* "stick": Ayr *ə-boray*, Ghd *ta-buri-t*, Ghat *ta-buray-t*, Ahg *tə-buri-t*.
Secondary *-*u*- after a labial.
Eg *bry* "sticks, canes" (n).
WCh **mV-bar-* "arrow": Zaar *mbara*, Zak *mbara*.
Prefix **mV-*.
CCh **baraw-* "arrow, bow": Msg *barau*, Masa *ḅaraw-ta*.
ECh *ʾ*a-bawar-* "arrow": Kera *aḅōro*.
Metathesis. Note prefix *ʾ*a-*.

Note the consonantal alteration *-*w*- ~ *-*y*-.

229 *baraw-/*baray-"equid"

ECh **baraw-/*baray-* "horse": Dng *boora*, Mig *borow*, Brg *booray*.
Metathesis in Dng.
Omot **baray-* "mare": Kaf *baraayee*, Mch *baaraye*.

Consonantal alternation **-w-* ~ **-y-*. Cf. CCh **bwar-* "donkey" (Log *mbūri*, Kus *bori*, Afd *boro*) and ECh **bur-* id. (Mkk *buuru*).

230 *bariḥ- "run, go"

Sem **bVriḥ-* "leave" 1, "run away" 2, "run in awe" 3: Phn *brḥ* 1 2, Pun *brḥ* 1 2, Hbr *brḥ* 2, Aram (Palest) *bᵉraḥ* 2, Arab *brḥ* 1 [*-a-*], Amh *bäräyyä* 3.
Sem **i* of the second syllable is typical of *verba movendi*.
WCh **HVbar-* "escape" 1, "go out" 2, "return" 3: Ang *bar* 1, Tng *bar* 2, Gera *bōrə-* 3, Glm *bar-* 3, Wrj *var* 2.
Metathesis.
ECh **bir-* < **barya-* "go": Dng *birē*, *bire*.
Dhl *bariy-* "go out, depart".
From **bariH-*?

231 *bariḳ- "shine, be bright"

Sem **bVriḳ-* "shine (of lightning)": Akk *barāqu*, Aram *bᵉrēq*, *bᵉraq*, Arab *brq* [*-i-*], Gz *brq*, Amh *bärräqä*.
Eg *bꜣḳ* "be light, be bright" (pyr).
Omot **[b]arik-* "shine": Mch *ṗariqq(i)-*.
Secondary *ṗ-* < **b-* influenced by **ḳ*?

The present root may be further related to **bar-/*bur-* "morning".

232 *barod- "beast of prey"

Sem **barad-/*barud-* "leopard": Hbr *bārōd*, *bārūd*, Arab *ʔabrad-*.
**b-* corresponds to WCh **b-*. Note a secondary formation in Arab.
WCh **bwadar-* "zorylla": Hs *bōdārī*, *būdārī*.
Metathesis.
LEC **marod-* "elephant" 1, "lion" 2: Som *maroodi* 1, Or *marode* 2.

Irregular **m-*.

Derived from **bar-* "beast of prey".

233 *barVᶜ- "give"

Sem **bVrVᶜ-* "give, yield": Arab *brᶜ*.
WCh **bar-* "give": Hs *bā*, Ank *pe*, Bol *bar*, Krk *bar*, Ngm *bar*, Krf *bar*, Gera *bar*, Glm *bar*, Pol *bu-*, *bi-*, Geji *bəl*, Brw *bar*, *bə*, Say *ḅər*, Grn *bər*, *bur*, Ngz *baru*.
CCh **bar-/*bir-* "give": Tera *vəri*, Dgh *bire*, Gdf *bar*.
ECh **baHir-* "give": Dng *bere*, Mig *biraw*, Jegu *bir*, Bid *bere-n*, Mubi *bāra*, Brg *biri*.
Metathesis of the laryngeal.

234 *barVṭ- "boy"

Berb **baraṭ-* "boy": Ghat *a-baraḍ*.
Dhl *ḅoreṯe* "boy".

Derived from **bar-* "child".

235 *bas- "cut"

Berb **bVwVs-* "be cut, be wounded": Ayr *busu*, Ahg *buis*.
Based on the original **bVs-*.
WCh **bas-* "cut off": Bol *bas-*.
CCh **bas-* "break": Masa *bas*.
Agaw **bas-* "cut (skin)": Xmr *bas-*.
Omot **bas-* "slaughter": Kaf *baš-*, Anf *baš-*.

236 *bas- "apron"

Eg *bsȝw* "apron" (MK).
Going back to **bVsaw-*.
CCh **bas-ay-* "apron" [1], "loin-cloth" [2]: Gis *basay* [1], Bch *basɛy* [2].
If not **ba-say-*.

237 *bas- "walk"

Sem **būš-* "go away" [1], "trample" [2]: Akk *bêšu* [1], Hbr *bwš* [2].

Extension of the original **bVš-*.
CCh **mV-ba[s]-* ''enter'': Mofu *mbəz-*, *mbaz-*.
A secondary voiced in Mofu? Prefix **mV-*.
ECh **bas-* ''come'': Mobu *bəse*, Ndam *basi*.

238 *bas- ''live, beget''

Sem **bVšVy-* ''be, exist'': Akk *bašû*, Phn *bšy*.
Based on the original **bVš-*.
Agaw **bas-* ''beget'': Kem *baas*.
An ancient causative?

239 *bat- ''move''

Sem **bVt-* ''go away'' [1], ''go quickly'' [2]: Arab *btt* [1], Tgr *bättä* [2].
WCh **bwat-* ''accompany'': Ang *bwot*.
Secondary labialization of the vowel?
ECh **bat-* ''return'': Tum *bād*.

240 *bat-/*bit- ''cut''

Sem **bit-/*but-* ''cut off, break off'': Arab *btt* [*-u-* ,*-i-*].
u-vocalism is secondary.
Berb **bVt-* ''cut off, chop off'': Ahg *ə-bət*, Ayr *ə- bət*.
ECh **bit-* ''strike'': Bid *bit*.

Alternation **a* ~ **i*. Cf. **baṭ-* ''pierce, cut''.

241 *baṭ- ''pierce, cut''

Sem **buṭ-* ''split, pierce'' [1], ''be split'' [2]: Arab *bṭṭ* [*-u-*] [1], Jib *bɔṭṭəṭ* [2].
Secondary **-u-*.
Berb **bVṭ-* ''pierce'' [1], ''divide'' [2]: Ahg *əbəḍ* [1 2], Twl *ibḍu* [2], Sml *ibḍu* [1], Ntf *bəḍḍa* [1], Izd *bḍu* [1], Izy *bḍu* [1], Snus *bəḍḍa* [1], Izn *ebḍa* [2], Kby *əβḍu* [1].
WCh **ɓat-* < **baṭ-* ''cut'': Bol *ɓot-*, Ngm *ɓat-*, Gera *ɓaḍ-*.
Note the shift of emphatization.
LEC **baṭ-* ''part; divide'': Som *baḍ-*.

242 *baṭ- "speak"

Sem *bVṭ- "chat": Ug *tbṭ*, Hbr *bṭy*, *bṭʾ*.
Various derivatives of the biliteral root.
WCh *baṭ-/*bayaṭ- "speaking, speak": Krf *baati*, Fyr *beet*. *bayaṭ- seems to be a secondary extension of *baṭ-.
CCh *mV-baṭ-/*mV-biṭ- "answer, speak": Gis *mbiḍ*, *mbəḍ-*, *buboḍ-*, Mofu *babaḍ-*, *mbaḍ*.
Omot *yibat- "speak": Kaf *yibat-*.
Prefix *yV- and irregular *t < HS *ṭ. Metathesis?

243 *baw-/*bay- "water"

Berb *bVw-bVw- "water": Sgh *bbubbu*.
Reduplication.
WCh *bay- "watering of horses": Hs *bai*, *bāyī*.
CCh *baʾi- "water": Nza *mbii*, *bii*, *mbiʾi*, Bata *mboy*, *bōye*.
Bata -o- < *-a- after a labial.
LEC *baw- "lake": Arb *baww*.
Rift *boʾ- "dew": Kwz *boʾ-uto*.
From *baw-?

Consonantal alternation *-w- ~ *-y-.

244 *baw-/*bay- "place, house"

Berb *bVw- "enclosure": Ayr *ə-biwa*, Twl *ə-biwa*.
Eg *bw* "place" (pyr).
WCh *bayi- "place" [1], "village" [2], "hut" [3]: Sura *pɛ:* [1], Ang *pi* [1], Mnt *bi* [1], Ank *bē* [1], Bol *beyi* [1], Krk *biyi* [1], Gera *bi* [1], Zak *bayi* [2], Geji *bi* [3], Ngm *beʾi* [1], *bi* [3].
CCh *baw- "place, house" [1], "yard" [2]: Bura *vi* [1], Boka *bi-ta* [1], Ngw *mbwɔ* [1], Wmd *mbwa* [1], Mofu *mbaw* [2], Log *mba* [1].
The variant *bi- in Boka may be a result of the morphonological development of *bay-.
ECh *ba- "place": Sok *ba*.
From *baʾ-?
HEC *bay- "place": Sid *bay-*, *baʾa*, Had *beeyo*, Kmb *bee-ccu*.
Had and Kmb -ee- < *-a- before *-y-.

Consonantal alternation *-w- ~ *-y-. Related to *bay- "build" and *bayit- "house".

245 *bawal- "urinate, flow"

Sem **būl-* "urinate": Arab *bwl* [*-u-*].
ECh **bawal-* "overflow": Bid *bolol.*
Partial reduplication.

246 *bawar- "lion, hyaena"

Berb **b(V)war-* "lion": Nfs *wär*, Ght ä-*ḅər*, Ayr *a-har*, Twl *a-har*, Zng *war.*
Note Berb **b-* > **β.*
WCh **bVwar-* "lion" [1], "hyaena" [2]: Sura *mbɔ:r* [1], Ang *bwār* [1], Pol *bwər* [2], Fyr *mbwār* [1].
CCh **bVwVr-* "lion": Gid *bōlu.*
Cf. Gis *mo-bor* "lion", Mofu *ma-bar* "panther".
ECh **b[a]w[a]r-* "hyaena": Dng *boori*, Mig *booru*, Mubi *bōri.*
LEC **warab-* "hyaena": Som *warab*, Or *warab-esa*, Rnd *waraba.*
Metathesis.
Wrz **warap-* "hyaena": Gaw *oraap-atte*, Hss *araap-icce*, Dob *araap-acce*, Gll *oraap-atte.*
Metathesis.
Dhl *ḅoora* "dangerous animal".
From **bawar-*?

Cf. **bar-* "beast of prey".

247 *bawVd- "sorcerer"

WCh **bad-* "sorcerer": Ngz *badə-ra.*
Frow **bawad-*?
Agaw **bawVd-* "witch-doctor" [1], "werwolf" [2]: Bil *bawda* [1 2], Xmr *buda* [1 2], Kem *buda* [1].
Contraction in Xmr and Kem.
SA **bud-* < **bVwVd-* "witch-doctor": Afar *buda.*
LEC **bawVd-* "witch-doctor": Som *bida*, Or *bawda.*
Som is irregular.
HEC **bud-* "who has evil eye": Sid *bud-akko*, Dar *buda*, Bmb *buda.*
Omot **bud-* < **bVwVd-* "witch-doctor": Kaf *budo*, Bwo *budo.*

248 *bawVḳ- "drop" (n.)

Sem **bawḳ-* "shower": Arab *bawq-*.
Agaw **buḳ-* < **bVwVḳ-* "drops" (pl.): Bil *boḳʷ*.

249 *bawVn- "rope, band"

Berb **baw(V)n-* "leather sack with strings": Ahg *a-bawn*.
Eg *wbn* "band (on mummy's forehead)".
Metathesis.
ECh **bwan-* "rape": Mkk *bonne*. From **bawan-*.

Related to **ben-* "tie". Note consonantal alternation **-w-* ~ **-y-* (in **ben-*).

250 *bay- "chief, king"

Eg *by.ty* "king of the Lower Egypt" (OK).
CCh **bay-* "chief": Mofu *bay*, Gis *boy*, Bld *aboy*, Mtk *bay*, Mafa *boy*, Daba *bəy*, Mus *bay*.

251 *bay- "back, hump"

Berb **ʔu-bay-* "camel's hump": Ghat *t-uhi*, Ayr *t- uhəy*, Ahg *t-uhə*, Twl *t-uhəy*, Sml *ta-yyu*.
Prefix **ʔu-*. Note Berb **b-* > **β-*.
Eg *byꜣ.t* "head, occiput, beard, breast, back" (n).
-ꜣ is a sign for a vowel. The meaning is uncertain.
WCh **bay-* "back": Hs *bāyā*, Bol *boy*, Krk *bai*, Ngm *be*, Maha *boy*, Glm *bi*.

252 *bay- "build"

CCh **bV-* "build": Lmn *b-*.
ECh **bay-* "build": Smr *bi*, Kwn *bay*, Mobu *baye*.

Archaic verb preserved outside Chadic in a derivative **bayit-* "house".

253 *bayit- ''house''

Sem **bayt-* ''house'': Akk *bītu*, *bētu*, Ug *bt*, Phn *bt*, *byt*, Pun *bt*, Moab *bt*, Hbr *bayit*, Aram (Palest) *baytā*, *betā*, (Nab, Palm) *byt*, Arab *bayt-*, SAr *byt*, Gz *bet*, Tgr *bet*, Tgy *bet*, Amh *bēt*, Gog *bet*, Mhr *bayt*, Shr *but*, Jib *bet*, Soq *beyt*.
WCh **bit-* < **bVyit-* ''hut, shelter'': Sura *bit*, Mpn *bit*.

Cf. Zgh *bat-iwe* ''hut'' < **bayVt-*? Derived from HS **bay-* ''build''.

254 *bayVᶜ- ''sell''

Sem **bīᶜ-* ''sell'': Arab *byᶜ* [*-i-*].
WCh **bay-* ''trade'' [1], ''sell'' [2]: Tng *paya* [1], Krf *bayi* [2], Glm *baya-* [2].
Complete loss of the auslaut laryngeal.
Rift **beᵓ-* ''buy, sell'': Kwz *beᵓ-*.
Irregular **-ᵓ-*.

255 *baʒ- ''tear off, skin''

Sem **buz-* ''tear off'': Hbr *bzz*, Arab *bzz* [*-u-*].
Secondary **-u-*.
WCh **HV-baʒ-* ''skin'' (v.): Paa *ḅuzu*, Jmb *vaz*.
A laryngeal prefix. Assimilation of vowels in Paa.

256 *baʒ- ''flow, be wet''

Berb **bVʒ-* ''be wet'' [1], ''pour'' [2]: Sha *bzi* [1], Kby *βeẓẓeᶜ* [2].
Cf. a derivative with suffix **-g-* in Izy *bzeg* ''be wet''.
Eg *bzy* ''flow out, sprinkle'' (MK).
-y is a suffix.
WCh **baʒ-* ''spit'': Ngz *baz-iyu*.

257 *baʒar- ''be torn, be peeled''

Berb **bVʒVr-* ''be peeled'': Ghd *βzər*.
WCh **baʒar-* ''related to torn (clothes)'' (adv.): Hs *bazar-bazar*.

Derived from **baʒ-* ''tear off, skin''.

258 *bel- "blood"

WCh *ʔVbyal- "vein": Ank *vel*.
Prefix implied by the anlaut in Ank.
CCh *byal- "blood": Gid *bēli*.
Cf. Msg *fel* id., Mba *fal* id.
Agaw *bill- "blood": Bil *bir*, Xmr *bir*, Xmt *bera*, Kwr *bir*, Dmb *bir*, Kem *birr*, Aun *beri*, Dmt *beri*.
SA *bil- "blood": Saho *biilo*, Afar *bil*.

259 *bel- "weapon"

WCh *HVbyal- "arrow": Kr *ḅelu*.
A laryngeal prefix.
ECh *byal- "axe" [1], "knife" [2]: Mig *bo:la* [1], Smr *bela* [2].
LEC *bil- "knife": Or *billaa*.
HEC *bil- "knife": Kmb *billawwa*.

260 *belal- "rivulet"

CCh *byalal- "rivulet": Gul *belle*.
In this case, the vowel is reconstructed in the second syllable as a single possibility in which the first syllable is not influenced.
ECh *byalal- "rivulet": Smr *bellali*.

Archaic reduplicative root widely preserved in derivatives, cf. *bolan- "rain, cloud". The original form of the root was *bVl- as it is continued in ECh *byal- "pond": Mubi *bēli*. See also *bol- "flow, be wet".

261 *ben- "build"

Sem *bVn- "build": Akk *banû*, Ug *bny*, *bnw*, Phn *bny*, Pun *bnʔ*, *bny*, Amor *bny*, Moab *bny*, Hbr *bny*, OAram *bny*, Aram (Emp, Nab) *bnh*, *bnʔ*, (Palm) *bnʔ*, (Mand) *bna*, Arab *bny* [-*i*-], SAr *bny*, Mhr *benû*, Jib *bene*, Soq *bene*.
Various triliteral formations based on *bVn-.
Berb *bVn- "build": Ghd *ə-bni*, Sml *bənna*, Izy *bnu*, Ntf *bnu*, Izd *bnu*, Izn *ə-bnu*, Snus *ə-βnu*, Sha *ə-bna*, Kby *ə-βnu*, Lib *bny*.
Manifested in individual languages as *bVnVy- or *bVnVw-.
ECh *byani(H)- "build": Kwn *baŋ*, Mubi *bēni*.

Kwn may reflect a secondary formation **byaniʔ-* similar to those of Sem and Berb.

262 *ben- "tie"

Berb **bVn-* "tie": Ghd *aβən*, Ahg *ahən*.
Note Berb **b-* > **β-*.
CCh **byan-* "tie": Log *ḅən*, *bən*, Bud *pēnai*, *fanai*.
Log *ḅ-* may reflect a possible laryngeal prefix.

263 *ben- "be bad"

Eg *byn* "bad, angry" (OK), Copt **bōʔōn* id.: Boh *bōn*, Shd *bōon*.
Inlaut *-y-* seems to be a sign for vowel.
WCh **ban-* < **byana-* "wrath" [1], "bad" [2]: Tng *bana* [1], Wrj *embəna* [2].
ECh **byan-* "bad": Sok *benā*.
Agaw **bin-* "lie" (n.): Bil *bin*.
LEC **ben-* "lie" (n.): Arb *been*.

264 *ben- "building"

Berb **byan-* "tent, house": Ghat *(ə)-yan-an*, Ayr *e-hən*, Ahg *ə-hən*, Twl *e-hən*, Tsl *e-hən*, Lib *bn*.
Note Berb **b-* > **β-*.
Eg *bnbn* "stela" (MK).
Reduplication.
WCh **byani(H)-* "upper floor" [1], "hut" [2]: Hs *bēnē* [1], Grk *pīn* [2], Ank *pīn* [2], Krk *ben* [2], Bele *bin* [2], Geji *biŋ* [2], Pol *biŋ* [2].
CCh **binVH-* "hut": Glv *veŋ*, Nak *vine*, Gis *veŋ*, Bld *viŋ*, Gudu *vīn*, Nza *vine*, Bch *vunεy*, Bata *vino*, Log *vəni*, Suk *bīna*.
ECh **byaHin-* "hut": Mig *beŋ*, Mkk *biino*, Bid *beena*.

A nominal formation corresponding to **ben-* "build". WCh and CCh forms contain C^3 = *-H-*. The latter may be a result of the Common Chadic development and not necessarily leads to the HS reconstruction of **beniH-*.

265 *ber- "cereal"

Eg *brry* "bread" (n).

-rr- may mean a partial reduplication or an orthographic peculiarity. In any case, *-y* stands for a vowel (of the first syllable?).

CCh **ba-byar-* ''maize'': Log *bāberā*.

Partial reduplication.

Omot **bar-* ''maize'': Mch *baaro*, Anf *baro*.

Omot **a* < HS **e* in certain conditions?

266 *ber- ''cut''

Sem **bVrVʔ-* ''cut, cut down'': Hbr *brʔ*, Arab *brʔ*.

Based on original **bVr-*.

Berb **bVrVy-* ''cut'': Sml *bri*.

Based on original **bVr-*.

CCh **byar-* ''cut off'': Tng *ber*.

Dhl *ḅiir-*''cut grass, mow''.

267 *ber- ''mouse''

Sem **birr-* ''mouse, rat'': Arab *birr-*.

Berb **bVr(r)-* ''pole-cat'': Sml *a-bərr-ān*.

ECh **byar-* ''mouse, rat'': Smr *dē-bere*, Tum *bə:r-āŋ*.

Prefix in Smr.

268 *beʒ- ''sun, day''

Eg *bzy* ''Sun-god'' (reg).

-y stands for a front vowel.

CCh **byaʒ-* ''day'': Msg *bezā*.

Rift **bes-* ''sunlight'': Kwz *bes-iko*.

Continuants of **ʒ* in Rift are not established. The present example may be decisive.

269 *beʒar- ''corn''

Sem **bizr-* ''seed'' [1], ''peppers'' [2]: Aram (Pehl) *bzr* [1], (Palest) *bizrā* [1], Arab *bizr-* [1], Hss *bezār* [2], Mhr *bezār* [2], Shh *bizɛr* [2].

Cf. denominative Arab *bzr* [-*i*-]''sow''.

WCh **baʒar-* ''corn'': Mbu *vazar*, Jmb *vazar*, Tala *bazr*.

From **byaʒar-*.

Etymologically connected with **baʒar-* ''be torn, be peeled'' (as far as semantic change is concerned, cf. IE: **g'rHnom* "something ground; grain").

270 *biʾ-/*bay- "be angry"

Eg *b* "evil" (l).
The final laryngeal is not preserved. Eg may reflect an archaic form of the HS stem that may be then reconstructed as **bi-*.
WCh **biʾ-* "be angry": DB *biʾ*.
CCh **biH-/*bay-* "angry" [1], "bad" [2]: Gaa *ḅiḅa* [1], Gbn *ḅiḅa* [1], FKi *ḅəy* [2], Bud *abi* [2].
Reduplicated forms in Gaa and Gbn may be related to CCh **bib-* "hot".
ECh **bVy-* "anger": Bid *beyo*.

Note the morphonological alternation in the root.

271 *biʾ-/*bay- "bread, flour"

Eg *by.t* "kind of bread" (med).
CCh **biʾ-* "millet": Gul *bio*, Afa *bio*, Kus *byo*.
Quite probably, a semantic archaism within the present root pointing to the original type of the cereal.
Bed *biʾ* "flour".
HEC **boy-* < **b[a]y-* "flour": Bmb *booya*.
Secondary change of vowel after a labial.

As far as morphonology of the root is concerned, cf. **biʾ-/*bay-* "be angry".

272 *biʾ- "pierce"

Eg *wbꜣ* "pierce, open" (pyr).
Initial *w-* may stand for a rounded root vowel or represent a suffix.
WCh **biʾu-* "pierce": Diri *ḅū*, Paa *ḅi*, Miya *ḅiya*, Kry *ḅiya*, Siri *ḅiyu*, Fyer *ḅoo*.
-y- in Miya, Kry and Siri is an innovation from *-ʾ- in contact with a front vowel.
CCh **biʾu-* "pierce": Daba *būh*, Bud *biu*, *bihu*.
Note *-h* in Daba.

273 *biʾak- "slave, servant"

Eg *bȝk* "servant" (OK).
WCh **biHak-* "slave": Pol *biyək*, Kir *ḅiyak*.
Kir *ḅ-* shows that WCh **-y-* goes back to a laryngeal after a front vowel. Under the influence of the vowel, the laryngeal yielded to *-y-*.
CCh **byak-* "slave": Gis *beke*, Mofu *beke*, LPe *byek*.
CCh **-ya-* < **-iya-* < **-iHa-*.

Related to **boʾ-* "slave, servant"?

274 *biʾan- "separate, divide"

WCh **ḅyan-* < **biʾan-* "separate": Sura *ḅen*.
Agaw **bin-* < **biyVn-* "divide": Bil *bən*, Kwr *bin*, Xmr *bin*, Aun *ben-əŋ*.

Cf. also Sem **bVyVn-* "separate": Arab *byn* [-*i*-].

275 *biʾan-/*biyan- "look, know"

Sem **bīn-* "know" [1], "notice" [2]: Ug *bn* [1], Hbr *byn* [2].
Sometimes compared with Sem **bayn-* "link (n.); between", see HS **bawVn-* "rope, band" and cf. also HS **biʾan-* "separate, divide".
WCh **baʾan-* "look": Pero *ḅaan*.
Assimilation of vowels.
ECh **ʾibin-* "know": Dng *ʾibine*, Mig *ʾibino*, Brg *ʾibini*, Sok *ibine*.
Metathesis and assimilation of vowels.

Note the alternation **-ʾ-* ~ **-y-*. Any connection with **biʾan-* "separate, divide"?

276 *biʾir- "pit, well; dig"

Sem **biʾr-* "balk" [1], "well" [2]: Akk *bīru* [1 2], Hbr *b^{e}ʾēr* [2], OAram *byrʾ* [2], Aram (Emp) *bʾr* [2], (Palest) *b^{e}ʾērē* [2], (Mand) *bira* [2], Arab *biʾr-* [2].
ECh **biʾir-* "dig": Lele *biir*.
LEC **biHir-* "bore, drill": Arb *biir-* .

Related to **buʾar-* "dig", **baʾVr-* "well, pit" as a morphonological variant.

277 *biʾVy- "snake"

Eg *byꜣ* "holy serpent" (gr).
Metathesis.
CCh **biʾVy-* "python": HGh *ḅiya*, FG *ḅiya*, Kap *mḅya*, HNk *bg'ye*, HB *wg'ye*.

278 *bibab- "goat, sheep"

Sem **bibb-* "wild sheep": Akk *bibbu*.
WCh **bVwab-* < **bVbab-* "he-goat": Ang *bwop*.
Unvoicing of **-b-* in Ang is regular.

Descriptive stem.

279 *biçur-/*piçur- "pudenda"

Sem **binVṭur-* "vulva": Akk *biṣṣūru*, Arab *bunẓur-*.
Metathesis in Proto-Sem and secondary *-u-* in Arab. Cf. also Hss *bešelēt* "clitoris", Mhr *beśselēt* id.
CCh **pičur-in-* "testicles": FJ *fčerin*, FM *fučuru*.
Metathesis in FG and Gude. The original stem seems to be **pičur-*.

Numerous phonetic irregularities are connected with the meaning of the word. Note more distant variants in CCh: HNk *subəle*, Kap *səpule*, FGl *spuɣli* etc. As far as the anlaut is concerned, see **ber-/*per-* "mouse, rat". As a whole, the word seems to be an ancient derivative of an otherwise unattested and unreliable stem.

280 *biĉ- "spit"

Eg *bšy* "spit" (pyr).
WCh **biĉ-* "spit": Ang *bis*, *bes*.
ECh **bVĉ-* "spit": Smr *bə:sə*.
Dhl *ḅuṯ'uʕ-* "spit".

The continuants of HS *-ĉ- in Dhl are not well established. -ṯ'- might reflect *-ĉ- in the intervocalic position. The root vowel -*u*- may be of a secondary origin.

281 *bid- "monkey"

Berb **bidd-Vw-* "monkey": Ghd *biddu*, Ahg *a-biddau*.
WCh **bid-* "monkey": Hs *biri*, Mnt *pit*, Ank *pit*, Grk *pit*, *pət*, Bol *bido*, Krk *bido*, Dera *bido*, Bele *bido*, Krf *biro*, Gera *biḍi*, Glm *birya*, Paa *vidi*, Jmb *vuda*.
Gera may reflect **bidVH-*.
CCh **biḍ-* "monkey": Tera *vidi*, Jara *vide*, Heba *mbeḍa*, Glv *ʔavda*.
CCh **biḍ-* < **bidVH-*? Prefix in Glv.

282 *biʕar- "burn"

Sem **bVʕVr-* "burn" (tr. and intr.): Ug *bʕr*, Hbr *bʕr*, Aram (Palest) *beʕār*, (Mand) *bar*.
WCh **biHar-* "heat": Mnt *biar*.
CCh **bar-* < **bVHar-* "burn": Tera *vara*.
ECh **bVHVr-* "warm up": Kera *boore*.
Secondary labialization of vowels after **b-*.
Agaw **ʔV-bVr-* "flame" (v.): Aun *əbr-əŋ*.

283 bihal- "be angry"

Sem **bVhal-* "curse" (v.): Arab *bhl* [-*a*-].
WCh **biHal-* "anger": Mnt *bial*.

284 *biH[o]d- "jump, run"

CCh **biHVd-* "go": Boka *biḍe-ḍi*.
LEC **bVHod-* "jump": Som *bood-*.
Omot **biHVd-* "jump": Bwo *biḍ-*.
Dhl *ɓuḏuw-* "run away".
-*uw*- may be a suffix.

285 *biHok- "rain"

WCh **biHVk-* "rain that succeeds sowing": Hs *bīko*.
LEC **bVHok-* "rain": Som *bokk-*, Or *booka*.

286 *bil- "butterfly"

WCh **bil-* "butterfly, bird": Hs *bilbilo*, Glm *ḅil-iwi*.
Reduplication in Hs. Glm may go back to **HV-bil-* > *ḅil-*.
Agaw **bil-* "butterfly": Xmr *bil*.
Rift **ba-bal-* "butterfly": Kwz *babal-iko*.
Partial reduplication causing a change of vocalism.

Related to **bal-* "wing, feather"?

287 bil- "door"

Sem **ˁabul-* "door, gate": Akk *ˁabullu*, Aram (Syr) *ˁābul-*.
Prefix **ˁa-*. Secondary **u* < **i* after a labial.
Agaw **bil-* "door" [1], "hole, window" [2]: Xmr *bila* [1], Kwr *bela* [2].
LEC **bal-bal-* "door": Or *balbala*.
Reduplication with modified vocalism.

288 *bin- "man, male relative"

Sem **bin-* "son": Akk *binu*, Ug *bn*, Phn *bn*, Pun *bn*, Moab *bn*, Hbr *bēn*, Aram (Nab) *bn*, Arab *bin-*, SAr *bn*, Hss *ḥe-būn* (pl.).
Hardly any connection with Sem **bar-* id.
WCh **mV-bVn-* "person": Buli *mbən*, *mban*.
Prefix **mV-*.
CCh **bin-* "brother": LPe *bin*.

289 *binVg- "bird"

Eg *bng* "kind of bird" (MK).
WCh **binVg-* "rough-coated fowl": Hs *bingi*.
CCh **byanVg-* "bird": Gid *benga*, *buŋga*.
Secondary vocalism in *buŋga*.

290 *bir- "metal"

Eg *byꜣ* "ore, copper" (XVIII).
Vocalic *-y-*.
CCh **HV-bir-* "iron": Mofu *bərey*, Gis *ḅire*.
Prefix **HV-* reflected in the Gis initial emphatic.
ECh **bir-* "iron": Smr *biri*.

Agaw **bir-* "metal": Kem *birr*.
LEC **bir-* "metal": Som *bir*.
HEC **bir(r)-* "silver": Bmb *birri*, Kmb *bira-ta*.
Omot **bir-* "metal": Kaf *bir-ewo*.

Cf. derivatives in SA **birit-* "iron" (Saho *birtaa*, Afar *birtaa*) and Rift (Kwz *belet-iko* id.).

291 *bir- "jump"

CCh **mV-bir-* "jump, fly": Daba *mbir*, Msg *mbir*.
Prefix **mV-*.
ECh **bir-* "jump": Kwn *bəre*.
Bed *bir* "jump".
Agaw **bir-* "jump" [1], "fly" [2]: Xmr *bir-* [1], Aun *berer-əŋ* [2].
Partial reduplication in Aun.
HEC **burr-* "jump": Bmb *burr-*.
**i* > **u* after a labial.

292 *bir- "finger"

WCh **bir-* "finger-nail": Sha *bər-ən*, Grn *mbil*.
Prefix **mV-* in Grn. Grn *-l-* < **-r-* is regular.
Omot **bir-* "finger": Ome *bir-aḍe*.

293 *bir- "bird"

Berb **bVr-* "quail": Twl *ta-bərr-ut*.
Eg *bꜣ* "kind of bird" (a).
WCh **bir-* "quail": Hs *birabirā*.
Reduplication in Hs. Note a parallel variant *buraburā*.

294 *birVg- "be high"

Berb **bVrVg-* "rise": Tua *burg-ət*.
Bed *birga* "high".

295 *bisVr- "plant"

Sem **bišr-* "onion" [1], "sprout, shoot" [2], "dates" [3]: Akk *bišru*, *bisru* [1], Arab *busr-at-* [2], Hss *beser* [3], Mhr *bēser* [3].

Arab *-u-* < **-i-* after a labial.
Eg *ỉbsꜣ* "plant" (MK).
Prefix **ʾ-* or a graphic sign for **-i-* of the first syllable.

296 *bit- "jump"

WCh **bit-* "jump": Bgh *pit*.
Bgh *p-* < **b-* is regular.
Omot **bitt-* "jump" [1], "fly" [2]: Kaf *bitt-* [1], Mch *biitti* [2].

297 *boʾ- "grass"

Berb **buʾ-* "grass": Izy *a-bu*, Gua *buho*.
WCh **bay-* < **baʾi-* "kind of wild grass": Hs *bayā*.
ECh **bwaʾi-* "grass": Bid *booʾibooʾi*.
Full reduplication.

298 *boʾ- "slave, servant"

Eg *wbꜣ* "servant" (MK).
Initial *w-* stands for a rounded vowel in the root.
WCh **bway-* < **bwaʾi-* "slave" [1], "servant" [2]: Hs *bāwa* [1], Bol *baya* [1], Ngz *baayi* [2].

299 *boʾVd- "vessel"

Sem **buʾd-* "implement": Akk *buʾdu*, *būdu*.
Unexpected HS **u* > **u* after a labial.
Eg *bꜣd.t* "dipper" (med).
ECh **bwaʾVd-* "gourd": Mkk *boode*, Bid *booda*.

300 *bod- "penis"

CCh **bwadVH-* "penis" [1], "vagina" [2]: Bch *vöḍu-to* [1], Gudu *vədə-cu* [2].
SA **bud-* "penis": Afar *buddaa*.

301 *bogur- "bird"

Eg *bḏꜣ* "duck" (OK).

-ḏ- < **-g-* after **o*.

ECh **bwagur-* "hen": Kwn *bogor-to*, *bugur-to*, Kera *də-bərgə*, (pl.) *ga-bgur*.

Various assimilations of root vowels in individual forms.

302 *boᶜ- "sun"

Eg *bᶜ* "Sun-god" (reg).

WCh **bwaH-* "sun": Bks *ḅwe*, DB *ḅwe*.

The emphatic anlaut reflects the lost laryngeal.

303 *boᶜ-boᶜ- "pour, drink"

Sem **baᶜ-baᶜ-* "gurgling of water": Arab *baᶜbaᶜ-t-*

Deverbative noun.

Eg *bᶜbᶜ* "drink" (pyr).

ECh **bwaH-b[wa]H-* "pour": Dng *boobe*, Jnk *boobo*.

Derived from HS **baᶜ-* "pour". Reduplication. May be an onomatopoeia.

304 *boḥ- "middle"

Sem **buḥ-buḥ-* "middle": Arab *buḥbūḥ-at-*.

Full reduplication.

CCh **bwaχ-* "middle": Bud *boho*.

305 *boḥVr- "sea, lake"

Sem **baḥr-* "sea, lake": Aram (Syr) *baḥrā*, Arab *baḥr-*, SAr *bḥr*, Gz *bāḥr*, Tgr *bähar*, Tgy *baḥri*, Amh *bahər*.

Regular Sem **-u-* > **-a-* after a labial.

WCh **bwaHVr-* "pond" [1], "rivulet" [2]: Sura *voɣor* [2], Grk *vor*, *voor* [1 2], Ang *fwor* [2].

ECh **bwar-* < **bwaHVr-* "sea, river": Kera *vor*.

306 *boḫ- "give birth"

Eg *bẖ* "give birth" (NK).

Conditions in which HS **ḫ* > Eg *ẖ* are unknown.

WCh **bwaH-* "give birth": Zaar *ḅwa*.

Emphatic in Zaar reflects a lost laryngeal.

CCh **mV-buh-* "give birth": Nza *mbuho*, FJ *mbu*.

307 *boHar- "be yellow, be gray"

CCh **bwaH[a]r-* "gray": Msg *bɔgɔraˁ*.

Since **bwaHwar-* with two middle vowels is morphonologically impossible, the reconstruction of **-a-* in the second syllable is inevitable.

LEC **boHor-* "yellow": Or *boora*.

Cf. Arb *burri* "red"? Assimilation of vowels.

HEC **bor-* "gray, brown": Kmb *bora*.

308 *boḳ- "rot, be rotten"

Sem **bVḳ-* "rot": Hbr *bqq*, Aram *bqq*, (Mand) *baq*.

WCh **ɓwak- < *bwaḳ-* "suppurate, fester": Sura *ɓwak*.

Shift of emphatization.

HEC **buḳ-* "rot": Bmb *buuḳ-*.

309 *boḳ- "goat"

CCh **ɓwak- < *bwaḳ-* "goat": Mafa *ɓokw*.

Shift of emphatization. *-kw < *-k-* appeared in the auslaut under the influence of the root vowel.

Bed *bok*, *book*.

Cf. ECh **bVk-* "kine": Kera *beke*.

310 *boḳar- "cattle"

Sem **baḳar-* "bull" [1], "cattle" [2]."cow" [3]: Akk *buqāru* [1], Phn *bqr* [2], Hbr *bāqār* [2], Aram (Palest) *bᵉqartā* [2], Arab *baqar-* [2], SAr *bqr* [2], Hss *beqār* [3].

In the first syllable, Sem **-a- <* HS **-o-* is regular after a labial. *-u-* in Akk is secondary.

Berb **bukVr-* "one year old camel": Twl *əbuɣer*.

CCh **bwakVr-* "goat": Tera *bokəra*, Tera-P. *pokər-ti*, Bch *bogər-ey*.

Derived from **boḳ-* "goat". On the other hand, cf. **baraḳ-* "ram, goat, calf".

311 *boḳVr- "rich, king"

Berb **bVḳVr-* "be rich": Ahg *bəγər*, Twl *baghar*.
LEC **boḳor-* "king": Som *boqor*.

The reconstruction of HS **boḳor-* implied by LEC is morphonologically improbable.

312 *bol- "flow, be wet"

Sem **bul-* "moisten" [1], "rain" [2]: Aram *bll* [1], Arab *bll* [-*u*-] [2]. Secondary **u*. Cf. Arab *wbl* [-*u*-] "fall (of rain)" (v.) and also a deverbative name in Hbr *yābāl* "heavy shower", Arab *wabl-* "shower".
CCh **HV-bwal-* "rain": Bch *ḅole*.
Prefix **HV-*.

313 *bol- "lead, follow"

Sem **wVbVl-* "lead": Hbr *ybl*, Aram *ybl*.
**wV-* may be a prefix.
WCh **byal-/*bwal-* "come" [1], "follow" [2]: Grk *bel* [1], Bol *bol* [2], Sha *bol* [1].
CCh **bul-* "run": HNk *mbule*, HG *mbule*, HB *mbulo*, HF *mbəlu*.

314 *bolan- "rain, cloud"

ECh **bVlan-* "rain" [1], "sky" [2]: Smr *belani* [1], Tum *bəlan* [1 2], Ndam *bəlān* [2].
LEC **bolan-* "cloud": Arb *boolan*.

Related to **belal-* "rivulet".

315 *bor- "eat"

Sem **bVrVy-* "eat": Hbr *bry*.
Based on biliteral **bVr-*.
ECh **HV-bwar-* "eat": Tum *ḅor*.
Prefix **HV-* reflected in the Tum anlaut.

316 *boriġ- "insect"

Berb *bVriγ- "mosquito" [1], "flying ant" [2]: Ayr *bərγu* [1], Twl *bərγu* [1], Kby *i-bərriq* [2].
CCh *bwarVg- "louse": Log *borgo-mī*.
*-g- may be irregular. A normal CCh reflex of HS *ġ (at least in the anlaut) would be *γ. Cf. also metathetic Msg *biggerui* id.
ECh *bVrVg- "water insect" [1], "caterpillar" [2]: Kera *abərgi-jiwjiw* [1], Tum *kərə-bəərg-ən* [2].
Composites both in Kera and Tum.

317 *bos- "fish"

Eg *bss* "kind of fish" (n).
Partial reduplication or a graphic peculiarity?
WCh *HV-bwas- "fish": Dok *p̣was*, Wnd *ḅas*, Bnd *bwas*.
Laryngeal prefix.
ECh *busi- "fish": Mig *būsu*, Jegu *bišo*, Sok *busī*.

318 *buᵓ- "pot"

Eg *bȝw* "vessel" (med).
Cf. also *bᶜ* id. (OK) implying a different laryngeal. *-w* seems to be a vocalic sign for *-u-.
WCh *buᵓ- "pot": Grk *bu*.
CCh *ḅu- < *buᵓ- "pot": Tera *ḅu-ya*, Hw *ḅu-ra*, Gbn *ḅu-ta*, Boka *ḅə-ta*.

319 *buᵓar- "dig"

Sem *bVᵓar- "dig (a well)": Arab *bᵓr* [-a-].
WCh *buHar- "dig": Zul *yabori*, Fyer *ḅur*, Bks *ḅor*, DB *ḅuur*.
LEC *boHVr- "dig": Som *boor-*, Or *bor-*.

320 *buᵓuḥ- "penis"

Sem *būḥ- "penis" [1], "votive phallus" [2]: Arab *būḥ-* [1], SAr *bḥ-t* [2].
*ū results from a contraction.
Eg *bȝḥ* "penis" (pyr).

321 *buç- "sand, earth"

Sem *bāṣ- "sand" 1, "mud" 2: Akk bāṣu 1, Hbr bōṣ 2.
Regular Sem *-a- < HS *-u- after a labial.
HEC *buc- "soil": Bmb bucca, Kmb bucca, Sid buššа.
Irregular *-c-.

322 *buçal- "plant"

Sem *baṣal- "onion": Hbr bāṣāl, Aram (Syr) beṣlō, Arab baṣal-, SAr bṣl, Hss beṣel, Mhr beṣāl, Shh beṣal.
Regular Sem *-a- < HS *-u- after a labial.
WCh *ḇucal- < *buçal- "kind of grass": Bks ḇušal.
Shift of emphatization.

Derived from *buç- "sand, earth"? For a semantic parallel see *caẖal- "grass".

323 *buč- "pudenda"

Sem *buṯ- "shame, shameful object": Ug bṯṯ, Hbr būšā, Aram (Emp) bwt, (Palest) bīhūtā.
Cf also Akk la būštu "shamelessness". Related to *bVṯ- "be ashamed" (Akk bâšu, Ug bṯ, Hbr bwš, Aram (Palest) b^{e}hēt). Unexpectedly preserved *-u- in the root. Does it imply a reconstruction of a parallel HS *bač-?
Berb *buč- "vagina" 1, "penis" 2: Siwa bašša 1, Sml bəšši 1, Ntf a-bəšši 1, Izn a-bətš-un 1, Kby a-bbuc 2.
Bed bus "podex, croupe".
SA *bus- "vulva": Saho bus, Afar bus, busuu.
HEC *bis(s)- "vagina": Had bisso.
Unexpected *i.
Omot *bos- "vulva": Yam boosaa.

324 *bud- "hate" (v.)

Sem *bVdVy- "express hate": Arab bdy.
Based on *bVd-.
ECh *bu-buḍ- "curse": Mobu bəbəḍe, Ngm bubbuḍḍe.
Reduplication. Unexpected emphatic -ḍ-.

325 *bud- ''stick''

Sem **bad(d)-* ''pole, stick, beam'': Hbr *bad*, Aram *badd-*, Arab *badd-*.
Berb **budid-* ''pole of a hut'': Kby *a-βuδiδ*.
Secondary **u* after a labial. Partial reduplication.
ECh **bVdVH-* ''stick'': Kera *bəḍ-uwa*.
Suffix *-*H*-.

Cf. partial reduplication in CCh **bV-bVdVH-* ''digging stick'': Mafa *bebeḍ*.

326 *buʕun- ''rain, sky''

Eg *bʕn* ''sky waters'' (pyr).
CCh **buHun-* ''rain'': Gid *būna*.
ECh **bun-H-* ''rain'' [1], ''sky'' [2], ''God'' [3]: Mig *bun* [1], Dng *buŋ* [2], Jegu *boŋ* [2 3], Bid *buŋ* [2 3], Mubi *bun* [2].
Metathesis.

327 *buhar- ''shine''

Sem **bVhar-* ''be clear, shine'': Hbr *bhr*, Aram (Palest) *šabhar*, (Mand) *bhʾr*, Arab *bhr* [*-a-*].
WCh **buHVr-* ''shine'': Tng *ḅɛr*, Bgh *ḅūr*.
CCh **buHar-* ''shine'': Msg *bara*, Bch *ḅura*.

328 *bul- ''hut, village''

CCh **bul-* ''village'': Bud *bula*.
ECh **bVl-bVl-* ''yard'': Bud *belbele*.
Reduplication.
Agaw *ʾ*a-bVl-* ''tent'': Bil *abluu*.
SA **bul-* ''village, town'': Afar *buḷaa*.
Secondary *-ḷ-* in Afar?
LEC **bul-* ''hut'': Som *bul*.

329 *bul- ''lake, river''

Sem **bal-* ''lake'': Gur *bal*.
Proto-Sem status of this word is subject to doubts.
Eg *wbn* ''spring, source'' (n).

-*n* goes back to HS *-*l*-. Initial *w*- stands for a rounded root vowel.

WCh **bul-/*buʾul-* "river": Zul *ḅwulaʾyi*, *bullai*, Bgh *ḅul*.
Infix *-ʾ-.

CCh **bul-ay-* "sea, lake": Gis *bulay*, Mofu *bəlay*.
Cf. reduplication in Bud *bilabila* "lake".

Related to **bol-* "flow, be wet", **belal-* "rivulet" and its cognates.

330 *bul- "dove"

Eg *bn* "kind of bird" (pyr), *bnw* "phoenix" (BD).
bnw reflects **bul-* or **bol-*.

WCh **buʾal-* "dove": Hs *bōlō*, Sura *mbul*, Ang *bul*, Ank *bel*, Chip *bul*, Bol *mbolo*, Tng *la-mbul*.
Several forms have prefix **mV-*.

CCh **mV-bwal-* "turtle-dove": Tera *mbole*.
Prefix **mV-*.

ECh **buʾal* "bird" [1], "dove" [2]: Bid *bulle* [1], Gabri *belu* [2], Kwan *bəlō-ki* [2].

LEC **bulal-* "dove": Or *bullale*.
Partial reduplication. Amh *bulall*, Gur *bulle* are borrowed from LEC.

Secondary formation with an inlaut laryngeal in Chadic.

331 *bul-bul- "pour, flow"

Eg *bnbn* "let flow, pour" (gr).

WCh **bul-bul-* "pour out": Hs *bulbulā*.

Reduplication connected with **bul-* "lake, river" and **bol-* "flow, be wet".

332 *bul-/*bulal- "pit, well"

Berb **bVlVl-* "breach, opening in the rock": Ahg *e-bələl*.
Partial reduplication.

CCh **bul-* "hole": Log *bulu*.

ECh **bul-* "hole": Bid *bullo*, Mig *būle*.

333 *bulaˁ- "throat"

Sem *balaˁ- "throat": Aram *bālaˁtā*.
WCh *bulaʾ- < *bulaˁ- "craw, goitre": Bks *buleʾ*.
Bed *balaʾa* "gullet".
Assimilation of vowels.

Afar *biliˁa* seems to belong to this root. However the vocalism of the word is not clear. Related to HS *baliˁ- "eat, swallow".

334 *bulul- "flow, be wet"

Berb *bVlul- "be liquid": Ahg *bəlulu*.
The first syllable may contain *-a-*.
LEC *bulul- "flow": Or *bulula*.

Partial reduplication connected with *bul-bul- "pour, flow" and *bol- "flow, be wet".

335 *bun- "monkey"

Eg *bnw* "baboon" (BD).
-w stands for a rounded vowel.
WCh *buni- "monkey": Paa *bun*, Siri *bini*.
CCh *buni- "monkey": Gude *mɔ-bin*, Bch *ma-bwən*.

336 *bur- "boat"

Eg *br* "kind of Nubian ship" (n).
ECh *bur- "boat": Ndm *burō*.

337 *bur- "earth, sand"

Sem *barr- "empty place" [1], "field" [2], "(dry) land" [3], "region" [3]: Akk *barru* [1], Hbr *bar* [2], Aram (Syr) *barra* [2], Arab *barr-* [3], SAr *br* [2], Tgr *barr* [4].
Regular Sem *-a- < HS *-u-* after a labial.
Berb *bVrVw- "valley": Izy *ταβλαυτ*.
Derivative in *-Vw-.
WCh *buHVr- "sand" [1], "dust [2]: Sura *ḅur* [1 2], Ang *bur* [1 2], Krk *bər-bər-ən* [2], Bks *ḅura* [2], DB *ḅura* [2].
Secondary laryngeal infix.

CCh *bur-* "sand" [1], "dust [2]: Log *būrā* [1], Bud *bur- bur* [2].
ECh *bar-H-* "field": Kwan *kō-ḅarā*.
Irregular vocalism. Secondary laryngeal suffix.
SA *bur-* "sand": Saho *buree*.
LEC *bur-* "dune" [1], "earth" [2]: Som *burᶜo* [1], Arb *boore* [2].
Cf. also Or *booruu* "muddy".
Dhl *ḅur-une* "dust".

338 *bur- "boil"

Eg *brbr* "boil" (n), Copt *berber* id.: Boh *berber*.
Reduplication.
Berb *bVr-* "boil": Mzab *abər*, Nfs *abər*.
CCh *mV-bur-* "boil": Mnd *mbur*.
Prefix *mV-*.

339 *bur- "penis"

Eg *bȝȝw* "potency" (MK).
-ȝȝ- continues HS *-r-*. In the auslaut, *-w* is a sign for a rounded vowel.
WCh *bur-* "penis": Hs *būrā*.
CCh *bur-* "penis": Bura *bura*.

340 *bur- "calf"

Sem *būr-* "calf": Akk *būru*.
Regular long *ū preserved after a labial.
HEC *bur-* "calf": Dar *bur-uusa*.

Related to *bur-* "goat, sheep"?

341 *bur- "goat, sheep"

WCh *mV-bur-* "sheep": Buli *am-bərə*, *mberra*, Tala *mburra*.
Prefix *mV-*.
CCh *bur-* "goat": Hil *burā*, Klb *bura*.
Mwl *bwāra* < *bura-*.
LEC *barar-* "lambs" (pl.): Som *baraar*.
Partial reduplication and changed vocalism in a plural form.
Mgg *abuur* "sheep".

342 *buraʾ- ''build''

Sem *bVraʾ- ''create'': Hbr *brʾ*, Aram *bᵉrā*, (Mand) *bra*, Arab *brʾ* [-*a*-].
WCh *bur- ''build'': Krf *buru-*, Glm *bər-*.

Related to *bür- ''fortified place, building''. It is also possible to reconstruct *büraʾ-.

343 *buram- ''(be) particolored, (be) yellow''

Sem *barm- ''particolored'': Akk *barmu*.
Berb *bVram- ''yellow straw'': Ayr *i-bram*.
WCh *burum- ''yellow'': DB *burum*.
Assimilation of vowels.

344 *b[u]ray- ''grain, corn''

Berb *bVray- ''pounded grain'' 1, ''flour'' 2, ''pounded barley'' 3: Bmr *bərri* 1, Sml *i-bri-n* 2, Sgh *i-brai-n* 2, Izn *a-brəi* 3, Snh *a-brəi* 3.
Eg *bꜣy* ''kind of pastry'' (MK).
-*ꜣ*- < HS *-*r*-. Cf. Eg *brry* s.v. *ber- ''maize''

Derived from *bar-/*bur- ''grain, cereal''.

345 *burġuč- ''insect''

Sem *burġuṯ- ''flea'': Arab *burġūṯ-*.
WCh *burġuč- ''mosquito'': Gera *bursi*, Dera *buruk*.
CCh *mV-bVrguč- ''louse'': Daba *mbərguč*.

Related to *boriġ- ''insect''.

346 *burog- ''stomach''

Sem *ʾargāb- ''intestines'': Arab *ʾargāb-*.
Results from a metathesis of *-*b*- in *burog-. Initial *ʾ- is non-etymological. On the other hand, cf. Arab *bugr-* ''swelled belly''.
CCh *bVrwag- ''intestines'': Mnd *brogue*.
ECh *burwag- ''stomach'': Tum *buroog*.

Derived from *bor- ''eat''.

347 *bus- "plant, grass"

Eg *wbs* "cabbage, greens" (gr).
w- is a vocalic sign.
WCh **bus-* "kind of plant": Hs *būšī*.

348 *but- "hut"

Berb **but-* "mud-house": Ntf *ta-but*.
Cf. Bmr *ta-but* "door".
WCh **but-* "hut": Bks *but*, Klr *ʾabut*.

Related to **bayit-* "house"?

349 *but- "vessel"

Sem **batt-* "bottle": Arab *batt-at-*.
Regular **-a-* < HS **-u-* after a labial.
WCh **buHat-* "gourd bottle": Hs *būta*, Gera *mboota*.
CCh **bVt-* "pot": HNk *pta*.
p- < **b-* in contact with unvoiced *-t-*.
SA **but-* "pot": Afar *buti*.
HEC **bot-* "big jar": Bmb *bota*.
Omot **bat-/*bot-* "gourd, calabash": Ome *batta*, Kaf *botoo*, Mch *boto*, Gim *bat*.

350 *buṭ- "belly"

Berb **buṭ-* "navel" [1], "belly" [2]: Awj *a-būṭ* [1], Ahg *tə-but-ut* [1], Twl *tə-būṭ-ut* [1], Sml *a-buḍ* [1], Ntf *a-buḍ* [2].
WCh **ḇut-* < **buṭ-* "belly, stomach": Sura *ḇut*, Ang *ḇwut*, Mnt *ḇət*, Fyer *ḇuto*.
Shift of emphatization.

351 *buṭ- "vessel"

Sem **baṭ(ṭ)-* "vessel": Akk *baṭû*, Arab *baṭṭ-at-*.
Regular **-a-* < HS **-u-* after a labial.
Berb **buṭ-* "bottom of a vessel": Ntf *a-buḍ*, Sgr *buḍ*.

352 *b[u]ṭin- "womb"

Sem *baṭn- "womb": Hbr *beṭen*, Aram (Emp) *bṭn*, (Palest) *baṭnā*, *biṭnā*, Tgr *bäṭn*, Hrr *bäṭni*.

Secondary *-i-* in Aram. Regular **-a-* < HS **-u-* after a labial.

Berb **biniṭ-* "navel": Ntf *i-biniḍ*.

Metathesis on the HS level? Cf. Eg reflex of HS **b[u]ṭun-*. On the other hand, in Berb cf. Kby *le-bden* "body".

Derived from HS **buṭ-* "belly".

353 *buwuṭ- "burn; ash"

Eg *wbd* "burn" (mag).

Metathesis or a graphic representation of Proto-Eg **bud*? *-d* < **-ṭ-* is regular.

WCh **buw(V)ṭ-* "ash": Bol *buto*, Krk *bəto*, Dera *bubute*, Bele *buto*, Krf *buto*, Gera *bəḍa*, Diri *butu*, Ngz *bəbət*.

Partial reduplication in Dera.

CCh **bVwuṭ-* "ash": LPe *bwut*.

ECh **but-* "ash": Mig *bitti*, Bid *buto*, Brg *buti*.

Assimilation of vowels in Mig.

Dhl *ḅuw-eeδ-* "boil" may reflect a HS verb **buw-* from which the present root was derived.

354 *buyaĉ̣- "egg"

Sem **bayṣ̂-* "egg": Hbr *bēṣā*, Aram (Syr) *bīʕtō*, Arab *bayḍ-*, Hss *bēṣ̂eh*, Mhr *bēṣ̂ayt*, Shh *beṣ̂*.

Regular **-a-* < HS **-u-* after a labial.

WCh **buyaĉ̣-* "egg": Pol *byaŝ*, Geji *mbuŝi*, Zem *mboŝ*, Brw *mbuŝ*, *mboŝ*, Say *mbuŝ*, Buli *mbiŝ*.

355 *buʒ- "be bad"

Sem **bVzVy-* "treat badly" [1], "scorn" [2]: Akk *buzzuʔu* [1], Hbr *bzy* [2], Aram (Palest) *bazzē* [2].

Based on **bVz-*.

CCh **buʒ-* "evil, bad": Zgh *buza*, Gvo *bəza*.

356 *bük- "bird"

Eg *byk* "falcon" (a).
-y- may be a sign for a front vowel.
CCh **bwak-* < **buka-* "vulture" [1], "hen" [2]: LPe *bwok* [1], Msm *bok* [1], Gis *bokoy* [2].
ECh **ʾa-buk-* "great bustard": Bid *ʾabuka*.
Prefix **ʾa-*.
Agaw **bik-* "kind of bird": Bil *bikaa*.

357 *bül- "cure"

Sem **bil-* "heal, cure": Arab *bll* [*-i-*].
CCh **mV-bul-* "cure": Gis *mboul*, Mofu *mbəl*.
Prefix **mV-*.
ECh **bVl-* "cure": Sbn *bələ*.

358 *bür- "door"

Sem **birr-* "grill, lettice (of doors, windows)": Akk *birru*.
Berb **bur-* "door": Ghd *ta-ββur-t*, Ghat *ta-wur- t*, Ahg *ta-hor-t*, Kby *ta-bbur-t*.
Note Berb **b-* > **β-*.
LEC **bor-* "back (of a house)": Or *boroo*.

Related to **bür-* "fortified place, building"?

359 *bür- "fortified place, building"

Sem **bīr-* "fortress, palace": Akk *bir-t-*, Hbr *bīrā*, Aram (Emp, Nab) *byrtʾ*, (Palest) *bīrtā*.
WCh **bur-* "place" [1], "hut" [2]: Paa *mbura* [1], Siri *bəri* [1], Buli *ibəri* [1], Fyer *bur* [2].
CCh **bur-* "town": Mnd *bəre*, Gudu *vura-čü*, Nza *vəra-či*, Mwu *vura*, Bch *vura-to*.

360 *büʒ- "breast, bosom"

Sem **bizz-* "breast" [1], "nipple" [2]: Aram (Pehl) *bz* [1], (Syr) *bezzā* [2], Arab *bizz-* [2].
Berb **buʒ-* "large breasts": Ahg *buhū-tən*.

A descriptive stem.

361 *bVĉir- "announce"

Sem *bVŝir- "announce (good news)": Akk *bašāru*, Ug *bšr*, Hbr *bŝr*, Aram (Palest) *b^eŝar*, Arab *bšr* [-*i*-], SAr *tbŝr*, Soq *bsr*, Hss *abēśer*, Mhr *abōśer*, Shh *ōśer*.
Berb *bVçVr- "announce": Ghd *i-βdər*, Sml *i-bdər*, Kby *yəβḍər*.
Berb reflects *-ĉ̣-.

Irregular correspondence of affricates.

362 *bVġ- "wish"

Sem *bVġiw-/*bVġiy- "look for" [1], "wish" [2]: Akk *buʾü,baʾü* [1], OAram *ybʿh* [2], Aram (Emp) *bʿh* [2], Arab *bġw* [-*i*-] [2], Hss *beġayt* [2], Mhr *beġayt* [2].
CCh *bVγ- "not wish": Log *bγ'a*.
Note the peculiar semantic development: "not wish" ? ← * "wish not to".

363 *bVʿon- "neck"

Eg *bʿn* "neck (of a bird)" (pyr).
This word may be also compared with HS *bulaʿ- "throat".
WCh *bVHwan- "neck": Pero *ḅwəŋ*.
-*ŋ* < *-*n*-*H*- as a result of the metathesis of the inlaut laryngeal.

364 *bVhVw- "shine"

Sem *bVhVw- "shine": Arab *bhw* [-*u*-].
CCh *bVHVw-/*bVHVy- "light" [1], "lightning" [2]: Dgh *ḅiya* [1], LPe *buwo* [2].
Vowels both in Dgh and LPe are secondary for morphological and/or phonological reasons.

365 *bVŝ- "dig, bury"

Sem *nVbuś- "dig out": Arab *nbš* [-*u*-]
Prefix *nV-. Secondary *-*u*- after a labial may go back to HS *-*a*-.
WCh *bVŝ- "bury": Ngz *bəẑu*, Bade *əbẑu*.
CCh *bVẑ- "bury": Bura *bẑa*.

366 *bVtVḳ- "cut"

Sem *bVtVḳ- "cut, chop": Akk *batāqu*, *badāqu*, Hbr *btq*, Arab *btq*. Eg *btk* "slaughter" (gr).

Late development of *ḳ > *k*.

367 *bVṭun- "be pregnant"

Sem *bVṭun- "be pregnant" 1, "have a big belly" 2: Hbr *bṭn* 1, Aram (Talm) *bᵉṭan* 1, Arab *bṭn* 2 [-*u*-], Hss *beṭīn* 2, Mhr *beṭayn* 2, Shh *beṭin* 2.

Secondary *-*u*-?

Eg *bnd* "difficult delivery" (med).

Metathesis. Cf. Berb reflexes of *b[u]ṭin-.

Derived from *b[u]ṭin- "womb".

368 *bVw-/*bVy- "cry, weep"

WCh *bVy- "cry, weep": Siri *biyi*, Kry *biy*.

Secondary *i before *y.

LEC *bo- < *bVw- "cry, weep": Or *boo-*.

Note consonantal alternation *-*w*- ~ *-*y*-.

369 *bVʒuḳ- "be wet, spit"

Sem *bVzuḳ- "spit": Arab *bzq* [-*u*-], Tgr *bozäqä*.

Berb *bVʒVḳ- "be wet": Ghd *bzəγ*, Sml *ibzəg*, Ntf *əbzəg*, Shn *ibzəg*, Kby *əβzəγ*.

*C

370 *caʾ- "tree"

WCh *caʾ- "kind of tree": Tng *saaye*, *saawe*.

Derivative in *-*ay*- or *-*aw*-.

CCh *cyaʾ- "wood": Gaa *šeʾa*.

Irregular vocalism.

ECh *sVw- "tree": Sok *səwi*.

Cf. also Sok *čui* id., *suo* "acacia"?
Rift *caˀ-* "tree": Kwz *caˀ-unko*.

371 *cabar- "stick"

Eg *sbr* "twig, branch" (med).
Cf. also *ỉsbr* "whip" (NK) where *ỉ-* may be a prefix.
WCh **cabar-* "wooden poles": Hs *ç̣abarā*.
Hs *ç̣-* < WCh **c-* is regular.

372 *cabel-/*ç̣abel- "wild cat, leopard"

WCh **cVḅyal-* < **ç̣Vbyal-* "wild cat": Sura *səḅɛl*, Ang *sōl*, Mpn *səbəl*.
LEC **šabel-* "leopard": Som *šabeel*, Boni *šuel*.
Boni reflects an earlier **šawel-* < **šabel-*.

Irregular correspondence in the anlaut.

373 *cag- "break"

Sem **sVgVʿ-* "pierce": Gz *sagʷʿa*, Tgy *sägʷʿe*.
Secondary formation based on **sVg-*?
Eg *sḏ* "break" (pyr).
-ḏ points out to a preceding vowel different from **a*.
WCh **cag-* "break, cut": Hs *ç̣āga*.

374 *cagaḥ- "bird"

Eg *sḏḥ* "kind of bird" (MK).
Unexpected palatalization may indicate a root vowel other than **a*.
WCh **cagag-* "ibis": Hs *ç̣agagi*.
Partial reduplication.
ECh **sagay-* < **sagaH-* "vulture": Kwan *sagay*.

375 *caʿaw-/*caʿay- "squeeze, press"

Sem **sVʿVy-* "squeeze": Akk *seˀû*.
WCh **cV-cVy-* "squeeze": Miya *asəsəyo*.
Partial reduplication.

ECh **saw-* "squeeze out pus": Ngam *sow*.
Secondary *-o-* < **-a-* before a labial.

Consonantal alternation **-w-* ~ **-y-*.

376 *cahVw- "plaited object"

Sem **sahw-* "curtain": Arab *sahw-*.
WCh **caw-/*cay-* "plaited cover for a door": Hs *ҫauyā, ҫaiwā, ҫayawa*.
The inlaut laryngeal left no traces.
Rift **caḫw-* "snare": Irq *caḫwe-li*, Kwz *caʾ-uko*.
Kwz seems irregular.

377 *caḥ- "herd"

Eg *sḥȝ.t* "herd of donkeys" (OK).
-ȝ denotes a root vowel.
WCh **caḥi-* "herd": Wrj *čiyə*, Siri *cagu*.
Wrj *-i-* influenced by WCh **i* of the second syllable.

378 *caḥ- "know, teach"

WCh **caw-* < **caHaw-* "teach": Bol *soow*.
Suffix **-aw-*.
Rift **caḥ-* "learn, know": Irq *in-caḥ-*, Asa *šah-*.

379 *caḫal- "grass"

Sem **saḫl-* "cresse": Akk *saḫlû*.
CCh **cahal-* "grass": Mofu *sahal*.
ECh **sVHVl-* "grass": Mkk *soole*.

Probably, should be reconstructed as **caqal-* and derived from **caq-* "earth, field" if the comparison with **buҫal-* "plant" ← **buҫ-* "sand, earth" is valid.

380 *calaḳ- "gather"

Sem **sVlVḳ-* "gather": Arab *slq*.
Eg *sȝḳ* "gather" (pyr).

Note HS *-*l*- > -*ꜣ*-.
CCh **caḳal*- "gather, collect": Mafa *cakal*, Mofu *čakal*.
Metathesis. Unexpected in *č*- Mofu.

381 *calaq̇- "lamb, goat"

Sem **saḫ̮l*- "lamb": Arab *saḫ̮l-at*-.
Metathesis.
Berb **cVlaγ*- "goat": Siwa *zalaq*, Ayr *ə-zolaġ*, Ahg *a-hulaġ*, Twl *e-zolaġ*, Sha *zalaġ*.
CCh **calak*- "gazelle": Msg *salak*, *salag*.
ECh **sakal*- "lamb": Mig *sakalle*.
Metathesis.

An alternative reconstruction may be **caq̇al*-.

382 *cam- "yellow, red"

Sem **sām*- "red": Akk *sāmu*.
CCh **ci-cim*- "yellow": Gude *šišima*, Boka *šumma*, Hil *mī-šišimə:*.
Partial reduplication with modified vocalism.

383 *camid- "grass"

Sem **samīd*- "spice plant, vegetable groats": Akk *samīdu*.
ECh **sVmVd*- "grass": Smr *semdē*.
Assimilation of vowels under the influence of auslaut -*ē*.

Derived from **cim*- "grass, plant".

384 *cap- "vessel"

Sem **sapp*- "kind of vessel": Akk *sappu*, Hbr *sap*, Phn *sp*.
Eg *sp.t* "vessel" (n).

A cultural loanword or an inherited HS term?

385 *caq- "earth, field"

Sem **saḫ̮ḫ̮*- "meadow" [1], "good land" [2] Akk *saḫ̮ḫ̮u* [1], Arab *saḫ̮āḫ̮*- [2].
Secondary formation in Arab based on **saḫ̮ḫ̮*-.

Eg *sḫ.t* "field" (pyr), Copt *soḫi* id.: Fym *šōši*, Shd *sōše*.
CCh **caqwa-* "field" [1], "ground" [2], "sand" [3]: Log *sχē* [1], Hwn *čəχwē-ra* [2], Boka *-soχi-tə* [3], Gaa *čəkw-itə* [3], Gbn *čiyək-tə* [3].
Agaw **cVχ-* "prairy": Kem *sēḫā*.

386 *car- "elder, chief"

Sem **sarr-* "chief": Arab *sarr-*.
May be a Persian loanword.
Eg *sr* "high official, elder" (pyr).
WCh **car-* "king": Wrj *cāra*.
ECh **sVr-* "adult": Tum *səri*.

Cf. Berb **cVwVr-* "precede, head, command" (Ayr *izar*, *əẓwər*, Kby *zwir-*, Ahg *əhwar*).

387 *car- "know"

Sem **wVsVr-* "remind" [1], "teach, instruct" [2]: Akk *asāru* [1], Ug *wsr* [2], Hbr *ysr* [2].
Derivative in **wV-*. Note that, semantically, Sem verb is a causative in relation to Eg and CCh.
Eg *sꜣꜣ* "know" (a).
-ꜣꜣ reflects **-r-*. It is less acceptable in the present case to treat inlaut *-ꜣ-* as a vocalic sign.
CCh **car-* "know" [1], "remember" [2]: Glv *sər* [1], Msm *sar* [2].

388 *car- "rope, tendon"

WCh **car-ak-* "rope, tendon": Hs * çarkiyā*, Sura *carka*, Mbu *caraku*.
Suffix **-ak-*.
Bed *sar* "tendon".

Note form with an inlaut laryngeal: WCh **ciʔVr-* "rope, tendon" (Siri *cīra*, Bks *sir*), ECh **siʔyar-* "thread, rope" (Smr *šire*, Mubi *sērī*).

389 *caram- "chief"

Sem **sVran-* "prince" [1], "Philistine chiefs" [2] Ug *srn* [1], Hbr *sᵉrānīm* [2].

Philistine loanword related to or preserved by Gk τυραννος? If not a loanword, it may go back to HS *sVran- assimilated from *sVram-, cf. WCh.
WCh *caram- "chief": DB saram.

Derived from *car- "elder, chief".

390 *caw- "faeces"

WCh *caw- "faeces": Ngz šau.
Ngz may, alternatively, go back to *caʔ-.
Agaw *caw- "faeces": Xmr cawaa, Kwr šäwaa.

391 *cawar- "dance" (v.)

Sem *sūr- "dance": Akk sâru, Hbr swr.
WCh *cwar- < *cVwar- "dance" (v.) [1], "dance" (n.) [2]: Gera swarri [1], Ngz suwaari [2].
Ngz -uwa- < *-(V)wa-.
ECh *sawar- < *saHar- "dance": Brg čaari.

392 *ceʔ- "speak, shout"

Sem *sVwVʔ- "cry (of pain)": Akk sâʔu.
WCh *cyaH- "speak" [1], "speech" [2]: Bgh še [1], Fyer se [2].
ECh *sway- "shout": Smr s(w)ōy, Jegu say.
A secondary formation based on *swaʔ-. The vowel may result from the influence of the second syllable.
Rift *ceʔ- "shout": Irq ceʔ-.

393 *cel- "female pudenda"

Berb *c(V)lul- "clitoris": Izn azlul.
Partial reduplication.
WCh *cyal- "vulva, female pudenda": Hs c̣ēle, Krk cele, Tng šeli.
LEC *sil- "vulva": Som siil.
Wrz *sil- "clitoris": Hss siil-akko.
HEC *c̣il- "vagina": Sid c̣iʔle, Kmb c̣ili-t.

394 *cilam- ‘‘tail’’

ECh **silVm-* ‘‘tail’’: Mkk *silme.*
Agaw **cimal(l)-* ‘‘tail’’: Bil *šəmar*, Xmr *ç̣imir*, Aun *cəmaro.*
Metathesis. Secondary emphatization in Xmr.

An alternative reconstruction is **cimal-*.

395 *cim- ‘‘grass, plant’’

Sem **sim-sim-* ‘‘sesame’’: Arab *simsim-.*
Reduplication.
Eg *sm.w* ‘‘cabbage’’ (pyr), Copt **sim* id.: Fym *sim*, Ahm *sim*, Bhr *sim*, Shd *sim.*
WCh **cim-* ‘‘steep herbs (for medicinal purposes)’’: Hs *ç̣ima.*
ECh **syam-* ‘‘hay’’: Mkk *seemi* (pl.).
Rift **cam-* ‘‘kind of grass’’: Irq *camo.*
Dhl *t̠aam-ine* ‘‘blade of grass’’.

Innovative **a* in Cush.

396 *cin-/*cun- ‘‘leg’’

Sem **sūn-* ‘‘lap, crotch’’: Akk *sūnu.*
Cf. Arab *sinʕ-* ‘‘joint (of fingers)’’ and *ʔsn* ‘‘kick with a foot’’.
Eg *ỉns* ‘‘leg’’ (med). Metathesis,
Agaw **sin-H-* ‘‘calf’’: Bil *siŋ.*

The laryngeal may be treated as a remainder of an archaic prefix moved to the end of the root (if so, the Agaw word may be compared with Chadic forms under **ʔa-cin-H-*) or as a secondary suffix.

Chadic forms with **ʔa-/*Ha-*, a prefix of body parts, see under **ʔa-cin-H-*.

397 *cinun- ‘‘bird’’

Sem **sinun-* ‘‘swallow’’: Akk *sinuntu*, Arab *sinīnī*, *sinūnū.*
Rift **cuʔunun-* ‘‘hawk’’: Asa *šuʔununu.*
Secondary **-uʔu-* < **i* due to assimilation.

398 *cip- ''sweep''

Sem **sVp-* ''rake up'' 1, ''purify, refine'' 2: Hbr *spy* 1, Gz *sff* 2.
Various formations based on biliteral **sVp-*.
Berb **cVf-* ''plane'' (v.) 1, ''wash'' 2: Ayr *zafat* 1, Kby *ucuf* 2.
WCh **cVp-* ''take off the top layers of washed corn'' 1, ''sweep'' 2, ''skim'' 3: Hs *ç̣āf-ače* 1, Diri *səfa* 2, Siri *cəfu* 2, Ngz *səpu* 3.
ECh **sip-* ''sweep'' 1, ''remove foam'' 2: Bid *sep* 1,Mkk *sippe* 2.
Bid may reflect **sipa-*.

399 *cir- ''pot''

Sem **sīr-* ''mug'': Hbr *sīr*.
WCh **cir-* ''small pot'': Ank *šir*.
CCh **cir-/*cur-* ''pot'': Zgh *šire*, Gava *sura*.
Traces of an ancient apophony?

400 *cir- ''pierce''

Sem **sVr-sVr-* ''sharpen'': Arab *srsr*.
Reduplication.
WCh **cir-* ''spit meat on skewers, pierce'': Hs *ç̣īre*.

Related to **cir-* ''thorn''.

401 *cir- ''thorn''

Sem **sīr-* ''thorn, hook'': Hbr *sīrīm* (pl.).
Eg *sr.t* ''thorn'' (BD).
ECh **sir-* ''roasting spit'': Bid *sīri*.

402 *ciway- ''pay''

Sem **sūy-* ''cost'' (v.): Arab *swy* [-*a*-].
WCh **ciya-* ''pay'': Wrj *ča*, Kry *čiy*, Miya *c-*, Mbu *c-* , Jmb *ši*, *ša*, Ang *ši*.
Transformation of an earlier **ciwya-/*ciway-*?

403 *coˀab- ''drink''

Sem **sVbVˀ-/*sVˀab-* ''draw water'' 1, ''drink'' 2, ''be satisfied

with drinking'' 3, ''buy wine in order to drink it'' 4: Akk *sāb-* 1, Ug *sʔb* 1, Hbr *sbꜣ* 2, Aram (Jud) *sbꜣ* 2, Arab *sꜣb* [*-a-*] 3, *sbꜣ* [*-a-*] 4.
Metathesis of *-ꜣ- within Sem.
CCh **cwaHab-* ''suck'': Mofu *-sasab-*, Gis *soḅ*, *suḅ*, Daba *seḅ*, Zime *soḅo*.
Emphatic *-ḅ-* reflects the lost laryngeal.
ECh **swaHVb-* ''suck'' 1, ''drink'' 2: Kera *soḅe* 1, Mubi *suva* 2.

404 *cok- ''pot, vessel''

Sem *ꜣ*asuk-* ''vessel for ointments'': Hbr *ꜣasuk*.
Prefix *ꜣ*a-*.
Eg *sṯ.t* ''baking form'' (OK).
Progressive palatalization of **k* > *ṯ* after HS **o*.
WCh **cwak-* ''calabash'': Ngm *šoko*.
CCh **swak-* ''pot'': FKi *šaka*, Zgh *sakə*, Glv *šəka*, FJ *šaku*, Bch *suk-to*, Log *skwa*, Ksr *sko*.

405 *coriy- ''plant, grass''

Eg *sꜣry* ''kind of plant'' (med).
-ꜣ- is a sign for a vowel.
WCh **cwari-* ''grass, thatching grass'': Hs *c̣āri*, Bol *saro*, Dera *šwari*, Kry *car*, Miya *car*, Cagu *cir-in*.
ECh **swariy-* ''kind of grass'': Mkk *soriyo*.

406 *cuḫVl- ''pierce''

Sem **sVḫVl-* ''pierce'': Akk *saḫālu*.
WCh **cul-* ''pierce'': Sura *sul*, Chip *səl*.
Contracted from **cuHVl-*.

407 *cuk- ''close''

Sem **suk-* ''stop up'' 1, ''cover'' 2: Akk *sakāku* 1, Hbr *skk* 2, Arab *skk* [*-u-*] 1, Jib *sekk* 2.
CCh **ca-cVkwa-* ''stop up'': Mofu *sasəkw*.
Partial reduplication.
HEC **c̣uk-* ''close (with a lid)'': Bmb *cuk-*.
Bmb *c-* is due to the orthographic peculiarities of the lexical sources.

408 *cVḥaḳ- "cut, break"

Sem *sVḥaḳ- "break, crush": Akk *sâqu*, *zâqu*, Arab *sḥq* [-*a*-], Jib *sḥaḳ*, Hss *seḥāq*, Mhr *seḥāq*.
Berb *cVḳ(ḳ)- "cut, pierce": Kby *ceqq*.

409 *cVmVk- "cover"

Sem *sVmVk- "cover": Akk *samāku*.
Eg *skm* "wrap" (gr).
Metathesis.

An alternative reconstruction is *cVkVm-.

410 *cVtVḥ- "bird"

Eg *stḥ* "kind of bird" (XXII).
CCh *cVt- "kite": Bch *soto*.

*ċ

411 *ċaʾal-/*ċawal- "jump"

Sem *ṣūl- "rush at, jump at" [1], "jump in fright" [2]: Arab *ṣwl* [-*u*-] [1], Jib *ṣell* [2].
WCh *ċal- < *ċaʾal- "jump": Hs *ċallē*.
ECh *saʾal- "jump": Lele *čaal*.
HEC *ċāl- < *ċaHal- "jump": Had *ċaall-*, Kmb *ċaal-*.

Consonantal alternation *-ʾ- ~ *-w-.

412 *ċad- "grind"

Berb *ċVḍ- < *ċVd- "grind": Ayr *əẓəḍ*, Kby *eẓḍ*.
Secondary emphatization of *-d-.
Omot *ċad- "pound": Ome *č̣aad-*.

413 *ċad- "be thirsty"

Sem *ṣVday- "be thirsty": Arab *ṣdy* [-*a*-].
Based on biliteral *ṣVd-.

CCh *caḍ- < *çad- "lick" [1], "drink" [2]: Mofu - səḍ- [1], Mafa caḍ.
Shift of emphatization.
ECh *saḍ-/*siḍ- "suck" [1], "lick" [2]: Mig ʾasiḍo, Sbn čada [2].
Shift of emphatization preceding the merger of HS *ç in ECh.

414 *çadaˤ- "cut"

Sem *ṣVdaˤ- "split, separate": Arab ṣdˤ [-a-].
ECh *sad- < *saHad- "cut": Tum sad.
Metathesis.

An alternative reconstruction is *çaˤad-.

415 *çag- "hair"

WCh *çag- "hair (in the horse's tail)" [1], "hair" [2]: Hs çagiyā [1], Cagu gəṣiye [2].
Metathesis in Cagu.
Rift *çag- "hair": Irq çaga.
Unexpected Irq ç-.

416 *çaˤ- "stick"

Eg ḏˤˤ "twig" (med).
Partial reduplication (of orthographic nature?).
WCh *çaH- "stick": Bol cāwa, zāwa, Klr coh.
CCh *nV-cah- "stick": Gis ǯaha.
*n(V)c- > ǯ-.

The following forms may be related to this root: (i) Sem *ˤaṣaw- "stick" (Arab ˤaṣā) with metathesis; (ii) Rift *caḥ- "arrow-tip" (Alg caḥi, Bur caḥiya).

417 *çaˤaḳ- "shout, ask"

Sem *ṣVˤaḳ- "shout" [1], "call" (v.) [2], "thunder" (v.) [3]: Hbr ṣˤq [1], Aram (Jud) ṣˤq [1], SAr ṣˤq [2], Arab ṣˤq [-a-] [3], Jib ṣaˤak [1].
Berb *[ç]VwVk- "sing": Kby cewweq.
Irregular anlaut.
Eg ḏˤk "call" (n).
Note loss of emphatization in -k < *ḳ.

CCh *cak- ''ask'': Gbn *čəχi*, Boka *saχa-ḍa*, Hwn *cake*.
Agaw *çaw(V)ḳ- < *çaH(V)ḳ- ''ask'': Xmt *čawḳ-*.
Omot *çVyVk-/*çVwVk- < *çVHVk- ''shout'': Ome *çäyk-* , Kaf *čook-*.

Dissimilation of *ḳ > *k as in Eg.

Cf. also Som *ḍawaaq-* ''shout caused by grief''?

418 *çaḥ- ''be white''

Sem *ṣVḥ- ''be white'' [1], ''shimmer'' [2], ''be clear'' [3]: Hbr *ṣḥḥ* [1], Aram *ṣḥḥ* [2], (Syr) *ṣaḥā* [3], Arab *ṣḥw* [-u-, -a-] [3], Gz *ṣḥw* [3], Tgr *ṣḥy* [3], Tgy *ṣäḥe* [3], Soq *ṣḥy* [3].

Various triliteral formations based on *ṣVḥ-.

CCh *cay-''shining'': Mafa *cayaᵓa*.

From *çaH-.

Omot *çaH- ''white'': Ari *çaa-mi*.

Cf. also Berb: Ghd *iḍua* ''light'' (adj.)?

419 *çaḥ- ''metal''

Eg *ḏḥ* ''kind of metal'' (XVIII).
CCh *caχ- ''iron'': FG *caχyi*.

Derived from *çaḥ- ''be white''? Cf. a similar type of semantic derivation in Lat *argentum* ''silver'' and the like.

420 *çaḥoraᵓ- ''sand''

Sem *ṣaḥraᵓ-''desert'': Arab *ṣaḥrāᵓ-*.
WCh *ç[aHwa]r- ''sand'': Klr *ᵓasoor*, DB *nǯoor*.

DB *nǯ-* < *nVç-.

CCh *cVγVl- < *çVγVr- ''sand'': Nak *səγle*, Mnd *šili*, Glv *səγəlu*, *svγvla*.

Cf. also HEC *šašar- ''sand'' (Had *šaššara*)? An old compound?

421 *çaḥ-çaḥ- ''field''

Sem *ṣaḥ-ṣaḥ-''plot of land'': Arab *ṣaḥṣaḥ-*.

Cf. non-reduplicated Jib *ṣεḥ*.

HEC *ḍaḍ- "field, land, soil": Bmb *ḍaḍdoo*.
From *çaç-, cf. HEC *ḍu-ḍuf- "python" < *çu- çuf- (see HS *çUfaᶜ- "snake").

Reduplication.

422 *çal- "rope; tie"

Sem *ṣVl- "join, attach": Hbr *ʾṣl*, Arab *wṣl*, *yṣl*.
Denominative formation.
WCh *çal- "tree used to make ropes" [1], "rope" [2]: Ang *sāl* [1], Bol *coli* [2].
CCh *cal- "rope": Mwu *saalu*.

423 *çap- "be clean"

Sem *ṣVpVʾ-/*ṣVpVw- "(be) clean": Arab *ṣfw* [-*u*-], Mhr *ṣōfi*, Hss *ṣāfi*, Jib *ṣefi*.
Based on *ṣVp-.
WCh *çap- "wash" [1], "be clean" [2], "well washed" [3]: Hs *çaf* [3], Sura *sugup* [1], Ang *sup* [1 2], Mpn *sūp*, *suwup* [1], Say *cap* [1], DB *sapa* [2].
CCh *caḅ- < *çap- "wash": Tera *šiḅ-ara*, Boka *sap-aḍa*, Hwn *cəbən*, Gbn *čəpən*, Gaa *čap-an-*.
Shift of emphatization.

424 *çat- "be warm"

Sem *ṣVt- "hot ashes" [1], "set fire" [2] Akk *ṣētu* [1], Hbr *yṣt* [2].
CCh *cat- "warm oneself": Mofu *-sət-*, *-zət-*.

425 *çat- "shout, speak"

Sem *ṣūt- "shout": Arab *ṣwt* [-*a*-, -*u*-], Gz *ṣwt*.
Based on *ṣVt-.
WCh *çat- "speak": Sura *sat*, Ang *sat*, Chip *sət*.

426 *çawad-/*çayad- "hunt"

Sem *ṣūd- "hunt (v.)": Akk *ṣādu*, Ug *ṣd*, Hbr *ṣwd*, Arab *ṣyd* [-*i*-, -*a*-].

-*i*- in Arab is secondary and induced by intervocalic -*y*-.

ECh **sawad-/*sayad-* "chase" [1], "hunt" (n.) [2]: Sbn *čwada* [1], Mubi *saiyad* [2].

HEC **sa[y]ad-* "hunt": Bmb *saad-*.

Unexpected *s*- indicating a possible borrowing from Sem.

Consonantal alternation **-w-* ~ **-y-*.

427 *çawaḥ-/*çayaḥ- "shout, ask"

Sem **ṣūḥ-* "shout, call, clamor": Akk *ṣāḫu*, Ug *ṣḥ*, Hbr *ṣwḥ*, Aram (Syr) *ṣwḥ*, Arab *ṣyḥ* [-*i*-], Tgy *č̣əwaḥ bälä*, Amh *č̣ohä*, Jib *eṣyeḥ*.

WCh **çVwVḥ-/*çVyVḥ-* "ask": Wrj *cəγ*, Kry *ṣiy*, Miya *ṣiy*, Cagu *ṣa*, Siri *ṣuw*.

HEC **çēḥ-*"call": Bmb *ceeh-*.

Bmb *c*- is an orthographic variant of *ç*-. HEC **-ē-* reflects a contraction of **-aya-*.

Consonantal alternation **-w-* ~ **-y-*.

428 *çawan- "flint, stone"

Sem **ṣawān-* "flint, quartz": Arab *ṣawwān-at-*.

WCh **çaw(V)n-* "hill, pile": Hs *çauni*.

429 *çawlag- "stick"

Sem **ṣawlag-* "stick": Arab *ṣawlag-ān-*.

Derivative in -*ān*-.

CCh **cugul-* "stick, beam": Masa *sugula*, Bnn *sugul-da*, Mafa *cagalay*.

Metathesis.

An alternative reconstruction is **çawgal-*. As far as vocalism in CCh is concerned, see HS **dawḫal-* "vessel".

430 *çeb- "look"

Sem **ṣVb-* "observe": Akk *ṣubbû*.

D stirpes in Akk.

WCh **çyab-* "look": Tng *sebi*.

431 *çef- "flow, soak"

Sem *ṣVpVw- "flow": Arab *ṣfw*.
Based on *ṣVp-. Cf. Hbr *ṣwp* "flow".
Berb *çVf- "weep": Ghd *eẓẓəf*.
HEC *çeff- "imbue, moisten": Ala *çeffo*, Kab *çeffo*, Kmb *çef-fo*.

432 *çepur-/*č̣epur- "bird"

Sem *ṣipār- "sparrow" 1, "bird" 2, "sandpiper" 3: Akk *ṣibāru* 1, Hbr *ṣippōr* 2, Aram (Syr) *ṣeprō* , Hss *ẓefār* 3.
Secondary ẓ- in Hss. Cf. Arab *ᶜuṣfur-* "sparrow".
WCh *č̣apur- < *č̣yapur- "guinea fowl": Wrj *č̣apur*.
*-ya- > *a after an affricate.
CCh *cipur- "guinea fowl": Mrg *cəvur*, Klb *civər*, Hil *civə:rə:w*, Bura *cəvur*, Chb *ʒuvura*.
ECh *sibVr- "guinea fowl": Smr *sibir*, Sok *sōir*.
May belong to HS *sa(m)bir-.

Irregular anlaut.

433 *çer- "speak, shout"

Sem *ṣir- "shout": Arab *ṣrr* [-i-].
WCh *çyaru- "speak": Bol *sor-*, Tng *seer-*, Pero *čeero*.

434 *çibVᶜ- "finger"

Sem *ṣibᶜ- "finger": Aram (Syr) *ṣēbᶜ-*, Tgr *č̣əbᶜ-it*.
Cf. a derivative in Ug *ʾuṣbᶜ*, Hbr *ʾeṣbāᶜ*, Arab *ʾiṣbaᶜ*, Gz *ʾäṣbaᶜ-*, Tgy *ʾaṣabəᶜ*, Jib *ʾiṣbaᶜ*, Soq *ʾəṣbaᶜ*, Amh *ṭat*.
Eg *ḏbᶜ* "finger" (pyr).

435 *çiç-/*çuç- "chick"

Sem *ṣūṣ- "chick": Arab *ṣūṣ-*.
LEC *çuç- "chick": Or *çuçoo*.
HEC *çiç- "chick": Had *çiiç-oola*, Kmb *çiiç-oorra*.

Descriptive root with an alternation of vowels.

436 *çig- ''flower''

Berb *çig- ''flower'': Sus *ažžig*.
WCh *çig- ''kind of tobacco flower'': Hs *çīgī*.
Agaw *çag-/*çig- ''flower'': Bil *č̣aga*, Kwr *ṣəge*, Xmr *ṣiya*.

437 *çihar- ''in-law''

Sem *ṣih(V)r- ''son-in-law'' [1], ''brother-in-law'' [2]: Arab *ṣihr-* [2], Soq *ṣeher* [1].
WCh *çVHVr- ''in-laws'': Sura *səgər*, Mpn *səər*.
Regular *-g-* in Sura.

438 *çil- ''snake''

Sem *ṣill- ''adder'': Arab *ṣill-*.
WCh *çil- ''tapeworm'': Hs *çīlā*.

439 *çilal-/*çilul- ''kite, hawk''

Sem *ṣalal- ''night bird'': Akk *ṣallalu*.
Assimilation of vowels.
HEC *çulul- ''kite'': Sid *č̣ululle*.
Assimilated from *çilul-. Borrowed in Or *č̣ulullee*.
Rift *cilil- ''cry of the hawk'': Irq *cilili*.
Assimilation of vowels.
Dhl *tsilala* ''hawk''.

440 *çin- ''sharp object''

Sem *ṣīn- ''thorn'': Hbr *ṣēn*.
WCh *çin-''sharp point'' [1], ''tooth'' [2]: Hs *çīnī* [1], Siri *çinna* [2].

441 *çin- ''nose''

WCh *ḥV-çin-''nose'': Hs *hanči*, Sura *pəgə-zin*, Mnt *kəzəŋ*, Grk *yiddiŋ*, Bol *wunti*, Krk *ʾuntin*, Dera *wariŋ*, Ngm *wunti*, Maha *wotiŋ*, Bele *unti*, Krf *wuttini*, Gera *wunčini*, Glm *wuzi*, Grm *umši*, Pol *išin*, Geji *ičin*, Brw *ngə- sən*, Say *nyi-cəŋ*, Dwot *ngu-zuŋ*, Buli *išin*, Fyer *šin*.
Prefix *ḥV-.

CCh *(χV-)cin-"nose": FKi *n-čən*, FG *k-šin*, Mtk *χə-can*, Daba *me-čiŋ*, Mus *mi-čiŋ*, Gude *šinə*, Gudu *čin*, Nza *činē*, Bch *šine*, Bata *činne*, Log *xsəni*, Bud *činne*, Kus *asen*, Msg *čunge*, *hantsiŋ*, Lame *čini*, Bnn *čina*.
   Prefix *χV- in several languages.
ECh *sin-um- "nose": Sbn *syan-*, Tum *hun*, Smr *sen-dum*, Nch *ǯinum-*.
   Suffix of body parts *-um-.

Archaic root preserved only in Chadic. Cf. *çin- "smell". Note prefix *ḥV- in WCh and CCh probably lost in ECh for phonetic reasons.

442 *çin- "smell" (v.)

Sem *ʔVṣVn- "smell": Akk *eṣēnu*.
   Cf. Arab *ṣnn* "have a bad smell", Gz *ṣnw* "be fragrant".
SA *sin- "odor": Saho *sin*.
HEC *çinç- "smell": Bmb *çinç-*.
   Partial reduplication.
Omot *çin-"smell": Kaf *çiin-*.

Derived from *çin- "nose".

443 *çir- "bird"

Sem *ṣir- "bird": Tgy *ṣir*, Amh *čəre*.
   Borrowed from Cush?
Eg *ḏry.t* "kite" (pyr).
   -y functions as a vocalis sign.
WCh *çir- "parakeet": Hs *çiryā*.
LEC *çir- "kind of bird": Or *çirrii*.
Omot *çer- "bird": Ome *čeraa*.

444 *çir- "cut"

Sem *ṣVr- "cut, split" [1], "separate" [2] Aram (Syr) *ṣry* [1], Arab *ṣwr* [1], Soq *ṣer* [2].
   Various derivatives based on the original *ṣVr- (*ṣVwVr-, *ṣVrVy-).
LEC *çir- "cut": Or *çira*.

445 *çiriḫ- "warm" (v.)

Sem *ṣVrVḫ- "warm" (v.): Akk ṣarāḫu.
Rift *ciriḥ- "glow": Irq ciriḥ-.
Reflexes of HS *ḫ are not quite clear.

446 *çirVᶜ- "gather, collect"

Eg ḏrᶜ "gather" (XX).
WCh *çīr- < *çiHVr- "pile up": Hs çīra.
Metathesis.

An alternative reconstruction could be *çiᶜVr-.

447 *çit- "be silent"

Sem *nVṣit- "be silent": Arab nṣt [-i-].
Prefix *nV-.
WCh *çit- "quiet, silent": Ang šit.

448 *çiwar- "flock"

Sem *ṣiwār- "flock (of wild kine or bulls)": Arab ṣiwār-, ṣuwār-, ṣiyār-.
Berb *çVrVw- "flock (of wild animals)": Tua asera, pl. i-serā-ten.
Metathesis.

449 *çoçof- "drip"

WCh *çaçaf- "bubble": Hs çaçafō.
Modified vocalism in a reduplicated form?
LEC *çoçof- "drip": Or çoççopa.
If Or -p- < HS *-f-.

Partial reduplication of *çof- "drop".

450 *çof- "drop"

Eg ḏf "drops" (n).
CCh *cVf- "sprinkle" (n.): Mafa čəffeʾa.
LEC *çof- "drop": Or çopa.
Note Or -p-.

Omot **çaf-çaf-* "drip": Kaf *čafčafoo*.
Full reduplication with changed vocalism.

Related to **çef-* "flow, soak".

451 *çoḥ- "dry up"

Sem **ṣVḥ-* "dry up" [1], "be dry" [2]: Hbr *ṣḥy* [1], Aram (Palest) *ṣḥʾ*.
Derivatives in C^3 = *y*, ʾ based on the original biconsonantal structure **ṣVḥ-*.
CCh **cwaH-* "dry up": LPe *čoʾ*, Masa *soya*, Msm *tchoʾo*, Bnn *soʾa-mo*.
Masa *-y-* < **-H-*.

452 *çor- "hair"

Sem **ṣVrr-* "whiskers": Akk *ṣerretu*.
Eg *ḏꜣꜣ* "plait" (of hair) (BD).
-ꜣꜣ may go back to **-r* or **-rr*.
WCh **çwar-* "hair": Hs *çōrō*.
The vowel may result from assimilation.

Cf. also Berb **[c]VˁVr-* "hair" (Kby *eccˁer*).

453 *çub- "cloth"

Eg *wḏb* "cloth" (XVIII).
Initial *w-* represents the root vowel.
WCh **suḅa-* < **çuba-* "cloth": Bol *suḅa*, Tng *seb*, Ngm *suḅa*.
CCh **cuḅ-* < **çub-* "cloth": Bch *suḅwe-to*.

454 *çul- "pour, drip"

Sem **mVṣul-* "drip": Arab *mṣl* [*-u-*].
Prefix **mV-*.
WCh **çul-* "pour": Hs *çula*.

455 *çur- "press together"

Sem **ṣVr-* "press together, wrap": Hbr *ṣwr*, Aram *ṣwr*, Arab *ṣrr*.
Secondary formation in Hbr and Aram based on **ṣVr-*.

ECh **sur-* "press, pack" 1, "be heavy , load" 2: Kbl *sər* 1, Bid *sur-ray* 1, Mig *sūra* 2.

Mig *-ū-* may reflect **-u-* or **-uwa-*.

456 *çuraᶜ- "throw"

Sem **ṣVraᶜ-* "throw": Arab *ṣrᶜ* [*-a-*], Soq *ṣer(r)*.

WCh **çVHVr-* "fall": Bol *soor*.

Metathesis.

ECh **suHVr-* "fall": Kera *suuri*.

Metathesis.

457 *çübur- "sharp instrument"

Sem **ṣibār-* "pointed tool": Akk *ṣibāru*.

Regular HS **u* > Sem **a* after a labial.

WCh **suḅur-* < **çubur-* "knife": Buli *səbər*, Say *subur*, Dira *suḅuri*, Pol *sərrəb*, Dwot *surup*.

Metathesis in Pol and Dwot.

458 *çüf(aᶜ)- "snake"

Sem **ṣipaᶜ-* "snake": Hbr *ṣepaᶜ*.

Cf. a derivative in Hbr *ṣipᶜ-ōnī* id.

Eg *ḏdf.t* "snake" (BD).

Note *ḏd-* as a reflex of **ç*.

HEC **ḍu-ḍuf-* "python": Sid *ḍuḍuufa*.

Partial reduplication. As far as **ḍ* < **ç* is concerned in a situation of two contacting **ç*, see HS **çaḥ-çaḥ-* "field".

459 *çVrVf- "burn"

Sem **ṣVrVp-*"burn": Akk *ṣarāpu*.

Eg *ḏɜf* "burn" (trans.) (NK).

-ɜ- reflects **-r-*.

*Č

460 *čabaḫ- ‘‘wing’’

Eg *sbḫ.t* ‘‘wing’’ (gr).
WCh **čaHab-* ‘‘wing’’: Sura *čaap*, Ang *čēp*, Chip *šəp*, Mpn *čāp*.
Metathesis.

An alternative reconstruction is **čaḫab-*.

461 *čabVḥ- ‘‘speak, shout’’

Eg *sbḥ* ‘‘shout’’ (pyr).
WCh **čab-*‘‘speak’’: Tng *saba*.
CCh **čab-*‘‘ask’’: Msm *tchab*.

462 *čad-/*čid- ‘‘breast’’

Sem **ṯady-* ‘‘breast’’: Hbr *šad*, Aram (Syr) *tᵉdā*, Arab *ṯady-*, Hss *ṯōdi*, Mhr *ṯōdi*, Shh *ṯodɛʾ*, Soq *todi*.
ECh **čid-* ‘‘breast’’: Ndam *sid*.

Alternation **a* ~ **i*.

463 *čaᶜ-/*čiᶜ- ‘‘catch’’

WCh **čiw-* ‘‘fish’’ (v.): Kry *čiwu*, Ngz *šuyu*.
Ngz *-uy-* < **-iw(V)y-*.
Dhl *ṯaᶜ-aaδ* ‘‘trap’’ (v.).

Alternation **a* ~ **i*.

464 *čaᶜlib-/*čuᶜlib- ‘‘fox, jackal’’

Sem **ṯaᶜlib-* ‘‘fox’’: Akk *šēlebu*, *šēlibu*, Ug *ṯᶜlb*, Hbr *šaᶜalᵉbīm*, Arab *ṯaᶜlab-*.
Assimilation of vowels in Arab.
CCh **či-čVlVb-* ‘‘jackal’’: Msg *čičelebe*.
Partial reduplication.
ECh **čulib-* ‘‘wolf’’: Mkk *sullibe*.

Derived from *čuᶜal- "beast" with suffix *- (i)b-. Alternation *a ~ *u.

465 *čaḥ- "bird"

Eg *sḥ.t* "kind of bird".
CCh **čah-* "kind of bird": Mafa *caha-caha*.
Reduplication in Mafa.

466 *čaḫar- "plan" (v. and n.)

Eg *sḫr* "idea, plan" (OK).
WCh **čaHar-* "intention, plan": Fyer *čoor*.
ECh **čaHar-* "imagine, predict": Bid *čaar*.

467 *čak- "plait"

Eg *sṯꜣ* "spin" (pyr).
ṯ < **k* must be followed by HS **e* or **o*. Eg *-ꜣ* seems to stand for the root vowel **a*.
WCh **čak-/*čaHVk-* "plait": Krk *čāku*, Ngz *čaakau*.
Secondary laryngeal?
CCh **či-čik-* "twist": Daba *čičiku*.
Partial reduplication with modified vocalism.

Cf. ECh **čaHak-* "loom" (Mig *čaaka*).

468 *čakam- "shoulders, nape"

Sem **ṯVkVm-* "shoulders, upper part of the back": Ug *ṯkm*, Hbr *šekem*.
LEC **sagam-* "nape": Som *sagan*, pl. *sagmo*.
Voiced **-g-* < **-k-* before a sonant? Final *-m* > *-n* is regular in Som.

469 *čakin- "net"

Sem **ṯikin-* "net": Akk *šikinnu*.
Secondary vocalism with assimilation.

WCh *čank- ''snare'': Hs čaŋkō.

In WCh the HS group *-kVn- is transformed into a cluster *-nk-. Cf. HS *čak- ''plait''.

470 *čaḳel- ''thigh''

Eg *sḏꜣ* ''leg'' (n).

Palatalization of *g > ḏ before *e. Note HS *l yielding to Eg -ꜣ.

CCh *čakyal- ''thigh'': Bud čakel.

An alternative set of comparisons may be suggested for Eg *sḏꜣ* ''leg'' if it is connected with *sḏḥ* ''shin'' (med). It could be identified with WCh *sag- ''leg'' (Miya šagu-hu) and CCh *sig- ''bone'' (Log šigo).

471 *čam- ''gather, join''

Sem *čum- ''collect, gather'': Arab *ṯmm* [-u-].

Secondary *-u-.

WCh *čam- ''link up, join'': Hs čamme.

472 *čamaʔ- ''eat, feed''

Sem *ṯVmaʔ- ''feed (with rich food)'': Arab *ṯmʔ* [-a-].

WCh *čam- ''taste, test'': Mpn čam.

Cf. WCh *čīm- < *čiHVm- ''food'': Hs čīmā.

CCh *čam- ''eat (hard food)'': Mubi čam.

473 *čapaḥ- ''catch''

Eg *spḥ* ''catch with a lasso'' (pyr).

WCh *čaHap- ''catch'': Hs čafe, DB syap.

Metathesis. DB -ya- < *-Vya- < *-aHa-.

ECh *čaHap- ''catch'' 1, ''fish'' (v.) 2: Smr šəbə 1, Bid čaap 2, ačap 1.

Metathesis. Voicing of *-p- in Smr is regular.

An alternative reconstruction is *čaḥap-.

474 *čar- ''throw''

Sem **ṯVr-* ''throw'': Aram *trtr*, Soq *trr*.
Reduplicative stem in Aram. Cf. Arab *nṯr* [*-u-*, *-i-*] ''disperse''.
WCh **čar-* ''throw, shoot'' [1], ''strike'' [2]: Hs *čara* [1], Sura *čar* [2], Ang *čar* [1], Mpn *čar* [1].
Dhl *ṯaaro* ''pierce''.

475 *čar- ''weapon''

Eg *šsr* ''arrow'' (pyr).
šs- is one of possible reflexes of HS **č-*.
Dhl *ṯaaro* ''spear''.

Derived from **čar-* ''throw''?

476 *čawVb-/*čayVb- ''clothes''

Sem **ṯawb-* ''kind of clothes'': Akk *šubtu*, Aram (Syr) *tawb-*, Arab *ṯawb-*, Sok *tob*.
Eg *sbby.t* ''clothes'' (gr).
Partial reduplication **čVbib-*.
WCh **čwab-* ''put on'': Pero *čobbo*.
From **čVwab-*.
ECh **čwab-* < **čVwab-* ''undress'': Sbn *čwəbə*.

Consonantal alternation **-w-* ~ **-y-*.

477 *čawVr-/*čVr- ''bull''

Sem **ṯawr-* ''bull'': Akk *šūru*, Ug *ṯr*, Hbr *šōr*, Aram (Syr) *tawrā*, Arab *ṯawr-*, Gz *sōr*, Hss *ṯawr*.
Eg *šsr* ''bull (for slaughtering)'' (pyr).
šs- continues HS **č-*.

Eg may represent the original form of the HS root while Sem reflects a secondary extension in **-w-*. Cf. WCh **tawVr-* ''bull'' (Hs *tōrō*); ECh **tawVr-* ''cow, antelope'' (Sok *tor*, Tum *tor̃*).

478 *če>- "pierce"

Sem **ṯV>ay-* "pierce, wound": Arab *ṯ>y* [*-a-*].
Derived from a biconsonantal **ṯV>-*.
CCh **čV-* "cut": Mofu *č-*.
ECh **čwa>-* "pierce": Kera *čo>e*.
Dhl *ṯi*ᶜ- "punch a hole".
The root vowel is not clear. The development of the laryngeal may be not quite regular.

479 *čem- "fog, rain"

Eg *sym* "fog" (sarc).
Vocalic *-y-*.
CCh **čyam-* "rain": Log *sema*, *sama*, Kus *sama*.
Cf. WCh **čam-* "rainy season": DB *čam*.

480 *čen- "house"

Eg *sn.wt* "palace" (pyr).
WCh **čyan-* "house": Sha *čen*, Klr *čyen*.
CCh **čin-* "house, compound": Bnn *sina*, *šina*.

481 *čer- "shine; light"

Eg *šsr* "shine" (gr).
šs- may reflect HS **č-*.
WCh **čyar-* "light" (n.): Buli *bə-šerə*, Wnd *čeri*, Geji *čil-ti*.
Prefix **bV-* in Buli.

482 *čer- "medicine"

Eg *syꜣ* "medicine" (med).
-ꜣ continues HS **-r-*.
CCh **čyarir-* "medicine": Bud *čerire*.
Partial reduplicaton.

483 *čer- "speak, shout"

Sem **ṯVr-ṯVr-* "chat": Arab *ṯrṯr*.

Reduplication.

Eg *šsr* "speak out" (MK).

šs- is one of possible reflexes of HS **č-*.

WCh **čyar-* "cry out" [1], "explain" [2]: Hs *čērā* [1], Ang *čīr* [2].

CCh **čir-* "shout": Mba *čiri*.

ECh **čyačyar-* "cry (of guinea-fowl)": Bid *čečer*.

Partial reduplication.

Descriptive stem?

484 *čeraʾ- "furrow"

Sem **ṯirʾ-* "furrow": Akk *šerʾu, širʾu*.

ECh **čaHar-* < **čyaHar-* "furrow": Bid *čaare*.

Metathesis.

The alternative reconstruction is **čeʾar-*.

485 *čin- "move"

Eg *syn* "hurry" (pyr).

-y- is a vocalic sign.

WCh **čin-* "go": Bol *čīna*.

486 *čir- "faeces, dirt"

Eg *sr* "dirt" (gr).

ECh **čir-* "faeces, dirt": Mkk *siiri*.

HEC **ç̣ir-* "faeces": Had *ç̣iro*.

Cf. also Bmb *sera* id.?

487 *čit- "throw, shoot"

Eg *sty* "throw, shoot" (OK).

-y denotes a front vowel in the root.

CCh **čit-* "shoot": Gbn *čitə-*, Boka *čett-*, Gaa *čiti*.

488 *čiw-/*čiy- "grass, plant"

Eg *sw* "kind of plant" (l).

WCh **čiy-* "grass": Hs *čiyāwa*.

Cf. Rift **caw-* "reeds" (Irq *cawo*)? Consonantal alternation **-w-* ~ **-y-*.

489 *čor- "be strong"

Sem **ṯVrVw-* "be considerable, be big": Arab *ṯrw*.
Based on **ṯVr-*.
Eg *wsr* "strong" (pyr).
WCh **čwar-* "strength": Gwn *čori*.

490 *čuᶜal- "beast"

Sem **ṯuᶜāl-* "fox": Hbr *šūᶜāl*, Aram *taᶜlā*, Arab *ṯuᶜāl-*, Jib *iṯᶜol*, Mhr *yeṯayl*, Hss *yeṯayl*, Shh *iṯᶜol*.
Dhl *ṯeele* "lion", *ṯaali* "lioness".
Assimilation of vowels.

491 *čumal- "creamy milk"

Sem **ṯumāl-* "milk skin": Arab *ṯumāl-at-*.
Cf. more archaic vocalism in Arab *ṯamīl-* "sour milk".
Eg *smr* "cream".
Note *-r* < HS **-l-*.

492 *čül- "seed"

Sem **ṯīl-* "seed": Arab *ṯīl-*.
Secondary formation in Arab *ṯayyil-* id.
WCh **čVl-* "seed": Tng *sala*.
CCh **čuli-* "seed": Klb *čuli*, Hld *čuli*, Wmd *čuli*, HNk *cili*, HBz *cəlu*.
ECh **čulwa-* "rice": Mubi *čulwayo*.

493 *čVbVḫ- "close" (v.)

Eg *sbḫ* "close" (XVIII).
ECh **čVb-* "close": Kera *čebe*.
Complete loss of the laryngeal.

494 *čVwaġ-/*čVyaġ- "shout, ask"

Berb **sVwVγ-* "shout": Kby *suġ*.
Irregular development of **č-*?
CCh **čyag- < *čVyaγ-* "ask": Bud *čega*.
Unexpected change of **-ġ-*.

Consonantal alternation **-w- ~ *-y-*.

*ç̌

495 *ç̌agan- "goat, boar"

WCh **ç̌ang-* "goat": Cagu *ṣaŋgen*, Mbu *ç̌angu*.
Suffix **-(y)an-* in Cagu.
ECh **ç̌ang-* "goat": Smr *čaⁿge*.
Agaw **ç̌yagan-* "boar": Aun *cyägänaa*.

Chadic word-structure of the present word is similar to the development in HS **čakin-* "net".

496 *ç̌aʕ- "catch, seize"

Eg *ḏʕ* "catch" (MK).
WCh **ç̌aw-/*ç̌ay-* "catch, seize": Krk *čaw*, Paa *čei*.
Phonetically developed from **ç̌aʕu-/*ç̌aʕi-*.
CCh **ča-/*či-* "catch, seize": Mtk *či*, Gis *ǯe*, Log *si*, Bud *ča*.

497 *ç̌a[ʕ]Vr- "snake, worm"

Sem **ṣV[ʕ]Vr-* "snake": Akk *ṣēru*.
Intervocalic **-ḥ-* is also plausible.
CCh **čar-* "worm": Log *čarē*.

498 *ç̌ahar- "show"

Sem **ṭ̱Vhar-* "appear, be evident": Arab *ẓhr* [*-a-*], Mhr *ẓahar*, Soq *ṭahar*.
CCh **čar-* "show": Klb *a-čäř*.
From **čaHar-*.

499 *çaḫut- "squeeze"

Sem **ṭVḫut-* "extract oil": Akk *ṣaḫātu* [-*u*-].
WCh **čūt-* < **čaHut-* "press, squeeze out": Glm *čuuz-*, Pero *čotto*.
Glm *-z-* < **-t-* is regular.
ECh **čēt-* < **čayVt-* "squeeze": Kera *čeete*.
Assimilation of vowels. ECh **-ayV-* < **-aHV-*.

500 *ça'-/*çi'- "bird"

ECh **čač-* "kind of bird": Bid *čeeču*.
Reduplication.
HEC **çi'-* "bird": Sid *çe'aa*, Dar *çi'a-*, Had *çi'a-*, Kab *çi'a-*, Bmb *çi'a-*, Kmb *çi'a-*, Tmb *çi'a-*.
Omot **ça'-* "bird of prey": Mch *ča'o*.

Alternation **a* ~ **i*. Irregular correspondences of CCh and Cush laryngeals.

501 *çak- "vessel"

Berb **çVk-* "plate for couscous": Ghd *a-ẓku*.
WCh **čakwa-n-* "pot": Wrj *čakwān-na*.
Suffix **-n-*.
CCh **čaχwa-* "pot": FG *caχwa*.
HS **k* > CCh **χ* under the influence of the originally emphatic **č*.
ECh **čwaka-* < **čakwa-* "big vessel": Bid *čook-iya*.

502 *çal- "locust"

Sem **ṭVl-ṭal-* "locust": Hbr *ṣᵉlāṣal*.
Reduplication.
WCh **čiHal-*"locust": Ang *čol*, Mnt *šiyel*, Tng *solo*.
Metathesis.

503 *çal-/*çil- "shadow"

Sem **ṭil(l)-* "shadow": Akk *ṣillu*, Ug *ẓl*, Hbr *ṣēl*, Aram *ṭullā*, Arab *ẓill-*, Gz *ṣelālāt*, Jib *ẓelɛl*.
WCh **(nV-)čila-* "shadow": Ang *ǯil*, Sha *čala*.

CCh **nV-ǯal-* < **nV-čal-* "west": Gis *nʒala*.
HEC **çal-* "shade": Sid *çaale*.
Dhl *ṯiilali* "shadow".
Partial reduplication.

Alternation **a* ~ **i*.

504 *čam- "think, know"

Sem **wVṯVm-* "think": Arab *wẓm*.
Prefix **wV-*.
CCh **čam-* "know": Pad *cam*, FM *čam*, Nak *cama-*, Nza *cəm-an*, Zgh *cama*.

505 *čamon- "think, know"

Sem **ṯun-* < **ṯVnVn-* "think": Arab *ẓnn* [-*u*-], Hss *ẓen*, Shh *εẓnin*.
Probably, with assimilation of the inlaut **-m-* > **-n-*.
WCh **čamwan-* "think, remember": Hs *çammāni*, Ang *čan*, Krk *čawan*.
Derived from **čam-* "think, know".

506 *čar- "look, see"

Sem **nVṯar-* "guard" [1], "look" [2]: Akk *naṣāru* [1], Ug *nġr* [1], Phn *nṣr* [1], Hbr *nṣr* [1], Aram *nṭr* [1], Arab *nẓr* [-*u*-] [2], SAr *nṭr* [1], Gz *nṣr* [2].
Prefix **nV-*.
Berb **çVr-* "see, look": Izn *ẓer*, Snh *ẓar*.
WCh **čar-* "guard": Hs *çare*.

Cf. Berb **çVr-* "pupil (of an eye)" (Twl *əẓẓəru*).

507 *čaw- "mouse, rat"

Berb **çVw-* "jerboa": Ayr *e-ḍəwi*, Twl *e-ḍəwi*.
WCh **čiy-* "field rat": Hs *çiyō*.
An old morphonological variant **čVy-*?
Agaw **ʔin-čaw-* "mouse": Bil *inšuwaa*, Xmr *iečuwaa*, Xmt *ačuwaa*, Kem *yešwaa*, Aun *ençaa*, Dmt *inçii*.
Prefix **ʔin-*.
Omot **ʔ[i]n-çaw-* "rat": Ome *uçaa*, Kaf *ičoo*, Bwo *inčoo*, Gim *uç*, *uč*.
Note fluctuations of vowels in the prefix.

506 *çawar- "neck"

Sem *ṭawār- "neck": Akk ṣawāru, Hbr ṣawār.
Eg wsr.t "neck" (pyr).
Metathesis.

509 *çen- "wind, cold"

Sem *ṭin- "cold" (n.): Hbr ṣinā.
WCh *čyan- "wind": DB čyen.

510 *çil- "tail"

Sem *ṭVl- "wag (of a tail)": Arab ẓll.
Denomiantive verb.
WCh *čila- "tail": Wrj čalai, Geji čil.
Omot *çell- "tail": Kaf čeero, Mch čeero, Maji čəru.

511 *çilam- "be dark"

Sem *ṭVlam- "be dark, be black": Akk ṣalāmu, Arab ẓlm [-a-], SAr ṭlm, Gz ṣalma, Tgr ṣälma, Tgy ṣällämä, Gaf ṣillämä, Amh čällämä, Arg čelläma, Har čēläma, Gur čällämä, Soq ṭlm.
Cf. Ug ẓlmt "darkness", Mhr ẓalem id.
CCh *čilVm- "dark" [1], "black" [2]: Bud čilim [1], Gul selem [2].

Derived from *čal-/*čil- "shadow". Cf. also LEC *ḍelam- "return of the cattle home in the evening" (Som ḍelan < *ḍelam, pl. ḍelmo) and ECh *čulum- "west" ← * "dark (side)": Mig čulum-ti.

512 *çotVḥ- "bird"

Eg stḥ "kind of bird" (XXII).
WCh *čwat- "bird": Mbu čoti.
Cf., on the other hand, Hs çīta id., Diri ačida id.
SA *ça-çut- "bird": Saho çaaçutta.
Partial reduplication.
HEC *çi-çut- "bird": Ala čičuta.
Partial reduplication.

513 *čupar- "fingernail"

Sem **ṭupr-* "fingernail": Akk *ṣupru*, Hbr *ṣipporen*, Aram (Palest) *ṭuprā*, Arab *ẓufr-*, Gz *ṣəfr*, Tgr *ṣəfər*, Tgy *ṣəfri*, Amh *ṭəfər*, Gaf *ṣəfra*, Arg *čuffər*, Gur *ṭəfər*, Soq *ṭifer*, Mhr *ṭayfer*, Shr *ẓefer*, Jib *ẓifɛr*.
Agaw **çifar-* "finger": Bil *çəfər*, Aun *tseefir*.
Metathesis in Kwr and Dmb. From Ethio-Sem?
HEC **ʒurup-* "finger": Bmb *ʒurup-mata*.
Unexpected **ʒ-*.
Omot **ǯafar-* "finger": Kaf *yafaroo*.
Assimilation of vowels. Irregular **ǯ-*. A common HEC ~ Omot innovation or a loanword? This innovation is partly shared by Agaw: Kwr *ǯerfa*, Dmb *zalfa*, not comparable immediately with other forms quoted above. If, however, these Agaw words *are* derived from Agaw **çifar-* > **çiraf-*, they may be believed to be the source of Omot and HEC.
Rift **čaraf-* "fingernail": Alg *čarafu*, Bur *čarafu*.
Metathesis.

Cf. phonetically close **çibVʕ-* "finger". The vocalism of the first syllable may be tentatively reconstructed as **a* ~ **i*.

514 *čur- "flint, flint knife"

Sem **ṯirr-/*ṯurr-* "flint" 1, "rock" 2: Akk *ṣurru* 1, Hbr *ṣōr* 1, Aram *ṭūr-* 2, Arab *ẓurar-*, *ẓirr-* 1, SAr *ẓwr* 2.
Berb **çVr-* "flint" 1, "rock" 2: Qbl *i-ẓra* 1, Ahg *a-ẓəru* 2.
WCh **čur-* "knife without handle": Hs *çūrā*.
CCh **čur(i)-* "hoe": FM *curu*, Gude *cəra*, FJ *čili*, FBw *cərən*.

Related to HEC **çar-* "whetstone" (Bmb *çar-aanco*)? Eg *wḏꜣ.t* "knife" (gr) may be connected with this root.

515 *čVHol- "shine, be bright"

Sem **ṯVhVl-* "shine": Hbr *ṣhl*.
LEC **çol-* < **çVHol-* "bright": Or *çollee*.

*ĉ

516 *ĉaˀ-/*ĉaw-/*ĉay- "move upwards"

Sem *nVŝaˀ- "rise, grow, raise": Akk *našū*, Ug *nšū*, Hbr *nŝˀ* [-*a*-], Arab *nšˀ* [-*a*-, -*u*-], Gz *nŝˀ*, Amh *nässa*.
Prefix *nV-.
Eg *šwy* "raise" (pyr).
Cf. also *zšy* "lift" with digraph *zš*- reflecting HS *ĉ-. In both cases, -*y* is a suffix.
WCh *ĉaˀ- "stand up": Wrj *ŝa*, Kry *ŝa*-, Diri *ŝa*- , Miya *ŝa*-, Paa *ŝu*, Cagu *ŝu*, Mbu *ŝa*-, Pol *ŝa*, *ŝi*, Geji *ŝa*, *ŝi*, Zem *ŝa*, *ŝi*, Brw *ŝe*, *ŝu*, Tala *iŝa*, Ngz *ŝa*, *ŝau*.
CCh *ŝaˀ-/*ŝay- "stand up, rise": Tera *ẑa*, Gaa *ŝeˀe*, Gbn *ŝaˀi*, Hwn *ŝi*, Mrg *ŝay*, Klb *ŝēy*, Chb *ŝāy*, HB *ŝa-vo*, FK *ŝa-tuˀ*, Lame *ŝi*-, LPe *ŝe*, Boka *ẑeˀi*.
ECh *ĉaw-/*ĉay- "stand up, rise": Smr *so*, Lele *sē*, Tob *say*.

Cf. Rift *ĉe-s- "lift, raise" (Irq *ĉes*-). Consonantal alternation *-ˀ- ~ *-*w*- ~ *-*y*-.

517 *ĉaˀ- "meat"

Sem *ŝāˀ-/*ŝēˀ- "sheep": Akk *šûˀu*, Ug *š*, Hbr *ŝē*, Aram *si-t*-, Arab *šā-t*.
Berb *[c]V- "meat": Ahg *isa-n*.
Irregular reflex of Berb *c- in Ahg.
WCh *ĉaw-/*ĉuˀ- "meat": Wrj *ŝū-na*, Kry *ŝiwi*, Miya *ŝiwiya*, Paa *ŝuwi*, Cagu *ŝu-n*, Siri *ŝuyi*, Geji *ŝu*, Zem *ŝau*, Brw *ŝau*, Say *ŝu*, Bgh *ŝaw*, Grn *ŝu*, Kir *ŝo*, *ŝu*, Tala *ŝu*, Ngz *ŝuwai*, Bade *saa*.
WCh *-ˀ- > *-*w*- in unknown conditions. Note also WCh *ŝa- "cow, bull".
CCh *ŝiw-/*ŝuw- "meat": Gbn *ŝuwe*, Hwn *ŝuwe*, Zgh *ŝuwe*, Lame *ŝiau*, *ŝeo*, Msm *ŝiou*, Bud *hu*, Glv *ŝuw*, HF *ŝū*, Mofu *aŝəw*.
Note CCh *(nV-)ŝa- "cow, bull".
ECh *ĉVw-/*ĉVy- "meat": Lele *sii*, Mkk *sey*, Jegu *su-ut*.
LEC *sow-/*soH- "meat": Som *soˀ*, Bay *soˀo*, Gel *so*, Kon *sowa*, Gato *soha*, Gdl *soha*.
LEC *-*o*- < *-*a*- before a labial?
Omot *(ˀa-)šaw-/*šaˀ- "meat" [1], "goat" [2]: Ome *aššwa*, *ašo* [1], Mao *šaa* [2].

Rift *ĉaʾ- "body": Asa *ŝaʾa*.
Semantic development is not quite reliable.

Consonantal alternation *-ʾ- ~ *-w- in several branches. WCh and CCh reflect a secondary development of the root vocalism.

518 *ĉaʾVb- "rain"

Sem *ŝaʾbab- "shower": Arab *šaʾbab-*.
Partial reduplication.
WCh *ĉaHVb- "rainy season": Krf *šaḇu*, Gera *saḇu*.

519 *ĉaʾVp- "foot"

Sem *ŝ[a]ʾp- "foot": Akk *šēpu*, Jib *ŝef*, Soq *ŝaf*.
Agaw *šanp- "foot, heel": Bil *šaanfi*, Kwr *šaanpaa*, Dmb *šanfa*, Kem *šaambaa*.
Secondary nasalization or a reflex of an early HS cluster *-mp- lost in Sem?

520 *ĉa[b]ir- "thigh"

Sem *ŝapr- "thigh": Akk *šapru*.
Irregular Sem *p < HS *b.
LEC *sabir- "back thigh (of camel)" [1], "thigh" [2]: Som *sibir* [1], Or *sarba* [2].
Assimilation of vowels in Som. Metathesis in Or.

521 *ĉad- "pit, well"

Eg *šd.t* "well" (OK).
WCh *ĉad- "pit": Hs *šaddā*.

May be derived from *ĉud-/*ĉaʾad- "harrow, till".

522 *ĉad-/*ĉaʾid- "field, land"

Sem *ŝād- "field, vacant land": Ug *šd*, Hbr *ŝāde*.
Eg *šdw.t* "field" (MK).
The function of -w is not clear. Is it a suffix?
ECh *ĉVHid- "earth": Kwn *čədo*, Mkk *siiḍo*.

Related to *ĉud-/*ĉaʔad- "harrow, till".

523 *ĉaf- "lake"

CCh *ŝaf- "lake": Mrg ŝafu.
Omot *šaf- "river, lake": Ome šafaa.

524 *ĉag- "mix"

Sem *mVŝug- "mix": Arab mšg [-u-].
Prefix *mV- and modified vocalism.
WCh *ĉag- "mix": Tng sāge.

525 *ĉaʕ- "cut"

Eg šʕ "cut" (pyr).
WCh *ĉaw- "scratch" [1], "cut" [2]: Wrj ŝaw [1], Paa ŝawo [1], Brm ŝuwe [2], Dwot ŝu-χ [2], Buli ŝo [2], Ngz ŝuwai [2].
*-w- goes back to intervocalic *-H- (before a rounded vowel).
CCh *ŝaH-/*ŝay- "cut": Chb ŝay, Mrg ŝa, FG ŝa-nti, HG ŝa-ve, HN ŝa-nte.
*ŝay- < *ŝaHi-.

526 *ĉaʕ- "begin"

Eg šȝʕ "begin" (MK), Copt *ša: Boh ša, Shd ša.
-ȝ- stands for HS *-a-.
WCh *ĉaH- "begin": Sura šɛɛ.
The development of the vowel is regular.

527 *ĉaʕ- "vessel"

Eg šʕ "vessel" (OK).
WCh *ĉayaʕ-/*ĉawaʕ- "pot": Sha šya, ša, Klr šwaʕi.
Based on *ĉaʕ-.

528 *ĉaʕar- "hair"

Sem *ŝaʕr- "hair" [1], "wool" [2]: Akk šārtu [1], Ug šʕrt [2], Hbr ŝēʕār, ŝaʕarā [1], Aram (Syr) šaʕrō [1], Arab šaʕr- [1], Gz ŝeʕert [1], Soq ṣaʕihor [1].

Cf. denominative Sem *ŝaˁar- "be hairy": Hbr *ŝˁr*, Arab *šˁr* [-*a*-].

WCh *ĉaHar- "hair on the chest of a ram" [1], "hair" [2]: Hs *šāri* [1], Bks *syaḥ* [2].

Bks -*ḥ* is regular.

Omot *šaHar- "hair": Maji *saaru*.

Assimilation of vowels.

529 *ĉaˁop- "hair"

Sem *ŝaˁap- "hairlock" [1], "hair" [2]: Arab *šaˁaf-at-* [1], Jib *ŝɔf* [2].

In the second syllable, HS *o > *a before a labial.

Berb *cVf- "hair": Izn *azäf*.

WCh *ĉaHwap- "hair": Sura *šwɔp*, Chip *šap*, Mnt *swεp*, Mpn *siwep*, Bol *šowɔ*, Maha *šofi*.

*-*iwa*- < *-*iHa*-.

LEC *sap- "pubic hair": Or *sap̣ii*.

Secondary Or -*p̣*- under the influence of the laryngeal.

HEC *sap- "hair, pubic hair": Dar *sap̣e*.

LEC loanword?

530 *ĉah- "wish, be able"

Sem *ŝVh- "wish" [1], "like" [2]: Arab *šhw*, *šhy* [-*a*-, -*u*-] [1], Jib *ŝuthi* [2].

CCh *ŝah- "be able, can": Mafa *ŝaha*.

As far as the development of meaning is concerned, cf. the semantic history of Germ *mag* and *darf*.

531 *ĉahar- "moon, star"

Sem *ŝahr- "new moon": Arab *šahr-*, Aram *saharā*, Mnd *sira*, Gz *ŝāhr*, Soq *ŝeher*, Jib *ŝεhər*.

WCh *ĉaHar- "star": Ank *sum-šar*, Tuli *ŝa-ŝur*, Zak *čā-zur*, Bot *ŝaar*, Grn *saar*.

Partial reduplication in Tuli and Zak.

532 *ĉaḫ- "grow"

Sem *ŝūḫ- "become high": Akk *šâḫu*.

Based on biconsonantal *ŝVḫ-.

WCh *ĉaH- "grow": Wrj *ŝa*, Sha *šoḥo*.

533 *ĉaḫ- "urine; urinate"

Sem **ŝuḫ-* "urinate": Arab *šḫḫ* [*-u-*].
Denominative formation?
WCh **ĉaH-* "urine": Bks *šaa*.
Agaw **šaγ-* "urine": Kem *šaγ*, Aun *čaγ-əŋ*, *čaq-əŋ*.
Aun *č-* appears to be regular.
Dhl *saaḥaw-* "urinate".
Unexpected *s-*. Cf. **saḫ-* "urine".

534 *ĉaḫür- "snore"

Sem **ŝVḫir-* "snore": Arab *šḫr* [*-i-*].
WCh **ĉa(n)Hur-* "snore": Hs *min-šāri*, Wrj *ŝər-mə*, Diri *ŝərma*, Paa *ẑur-guna*, Ngz *ẑankor*.
Secondary cluster **-nH-*.

535 *ĉakin- "knife"

Sem **ŝakīn-* "knife": Hbr *ŝakkīn*, Aram (Syr) *sakkīnō*.
WCh **ĉ[a]nk-* "knife": Krf *šonge*, Glm *čonga*.
Metathesis. The development of the original morphonological structure is parallel to WCh reflex of HS **čakin-* "net".
Dhl *hlakane* "sharp (knife)".
Assimilation of vowels.

Derived from **ĉuk-* "cut, pierce".

536 *ĉalaḫ- "break"

Sem **ŝVlaḫ-* "split": Arab *šlḫ* [*-a-*].
WCh **ĉaHal-* "crush": Tng *seele*.
Metathesis.
ECh **ĉaHal-* "break": Dng *saale*.
Metathesis.

An alternative reconstruction could be **ĉaḫal-*.

537 *ĉalay- "hail" (n.)

Eg *šny.t* "hail" (pyr).
Note *-n-* < HS **-l-*.

CCh *ŝa-ŝalay- ''hail'': Gis *ŝaŝalay*.
Partial reduplication.

538 *ĉaluḳ- ''cut, slaughter''

Sem **ŝVluḳ-* ''cut, split'': Akk *šalāqu*, Arab *šlq* [*-u-*].
WCh **ĉalVḳ-* ''opening a vein (in the leg of an animal)'': Hs *salkā*.

Cf. **ĉalaḫ-* ''break''.

539 *ĉambar-/*ĉambir- ''flute''

WCh **ĉambar-* ''kind of flute'': Hs *samḅara*.
Emphatic *-*ḅ*- seems to have no phonological justification.
Omot **šumbir-* ''shepherd's flute'': Mch *šumbiro*.
Secondary **u* before a labial.

540 *ĉap- ''leaf''

WCh **ĉaHVp-* ''leaf'': Siri *ŝāpi*, Miya *ŝepi*.
Metathesis from **ĉapVH-*? Cf. CCh.
CCh **ŝapVH-* ''leaf'': Lame *ŝapa*, LPe *ŝap*, ZBt *ŝab*, Masa *ŝaḅ*.
-b- < *-ḅ-* results from the emphatization of *-*p*-.
LEC **šaf-* ''leaf'': Or *šafo*.
HEC **šaf-* ''leaf'': Had *šäf-ita*, Kab *šäf-ita*, Dar *šafa*.

541 *ĉar- ''cut, saw''

Sem **wVŝVr-* ''saw'': Arab *yšr*, *wšr*, Gz *wšr*, Mhr *wuŝor*, Jib *ʾŝr*.
Prefix **wV-*.
WCh **ĉar-* ''cut (trees)'': Hs *sārā*.
CCh **ŝar-* ''adze, shave'': Gis *ŝar*, Mofu *ŝər*.
LEC **sar-* ''cut'': Som *sar*.

542 *ĉar- ''tree''

Eg *šꜣ* ''tree'' (XVIII).
-ꜣ continues HS *-*r*-.
ECh **ĉar-* ''tree'': Bid *čaro*.

543 *ĉar- "buy, sell"

Sem *ŝVrVy- "buy, sell": Arab šry [-i-].
Derived from *ŝVr-.
WCh *ĉar- "buy (in order to sell)": Hs sārā.

544 *ĉar-/*ĉaʕVr- "barley"

Sem *ŝaʕār-/*ŝaʕīr- "barley": Ug šʕr, Hbr ŝeʕorā, Aram (Syr) səʕārətā, Arab šaʕīr-, Sab ŝʕr.
Derivative vocalism in Arab. The original form might have been *ŝar- influenced by or contaminated with *ŝaʕar- "be hairy".
Eg šr.t "barley" (MK).

545 *ĉariʕ- "road"

Sem *ŝāriʕ- "road": Arab šāriʕ-.
ECh *ĉaHVr- "path": Dng sāre.
Metathesis.

The alternative reconstruction is *ĉaʕir-.

546 *ĉeʔ- "faeces"

Eg šꜣ.w "faeces" (med).
CCh *ŝyaʔ- "faeces": Hwn ẑe, ŝe.
Omot *šiy- "faeces": Ome šiyaa.
From *šiʔa-.
Rift *ĉaʔ- "faeces": Irq ĉaʔe.

547 *ĉeʕ- "sand"

Eg šʕy "sand" (pyr), Copt *šō: Akh šou, Boh šō, Shd šō.
-y stands for a front vowel of the root.
WCh *ĉyay- < *ĉyaH- "sand": Bgh šey.

548 *ĉeḥaṭ- "squeeze"

Sem *ŝVḥaṭ- "squeeze": Hbr ŝḥṭ [-a-].
WCh *ĉyaHVṭ- "squeeze": Krf šeetu, Gera šeeḍ.

Cf. *ç̌aḫut- "squeeze".

549 *ĉeḳ- "smell" (trans.)

Sem *nVŝaḳ- "smell": Arab nšq [-a-].
Prefix *nV- and modified vocalism.
WCh *ĉyaḳ- "smell": Hs šēḳa.

550 *ĉem- "go, enter"

Sem *ŝīm- "enter": Arab šym [-i-].
Based on biconsonantal *ŝim-.
Eg šm "go" (pyr).
ECh *ĉyam- "enter" [1], "run" [2]: Kwan seme [1], Mobu səme [2], Ngm seme [2].

551 *ĉer- "root"

Sem *śVrś-"root": Akk šuršu, Ug šrš, Hbr šoreš, Aram (Syr) šeršō.
Partial reduplication. No reduplication is attested in Gz ŝərəw, Tgr sər, Tgy sər, Amh sər, Gaf sər, Gur sər, Soq ŝeraḥ.
Berb *car- "root": Kby azař.
WCh *ĉyarwa-"root": Hs saiwā, Bol sori-, Ngm šori, Maha sar-om, Krf sooriyo, Gera suurə-na, Glm surya, Grm sūra, Miya ŝerwa, Paa ŝari, Siri ŝūra, Mbu ŝar-nani, Jmb ŝera, Pol ŝər-tə, Geji ŝar-ki, ŝer-ki, Say ŝər-tə, Kir ŝəri, Tala ŝəri, DB ŝure.
CCh *ŝar- "root": Mtk ⁿẑoⁿẑor, Dgh ŝəla, Glv ŝali, Zime ŝōr.
*-a- < *-ya- after an affricate?
ECh *ĉyar-aw- "root": Tum heraw, Ndam sirwe, Lele sara, Kera kə-sar, Bid čāra, Mig čāru.
Agaw *sVr- "root": Kem sər, Kwr sər.

552 *ĉiʾ-/*ĉiw- "darkness"

Sem *ŝiw- "evening": Akk šiwītu.
Eg šw.t "shadow" (pyr).

Cf. LEC *ḍiʾ- "become dark": Or ḍiʾa. Note the consonantal alternation *-ʾ- ~ *-w-.

553 *ĉid- "vessel"

Sem **ŝidd-* "kind of vessel": Akk *šiddatu*.
Eg *šdy* "vessel" (med).
-y is a vocalic sign.

554 *ĉid- "squeeze"

Sem **ŝid-/*ŝud-* "squeeze" [1], "load, put on: Arab *šdd* [*-i-*, *-u-*] [1], Jub *ŝedd* [2].
ECh **ĉidVH-* "squeeze, press": Smr *šiḍə*.
Suffix **-VH-*.

Cf. HS **ĉeḥaṭ-* "squeeze".

555 *ĉiḫar- "grow, be long"

Sem **ŝVraḫ-* "grow": Arab *šrḫ* [*-a-*].
Metathesis.
WCh **ĉiHVr-/*ĉuHVr-* "grow" [1], "high, tall" [2]: Bol *siir* [1], Ank *sur* [1], Sha *šoḥo* [1], Tng *soori* [2].
Rift **ĉeHVr-* "long": Gor *ĉeer*, Alg *ĉeer*, Bur *ĉeedu*.

Cf. LEC **ḍēr-* < **ḍeHVr-* "long, tall": Som *ḍeer*, Or *ḍeeraa*, Rend *dɛr*.

556 *ĉin- "speak"

Eg *šny* "speak" (MK), Copt **šini* id.: Fym *šini*, Ahm *šine*, Bhr *šini*, Shd *šine*.
-y stands for a front vowel of the root.
WCh **ĉin-* "speak": Dik *ŝin*, Mng *ŝin*.

557 *ĉip- "moisten, be wet"

Sem **nVŝap-/*nVŝup-* "absorb (of liquids)": Arab *nšf* [*-a-*, *-u-*].
Prefix **nV-*. Secondary development of the vowel in a derivative.
ECh **ĉip-* "moisten": Bid *čiip*.

558 *ĉiwam-/*ĉiyam- "rat"

Sem **ŝiyām-* "rat": Arab *šiyām-*.
ECh **ĉVwVm-* "rat": Tum *soom*.

Consonantal alternation **-w-* ~ **-y-*.

559 *ĉoᶜ- "cereal"

Eg *šᶜ.t* "kind of bread" (med).
Cf. reduplicated *šᶜšᶜ* "kind of corn" (l).
WCh **ĉwaH-* "millet" [1], "meal made of millet" [2]: Hs *çāwā* [2], Sura *šwaa* [1], Ang *šwe* [1], Mnt *sua* [2], Ank *sua* [2], Siri *ŝawi* [2], Tng *sau* [1].

560 *ĉogar- "tree"

Sem **ŝagar-* "tree": Arab *šagar-at-*.
Assimilation of vowels. Cf. Hss *śegerēt* "plant name".
CCh **ŝwagVr-* "palm tree": Sok *soger*, *sogor*.
Secondary vowel of the second syllable.

561 *ĉoᶜid- "cut, scratch"

Eg *šᶜd* "cut" (med).
WCh **ĉwaHid-* "tatoo" [1], "scratch" [2]: Ang *līt* [1], Cagu *ŝēḍ-* [2], Jmb *ŝinḍ-* [2], Klr *šut* [2], Ngz *ŝaaḍu* [2].
CCh **ŝwadVH-* "chop": Zgh *ŝoḍaya*.
Metathesis.

562 *ĉohVr- "fall"

Eg *šhr* "throw down" (pyr).
Semantically, Eg is a causative in relation to Chadic forms.
WCh **ŝwaHVr-* "fall": Bol *soor*.
ECh **ĉuHVr-* "fall": Kera *suuri*.

Cf. Sem **ŝVrVy-* "put flatwise" (Akk *šerû*).

563 *ĉom- "pot"

Eg *wšm* "pot" (XVIII).

w- is a sign for a rounded vowel.
ECh **ĉwam-* "pot": Kera *soma*.

564 *ĉor- "become dry"

Eg *wšr* "become dry" (MK).
w- is a vocalic sign.
WCh **ĉwar-* "become dry": Krk *səwru*.

565 *ĉorah- "swallow"

Sem **ŝVrah-* "glut": Arab *šrh* [-*a*-].
Note the semantic development.
LEC **sōr-* < **soHVr-* "feed": Or *soora*.
Metathesis.

566 *ĉud-/*ĉaʾad- "harrow, till"

Sem **ŝud-* "harrow, till": Hbr *šdd*.
Eg *šȝd* "dig, till" (OK).
WCh **ĉaHVd-* "till, plough": Wrj *ŝaḍ-*, Kry *ŝeyasēḍ*, Miya *ŝaḍ-*, Paa *ŝaḍu*, Siri *ŝaḍa*.
Dhl *hlaḍ-* "sweep ground".
-ḍ- seems to reflect a lost laryngeal.

Note a parallel form of the root with an inlaut laryngeal.

567 *ĉuʿ- "knife"

Eg *šʿ.t* "knife" (pyr).
CCh **ŝuw-* "knife": Gis *ŝuw-eḍ*, Bld *ŝuw*, Mofu *ŝuw-eḍ*.
From **ĉuH-*.
ECh **ĉuw-* "knife": Mkk *suwo*.
From **ĉuH-*.

Related to **ĉaʿ-* "cut".

568 *ĉuḫat- "be afraid"

Sem **ŝVḫat-* "be afraid": Akk *šaḫātu* [-*a*-].
WCh **ĉuHat-* "be afraid": Fyer *šušwet*, Tng *soode, suude*.

Partial reduplication in Fyer.

569 *ĉuk- "cut, pierce"

Sem **ŝuk-* "pierce (with a spear)" [1], "skewer" [2]: Arab *škk* [*-u-*] [1], Jib *ŝekk* [2].
WCh **ĉuk-* "pierce, slaughter": Hs *sōka, sūka*.
Omot **šuk-* "slaughter": Ome *šuk-*, Yam *šuk-*, Kaf *šuk(k)-*, Bwo *šuk-*, Gim *šuk-*.

570 *ĉuk- "sharp weapon"

WCh **ĉuk-* "knife": Sha *šuk*, Klr *suk*.
CCh **ŝuk-* "knife": Tera *ŝug-di*, Boka *ŝəχ-tə*.
Boka *-χ-* < **-k-* in contact with an unvoiced stop.
HEC **šuk-* "big knife": Bmb *šuko, šuuko*.

Derived from **ĉuk-* "cut, pierce".

571 *ĉun- "sorcery, magic"

Eg *šn.w* "sorcerer" (NK).
ECh **ĉun-* "magic, medicine" [1], "fetish" [2]: Kwn *sɔ:nɛ* [1], Sok *sune* [2].

572 *ĉup- "lip"

Sem **ŝap-* "lip": Akk *šaptu*, Ug *šp-t*, Hbr *ŝāpā*, Aram (Syr) *sep^etō*, Arab *šaf-at-*.
**-u-* > **-a-* before a labial.
Rift **ŝuf-* "lip": Irq *ŝufi*, Bur *ŝufi*, Kwz *ŝifi- to*.
Initial **ŝ-* is irregular.

Cf. also Eg *sp.t* "lip" (pyr)?

573 *ĉur- "make warm"

Sem **ŝur-* "keep in the sun": Arab *šrr* [*-u-*].
Eg *ꜣšr* "roast" (pyr).
Eg *ꜣ-* may reflect prefix **ʔV-*.

574 *ĉuram- "big vessel"

Sem **ŝurām-* "big vessel": Akk *šurāmu*.
Eg *šꜣm.w* "big mug" (OK).
Note *-ꜣ-* < **-r-*.

Probably, a *Wanderwort*.

575 *ĉVmVm- "be ill"

Sem **ŝVmVm-* "become weak": Akk *šamāmu*.
Eg *šmm*, *šm* "be feverous" (med).

576 *ĉVpVṭ- "be angry"

Sem **ŝVpVṭ-* "threaten": Akk *šapāṭu*, *šapātu*.
Eg *špt* "wrath" (BD).
Eg *-t-* is one of regular continuations of HS **-ṭ-*.

*Ç̂

577 *ç̂abaʾ- "army, people"

Sem **ṣ̂abaʾ-* "army, soldiers": Akk *ṣābu*, Ug *ṣbʾ*, Phn *ṣbʾ*, Hbr *ṣābā(ʾ)*.
Eg *ḏbꜣ* "army".

Related to **ç̂abaʾ-* "wage war".

578 *ç̂abaʾ- "wage war"

Sem **ṣ̂Vbaʾ-* "attack" [1], "wage war" [2], "fight" [3]: Akk *sabāʾu* [2], Hbr *ṣbʾ* [2], Arab *ḍbʾ* [-*a*-] [1], SAr *ḍbʾ* [1], Gz *ṣbʾ* [2], Tgr *ṣbʾ* [3], Tgy *ṣbʾ* [3].
Agaw **šab-* "wage war": Bil *šab-*, *šib-*, Kwr *sab-*.

579 *ç̂afir- "plaiting"

Sem **ṣ̂apīr-* "plaiting" [1], "braid" [2]: Arab *ḍafīr-* [2], Gz *ḍəfr* [2], Jib *ḍəfre-t* [1], Soq *ḍafr-əh* [1].

Cf. Sem *ṣ̂VpVr- "plait, twist": Arab ḍfr, Gz ḍfr, Jib ḍɔfɔr.

ECh *ç̂yapir- < *ç̂apir- "kind of pubic hair": Bid ḍyeepir.

*-ya- < *-a- influenced by the front vowel of the following syllable.

LEC *çif(V)r- "women's hairdo" [1], "braid" [2]: Or çifra [1], Kon çirf- [1], Gid č̣irf- [2].

Metathesis in Kon and Gid. Unexpected *i resulting from the assimilation of vowels.

Related to *ç̂ef- "plait, comb".

580 *ç̂am- "be bitter"

WCh *ç̂amam- "(be) bitter": Hs çāmi, Siri ṣ̂āmāmu, Cagu ṣ̂emama, Paa ṣ̂ammā.

Partial reduplication.

ECh *ç̂yam- "bitter": Jegu ʾǯeema.

*ç̂yam- < *ç̂ami-.

Omot *çam- "(be) bitter": Ome č̣aam-, Kaf č̣aamm-, Mch č̣ammo.

Ome and Kaf may reflect a secondary formation with an inlaut laryngeal *çaHam-.

581 *ç̂amb- "lizard, frog"

Sem *ṣ̂abb- "turtle" [1], "lizard" [2]: Hbr ṣāb [1], Arab ḍabb- [2], Hss ḍōb [2], Mhr ḍōb [2], Shh ḍob [2].

*-b(b)- continues a prenasalized HS cluster *-mb-.

WCh *ç̂umb- "frog": Hs çumbō.

Secondary *-u- before a labial.

Rift *ĉamb- "frog": Alg ĉembeʿu, Bur ĉambeʿu.

582 *ç̂ap- "marry"

Berb *çVp- "marry": Ayr əṭṭəf.

Rift *ĉap- "pay bridewealth": Kwz ĉap.

583 *ç̂ar- "enemy"

Sem *ṣ̂arr- "enemy": Akk ṣerru, ṣēru, Ug ṣr-t, Hbr ṣar, Aram ʿār, Gz ḍar, Tgy ṣär.

Eg ḏꜣḏꜣ "enemy" (pyr).

Reduplication. Note *-ȝ* < HS **-r-*.

Related to **ĉir-/*ĉur-* "be hostile"

584 *ĉayVp- "stranger, guest"

Sem **ṣ̂ayp-* "guest": Arab *ḍayf-*, Hss *ḍayf*, Mhr *ḍayf*.
Cf. a denominative verb **ṣ̂VyVp-* in Arab *ḍyf* [-*i*-] "be a guest", Jib *eḍef* "give hospitality".
WCh **ĉay(V)p-* "friend" [1], "pilgrim, stranger" [2], "guest" [3]: Sura *mi-zɛp* [2], Chip *mə-zɛp* [1], Mnt *mɛ-zɛp* [2], Ank *mos* [2], Grk *mɛ-dap* [2], Krk *ŝapa* [1], Pero *mi-ẑiva* [3], Krf *n- zafe* [1].
CCh **mi-ŝip-* "guest": Mrg *miŝipi*, Chb *məŝəbi*, Wmd *miŝibi*, Klb *mihibi*.
Prefix **mi-*. Voicing of **-p-* in individual languages is regular.

585 *ĉef- "plait, comb" (v.)

Sem **ṣ̂Vp-ṣ̂Vp-* "plait (hair)": Arab *ḍfḍf*.
Reduplication.
WCh **ĉyaf-* "comb (beard)": Hs *ç̣ēfe*.

586 *ĉim- "tie, sew"

Sem **ṣ̂um-* "join, bind": Arab *ḍmm* [-*u*-], Gz *ḍmm*.
**-u-* < HS **-i-* influenced by the following labial.
WCh **ĉim-* "sew": Siri *ṣ̂im*, Jmb *ŝim*, Geji *ŝim-vi*, Buli *ŝemu*.
ECh **ĉim-* "sew": Mig *ḍyimmo*, Mubi *ʾʒeme-ge*.

587 *ĉur- "be hostile"

Sem **ṣ̂ur-* "be hostile" [1], "inflict harm" [2]: Ug *ṣrr* [1], Arab *ḍrr* [-*u*-] [1], Sar *ḍrr* [1], Jib *ẓerr* [2].
Cf. also Hbr *ṣwr* "be hostile".
Eg *ḏȝy* "be hostile" (pyr).
Suffix *-y*. Note HS **-r-* > *-ȝ-*.
WCh **ĉVr-* "ostracizing": Hs *ç̣iri*.
Assimilation of vowels.

588 *çüb- "flow, rain" (v.)

Sem **ṣib-* "flow" (v.): Arab *ḍbb* [-*i*-].
Rift **ĉub-* "rain (v.)": Irq *ĉuw-*, Bur *ĉub-*, Kwz *ĉub-*.
Dhl *luβ-* "rain (v.)".

*d

589 *daʾ- "child"

WCh **daʾ-* "child": Hs *ḍa*.
ḍ- < **d-* under the influence of the laryngeal.
ECh **dwaʾ-* "son, child": Smr *doi*.
Unexpected **-wa-*, probably resulting from the interaction with the lost vowel of the second syllable.
LEC **daʾ-* "baby, child": Or *daaʾ-ima*.

Related to **daʾ-/*daw-* "man, chief"? As far as the development of meaning is conserned see s.v. **bar-* "man".

590 *daʾ- "worm, snake"

WCh **daʾ-* "snake": Hs *ḍa*.
Hs *ḍ-* < **d-* under the influence of the laryngeal.
Cf. Ang *dū* "lizard".
Bed *dʾa*, *doʾo* "worm".

591 *daʾ- "urinate, ejaculate, perspire"

Berb **dVH-* "perspiration": Izy *τiδi*.
Eg *dȝ* "ejaculate".
Bed *daʾ-* "urinate".

Related to **daʾ-/*daw-* "be wet"? The present word seems to be a generalized term for liquid excreta.

592 *daʾ- "place, house"

Berb **daH-* "place": Ghd *-dā-*, Sml *i-dā*.
WCh **daH-* "place" [1], "town" [2]: Sha *ḍa* [1], Ngz *ḍā* [2].

ḍ- < *d- under the influence of the laryngeal.

CCh *dayi- "town": Bura *di*, Ngw *dey*, *di*.

From *daʾi-.

ECh *daH- "house": Sok *dā*.

LEC *daʾ- "hiding place": Or *daʾoo*.

Rift *daʾ-/*diʾ- "place": Irq *di*, Bur *da*, Alg *di* (pl.).

Cf. also Irq *do* "house", Alg *doʾo* id. Unexpected *-i-* in Irq and Alg may reflect the vocalism of plural.

593 *daʾ- "move"

Berb *dV(w)- "go, walk": Izy *eddu*, Kby *ddu*, *əddu*.

Eg *dȝ* "run, run away".

WCh *daʾ-/*diʾ- "go" 1, "come" 2, "follow" 3: Ang *dā* 1, Miya *ḍiy* 2, Kry *ḍə* 3.

Miya *-iy-* < *-iʾ-.

CCh *daʾ-/*diʾ- "run" 1, "lead" 2, "migrate" 3: Tera *ḍa* 1, Hwn *ḍa* 1, Log *da*, *di* 2.

HEC *dV- "come": Sid *d-*.

Dhl *d̠aaʿ-* "leave in a hurry".

Unexpected laryngeal.

Omot *doH- "return" (Ome *doh-*) and Rift *dah- "come, enter" (Irq *dah-*, Kwz *dah-*, Asa *dah-*) may also belong to this root.

594 *daʾ-/*daw- "be wet"

Sem *nVdaw-/*naday- "be wet": Arab *ndw*, *ndy* [-*a*-].

Prefix *nV-. Cf. Sem *dVy- "rain" (n.) (Eja *dəyyä*, Gog *diyä*).

Berb *dVw- "soak": Ahg *ə-du*.

WCh *daʾ- "pour" 1, "be wet" 2: Sura *ḍō* 1, Ang *dō* 1, Kry *ḍā* 2, Jmb *daʾā* 2.

Agaw *du- "pour": Aun *du-ŋ*.

LEC *daʾ- "rain" (v.): Som *daʾ-*.

Cf. also reduplication in SA *dad- "rainy season" (Saho *dada*). Consonantal alternation *-ʾ- ~ *-w-.

595 *daʾ-/*daw- "man, chief"

Berb *dVw- "men": Fgg *i-du*.

Cf. also Nfs *i-wd-an*, Sha *i-wd-an* id. continuing **wVd-*.
WCh **daʾ-* "chief": Sura *n-daa*, Ang *dē*.
CCh **daʾi-* "man" [1], "people" [2]: Mba *ʾḍiya* [1], Msg *dai* [2].
Rift **daH-* "stranger": Irq *dahay-mo*, Bur *daha*, Asa *deʾ-imu*.

Consonantal alternation **-ʾ-* ~ **-w-*. Related to **daʾ-* "child"? Note **nV-da-* "person; father" in WCh and CCh.

596 *daʾap- "follow"

WCh **daʾap-* "follow": Sura *tap*, Bol *ḍapp-*, Krk *dāf-*.
HEC **daHap-* "reconnoitre, spy": Had *daap*.

597 *daʾaw- "move"

Sem **dVʾaw/*dVʾay-* "sneak (of a wolf)": Arab *dʾw*, *dʾy* [-*a*-].
Berb **dVw-* "arrive in the afternoon": Ayr *adwu*.
WCh **daʾaw-* "return" [1], "come" [2]: Hs *dāwō* [1], Paa *dav* [2].
Cf. also Miya *ḍiy* "follow" reflecting **dVʾVy-*, probably, corresponding to Arab *dʾy*.

Derived from **daʾ-* "move".

598 *daʾud- "trample"

ECh **dVʾud-* "trample": Mkk *dūḍ-*.
Agaw **dad-* "trample": Bil *dad-*, Kwr *dad-*, Dmb *dad-*, Kem *dad-*.

Reduplication of **daʾ-* "move".

599 *daʾüm- "spear"

Sem **daʾīm-* "spear": Akk *daʾīmu*.
Secondary inlaut laryngeal?
CCh **ʾudum-* "spear": FJ *wudumi*, Gude *ʾuduma*.
Assimilation of vowels and metathesis.

600 *dab- "follow"

CCh **daʾVb-* < **HV-dab-* "follow": Dgh *ḍaba*, Mnd *ḍaba*.
Metathesis of the laryngeal prefix.
Omot **dab-* "follow": Ome *dab(b)-*.

Cf. Sem *dib- "crawl, walk slowly": Arab *dbb* [-*i*-].

601 *dab- "vessel, box"

Sem **dabb-* "vessel for oil": Arab *dabb-at-*.
Eg *db* "box" (n).
LEC **dob-* "vessel for oil": Som *dobi*.
**-o-* < HS **a* before a labial consonant.

602 *dab- "trample"

Sem **dVb-dVb-* "trample": Arab *dbdb*.
Reduplication.
WCh **dabVH-* "trample (floor)": Hs *daḅa*.
Laryngeal suffix?

603 *dab- "big animal"

Sem **dabb-/*dubb-* "bear": Akk *dabbu*, Amor *dabbu*, Hbr *dōb*, Aram (Syr) *debb-*, Arab *dubb-*, Gz *dəb*, Tgr *dəb*.
**dubb-* is a secondary variant of **dabb-*.
Eg *db* "hyppopotamus" (OK).
Dhl *ḏaβi* "animal, meat".

604 *dab- "skin, hide"

ECh **daḅ-* < **dabaH-* "skin": Kwn *daḅa*.
Irregular emphatic.
Agaw **dabb-* "tanned hide": Bil *dabba*.
Derivative in **dVbVl-* "hide": Bil *dəbbəla*, Kwr *dəbəlaa*, Kem *dəbəlaa*.
LEC **dub-* "skin": Som *dub*.
Secondary **u*.
Omot **dabb-* "clothes made of bull-hide": Kaf *dabboo*.

Cf. Bed *adeeb* "skin, hide" < **ʾa-daHab-*. As to *-ee-* < **-aHa-*, see s.v. **daḥar-* "drive away".

605 *dab-/*dib- "break, beat"

WCh **dab-* "break": Sura *tɛp*, Ang *tap*, *tep*, Mnt *tep*, Krk *dabu*, Ngm *dap*, Glm *dw-*.
SA **dib-* "whisk, beat": Afar *dibe*.

Alternation **a* ~ **i*. Connected with **dab-* "trample"?

606 *daba'- "insect"

Sem **dabaʾ-* "small locust": Arab *dabā(ʾ)-t-*.
CCh **daḅ-* < **dabaʾ-* "termite": Lame *daḅ*, *dəḅai*.
ECh **dVb-dVb-* "tsetse": Kera *adəbdəbə*.
Reduplication.

607 *dabaʒ- "pound, grind"

Berb **dVbVʒ-* "thresh": Zng *dəbəz*.
WCh **dabaʒ-* "coarsely ground flour": Hs *dābāza*.
Nominal derivative of the original verbal root.

608 *dabin- "fence, trap"

Sem **dibn-* "enclosure": Aram (Syr) *debn-*, Arab *dibn-*.
**dibn-* may result from a modification of **dabin-*?
LEC **dabin-* "trap": Som *dabin*.

609 *dabur- "insect"

Sem **dabr-* "bee" [1], "wasp" [2]: Hbr *dᵉbōrā* [1], Aram (Jud) *dᵉbōrā* [1], Arab *dabr-at-* [2], *dabbūr-* [2].
CCh **dVbur-* "termite": Bata *dəvuř-ŋən*.
LEC **darab-* "earth-worm": Or *darabii*.
Metathesis and assimilation of vowels?

Derived from or related to **dabaʾ-* "insect".

610 *dac- "flint knife"

Eg *ds* "knife, flint" (pyr).
ECh **das-* "knife": Gbr *dase-n*, Kbl *dasi*, Dor *dosi-n*.

HS *-*c*- (and not **s*) is reconstructed on the basis of the related **dac*- ''cut, chop'' where it is definitely attested in WCh and CCh.

611 *dac- ''cut, chop''

Eg *ds* ''cut'' (t).
WCh **dac*- ''cut'': Hs *dāc̦a*.
Cf. Zem *ducə* ''kill''.
CCh **dVc*- ''chop'': Log *dəsə*.
ECh **daHis*- < **Hi-das*- ''cut'' [1], ''cut hair'' [2]: Sbn *d̦yəs* [1], Sok *dis* [2].
Metathesis of the laryngeal prefix.

Related to **dac*- ''flint knife''.

612 *dad- ''mother''

Sem **dad*- ''nursing mother'': Arab *dada(h)*.
WCh **dad*- ''mother, sister'': Ngz *daadu*.
May go back to **daHad*-.
CCh **dad*- ''mother'': Gis *dada*.

Descriptive root.

613 *dad- ''man, boy''

Berb **dad*- ''people'' [1], ''brother, uncle'' [2]: Izy *mi-dd-en* [1], Kby *dadda* [2].
Kby is also used as a term of respect.
WCh **dad*- ''boy'': Bol *dāde*.
LEC **dad*- ''men, people'': Som *dad*, Boni *dad*.

Descriptive root? Reduplication of **daʔ*-/**daw*- ''man, chief''?

614 *dad- ''flow, be wet''

Eg *dȝdȝ* ''flow away''.
WCh **dVd*- ''be wet'': Wrj *dəd*, Diri *dəd*.
LEC **dad*- ''flow of water'': Som *daad*.
HEC **dad*- ''flow'': Had *daadd*-.

Reduplication of HS **daʾ-/*daw-* "flow, be wet".

615 *daf- "heat, sweat"

Berb **dVf-* "warmth": Aks *ddfa*.
WCh **daHVf-* "sweat": Ngz *ḍaafau*.
CCh **(mu-)daf-* "sweat": Ngw *mu-ḍufa*, Glv *ŋgu-dəfa*, Gava *ŋgʷu-ḍufa*, Log *mu-ṭfu*, Kus *n-dafy*.
Kus *n-* is assimilated from **mV-*.
Bed *duf* "sweat".
-u- < **a* before a labial.
Agaw **dif-* "sweat": Bil *dif*.
Irregular vocalism.
HEC **daff-* "sweat": Dar *daffa*.
Omot **duf-* "sweat": Hmr *duf*, *duuf*.
-u- < **a* before a labial.

Related to **dafaʾ-* "be hot, perspire".

616 *dafaʾ- "be hot, perspire"

Sem **dVpaʾ-* "be hot": Arab *dfʾ* [*-a-*, *-u-*].
CCh **daf-* "hot, warm": Kus *ndafu*, Mus *dafu*.
Cf. Mtk *ḍuf-* "warm (water)" (v.).
HEC **daf(f)-* "perspire": Dar *daff-*.

Cf. WCh **daf-* "cook" (v.): Hs *dafaʔ*. Related to **daf-* "heat, sweat".

617 *dag- "forget, lose"

ECh **dag-* "get lost": Mkk *daggiya*.
Suffix *-iya*.
LEC **dag-* "forget": Or *daga*.

618 *dag- "see, know"

Eg *dgy* "see, look".
Suffix *-y-*.
ECh **ḍVg-* "think": Kera *ḍigi*.
Irregular emphatic.

SA *(HV)dag- "know, learn": Saho -ḍag-, -ḍig-, - ḍeg-, Afar dag-, ḍag-.
HEC *dag-/*deg- "know": Kmb dag-, deg-.

619 *dag-/*dig- "go"

Sem *dig- "go slowly" [1], "be slow" [2]: Arab dgg [-i-] [1], Gur dəg, dəg [2].
Eg dgꜣ "go" (n).
-ꜣ stands for *a of the root syllable.
Agaw *dig- "come close": Aun dig-əŋ.
HEC *dag- "come" [1], "go" [2], "escape" [3]: Sid dag- [1], Dar dag- [2], Bmb dag- [3].

Alternation *a ~ *i.

620 *dagan- "corn"

Sem *dagan- "corn": Ug dgn, Phn dgn, Hbr dāgān.
WCh *dang- "corn": Ang tang.
The development of the original structure in Chadic is parallel to similar structural changes in HS *ĉakin- "knife"and *čakin- "net".

621 *dagir-/*dagur- "beans, millet"

Sem *digr- "haricot" [1], "bean" [2]: Arab digr- [1], Soq digir [2].
Assimilation of vowels from *dagir-. Cf. also Arab dagr-, dugr- id.
ECh *dagir- "millet": Sok dagir.
Agaw *ʔa-da(n)gur- "bean": Xmr adogur, Dmt adanguari, Aun adanguari.
Prefix *ʔa-.
SA *ʔa-dagur- "bean": Saho adogur.
Prefix *ʔa-.
LEC *digir- "bean": Som digir.
Assimilation of vowels. A Sem loanword?

622 *da^{c}-/*di^{c}- "look, know"

WCh *diH-/*diw- "see": Cagu duw-, Fyr ḍi.

Secondary **-w-* < **-H-* before a rounded vowel (cf. also its influence upon the root vocalism in Cagu).

SA **daᶜ-/*diᶜ-* ''know, be able'': Saho *diᶜ-*, *daᶜ-*, *ḍiᶜ-*, *ḍaᶜ-*, Afar *diᶜ-*, *daᶜ-*, *ḍaᶜ-*.

LEC **daᶜ-* ''understand'' [1], ''see'' [2]: Som *daᶜ-*, *ḍaᶜ-* [1], *daay* [2], Bay *d-* [2].

Dhl *d̲aaw-at̲-* ''look after''.

-w- < **-ᶜ-*?

Rift **daʾ-* ''watch, gaze'': Kwz *daʾ-am-*.

Note Rift **-ʾ-* < **-ᶜ-*.

Cf. reduplications in Dhl *d̲iid̲-* ''inspect'' and Rift **did-* ''remember'': Kwz *did-*.

623 *daham- ''vessel, container''

Sem **dahmay-* ''pan'': Arab *dahmā-*.

Derived from **dahm-*.

WCh **Ha-dam-* ''bag'': Sura *daam*.

Metathesis. Cf. Hs *madāmi* ''pot'' < WCh **ma-daHam-*.

624 *dahun- ''lie, deceive''

Sem **dVhun-* ''deceive'': Arab *dhn* [*-u-*].

WCh **danuH-* < **daHun-* ''lie, deceive'': Chip *ḍuŋ*, Bks *daŋ*.

Metathesis.

625 *daḥ-/*diḥ- ''fall''

Sem **dVḥ-* ''push'': Akk *daḫû*, *deḫû*, Phn *dḥy*, Aram (Syr) *deḥaʾ*, (Mand) *dhʾ*, Arab *dḥw*.

Various derivatives based on a biconsonantal stem.

WCh **daH-* ''fall'': Siri *da*, Cagu *dā-*, Mbu *dā-*.

CCh **diH-* ''fall'': Chb *ḍi*.

ECh **daHwa-* ''fall'': Kwn *ḍawē*, Mobu *ḍawe*.

Omot **dih-* ''fall'': Mch *dihi(ye)*.

Note **-h-* < **-ḥ-*.

626 *daḥar- ''drive away''

Sem **dVḥar-* ''drive away'' [1], ''divorce'' [2]: Arab *dḥr* [*-a-*] [1], Gz *dḥr* [2].

Bed *deer* "drive away".
-ee- < **-aHa-*.
SA **daHar-* "drive away": Afar *daʔar*.
Unexpected **-ʔ-*.
LEC **day(V)r-* "drive away" [1], "send": Som *dayri-* [1], *dir-* [2].
**-y-* may reflect an intervocalic laryngeal.

Any connection with **dVhar-* "hunt" (v.)? As far as the meaning is concerned, cf. Slav **gъnati* "hunt, drive away". Derived from **dar-* "drive away".

627 *daḥiç̣- "press, squeeze"

Sem **dVḥVṭ-* "oppress" [1], "trample over" [2]: Akk *daṣû* [1], Tgr *dähaṣa* [2], Tgy *däḥaṣä* [2], Amh *daṭä* [2], Gur *datä* [2].
CCh **daHič-* "squeeze": Gis *doč*, Mofu *ḍač*, Daba *ḍič*.

628 *daḥVr- "skin"

Eg *dḥr* "skin" (MK).
ECh **dar-* "skin": Tum *dar*.

629 *daḫ- "stone"

Berb **dVɣ(Vɣ)-* "stone": Kby *adɣaɣ*.
Partial reduplication.
Eg *dḫ.w.t* "stone block" (n).
WCh **daHya-* "stone": Jmb *ḍaya*, Dwot *ḍayi*.
ECh **dVHVy-* "stone, rock": Tum *dəə:y*.

630 *daḫ- "smoke"

Sem **duḫ(ḫ)-* "smoke": Arab *daḫḫ-*, *duḫḫ-*.
Secondary vocalism in *duḫḫ-*.
CCh **dyaH-* < **daHi-* "smoke": LPe *dēoka*, Msm *deu*.

631 *daHir- "press, squeeze"

Berb **dVr-* "press": Ahg *a-dər*.
WCh **daHir-* "crack" [1], "thresh" [2]: Hs *dāre* [1], Bol *diir* [2], Wrj *dər* [2], Kry *dər* [2], Miya *dər* [2], Cagu *dar* [2],Mbu *dər* [2], Jmb *dira* [2].

If Hs does not belong here, it is quite plausible that the original form of the root was **dir-*.

632 *dak- "niche, stair"

Sem **dak(k)-* "bench" [1], "staircase" [2]: Arab *dakk-at-* [1], Tgr *dəkka* [1], Mhr *dekk-īt-* [1], Soq *dekk-oh* [2].
Berb **dVwVk-* "niche": Ghd *a-ddūk*.
Secondary formation based on **dVk-*.

633 *dak-/*duk- "beat, pound"

Sem **duk-* "pound": Akk *dakāku*, Arab *dkk* [*-u-*].
Cf. Sem **dVkaʾ-* "pound, push": Akk *dakû*, Hbr *dkʾ*.
WCh **dak-/*duk-* "pound": Hs *daka*, Bol *dak-*, Tng *tug-*.
CCh **dak-* "trample" [1], "strike" [2]: Mba *dak* [1], Log *tku* [2].

Alternation **a* ~ **u*. Cf. **daḳ-/*duḳ-* "break, pound".

634 *daḳ- "clay, sand"

Berb **dVḳ(ḳ)-* "clay": Sus *idəḳḳi*.
WCh **daḳ-* "clay soil": Hs *daḳo*.
Bed *dekʷa* "dust".
Irregular *-k-* < **-ḳ-*. The development of the vowel is not quite clear.
Agaw **daḳu-* "clay": Kwr *daχʷa*.

635 *daḳ-/*duḳ- "break, pound"

Sem **duḳ-* "crush" [1], "break, beat" [2]: Hbr *dqq* [1], Arab *dqq* [*-u-*] [2].
Berb **dVḳ-* "strike, pound": Kby *duqq*.
WCh **ḍak-* < **daḳ-* "pound": Hs *dan-daḳā*, Ngz *ḍəku*.
Dhl *ḍukʼ-uδ-* "destroy".

Alternation **a* ~ **u*.

636 *dal- "buttocks"

Sem **dall-* "buttocks, hips": Gz *dālle*, Amh *dalle*.
CCh **dal-* "buttocks": Mrg *ta-dal*, Hld *ndə:lu*, Klb *ndɛl*.

Prefixes **ta-* and **nV-*.

637 *dal- "be weak, be tired"

Sem **dall-* "small, inferior" [1], "weak" [2], "imperfect" [3]: Akk *dallu* [1], Ug *dl* [2], Pun *dl* [3], Hbr *dal* [2].
LEC **dal-* "be tired": Som *daal-*.
Omot **dall-* "become meager": Kaf *dalli-*.

638 *dalaḥ- "go, walk"

Sem **dVlaḥ-* "walk slowly": Arab *dlḥ* [-*a*-].
CCh **dal-* "go (away)": Glv *dal-*, Gdf *dala*, Nak *adala*, Gis *ndal*.
Cf. Zgh *dile*. Prefix **nV-* in Gis. Complete loss of the auslaut laryngeal.
ECh **dal-* "go": Mobu *dale*.

639 *dam- "blood"

Sem **dam-* "blood": Akk *dâmu*, Ug *dm*, Hbr *dām*, Aram (Syr) *dəmō*, Arab *dam-*, Gz *dam*, Tgr *däm*, Tgy *däm*, Amh *däm*, Gaf *dämʷä*, Hrr *däm*, Gur *däm*.
Berb **dam(m)-* "blood": Ghd *dəmm-ən*, Nfs *i-dəmm-ən*, Siwa *i-damm-ən*, Zng *dəmm-ən*, Sml *i-damm-ən*, Izd *i-damm-ən*, Mzab *i-dam-ən*, Shn *i-δam-ən*, Sha *i-δam-ən*, Kby *i-δam-ən*, Izn *iδammen*, Snh *eddem*.
The above forms are generalized pl. Sg. indicates **dim-*, cf. Kby *iδim*.
WCh **dam-* "blood": Sura *tɔγɔm*, Ang *tom*, Ank *tiyem*, Bol *dom*, Tng *tɔm*, Ngm *dom*, Maha *dom*, Bele *dom*, Krf *n-daame*, Gera *n-dooma*, Ngz *dədəm*.
Omot **dam-* "blood": Kaf *damoo*, Mch *damo*.

640 *dam- "flow (of blood)" (v.)

Sem **dVm-* "wound" (v.): Aram *dmm*.
Eg *dmȝ* "coagulate" (med).
Eg *-ȝ* may indicate HS **a*.

Derived from **dam-* "blood".

641 *dam- "equid"

Sem **dam-dam-* "mule": Akk *damdammu*.
Reduplication.
Berb **dVm(m)-* "mule": Ayr *edəmi*.
ECh **gV-dam-* "horse": Kera *gədaamo*.
Prefix **gV-*.
SA **dam-* "zebra": Afar *daami*.

642 *dam- "break, press"

Berb **dVm-* "press, squeeze": Zng *a-δammi*.
WCh **daʔVm-* "beat": Hs *ḍāmā*.
ECh **diʔim-* "break": Jegu *ḍimm-*, Mkk *diʔimu*, Mig *ḍiimo*, Dng *ḍyiime*.
Rift **dam-* "knead": Kwz *dam-*.

Secondary laryngeal infixes in WCh and ECh. An alternative reconstruction is **daʔim-*.

643 *dam- "live, last, sit"

Sem **dVm-/*dūm-* "dwell" [1], "last" (v.) [2], "stay a long time in one place" [3]: Ug *dm* [1], Arab *dwm* [-*u*-] [2], Hss *adīm* [3], Mhr *adyīm* [3], Shh *εdyim* [3].
Secondary derivative from **dVm-* morphologically identical with HS **dVwVm-* "drip, flow" formed on the basis of **dam-* "cloud".
Eg *dmꜣ* "lie".
-ꜣ is a vocalic sign.
WCh **dam-* "dwell" [1], "sit" [2]: Bgh *tam* [1], Geji *dem-owi*, *dəm* [2].
Secondary *-e-*.
ECh **dam-* "dwell, live, sit": Smr *dam*, Sbn *dama*.
Rift **dam-* "wait": Irq *dam-*.

644 *dam- "knife"

Eg *dm.t* "sword" (MK).
CCh **dam-dam-* "knife": Mafa *damdam*.
Reduplication.

Related to **dam-* "break, press"?

645 *dam- "cloud"

Sem **damm-/*dimm-* "light fog with dew" [1], "rainless cloud" [2]: Aram (Syr) *dīm-ət-* [1], Arab *damm-*, *dimām-* [2].
Cf. **dVmaᶜ-* "rain" (v.): Arab *dmᶜ* [*-a-*].
WCh **ʾa-dam-* "cloud": Tng *adam*.
Prefix **ʾa-*.

Cf.Berb **ʾadVm-* "drip" (Izy *addum*).

646 *damik- "hare"

Sem **dVmVk-* "run quickly (of a hare)": Arab *dmk*.
Denominative verb.
WCh **damik-* "hare": Paa *damiki*.

647 *dan- "family"

Eg *dn.w.t* "family" (XVIII).
WCh **dan-H-/*Ha-dan-* "family, clan, people": Hs *dangi*, Sura *daŋ*, Ang *deng*.
Originally, **Ha-* is a prefix.

Cf. also Rift **dan-H-* "twins" (Irq *dangi*).

648 *danaḫ- "go, walk"

Sem **dVnaḫ-* "walk slowly (carrying a load)": Arab *dnḫ* [*-a-*].
WCh **dan-H-* "go" [1], "come" [2]: Bgh *dang* [1], Buli *dang* [2].
CCh **din-H-* "go": Mwl *udiŋ-ən*, Kus *ndīnga*.
Irregular vocalism results from the influence of a lost vowel preceding **-H-*.
ECh **dan-H-/*daHan-* "run away" [1], "go away" [2], "follow" [3]: Kera *deŋe* [1], Jegu *daŋ* [2], Mkk *daane* [3].
Metathesis in Mkk.

649 *dand- "run away"

WCh **dand-* "emigrate": Hs *dandī*.
Agaw **dand-* "run away": Kwr *daand-*.

650 *dan(g)- "elephant"

HEC **dan-* "elephant": Sid *daan-icco*, Had *daane-cco*, Kmb *dani-eččoa*.
Omot **dang-* "elephant": Kaf *dangiyo*, Mch *däŋgao*, Anf *dang-eččo*, Bwo *dang-as*.
Dhl *ḏannaβa* "female elephant".
Rift **dang-* "elephant": Irq *dangw*.

This root serves as a base for HS derivatives attested outside Cush and, thus, may be a HS archaism. Cf. also SA **dakan-* "elephant" (Saho *dakaano*, Afar *dakaano*), LEC **dagon-* id. (Som *dagon*, Dhl *dokomi* id.).

651 *da(n)ger- "monkey"

CCh **dagyal-* "monkey": Bud *dägel*.
Spontaneous change of **r* > **l*.
ECh **dVgVr-* "monkey": Ndm *də:gre*.
LEC **danger-* "monkey": Som *daŋer*, Boni *dašer*.
HEC **dager-* "monkey": Had *dagieraa*, Kmb *dagieraa*.

652 *dangol- "elephant"

ECh **dVng[wa]l-* "trunk" [1], "elephant" [2]: Dng *dugulo* [1], Mig *diŋgillu* [1], Sok *dogol* [2].
Omot **dongor(r)-* "elephant": Ome *dongor*.
Assimilation of vowels.

Derived from **dan(g)-* "elephant". The reconstruction of **-a-* in the first syllable is tentatively based on the vocalism of **dan(g)-*.

653 *dankal-/*dankul- "bean"

WCh **dankal-* "sweet potato": Hs *dankali*.
Cf. Kanuri *dangali*.
Agaw **ʔa-dangwal-* "beans": Bil *adängʷal*.
Prefix **ʔa-*.
LEC **dangul-* "beans": Or *daangulle*.

Connected with **dagir-/*dagur-* "beans, millet"? Cush shows voicing of the postnasal stop.

654 *daparan- "tree"

Sem **daparan-* "juniper": Akk *daparānu*, Ug *dprn*.
CCh **dapVrVn-* "acacia": Mofu *davərna*.
Voiced *-v-* < **-p-* between two vowels?

An ancient composite? For the first component cf., probably, WCh **da[p]-* "leaf" (Krk *dafo*, Ngm *daho*, *davo*).

655 *daq̇- "fall, push"

Eg *dḫ* "fall" (XIX).
WCh **ḍak-* < **daq̇-* "upset": Tng *ḍako*.
Shift of emphatization.
CCh **dVq̇-* "push": Mofu *-dəg-*.

656 *dar- "run"

Sem **dVr-* "run freely" [1], "run tirelessly" [2]: Akk *darāru* [1], Arab *drr* [2].
Berb **dVrVᶜ-* "gallop": Kby *dreᶜ*.
Secondary **-ᶜ-*.
CCh **dar-* "run": Tera *dara*, Glv.
Prefix **mV-* and modified vocalism in Glv.

657 *dar- "road"

Sem **darar-* "straight way": Arab *darar-*.
Partial reduplication.
WCh **darVH-/*daHVr-* "road": Grk *der*, Krk *ndaru*, Maha *ḍore*, Miya *darhi*, Mba *dēri*, Jmb *dāru*.
Secondary inlaut laryngeal. Prefix **nV-* in Krk.
Mgg *dar* "way, road".

Derived from **dar-* "run". For the semantic development, cf. Gk *ὅδος* "road" ~ Slav **xoditi* "walk" and many other similar formations in IE.

658 *dar- "dwelling place"

Sem *dār- "dwelling" [1], "house" [2], "granary" [3]: Hbr *dōr* [1], Aram *dāra(ʔ)* [1], Arab *dār-* [2], Hrr *dēra* [3].
Berb *dar- "room" [1], "house" [2], "village" [3]: Rif *tha-ddar-t* [1], Izn *thi-ddar-t* [1], Snus *ṯa-ddar-t* [2], Kby *τa-ddar-τ* [3].

659 *dar- "man, master"

CCh *dar- "bridegroom": Msg *darai*.
Rift *dar- "master": Gor *daari*.

Cf. also Sem *dār- "generation, family" (Akk *dāru*, Ug *dr*, Phn *dr*, Hbr *dōr*)?

660 *dar- "drive away"

Sem *dVr- "drive away, make go": Arab *drʔ*, Soq *ʔedre*.
Eg *dr* "drive away" (pyr).
Comparison with Arab *ṭrr* "drive" is also possible.
Omot *dar- "drive away": Kaf *dar*.

Cf. *daḥar- "drive away".

661 *daraḳ- "shield"

Sem *daraḳ- "leather shield": Arab *daraq-at-*.
ECh *darag- "shield": Mubi *daraga* (from Arab?).

662 *darib- "road"

Sem *dar(V)b- "road, street": Arab *darb-*, Mhr *darb*.
CCh *darVb- "road": Log *darba* (< Arab?).
Bed *darib* "road".
Agaw *darib- "road": Bil *därib*.
SA *darib- "road": Saho *darib*, Afar *darib*.
LEC *darab- "enclosure": Or *darabaa*.
Assimilation of vowels.

Derived from HS *dar- "road". Some of the above Cush forms may be Arab borrowings.

663 *das- "vessel"

Eg *ds* "clay jug" (pyr).
WCh **das-* "kind of calabash": Hs *dasa*.
CCh **dasya-/*daswa-* "pot, calabash": Mofu *des*, Gude *dosa*.

664 *daw- "day"

Eg *dwȝ.w* "morning" (MK), Copt **towi* id.: Bhm *tooui*, Shd *tooue*. -*ȝ* stands for a vowel.
ECh **daw-* "day" [1], "sun" [2]: Smr *dawa* [1 2], Sbn *dawa* [1 2], Tum *dəw* [2], Kera *dāway* [1].

665 *daw-/*day- "arrow"

WCh **dVyiw-* "arrow" [1], "knife" [2]: Jmb *dīwa* [1], Tng *diya* [2]. Contraction.
ECh **dVw-* "dart" (n.): Tum *dəəw*.
LEC **daw-* "arrow": Bay *dawwe*.
HEC **day-* "arrow": Bmb *daaya*.
Traces of HS consonantal alternation **-w-* ~ **-y-*.

Rift **daʾ-* "quiver" (*daʾa-*) may also belong here.

666 *dawaʾ-/*dayaʾ- "be ill"

Sem **dūʾ-/*dūy-* "be ill, be weak": Ug *dw*, *dwy*, Hbr *dāwe*, Aram (Syr) *dᵉwī*, Arab *dwʾ* [-*a*-].
CCh **daʾVw-* "illness": HNk *ḍəwa*, Kap *ḍawa*, HF *ḍawa*.
ECh **dVw-* "weak": Kera *dewe*.
LEC **dayaʾ-* "be hurt badly": Or *dayyaʾa*.

Consonantal alternation **-w-* ~ **-y-*.

667 *dawak- "equid"

WCh **dawak-* "horse": Hs *dōki*, Bol *dōso*, Krk *dōku*, Dera *dok*, *dōwi*, Ngm *doku*, Bele *dōšo*, Krf *dūšo*, Gera *dūša*, Grm *dūsa*, Miya *duwakə*, Cagu *dākə-n*, Siri *dukwi*, Mbu *dāku*, Jmb *dakwa*, Ngz *dūka*.
Rift **da[ḳ]way-* "donkey": Irq *daqwai*, Alg *ndagʷai*, Bur *daqʷe*, Kwz *dagwagwai-ko*.

Secondary *ḳ. Metathesis.

Agaw *dikwar- "donkey" (Kem *doχwaraa*, Kwr *dekoraa* etc.) seems to be derived from this stem.

668 *dawal- "big vessel"

Sem **dal(V)w-/*dal(V)y-* "bucket": Akk *dalu*, Hbr *dᵉlī*, Arab *dalw-*, Hss *dōlew*, Mhr *dēlew*, Shh *dɛlɛ*.
Metathesis. Cf. Aram *dlw* "draw water", Gz *dlw* id.
ECh **dal-* "pot": Dor *dali*.
No traces of contraction.

LEC **dawVl-* "measure of weight" (Or *daawlaa*) may also belong to this root.

669 *dawal- "go, enter"

Sem **dūl-* "go around": Akk *dâlu*.
ECh **dawal-* "enter": Lele *dool*.
Contraction of *-*awa*- > Lele -*oo*-.

670 *dawḫ̮al- "vessel"

Sem **dawḫ̮al-* "basket": Arab *dawḫ̮al-at-*.
WCh **duHVl-* "pot": Sura *tugul*, Ang *tūl*.
WCh **u* may go back to HS *-*aw(V)*-.
CCh **dawγVl-* "pot, calabash": Log *ḍōli*, Mofu *dagəlu*.
ECh **d[u]gVl-* "basket" [1], "pot" [2]: Kbl *dugul* [1], Nch *degele* [2].
ECh **g* is a possible reflex of HS *ḫ̮.

Any connection with **dawal-* "big vessel"?

671 *dawul- "fence"

Sem **dawl-* "vicinity": Arab *dawl-*.
WCh **wVdul-* "goat pen, sheep fold": Ang *dul*.
Voiced Ang *d-* in the anlaut proves the existence of a preceding syllable. Note metathesis.
ECh **dVlVw-* "fence": Tum *dələəw*.
Metathesis.

The alternative reconstruction is **wadul-*.

672 *dawVḥ- ‘‘tree’’

Sem **dawḥ-* ‘‘high tree’’: Arab *dawḥ-at-*.
WCh **daw(VH)-* ‘‘kind of tree’’: Hs *dauye*.
CCh **duw-* < **duHVw-* ‘‘kind of tree’’: Gis *ḍuway*.
Cf. Dgh *daḍa* ‘‘branch’’ with reduplication.
ECh **daH-* ‘‘tree’’: Nch *dā*.

673 *day- ‘‘put’’

Eg *wdy* ‘‘put’’ (pyr).
Eg *w-* may be a prefix.
CCh **day-* ‘‘put’’: Log *de-he*.
ECh **daH-* ‘‘put (down)’’: Mubi *da*.
Cf. a reduplication in Sok *doudoi* ‘‘lie down’’.
Dhl *ḍaᶜ-* ‘‘put into, insert’’.

674 *dayas- ‘‘trample, beat, push’’

Sem **dūš-/*dīš-* ‘‘trample’’: Akk *dâšu*, Hbr *dwš*, *dyš*, Aram (Syr) *dwš*, Arab *dws*, *dys* [*-u-*], Gz *dsy*, Mhr *dōs*, Shh *dos*, Hss *dōs*.
Metathesis in Gz. The vocalism of the first syllable is conditioned by intervocalic **-y-*.
WCh **dyas-* < **dayas-* ‘‘pound’’ [1], ‘‘beat, strike’’ [2]: Geji *dɛsi* [1], DB *daš* [2].
HEC **dayas-* ‘‘split’’: Kmb *dayyaas-*.
Assimilation of vowels. Borrowing from Sem?

675 *deḫan- ‘‘smoke’’

Sem **dVḫan-* ‘‘be smoked’’ [1], ‘‘dark-colored’’ [2]: Arab *dḫn* [*-a-*] [1], Shh *edḫān* [2].
Secondary vocalism in a derivative.
CCh **dyaHVn-* ‘‘smoke’’: Gudu *mi-ḍeni*.

Derived from **daḫ-* ‘‘smoke’’.

676 *deḫul- ‘‘go, enter’’

Sem **dVḫul-* ‘‘enter’’: Arab *dḫl* [*-u-*].

WCh **dyaHul-* "enter" [1], "go out" [2]: Sura *ḍɛl* [1], Chip *ḍɛɛl* [1], Mnt *del* [1], Pol *ḍeli* [2], Geji *ḍeli* [2], Diri *ḍulə* [2].
ECh **dul-* "go out": Jegu *dul*.

677 *deḳ- "shave, cut hair"

ECh **ḍVk-* "cut hair": Mkk *ḍik-*.
Shift of emphatization.
Rift **deḳ-* "shave bald": Irq *deḳw-*.

678 *deman- "cloud, rain"

WCh **dyaman-* "rainy season" [1], "rain" [2]: Hs *dāmunā*, *dāminā*, *dāmanā* [1], Bade *demanu* [2], Ngz *dəman* [1].
Secondary vowels in the second syllable in Hs.
CCh **dyaman-* "rainy season": Gude *dɛvən*, Log *dēman*, Kus *deman*.
Dissimilation of nasals in Gude.
Agaw **dimin-* "cloud": Bil *dɛmna*, Xmr *dimmena*.
Reflects HS **demin-*?
HEC **duman-* "cloud": Dar *duuman-ca*, Bmb *dumman-ci*.
Labialization of the vowel in the first syllable.
Omot **daman-* "cloud": Ome *dämmänaa*.
Assimilation of vowels.

Derived from **dam-* "cloud".

679 *deman- "insect"

Sem **diman-* "insect": Akk *dimānu*.
Eg *dnm* "worms" (BD).
Metathesis.
WCh **dyaman-* "spider": Hs *dāmanā*.
de- is a forbidden sequence in Hs.

Derived from **dim-* "insect".

680 *den- "stone"

Eg *dny* "stone block" (n).
-y is a vocalic sign.
WCh **dyan-H-* "whetstone": Bks *ʾa-deŋ*, *ma-deŋ*.

Suffix *-H-.
ECh *dVn-H- "stone": Tum dəŋ.
Suffix *-H-.

681 *den- "dwell, remain"

Sem *dūn- "remain": Hbr dwn.
Modification of biconsonantal *dVn-.
WCh *dyan- < *dyaHVn- "sit": Ngm ḍeno, Maha ḍena.
ECh *dyan- "dwell": Kbl den.
SA *din- "sleep": Saho diin, Afar diin.

682 *der- "dress" (v.)

Eg dr "put on (clothes)" (gr).
WCh *dyar- "put on (clothes)": Kera dere.
ECh *dyar- "take off (clothes)": Lele der.

683 *der- "bird"

ECh *dyar- "dove": Mkk deere, Kwn dere.
Agaw *dir(u)- "hen": Bil diruwa, Kwr dirwa, Aun dur-.
Aun -u- < *-i- under the influence of the rounded vowel in the
second syllable.
Omot *der- "rooster": Ome deeraa.

684 *diʾ- "sickness"

Sem *diʾ- "sickness": Akk diʾu.
Rift *diʾ- "sick person": Kwz diʾ-ako.

Related to *dawaʾ-/*dayaʾ- "be ill".

685 *diʾay- "fly" (v.)

Sem *dVʾVy- "fly" (v.): Ug dʾy, Hbr dʾy.
WCh *diyaH- "fly" (v.): Krk diyau.
Metathesis.

Related to *diʾVw-/*diʾVy- "bird".

686 *diʾim- "be red"

Sem **dVʾVm-* "be dark red" [1], "red" [2], "brown" [3]: Akk *dʾm* [1], Amh *dama* [2], Hrr *dāma* [3].
Eg *ỉdmy* "red cloth" (pyr).
Metathesis. A Sem loanword?
Agaw **dVm(m)-* "(be) red": Aun *dəmma*.
SA **dum-* "red": Saho *duma*.
**-u-* < **-i-* before a labial.
LEC **diHim-* "red, red-brown": Or *diimaa*.
HEC **diHim-/*diHum-* "red" [1], "become red" [2]: Sid *dáama* [1], *duumo* [1], *duuʾm-* [2], Dar *diimma* [1].
Secondary vocalism in Sid?
Rift **dim-ay-* "red": Kwz *dimayi-*.

687 *diʾVw-/*diʾVy- "bird"

Sem **daʾ-/*day-* "vulture": Ug *dʾiy*, Hbr *dayyā*.
Secondary *-a-* in Sem.
WCh **ḍway-* < **dVway-* < **dVHay-* "bird": Bgh *ḍway*.
CCh **ḍiyaw-* < **diʾaw-* "bird": Gis *ḍiyew*, Bld *ḍiyaw*.
ECh **dVHaw-* "night bird": Tum *doo*.
Assimilation of vowels.

Related to **diʾay-* "fly" (v.).

688 *dib- "take"

Eg *dbdb* "grasp, take back" (XXI).
Reduplication.
WCh **diHab-* "take out, pluck, gather": Hs *ḍība*.
Secondary inlaut laryngeal? The original root was **dib-*.
LEC **deb-* "grasp" [1], "give back" [2]: Som *dab* [1], Or *deebisa* [2].

689 *dibin- "round container"

Eg *dbn* "round box; ring" (OK).
CCh **dibin-* "basket": Gude *divin*.

Cf. **dabin-* "fence, trap" ← * "round structure"?

690 *dič- "sneeze"

Sem *d*a*t̲t̲*- "cold, catarrh": Arab *dat̲t̲-at-*.
Deverbative.
WCh **dič-* "sneeze": Sha *dəš*, DB *diš*.

691 *di(m)bur- "back"

Sem **dubr-* "back": Hbr *dᵉbīr*, Arab *dubr-*.
Secondary formation in Hbr. Assimilation of vowels.
CCh **di(m)bur-* "buttocks": WMrg *dimbur*.

From **dub-* "back, tail".

692 *did- "elder"

Sem **did-* "honorable title": Mhr *ḥa-dīd*, Shh *edid*, *did*, Soq *dedo*.
WCh **did-* "chief's title": Ang *didē*.
Cf. Miya *didi* "in-law".
CCh **did-* "grandparent": Gis *dide*.

Descriptive stem?

693 *did- "bee"

WCh **did-* "fly" (n.): Bol *didi*, Krf *di:di*, Gera *didi*, Ngm *didi*.
Agaw **did-* "honey": Kem *didaa*.
SA **did-* "wasp": Afar *diidaa*.
HEC **did-* "bee, honey": Dar *diida*, Bmb *diida*.

Descriptive stem. Reduplication?

694 *did- "clothes"

Sem **dīd-* "kind of clothes": Akk *dīdu*.
WCh **HV-did-* "shirt": Ang *did*.
Prefix **HV-*.

695 *dif- "vessel"

Eg *dfy* "vessel" (OK).
-y is a vocalic sign.

CCh *dif- "pot": Mwu *deevo*, Nza *dəvə*, FBw *divə-n*, FMch *divu*.
Omot *dip-* "gourd": Ome *dip̣ʾee*.
Note emphatic *-p̣-*.

696 *diᶜ-/*duᶜ- "speak, call"

Sem *duᶜ-* "call" [1], "be called" [2]: Arab *dᶜw* [*-u-*] [1], Tgr *dᶜy* [2].
Various triconsonantal formations based on *duᶜ-.
CCh *diHya-* "call, say": Lame *ḍe*, Masa *dɛʾɛ*, Msm *de*, *ḍe*, *ḍi*, Bnn *diye*.
ECh *diy-*"say": Dng *diye*.
Probably, from *diHya-* as in CCh.
Bed *di* "speak, call".
SA *daᶜ-* "call": Saho *daᶜ*, Afar *daᶜ*.
The root vowel is not clear.

Alternation *i ~ *u.

697 *diᶜas- "walk"

Sem *dVᶜaš-* "trample" [1], "tread down" [2]: Arab *dᶜs* [*-a-*] [1], Tgr *dähasa* [2].
Cf. also Tgy *dähasä*, Gur *dasä* "destroy" with different laryngeals.
WCh *diHVs-* "follow": DB *ḍis-*.
CCh *dVHVs-* "enter": Gbn *ḍəsi*.

Cf. *dayas-* "trample, beat, push".

698 *diḥas- "cut, skin" (v.)

Sem *dVḥaš-* "skin, peel off": Arab *dḥs* [*-a-*], Tgr *däḥsa*, Shh *dḥas*, *dḥaš*, Soq *dōḥes*.
WCh *diHVs-* "cut, skin": Bol *ḍiss-*.

699 *diḥus- "hide, skin"

Berb *dVs-* "tanned leather": Ahg *te-dəse*, Ayr *te-dase*.
No traces of the inlaut laryngeal.
WCh *diHus-* "hide, skin": Ngm *ḍiši*, Gera *ḍīsi*, Grm *ḍuči*, Bol *ḍiši*.

Related to *diḥas-* "cut, skin".

700 *diHab- "enter, return"

ECh **diyab- < *diHab-* "enter" [1], "run away" [2]: Kbl *diyabə* [1], Kera *debe* [2].
LEC **deHeb-* "return": Or *deebiʔa*.
Contracted from **diHab-*.

Cf. HS **diHVp-* "enter".

701 *diHVp- "enter"

Berb **dVf-* "enter": Izn *a-def*.
CCh **diHVp-* "enter": Hwn *ḍəf-ən*.

LEC **daf-* "hurry, hasten" (Or *daf-*) may also belong here. Cf. HS **diHab-* "enter, return".

702 *dik- "bird"

Sem **dīk-* "rooster": Aram (Syr) *dīk-*, Arab *dīk-*.
ECh **dik-* "rooster": Mubi *dīk*.
Bed *diik* "rooster".

703 *diḳ- "build"

Sem **nVdVḳ-* "build": Gz *nadaqa*, Tgr *nadqa*, Tgy *nadaqa*, Amh *näddäqä*.
Prefix **nV-*.
WCh **ḍik- < *diḳ-* "build": Sura *ḍik*, Chip *ḍik*.
Shift of emphatization.

704 *diḳ- "be small, be thin"

Sem **diḳ(ḳ)-* "be small" [1], "be thin, fine" [2]: Akk *daqāqu* [1], Ug *dq* [2], Arab *diqq-* [2], Gz *dqq* [2], Soq *dqq* [2].
LEC **diḳ(ḳ)-* "become faint, tenuous" [1], "small" [2]: Som *dīq-* [1], Or *diqqa* [2].

Related to **daḳ-/*duḳ-* "break, pound".

705 *diḳar- "pot"

Sem *diḳār- "pot": Akk *diqāru*.
CCh *digyar- < *digar- "pot, jar": Mofu *dəger*, Gis *diger*.
CCh *-g- may reflect earlier intervocalic *ḳ.

706 *dim- "voice"

Sem *dimm- "moan" (n.): Arab *dimm-at-*.
WCh *ḍim- "sound of voice": Hs *ḍimī*, *ḍumī*.
u < *i* under the influence of the labial. Irregular Hs and WCh *ḍ-* < *d- reflects an original prefix *HV-.
CCh *dim- "song": Gis *dim-es*.

Related to *dVm- "utter".

707 *dim- "go, run"

Sem *dVm-dVm- "march": Tgr *dmdm*.
Reduplication.
Berb *dVm- "pant (when running)": Ahg *əddəm*.
The meaning makes the comparison dubious.
Eg *dmy* "move" (pyr).
-y is an infinitive suffix.
CCh *dim- "enter" [1], "go out" [2]: Mnd *dəm-* [1], Bch *dəmə* [2], Gudu *dəmu* [2], Mwu *udima* [2].
Prefix *ʾu- in Mwu.
ECh *dVm- "enter": Sbn *də:mə:*.

708 *dim- "insect"

Sem *dimm- "locust" [1], "louse, ant" [2]: Akk *dim-ī-tu* [1], Arab *dimm-at-* [2].
CCh *da-daHVm- "locust": Mofu *ḍa-ḍamiy-daw*.
Partial reduplication. Note the inlaut laryngeal and the secondary vocalism.

709 *dim- "dwelling, place"

Sem *dim- "tower" [1], "borough" [2]: Akk *dim-atu* [1], Ug *dm-t* [2].

Eg *dmy* "town" (pyr), Dem *dmy* id., Copt **tmi* "village": Boh *τmi*, Shd *τme*.

Copt shows that Eg *-y* continues a suffix.

710 *dimb- "gourd (vessel)"

WCh **dimb-* "gourd": Krf *dimbi*.
LEC **dibb-* "gourd, gourd vessel": Or *dibbe*.
HEC **dibb-/*dimb-* "drum": Sid *dibbe*, Had *dibbeʔe*, Dar *dibbe*, Kab *dibb-ita*, Bmb *diimba*.

711 *din- "cloud, rain"

Sem **dīn-* "long rain": Arab *dīn-at-*.
WCh **din-* "cloud": Mnt *tīn*.

712 *din- "vessel"

Eg *dny.t* "bowl, basket, vessel" (MK).

-y stands for a front vowel.

CCh **din-* "cooking pot": Lame *dinai*, LPe *dənai*.

Suffix *-ay-* in individual forms.

713 *din- "be weak"

Sem **dūn-* "be weak": Arab *dwn*.

Based on biconsonantal **dVn-*.

Berb **dVn-* "be weak": Zng *a-dən*.
Rift **din-* "get old": Irq *diin-*.

714 *ding- "bird"

WCh **ding-* "guinea fowl": Grm *dingi*.
Rift **ding-* "stork": Irq *dingi*.

It is difficult to say whether **-ng-* is an original HS cluster or the result of the loss of a vowel in the second syllable (if a reconstruction **dinVg-* is suggested).

715 *dink- "dwarf"

Eg *dng* "dwarf" (pyr).
**-nk-* > Eg *-ng-* in a contact position.
LEC **dink-* "dwarf": Or *dinki*.
HEC **dink-* "dwarf": Kmb *dənka*, Tmb *dinka*.

A borrowing LEC → HEC or HEC → LEC? On **-nk-* see HS **ding-* "bird".

716 *dinkar- "lizard"

WCh **dVnkar-* "lizard": Krk *dənkara*, Ngm *dəkura*.
Cf. Msg *diŋidiŋī* id., Hs *ḳadangara* id.
Omot **dingar-* "lizard": Kaf *dingaro*, Gim *dingar*.
Omot **-ng-* may be a regular reflex of HS **-nk-*.

Somehow connected with **dink-* "dwarf"?

717 *dinVy- "divide"

Eg *dny.t* "part" (n), Copt **toy(i)*: Boh *toi*, Shd *toe*.
ECh **ʾi-dinVy-* "divide": Dng *idinye*.
Prefix **ʾi-*.

718 *dir- "learn, remember"

Sem **dVrVy-/*dVrVy-* "learn, understand": Arab *dry* [*-i-*].
Based on biliteral **dar-/*dir-*.
CCh **HV-dir-* "remember": Lame *ḍir-*.

719 *dirac-/*diraç- "press, beat"

Sem **dVrVs-* "force out, trample": Akk *drs*, Aram (Jud) *drs*, Arab *drs* [*-i-*, *-u-*].
Irregular vocalism of the second syllable.
WCh **dirVç-* "press down": Hs *dirçe*, Kry *dərcə*.
CCh **dVrac-* "push (away)": Mofu *dəras*.

Sem ~ WCh correspondence is irregular as far as the affricate is concerned. CCh **-c-* is inconclusive.

720 *diŝar- "cereal"

Sem **diśar-* "wild growing cereals": Akk *dišarru*.
Eg dšr "corn" (OK).

A cultural loanword?

721 *diway- "fly" (n.)

Sem **dawVy-* "Spanish fly": Aram *dāwəy-at*.
Assimilated from **diway-*?
WCh **diyaw-* "fly": Krk *diyəw*, Pero *tiyo*.
Metathesis from **diway-*?
CCh **dVʔVy-* "fly": Hwn *ḍe*, Gbn *ḍeya*.
ECh ***diw-* "fly": Dng *duwo*, Jegu *diwo*, Brg *diwo*, Mig *duwwu*, Mubi *ḍuwo*, Sok *dōu*.
Unexpected emphatic in Mubi.

722 *diy- "plant"

Eg *dy* "cabbage" (gr).
ECh **Hwa-diy-* "grass": Mkk *oḍiyu*.
Prefix **Hwa-*.

723 *dob- "water"

Sem **dVbb-* "ocean": Ug *dbb*.
Omot **dob-* "rain": Ome *dubi*, Dime *dobi*, Kar *dobi*.

Semantically, the HS word seems to denote abundance of (flowing) water. As far as the meaning of Sem is concerned, cf. OIr *ler* "sea" ~ Slav **liti* "pour, flow".

724 *dob- "speak, call"

Sem **dub-* "speak": Akk *dabābu*.
WCh **dwab-* "call": Tng *dobi*.
LEC **deb-* "answer": Or *deeb-isa*.
Unexpected vowel.

725 *dog- "forge, beat"

Sem **dug-* "grind (to a powder)": Arab *dgg* [*-u-*].
Berb **dVg-* "forge": Aks *dəg*.
CCh **dwag-* "smith": Bid *dōgei*.
ECh **dwag-* "forge": Mubi *dogga*.
HEC **dug-* "tan": Sid *duug-*, Had *duug-*, Bmb *duug-*.
A typical case of tanning described as beating. Cf. another possible cognate: HEC **dig-* "demolish, destroy" (Sid *diig-*, Dar *diig-*).

726 *dohan- "fat, grease"

Sem **duhn-* "fat, grease": Aram (Palm) *dhn*, (Syr) *dūhān-*, Arab *duhn-*.
Berb **dun-* "fat, grease": Sml *ta-dun-t*, Znt *ꞇa-δun- t*, Snus *ꞇa-δun-t*, Ahg *t-adən-t*, Twl *tā-dhən-t*, Tsl *ta-dhən-t*, Zng *tə-dun-t*, Izy *ꞇadunn*.
WCh **dwan-H-* "fat, grease": Sura *ḍɔŋ*.
Metathesis.

727 *doḫVn- "millet, grain"

Sem **duḫn-* "sorghum": Akk *duḫnu*, Hbr *dōḥan*, Aram (Syr) *duḥnā*, Arab *duḫn-*.
CCh **dwan-* "corn": Mtk *dawna*.
From **dwaHVn-*.

728 *don- "stand up"

Eg *dwn* "stand up" (med).
-w- stands for a rounded vowel.
WCh **dwan-H-* "stand up": Fyer *ḍwaŋ*.
Secondary **-H-*, probably, functioning as a suffix.

729 *don- "be strong"

Sem **dVn-* "be strong": Akk *danānu*.
Eg *wdn* "be strong, be heavy" (XVIII).
w- is a vocalic sign.
CCh **dwanu-* "strong, strength": Chb *dəna*, Wmd *duno-ma*, Ngw

dina, Mrg *dəna-ma*, Mba *dono*, Log *donō*, Bud *dunoa*, Gul *dunu*, Kus *dunu*.
ECh **dwanu-* "strong": Smr *dwana*, Sok *duno*.

730 *dub- "horn"

Eg *db* "horn" (med), Copt **tap* id.: Boh *tap*, Shd *tap*.
ECh **ba-dub-* "horn": Tum *ba-dubo*.
Prefix **ba-*.

731 *dub- "back, tail"

WCh **dub-* "tail": Ang *tup*.
CCh **dub-* "back" [1], "buttocks" [2]: Mofu *duba* [1], Gis *dəba* [1 2], Daba *dədəba* [2], Msg *dəba* [1], Gid *dubo* [1], Zime *duḅu* [1], FJ *ḍuba-kuⁿ* [2].
LEC **dib-/*dub-* "tail" [1], "buttocks" [2]: Som *dib* [1], Or *duboo* [1], Rnd *dub* [1], Arb *dub* [2].
Cf. also Som *dabo* "tail, buttocks", Bay *däbe* id.
HEC **dub-* "tail (of sheep)": Dar *duba*.
Omot **dup̣-* < **duHVb-* "tail": Ome *duup̣iya*.
The development of HS **b* to Omot **p̣* is not quite clear. It may be explained by the influence of an intervocalic laryngeal.

CCh (Zime, FJ) and Omot may indicate HS **duHVb-*. It is not clear whether the present root is also connected with Agaw **danb-* "back, bottom" (Bil *dänbi*) and Omot **damb-* "anus, back" (Kaf *dambo*, Anf *dombo*).

732 *dubar- "speak"

Sem **dVbur-* "speak" [1], "retell" [2]: Phn *dbr* [1], Hbr *dbr* [1], Arab *dbr* [*-u-*] [2].
Secondary **-u-*.
ECh **duwVr-* < **dubwar-* "speak": Kbl *duwər*.
Secondary **wa* after a labial?
HEC **dabar-* "answer": Had *dabar-* "answer".
Assimilation of vowels.

Derived from **dob-* "speak, call".

733 *duč- "push, beat"

Sem *dVṯ- "beat, push": Ug dṯ, Arab dṯṯ.
WCh *duč- "push" [1], "pound" [2]: Ang *tus* [1], Dera *duše* [2].

734 *dud- "vessel"

Sem *dūd- "pot, cauldron": Akk *dūdu*, Ug *dd*, Hbr *dūd*, Aram (Syr) *dūd-*.
Eg *dd.t* "pot, cauldron".
WCh *dud- "calabash": Sura *tū*, Ang *tūt*.

Reduplication?

735 *dud- "bird"

Sem *dūd- "bird": Akk *dūdu*.
ECh *dudi- "bird": Smr *dudi*, Sbn *dudi*, Dng *ḍuḍa*, Mig *ḍiḍu*, Sok *didī*.
Secondary emphatization in Dng and Mig.

Descriptive stem, cf. *did- "bee".

736 *dug- "bird"

Sem *dugg- "thrush": Arab *dugg-*.
CCh *dug- "kite": Chb *dugu*.
Cf. also *kwa-dig-/*kwa-dug- "vulture" (FK *kwadəgu*, HF *wadəɣu*, Klb *kwadiga*, Gudu *kadugwa*).

737 *dugan- "darkness, night"

Sem *dugn- "darkness": Arab *dugn-*.
ECh *dugVn- "at night": Kera *duugŋ*.
LEC *dukan- "darkness": Or *dukkana*.
Unexpected *-k- < HS *-g-.
HEC *dukan- "darkness, cloud": Bmb *dukkani*.
Unexpected *-k- < HS *-g-.

*-k- seems to be a common Cush innovation in this word.

738 *duham- "be dark"

Sem **duhm-* "black": Arab *duhm-*.
ECh **dVHam-* "darkness": Gbr *damā*, Kbl *dama*.
A reduplication in Mubi *deḍem* id. with *-e-* in the root continuing **-uHa-*.
SA **dum-* "be dark": Saho *dum*, Afar *dum*.

739 *duk- "bury"

CCh **dVk-* "bury": Gis *dik*, Mafa *da-dɛg-*.
Secondary *-i-* in Gis.
Omot **duk-* "bury": Ome *duk-*, Kaf *dukki*, Mch *duukki*, Bwo *duk-*, Anf *duk-*, Gim *duk-*.

740 *dum- "destroy"

Sem **dum-* "destroy": Hbr *dmm*.
LEC **dum-* "be destroyed": Som *dum*.

Any connection with **dum-* "split, pierce"?

741 *dum- "worm, snake"

Eg *dm* "worm" (NK).
WCh **dum-* "eel, water snake"[1], "snake" [2]: Hs *dumiya* [1], Krk *ʾadəmo* [2], Krf *duma* [2].
Prefix **ʾa-* in Krk.
CCh **dum-* "ascarid": Mba *dum-say*.
HEC **dum-* "roundworm": Bmb *duma*.
Omot **dVm-* "python": Mch *dämo*.

742 *dum- "antelope"

Berb **dVmVw-/*dVmVy-* "gazelle": Ahg *a-dmū*, Twl *te-dəmi-t*, Zng *dāmi*, *dəmma*, Sha *ɽa-dəmu-ɽ*.
Derivatives of **dVm-*.
Omot **dum-* "kind of antelope": Yam *dumaa*.

743 *dum- "split, pierce"

Berb **dVm-* "split": Rif *əddəm*.
Eg *dm* "sharpen, pierce" (l).
WCh **dum-* "plunge a weapon (into a person)": Hs *duma*.

744 *dumb- "ring"

WCh **dumb-* "bracelet": Hs *dumbā*.
LEC **dub-* "ring": Som *duub*.
**-b-* seems to continue **-mb-*.

745 *dun- "sing, murmur"

Sem **dun-* "buzz": Arab *dnn* [-*u*-].
Cf. also Arab *dndn* id.
Berb **dVn-dVn-* "sing": Snus *dəndən*.
Reduplication.

Related to **dün-* "sound, voice". A reduplication **dVn- dVn-* may be reconstructed.

746 *dun- "be bent"

Sem **dVn-* "be bent": Arab *dnn*, *dnʾ*.
Formations based on biliteral **dVn-*
Berb **dun-* "squat, be bent": Ahg *dun-ət*.

747 *dur- "flow"

Sem **dir-/*dur-* "drip" [1], "flow abundantly" [2]: Hbr *drr* [1], Arab *drr* [-*u*-, -*i*-] [2].
Eg *dr* "prevent water from flowing down" (med).
WCh **duHwar-* "pour": Hs *ḍūra*, Tng *ḍer*, Pol *ḍurəw*.
Secondary laryngeal. Probably, **duHwar-* < **Hwadur-*.

Cf. nominal derivatives in WCh **dVHar-* "river" (Gera *doora*, Bks *ḍara*, DB *ḍeer*, *ḍiyar*), CCh **nV-dwar-* "rainy season" (Msm *ndor*) and SA **darur-* "rain-cloud" (Saho *darur*, Afar *darur*).

748 *dur- "bird"

Sem **durr-* "parrot": Arab *durr-at-*.
WCh **durwa-* "quail": Hs *durwā*.
ECh **dur-* "hen": Smr *durē*.

749 *dü'Vč- "grass"

Sem **diṯ'-* "grass, new grass" [2]: Akk *daš'u, diš'u, dīšu*, Hbr *deše'*, Aram *diṯ'ā*, SAr *dṯ'*.
Metathesis.
WCh **du'Vč-* "thatching grass": Hs *ḍūsā*.

750 *düm- "vessel"

Eg *dmy* "vessel" (n).
-y stands for a vowel.
WCh "bottle-gourd": Hs *dumā*.

751 *düm- "feline"

Sem **dimm-* "cheetah" [1], "cat" [2]: Akk *dumāmu* [1], Arab *dimm-at-* [2], Gz *dəmm-at-* [2], Tgr *dəmmu* [2], Tgy *dəmmu* [2], Amh *dəmm-ät-* [2].
Secondary formation in Akk.
WCh **dum-* "hyaena": Sura *ndumu*, Grk *domu*, Ank *tumu*.
Agaw **dam-Vy-* "cat": Kwr *damyaa*, Kem *daməya*.
**a* in the root is not quite clear. Maybe **dumay-* > **damay-*?
SA **dumm-* "cat": Saho *dummu*, Afar *dumoo*.
Rift **du'um-* "leopard": Irq *du'uma*, Bur *du'uma*, Alg *du'uma*, Kwz *du'umayi*, Asa *du'umok*.
The original root structure is modified in Rift with an innovative inlaut laryngeal.

752 *dün- "sound, voice"

Sem **dinn-* "reverberation" [1], "bang, noise" [2]: Mhr *den* [1], Hss *dennēt* [2].
Berb **dun-* "rough voice": Ahg *a-dûn-a*.
Eg *dny.w.t* "howl" (n.) (MK).

Related to **dun-* "sing, murmur".

753 *düp- "push"

Sem *dVp- "push": Hbr *dpy*, Hss *dōfa*, Mhr *dōfa*, Shh *defaʿ*.
Cf. also Sem *dVḥVp- "push away" (Akk *daʾapu*, Hbr *dḥp*) and *nVdVp- "push": Hbr *ndp*, Arab *ndf*.
WCh *dup- "push": Sura *tup*.
Rift *dif- "beat, fight": Alg *dif-*, Bur *dif-*.
Omot *dup- "throw": Kaf *dup-*.

754 *dVʾVʒ- "bow" (n.)

Eg *dȝz* "bow-string" (sarc).
ECh *dVʾVs- < *dVʾVʒ- "bow": Smr *ḍese*, Kbl *ḍəsə*.
Smr and Kbl *-s-* may also reflect ECh *-ʒ-.

755 *dVbVḥ- "pot"

Eg *dbḥ.w* "crockery" (OK).
CCh *dVHVb- "pot": Gul *ḍɛbɛy*.
Metathesis.

An alternative reconstruction is *dVḥVb-.

756 *dVg-dVg- "trample, press"

Sem *dVg-dVg- "trample down" [1], "press, squeeze" [2], "tap" [3]: Tgr *dägdägä* [1], Tgy *dägdägä* [1], Amh *dagäddägä* [1], Gur *dəgädägä* [2], Jib *edəgdəg* [3], Shh *adagdeg* [3].
Berb *dVg-dVg- "break": Ghat *dəgdəg*, Ahg *dəgdəg*, Twl *dagdag*, Kby *ddegδeg*.
Eg *dgdg* "press, squeeze, trample" (XX).

Reduplication in most HS branches. The root vowel may have been *i. Cf. *dog- "forge, beat"?

757 *dVgol- "look, see"

Sem *dVgVl- "look": Akk *dagālu*.
Cf. Aram (Syr) *dəgil-ūt-*.
Eg *dgȝ* "see" (gr).
May be identical with *dgy* "see, look" < *deg- or represent *dVgVl- with *-l- > *-ȝ*.

CCh **dVgwal-* "look": Msg *dəg^{w}ələ*.

Derived from **dag-* "see, know".

758 *dVgVy- "hide"

Sem **dVgVy-* "cover": Arab *dgy*.
Eg *dgy* "hide" (MK).

759 *dVˁVc- "pound, grind"

Sem **dVˁVs-* "grind": Arab *dˁs*, Amh *dasä*.
Berb **dVc-* "pound": Ahg *əddəh*, Twl *əddəz*, Zng *əddəž*, Sgr *əddəz*, Kby *əddəz*.

760 *dVhar- "hunt" (v.)

Sem **dVhVr-* "hunt": Hbr *dhr*.
CCh **dar-* < **dVHar-* "hunting": Masa *dara*.

761 *dVm- "utter"

Sem **dVm-* "moan" (v.): Ug *dmm*.
Eg *dm* "announce, pronounce" (OK).
WCh **dVm-* "swear": Ngz *dəma*.

762 *dVn- "cut off"

Sem **dVn-* "cut off": Tgr *dnn*.
Eg *dn* "cut off (head), kill" (XVIII).

763 *dVpir- "squeeze, push"

Sem **dVpVr-* "squeeze" [1], "push away" [2]: Akk *dpr* [1], Arab *dfr* [2], Shh *defōr* [2].
Berb **dVfir-* "squeeze": Zng *edfir*.

Derived from **düp-* "push"?

764 *dVr-dVr- "turn, rotate"

Sem **dVr-dVr-* "turn, rotate": Hbr *drdr*, Arab *drdr*.
Agaw **dVr-dVr-* "turn, rotate": Aw *dərdər*.

Full reduplication.

765 *dVwVd-/*dVyVd- "worm, snake"

Sem **dud-* < **dVwVd-* "worms": Arab *dūd-*.
Cf. also Arab *dwd* "swarm (of worms)" (v.).
Berb **dVy-dVy-* "kind of worm": Izy *aδiuδiu*.
Eg *ddy* "snake".
-y stands for a front vowel.
CCh **dVd-* "kind of snake": Mofu *dedew*.
-ew- is a suffix.

Reduplication. Cf. WCh **daw-day-* "kind of snake" (Hs *daudai*). Derived from HS **daʔ-* "worm, snake"?

766 *dVwVm- "drip, flow"

Sem **dūm-* "moisten, rain continuously": Arab *dwm* [*-u-* , 1].
Berb **dVwVm-* "ooze, flow": Izy *addum*, Sml *əddəm*, Rif *udum*, Kby *iδim*.

Derived from **dam-* "cloud". Cf. CCh **ta-dam-* "wet" (Kus *tadām*, Gul *tadam*).

767 *dVwVn- "register, count"

Sem **dūn-* "register": Arab *dwn*.
Berb **dVwVn-* "count" [1], "compare, estimate" [2]: Ahg *ədwən* [1], Zng *uddən* [1], Ayr *ədwən* [2].
Eg *wdn* "register" (NK).
Metathesis.

768 *dVwVr- "turn"

Sem **dūr-* "turn": Arab *dwr* [*-u-*], Hss *dawr*, Mhr *dawr*, Shh *dεbr*.
ECh **wVdVr-* "turn": Kbl *wədəra*.
Metathesis.

An alternative reconstruction is **wVdVr-*.

*f

769 *faˀVl- "foretell"

Sem *pVˀVl- "foretell fortune": Arab *fˀl*, Gz *fwl*.
Cf. Hbr *plˀ* "make miracles"
HEC *faˀVl- "deceive": Had *faˀl-*.

Related to *fal-/*faˀVl- "magic word, omen".

770 *faᶜ- "hit, strike"

WCh *fay- < *faHya- "strike": Bks *fayi*.
Rift *faˀ- "hit": Kwz *faˀ-am-*.
*-ˀ- < *-ᶜ- as in a number of other Rift words.
Dhl *faaᶜ-* "smash"

771 *faḫat- "dig, pierce"

Sem *paḫat- "pierce": Aram (Syr) *fḥt*, Arab *fḫt* [-a-, 1].
Dhl *faaṭ-* "dig".

772 *faḳ- "pierce, tear"

Sem *pVḳaˀ- "pierce, open, tear out (eye)" [1], "break" [2]: Arab *fqˀ* [-a-, 1] [1], Gz *fqˀ* [2].
Based on *pVḳ-.
Eg *fḳ*, *fḳw* "of a lion tearing its prey" (XX).
-w may be a suffix.
Agaw *faḳ- "tear": Bil *faḳ-*.
Dhl *pak'k'-eeδ-* "uncover".
Irregular *p-*.

Cf. SA *fak- "open" (Saho *fak*, Afar *fak*) and HEC *foḳ- "open" (Had *fooḳḳ-*).

773 *fal- "bone, leg"

WCh *falal- "middle bone of an animal's foreleg": Hs *fālālā*.
Partial reduplication.

CCh **fVl-* ''foot'': Bud *fɛle.*
Bed *fil-ik* ''top of the shin-bone''.
The comparison is valid if the Bed word may be segmented as *fil-ik*. The vowel of the first syllable is assimilated.
Rift **falaʔ-* ''bone'': Kwz *falaʔa-to*, pl. *falala.*
Assimilation of vowels.

Note the grammatical function of the partial reduplication in Rift in view of WCh.

774 *fal-/*faʔVl- ''magic word, omen''

Sem **faʔl-* ''omen'': Shh *fol*, Mhr *fōl*, Hss *fōl.*
Eg *fnn.wy* ''magic words'' (pyr).
Partial reduplication.
Agaw **fal-* ''omen'': Bil *faal.*
SA **fal-* ''omen'': Saho *faal.*
LEC **fal-* ''omen'': Som *faal.*

Related to **faʔVl-* ''foretell''.

775 *fal-/*ful- ''liver, lungs''

WCh **ful-* ''lungs'': Mpn *ful-fuk*, *flok*, Ang *fwolok*, Sura *fəlok*, Ank *fələl.*
Partial reduplication in Ank.
CCh **fa-ful-* ''lungs'': Bch *faful-awey.*
Partial reduplication.
HEC **ʔa-fal-* ''liver'': Sid *affale*, Bmb *affala*, Kmb *afɛl-ita.*
Prefix **ʔa-*.
Omot **ʔa-fall-* ''liver'': Mch *ap̄aaro*, Anf *afaaro*, Bwo *afaara.*
Prefix **ʔa-*. Note Mch *-p̄-*.

776 *faliy- ''insect''

Sem **pāliy-* ''scarabeus'': Arab *fāliy-at-.*
CCh **fili[y]-* ''spider'': Hil *ma-fīlī*, Wmd *pəla-tagu.*
Assimilation of vowels. Prefix **ma-* in Hil.

777 *fan- "look for, watch"

ECh **pan-* "seek, look for": Mubi *fān*, *hu-bān*.
LEC **fan-* "watch, follow": Or *fana*.

778 *far- "bone, leg"

WCh **far-/*fuwar-* "leg": Klr *far-aw*, Bks *ʾa-foor*, Fyer *furu*, DB *fuur*.
As it may be concluded from Klr, **fuwar-* is a metathesis from **fur-aw-*.
Rift **far-* "bone": Irq *fara*, Ala *fara*, Bur *fara*.

779 *far- "clay, earth"

WCh **far-* "arid soil": Hs *farā-farā*.
Reduplication.
HEC **far-* "clay": Gel *faara*.

780 *far- "equid"

Sem **paraʾ-* "onager": Akk *parû*, Ug *pri*, Hbr *pereʾ*, Arab *faraʾ-*.
SA **farar-* "horse": Saho *farar*, Afar *farar*.
Partial reduplication.
LEC **faraw-* "zebra": Som *faraw*, Arb *faraw*.
Omot **far-* "horse": Ome *faraa*.

781 *far- "climb"

Sem **pVrVʿ-* "climb": Arab *frʿ* [-*a*-, 1].
Sem **-ʿ-* finds no support in other branches of HS.
Berb **fVr-* "fly": Izy *afλu*.
Eg *fꜣy* "raise high".
May belong to **fay-*.
ECh **par-* "climb": Mobu *pare* (pl.).
SA **far-* "climb": Saho *for*, Afar *fär*.
Secondary *-o-* in Saho.

Partial reduplication in Berb **fVrir-* "be elevated" (Qbl *i-frir*).

782 *fat- "wish, desire"

Sem *pVtVw- "desire, seek" [1], "decide on a plan" [2]: Gz *ftw* [1], Hss *aftō* [2], Mhr *heftō* [2], Shh *ɛfte* [2].
Based on biconsonantal *pVt-.
WCh *fat- "wish well to person, pray": Hs *fātā*.

783 *fat-/*fit- "move"

Sem *pūt- "pass, go (of time)": Arab *fwt* [-*u*-, 1, 8].
Modification of the original biliteral structure *pat-.
Berb *fVt- "walk" [1], "pass (of time)" [2], "having passed" [3]: Sml *i-ftu* [1], Izy *faт* [2], Mns *i-fuт-ən* [3].
Izy and Mns may be loanwords from Arab.
WCh *fat-/*fit- "go out" [1], "come" [2]: Hs *fita* [1], Bol *fat* [1], Krk *fat* [1], Dera *pori* [1], Tng *pod-* [1], Ngm *hata* [1], Bele *feti* [1], Gera *fid-* [1], Glm *paz-* [1], Wnd *fut-* [2].
Agaw *fat-/*fit- "go away": Bil *far*, Xmt *fit-*, Aun *fat-*.
Bil -*r*- < *-*t*- occurs in a number of Agaw forms.
Rift *fit- "drive, run after": Irq *fiit*.

A reduplication of the original *fat-/*fit- is, probably, also reflected in Eg *ftft* "jump, spring" (med). Note the alternation *a ~ *i.

784 *fatVq- "pierce, split"

Sem *pVtVḫ- "pierce": Akk *patāḫu*.
CCh *patVk- "split": Mofu *pətkw-*.
*-*wa*- may be reconstructed in the 2nd syllable.

785 *faṭ- "tear"

WCh *faṭ- "tear, rip": Hs *fatta*, Diri *fəta*.
Omot *feṭ- "tear" [1], "rags" [2]: Omet *peḍ-* [1], Kaf *heeṭo* [2].
Innovative Cush *-*e*- in verbs.

786 *faṭaḳ- "tear"

Eg *fdḳ* "tear off" (MK).
-*d*- < *-*ṭ*- is regular.

WCh **faṭaḳ-* "lacerate": Hs *fatattakā*.
ECh **pVtVk-* "pull by": Dng *petke*.
Dng *-e-* is secondary.

787 *fay- "lift, go up"

Eg *fꜣy* "lift, carry" (OK).
-ꜣ- stands for **-a-*.
ECh **pay-* "fly, go up": Kera *fe*.

788 *feʾ- "arrow"

WCh **nV-fyaʾ-* "arrow": Bks ⁿ*vya*, DB ⁿ*vyah*.
Prefix **nV-*.
LEC **fiʾ-/*fuʾ-* "arrow": Or *fia*, *fue*.
Rift **fay-* "arrow": Alg *fayu*, Bur *fayu*.
Rift may continue a HS form **fey-* as a variant of **feʾ-*.

Cf. also Sem **piʾ-/*paʾ-* "edge": Hbr *pēʾā*, Aram *pâʾ-t-*?

789 *feč- "blow"

Sem **(nV-)piṯ-* "blow": Akk *pašû*, Arab *nfṯ* [*-i-*, *-u-*].
In Arab, a formation using prefix **nV-*.
WCh **fyač-* "blow": Cagu *fēs*, Diri *fəču*, *fuču*.
Diri *-u-* in *fuču* results from an assimilation.
CCh **fič-* "blow": Mba *pise*.

790 *fed- "tear"

Eg *fdy* "pluck off" (pyr).
-y reflects a front vowel in the root.
HEC **fed-* "tear (cloth)": Bmb *feedi-*.

791 *fediḳ- "split"

Eg *fdḳ* "divide, split" (MK).
Bed *feḍig* < **fediḳ-* "split, separate".

Related to **fed-* "tear"?

792 *fer- ''scratch, peel''

Sem **pVr-* ''scratch, cut wood, husk'': Amh *farä*.
WCh **fyar-* ''pare off outer surface of rind'' [1], ''scratch'' [2]: Hs *fēra* [1], Ang *fir* [2].
ECh **pir-* ''peel'' (v.): Bid *pir*, Mig *pir-aw*.

793 *feras- ''fall''

ECh **par-* < **pyar-* ''fall (from a tree)'': Mkk *parso*.
Bed *feraas* ''fall''.
Agaw **firaš-/*firiš-* ''fall'': Bil *feras*, Xmr *feriš*.

794 *feriḳ- ''dig, divide''

Sem **pVriḳ-* ''split'' [1], ''divide'' [2], ''break'' [3]: Akk *parāqu* [1], Ug *prq* [3], Aram (Syr) *prq* [2], Arab *frq* [*-i-*, *-u-*] [1 2], Gz *frq* [2].
Secondary **u* as a variant of **i* in Arab.
ECh **pVrVg-* ''dig'': Kera *fərgi*.
-g- may continue **-ḳ-* in the intervocalic position.
Bed *feriḳ* ''dig''.

Cf. **fediḳ-* ''split''.

795 *fet- ''break, cut''

Sem **pVt-* ''break'' [1], ''destroy'' [2]: Hbr *ptt* [1], Arab *ftt* [*-u-*] [2], Gz *ftt* [1].
WCh **fyat-* ''slaughter'': Sura *fɛt*.
CCh **fVt-* ''cut'': Mofu *fət-aḍ*.

796 *feṭ- ''sweep''

WCh **fyaṭ-* ''sweep'': Sura *fet*, Ang *fet*.
CCh **fyaṭ-* ''sweep'': Gudu *mi-fīḍa*, Mwu *ufeḍō*.
HEC **fiṭ-* ''sweep'': Sid *fiṭ-*.
Omot **fiṭ-* ''sweep'': Ome (Koyra) *fit-*.
Dhl *fit'a* ''plaster wall with mud and dung''.

797 *fiʾ- "blow"

Sem **pVʾVy-* "blow off": Hbr *pʾy*.
Based on **pVʾ-*.
WCh **fiʾ-* "blow": Sura *fī*, Ang *fī*.
CCh **faʾ-/*fiʾ-* "blow": Bura *fia*, Mrg *fi*, Gis *fe*, Bud *pha*, ZBt *foʾo*.
Gis may go back to CCh **fay-* < **faʾVy-* identical with Sem **pVʾVy-*.
Rift **fiʾ-/*fuʾ-* "catch one's breath, rest" [1], "sniff, snuff up" [2]: Asa *fuʾ-it-* [1], Kwz *fiʾ-* [2].
Secondary **-u-*.

798 *fiç̣- "be wet"

CCh **fič-* "wet, soak": Mrg *fiču*.
LEC **finç̣-* "flow": Or *finç̣aa^{w}a*.
**-n-* may be an infix.
HEC **faç̣-/*fiç̣-* "sprinkle": Dar *fiṭ-*, Bmb *fac-*.
Traces of the *a*-grade in Bmb.

799 *fidaḫ- "break, cut"

Sem **pVdaḫ-* "break (skull)": Arab *fdḫ* [*-a-*, 1].
WCh **fidaH-* "cut open, wound": Tng *pide*, Pero *peḍḍo*.
**-a-* of the second syllable explains *-e-* in Pero.
CCh **fidaH-* "cut, carve": Mafa *fiḍ-*, Bch *fyeḍo*, Dgh *piḍa*.

800 *fiʿ- "speak, shout"

Sem **pVʿVy-* "cry, shout": Hbr *pʿy*.
Based on **pVʿ-*.
WCh **fi-* "speak": Sha *fi*.
CCh **fVy-* "call": Bud *fe*.
From **fVHVy-* or **fVHi-*.
Agaw **fiw-* "cry": Kw *few-*, Dmb *fuu-*.
Continuation of **fiHw-*?

801 *fil- "skin, rub"

Sem **wVpVl-/*yVpVl-* "skin, peel" (v.): Arab *wfl*, *yfl*.
Prefix **wV-/*yV-*.

WCh **fyal-* < **fila-* "skin" (v.) [1], "rub" [2]: Sura *fēl*, Ang *fil*, Bks *fyal* [2].
CCh **fil-* "rub": Dgh *fila*.
ECh **pil-* "skin" (v.): Bid *pil*, Smr *pəl*.

802 *fin- "nose; smell"

Berb **fun-fan-* "muzzle, nose" [1], "nostrils" [2]: Ahg *a-fun-fan* [1], Twl *i-fūfan-ən* [2].
Reduplication with modified vocalism.
Bed *fin* "scent, smell" (v.).
Agaw **fin-* "scent, smell" (v.): Bil *fin*.

803 *finaḫ- "opening"

WCh **finaḫ-* "hole" [1], "mouth" [2]: Sura *fuŋ* [1], Ang *fuŋ* [1], Wrj *vinahə-na* [2], Kry *vinahə* [2], Diri *vəna* [2], Paa *vingi* [2], Mbu *vəŋhu* [2], Miya *vun* [2], Cagu *vehe* [2], Siri *vengi* [2], Jmb *vina* [2], Fyer *fuŋ* [1].
CCh **fun-H-* "mouth": HG *fuŋe*, Bnn *funa*, LPe *vun*, Masa *funano*.
Partial reduplication in Masa.
Omot **pin-H-* "opening, hole": Ome *pinge*.

Related to **finaḫ-* "break". Thus, "opening" ← * "breach" as ON *rauf* "hole" ~ *rjūfa* "break".

804 *finaḫ- "break"

Sem **pVnaḫ-* "damage (of a bone)" (v.): Arab *fnḫ* [-*a*- , 1].
Berb **fVnVḥ-* "beat": Kby *s-funneḥ*.
WCh **fin-H-* "break": Klr *fiŋy-*.

805 *fir- "monkey"

Eg *nfry* "monkey" (gr).
Is *n-* a prefix? *-y* stands for a front vowel.
WCh **fir-* "red monkey": Fyer *fiir*.
CCh **fir-* "monkey": Mba *fre*, Masa *fira*, Gis *vri*, Lame *vir*, Masa *fira*.
Cf. also Msg *afri*, *afrig* id.

806 *fir- "be good"

Sem **purr-* "best ones, elite": Arab *furr-*.
Deverbative formation with a secondary vowel.
Berb **fVrVr-* "be good": Ahg *i-frar*.
Partial reduplication based on **fVr-*.
Eg *nfr* "good, beautiful".
Prefix **nV-*.
Agaw **fir-* "best": Bil *feraa*.
SA **fer-* "best": Saho *feer*.

807 *fir-ut- "insect"

WCh **mV-firut-* "mosquito": Jmb *avirvir*, Kry *aviltu*, Paa *vituwi*, Sura *mfut*, Ang *fut*.
CCh **f[i]r-ut-* "mosquito": Daba *vərrut*.
Vocalism and segmentation are indicated by CCh **fir-/*fur-* "mosquito": Gaa *fir-ḍa*, Gbn *gər-dič̆a*, Boka *fir-ḍaʾa*, Bnn *furu-na*, Masa *furu-tna*, Msm *vursu*.
Agaw **firrut-* "insect(s)": Bil *filuta*, Xmr *felta*, Kem *felät*.

808 *firVṭ- "tear off, pluck"

Sem **pVrVṭ-* "pluck (fruit)" [1], "knock fruit down from the tree" [2] : Akk *parāṭu* [1], Aram (Syr, Jud) *prṭ* [1], Arab *frṭ* [-*u*-, 26] [2].
CCh **firVṭ-* "tear": Bud *firte*.

809 *fit- "land"

Sem **pitt-* "area, region": Akk *pittu*.
CCh **fVt-* "earth": Msg *futi*, *fate*, *feti*.

810 *fit-/*fut- "jump"

Eg *ftft* "jump, spring" (med).
Reduplication.
WCh **pit-* "jump": Bgh *pit*.
Irregular **p-*.
LEC **fut-* "spring back": Or *futtaʾa*.

Alternation **i* ~ **u*.

811 *fitaʾ- "forget"

Sem **pVtaʾ-* "forget": Arab *ftʾ* [*-a-*, 1].
CCh **fit[a]H-* "forget": Gudu *fitei*.
**-aHi-* > *-ei* in the auslaut.

812 *fiṭaʾ-/*fiṭay- "destroy"

Sem **pVṭaʾ-* "break": Arab *fṭʾ* [*-a-*, 1].
Berb **fVṭVy-* "be pierced": Ahg *fəḍəi*.
Bed *fədi(y)* "split, separate".
LEC **fiṭ-* "destroy": Or *fiṭa*.

Consonantal alternation *-ʾ- ~ *-y-*.

813 *fiwaḥ- "smell, blow" (v.)

Sem **pūḥ-* "spread (of smell)": Arab *fwḥ*.
Berb **fVwVḥ-* "stink, smell": Kby *fuḥ*.
WCh **f[i]w[a]ḥ-* "blow": Bks *fuʾ*, Sha *fyah*, DB *fuʾ*.
-ya- in Sha results from **-iʾa-* < **-iwa-*.
CCh **fiyaH-* "smell": Mnd *ʾifiyaʾa*.
**-iya-* < **-iwa-*.
ECh **pwaH-* < **pVwaH-* "blow": Tum *po*.
Rift **faḥ-* "blow": Alg *faḥ-*.
Contraction of **-iwa-* > **-a-* or a more archaic form of the original root?

Cf. **fiwaq-* "blow".

814 *fiwaq- "blow"

Sem **pūḫ-* "blow": Hbr *pwḥ*, Aram *pwḥ*, Arab *fwḫ*.
WCh **fiqu-* "blow": Paa *fuki*, Siri *fikuu*, Sha *fuk*, Fyer *vivik*.
Partial reduplication in Fyer.
CCh **fuqu(w)-* "blow": Mafa *fukuw*, Lame *fuku*, Msm *fok*.
Secondary vocalism after a labial.
ECh **pu[w]uk-* "breathing": Mkk *puukiyo*.
-uu- results from assimilation (and contraction?).
Agaw **fiχw-* "blow, breathe, rest": Bil *fiγʷ*, Kem *fiγʷ*, Aun *fiγ-uŋ*.
Dhl *fookʾ-* "catch one's breath, rest".
Contraction of **-iwa-* yielding to *-oo-*.

Cf. **fiwaḥ-* "smell, blow". The alternative reconstruction is **fiqaw-*.

815 *fiyal- "cook, boil"

Berb **fVl-fVl-* "boil": Izy *fḷufell.*
Reduplication.
WCh **fiyal-/*fuwVl-* "boil": Ang *fīl*, Chip *fiyəl*, Ank *fial*, Bol *pūlō*, Pol *fula*, Geji *huluwi*, Brm *fule*, Buli *fulu*.
**fuwVl-* goes back to a co-variant **fiwal-*.
LEC **ʔa-fēl-* "cook" (v.): Or *affeela*.
Contraction of the original cluster **-iya-* > **ē*. Prefix **ʔa-*.

816 *foʔ- "sand, dust"

Eg *fꜣ.t* "dust (?)" (pyr).
The meaning is not certain.
WCh **fwaʔ-* "sand": Dera *pwa*.

817 *fo(ʔ)- "mouth"

Sem **pa(ʔ)-/*pi(ʔ)-* "mouth" [1], "forehead" [2], "face" [3]: Akk *paʔu*, *pû* [1], Ug *p* [1], Hbr *pe* [1], Aram (Syr) *pa-t* [2], Arab *fiʔ-at-* [2], *fūw-*, *fūh-at-* [1], Amh *fi-t* [2 3], Soq *fio* [2 3].
**-a-* < **-u-* after a labial. The stem has an irregular structure in which *-ʔ-* of Arab may be a result of a late analogical modification.
WCh **fwa(H)-* "mouth": Fyer *fo*, Bks *fo*, DB *fo*, *foh*.

Related to **fiʔ-* "blow"?

818 *foc- "roast, cook"

Eg *fs* "cook" (a), Copt **fisi* id.: Boh *fisi*, Shd *pise*.
Copt may reflect HS **-e-*.
WCh **fwac-* "burn" [1], "cook" [2], "roast" [3]: Fyer *fwaš* [1], Bks *fos* [2], Sha *fos* [2], DB *faš* [3].
DB *-a-* < **-wa-* after a labial.

819 *foḥ- ''fire; burn''

Eg *wfḥ* ''burn'' (l).
w- stands for a rounded vowel.
CCh *ʾa-f[wa]-* ''fire'': Log *fo*, Msg *afu*, Gid *afa*, Mba *fẽ*.
Irregular vowels in individual languages may continue *-*yaHu-*/*-*waHu-*.

820 *fosaḫ- ''be bad''

Sem **pašaḫ-* ''be bad, be spoilt'': Arab *fsḫ* [-*a*-, 4].
*-*a-* of the first syllable is a regular reflex of Sem *-*u-* < HS *-*o-* after a labial.
WCh **fwas-* ''bad'': DB *fwaš*.

Related to **fus-* ''be angry''.

821 *fos[i]ʾ- ''breathe''

Sem **pVšVʾ-* ''breathe, blow'': Akk *pašû*.
HEC **fošeʾ-* ''breathe'': Kmb *foošeeʾ-*.
From **fošiʾ-*?

822 *fot- ''wipe, scrape''

Sem **pVt-* ''wipe oneself with small stones after excreting'': Jib *fett*.
An isolated archaism?
Eg *ftt* ''erase (inscriptions)''.
WCh **fwat-* ''scratch ground'': Ang *fwot*.
Omot **fut-* ''oil'' (v.): Kaf *hut*.
h- < **f-*, cf. Kaf *futo* ''ointment''.

823 *foy- ''cloth''

Eg *fy* ''cloth'' (NK).
CCh **fway-* ''loincloth'': Mwu *fwoyi*.

824 *foyaʒ- ''mouse, rat''

Sem **pVyaz-* ''mouse'': Akk *piazu*.
WCh **fwayaʒ-* ''rat'': DB *fwyaš*.

An archaic separate isogloss replaced in the majority of languages with such innovations as *ʾantuʾ-/*ʾantaw- and *ber-/*per- "mouse, rat".

825 *fuʾon- "meat, flesh"

LEC *foHon-* "meat, flesh": Or *fon*, *foon*.
Rift *fuʾun-* "meat": Irq *fuʾuni*, Bur *fuʾunai*.

Note Arab *ˁfn* [-*i*-] "make meat rot".

826 *fuf- "lung, breast"

Berb *fVf-* "breast": Ghd *i-fef*, Siwa *i-fiff-an*, Ghat *i-fef*, Ahg *e-fef*, Twl *ă-faf*, Zng *i-fəffi*, Sml *t-iffī-t*, Ntf *i-ff*, Izy *i-ff*, Mzab *i-f*, Wrg *i-f*, *i-ff*, Fgg *i-f*, Snus *i-fef*, Kby *i-f*.
WCh *fuf-* "lung" [1], "breast" [2]: Hs *fūfū* [1], Mpn *fufu* [2], Fyer *fuf* [2], Bks *fof* [2], Klr *fuf* [2].
CCh *fif-/*fuf-* "lung": Tera *fufuf*, Gaa *pipifa*, Hwn *pufə*, Bura *fufu*. Tera and Gaa reflect a "double" reduplication by adding one more syllable in the anlaut.
ECh *pupi-* "breast": Brg *fīfo*, Mig *pūpu*, Bid *pūpa*.

Any connection with Sem *pawp-* "bull's bladder" (Arab *fawf-*)? Reduplication of *f[ü]ʔ-* "lungs, belly".

827 *fuġVr- "open" (v.)

Sem *pVġVr-* "open wide": Hbr *pˁr*, Aram (Syr) *pˁr*, Arab *fġr*.
LEC *fur-* "open, free, untie": Som *fur-*, Or *fur-*, Rnd *fur-*, Boni *fur-*, Kon *fur-*, Gid *fur-iyy-*.
Inlaut *-ġ- lost without leaving any traces.

828 *fuˁun- "thigh, leg"

Sem *pVˁVn-* "thigh, leg": Akk *pēnu*, Ug *pˁn*.
WCh *fun-H-* "knee": Fyer *fuŋ*.
Metathesis.
CCh *pun-* "thigh": FK *punuʾ*.
Metathesis. Irregular *p-.

An alternative reconstruction is **funuʿ-*. Cf. also Akk *pēmu* ''thigh'', Hbr *paʿam* ''foot'', Shh *faʿm*, Hss *fām*, Mhr *fēm* (< **pVʿVm-*) and Kwz *paʾam-uko* ''foot'' (< Rift **paHam-*), eventually pointing out to HS **paʿam-* with initial **p-*!

829 *ful- ''go up, mount''

CCh **ful-* ''mount'': Chb *fəl-ti*, Klb *afül-tü*.
Prefix **ʾa-* in Klb.
HEC **ful-* ''go up, go out'': Sid *ful*, Dar *ful*, Kmb *ful*.

830 *ful- ''bore a hole''

ECh **pul-* ''big hole'': Tum *pūl*.
Deverbative.
LEC **ful-* ''break through, pierce through'': Or *full-aʾa*.
Rift **ful-* ''bore a hole'': Irq *ful-*.

831 *ful- ''hide, husk''

ECh **pulVl-* ''shell'': Tum *puləl*.
Partial reduplication.
Rift **fal-/*ful-* ''hide'': Bur *fala*, Asa *fulo*.
a-vocalism may be a Rift innovation or an assimilation in Bur.

832 *funVg- ''nose''

Eg *fnḏ* ''nose'' (pyr).
Eg *ḏ* < **g* palatalized before a middle vowel (**o* or **e*).
LEC **fung-* ''nose'': Or *fuññ-aan*.

Cf. **finaḫ-* ''opening'' (and also ''mouth''!) and, on the other hand, **fin-* ''nose; smell''. **-Vg-* may be a suffix.

833 *furVh- ''fear'' (v.)

Sem **pVrVh-* ''fear'': Gz *frh*, Amh *färra*.
An Ethio-Sem archaism?
LEC **fūr-* < **fuHVr-* ''fear'': Kon *fūr*, Gid *hūr*.
Metathesis.

834 *furVk- "skin, bark"

Berb **fVrVk-* "bark": Ahg *ta-fərk-it*, Twl *ti-frăk- ăwin*, Sml *ti-fərk-īt*, Ntf *ti-fərk-it*.
ECh **purVk-* "bark": Sok *furkia*.

Derived from **fuwar-* "skin, bark".

835 *fus- "be angry"

Sem **pūš-* "be angry": Akk *puāšu*.
Based on the original HS **fus-*.
WCh **fus-* "anger": Hs *fuši*, Gwn *hušī*, *puši*.

836 *fut- "hole, vulva"

Sem **put-* "vulva": Hbr *pot*.
WCh **fut-* "hole": Ang *fut*.
LEC **fut-* "vulva" [1], "anus" [2]: Som *futo* [1], Or *futee* [2].

Cf. Eg *wft* "pierce".

837 *fut- "vomit"

WCh **fut-* "vomit": Sura *fūt*, Ang *fut*, Ank *fūt*, Mpn *fūt*.
Wrz **fat-* "vomit": Gaw *fač-fat-*.
Reduplication with modified vocalism.

838 *fuwar- "skin, bark"

Sem **parw-* "skin" [1], "fur" [2], "shell, husk" [3]: Akk *pāru*, *parru* [1], Hbr *parwā* , Arab *farw-* [1], Gz *farra* [3].
Metathesis. Regular Sem **-a-* < **-u-* after a labial.
Berb **fVwVr-* "skin disease" [1], "bark" [2]: Ahg *tafūre* [1], Zng *ta-ffrāh* [1], Sml *ta-fāri* [1], Ntf *ta-fura* [1], Ghd *ti-fra* [2].
WCh **fuwar-* "skin of monkey-nuts" [1], "peel" [2], "bark" [3]: Hs *fūrū* [1], Tng *paara* [2], Diri *fu-fur* [3].
Reduplication in Diri.
ECh **pVr-* "shell": Kera *ke-fre*.
Prefix **kV-*.

839 *fuwaṭ- "cloth"

Sem **puwaṭ-* "table-cloth": Arab *fūṭ-at-*, pl. *fuwaṭ-*.
WCh **fVwaṭ-* "cloth" [1], "loin-cloth" [2]: Sura *fwat* [1], Ang *fwet* [2], Mpn *fwāt* [2].
Cf. DB *fataʔu* "cloth".

840 *fuy- "chaff, shell"

Sem **puy-* "chaff": Akk *pû*.
WCh **fwaf-* "shell": Ang *fwop*.
Partial reduplication.
CCh **puy-* "bark": Bch *puyey*.
Suffix **-ay-* > Bch *-ey*.

841 *f[ü]ʔ- "lungs, belly"

Eg *wfꜣ* "lungs" (BD).
Initial *w-* reflects a labial root vowel.
Bed *fiʔ* "belly".
LEC **fiʕ-* "belly": Som *fiiʕ*.
Unexpected *-ʕ- < *-ʔ-.

Related to **fiʔ-* "blow". Note the semantic evolution in Cush.

842 *füç̣- "sweep, clean"

WCh **fuç̣-* "clean, wash": Tng *puḍe*.
CCh **fuč-* "sweep": Mofu *fəč*, Gis *fuča*.
Rift **fiç̣-* "sweep": Irq *fiç̣-*, Alg *fiç̣-*, Bur *fič-*.

Cf. **feṭ-* "sweep".

843 *fVḥVḳ- "scrape, scratch"

Sem **pVḥVḳ-* "scrape, scrub": Gz *fḥq*, Tgy *fäḥaqʷä*, Hrr *fēḥaqa*.
WCh **fuḳ-* "scrape, polish": Ang *vuk*.
Agaw **faḳ-* "scrape": Xmr *faq-*, Aun *faki*.
SA **fik-* "scratch": Saho *fik*.
LEC **fiḳ-* "scratch": Som *fiiq-*.

Various contractions in Chadic and Cush.

844 *fVḳir-/*fVḳur- "pierce, tear"

Sem *pVḳir-/*pVḳur- "pierce, dig, tear out (eye)": Arab *fqr* [-*i*-, -*u*-].
Eg *fḳꜣ* "tear off" (n).
-*ꜣ* goes back to *-*r*-.

Derived from **faḳ*- "pierce, tear".

845 *fVl- "divide, pierce"

Sem **pVl*- "divide" 1,"(be) split" 2: Hbr *ply* 1, Aram (Jud) *ply* 1,Gz *fly* 1 2, Tgr *fäla* 2, Tgy *fly* 2, Amh *fälläl* 2.
The original biliteral stem **pVl*- is represented either as **pVlVy*- or as **pVlVl*-.
Berb **fVlVw*- "pierce": Kby *flu*.

846 *fVr- "boil"

Sem **pūr*- "boil": Arab *fwr* [-*u*-].
Eg *ꜣfr* "boil" (gr).

Both in Sem and Eg derivatives of **fVr*- are presented. Probably, the original root should be reconstructed as **fVwVr*-/ **fVʾVr*- or *ʾ*VfVr*-/**wVfVr*-.

847 *fVt- "feel aversion, ignore"

Sem **pūt*- "go round, avoid": Arab *fwt*.
Eg *ft* "feel aversion, boredom".

Connected with **fut*- "vomit"?

848 *fVṭ- "pull out, take (out)"

WCh **faṭ*- "pull out": Bol *foḍu*, Gera *faḍ*-, Ngz *fəta*.
LEC **fuṭ*- "take": Or *fuuḍa*.

Irregular vocalism. If -*o*- in Bol is a reflex of *-*wa*-, HS should be **foṭ*-. Cf. Dhl *fir*- "take out"?

*g

849 *ga'- "rise"

Sem *gV'Vy- "rise" [1], "be high" [2]: Hbr *g'y* [1], Aram *gᵉ'ā* [2].
Triliteral formation based on *gV'-.
ECh *ga'ay- "increase": Bid *gāya*, Mig *gāyo*.
Derivative from *ga'- similar to the Sem formation in *-y-.
Agaw *gwi'- "be high": Bil *gwe*, Xmr *gwe*, Kwr *gwe*, Dmb *gwe*, Kem *gwee*.
Unexpected vocalism reflecting HS *ü.

850 *ga'ab- "dwelling"

Eg *gbꜣ* "side of a room" (Westc.).
Metathesis.
WCh *ga'ab- "room": Bol *gabi*, Dera *gawi*, *gaḅi*, Tng *kaabi*, Krf *kaafi*, Gera *gawa*, Glm *gaabu*.

Connected with *gab- "wall, dwelling".

851 *ga'id- "face"

WCh *ga'id- "face": Bol *gaido*.
Bed *gedi* "face, eye".

Composite of prefix *ga- and *'id- "eye". For a similar semantic development cf. Goth *and-augi* "face" ← *augo* "eye".

852 *ga'ur- "wall, yard"

Sem *'igār- "wall" [1], "roof" [2]: Akk *'igāru* [1], Aram *'gr* [1], Arab *'iggār-* [2].
Metathesis.
WCh *gar-gar- "low wall or mount": Hs *gargarī*.
Reduplication.
CCh *ga'ur- "shed": Log *gaura*.
ECh *ga'Vr- "pricky fence": Mkk *gāra*.
Bed *ga'ra*, *gaar'a* "yard".
Assimilation of vowels.
Rift *garV'- "wall of the verandah": Irq *gar'ai*.
Metathesis.

853 *gaʾuǯ-/*gawuǯ- "calabash, basket"

Berb **gaʒVw-* "calabash": Ghd *ta-gazu-t.*
Metathesis.
WCh **gaʾuǯ-* "calabash": Hs *gōǯī.*
ECh **guǯ-* "calabash" [1], "basket" [2]: Kbl *guǯe-gā* [1], Tum *gəǯ* [2].
Contraction.

Consonantal alternation **-ʾ-* ~ **-w-*.

854 *gab- "wall, dwelling"

Sem **gabb-* "entrance, vestibule" [1], "enclosure" [2]: Gz *gabgab* [1], Gur *gəbbi* [2].
Reduplication in Gz.
Eg *gb.w* "palace" (NK).
ECh **gab-* "wall": Tum *gab*, Ndam *gaba.*

855 *gab- "weapon"

Sem **gabāb-* "sling": Akk *gabābu.*
Partial reduplication. Cf. Akk *kapāpu* id.
HEC **gab-* "bow and arrow": Dar *gabe.*

856 *gab- "side, bank, beach"

WCh **gaḅ-* < **gabVʾ-* "bank": Hs *gāḅa.*
Suffix **-Vʾ-*.
Bed *gäb, geb* "side".
From **gabi-*?
Agaw **gab(b)-* "side": Bil *gaf*, Xmr *gəba.*
LEC **geb-* "bank": Som *gebi.*
Secondary **e*. Cf. Bed.
HEC **gab-* "side": Bmb *gaba.*

Cf. Sem **ganb-* "side (particularly, of the body)" (Aram (Syr) *gabba*, Arab *ganb-*), presumably, a deverbative related to Arab *gnb* "be near smb.". Cf. also Eg *wḏb* "bank" (pyr) that could be a reflex of **gob-*.

857 *gab- "earth, clay"

Sem **gabīb-* "ground, earth": Akk *gabību*, Arab *gabīb-*, *gabūb-*.
Partial reduplication.
Eg *gbb* "earth, Earth-god" (pyr).
Partial reduplication.
CCh **gVb-* "field": Gis *guva*.
Secondary *-u-* in Gis before a labial.
ECh **gab-* "clay": Tum *gab*, Ndam *ga:b*.

858 *gab- "front"

Sem **gabh-* "forehead, front, brow": Arab *gabh-at-*, Jib *gəbh- εt*, Hss *yabheh*, Shh *gebhat*.
Secondary derivative in **-h-*? Cf. also **gabb-* "part of the body, (?) brain": Akk *gabbu*.
WCh **gab-* "physical front of a person" [1], "breast, chest" [2]: Hs *gabā* [1], Say *gəp* [2], Dwot *gup* [2], Ngz *bo- gaba* [2], Bade *bo-gawa* [2].
Prefix **bwa-* in Ngz and Bade. Dwot *-u-* may be explained if WCh **gabu-* is reconstructed.

859 *gabaʾ- "hand, arm"

Eg *gbꜣ* "arm".
WCh **gaḅ-* < **gabaʾ-* "joint, limb": Hs *gaḅa*.
SA **gab-* "hand": Saho *gabaa*, Afar *gaba*, *gabaa*.

860 *gabar- "male"

Sem **gabr-* "man": Phn *gbr*, Moab *gbrn*, Hbr *geber*, Aram (Mand) *gabra*.
WCh **gwar-* < **gVbar-* "man": Sura *gwar*, Bol *gwor-zo*, Krk *gworzo*, Ngm *gwor-zo*.
LEC **garVb-* "slave": Or *garba*.
Metathesis.
HEC **gabar-* "slave, farmer": Bmb *gabari*, Kmb *gabare*.
Dhl *gaβara* "male lion".
Note the meaning, presumably, from *"male".

861 *gabVḥ- "be weak"

Sem *gVbVḥ- "be weak" [1], "soften" [2]: NSyr *gāwiḥ* [1], Tgr *gäbḥä* [2], Tgy *gäbḥe* [2].
Eg *gby* "be weak" (n).
Late Eg loss of the laryngeal (substituted by *-y*?).
CCh *gaḅ- < *gabaH- "weakness": Lame *gaḅa*, LPe *gaḅ*, Msm *gab*.
LEC *ga-gab- "be exhausted": Or *gaggaba*.
Partial reduplication.

Cf. WCh *gāb- < *gaHab- "febrile cattle disease": Hs *gābu*.

862 *gac- "bank, side"

Eg *gs* "side" (pyr).
WCh *gač- "bank": Hs *gači*.

Isolated parallel, probably, of archaic provenance.

863 *gac-/*gic- "face"

Eg *d̲s* "person" (pyr).
*d̲- < *g-* before *e or *o. For the semantic development, cf. Lat *persōna*.
Agaw *gac- "face" [1], "figure" [2]: Bil *gaš* [1], Xmr *gaç* [1], Kwr *gaš* [1], Dmb *gaš* [1], Kem *gaṣ*, *gäš* [1 2].
LEC *gos- "chin, beard": Arb *goos*.
Reflects one more HS variant *goc-?
Rift *gic- "face": Irq *gitsaʕa*.

Reconstruction of vocalism is very shaky. Note parallel forms *gaǯ-/*gawaǯ- "cheek, chin", *gaĉ-/*guĉ- "cheek, chin". Note an alternative comparison for Eg *d̲s* ~ WCh *das- "man" (Sura *dās*, Ang *des*) implying a tentative phonological correspondence Eg *d̲* ~ WCh *d 'see *pVʔud- "knee").

864 *gač- "spear"

WCh *gač- "spear": Ang *gašī*, Krk *agači*, Dera *gai*, Gera *gossa*, Glm *gass*, Pol *gəs*, Geji *gəsi*, Buli *gəs*, Ngz *ngas*.
Gera *-o-* may reflect a rounded vowel of the second syllable.
CCh *gač- "spear": Tera *gas*, Jara *gas*.
SA *gaš- "spear": Saho *gaša*.

865 *gaĉ- ''be wet''

Eg *g3š* ''pour out'' (n).

-3- is a sign for **-a-*.

WCh **gaĉ-* ''wet'': Ngz *gāŝa*, *gaẑa*

866 *gaĉ̣- ''cheek, chin''

Berb **[g]aç-* ''cheek'': Ahg *aγaẓ*.

Irregular reflex of **g-*.

WCh **gaĉ̣-/*guĉ̣-* ''cheek'': DB *gaŝ-am*, Jmb *guṣa*.

CCh **guŝwa-* ''cheek'': Zime *ŋguŝo*, Bnn *ŋgoŝo-no*.

Cf. Mofu *gwaŝ* ''molar'' ← ''cheek tooth''. **-u-* seems to be secondary as well as in WCh.

ECh **gaĉ̣-* ''cheek'': Bir *gaḍayo*, Bid *gəḍe-ma*, Mig *gaḍu-mo*, Jegu *gede*.

HEC **gaç-* ''chin, jaw'': Sid *gaččo*, Bmb *gaçço*, Kab *geča*.

Omot **gaṭ-* ''chin'': Mch *gaṭ-ano*.

Dhl *gaṯ'a* ''beard''.

Confusion of two meanings, ''chin'' and''beard'', is typical of IE **smek'ru-*.

Cf. **gac-/*gic-* ''face''.

867 *gad- ''be old; elder''

Sem **gad-* ''be considerable, be respectable (of men)'': Arab *gdd* [*-a-*].

Note a nominal derivative of this verb in Arab *gadd-* ''grandfather, ancestor''.

ECh **gaḍ-* ''old'': Kwn *gāḍ-atē*, Ngm *gaḍe*.

Originally, from **gad-VH-*.

HEC **gad-* ''age group, generation'': Bmb *gada*.

Rift **gad-* ''old man'': Alg *gar-mo*, Bur *gad-uwa*.

If Alg reflects a different root **garVm-* it might be compared with CCh **gurVm-* ''become old'': Mofu *gurm*.

868 *gad- ''cut, split''

Sem **gVd-* ''cut off'': Aram (Syr) *gdd*, SAr *gdd*.

ECh **gad-* ''split'': Tum *gād*, Ndm *gəda*.

869 *gad- "river"

Sem **gad(y)-* "river-bank": Hbr *gādā*, Aram (Mand) *gada*, *gida*, Arab *gady-at-*.
WCh **g[a]daw-* "lake": Ngm *godo*.
Assimilation of vowels.
CCh **nV-gad-* "river": Bud *ŋgada*.
Prefix **nV-*.
Agaw **gad-* "river-bed": Bil *gadi*.
SA **gad-* "river, stream": Saho *gadee*.

870 *gadeb- "stomach"

WCh **gadyab-* "kidneys": Hs *gažēbā*.
CCh **gVdVb-* "belly": Gdr *gədəf*.
Unvoiced *-f* in the auslaut.
HEC **godeb-* "belly": Sid *godoba*, Ala *gɔddɛba*, Kmb *gʷɔdɛɛba*, *godaba*, Dar *godaba*, Had *godabo*.
Irregular **-o-* of the first syllable.

871 *gadel- "fertile soil"

Sem **gadīl-* "land, beach": Arab *gadīl-*.
Secondary formation?
Eg *ḏdꜣ* "fertilize (field)" (gr).
Denominative verb reflecting **godVl-* with **-l-* > Eg *-ꜣ*.
ECh **gVdyal-* "(clay) earth": Kera *gedel*.
Assimilation of vowels.

872 *gadum- "cut; axe, hoe"

Sem **gVdVm-* "cut off": Akk *gadāmu*, Aram *gdm*, Arab *gdm*.
Bed *gaduum* "axe".
SA **godum-* "axe": Saho *gɔdumaa*.
**o* < **a* is influenced by **u* of the second syllable.
LEC **gudum-* "axe": Som *guddum*.
Assimilation of vowels.

Derived from **gad-* "cut, split". **gadum-* as a nominal stem appears to be a common Cush innovation.

873 *gag- ''roof''

Sem *gag-* ''flat roof'': Akk *gaggu*, Ug *gg*, Hbr *gāg*.
Berb *gVg-* ''arch supporting a tent'': Ayr *a-gəgu*, Twl *a-gəgu*.

Reduplication?

874 *gaʿ- ''be empty''

Eg *ḏʿ* ''be deserted'' (XIX).
Irregular *ḏ-* < *g-* implies the influence of *e* or *o* in the original HS verb.
WCh *gay-* ''empty'': Tng *gayɛ*.
From *gaHi-*.
ECh *gay-* ''desert'': Tum *gay*.
A deverbative formation.

875 *gaʿ-/*giʿ- ''dig, bury''

WCh *giH-* ''dig'': Zaar *gi*.
CCh *gaH-* ''bury'': Bud *gau*.
ECh *gay-* ''bury'': Kera *ge (ti tiŋ)*.
From *gaHi-*.
SA *gaʿ-* ''bury'': Afar *gaʿ*.

Cf. Eg *ḏɜt* ''tomb'' (NK)?

876 *gaʿad- ''dog, wolf''

Sem *gaʿd-* ''wolf'': Arab *gaʿd-at-*, *gaʿād-at-*.
Berb *gVd-* ''dog'': Kby *agdi*.
CCh *gVd-* ''dog'': Mofu *gədey*.
Suffix *-ay-* > Mofu *-ey*.
ECh *gad-* ''dog'': Mkk *gede* (masc.), *gada* ((fem.), Smr *do-gədi*.
Prefix *dwa-* in Smr.

Cf. a derivative in LEC *ged-al-* ''jackal'' (Or *gedallo*).

877 *gaḥun- ''stomach''

Sem *gaḥun-* ''belly'': Hbr *gāḥōn*.
CCh *guHan-* ''stomach'': Log *ŋgun*, Bud *ŋun*, Kus *nguen*, Glf *um-guen*.

Metathesis of vowels. Prefix **mV-/*nV-*.
ECh **gya-gVHVn-* "stomach": Tum *gegə:n*.
Partial reduplication.

878 *gal- "vessel"

Eg *gn.t* "vessel" (NK).
Note *-n* < **-l-*.
WCh **gal-* "calabash": Wrj *galiya*, Kry *gali*, Geji *gale*, Brm *kal*, Buli *gal*, Wnd *gal*.
Suffix *-iya* in Wrj.
CCh **gal-* "pot": Bnn *gala*.

879 *gal- "go, enter"

Sem **gūl-* "go, travel": Arab *gwl* [*-u-*].
Secondary interfix *-w-*. Cf. Arab *glw* "migrate, resettle".
Berb **gVl(Vw)-* "go": Kby *glu*.
WCh **gal-/*gul-* "run" [1], "follow" [2]: Sha *gal* [1], *gulay* [2].
Note WCh alternation **a* ~ **u*.
ECh **gal-* "go out": Ndam *gal-ǯoyo*, Mobu *gale*.
SA **gal-/*gil-* "run" [1], "go" [2]: Saho *gil* [1], Afar *gaḷ* [2].
SA reflects an alternation **a* ~ **i*.
LEC **gal-* "enter": Som *gal-*, Or *gala*, Arb *gal-*.
HEC **gal-* "enter": Bmb *gal-*.
Omot **gal-* "enter": Ome *gal-*, Anf *gal-*.

880 *gal- "throw"

Sem **gVlaʾ-* "throw, overturn": Arab *glʾ* [*-a-*].
Formation based on **gal-*. Cf. also Arab *ngl* [*-i-*].
WCh **gal-* < **giHal-* "throw": Klr *gyol*.
ECh **gVl-* "throw": Ndm *gəla*.

881 *gal-/*gaʾil- "egg"

CCh **gal-/*gaʾil-* "egg": Gaa *geʾila*, Gbn *ngeʾele*, Boka *ngala*, Hwn *ŋgala*, Tera *ngərli*.
Secondary laryngeal in some CCh forms. Note prefix **nV-* in Boka, Hwn and Tera.

ECh *giʔil- "lay eggs": Jegu *giil*.
Denominative verb .
SA *gVlVl- "egg": Afar *gələlo*.
Partial reduplication.

882 *galab- "give"

Sem *gVlVb- "procure": Arab *glb* [-*i*-, -*u*-].
The vowels of the second syllable may be secondary.
WCh *galab- "give": Mnt *gallap*.
*-b- is unvoiced in the final position.

883 *galam- "ram"

Sem *galam- "ram with long legs": Arab *galam-*.
CCh *gamal- "ram": Lame *gəmla*, Bnn *gamala-na*.
Metathesis.
ECh *gamVl- "ram": Kera *gamla*.
Metathesis.
Dhl *ngolome* "buffalo".
Secondary vocalism and prefix *nV-.

884 *gal-an- "river, lake"

CCh *galan-H- "swampy river-branch": Mba *goloŋay*.
Secondary vocalism.
LEC *galan- "sea": Or *galaana*.
HEC *galan- "river": Dar *galaana*.

Cf. Sem *gal- "wave" (Hbr *gal*) that may reflect HS *gal- "river, wave" from which the present root is derived.

885 *gal-gal- "hunger"

Sem *gal-gal- "hunger": Akk *galgaltu*, *galgallatu*.
HEC *gar-gal- "famine": Bmb *gaargale*.
Dissimilation of liquids.

Reduplication?

886 *gal-gal-/*gal-gil- "thunder"

Sem **gal-gāl-* "continuous thunder": Arab *galgāl-*.
ECh **gal-gil-* "thunder": Mig *galgilo*.

A descriptive reduplicated stem.

887 *gam- "vessel"

Sem **gām-* "bowl": Arab *gām-*.
ECh **gVm-* "clay pot": Tum *gəmi*.

Cf. HEC **gamb-* "jar" (Had *gamboʾo*).

888 *gam- "be full"

Sem **gim-/*gum-* "be full": Arab *gmm* [*-i-*, *-u-*].
Secondary vocalism?
WCh **gamu-* "fill, be full": Sura *gam*, *kum*, Ang *gam*, Mnt *gum*, Ank *gam*, Grk *kum-pan*, Bol *gom*, Krk *nǯamū*, Pero *kem*, Ngm *ŋgama*.

Cf. Berb **gVm-/*gVwVm-* "scoop, draw (water)" (Kby *agʷem*)?

889 *gamaḥ- "wait"

Eg *gmḥ* "wait" (MK).
ECh **gam-* "wait": Smr *gam*, Sbn *gam-*.
No traces of the auslaut laryngeal.

890 *gan- "field"

Sem **gann-* "garden": Hbr *gan*, Arab *gann-at-*.
Berb **gVn-* "plateau": Kby *agʷni*.
Note labialization, probably reflecting an earlier **gVwVn-* (cf. WCh!).
WCh **gaHwan-* "field": Hs *gōnā*, Tng *kaŋ*, Fyer *haⁿgon*, Sha *goŋ*, DB *goŋ*.
Sha and DB reflect the secondary metathesis of laryngeal yielding to *-ŋ-* in contact with **-n-*.
ECh **gaHan-/*gan-H-* "field": Mig *gaan*, Bid *gaŋ*.

Secondary laryngeal in WCh and ECh.

891 *gan- ''leg''

CCh **gwan-* < **ganu-* ''leg'': Bata *gwɔnɛ*.
ECh **ganu-* ''leg'': Dor *de-ganu*, Nch *guan-ung*.
Prefix in Dor.
Omot **gan-* ''leg'': Mch *gano*.

An isolated archaic formation that may be somehow connected with **gonVḥ-* ''elbow, shoulder, wing'' as a word for ''extremity, limb''.

892 *gan-/*gin- ''go''

Sem **gVn-* ''come'' (imperative): Akk *gana*.
WCh **gan-* ''go'': Fyer *gan*.
ECh **gin-* ''go out'': Sok *ginē*.

Alternation **a* ~ **i*.

893 *ganaḥ- ''bend''

Sem **gVnaḥ-* ''bend'': Arab *gnḥ* [*-a-*].
WCh **ma-gan-* ''bend'': Sha *magan*.
Prefix **ga-*.
CCh **gan-* ''bend'': Zime *gan*.

894 *gar- ''container, vessel''

Sem **garr-* ''box'' [1], ''jug'' [2]: Akk *garru* [1], Arab *garr-at-* [2].
Berb **gVr-* ''small wooden vase'': Izy *ɾa-gλa*.
WCh **gar-* ''tin container'': Hs *garwa*.
CCh **gVr-* ''pot'': Gude *gəra*, Nza *gəra*.

895 *gar- ''boat, ship''

Sem **gāriy-* ''ship'': Arab *gāriy-at-*.
WCh **gVr-* ''boat'': Krf *gerre*.
The vocalism of the first syllable in Krf is induced by the final *-e*.
ECh **gar-* ''boat'': Kwn *ga:r*.

Etymologically identical with **gar-* ''container, vessel''?

896 *gar- “calf, bull”

Eg *ḏr* “calf” (MK).
ḏ- < *g*- usually before **e* or **o*.
CCh **gar*- “bull”: Msg *gari*.

897 *gar- “be angry”

Sem **gūr*- “be unjust” [1], “be audacious” [2]: Arab *gwr* [-*u*-] [1], Tgr *gawärä* [2].
Secondary *-*w*-?
Berb **gVr*- “be enraged”: Kby *egru*.
CCh **gar*- “angry, anger” [1], “evil” [2]: Mnd *gər-ha* [1], Lame *ngar* [2].
Prefix **nV*- in Lame.

898 *gar-/*gawar- “antelope”

WCh **gar*- “oryx”: Cagu *gāre*, Mbu *gāri*.
Cf. Paa *gur-maŝi* “antelope”, Siri *zəb-gəri* id.
CCh **gar*- “antelope”: Log *garia*.
ECh **gawar*- “antelope”: Tum *gəru*, Kwn *gowor-to*.
Bed *gar-uwa* “kind of antelope”.
Omot **gar*- “kind of antelope”: Ome *gaaraa*.
Rift **gwar*- “antelope”: Irq *gwaraay*.
Reflects HS **gVwVr*-?

In ECh and Rift, a characteristic innovation: C^2 = -*w*-.

899 *garab- “disease”

Sem **garab*- “lepra, scabies”: Akk *garābu*, Hbr *gārāb*, Aram (Syr) *garᵉbō*, Arab *garab*-.
ECh **gabyar*- < **gabari*- “syphilis”: Smr *gaberi*.
Metathesis.

An alternative reconstruction is **gabar*-.

900 *garaˤ- “cut”

Sem **gVrVˤ*- “cut (hair)”: Hbr *grˤ*, Jib *geraˤ*, Soq *garaˤ*.
SA **garaˤ*- “cut, strike”: Saho *garaˤ*-, Afar *garaˤ*- .

LEC *garaᶜ- "cut": Or garaᶜ-.
Cf. Som gur- id.

901 *gas- "container"

Eg gsꜣ "sack" (pyr).
Auslaut -ꜣ reflects the root vowel.
CCh *mi-gis- "basket": Suk migisa.
Prefix *mi-. Assimilated from *mi-gas-.

Cf., probably, a reduplicated stem in ECh *gVsas- "bottle" (Kera gəsasi).

902 *gas-/*gus- "move"

WCh *gusya- "move": Hs gusa, Sura gyes.
LEC *goš- "ply between two places": Som goš-.
Rift *gus- "drive (away)": Irq gus-, Alg gus-im-.

Cf. Omot *gaš- "drive": Kaf gaš-.

903 *gasoʾ- "antelope"

Eg gsꜣ "antelope" (OK).
WCh *gas- "kind of antelope": Ngz gas-ka.
ECh *gawas- "antelope": Ndam gōs, Smr gawsa.
From *gaHwas-?
LEC *gu-guš- "antelope": Or guguf-to.
Partial reduplication. Note Arb gasar "buffalo". Note Or -f- continuing a sibilant.
Rift *ga-gVs- "antelope": Irq gagəs.
Partial reduplication.

904 *gaṭ- "hunt"

WCh *gaṭ- "hunt": Gera gaḍə, Sha gəḍ.
LEC *ʾu-gaṭ- "hunt": Som ugaaḍ-s-.
Denominative formation. Prefix *ʾu-.
HEC *ʾu-gaṭ- "hunt": Sid ugaaṭ-.
Identical with LEC.

905 *gaw- "bull, buffalo"

Berb **gaw-* "bull": Izy *ayuǧu*, pl. *iyuǧ^{w}awen*.
Eg *gw* "bull" (MK).
ECh **gVwVy-* "bull": Tum *guūy*.
Omot **gah-* "buffalo": Kaf *gahoo*.
As in some other cases, it is not clear whether *-h-* is a part of the root.

906 *gaw- "man, people"

Sem **gaw-* "people": Akk *gaʔ-*, *gaw-*, Hbr *gōy*, SAr *gw*.
WCh **nV-gaw-* "man": Sura *ŋgɔ*, Ang *go*, Krk *ŋgā*, Ngm *ŋgo*.
Prefix **nV-*.
ECh **ga-* "friend": Bid *gee-* (masc.), *gaa-* (fem.).
Bed *gaw* "tribe, family".
Wrz **ʔi-kaw-*"clan": Hrs *iko*.
Prefix **ʔi-*.

907 *gaway- "body"

Sem **gVwy-* "body, belly": Hbr *g^{e}wiyyā*, Aram (Palest) *giwy^{e}tā*.
Cf. reduplicated **guʔ-* in Arab *guʔguʔ-* "chest".
WCh **gaw-* "corpse": Hs *gāwā*.
Probably, reflects original HS **gaw-*.
ECh **gway-* < **gaway-* "corpse": Sok *goy*.

Related to **gaw-* "man, people"?

908 *gawaʒ- "go, walk"

Sem **gūʒ-* "pass, go": Hbr *gwz*, Aram (Syr) *gāz*, Arab *gwz* [*-u-*], SAr *gz*.
Berb **gaʒ-* "go away": Kby *ggaǰ*.
Agaw **gaʕVʒ-* "depart": Bil *gaʕd-*.
Unexpected **-ʕ-*. A reflection of **-w-*?

The original form of the root could be **gaʒ-*.

909 *gawVf- "interior"

Sem **gawp-* "body" [1], "heart, middle, interior" [2]: Hbr *gūp* [1], Arab *gawf-* [2], Tgr *gof* [2].

CCh *gu-guf- "heart" [1], "lungs" [2]: Klb guguvi [1], HNk gugufɛ [1], FKi gugufi [2], Gude guguf-in [2], FM gugufi [2], FBw guguf-in [1].
Partial reduplication. Contraction of the inlaut cluster *-awV- > *u.

910 *gay- "move"

Sem *gīˀ- "come": Arab gyˀ [-i-].
Cf. Gz gʷayya "run". Based on *gVy-.
WCh *gay-/*guy- "ride, run away": Bol gay, Krk guy.
CCh *gway- "enter" [1], "return" [2], "follow" [3]: Klb gwa [1], Mrg gwa [1], Glv gwi [2], Bud gya [3], Masa gɔio [1].
The original form of the root was *gaywa-.
ECh *giy- "come": Kbl giyə.
Secondary *i before *y.
SA *gay- "arrive": Afar gay-.
LEC *gay- "arrive": Or gaya.
HEC *ge(ˀ)- < *gay- "arrive": Dar ge-.

Cf. Rift *gow- "run away": Irq gow-.

911 *gay- "say"

Eg d̲wy "call, say" (pyr).
Causes of palatalization are not clear.
WCh *gay- "tell": Hs gaya.
CCh *ga- "speak": Tera ga.
Omot *gay- "say": Shk ge, Dime gee-mu, Gll gay, Ari gai-.

Cf. Sem *gVᶜVy- "shout": Hbr gᶜy.

912 *gayVᶜ- "work"

Sem *yVgVᶜ- "be tired" [1], "work" [2]: Akk egû [1], Hbr ygᶜ [1 2].
Metathesis.
Berb *gVH- "make, put": Izy iga, Kby əgg.
CCh *gaH-/*gay- "do, make" [1], "build" [2]: Gis ge [1], Mwl ugo [1], Log gaˀe [2].
ECh *giy- "work" (n.): Smr giya.
Deverbative. Cf. Kera geye "be tired" < *g[a]y-.

913 *gaʒaw- "tumor, paunch"

Sem **gVzVw-* "tumor": Tgr *gəzwa*, Tgy *gəzwa*.
Berb **gaʒaw-* "paunch, offal": Ayr *ši-gəza*, Twl *te-gazaw-t*.

914 *gaǯ-/*gawaǯ- "cheek, chin"

ECh **gaǯ-/*gwaǯ-* "cheek": Smr *gaǯe*, Kbl *kwaǯi*.
**gwaǯ-* < **gawaǯ-*.
Bed *g^w^aǯ* "face".
Phonetic development similar to ECh.
SA **gaʒ-* "face": Saho *gazaa*, *gadaa*.
LEC **gaǯ-*"chin": Som *gaǯ*, *gaḍ*.

A typical *CVC-* ~ *CVwVC-* root pattern.

915 *gelal- "be weak"

Eg *gnn* "be weak" (OK).
Note *-n-* < **-l-*.
ECh *gyalal-* "weak": Gbr *gelāle*.

Partial reduplication?

916 *genaᶜ- "hand"

ECh **gyan-* "hand": Tum *geny-*.
LEC **gen-* "hand": Som *ǯini*, Bay *gɛne*.
Som *ǯ-* < *g-* before *-i-*.
Bed *ganaʾa*, *ganʾa* "hand".
Assimilation of vowels.
SA **genaᶜ-* "hand, palm": Saho *ginaᶜ*, Afar *genaaᶜ*.
Note **-ᶜ-* < **-ḥ-*.
LEC **gaᶜan-* "hand, arm": Som *gaᶜan*, Or *gana*, Boni *kaᶜan*.
Metathesis and assimilation of vowels.
Wrz **kanaᶜ-* "hand" [1], "palm" [2]: War *kanɛɛʾe* [1], Gaw *kanᶜate* [2], Hrs *kanaᶜᶜe* [2].
Assimilation of vowels.
Mgg *kinnɛʾ-* "hand".

917 *ger- "dog, cub"

Sem **gVrw-* "wild animal's cub" [1], "cub, puppy" [2]: Akk *gerru* [1],

Hbr *gūr* [2], Aram (Syr) *guryō* [2], Arab *garw-*, *girw-*, *gurw-* [2], Hss *yeru* [2].
ECh **gyara-* "dog": Nch *gera*, Lele *gira*, Kbl *gara*.

Cf., probably, HEC **giraw-* "cat" (Bmb *giraaʾwee*).

918 *giʾ- "see, look"

Eg *gȝgȝw* "look" (XVIII).
Reduplication.
WCh **giy-* < **giH-* "look": Bol *giy*.

919 *gid-/*gud- "be big, be numerous"

Sem **gidd-* "many, much": Arab *gidd-*.
Berb **gVwVd-* "be numerous": Izy *egguδ*.
Based on **gud-*.
WCh **gVd-* "many": Bol *godo*.
Secondary vocalism influenced by the auslaut vowel.
LEC **gud(d)-* "large": Or *guddaa*.

Alternation **i* ~ **u*.

920 *gidol- "be big"

Sem **gVdVl-* "big" [1], "be big" [2], "become big, strong" [3]: Ug *gdl* [1], Hbr *gdl* [2], *gādōl* [1], Aram *gᵉdal* [2], Arab *gādil-* [1], *gdl* [3].
CCh **digwal-* "big": Klb *dügōlu*, Mrg *digal*.
Consonantal metathesis.

Derived from **gid-/*gud-* "be big, be many".

921 *gif- "strike, pierce"

Sem **nVgVp-* "strike, push, shake": Hbr *ngp*, Gz *ngf*.
Prefix **nV-*.
ECh **gif-* "strike (with a sword)": Sok *gifē*.

922 *giᶜ- "beer"

Sem **giᶜ-* "beer": Arab *giᶜ-at-*.
WCh **giy-* < **giHya-* "beer": Hs *giya*.

923 *giᶜar-/*giᶜur- "seek"

Eg *d̲ᶜr* "seek" (MK).
CCh **giHar-* "seek": Daba *gir*, Mus *gər*, Masa *gar*, *gāra*.
SA **gVHur-* "seek": Saho *guur*.

924 *giHad-/*giyad- "neck"

Sem **gīd-* "tendon" [1], "muscle" [2], "nerve" [3], "neck" [4]: Akk *gīdu* [1 2], Hbr *gīd* [1 3], Aram *gᵉyādā* [1 3], Arab *gīd-* [4], Soq *žid* [3].
Contraction of **giyVd-*.
WCh **nV-giḍ-* < **nV-giHVd-* "neck": Krf *ngiḍo*, Glm *ngirya*.
Prefix **nV-*.
ECh **giHad-* "neck": Dng *gaaḍya*, Tum *geer*, Ngam *ger-*, Sok *get-im*, *gere*.
Contraction in individual languages.

Consonantal alternation of a laryngeal (presumably, **-ʾ-*) and **-y-*. Cf. also another possible cognate in LEC **gaHad-* "breast": Som *gaaddo*. The semantic variety of Sem makes the whole comparison dubious.

925 *gil- "cloud, dew"

Sem **ʾigVl-* "drops (of dew)": Hbr *ʾēgel*.
Prefix **ʾi-*.
WCh **nV-gil-* "cloud" [1], "sky" [2]: Krf *ngilla* [1], Glm *ngəla* [2].
Prefix **nV-*.

Forms with prefixes in both Sem and WCh.

926 *gim- "receive"

Eg *gmy* "receive, find" (NK), Copt **t̲imi* id.: Boh *t̲'imi*, Shd *t̲ime*.
Copt **-i-* reflects HS **-i-*.
WCh **gVm-* "get": Cagu *gəm-*.

927 *gin- "grind, pound"

Eg *d̲n* "grind" (med).
Palatalization of **g-* before a front vowel.
ECh **gin-* "pound": Smr *gine*, Tum *gən*, Ndm *gəna*, Dng *igina*.

928 *gin- ‘‘fire’’

Eg *ḏnḏn.t* ‘‘fire’’ (sarc).
Reduplication.
CCh **gin-* ‘‘roast’’: Mafa *gin-*.
Denominative formation.

929 *gin-/*gun- ‘‘build’’

Berb **gVn-* ‘‘set up (house), lay off (garden)’’: Ghd *ə-gnu*.
WCh **gin-* ‘‘build’’: Hs *gina*.
CCh **gun-* ‘‘build’’: Log *gun-*.

Alternation **i* ~ **u*.

930 *gir- ‘‘fire’’

Sem **gir-* ‘‘fire, deity of fire’’: Akk *giru*, *girru*.
Eg *ḏr* ‘‘fire’’ (gr).
Palatalization of **g-* before a front vowel.
SA **gir-* ‘‘fire’’: Saho *gira*, Afar *giraa*.
HEC **gir-* ‘‘fire’’: Sid *giira*, Dar *giira*, Had *giira*, Kmb *giira*.
Cf. Rift **giʔir-* ‘‘embers’’ (Irq *gilˀi*, Bur *giʔiru*, Alg *giʔiru*).

931 *gir- ‘‘be hot’’

WCh **gir-gir-* ‘‘hot’’: Maha *girgir*, Dera *gərgət*.
Reduplication. Dera < **gərgər*. Cf. Hs *gūra* ‘‘set fire’’.
CCh **gVr-gVr-* ‘‘hot’’: Tera *gərgər*, Bura *gərgər*.
Reduplication.
HEC **gir-* ‘‘burn’’: Sid *giir-*, Had *giir-*.

Related to **gir-* ‘‘fire’’.

932 *gir- ‘‘live’’

Sem **gūr-* ‘‘live’’ [1], ‘‘be close by’’ [2]: Hbr *gwr* [1], Arab *gwr* [2].
Based on **gVr-*.
LEC **gir-* ‘‘be, exist’’: Som *gir-*, Or *gir-*, Rnd *gir-*, Bay *gir-*.

933 *gir-/*giʾur- "corn"

Sem *gir-* "bean, corn": Hbr *gērā*.
WCh **giʾur-* "millet": Hs *gērō*, Sura *gor*, Diri *agyura*, Say *gyoro*.
Secondary laryngeal in the inlaut.
CCh *-*gur-* "bean": Mnd *ⁿgire*, Zgh *ŋgure*, Glv *ʾagura*, Gvo *ŋgəre*, Log *māgurē*.
Various prefixes in individual languages.
ECh **gir-* "bean": Smr *giri*, *ǯiri*, Jegu *giri*, *giri-k*.

A root pattern including a morphonological variant with C^2 = -ʾ-.

934 *gir-/*gur- "go, run"

Sem **gVrVy-* "run, flow" 1, "pass": Arab *gry* [-*i*-] 1, Hss *gerō* 1, Mhr *gerō* 2.
Derived from biconsonantal **gVr-*.
Berb **gVwVr-* "go, walk": Rif *uġur*, Izn *uγur*.
Based on **gVr-*.
WCh **guraʾ-* "come" 1, "go around" 2: Dera *gur-* 1, Bks *garaʾ* 2.
Suffix *-*aʾ*-.
CCh **gwar-* < **gura-* "go (into)" 1, "return" 2, "follow" 3: Tera *gəri* 2, Hil *gwər* 1, Log *gər* 1, Bnn *gwərə* 3.
ECh **gVr-* "come": Sbn *gər*.
Bed *agir* "return".
Metathesis of **giraʾ-*, cf. WCh.
HEC **geHer-* "run": Had *geer-*.
Metathesis from **giʾar-*, cf. WCh.

Alternation **i* ~ **u*. In WCh and Cush, similar derivatives in *-*aʾ*- are worth notice.

935 *go- "stone, mountain"

Eg *ḏw* "mountain" (pyr), Copt **[ṯ]ōw*: Boh *tōou*, Shd *toou*.
There are no traces of a laryngeal in Eg.
CCh **gwaʾ-* "stone": Lame *ngwai*, LPe *gwoiʾ*, Zime *gwoʾ*.
Secondary *-ʾ-. **gwaʾ-* may go back to **gwa-iʾ-*.

936 *goꜣ- "sing"

Eg *gꜣ* "sing" (n).
The palatalization of **g* is unmarked in late Eg.
CCh **gwaꜣ-* "sing": Bata *goo*.
LEC **goꜣ-* "moan": Or *goꜣa*.
Note a reduplication in WCh deverbative **gwag-* "song, dance": Mpn *kook*.

937 *goꜣVy- "carry"

Eg *ḏꜣy* "bring" (gr).
Regular palatalization of **g-*.
WCh **gwaꜣVy-* "carry (on one's back)": Hs *gōyā*.

938 *gob- "bend"

Eg *gb* "stoop" (gr).
No traces of palatalization in late Eg.
CCh **gwaḅ-* "bend": Gis *goḅ-*, Mofu *gəḅ*.
Unexpected emphatic **ḅ*. A trace of a laryngeal, also indicated by the vowel length in SA?
ECh **gwab-* "bend": Kera *gobe*.
SA **gub-* "be bent": Afar *guub*.

Cf. LEC **goṗ-* "hunchback" (Or *gooṗṗo*)?

939 *goĉal- "ant"

Sem **gaŝl-* "ant": Arab *gašl-at-*.
From HS **goĉal-* with assimilation of vowels.
WCh **gwaĉal-* "ant": Wrj *gwaŝala-na*.

940 *godaꜥ- "injure, damage"

Sem **gVdaꜥ-* "mutilate (of nose or lips)" [1], "cut" [2], "beat" [3], "damage" [4]: Hbr *gdꜥ* [2], Aram (Syr) *gdꜥ* [1 2], Arab *gdꜥ* [-*a*-] [1], Gz *g^w^dꜣ* [3], Tgr *gdꜣ* [3], Tgy *g^w^dꜣ* [3 4], Amh *g^w^dd* [4], Arg *g^w^dd* [4].
Labiovelars in Ethio-Sem may reflect an earlier rounded vowel of the first syllable. Note Ethio-Sem -ꜣ-.
Agaw **gwad-* "injure": Bil *g^w^ət-*, Kwr *g^w^ad-*, Kem *gäd y-*, Aun *g^w^əd-*.

Omot *gond- "injure" [1], "be bad" [2]: Kaf gond- [1], Mch gondo [2], Bwo gondo [2].

Nasal infix?

941 *godVn- "ant"

ECh *gwadVn- "ant": Kera godnoy.
LEC *gonVd- "ant": Or gondaa.
Metathesis.

Cf. HEC *goṭan- "termite" (Sid goṭan-čoo) and Omot *gutun- "worm" (Ome gutune).

942 *go-go- "skin"

CCh *gwa-gwa- "skin": Mnd gwogwa.
LEC *gog- "skin": Or googa.
HEC *gog- "skin": Sid googa, Bmb goga, gogaa, Dar goga, Kmb goga.
Omot *gog- "skin" [1], "bark" [2]: Yam goŋa [1], Kaf goggo [1], Bwo gooḳa, gooḳaa [1], Nao gogu [2].

Reduplication?

943 *go-gor- "bird"

CCh *gwa-gwar- "hen": Mofu gwagwar.
ECh *gu-gur- "hen": Kera guugur.
LEC *go-gor- "guinea fowl": Or gogorrii.

Partial reduplication. A descriptive stem. Cf. *guray- "hen".

944 *goʿad- "stick"

Eg ḏʿdd "stick" (n).
Note the palatalization of *g-.
WCh *gwaHad- "stick": Paa dan-gwaḍi, Mbu gwadə.
Prefix in Paa.
CCh *gad- "stick": Mafa gada.

945 *goḥ-goḥ- "monkey"

Eg ḏḥḏḥ "monkey" (reg).

WCh *gwagu- < *gwaH-gwaH- "baboon" [1], "monkey" [2]: Hs *gōgo* [1], Sha *gugwa* [2], Klr *guga* [2].
Reduplication.

946 *goḥas- "scratch"

Sem *gVḥaš- "skin" (v.): Arab *gḥs* [-*a*-].
WCh *nV-gwas- < *nV-gwaHVs- "scratch": Sha *ⁿgos*.
CCh *nV-gas- < *nV-gVHas "mark, make scratches on pottery": Mafa *ngas*.

Prefix *nV- in Chadic.

947 *gol- "cloud, water"

Berb *gVl-gVl- "quiet water": Izy *igḷugeḷ*.
Reduplication.
Eg *wgꜣ* "waters" (n).
w- stands for a rounded root vowel. No traces of palatalization in a late Eg form.
WCh *gwal- "cloud": Ang *gwal*.

Related to *gil- "cloud, dew".

948 *gol- "be round, go around"

Sem *gVl- "go around" [1], "roll" [2]: Akk *galālu* [2], Arab *gwl* [1], Amh *gʷll* [2].
Infix *-*w*- in Arab and a labiovelar in Amh may reflect an original back (rounded) vowel of the first syllable.
Berb *gVlVl- "be round": Tua *gelellet*.
Partial reduplication.
CCh *gwal- "round": Log *ŋgolō*.
Prefix *nV-.

949 *gol- "vagina"

CCh *gwal- "vagina": Glv *γwala*, Nak *γwala*, Bch *gwuley*.
LEC *gul- "genitals": Or *gula*.
Cf. Rnd *gɛl* "vagina", Arb *gel* id.
Rift *gwal- "vagina": Irq *gwalay*, Gor *golay*, Kwz *gulaʾ-iko*.

950 *golaḥ- "be bald"

Sem *gVlaḥ- "make bald" [1], "become bald" [2]: Hbr *glḥ* [1], Arab *glḥ* [-*a*-] [2].
Bed *gʷɔʔa* "baldness".
Agaw *gwalVh- "be bald": Bil *gʷalh-ay-*.
LEC *golaḥ- "bald spot, baldness": Som *gɔlaḥ*, *galaḥi*.

951 *golan- "soup, sauce"

Eg *gnn* "kind of food" (n).
Note *-*l*- > Eg -*n*-.
ECh *gwalan- "soup": Jegu *goloŋ*.
Secondary vocalism of the second syllable.

Cf. CCh *[g]unan- "soup" (Log *ɣunan*) with assimilation of sonants and irregular anlaut.

952 *gomaʕ- "gather, meet"

Sem *gVmaʕ- "gather": Arab *gmʕ* [-*a*-], Hss *egtōma*, Mhr *gatmaʔ*, Shh *gotmaʕ*.
T stirpes in Hss, Mhr and Shh.
WCh *gwama- < *gwamaH- "meet together": Hs *gamu*, Ang *gwom*, Mnt *kwam*, Bol *gom*, Krk *gam*, Tng *komb-*, Bade *gam-*.
Secondary -*mb*- < *-*m*- in Tng.

953 *gon- "poultry"

Eg *d̠nd̠n* "poultry" (MK).
Reduplication.
WCh *gwan- "rooster": Fyer *gwene*.

954 *gonVḥ- "elbow, shoulder, wing"

Eg *d̠nḥ* "wing" (pyr).
WCh *ḥVgwan- "shoulder, wing" [1], "arm" [2]: Sura *kəgɔn* [1], Ang *gwon*, *gwong* [1], Dwot *kuɣun* [1], Bks *koŋ* [2], Sha *ⁿgaan* [2].
Metathesis of the laryngeal.
CCh *gwan- "elbow": Msg *gono-gone*.
Reduplication.

HEC **gon(n)-* "wing": Kmb *gonna-ta.*
Rift **gon(g)oḫ-* "elbow": Irq *goŋgoḫi.*
Unexpected inlaut *-g-*.

Cf. a secondary deverbative formation in Sem **gināḥ-* "arm" [1], "wing" [2]: Arab *ginā̄ḥ-*, *ganāḥ-* [1], Mhr *ginaḥ* [2]. The root is, probably derived from **ganaḥ-* "bend", cf. Lat *ulna* "forearm", OIr *uilind* "elbow" derived from **elə-* "bend".

955 *gor- "back"

Sem **gur-* "back of the house": Tgr *gəray*, Tgy *g^w^aro*, Amh *g^w^aro*, Gur *g^w^aro.*
HEC **gor-* "back": Bmb *gooroo.*

956 *gor- "wall, house, dwelling"

Eg *ḏry.t* "dwelling" (gr), *ḏrw* "part of house" (MK), *ḏry* "wall", Copt **ḏoye* id.: Boh *ḏoi*, Shd *ḏoie.*
According to Copt, *-y* reflects a suffix while **g-* > Eg *ḏ-* before HS **o.*
LEC **gor-* "house" [1], "wall" [2]: Som *guri*, *guuri* [1], Or *goorroo* [2].
HEC **gor-* "shed": Bmb *goore*, Dar *gooʾre.*
Omot **gorr-* "house": Ome *guolle.*

957 *gor- "catch"

Eg *nḏry* "catch" (a), *nḏr* "seize" (XVIII).
n- is a prefix.
ECh **gwar-* "catch": Ndam *gōre*, Sok *gɔurē.*

958 *gor-gor- "plant, leaf"

Sem **gur-gur-* "plant": Akk *gurgurru.*
Eg *ḏrḏr* "leaf" (Amar).
WCh **gwar-gwar-* "kind of grass": Hs *gōragōra.*

Reduplication. HS **o* is corroborated by the palatalization in Eg. Cf. LEC **gor-* "fruit found in the forest" (Or *goraa*).

959 *goraf- "friend, servant"

WCh **ma-gwaraf-* "friend": Bol *gworavi*, Krk *nǯarafu*, Ngm *ngɛrfo*, Ngz *magirəf*, Bade *magərav-an*.

Unexpected *-i-* in Ngz.

Agaw **gwirrVf-* "servant": Bil *gʷəlf-aaraa*.

960 *goraᶜ- "throat, neck"

Sem **gVrᶜ-* "throat": Gz *gʷərᶜē*, Tgy *gʷärära*.

The vowel of the first syllable may be reconstructed as **-u-* causing labialization of the initial velar.

WCh **gwar(VH)-* "throat": Hs *-gwarō*.

In a compound.

CCh **gwar-* "neck": Tera *gura*, Pad *guara*, Mba *gur- ḍoy*.

SA **garaᶜ-* "throat": Saho *garaᶜ*, Afar *garaᶜ*.

Assimilation of vowels.

LEC **g[o]raᶜ-* "throat": Som *gawraᶜ*.

Is *-aw-* a reflex of **o*?

Cf. compounds with the same element in Agaw **gwir-gum-* "throat, neck" (Bil *gurgumaa*, Aun *gʷergum*, Dmt *gʷergem*) and SA **gur-dum-* "throat" (Saho *durgumaa*, Afar *gurdumee*).

961 *gorum- "young man"

Eg *ḏȝm* "young man" (MK).

Palatalization of **g-*.

WCh **gwarum-* "slave": Sura *kurom*, Mpn *krom*, Ang *kwarm*, Bol *ngaru*, Krk *nčarum*.

Prefix **nV-* in Bol and Krk.

LEC **gorom-* "young man": Som *gorom-saa*.

Assimilation of vowels.

Rift **garVm-* "boy": Irq *garma*.

Unexpected **-a-*.

962 *gorun-gorun- "knee"

ECh **gwarun-gwarun-* "knee": Sok *gorungorun-du*.

Rift **gurun-gu(n)d-* "knee": Irq *gurungura*, Alg *gurunguda*, Bur *guruguda*.

Haplology and dissimilation from **gurun-gurun-*.

Reduplication.

963 *gos- "fish"

Eg *ḏs* "kind of fish" (n).
Palatalization of **g-*.
WCh **gwasi-* "fish": Zem *giši*, Say *gwusi*, Bks *guše*, Sha *gwaše*.

Cf. ECh **gwas-* id. (pl.): Sib *gose* (sg. is *dose*!).

964 *gos- "be small"

Eg *nḏs* "small" (pyr).
Prefix **nV-*. Note the palatalization of **g-*.
CCh **gwasi-* "short": HF *gusi*, FKi *gwusu*, Gude *gwus*, Nza *gus*, FJ *gwus*.

965 *goy- "bird"

Eg *ḏwy.t* "kind of bird" (sarc).
-w- stands for a rounded vowel.
CCh **gya-* < **gVya-* "hen" [1], "bird" [2]: Gude *gyagya* [1], Mnd *giye* [2].
Reduplication in Gude. Secondary *-i-* under the influence of *-y-* in Mnd.

966 *goʒ- "woman"

Sem **ʿagūz-* "old woman": Arab *ʿagūz-*.
Cf. Arab *ʿgz* [*-u-*]"become old (of a woman)". Prefix **ʿa-*.
CCh **nV-gwaʒ-* "woman": Gis *ŋgos*, Bld *ŋgas*, Mtk *ŋgwaz*.
Prefix **nV-*. Unvoicing of final **-ʒ* in Gis and Bld.

Prefixes both in Sem and CCh.

967 *guʾ- "container"

Eg *gwɜ.t* "box" (MK).
-w- stands for a rounded vowel.
WCh **guʾ-gaʾ-* "pail": Sura *guugaa*.

Reduplication.
CCh *guʾ- ''pot'': Gul *guā*.
ECh *guʾ- ''basket'': Kwn *gu*.
Cf. reduplication in Tob *gīgū*.

968 *gub- ''fish''

Eg *gb.t* ''kind of fish'' (OK).
ECh **gub-* ''fish'': Tob *gubü*.

969 *gub- ''clothes''

Sem **gubb-* ''jubba, kind of clothes'': Arab *gubb-at-*, Tgr *gäbbät*.
CCh **gVb-* ''man's clothes'': Gava *gəbəya*.
Suffix *-əya*.

970 *gub- ''hole, well''

Sem **gubb-* ''well'' (n.) [1], ''moat'' [2]: Akk *gubbu* [1], Hbr *gēb* [2], Aram *gubbā* [2], Arab *gubb-* [1], Gz *gəbb* [2], Tgr *gəbb* [2].
ECh **gub-* ''hole'': Smr *gubu*.

971 *gub- ''burn''

Sem **gVb-* ''roast'': Akk *gubbubu*.
D stirpes in Akk.
LEC **gub-* ''burn'': Som *gub-*, Or *gub-*, Rnd *gub-*, Boni *kub-*.
Dhl *guβ-* ''burn'' (trans.).

972 *guĉ- ''fingernail''

CCh **nV-giŝ-* ''fingernail'': Gude *gəŝa*, Zime *ngiŝē*.
Prefix **nV-*. The above form may go back to **niguŝ-*.
Omot **guš-* ''fingernail, claw'': Dime *guš*, Ari *gəšaa*, Karo *gušo*.

Cf. ECh **gus-* id.: Kbl *guse-maŋ*.

973 *gud- ''house''

Sem **gudd-* ''djedda, town'': Arab *gudd-at-*.
CCh **gud-* ''house'': Glv *guda*.

LEC **god-* "hut": Or *godoo*.
HEC **god-* "place, cattle-pen": Bmb *godoo*, Dar *gooḍe*.
Wrz **kot-* "house": Hrs *koto*, Dob *koto*.

Tgy *g^{w}ada*, Amh *g^{w}ada* are borrowed from Cush.

974 *gud- "find, seek"

Sem **wVgVd-* "find, meet": Arab *wgd*.
Prefix **wV-*.
CCh **gud-* "seek anxiously": Mafa *gud-*.

975 *gud- "soil"

Sem **gad-* "soil, ground": Arab *gadad-*.
Secondary formation based on the otherwise unattested root.
Innovative vocalism.
ECh **gVd-* "fertile soil": Sok *gede*.
Assimilation of vowels in Sok.
Dhl *gud̲d̲e* "land".

976 *gudin- "axe, hoe"

ECh **gidin-H-* < **gudin-H-* "hoe": Kera *gidiŋ-*.
Assimilation of vowels.
LEC **gudin-* "axe": Som *gudin*.

Cf. HS **gadum-* "cut; axe, hoe".

977 *guᶜal- "divide"

Sem **gVᶜVl-* "divide": Arab *gᶜl*.
ECh **gal-* < **gVHal-* "part, side": Kera *gal*.
Nominal derivative of the original HS verb.
Agaw **guHal-* "divide": Kwr *golee*, Dmb *golee*, Kem *gualəy*.
Contraction in Kwr and Dmb.

978 *guᶜal- "insect"

Sem **guᶜal-* "scarabeus": Arab *guᶜal-*.
WCh **nV-gal-* "termite": Bks *^{n}gal*.

Prefix *nV-.

CCh *nV-gVl- ''termite'': Nz *ngəle*.

Prefix *nV-.

Contraction of *-uHa- > *-a- in Chadic.

979 *gulul- ''vessel''

Sem *gull- ''bowl'': Akk *gullu*, *gullatu*, Hbr *gullā*.
CCh *gulVl- ''straw bottle'': Msg *gullai*.
Rift *gudul- ''water jug'': Irq *gudulia*.
Dissimilation of liquids?

Etymologically identical with *gulul- ''ball''?

980 *gulul- ''ball''

Sem *gull- ''round object'': Arab *gull-at-*.
WCh *gulul- ''ball'': Hs *gulūlu*.

Derived from *gol- ''be round, go around''.

981 *gum- ''cut''

CCh *gum- ''cut off'' 1, ''carve'' 2: Mofu *ngəm* 1, Gis *ŋgom* 1, Mtk *gum* 2, Hld *gum-na* 2.
Prefix *nV- in Mofu.
Rift *goʔim- ''carve'': Irq *goʔim*.
Secondary inlaut *-ʔ-. The original form could be *gom- .

982 *gun- ''occiput''

CCh *gun- ''occiput, neck'': ZBt *guno*, Bud *ŋguni*, FG *gona*.
Prefix *nV- in Bud.
ECh *gun- ''occiput'': Smr *gəgəne*, Lele *tu-gna*, Ndam *da-gən*, Tum *gun kumu*, Kera *kənə-g*, Kwn *ku-kīn*.
Partial reduplication in Smr and Kwn. Prefixes in Lele and Ndam.
Omot *gon- ''nape'': Ome *gonno*.

983 *gup-/*gump- "knee"

ECh **gupi-* "knee": Smr *gube*, Tum *gub*, Ndam *gub*, Dng *gipi*, Mig *gippi*, Br *gifi*, Jegu *gifo*, Mubi *gip*.
Bed *gumba* "knee".
Omot **gumb-* "knee": Sezo *gubbi*, Nao *gum-ta*.

It seems that ECh lost the nasal element of *-*mp*- cluster. On the other hand, *-*mb*- cannot be reconstructed in order to explain Cush because of the unvoiced in ECh. A very difficult case. Cf. also HEC **gub-* "thigh" (Bmb *gub-eedi*)?

984 *gur- "house, place"

Berb **gVrur-* "enclosure" [1], "wall" [2], "place, yard" [3]: Nfs *a-grur* [1 2], Ahg *a-gror* [1], Ish *a-grur* [2], Tzr *a-grur* [3], Gua *ta-goror* [3], Sus *a-grur* [1 2], Kby *agrur* [1].
Partial reduplication.
WCh **gur-* "place": Hs *gure*.
CCh **gur-* "enclosure": Mba *guru*.

985 *gur- "pull"

Sem **gur-* "pull": Hbr *grr*, Arab *grr* [-*u*-], Jib *gerr*, Hss *ger*.
CCh **gur-* "pull": Mofu *-gur-*.

986 *gur- "ash"

Sem **gurār-* "hot ash": Akk *gurāru*.
Cf. Akk *kirāru* id. A secondary formation.
WCh **gur-* "ash": Sura *kuur*, Ang *kur*.
ECh **gur-* "coal": Ndm *gurē*.

Related to **gir-* "fire".

987 *gur- "hole"

Sem **gūr-* "cavity": Hbr *gōr*, Arab *gūr-at-*.
ECh **gur-* "hole": Smr *gurō*.
-ō goes back to *-*aw*-.

988 *guray- "hen"

Eg *gry* "poultry" (n).
The final *-y* may be a suffix, cf. ECh (Sbn).
CCh **yVgur-* "hen": Mnj *yugur*, Msg *yugur*, *igur*.
Metathesis of **gurVy-*. Assimilation of vowels in Msg.
ECh **gur(Vy)-*"hen, rooster": Sbn *gəray*.

989 *gut- "container"

Eg *gt* "box" (n).
CCh **guta-* "calabash": Bnn *gwətə*, BM *nguta*.
Prefix **nV-*.

990 *guy- "chin"

Eg *wgy.t* "lower jaw" (pyr).
w- is a vocalic sign.
CCh **guyi-* "chin, beard": Lmn *goyo*, Zgh *gwiye*, Glv *g^{w}iya*, Gava *g^{w}uya*, Nak *g^{w}iya*.

991 *guǯ- "stomach"

WCh **guǯ-* "internal organ (of a bird)": Hs *guǯiyā*.
ECh **giǯ-/*guǯ-* "belly": Ndm *gūǯ*, Kera *giidə*.
Agaw **gwiz-uk-* "stomach": Xmr *gizuu*, pl. *gizuk*, Xmt *gizuu*, Kwr *gwazgu*, Dmb *gozgw*, Kem *gwazguu*, Aun *gwezguii*.
Generalized pl. in **-uk-*?
SA **guǯ-* "belly": Afar *gudee*.
LEC **guǯ-* "intestines": Som *guudo*.

992 *güba^{c}- "mountain"

Sem **gab^{c}-/*gib^{c}-* "hill, height": Akk *gab^{ɔ}u*, Ug *gb^{c}*, Hbr *gib^{c}ā*, Amh *guba*.
a-vocalism seems to be secondary.
CCh **guḅa-* < **gubaH-* "mountain": Glv *γoba*, Gava *γuḅa*, Msm *gəbəy*.
LEC **gubb-* "summit": Or *gubba*.
HEC **gubb-* "highland": Bmb *gubba*.
Dhl *guβa* "plains".

993 *gül-/*gül-ib- "knee"

ECh **gVl-* "knee": Sok *der-gel-*, *bo-golo*.
der- and *bo-* are prefixes.
CCh **gVl-* "thigh": Mofu *gəl-aw*.
Msg *gurfa* "knee" may be connected with a different Chadic root for "knee", **gVr-*.
Agaw **gwillib-* "knee": Bil *girib*, Xmr *girb*, Xmt *gərəb*, Kwr *gerb*, Dmb *gulviɛ*, Kem *gərbii*, Dmt *gereb*, Aun *gerbii*.
SA **gulub-* "knee": Saho *gulub*, Afar *gulub*.
LEC **gilib-* "knee": Som *ǯilib*, Or *ǯilba*, Rnd *ǯələb*, Bay *gilib*.
HEC **gilub-/*gulub-* "knee": Sid *guluppo*, Dar *gulubo*, Had *gurubbo*, Kab *gulubi-ta*, Bmb *gilba*, Kmb *gulubi- ta*, Tmb *gulubi-ta*.
Wrz **kilVp-* "knee": Gaw *kilpayho*, Hrs *kilpayo*, Dob *kilpayo*.
Omot **gul(l)Vb-* "knee": Ome *gulb-ata*, Bwo *guubra*.
Metathesis in Bwo.
Dhl *gilli* "knee".

The dominating Cush form is derived from **gül-* with suffix **-ib-*.

994 *gün- "bend"

Sem **ḥVgin-* "become curved": Arab *ḥgn* [*-i-*].
Prefix **ḥV-*.
WCh **nV-gun-* "bend": Bol *ŋgūn*, Krk *ŋgun*, Wrj *ngunai*, Kry *ngun*.
Prefix **nV-*.

Prefixes in both branches of HS. Related to **ganaḥ-* "bend"?

995 *güriʾ- "stomach"

Sem **giriʾ-* "stomach (of a bird)": Arab *girīʾ-at-*, *giriyy- at-*.
ECh **gur-* "stomach": Lele *gūr-mu*, Mig *gur-mūḍu*.
Agaw **gir(r)-* "stomach" [1], "intestines" [2]: Bil *gir*, *ǯir* [1], Xmr *zillaa* [1], Xmt *ziilaa* [1], Kwr *ǯir* [1], Kem *ǯər* [2].
Palatalization of **g-* in most Agaw forms.
LEC **gereʾ-* "belly": Arb *gereʾ*.
Assimilation of vowels.
Rift **gurVʾ-* "belly": Irq *gura*, Alg *guraʾa*, Bur *guraʾa*.
Secondary **-a-* of the second syllable.

996 *gVbVl- "edge"

Sem **gVbul-* "edge": Phn *gbl*, Hbr *gᵉbūl*, Aram *gbl*.
Eg *gbꜣ* "side of a room" (westc.)
WCh **gVlVb-* "edge": Dera *gəlba*.
Metathesis.

997 *gVsVy- "go, move"

Sem **gīš-* "go (home)": Akk *gâšu*.
Metathesis.
Eg *gsy* "run" (XVIII).

Derived from **gas-* "move".

998 *gVwVb-/*gVyVb- "call, answer"

Sem **gūb-* "answer": Aram *gawwēb*, Arab *gwb*, Hss *yewāb*.
ECh **gyab-* < **gVyVb-* "call": Nch *geba*.

Consonantal alternation **-w-* ~ **-y-*.

999 *gVwun- "be black"

Sem **gūn-* "be black": Arab *gwn* [*-u-*].
If not related to Aram *gawnā* "color" borrowed from Iranian.
WCh **[wV]gun-* "dirty": Ang *gun*.

An alternative reconstruction is **wVgun-*.

1000 *gVʒim- "cut"

Sem **gVzim-* "cut": Hbr *gzm*, Arab *gzm* [*-i-*].
Cf. Arab *gḏm* id.
Berb **gVʒVm-* "cut": Izy *gezzem*, Kby *egzem*.

*ġ

1001 *ġa'-/*ġo'- "stone"

Eg *ʿꜣ.t* "stone" (OK).
WCh **ġay-* < **ġa'i-* "rock, stone": Gera *giiwi*, Glm *gigai*, Grm *gii*, Sha *wa-ḥay*, DB *hayi*.

Partial reduplication in Glm. Prefix in Sha.

CCh *γwaʾ- "mountain": Ngw *γwa*, Lmn *χwa*, Zgh *χwaʾa*, Glv *γwa*.

Alternation *a ~ *o?

1002 *ġabur- "dust"

Sem *ġabar- "dust": Arab *ġabar-at-*, *ġubār-*, *ġubr-at-*, Hss *ġebār*.

Seconary vocalism in *ġubār-*, *ġubr-at-*. *-u- > *-a- after a labial is regular.

WCh *ġabVr- "dust": Hs *habrā*.

CCh *γurVḇ- "sand": Mofu *ma-hurḇay*.

Metathesis. Secondary emphatization of *-b-* > *-ḇ-* influenced by the initial *γ.

Derived from *bur- "earth, sand"?

1003 *ġaḳ- "crow"

Sem *ġāḳ- "raven": Arab *ġāq-*.

WCh *ġaġ- < *ġaḳ- "crow": Paa *gāga*.

Assimilation.

CCh *γak- "crow": Dgh *γaga*, Gis *mu-ghak*, *ma-gaga*, Mofu *mangahak*, Log *γake*, Bud *ngage*.

Mofu reflects *γaHak-, cf. ECh. Prefix *ma(n)- in Gis and Mofu.

ECh *gak- "crow": Mubi *gak*, Bid *gaaga*, Kwn *gāga*.

Bid may reflect *gaHak-.

Dhl *ʾaak'ak'o* "crow".

Partial reduplication.

A descriptive stem, possibly, of reduplicative nature (*ġaḳ- < *ġaġ-, cf. WCh).

1004 *ġal- "kill"

Sem *ġūl- "make smb. perish quickly": Arab *ġwl* [-*u*-].

Based on the original *ġVl-.

CCh *γal- "kill": Log *γəla*, Bud *hala*.

1005 *ġaluç̌-/*ġiluç̌- "be heavy, be thick"

Sem **ġaliṯ-/*ġaluṯ-* "be fat, be bulky": Arab *ġlẓ* [*-i-*, *-u-*], Hss *ġeleẓ*, Mhr *ġelayẓ*.
SA **ʿilVs-* "heavy": Afar *ʿilsi*.
LEC **ʿiluč-/*ʿuluč-* "heavy": Som *ʿulus*, Or *ʿulf-ata*, Kon *uls*, Arb *ilč-iyda*.
**ʿuluč-* from **ʿiluč-* as a result of the assimilation of vowels. Alternation **a* ~ **i*. Cush forms reflect HS **ġiluc-* with an irregular correspondence of **c* to HS **ç̌* > **ṯ*.

1006 *ġar- "army, raid"

Sem **ġār-* "army": Arab *ġār-*.
WCh **ġar-* "raid": Hs *harā*.

1007 *ġar- "skin"

Sem **ġar-* "skin, hide, fur": Ug *ġr*, Hbr *ʿor*.
Cf. Hss *ġerēret* "bag, sack"?
CCh **γar-* "skin": Gis *gar-ak*.
Suffix *-ak* in Gis.
ECh **gar-* "skin": Smr *gare*, Ndam *gari*.

1008 *ġarub- "darkness"

Sem **ġarb-* "sunset, evening": Akk *erbu*, Hbr *ʿereb*, Gz *ʿarab*, Hss *ġarb*.
Cf. **ġVrVb-* "be dark": Arab *ġrb*, Gz *ʿrb*.
WCh **rubaH-* "darkness": Sura *rap*, Ang *rāp*, Say *rub-gir*, Dwot *rup-ǯur*.
Metathesis.
CCh **rub-* < **rubVH-* "darkness": Mtk *ruva*.
Metathesis.

Note that **ġurab-* "raven, crow" and **ġarub-* "darkness" may be etymologically connected. Cf. Slav **vornъ* "raven, crow" = **vornъ* "black".

1009 *ġawaʾ- "deceive"

Sem **ġūʾ-* "deceive, tempt": Arab *ġwʾ* [*-a-*].
CCh **γaw-* "lie" (n.): Chb *χawi*.
Deverbative formation.

1010 *ġawaġ- "locust"

Sem **ġawġ-aʾ-* "locust (beginning to fly)": Arab *ġawġāʾ-*.
WCh **nV-ġwaġ-* < **nV-ġVwaġ-* "locust": Ang *gwok*, Ank *ngok*.
Prefix **nV-*.

Reduplication?

1011 *ġaʒ-/*ġuʒ- "keep, gather"

Sem **ġuz-* "keep, cling to": Arab *ġzz* [*-u-*].
CCh **γaʒ-* "collect, gather (in big amounts)": Mafa *haz-*.

Alternation **a* ~ **u*.

1012 *ġer- "town"

Sem **ġīr-* "town": Hbr *ʿīr*.
ECh **gyar-* "house" [1], "village" [2]: Dng *ger* [1], Mig *ger* [1], Jegu *gēr* [2], Mubi *gir* [1], Bid *geeru* [1], Jegu *geer* [2].
Cf. partial reduplication in Mig *gēger* "village".

1013 *ġič- "be bad"

Sem **ġaṯ-/*ġiṯ-* "be thin, be bad": Arab *ġṯṯ* [*-a-*, *-i-*].
Traces of *a*-grade?
CCh **γič-* "be insufficient": Mafa *hič-*.

1014 *ġor- "punish"

WCh **ġwar-* "discipline (a person), break in (a horse)": Hs *hōrā*.
Rift **ḫwar-* "beat hard" [1], punish" [2]: Irq *ḫwar-* [1], Asa *har-* [2].

1015 *ġor- "crow"

WCh **ġwar-* "crow": Sura *gɔɔrɔɔ*.

CCh *γVr-* "crow"; Glv *(γaγa-)χəra*.
ECh **gVr-* "crow": Ndam *ʾagra*.
Agaw **χur-* "crow": Kem *χorai*.
Rift **ḫwaʾar-* "crow": Irq *ḫwaʾari*, Bur - *ḫwarariya*, Asa *ḫoḫoraʾi*.
Secondary inlaut laryngeal.

Descriptive root.

1016 *ġuf- "grain, flour"

Sem **ġVpVy-* "clean, hull (grain)": Arab *ġfy*.
Denominative verb.
CCh **γup-* "flour": FK *uγupu*, FG *χupwu*, Glv *ʾaχupiya*, Zgh *kufe*, Gava *χupiya*, Nak *χaχpiya*, Mtk *gwufa*, Log *mu-χbī*.
Partial reduplication in Nak.

1017 *ġufir- "antelope"

Sem **ġupr-* "young gazelle" [1], "young of deer" [2]: Hbr *ʿōper* [1], Arab *ġufr-* [2].
WCh **fir-* < **ġVfir-* "antelope": Ang *fir*.

Any connection with MMs **ʾafor-* "antelope" (Asa *ʾofor-ok*, Kwz *aful-atu*)?

1018 *ġulum- "young man"

Sem **ġulām-* "young man, young slave": Hbr *ʿelem*, Aram (Syr) *ʿelaymō*, Arab *ġulām-*.
**u* > **a* in contact with a labial. Arab *ġlm* "be lascivous" may be a secondary derivative from the present noun.
ECh **hulum-* < **ġulum-* "man": Kera *hulum*.
Note the irregular development of the initial **ġ-*.

Cf. HS **ġol-* > CCh **γwal-* "child": Log *γ'oli*, Bud *ūli*?

1019 *ġum- "cover, shut"

Sem **ġum-* "cover": Arab *ġmm* [-*u*-].
WCh **ġum-* "shut": Mnt *gwum*.

1020 *ġurab- "raven, crow"

Sem *ġurāb- "raven" [1], "Egyptian vulture" [2]: Arab ġurāb- [1], Hss ye-ġerēb [1], Mhr yeġerayb [1], Shh εġereb [1], Soq aʕreb [2].

Different vocalism is represented in Akk āribu, Hbr ʕōreb.

ECh *gurVb- "crow": Jegu gurb-aak.

HEC *gurub- "crow": Bmb gurruba.

Assimilation of vowels.

Cf. CCh *γVrVb- "dove" (HGh χərbe)? The root is derived from *ġor- "crow".

1021 *ġural- "genitals"

Sem *ġurl- "foreskin": Akk urulla, Hbr ʕorlā, Aram (Syr) ʕurlūtō, Arab ġurl-at-.

Assimilation of vowels.

ECh *gural- "testicles": Mubi gurli, Brg gulaali, Jegu gulle, Dng gulla, Bid gulal, Mig golile.

Assimilation to *gulal- in most languages.

Rift *gulal- "testicles" (Kwz gulala, Asa gulala) was borrowed from ECh.

1022 *ġuwuṭ- "dig"

Sem *ġūṭ- "dig": Arab ġwṭ [-u-].

WCh *ġu[w]uṭ- "dig, scratch": Ngz guutu.

CCh *nV-γuṭ- "dig": Gude ŋguḍ-, Mwl uŋgəḍi, Gudu guḍān.

Prefix *nV-. Note that in Gudu the root is preserved without a prefix.

1023 *ġVpar- "clothes"

Sem *ġVpar- "kind of clothes": Akk epartu.

Cf. Akk apāru, epēru "cover the head", Arab ġfr "cover".

Eg ʕpr "clothes" (gr).

A cultural *Wanderwort*?

1024 *ġūr- "raid, plunder"

Sem **ġVwVr-* "raid, attack" (v.): Arab *ġwr*, Hss *šew-ġōr*.
Eg *ᶜwȝy* "plunder".
**-r-* > Eg *-ȝ-*
CCh **γVr-* "kill": Mofu *hər*.

Related to **ġar-* "army, raid".

*ᶜ

1025 *ᶜab- "be big"

Sem **ᶜVbVy-* "be thick" [1], "be big" [2]: Akk *ebû* [1], Hbr *ᶜābe* [1], Aram (Syr) *ʾebī* [2], Arab *ᶜby* [1], Gz *ᶜabiy* [2].
Formation based on **ᶜVb-*.
HEC **ᶜabb-* "be big": Kmb *abba*.

1026 *ᶜab- "tree"

Eg *ᶜȝb* "tree" (pyr).
-ȝ- stands for a vowel.
ECh **ʾab-* "tree": Brg *ʾabi*.

1027 *ᶜab- "drink"

Sem **ᶜVb-* "gulp, swallow in one draught": Arab *ᶜbb*.
SA **ᶜab-/*ᶜub-* "drink": Afar *-aᶜab-*, *-aᶜub-*, Saho *-ōᶜob-*.
LEC **ᶜabb-* "drink": Som *ᶜabb-*.

Cf. CCh **Hub-wak-* "drink": Nak *χuboka*?

1028 *ᶜabal- "be big, be thick"

Sem **ᶜVbal-/*ᶜVbul-* "be thick": Arab *ᶜbl* [*-a-*, *-u-*].
Secondary **-u-*.
WCh **baHal-* "big" [1], "be abundant" [2]: Bks *ḅal* [1], DB *ḅal* [2].
Metathesis.
ECh **bVHVl-* "big": Smr *ḅəllē*, Ndm *ḅə:l*.

Metathesis.

Cf. also partial reduplications in CCh **ba-bal-* "big" (Msg *bobolo*) and ECh **bwa-bVl-* "big" (Kera *boblo*).

1029 *ᶜabod- "slave"

Sem **ᶜabd-* "slave": Hbr *ᶜebed*, Aram (Syr) *ᶜabdō*, Arab *ᶜabd-*, SAr *ᶜbd*.
**ᶜVbVd-* "work" (v.) seems to be a denominative.
WCh **bawad-* < **baHwad-* "slave": Zar *bad-am*, Say *bawəd-n*.
Zar *-a-* is a result of contraction. Metathesis.
CCh **buḍ-* < **buHVd-* "slave": Lmn *vəḍa*, Dgh *vḍa*, Zgh *vuḍa*.
Metathesis.

An alternative reconstruction is **baᶜod-*.

1030 *ᶜabül- "leaf"

Sem **ᶜVbil-* "fall (of leaves)": Arab *ᶜbl* [*-i-*].
Denominative verb.
CCh **bVʾul-* "grass, leaf": Zgh *ḅule*.
LEC **baHal-* "leaf": Or *baala*, Arb *baal*.
Metathesis and assimilation of vowels.

Cf. also WCh **bVl-* "flower" (Dera *bəlei*) and ECh **bil-* "flower, grass, leaf" (Kwn *bə:le*, Mubi *bil-bil-ič*, Mkk *-bile*).

1031 *ᶜacem- "leg"

Eg *smᶜ* "leg (of falcon)" (pyr).
Metathesis.
WCh **ᶜacVm-* "leg": Kry *cuma-kə*, Diri *ašəma*, Paa *cim-un*, Siri *cuma*, Mbu *cəma*, Pol *asəm*, *asən*, Zem *asəm*, Kir *wasəm*.
CCh **cyam-* "leg": LPe *šem*, Zime *sam*, Msm *sem*, Bnn *siyema*.
First syllable lost.

Phonetic variant of **ᶜač̣em-* "bone"?

1032 *ᶜacib- "pile up"

WCh **(HV)cib-* "pile up": Hs *ç̣iba*.

Agaw *ᵓacib- ''pile up'': Bil *ašib-*.
Note *ᵓ- as one of two reflexes of HS *ᶜ- in Agaw.
SA *ᶜasab- ''add'': Saho *ᶜasab-*.
Assimilation of vowels.

1033 *ᶜaçar- ''year''

Sem *ᶜaṣr- ''time, age'': Arab *ᶜaṣr-*.
WCh *çar- ''year'': Tng *sɔr*.
CCh *car- ''time'': Glv *sar-ta*, Mnd *sar-te*.

*ᶜa- may be a prefix.

1034 *ᶜačuč- ''insect''

Sem *ᶜaṯṯ- ''moth'': Akk *ašāšu*, Hbr *ᶜāš*, Aram *ᶜaššā*.
Assimilation of vowels.
WCh *ᶜučač- ''ant'': DB *ᵓušaaš*.
CCh *čači- ''louse'': Mnd *čača*, Glv *čača*, Zgh *čiči*, Glv *cica*.
Loss of the initial laryngeal.
ECh *ᵓačuč- ''ant'': Kera *ačuči*.

Metathesis of vowels in WCh and CCh.

1035 *ᶜaĉab- ''container''

Sem *ᶜaṱab- ''vessel'': Hbr *ᶜaṣab*, Arab *ᶜaẓab-*.
WCh *čab- ''bag'': Ang *čep*.
LEC *çaHab- ''bowl'': Or *çaabii*.
Metathesis.

1036 *ᶜaĉem- ''bone''

Sem *ᶜaṱm- ''spine'' 1, ''bone'' 2, ''back'' 3: Akk *eṣem-sēru* 1, Ug *ᶜẓm* 2, Hbr *ᶜeṣem* 2, Aram (Jud) *ᶜiṭmā* 2, Arab *ᶜaẓm-* 2, Gz *ᶜäṣm* 2, Hss *ᵓaẓemet* 3, Mhr *ᵓāẓemēt* 3.
WCh *čyam- ''bone'' 1, ''shin-bone'' 2: Brw *cem* 1, Fyer *sem* 2.
No traces of the anlaut laryngeal.

*ᶜa- may be a prefix.

1037 *ᶜaĉ- "bird"

Eg *ᶜš3* "kind of bird" (MK).
-3 stands for a vowel.
WCh **yaĉi-* "bird": Say *yaŝi*, Buli *iŝ*, Geji *yaẑi*.
**y-* < **H-*.
CCh **ʾaŝ-* "turtle dove": Chb *ʾaẑa*.

1038 *ᶜaĉer- "clan, member of the clan"

Sem **ᶜaŝīr-* "clan" [1], "friend" [2], "family" [3]: Arab *ᶜašīr-* [1 2 3], SAr *ᶜŝr-t* [1].
WCh **HVĉ(y)ar-* "person of the same age" [1], "friend" [2]: Hs *çārā* [1], Sura *šār* [2], Ang *šēr* [2], Mnt *čai-na* [2], Dera *šer* [2], Tng *sɛr* [2], Glm *čor* [2].

Cf. Eg *šr*, *šry* "friend" (pyr) reflecting no laryngeal in the anlaut.

1039 *ᶜaĉ̣- "bite"

Sem **ᶜaṣ̂-* "bite": Arab *ᶜḍḍ* [*-a-*].
WCh **ᶜaĉ̣wa-* "bite" [1], "eat" [2]: Hs *gāçā* [1], Sura *at* [1], Ang *at* [1], Krk *haḍu-* [2], Dera *aʾḍe* [2], Tng *ʾeḍ-* [2], Ngm *haḍ-* [2], Bele *oḍu-* [2], Krf *aḍḍu-* [2], Gera *haḍ-* [2], Glm *ary-* [2], Grm *aḍ-* [2], Fyer *ʾet-* [2], Klr *wod* [1].

Cf. Eg *wšᶜ* "eat, chew" (med)?

1040 *ᶜaĉ̣ed- "hand, arm"

Sem **ᶜaṣ̂id-/*ᶜaṣ̂ud-* "arm": Arab *ᶜaḍid-*, *ᶜaḍud-*.
CCh **ŝyaḍa-* "hand, arm": Log *ŝaḍe*, Gul *χ̂ede*, Kus *sedē*.
From **(HV)ĉ̣ed-*, with a shift of emphatization.

1041 *ᶜaĉ̣ib- "sharp weapon"

Sem **ᶜaṣ̂b-* "sabre": Arab *ᶜaḍb-*.
ECh **cib-* "knife": Lele *sibi*, Kwn *sibi*.
Initial **HV-* is lost.

**ᶜa-* may be a prefix.

1042 *ᶜad- "go"

Sem *ᶜ*adaw*- "run" [1], "cross over, pass by" [2]: Arab ᶜ*dw* [-*u*-] [1], Gz ᶜ*dw* [2].
Based on *ᶜ*ad*-.
ECh *ʾ*ad*- "follow" [1], "go out" [2]: Dng *ā*ḍ*e* [1], Mkk ʾ*u*ḍḍ*e* [2].
Emphatization caused by the anlaut laryngeal *-ᶜ- > *- ʾ-.
LEC *ʾ*ad*- "go": Som *aad*-.
HEC **had*- "go": Sid *haadi*.
Note **h*- < *ᶜ-.
Omot *ʾ*a*ḍ- "go": Ome *aa*ḍ-, Ari *ada*.
Emphatic **d* may reflect an old *ᶜ > *ʾ.
Rift *ᶜ*ad*- "go, tread": Irq *ada-ha*, Asa *adi*.

Berb *ᶜ*Vd*- "pass" (Kby ᶜ*eddi*) may be borrowed from Arab.

1043 *ᶜadas- "bean, seed"

Sem *ᶜ*adaš*- "lentil": Hbr ᶜ*ᵃdāšā*, Arab ᶜ*adas*-.
CCh **HVda[s]*- "seed": Bch ḍ*as-ito*.
If not **daʒ*-, cf. Mwl *dazo* id.

1044 *ᶜadaw- "fish"

Eg ᶜ*dw*, ᶜ*ȝdw* "kind of fish" (XVIII).
ECh **daw*- "fish": Tum *doo*, Kwn *do*.
From **HVdaw*-?

*ᶜ*a*- may be a prefix.

1045 *ᶜadil- "be true, be just"

Sem *ᶜ*Vdil*- "be just": Arab ᶜ*dl* [-*i*-].
CCh **diyal*- < **diHal*- "truth": Bch *diyalo*, Daba *ma-delele*.
Metathesis. Partial reduplication and prefix **ma*- in Daba.

An alternative reconstruction is **di*ᶜ*al*-.

1046 *ᶜaf- "grass, plant"

Sem *ᶜ*ap*- "rush, reed": Akk *apu*.
Eg ᶜ*f.t* "kind of plant" (med).
CCh *ʾ*af*- "grass": Mba ʾ*af*.

1047 *ˤaf- "health"

Sem *ˤ*āpiy*- "health": Arab ˤ*āfiy-at*-, Hss ʾ*āfyet*, Mhr ʾ*āfyēt*, Shh ˤ*afyet*.
ECh *ʾ*af*- "health": Mubi *afi*.

Both Sem and ECh may be deverbative formations going back to HS *ˤ*uf*- "be healthy".

1048 *ˤafur- "dust, sand"

Sem *ˤ*apar*- "dust, earth": Akk *eperu*, Ug ˤ*pr*, Hbr ˤ*āpār*, Aram (Syr) ˤ*aprō*, Arab ˤ*afar*-, ˤ*afr*-, Har *afär*.
*-*u*- > *-*a*- after a labial.
CCh **Hafur*- "ground": Boka *fur-ta*, Gaa *fər-ta*, Mafa *vara*.
In Mafa *v*- < **H(V)f*-.
Derived from **far*- "clay, earth".

1049 *ˤafaw-/*ˤafay- "leaf, plant"

Sem *ˤ*upVy*- "twig, foliage": Hbr ˤ*opī*.
Secondary *-*u*-.
Eg ˤ*fꜣy.t* "kind of plant" (med).
-*ꜣ*- stands for *-*a*-.
WCh *ˤ*af*-ˤ*afaw*- "leaf": Klr ʾ*afafaw*.
Partial reduplication.

Derived from *ˤ*af*- "grass, plant". Consonantal alternation *-*w*- ~ *-*y*-.

1050 *ˤafüc̣- "be bitter"

Sem *ˤ*apiṣ*- "bitter": Arab ˤ*afiṣ*-.
CCh **fuc*- "salt": Ngw *fəca*.
Hwn reflects a CCh word for ash.

*ˤ*a*- may be a prefix.

1051 *ˤag- "strike"

Eg ˤ*ꜣg* "strike" (MK).
-*ꜣ*- reflects HS *-*a*-.
ECh *ʾ*ag*- "drum" (v.) [1], "beat" [2]: Ndm *age* [1], Mkk ʾ*igg*- [2].

1052 *ᶜagom- "tree"

Sem *ᶜ*agm-* "palm tree": Arab ᶜ*agm-at-*.
WCh *ᶜ*agwam-* "mahogany" [1], "Balantes egypt." [2]: Miya *agam* [2], Jmb *agwama* [1], Ngz *aguma-k* [1].
LEC *ʾ*agam-* "kind of bush": Or *agam-sa*.
Assimilation of vowels.

Cf. CCh **gwagwam-* < *ᶜ*agwam-* "bread tree" (Msg *gogom*) with assimilation ᶜ – *g* > *g* – *g*.

1053 *ᶜagor- "bird"

Sem *ᶜ*agūr-* "crane": Hbr ᶜ*āgūr*.
ECh **gwar-* "heron": Smr *gwara*.
No traces of the anlaut laryngeal.

1054 *ᶜaḥ- "earth, field"

Eg ᶜ*ḥ.t* "field" (OK).
CCh **χaχ-* "earth" [1], "clay" [2]: Gbn *χaχa* [1], FKi *χaχəy* [1], Gis *hahay* [2].
Assimilation of laryngeals.

1055 *ᶜak- "be hot; fire"

Sem *ᶜ*ik-*/*ᶜ*uk-* "be hot": Arab ᶜ*kk* [*-i-*, *-u-*].
Secondary vocalism?
WCh *ᶜ*akwa-* "fire": Diri *akuwa*, Miya *aku*, Cagu *ākwe*, Jmb *akwa*, Ngz *aka*.
CCh *ʾ*Vkk-* "hot": Log *kku*.
ECh *ʾ*ak(k)wa-* "fire": Mig *okko*, Jegu ʾ*ook*. Bid *ako*, Brg ʾ*aku*, Sok *oko*.
Nominal formation.

1056 *ᶜaḳ- "know, see"

Eg ᶜ*ḳ* "learn" (a).
Agaw *ʾ*aḳ-* "see, know": Kwr *aχ-*, Dmb *aχ-*, Kem *aχ-*, Aun *-aq-*, Dmt *-aḳ-*.
LEC **Hak-* "know" [1], "see" [2]: Gel *ɔk-* [1], Kon *-ak-* , *-yak-* [2], Bus *haake* [2], Gdl *-ak*, *-aki* [2].

Irregular laryngeal reflexes as well as unexpected non-emphatic *-*k*-. Is this really a continuation of *ᶜ*aḳ*-?

1057 *ᶜaḳab- "hill, stone"

Sem *ᶜ*aḳab*- "hill": Arab ᶜ*aqab-at*-.
WCh **kaḅ*- < **ḳab*- "polishing stone": DB *kaḅu*.
Shift of emphatization.

*ᶜ*a*- may be a prefix. Semantically dubious.

1058 *ᶜaḳid- "bind, spin"

Sem *ᶜ*Vḳid*- "bind" [1], "knot" [2]: Hbr ᶜ*qd* [1], Arab ᶜ*qd* [-*i*-] [2].
CCh **kiyad*- < **kiHad*- "plait": Bnn *kiyedu*.
Metathesis.
ECh **kVd*- "untie": Ndam *kədə*.
From **kVHVd*- as in CCH?

An alternative reconstruction is **ḳi*ᶜ*ad*-.

1059 *ᶜal- "leaf"

Sem *ᶜ*al*- "leaf, foliage": Hbr ᶜ*āle*, Aram ᶜ*elw*- (Syr).
WCh *ᶜ*al*- "leaf": Pero *alaw*, Jmb *alu-hu*.

1060 *ᶜal- "rise"

Sem *ᶜ*VlVy*- "rise, climb": Hbr ᶜ*ly*.
Based on biconsonantal *ᶜ*Vl*-.
Berb *ʾ*al*- "be suspended": Ahg *ali*.
CCh *ʾ*al*- "jump": Masa *halla*.
Irregular Masa *h*-.
ECh *ʾ*al*- "climb": Kwn *ale*, Kera *li*.

Related to *ᶜ*al*- "top".

1061 *ᶜal- "top"

Sem *ᶜ*al*- "top, height, upper part": Hbr ᶜ*āl*, Arab ᶜ*al*-.
SA *ʾ*al*- "mountain": Saho ʾ*al*.

LEC *ᶜ*al-* "mountain": Som ᶜ*al-*, Rnd *ḥal-*.
Note Rnd *ḥ-*.

1062 *ᶜalaḳ- "tie, untie"

Sem *ᶜ*Vlaḳ-* "be attached" [1], "hang, be suspended": Arab ᶜ*lq* [-*a*-] [1], Hss ᶜ*ayleq* [2].
WCh **laḳ-* "untie": Dera *lake*.

*ᶜ*a-* may be a prefix.

1063 *ᶜalal- "drink, chew"

Sem *ᶜ*VlVl-* "drink for the second time": Arab ᶜ*ll*.
LEC 2*ᶜ*alal-* "chew": Som ᶜ*alaal-*, Kns *alal-*, Gid *alal-*.

Reduplication?

1064 *ᶜam- "eat"

Eg ᶜ*m* "swallow" (n).
Rift *ʾ*am-* "chew": Kwz *am-*.
Cf. Irq *ayim* id.

Descriptive stem.

1065 *ᶜam- "relative, friend"

Sem *ᶜ*amm-* "relative" [1], "uncle" [2], "ancestor" [3]: Hbr ᶜ*am* [1], Arab ᶜ*amm-* [2], Hss ʾ*ōm* [3], Mhr ʾ*ōm* [3], Shh ᶜ*om* [3].
CCh *ʾ*wam-* < *ʾ*amu-* "guest": Bch ʾ*omey*, Nz *womɛ*.
Dhl ʾ*ame* "uncle".

1066 *ᶜam- "people"

Sem *ᶜ*amm-* "people" [1], "crowd" [2]: Akk *ummānu* [1], Hbr ᶜ*am* [1], Arab ᶜ*amm-* [2].
Derivative in Akk.
Rift *ʾ*Vm-* "people, crowd": Irq *imi*, Alg *imi*.
Assimilation of vowels.

Connected with *ᶜ*am-* "relative, friend"?

1067 *ᶜamVw- "plant"

Sem *ᶜamVw- "kind of plant": Akk *amû*.
Cf. Arab *ᶜam-at-* id.
Eg *ᶜȝmw.t* "field plant" (XVIII).
-ȝ- stands for *-a-.

1068 *ᶜan- "be tired, be ill"

Sem *ᶜVnaʾ-/*ᶜVnay- "be tired": Arab *ᶜnʾ*, *ᶜny* [-a-].
Based on *ᶜan-.
WCh *ᶜan- "ache" (v.): Bks *han*.
ECh *ʾani- "illness": Mkk *ʾeni*.
Mkk *-e-* < *-a- under the influence of *-i*.

Related to *ᶜVnaw-/*ᶜVnay- "work, make"?

1069 *ᶜan-/*ᶜin- "exist"

Sem *ᶜin-/*ᶜun- "appear": Arab *ᶜnn* [-i-, -u-].
Agaw *ʾan-/*ʾin- "be": Bil *en-*, *in-*, Xmr *an-*, Kwr *en-*.
Bed *ʾan-* "be".
SA *ʾan-/*ʾin- "be": Saho *-in(n)-*, *-an-*.
HEC *yon- "be": Had *yon-*, Kmb *yon-*.
Phonetically not quite clear. Probably, from *ʾi-ʾon-?

1070 *ᶜanaʒ- "goat, ram"

Sem *ᶜanz- "she-goat": Akk *enzu*, Ug *ᶜz*, Hbr *ᶜēz*, Aram (Syr) *ᶜezzā*, Arab *ᶜanz-*.
WCh *ᶜaʒan- "ram": Bks *ʾazan*.
Metathesis.

An alternative reconstruction is *ᶜaʒan-.

1071 *ᶜanduk- "navel, nipple"

WCh *HVnduk- "heart": Fyer *ⁿduk*.
CCh *bu-ʾinduk- "heart, chest": Lame *vəinduku*, *vunḍuku*.
Prefix *bu-. The root vowel *-i- is not clear.
SA *hondub- "navel": Saho *hondub*, Afar *hondub*.
Unexpected *-b and irregular *h-*. A loanword?

HEC *mudukk- < *mu-ˀVdu(n)k-, *haṇḍur- "navel": Sid *mudukko*, Bmb *haṇḍura*.

Prefix *mu- in Sid. Bmb looks like a loanword (from SA?).

Wrz *ᶜadunk- "nipple, breast": War *aadunku*, Gaw *ᶜaḍunko*, Cam *aḍunku*.

*d > ḍ is influenced by *ᶜ-.

Rift *mudung- < *mu-ˀVdung- "navel": Gor *murungu*, Alg *murungu*.

In Cush the prototype is reconstructed as *ᶜadunk- which may be also an alternative HS reconstruction. At least, some of the Cush forms were borrowed and reborrowed. A very irregular and problematic root.

1072 *ᶜanon- "breast, chest"

Eg *ᶜnn.t* "part of the body" (pyr).

The meaning is not definite.

WCh *nwan- "breast": Hs *nōno*.

From *HVnwan-.

HEC *ˀanon- "breast": Sid *ununa*, *unuuna*, Dar *unuuna*, Had *anoona*, Ala *onoona*, Bmb *ununa*, Kmb *anuuna*.

Various assimilations of vowels in individual languages.

1073 *ᶜar- "stone, rock"

Eg *ᶜr* "small stone" (n).

Cf. also *ᶜꜣ.t* "precious stone" (a).

ECh *ˀar- "rock": Kbl *arra*.

1074 *ᶜareḳ- "see, understand"

Eg *ᶜrḳ* "understand" (XVIII).

Agaw *ˀariḳ- "understand, know": Xmr *areḳ-*, Xmt *arek*, *aarqʷ*.

LEC *ˀare[ḳ]- "see": Som *ark-*, *areg-*, Or *arga*, Boni *ark-*, Gel *argiyɛ*.

Unexpected reflexes of *ḳ.

1075 *ˀariw- "tree"

Eg *ᶜrw* "tree" (med).

WCh *ᶜariway- "tree": Bol *rewe*, Tng *riya*, Ngm *roya*, Siri *aruwai*, Kry *riwai*.

Derivative in *-ay-*.

CCh *ˀariway- "tamarind": Gava *riwe*, Zgh *arwe*, Nak *iriwey*.

Derivative in *-ay-*. Assimilation of vowels in Nak.

1076 *aṭuw- "give, pay"

Sem *ˁVṭVw- "give (a present)": Arab *ˁṭw*.

ECh *ˀatuw- "pay": Ndm *atuwe*.

1077 *ˁaw- "goat, bull"

Eg *ˁw.t* "sheep and goats" (OK).

CCh *ˀaw- "she-goat": Gis *ˀaw*, Bld *ˀawa*.

Rift *ˀaw- "bull": Irq *aw*, Alg *aw*, Bur *aw*.

1078 *ˁawag- "roast"

Eg *ˁwg* "roast" (BD).

ECh *waHag- "roast, burn": Ndam *woga*, Kwn *wage*, Ndam *wuga*, Dng *ogiye*, Tum *waag*.

Metathesis.

*ˁV- may be a prefix. Cf. also Dhl *hag*^{w}- "boil" < *HagVw-.

1079 *ˁawan- "palm tree"

Sem *ˁawān- "big palm": Arab *ˁawān-at-*.

CCh *hawan-H- "date palm": Gis *huwaŋ*, Mafa *hawan*.

Unexpected initial *h-. Probably, the original form contained a prefix: *ha-ˁawan-? Secondary *-u-* in Gis.

1080 *ˁawar- "give back, return"

Sem *ˁūr- "pay debts": Arab *ˁwr* [-u-].

WCh *waHar- "give back, lend": Tng *warɛ*, DB *weer*, Bol *ˀar*.

Metathesis.

An alternative reconstruction is *waˁar-.

1081 *ᶜawar-/*ᶜayar- "donkey"

Sem *ᶜayr- "donkey" [1], "young donkey" [2]: Ug ᶜr [1], Hbr ᶜayir [2], Aram ᶜēr- [1], Arab ᶜayr- [1].
Eg ᶜꜣ "donkey" (OK).
Sem loanword? In any case, the inlaut sonant is not graphically expressed. -ꜣ- < *-r-.
Omot *ʔawar- "horse": Kaf *awaroo*, Mao *wɔɔre*.

Consonantal alternation *-w- ~ *-y-.

1082 *ᶜawil- "genitals"

WCh *yawil- < *ᶜawil- "testicles" [1], "vulva" [2]: Krk ʔ*ilaa* [1], Dera *yiwulu* [1], Say *wəla* [1], Fyer *wul* [2].
Secondary vocalism in Dera.
Bed ʔ*awil* "vagina".
Agaw *ᶜawil- "vagina": Bil ᶜ*awil-too*.

1083 *ᶜawur- "hole"

Sem *ᶜawr- "cleft": Arab ᶜ*awr-at-*.
CCh *wur- "hole": HNk *wuřɛ*.
*HV- lost.

*ᶜa- may be a prefix. Cf. WCh *wur- "dig (a hole)": Tng *wure*.

1084 *ᶜayVn- "eye"

Sem *ᶜayn- "eye": Akk *īnu*, Ug ᶜ*n*, Hbr ᶜ*ayin*, Aram (Syr) ᶜ*aynō*, Arab ᶜ*ayn-*, Gz ᶜ*ayn*.
Eg ᶜ*n*, ᶜ*yn* "eye" (a).
Borrowing from Sem?
Omot *ʔan- "eye": Gim *an*.
Regular develpoment from *ᶜayn-?

1085 *ᶜaǯ- "fish"

Eg ᶜ*ḏ*, ᶜ*ḏw* "kind of fish" (BD).
ECh *ʔač- < *ʔaǯ- "sardine": Kera *ačo*.
Irregular unvoicing of the affricate.

Agaw *ᶜaʒ- "fish": Bil ᶜaʒaa, Xmr χazaa, Kwr azaa, Kem azaa, asaa, Aun asi, Dmt asii.
SA *ᶜaʒ- "fish": Saho ᶜaazaa.
Note SA *-ʒ- < HS *-ǯ-.

1086 *ᶜaǯ- "sun"

Eg ᶜḏ "sun" (gr).
CCh *ᵓaǯ- "sun": Bud āǯi.
LEC *ᵓaʒ- "sun": Or aduu.
Note LEC *-ʒ- < HS *-ǯ-.
Dhl ᵓaḏo "sun".

1087 *ᶜaǯ-/*ᶜiǯ- "river"

Eg ᶜḏ "waters" (BD).
WCh *ᶜaǯ- "rivulet": Klr ᵓaǯi.
CCh *ᵓiǯ- "river": Lame iže.

Alternation *a ~ *i.

1088 *ᶜeb- "bird"

Eg ᶜbw "kind of bird" (MK).
Suffix -w.
WCh *Hyabi- "hen" [1], "chicken" [2]: Bol yawi [1], Dera yāwe [1], Tng yabe [1], Pero yabe [1], Ngm yabi [1], Krf yibbi [2], Gera yībi [2], Glm yīwu [2], Grm ibbi [2].

1089 *ᶜel- "see"

Berb *ᶜVl- "see": Izy aᶜḷu.
Unexpectedly preserved HS *ᶜ-.
WCh *yal- "see": Zar yɛl, Dwot yeliy, Wnd yɛle.
From *Hyal-.
ECh *Hyal- "look": Brg heeli.
Brg h- < *ᶜ- is not regular. The form may continue a prefixal pattern *HV-ᵓyal-.
LEC *ᵓil- "look!" (imper.): Or ilaa.
Dhl ᵓeley- "know".

1090 *ᶜelal- "look"

ECh *ᵓyalVl-/*ᵓwalVl- "look": Mig *ᵓello*, Mkk *woll-* .
Agaw *ᶜalal- "look": Bil *ᶜaläl*.
    Assimilation of vowels.
SA *ᵓilal- "wait" [1], "look" [2]: Saho *ilaal-* [1], Afar *ilal-* [2].
LEC *ᵓilal- "watch" [1], "look" [2]: Som *ilaali-* [1], Or *ilaala-* [2].

Partial reduplication of *ᶜel- "see". It is quite possible that some of the Cush forms result from cross-borrowings.

1091 *ᶜen- "vessel"

Berb *yVn- < *HVyVn- "plate": Ghd *ta-yyin-t*.
    Loss of *H-.
Eg *ᶜn* "vessel" (OK).
CCh *ᵓyani- "pot": Hwn *ᵓina*, Daba *yen*.

1092 *ᶜen-ᶜen- "monkey"

Eg *ᶜnᶜn* "baboon" (pyr).
WCh *ᶜyamyan- "monkey": Fyer *yamēn*, Sha *amen*, Klr *rimen*.
    Probably, goes back to *ᶜyan-ᶜyan- with dissimilation of nasals.

Reduplication. A descriptive stem?

1093 *ᶜeray- "river"

Eg *ᶜry* "waters" (gr).
CCh *ᵓyaray- "river": Mba *re*, Msg *erē*.

1094 *ᶜib-/*ᶜub- "breast, bosom"

Berb *ᵓab- "breast": Ghat *abbui*.
    Secondary *a before a labial?
CCh *ᵓub- "breast": Dgh *uḅa*, Mnd *ube*, Glv *uba*, Gdf *uḅa*.
LEC *ᶜib- "nipple": Som *ᶜib*.

Alternation *i ~ *u. Descriptive stem?

1095 *ˁi-çir- "bird"

Sem *ˁ*iṣur-* "bird": Akk ʾ*iṣṣuru*, Ug ˁ*ṣr*.
Secondary *-*u*-? Cf. **çepur-*.
Rift **cira*ˁ- "bird": Irq *tsir*ˁ*i*, Alg *cira*ˁ*a*, Bur *cira*ˁ*a*, Asa *šira*ʾ*a*.
Metathesis.

Derived from **çir-* "bird".

1096 *ˁiçVd- "harvest" (v.)

Sem *ˁ*VṣVd-* "harvest" (v.): Akk *eṣēdu*, Gz ˁ*ṣd*.
ECh **siHVd-* "harvest" (v.): Dng *siḍe*.
Metathesis.

An alternative reconstruction is **çi*ˁ*Vd-*.

1097 *ˁiĉ- "do, make"

Sem *ˁ*VŝVy-* "do, make": Ug ˁ*š*[1]*y*, Hbr ˁ*ŝy*, SAr ˁ*ŝy*.
ECh *ʾ*iĉ-* "do, work": Mkk ʾ*ise*.
Agaw *ʾ*iš-* "do, make": Bil *es-*, *is-*, Xmr *ieš-*, Kwr *iš-*, Dmb *es-*.
SA *ʾ*is-* "do, make": Saho *is-*, *iš-*, Afar *is-*.
HEC *ʾ*is-* "do": Bmb *iss-*.
Rift *ˁ*es-im-* "do, act": Alg ˁ*isim-*, Bur ˁ*esim-*.
Irregular *-*s*-. Rift may be borrowed from one of Cush branches.

1098 *ˁidar-/*yadar- "flock, herd"

Sem *ˁ*Vdr-* "flock, herd": Hbr ˁ*ēder*.
Eg *ỉdr* "flock, herd" (OK).
Borrowed from Sem?
SA **wadar-* "cattle": Afar *wadar*.
An ancient alternation **y-* ~ **w-* in the anlaut or an irregular development of **y-* > **w-* in SA?

All correspondences in the anlaut are irregular. Cf. also WCh **nV-dur-* "ram": Sha *ⁿdur*, DB *ⁿduur*, Bks ʾ*aⁿdur*.

1099 *ˁig- "fat, grease"

Eg ˁ*ḏ* "fat, grease" (OK).

Progressive palatalization of **g*.
CCh **ᵓig-* "fat": Bud *ma-ige*.
Prefix *ma-*.
ECh **ᵓyag-ay-* "fat, grease": Mkk *ᵓegey*.
From **ᶜig-ay-*.

1100 *ᶜigal- "cow, calf"

Sem **ᶜigl-* "calf" 1, "young of animals" 2: Ug *ᶜgl* 1, Hbr *ᶜēgel* 1, Aram (Syr) *ᶜegl-* 1, Arab *ᶜigl-* 1, Gz *ᶜəgʷəl* 2, Tgr *ᵓəgal* 1.
CCh **gyal-* "cow": Bura *gyɛl*.
Probably, from **giᶜal-*.
Agaw **gall-* "calf": Bil *gär*, Kwr *gär*, Kem *gär*, Aun *gara*.
Omot **gal-* "calf": Ome *gallua*.

**ᶜi-* may be a prefix unatttested in Cush. Cf. HEC **gal-* "camel" (Bmb *gaale*)?

1101 *ᶜil- "eye"

CCh **ᵓil-* "eye": Bud *yel*, *yil*, Gul *el*, Lmn *ili*.
Agaw **ᶜil-* "eye": Bil *ᶜil*, *ᶜel*, Xmr *el*, *iel*, Xmt *əl*, Kwr *el*, *yel*, Dmb *il*, *yil*, Kem *yil*, Aun *el*, *əll*, ill.
LEC **ᵓil-* "eye": Som *il*, Or *ila*, Bay *il*,*ili*, Arb *ille*, Gel *iil*, Kon *il-da*, Bus *il-ča*, Gdl *il-ta*.
HEC **ᵓill-* "eye": Sid *illee*, Dar *ille*, Had *illi*, Ala *ille*, Bmb *ille*, Kmb *ille*.
Dhl *ᵓila* "eye".
Mgg *ila* "eyes".
Rift **ᵓil-* "eye": Irq *ila*, Alg *ila*, Bur *ila*, Asa, *ᵓilat*, Kwz *ilito*.

1102 *ᶜilay- "rise"

Sem **ᶜVlaw-/*ᶜVlay-* "be high" 1, "rise" 2, "cross" 3: Akk *elû* 1, Ug *ᶜlw*, *ᶜly* 1, Hbr *ᶜlw*, *ᶜly* 1, Aram *ᶜlw*, *ᶜly* 1, Arab *ᶜly* [*-a-*] 1 2, SAr *ᶜly* 3, Gz *ᶜlw* 2.
Eg *iᶜr* "ascend" (1).
Metathesis.
WCh **yiᶜal-/*ᶜilay-* "stand up": Sura *yaɣal*, Ang *yal*, Tng *ᵓil*, Geji *hilya*.

Metathesis.

Derived from *ᶜ*al*- "rise".

1103 *ᶜim- "know, see"

Eg ᶜ*m* "know" (n), Copt *ᵓ*imi* id.: Fym *imi*, Boh *emi*, Shd *eime*.
WCh *ᶜ*im*- "think": Tng *yim*-, Pero *yim*.
CCh *ᵓ*um*- "teach": LPe *wum*.
ECh *ᵓ*um*- "see": Mubi ᵓ*um*.

Secondary **u* in CCh and ECh.

1104 *ᶜiw-/*ᶜiy- "cry"

Sem *ᶜ*ūy*- "cry": Arab ᶜ*wy*, Jib ᶜ*wy*.
Based on *ᶜ*Vw*-.
LEC *ᶜ*iy*- "cry": Som ᶜ*iyy*-, Bay *iy*-, Or *iyy*-.

Consonantal alternation *-*w*- ~ *-*y*-.

1105 *ᶜiǯ- "man, child"

Berb *ᵓ*iʒ*- "men" (pl.): Zng *iǯ*.
Eg ᶜ*d̲d* "young one" (n).
The cluster *d̲d* stands for an affricate **ǯ*.

1106 *ᶜog- "dig, cut"

Eg ᶜ*d̲* "hoe" (v.) (pyr).
Palatalization of *-*g*- after a middle vowel.
ECh **yuwag*- "hoe" (v.) [1], "plough" (v.) [2]: Smr *yīgə* [2], Tum *yəg* [1], Ndm *yə:gə:* [1], Lele *yagi* [1], Kbl *yuwege* [2].
ECh **yuwag*- may go back to **ywag*- < **Hwag*-.

1107 *ᶜog- "shout, call"

Sem *ᶜ*Vg*-ᶜ*Vg*- "shout": Arab ᶜ*g*ᶜ*g*.
Reduplication.
ECh *ᶜ*wag*-/*ᶜ*wak*- "call": Smr ᵓ*wōgo*, Sbn ᵓ*waga*, Tum *wəg*, Kwn ᵓ*oge*.
Irregular consonantism. Two different roots?

1108 *ᶜoḳab- "vulture"

Sem *ᶜ*uḳāb-* "vulture": Arab ᶜ*uqāb-*, Hss ʾ*aqāb*, Mhr ʾ*āqāb*, Shh ᶜ*eqεb*.
CCh **kwaḅ-* < **ḳwab-* "kite": Boka *koḅi*.
Shift of emphatization. The original source was **Hu-ḳab-*.

Cf. ECh **kwamb-* "eagle": Kera *kombe*.

1109 *ᶜol- "be ill"

Sem *ᶜ*Vl-* "be ill": Arab ᶜ*ll*.
CCh **wal-* < **Hwal-* "ache" (v.): Bud *wel*.

Cf. WCh **la-* "ache" (v. and n.): Sura *laa*, Ang *le*.

1110 *ᶜol- "snake, leech"

CCh *ʾ*wal-* "snake": Msg *wala*.
ECh *ʾ*yala-* "snake": Brg ʾ*eli*, Jegu ʾ*illo*, Dng ʾ*aalo*, Bid ʾ*aalo*.
From *ʾ*wala-*?
LEC *ᶜ*ola-*ᶜ*ol-* "leech": Som ᶜ*olaa*ᶜ*ol*.
Reduplication.
Omot *ʾ*ul-* "leech": Ome *ulo*.

1111 *ᶜor- "grain, corn"

Eg ᶜ*wȝȝ* "bread" (NK).
Vocalic *-w-*.
ECh *ʾ*war-* "corn": Mubi *wār*.
Mubi may also reflect **waHVr-*.

1112 *ᶜor- "goat"

Eg ᶜ*r* "she-goat" (med).
WCh *ᶜ*waru-* "he-goat": Mnt *ur*, Grk *ur*, Klr *war*.
ECh *ʾ*war-* "goats" (pl.): Lele *ōrē*.

1113 *ᶜoreb- "mix"

Sem *ᶜ*VrVb-* "mix": Hbr ᶜ*rb*.
WCh **ryab-* "mix": Fyer *rep*.

**-b- > -p* in the auslaut.

ECh **HwarVb-* ''mix'': Kera *horḅe*.

Irregular *h-*, cf. ECh s.v. **ᶜel-* ''see'' and **ᶜoruk-* ''rub''.

**o* and **e* are generally incompatible within one root.

1114 *ᶜoruk- ''rub''

Sem **ᶜVruk-* ''rub'': Arab *ᶜrk* [*-u-*].

ECh **HwarVk-* ''rub'': Kera *horke*.

Irregular *h-*.

1115 *ᶜoṭis- ''sneeze''

Sem **ᶜVṭiš-* ''sneeze'': Hbr *ᶜṭš*, Arab *ᶜṭs* [*-i-*, *-u-*], Gz *ᶜṭs*, Jib *ᶜɔṭəš*.

WCh **ᶜaṭus-/*ᶜwaṭus-* ''sneeze'': Hs *atušāwa*, Ngz *waatəši*.

Unclear **-u-*.

CCh **ʾwaṭis-* ''sneeze'': Dgh *wdisa*, Log *ḍisa*, Bud *wattisi*.

ECh **Hwaṭis-* ''sneeze'': Mig *haddiso*, Mubi *attaša*, Brg *waḍḍase*, Mkk *waddiso*.

Assimilation of vowels in Mubi and Brg.

LEC **haṭis-* ''sneezing'': Or *haṭṭissoo*.

Omot **haṭis-* ''sneeze'': Mch *häṭṭissi(ye)*.

Cush forms go back to **ḥaṭis-*. Dhl *ḥaaḏiδ-* id. is a loanword from LEC or Omot.

1116 *ᶜub- ''dirt''

Sem **ᶜVb-* ''dung'': Gz *ᶜəbā*, Tgr *ᶜiba*, Amh *əbät*.

Eg *ᶜbw* ''dirt'' (sarc).

-w reflects a rounded vowel of the root.

CCh **ʾubi-* ''faeces'': Mrg *ubi*, Klb *ibi*, Hld *ʾubī*, Kap *uvye*.

1117 *ᶜubub- ''fish''

Eg *ᶜwbbw* ''kind of fish'' (reg).

In both cases, *w* is a vocalic sign.

WCh **ᶜVbub-* ''fish'': Ang *bup*.

Reduplication in Sura *pupwap* id. Fyer *pupwap* id. may be borrowed from Sura.

1118 *ʿučan- "burn"

Sem **ʿVṯun-* "smoke (of fire)" (v.): Arab *ʿṯn* [-*u*-].
WCh **čan-* "burn": Sura *čan*, Chip *šan*, Mpn *čān*.
No traces of the anlaut laryngeal.

A denominative verb in Sem?

1119 *ʿud- "count"

Sem **ʿud-* "count": Arab *ʿdd* [-*u*-], Hss *ʾadōd*, Mhr *ʾed*, Shh *ʿed*.
ECh **ʾVd-* "count": Brg *ʾeddi*.
Brg -*e*- is secondary.

1120 *ʿuf- "heal, cure"

Sem **ʿVpVw-* "heal, cure": Arab *ʿfw*.
Based on **ʿVp-*.
CCh **ʾuf-* "heal, care": Gava *ʾufa*, Nak *wufa*.

1121 *ʿufan- "vessel"

Sem **ʿupun-* "vessel": Akk *uppunu*.
Secondary **u* after a labial.
Eg *ʿfn* "vessel" (gr).
WCh **fVn-* "calabash": Ngz *funa*, *fəna*.
Ngz -*u*- < -*ə*-.
CCh **fan-* "pot, calabash": Mba *fanay*.
Suffix **-ay-*.

1122 *ʿum-ʿam- "animal"

Sem **ʿumām-* "animals": Akk *umāmu*.
From **ʿum-ʿam-*?
Eg *ʿmʿm.w* "animal" (med).

Reduplication.

1123 *ʿupel- "hill, stone"

Sem **ʿup(V)l-* "bulge, hill": Hbr *ʿopel*.
Cf. Akk *pīlu* "limestone"?

CCh *pyal- "hill" [1], "stone" [2]: Bura *pyɛla* [1], Mofu *pəlay* [2].
Suffix *-ay* in Mofu.

*ʿu- may be a prefix.

1124 *ʿupVl- "insect"

Sem *ʿupl- "louse": Akk *uplu*.
Eg *ʿpnn.t* "worm" (med).
Cluster *-nn* seems to reflect *-l-.

1125 *ʿurag- "be lame"

Sem *ʿVrag- "be lame": Arab *ʿrg* [-a-].
Assimilation of vowels
WCh *ʿurVg- "lame person": Hs *gurgu*.
Deverbative formation with different vocalism.

1126 *ʿüĉ- "tree"

Sem *ʿiŝ- "tree": Akk *iṣu*, *iṣṣu*, Ug *ʿṣ*, Hbr *ʿēṣ*, Gz *ʿeḍ*.
Cf. Arab *ʿiḍ-at-* "kind of acacia".
ECh *ʾuĉ- "fig tree": Sok *ussē*.

1127 *ʿVbar-/*ʿVbir- "run, walk"

Sem *ʿVbur- "cross over": Akk *ebēru*, Hbr *ʿbr*, Arab *ʿbr* [-u-], SAr *ʿbr*.
*-u- < *-a- after a labial.
CCh *bar- "run": FJ *varu*.
ECH *bir- "go": Dng *birē*.
Dhl *ḅariy-* "go out, depart".
ḅ- < *b- after a laryngeal?

*ʿV- may be a prefix.

1128 *ʿVboʾ- "light, shine"

Eg *ʿbȝ* "light" (gr).
WCh *ḅway- < *bwaH- "sun, day": Bks *ḅwe*, DB *ḅwe*.
CCh *ḅiy- < *biH- "shine": Dgh *ḅiya*.

Secondary *-i-* before **y*?

*ᶜ*V-* may be a prefix.

1129 *ᶜVf- "give"

Sem *ᶜ*VpVw-* "give": Arab *ᶜfw*.
Based on *ᶜ*Vp-*.
WCh **fa-* "give": Fyer *fa*, Bks *fa*.
CCh **fa-/*HVfa-* "give": Gul *fā-re*, Log *va*, Mafa *va*, Bud *we*.

1130 *ᶜVgaʒ- "be weak"

Sem *ᶜ*Vgaz-/**ᶜ*Vgiz-* "be unable, be weak" [1], "be lazy" [2]: Arab *ᶜgz* [-*a*-, -*i*-] [1], Hss *ᵓāgōz* [2], Mhr *ᵓāgōz* [1], Shh *ᶜagoz* [2].
WCh **gaʒi-* "be tired": Hs *gaǯi*.
No traces of the original laryngeal.

1131 *ᶜVḥaᶜay- "maid"

Eg *ᶜḥᶜy.t* "maid" (MK).
WCh **ḥayay-* < **ḥaᶜay-* "maid": Cagu *hayai*, Mbu *γaya*, Jmb *γaya*.

*ᶜ*V-* may be a prefix. Note an unusual morphonological structure of this word. Is it an old compound?

1132 *ᶜVkaw-/*ᶜVkay- "tie, bind"

Sem *ᶜ*VkVw-* "make a knot (on the horse tail)": Arab *ᶜkw* [-*u*-].
ECh **kay-* "weave": Kwn *ke*, Kera *kɛ*.

*ᶜ*V-* may be a prefix. Consonantal alternation **-w-* ~ **-y-*.

1133 *ᶜVküs- "turn"

Sem *ᶜ*Vkiš-* "turn upside down": Arab *ᶜks* [-*i*-].
ECh **kus-* "turn": Kbl *kusu*.

*ᶜ*V-* may be a prefix.

1134 *ᶜVḳal-/*ᶜVḳil- ‘‘teach, be clever’’

Sem *ᶜ*Vḳil-* ‘‘be clever’’: Arab *ᶜql* [-*i*-].
ECh **HVkal-* ‘‘teach’’: Smr *gəl*, Tum *kəl*, Kbl *gələ*, Kwn *gal*.
g- < **ḳ* in the originally intervocalic position?

The root may be connected with or derived from *ᶜ*Vḳeʾ-* ‘‘be right, be true’’. *ᶜ*V*- may be a prefix.

1135 *ᶜVḳeʾ- ‘‘be right, be true’’

Eg *ᶜḳꜣ* ‘‘right, true’’ (MK).
CCh **kyaʾ-* ‘‘correct’’: Boka *keʾkeʾ*, Gaa *keʾkeʾ*.
Reduplication.

*ᶜ*V*- may be a prefix. The correspondence is valid only if Eg -*ꜣ* continues HS *-ʾ-. Otherwise, if -*ꜣ*- reflects HS *-*l*-, Eg *ᶜḳꜣ* should be placed together with cognates grouped under *ᶜ*Vḳal-*/ *ᶜ*Vḳil-* ‘‘teach, be clever’’.

1136 *ᶜVḳüp- ‘‘weave, sew’’

Sem *ᶜ*Vḳip-* ‘‘twist’’: Arab *ᶜqf* [-*i*-].
WCh **ḳup-* ‘‘weave’’: Zar *kʋp*.
CCh **kap-* ‘‘sew’’: Lame *kap*-.
Secondary vocalism?
ECh **kup-* ‘‘sew’’: Tum *kup*.

*ᶜ*V*- may be a prefix.

1137 *ᶜVlal- ‘‘do, build’’

Sem *ᶜ*VlVl-* ‘‘do, act (severely)’’: Hbr *ᶜll*.
WCh **lal-* ‘‘build’’: Tng *lal*.

Reduplication of *ᶜ*al-*/*ᶜ*il-* preserved in CCh *ʾ*il-* ‘‘build’’ (Dgh *ʾila*) and ECh *ʾ*al-* ‘‘make’’ (Smr *ʾal*).

1138 *ᶜVlič- ‘‘mix’’

Sem *ᶜ*Vliṯ-* ‘‘mix’’: Arab *ᶜlṯ* [-*i*-].
ECh **lič-* ‘‘mix’’: Kwn *lise*, Ngm *lise*.

*ᶜ*V*- may be a prefix.

1139 *ᶜVn- "turn"

Sem *ᶜ*Vn-* "displace": Akk *enû*, Arab ᶜ*nn*.
Eg ᶜ*n* "turn" (MK).

1140 *ᶜVnaw-/*ᶜVnay- "work, make"

Sem *ᶜ*VnVw-* "produce (of land)": Arab ᶜ*nw* [-*u*-].
WCh **nVy-* "work": Fyer *nyi*.
CCh **naH-* < **nay-* "do, make": Tera *nna*, Bud *na*.
ECh **nay-* "work": Lele *ne*.

*ᶜ*V-* may be a prefix. May be derived from *ᶜ*an-* "be tired, be ill", cf., from the semantic point of view, cf. the history of Fr *travail*.

1141 *ᶜVnVʒaw- "day, sunshine"

Eg ᶜ*nḏw* "sunshine" (pyr).
CCh **nVǯaH-* < **nVǯaw-* "day": Mba *nǯā*.
ECh **nVǯaH-* < **nVǯaw-* "day": Tum *nǯā*, Ndm *ǯā*, Kbl *ǯɛ*.

*ᶜ*V-* may be a prefix.

1142 *ᶜVru- "near"

Eg ᶜ*rw* "closeness" (MK).
WCh **ru-ru-* "near, close": Krk *ruru*.
Reduplication.

*ᶜ*V-* may be a prefix.

1143 *ᶜVtuḳ- "go"

Sem *ᶜ*VtVḳ-* "cross": Akk *etēqu*.
WCh **tuḳ-* "go away": Hs *tuḳa*.
No traces of **HV-*.

*ᶜ*V-* may be a prefix.

1144 *ᶜVtun- "push"

Sem *ᶜ*Vtun-* "push": Arab ᶜ*tn* [-*u*-].

WCh **tVHun-* "push": Mpn *tūn*.
Metathesis.

An alternative reconstruction is **tVˁun-*.

1145 *ˁVṭiʾ- "be dark"

Sem **ˁVṭVʾ-* "be dark": Akk *eṭû*.
LEC **ṭiʾ-* "become evening": Or *ḍiʾa*.

**ˁV-* may be a prefix.

1146 *ˁVǯimb- "be sweet"

Sem **ˁVḏub-* "be sweet": Arab *ˁḏb* [*-u-*].
**u* < **i* before a labial. **b* seems to be a regular Sem reflex of HS cluster **-mb-*.
ECh **ʾVǯimb-* "honey, bee": Mig *ʾǯimbe*.
Deverbative noun. Note the cluster **-mb-*.

*h

1147 *haʾ-/*hay- "take"

Eg *hꜣy* "capture" (MK).
-ꜣ- stands for HS **-a-*.
WCh **haʾ-* "catch": Bks *haʾ*.
ECh **hay-* "take": Kera *he*.

Consonantal alternation **-ʾ-* ~ **-y-*.

1148 *haʾ-/*haw-/*hay- "be, exist"

Sem **hūy-* "be, become": Akk *ewû*, Amor *hwy*, Hbr *hwy*, Aram *hwy*.
Based on **hVw-*.
Berb **hVʾ-* "be, stay": Ahg *ihâ*, Ayr *iha*.
CCh **hay-* "live": Bud *aiyu*.
ECh **hay-* "be": Mig *ʾay*.
Bed *haay-* "live".

SA **hay-* "live": Saho *hay*, Afar *hay*.
LEC **ˀa-hay-* "be": Som *ahay*.

Consonantal alternation **-ˀ-* ~ **-w-* ~ **-y-*.

1149 *haˀad- "be weak"

Eg *ꜣhd* "weak" (med).
Metathesis.
ECh **haˀad-/*hawad-* "weak" [1], "sick" [2]: Tum *hād* [1], Mubi *huwade* [2].

An alternative reconstruction is **ˀahad-*.

1150 *haˀem-/*haˀom- "tent, room"

WCh **ˀahwam-* "room": Bks *ˀahom-*.
Metathesis.
Rift **hēm-* < **haˀem-* "tent": Irq *heema*.
Assimilation of vowels.

An alternative reconstruction is **ˀahem-/*ˀahom-*.

1151 *hab- "cut, split"

Sem **hub-* "cut": Arab *hbb* [*-u-*].
Secondary **-u-*?
Dhl *haβ-* "split firewood".

1152 *habiṭ- "fall"

Sem **hVbiṭ-/*hVbuṭ-* "fall": Arab *hbṭ* [*-i-*, *-u-*].
WCh **habiṭ-* "fall": Hs *gabta*, Bol *biḍ-*, Krk *biḍ-* , Krf *bito*, Gera *bad*, Glm *bəz-*.

1153 *had- "take"

Sem **hīd-* "rob, take by force" [1], "be taken away" [2]: Gz *hyd* [1], Amh *hedä* [2].
Secondary formation based on biconsonantal **hVd-*.
Eg *hd* "grasp, seize" (MK).
WCh **had-* "take" [1], "carry" [2]: Tng *adi* [1 2], Fyer *ˀat* [1].

1154 *had- "thorn"

Eg *hd.t* "thorn" (med).
CCh **had-* "thorn": Gis *had-aw*.

Related to **had-* "cut".

1155 *had- "cut"

ECh **hVd-* "cut with a sickle": Kera *heḍe*.
Secondary emphatization of *-*d*-.
Agaw **ʔad-* "divide": Xmr *ad-ey-*.
LEC **had-* "cut, shave": Or *haada*.
HEC **had-* "shave": Bmb *haad-*, *haaḍ-*.

1156 *ham- "water"

Sem **hVmVw-*/**hVmVy-* "pour": Arab *hmw*, *hmy* [-*i*-, -*u*-].
Denominative verb based on **hVm-*.
WCh **ham-* "water": Sura *am*, Ang *am*, Mnt *ham*, Ank *ham*, Grk *ɣam*, Bol *ʔamma*, Krk *amo*, Ngm *ham*, Maha *amma*, Bele *amma*, Krf *amma*, Gera *hama*, Glm *ama*, Grm *amma*, Fyer *ham*, Bks *ham*, Sha *ham*, Klr *ʔaam*, Ngz *am*, Bade *ʔam-*.
ECh **ham-* "water" 1, "rain" 2: Dng *ammi* 1, Jegu *ʔam* 1, Mubi *ʔaame* 2, Brg *aame* 1.

1157 *ham- "eat"

Sem **nVham-* "be insatiable": Arab *nhm* [-*a*-].
Prefix **nV-*.
WCh **hVm-* "eat": Paa *ʔmma*.
CCh **ham-* "eat" 1, "chew" 2: Bud *ham* 1, Daba *həmu* 1, Mus *ḥam* 2.
ECh **ham-* "eat": Kera *hamɛ*, Smr *ʔəm-*.
Dhl *ham-* "toss a portion of food in the mouth".

Descriptive stem.

1158 *ham-/*him- "go, walk"

WCh **yim-* < **Him-* "return": Krk *yim*.
ECh **him-* "go in" 1, "go out" 2: Tum *him* 1, Mig *ʔo:mo* 2.

HEC **ham-* "go, walk": Sid *ham-*.
Omot **ham-* "go, walk": Ome *ham-*, *haam-*, Yam *ham-*, Kaf *ham-*, *hamm-*, Mch *hammi*, Anf *ham-*, Bwo *haam-*, *aam-*, Gim *hamu*, Shk *ham*, *am*.
Rift **hiʔim-* "walk": Irq *-hiʔim-it-*.
Secondary intervocalic laryngeal.

Alternation **a* ~ **i*.

1159 *har- "back"

Sem **harVw-* "back": Akk *erûtu*, *arûtu*.
WCh **har-* "back": Cagu *āri*.
ECh **har-* "back": Mubi *har*, Brg *ʔara*.

1160 *haram- "river"

Eg *hnm.t* "spring, source" (med), Copt **halme* id.: Lyc *halme*.
According to Copt data, Eg *-n-* < **-l-*.
WCh **haram-* "river": Klr *haram*.

Irregular correspondence of *liquida*.

1161 *haraw-/*haray- "wild boar"

Berb **rVy-* "wild boar": Rif *a-ruy*.
From **HVrVy-* or **HVrVwVy-*?
Bed *harawya* "wild boar".
Agaw **ʔarw-* "wild animal": Bil *arwee*.

Consonantal alternation **-w-* ~ **-y-*.

1162 *haw- "want"

Sem **hVw-* "wish" (n.) [1], "want" [2]: Ug *hwt* [1], Arab *hwy* [2].
Represented as triliteral **hVwVy-* in Arab.
LEC **haw-* "wish" (n.) [1], "want" [2]: Som *hawo* [1], Or *haw-* [2].

1163 *haw-/*hay- "fall"

Sem **hVw-/*hVy-* "fall (upon)": Arab *hwy* [-*i*-], Jib *hē*, Hss *hewō*.
Berb **hVy-* "fall (upon)": Ahg *ihi*.

Eg *hꜣy* "descend, fall, return" (OK), Copt **hey* id.: Boh *hey*, Shd *hey*.

Vocalic -*ꜣ*-.

WCh **hay*- "fall": DB *hay*.

CCh **hay*- "descend": Bud *hai*.

Rift **huʔ*- < **hVw*- "fall": Irq *hu*-, Alg *hu*-, Bur *hu*-.

Consonantal alternation *-*w*- ~ *-*y*-. If Eg *hꜣy* "return" is a separate word (only homonymic with Eg *hꜣy* "descend, fall"), it should be compared with CCh **hway*- "return" (Mba *hoy*), both Eg and CCh being reflexes of HS **hoy*- "return".

1164 *hawag-/*hayag- "lift"

Sem **hīg*- "be lifted": Arab *hyg* [-*i*-].

ECh **hawag*- "climb" [1], "lift" [2]: Smr *hagə* [1], Tum *ag*- [1], Ndam *ʔəga* [1], Tob *hoge* [2].

Consonantal alternation *-*w*- ~ *-*y*-.

1165 *haway- "blow"

Sem **hūy*- "blow": Arab *hwy* [-*i*-].

CCh **haway*- "wind": Bch *hawɛy*, Bata *haue*.

Deverbative noun.

1166 *hay- "building, town"

Eg *ỉhy* "building" (sait).

Orthographic representation of **hVy*-.

WCh **hay*- "town": Bade *he*.

CCh **haʔ*-/**hay*- "town, place" [1], "compound" [2]: Tera *he* [1], Gude *χa* [1], Gudu *hā-čü* [1], Bch *ha* [1], Gis *hay* [2].

Rift **ʔay*- "neighborhood" [1], "dwelling" [2]: Irq *aya* [1], Bur *aya* [1], Asa *ayo* [2], Kwz *ayo* [2].

Irregular *ʔ-.

1167 *hay- "cereal"

Eg *ỉhy* "cereal" (OK).

Orthographic representation of **hVy*-.

WCh **hay-* "corn" [1], "kind of millet" [2]: Ang *he* [1], Fyer *hay* [2], Bks *hay* [2].

Cf. CCh **χay-* "corn, guinea corn" (Zgh *χiya*, Glv *χiya*, Gudu *χəi*, HNk *χa*, Kap *χa*, FK *χa*, Gdr *hay*) with a different laryngeal **ḥ-*.

1168 *hay- "give birth"

Eg *hꜣy* "be born" (MK).
Vocalic *-ꜣ-*.
CCh **hay-/*hiy-* "give birth": Klb *aya*, Mrg *iya*, HNk *yε*, HGh *iʾya*, FKi *ya*, Kap *ya*, Tera *hya*.
ECh **hVy-* "birth": Mkk *ʾeʾiyo*.

1169 *hay- "speak"

Eg *ỉhy* "shout" (pyr).
Orthographic representation of **hVy-*.
Bed *hay-* "say".
LEC **hay-* "say": Som *hay-*.
HEC **hay-/*hiy-* "say": Dar *hiyy-*, Bmb *hay-εn-*.
Omot **hiʾ-* < **hVy-* "say": Ome *hii-*.

Cf. also Dhl *ḥaaw-* "name" (v.).

1170 *haʒin- "heart, intestine"

WCh **hanʒ-* < **haʒin-* "guts": Hs *hanǯī*, Bol *azin*, Krk *azi*, Ngm *hazi*, Krf *aǯǯo*, Gera *haza*, Glm *ašiⁿ*, Sha *ʾaǯi*.
Cf. the development of the root structure in HS **ĉakin-* "knife" and **čakin-* "net".
Agaw **ʾVʒin-* "heart": Xmt *əəzεn*.

1171 *her- "feline"

Sem **hirr-* "cat": Arab *hirr-*.
CCh **ʾa-hyar-* "leopard": Msg *aharau*, *aχerau*.
Prefix **ʾa-*.

1172 *her- "sheep, goat"

Berb **hVr-* "ram" [1], "sheep" [2], "sheep and goats" [3]: Ayr *e-hərə* [1], Ahg *e-hərə* [3], Twl *e-hərə* [1], Sml *a- hru* [1], Gua *hara* [2].
Dhl *heeri* "goat, sheep".

1173 *heraw-/*heray- "day"

Eg *hrw* "day" (pyr), Copt **hrew*: Akh *hreu*.
CCh **hyaraw-* "day": Bud *yīrow*.
Bud *-ow-* < **-aw-*.
ECh **hyariy-* "noon": Dng *ʾeriyo*.
Secondary **-i-* before **y*.

Consonantal alternation **-w-* ~ **-y-*.

1174 *hey- "man"

Eg *hꜣy* "husband, nobleman" (pyr), Copt **hay* id.: Boh *hai*, Shd *hai*.
-ꜣ- stands for a vowel.
Bed *hiyo* "man, husband".
SA **hey-* "man": Saho *heyoo*, Afar *heyoo*.
Rift **he-* "man": Irq *hεε*, Gor *hee*.

The root may be related to HS **hay-* "give birth".

1175 *hiʕir- "excrement"

Eg *hʕyr.t* "excrement".
Vocalic *-y-*.
ECh **hiʔir-* "faeces": Mkk *ʔiiri* (pl.).

Cf. Rift **hor-* "dung": Bur *hori*.

1176 *hilal- "moon"

Sem **hilāl-* "new moon": Ug *hll*, Arab *hilāl-*, Gz *helāl*.
Berb **HalVl-* "moon": Ahg *t-alli-t*.
Assimilation of vowels.

1177 *himal- "tear" (n.)

Sem **hVmVl-* "shed tears": Arab *hml* [-*i*-, -*u*-].
Denominative verb with a new vocalic pattern.
CCh **himal-* "tear" (n.): Bud *himālo*.

Cf. metathetic HEC **Hil(V)m-* "tear" (Bmb *ilma*)?

1178 *himis- "go"

Sem **hVmiš-* "walk day and night": Arab *hms* [-*i*-].
CCh **yimVs-* < **Himis-* "enter": Tera *ayimsi*, Boka *yimsi*.

Derived from **ham-/*him-* "go, walk".

1179 *hin- "head"

Eg *hn* "head" (gr).
CCh **hin-* "head": Tera *yin*, Gudu *yin*, FJ *γin*, Mwu *həne-gi*, Msm *yano*, Gbn *in-ḍa*, Gaa *in-da*, Bch *nne*.
y- < **h-* in individual languages.

1180 *hinVn-/*ḫinVn- "child"

Eg *nḫn* "child" (pyr).
Metathesis.
WCh **hinVn-* "child": Cagu *hīnən*.

Irregular correspondence of laryngeals.

1181 *hiw- "enclosure"

Eg *ỉhw* "enclosure" (n), Copt **ʾohi* id.: Fym *ahi*, Akh *ohe*, Boh *ohi*, Shd *ohe*.
ECh **hiw-* "enclosure": Kera *hiw*.

Eg and Copt may indicate a different prototype **ʾVhiw-* (with a prefix?), also possible for ECh.

1182 *hiʒ-/*huʒ- "child"

CCh **huʒ-* "child": Lmn *uuza*, Zgh *uza*, Gis *za*.
HEC **hiʒ-* "brother": Kmb *hizo*, Tmb *izo*.

Alternation **i* ~ **u*.

1183 *hob- "give, send"

Sem **wVhVb-* "give": Aram *yhb*, Arab *whb*, SAr *whb*, Gz *whb*.
Prefix **wV-*.
Eg *hꜣb* "send".
The function of *-ꜣ-* is not clear.
WCh **hwab-* "lend, borrow": Sura *hwɔp*.

Cf. Berb **hub-* "drag, pull along" (Ahg *hub-ət*, Ayr *hub-ət*)?

1184 *hoh- "burn; heat"

Eg *hh* "heat" (med).
WCh **hwah-* "burn": Sha *hwoh*.

Possible reduplication of **haʾ-/*haw-* "fry", cf. in CCh: Msm *haou*, LPe *hao*.

1185 *hor- "rest" (n.)

Eg *hr.t* "rest, peace" (OK).
ECh **hwar-* "rest": Tum *hōr*, Sbn *wara*.

1186 *hos- "grind"

Sem **huš-* "break into small fragments": Arab *hss* [*-u-*].
WCh **Hyas-/*Hwos-* "grind": Sura *ʾɛ:s*, Chip *ʾɛɛs*, Ank *es*, Bol *ʾoss*, Krf *ʾyasu*, Gera *yaso*, Grm *es-*.

1187 *hot- "fire"

Eg *hwt* "fire" (sarc).
Vocalic *-w-*.
WCh **Hwatu-* "fire": Hs *wutā*, Tng *wəti*, Geji *wutu*, *wuti*, Brw *wut*, *wutu*, Brm *wut*, Say *wut*, Dwot *ʾutu*, Kir *wut*, Tala *wudi*.
CCh **hwat-* "fire": Gbn *wəte*, Boka *χwətə*, Gaa *wəta*, Tera *wəti*.

1188 *hoṭ- "fence, enclosure"

CCh **hwaḍ-* < **hwaṭ-* "compound": Gudu *hwod-očü*, Nza *hwaḍɛ*, Bch *wəḍiy*.
HEC **huṭ-* "fence, enclosure": Sid *huṭa*.

1189 *hoṭaʾ- "go"

Sem **hVṭaʿ-* "go ahead in awe": Arab *hṭʿ* [*-a-*].
WCh **hwaṭa-* "come" [1], "enter" [2], "go" [3]: Tng *wato* [1], Pero *wat* [1], Zem *wutə* [1], Say *wət* [2], Kir *wad* [2], DB *hat* [3].

Connected with Rift **hVʾVt-* "march, go" (Irq *hiʾiit-* , Alg *haʾut-*) and Dhl *hu<u>t</u>'-* "follow"?

1190 *hoṭar- "fortified site"

Berb **hu[ṭ]ar-* "fortified site": Gua *a-χodar*, *a-jodar*.
Is Gua *d* a reflex of Berb **ṭ*?
HEC **hoṭor-* < **hoṭar-* "yard": Had *ooṭoro*.
Assimilation of vowels.

Derived from **hoṭ-* "fence, enclosure".

1191 *hoʒ- "sleep"

Sem **hV<u>d</u>-* "sleep" [1], "be delirious" [2]: Hbr *hzy* [1], Arab *h<u>d</u>y* [*-i-*] [2].
ECh **hwaǯ-* "sleep": Mig *ʾōḍyo*, Bid *ʾōḍy*, Brg *ōḍyi*, Dng *weḍye*, Ndam *ʾəǯa*.

Cf. Dhl *ha<u>d</u>uura* "sleep"?

1192 *hubag-/*hubig- "strike"

Sem **hVbag-* "strike": Arab *hbg* [*-a-*].
WCh **hubag-* "beat": Hs *buga*, Ang *bak*.
ECh **mV-big-* "slap": Tum *mbig*.
Prefix **mV-*.
Bed *bag-* "slap".
LEC **bog-* "slap": Som *bog*.
Secondary labialization of the vowel.

1193 *hud- "break"

Sem **hud-* "break": Arab *hdd* [-*u*-].
Eg *hd* "break" (MK).
CCh **hVd-* "break": Msg *ḥada*.

WCh **hya[d]-* "strike" (Ank *het*) also may belong to this HS root. Berb **hVd-* "destroy" (Kby *hudd*) may be borrowed from Arab.

1194 *hu-dam- "utter"

CCh **hu-dVm-* "swear": Gis *hudom, hudum*.
Gis *-o-* < **-a-* before a labial.
LEC **dam-* < **HV-dam-* "communicate": Or *ḍaam-*.

**hu-* is a prefix. The word is derived from **dVm-*"utter".

1195 *hulim- "child, man"

ECh **hulum-* "man, person": Kera *hulum*.
Assimilation of vowels.
Rift **holim-* "child": Alg *holimo*, Bur *χwaylimo*.
Unexpected *-ay-* in Bur.

1196 *hulüb- "soak"

Sem **hVlib-* "soak, be wet": Arab *hlb* [-*i*-].
WCh **luḅ-* < **luHub-* "sogginess": Hs *luḅuluḅū*.
Reduplication.
CCh **luḅ-* < **luHub-* "wet" (v.): Hld *lūḅu-ri*, Klb *ālub-tū*, Chb *lup-ti*, WM *ləb-di*, Wmd *lub-ta*, FGl *luḅwi-ti*, Kap *luḅi-ke*, Gava *luḅ-*, Daba *lub*.
ECh **lub-* "soak": Kera *lubi*.

The alternative reconstruction reflected by all Chadic branches is **luhub-*.

1197 *humac- "grass, straw"

Sem **humṣ-* "tough grass": Akk *umṣatu*.
CCh **humac-* "straw": Mofu *humas*.

1198 *hunay- "(be) small"

Sem **hunay-* "a little": Arab *hunayy-at-*.
ECh **hVnay-* "small": Smr *hnye*.

1199 *hur- "pierce"

ECh **hVr-* "pierce": Tum *hər*.
LEC **hur-* "pierce": Or *hura*.

1200 *hur- "be pregnant"

Sem **hVrVy-* "be pregnant": Akk *arû*, Ug *hry*, Hbr *hry*.
Based on biconsonantal **hVr-*.
ECh **hur-* "be pregnant": Ndam *ʾəra*, Tum *urər*.
Reduplication in Tum.

1201 hut- "dig"

Eg *htht* "dig" (BD).
CCh **hwa-hut-* "dig": Mofu *hwuhut*.

Different types of reduplication.

1202 *hüw- "snake"

Eg *hyw* "snake" (pyr).
Vocalic *-y-*.
CCh **hu[w]-* "snake": Zime *huu*.

1203 *hVban- "gazelle"

Eg *hbn* "gazelle" (MK).
WCh **ban-* "gazelle": Dwot *bani*.
The anlaut laryngeal is lost.

**hV-* may be a prefix.

1204 *hVbat-/*hVbit- "throw down"

Sem **hVbit-* "throw down, beat, destroy": Akk *abātu*, Arab *hbt* [-*i*-].

WCh **HVbat-* "push, throw down": Ang *bat*, Sura *bet*.

Cf. LEC **HVbot-*: Or *aboota* "give a blow".

1205 *hVben- "vessel"

Eg *hbn.t* "big mug" (OK).
WCh **HVbyan-* "gourd, gourd bottle": Sura *been*, Mpn *been*.
Voiced anlaut in Sura reflects the lost laryngeal.
ECh **byanu-* "pumpkin": Kbl *tə-bəni*, Gbr *ti-bini*, Kwn *bone*.

1206 *hVdag- "go"

Sem **hVdig-* "go trembling": Arab *hdg* [-*i*-].
The source of the vowel in the second syllable is not clear. The meaning is questionable.
WCh **ḍag-* < **HVdag-* "go away" [1], "follow" [2]: Hs *ḍaga* [1], Ngz *ḍəgu* [2].

Derived from **dag-/*dig-* "go". Cf. also ECh **HVdug-* "enter" (Ndm *ḍuge*) with a metathesis of vowels.

1207 *hVlak- "go, drive"

Sem **hVlVk-* "go": Akk *alāku*, Hbr *hlk*.
CCh **lakwa-* "enter" [1], "drive" [2]: Bura *lukwa* [1], Chb *lukwa* [1], Glv *lagʷa* [2], Gvo *lakʷə-la* [2].

**hV-* may be a prefix.

*ḥ

1208 *ḥaʾ- "head"

Eg *ḥꜣ* "occiput" (pyr).
WCh **ḥa(ʾ)-* "head": Geji *ga*, Buli *ga*, Wrj *γa-may*, Kry *γa-m*, Diri *a-ma*, Paa *ḥa-ma*.
Forms in *-m-* may go back to possessives.

1209 *ḥaʔ-/*ḥaw- "vessel"

Eg *ḥw.t* "vessel" (OK).
CCh **χa-* < **χaʔ-* "pot": Mrg *χa*, Hld *χa*.

Consonantal alternation **-ʔ-* ~ **-w-*.

1210 *ḥab- "cereal"

Sem **ḥabb-* "grain, corn": Arab *ḥabb-*.
CCh **ma-χab-* "sorghum": Mba *mahaḇ*.
Prefix **ma-*. Note the emphatization of **-b-*.

1211 *ḥabuʔ- "fish"

Sem **ḥabuʔ-* "fish": Akk *abūtu*.
Dialectal development of a vowel after **ḥ-* in Akk.
Eg *ḥbꜣ* "fish" (OK).

1212 *ḥaçaʔ-/*ḥaçay- "count"

Sem **ḥaṣy-* "number": Arab *ḥaṣy-*.
Deverbative noun.
ECh **ʔasay-* "count": Smr *ʔāsē*, Sbn *ʔāsā*.

Consonantal alternation **-ʔ-* ~ **-y-*.

1213 *ḥaçir- "press, squeeze"

Sem **ḥVṣir-* "press, squeeze": Arab *ḥṣr* [*-i-*, *-u-*].
ECh **ʔasir-* "press, squeeze": Kbl *sər*, Dng *assire*.

1214 *ḥaĉar- "fence, enclosure"

Sem **ḥaṣ̂ar-* "enclosure" [1], "camp" [2], "yard" [3], "area" [4]: Akk *ḫaṣāru* [1], Phn *ḥṣr* [3], Hbr *ḥāṣer* [2 3], Aram (Syr) *ḥəṣārā* [3], Arab *ḥaḍar-* [4], SAr *ḥṣwr* [4], Gz *ḥaṣur* [1].
Irregular *ḫ-* in Akk.
WCh **ĉVr-* "fence": DB *siri*.
Assimilation of vowels. Cf. DB *saar* "fence" (v.).
CCh **ḥaẑar-* "fence": Mofu *ẑaẑar*, Mafa *gəẑar*.
Partial reduplication in Mofu.

Bed *eseer* "enclosure".

Assimilation of vowels. *-ee-* seems to reflect **-aHa-*.

Any connection with LEC **ᵓaraʒ-* "dwelling" (Or *areddaa*)?

1215 *ḥadur- "go down"

Sem **ḥVdir-/*ḥVdur-* "descend": Arab *ḥdr* [*-i-*, *-u-*].
WCh **dwar-* < **daHur-* "descend": DB *dor*, Bks *dōr*, Klr *doro*.
Metathesis.

1216 *ḥaf- "bank"

Sem **ḥāpp-* "bank": Hbr *ḥōp*, Arab *ḥāff-at-*.
WCh **ḥa-ḥaf-* "bank": Hs *gaggāfā*.
Partial reduplication.

1217 *ḥafal-/*ḥafil- "be full"

Sem **ḥVpil-* "rise (of water)": Arab *ḥfl* [*-i-*].
WCh **fal-* < **HVfal-* "full (of vessel)": Hs *fal*.

**ḥa-* may be a prefix.

1218 *ḥaᶜ- "child"

Eg *ḥᶜꜣ* "child, boy" (pyr).
Cf. *ᶜᶜy* "child" (l). *-ꜣ* is a vocalic sign.
CCh **χwaᵓ-/*χway-* "boy, son": Boka *χweya*, Gbn *wa*, Gaa *wa*, Tera *wi*.
Cf. **χway-* "give birth": Log *ɣwe*, Chb *ya*, Klb *aya*, Tera *hya*, HNk *ye*, FKi *ya*, HGh *iᵓya*.
Rift **haᵓ-/*haw-* "children": Alg *haᵓay*, Bur *yaᵓay*, Asa *hawa*, Kwz *yawa*.

1219 *ḥaᶜ-/*ḥuᶜ- "move upwards"

Eg *ᶜḥᶜ* "stand up" (pyr).
ᶜ- may be a prefix.
WCh **ḥaᶜ-* "raise": Bks *haᵓ*.
CCh **χu-* "lift": Klb *hü*, Mrg *χu*.

ECh *ʾu- "lift": Smr ʾ*u*.

Alternation *a ~ *u.

1220 *ḥak- "stone"

Eg *ḥṯ* "stone" (n).
*k > ṯ, presumably, before *o, cf. CCh *χakwa-.
WCh *ḥVk- "stone": Sura *γək*, Ang *γük*, *γk*.
CCh *χakwa- "stone": FG *hakwu*.

1221 *ḥakam-/*ḥakum- "rope"

Sem *ḥakam- "martingale": Arab *ḥakam-at-*.
Rift *ḥagum- "trap" [1], "rope" [2]: Alg *hagumo* [1], Bur *ḥaguumɔ* [2].
Unexpected *-g-.

Irregular correspondence of vowels in the second syllable.

1222 *ḥaḳVl- "earth, field"

Sem *ḥaḳl- "field": Akk *eqlu*, Aram (Syr) *ḥaqlā*, Arab *ḥaql-*, Gz *ḥaql*.
ECh *kVl- "earth": Tum *kələ*.
Loss of the anlaut laryngeal.

1223 *ḥaḳür- "be angry"

Sem *ḥVḳir- "despise": Arab *ḥqr* [-*i*-], Gz *ḥqr*.
WCh *Haḳur- "be angry": Paa *akwar*, Siri *aḳur*, Jmb *ḳwar*.

1224 *ḥaḳVw- "hip, thigh"

Sem *ḥaḳw- "loins, hip": Hbr *ḥeq*, Arab *ḥaqw-*, Gz *ḥaq*^{w}*e*.
LEC *ḥVwVg- "hip, thigh": Som *ḥoog*.
Note HS *-ḳ- > LEC *-g-. Metathesis.
Omot *hakVw- "hip": Kaf *hakkoo*.
Note HS *ḳ > Omot *k. Cluster *-aw- > -oo- in Kaf.

1225 *ḥal- "be sweet"

Sem *ḥVlaw-/*ḥVlaw- "be sweet": Arab *ḥlw* [-*a*-].

Based on biconsonantal *ḥal-.

WCh *ḥal- "sweet juice sucked from the abdomen of a hornet": Hs *galla*.

Deverbative noun.

CCh *χal- "sweet": Bud *alli*.

Rift *hal- "sweet": Kwz *hal-am-*.

1226 *ḥal- "wash"

Sem *ḥVl- "clean (adj.)" [1], "wash, clean" [2]: Akk *ellu* [1], Aram (Syr) *ḥll* [2].

LEC *ḥal- "wash": Som *ḥal-*.

1227 *ḥal- "spleen, liver"

ECh *ʔVl- "spleen": Mkk *ʔell-eso*.

Secondary root vowel influenced by *-e-* of the suffix.

LEC *ḥal- "liver": Rnd *ḥal-esi*.

1228 *ḥal-/*ḥil- "go"

Eg *ḥn* "go" (n).

Cf. also *ḥry* "move away" (pyr)? Note *-n* < *-l-.

CCh *χal-/*χil- "go": Mba *hili*, Msg *ḥala*.

SA *hal- "enter": Saho *haḷ*, Afar *hal*.

LEC *ḥil- "enter": Arb *hil-*.

Alternation *a ~ *i.

1229 *ḥalaḳ- "be smooth"

Sem *ḥalaḳ- "smooth": Hbr *ḥālāq*.

WCh *ḥalaḳ- "smooth": Tng *halak-halak*.

Reduplication.

1230 *ḥalib- "milk"

Sem *ḥalīb- "milk" [1], "fresh milk" [2]: Akk *ḫilpu* [1], Hbr *ḥālāb* [1], Ug *ḥlb* [1], Aram (Syr) *ḥalᵉbā* [1], Arab *ḥalīb-* [1], *ḥalab-* [2], Gz *ḥalīb* [1].

Irregular *ḫ* in Akk.

Rift *ʔilib- "milk": Irq *ilwa*, Ala *iliba*, Bur *iliba*, Asa *liba*.

Assimilation of vowels. Unexpected *ʾ-, see Rift s.v. *ḥanVĉ- "tooth".

1231 *ḥam- "salt"

Eg *ḥmꜣ.t* "salt" (med).
Vocalic *-ꜣ*.
WCh *ḥam- "salt": Fyer *ʾama*.
CCh *χwam- < *χam- "salt": Msg *ḥɔm*.
Secondary vowel before a labial.

1232 *ḥam-/*ḥim- "be black"

Sem *ḥam- "become black": Arab *ḥmm* [-*a*-].
HEC *hem- "be black": Had *heem-*.
Dhl *himm-aṯe* "black".

Alternation *a ~ *i.

1233 *ḥan- "tumor"

Eg *ḥnḥn.t* "tumor" (med).
Reduplication.
ECh *ʾan- "tumor": Tum *ān*.

1234 *ḥankar- "throat"

Sem *ḥangar- "larynx": Arab *ḥangar-at-*.
Is the development of HS *-nk- into *-ng- regular?
Bed *hankar* "throat".
SA *ʾanḳar- "throat": Saho *anḳar*, Afar *enḳaraa*.
Afar *e-* and emphatic *ḳ may be traces of the lost *ḥ.
Dhl *ḥank'ara* "hard palate".
As well as SA, Dhl reflects emphatic *-ḳ-.

1235 *ḥanVĉ- "tooth"

Eg *nḥḏ* "tooth, fang" (OK).
Metathesis.
Rift *ʾanĉ- "tooth": Irq *anĉ-amo*, Bur *aaĉ-imo*.

Unexpected *ḥ- > *ʔ-.

Related to Dhl *ḥunĉ-* "chew".

1236 *ḥap- "plant, grass"

Eg *ḥp* "kind of plant" (gr).
CCh **χap-* "grass": Bud *hāpu*.

1237 *ḥap- "close, cover"

Eg *ḥɜp* "cover" (MK).
Vocalic *-ɜ-*.
WCh **Hap-* "close": Tng *opɛ*.
Tng *o* is a regular reflex of **a*.
ECh **ʔVp-* "close, cover": Mkk *ʔipp-*.

1238 *ḥapat- "arm, wing"

Eg *ḥpt* "arm, wing" (MK).
WCh **ḥapVt-* "arm, wing": Ngz *gapta*, Bade *gapt-on*.
CCh **pVt-* "wing": Bud *fefeto*, Daba *pɛtɛ*.
Partial reduplication in Bud. Assimilation of vowels.
ECh **pat-* "arm": Sok *patu*, Jegu *poto*.
Secondary *-o-* in Jegu.

1239 *ḥapur- "pit"

Sem **ḥapr-* "big well" [1], "hole, cavity" [2]: Arab *ḥafr-* [1], Jib *ḥfər-ɛt* [2].
WCh **pur-* "tomb": Tng *pure*, Pero *pure*.
Loss of the anlaut laryngeal.

1240 *ḥapüd- "go"

Sem **ḥVpid-* "hurry, take pains": Arab *ḥfd* [-*i*-].
WCh **pVḍ-* < **pVHVd-* "go": Dera *poḍ-owu*, Ngm *poḍ-owu*.
Metathesis.
CCh **paHud-* "go" [1], "return" [2]: Gaa *puḍi* [1], Gbn *pədi* [1], Daba *pāḍ* [2].

Metathesis.

An alternative reconstruction is **paḥüd-*. Cf. **ḥupet-* "go".

1241 *ḥar- "sky"

Eg *ḥr.t* "sky" (pyr).
WCh **ḥar-* "sky": Hs *gārī*, Sha *ʾare* id.
Irregular ʾ- in Sha.

Cf. LEC **haror-* "cloudy weather" (Or *haroor-essa*).

1242 *ḥar- "arm"

CCh **χar-* "arm": Tera *χar*, Gaa *heřa*, Hwn *hara*, Gis *har*.
Cf. also Log *γʾar-zeni* "wrist".
Bed *har-ka* "arm".
SA **ḥar-* "arm": Saho *ḥaraa*.
LEC **ḥar-k-* "arm, hand": Or *harkka*, Kns *harga*.
Wrz **χar-k-* "hand": War *ḥarko*, Gaw *ḥarko*.

1243 *ḥar- "intestines"

Sem **ḥVrr-* "gut": Akk *erru*.
CCh **χar(wa)-* "intestines": Gis *hor*, HNk *χəři*, Kap *χaři*, FG *χař*, Bura *χyel*, Klb *hali*, Mrg *γali*, Hil *χali*.
-l- in Bura and other languages is regular.

Cf. Eg *ḥrr* "part of the body" (NK)?

1244 *ḥas- "roast"

Sem **ḥVš-ḥVš-* "roast": Arab *ḥsḥs*.
Reduplication.
WCh **ḥas-* "roast, bake": Hs *gasa*.

1245 *ḥas- "seek, look for"

CCh **χas-* "look for, search": Mafa *has*.
HEC **has-* "seek, look for": Sid *haas-*, Dar *has-*, Had *hass-*, Ala *has-*, Kmb *has-*.

1246 *ḥasar- "hand, arm"

Eg *ḥsr* "arm" (gr).
WCh **saHar-* "hand, arm": Sura *sar*, Ang *sār*, Chip *saar*, Mnt *sai*, Ank *sar*, Bol *sara*, Krk *sara*, Ngm *sara*, Maha *sara*, Krf *šara*, Gera *šara*, Glm *šara*, Grm *saraŋ*.
Metathesis.

1247 *ḥasek- "cereal"

Sem **ḥašīk-* "barley": Arab *ḥasīk-at-*.
CCh **syak-* "millet": Gaa *šek-ita*, Gbn *sek-ete*, Boka *šek-taʾa*.
Loss of the anlaut laryngeal.

**ḥa-* may be a prefix.

1248 *ḥaŝ-/*ḥuŝ- "cut"

Sem **ḥuś-* "cut": Arab *ḥšš* [-*u*-]
Rift **ḥaŝ-* "carve wood": Irq *ḥaŝ-*.
Dhl *haṯʼ-* "butcher meat".

1249 *ḥat-/*ḥut- "rub off, sweep"

Sem **ḥut-* "rub off": Arab *ḥtt* [-*u*-].
LEC **ḥaṭ-* "sweep" [1], "rub" [2]: Som *ḥaaḍ-* [1], Or *ḥaaḍ-* [2].
**-ṭ-* < **-t-* under the influence of **ḥ-*.

1250 *ḥaw-/*ḥaway- "return, go"

Eg *ḥwy* "go" (MK).
CCh **χway-* < **χaway-* "return": HGh *χwe*, Mba *hoy*.
Dhl *haʿ-*"come, arrive".
Irregular *-ʿ-*.
Rift **ḫaw-* "come": Irq *ḫaw-*, Alg *ḫaw-*, Bur *ḫaw-*.
Irregular **ḫ-*.

No traces of **-ay-* in Cush forms.

1251 *ḥaw-/*ḥay- "stomach"

Sem **ḥawīy-* "intestines": Arab *ḥawīy-at-*.

WCh **ḥaw-/*ḥay-* "belly": Bol *awo*, Ngm *hawo*, Gera *hawi*, Krf *awo*, Glm *awa*, Fyer *hye*, Bks *hihye*.
Partial reduplication in Bks.
CCh **χwa-/*χay-* "stomach": Wmd *χay*, Chb *ɣəy*, HF *χwi*, Kap *χwu*, Masa *haya*.
**χwa-* goes back to **χaw-*.
ECh **ʾVy-* "breast": Jegu *ʾoyo*.
Secondary vocalism.

Consonantal alternation *-*w*- ~ *-*y*-.

1252 *ḥaw-/*ḥay- "food"

Eg *ḥw* "food" (pyr).
ECh **ʾay-* "food": Smr *haye*, Ndam *a:y*.
Rift **hay-* "food": Asa *hay-uk*.
Irregular laryngeal.

Consonantal alternation *-*w*- ~ *-*y*-. Cf. verbal derivative in ECh **ʾay-* "eat" (Lele *ai*).

1253 *ḥaw-/*ḥay- "man"

WCh **ḥaw-* "chief": Gera *hawi*.
CCh **χuy-* < **χawVy-* "husband": Log *χūy*.
Dhl *ḥaayo*, pl. *ḥaaʿi* "man, husband".
-ʿ- in pl. is not clear.
Rift **ḥaw-* "man, husband": Irq *ḥaw-ata*, Alg *ḥaw-ata*, Bur *ḥawata*.

Consonantal alternation *-*w*- ~ *-*y*-. Cf. also Rift **ḥiy-* "brother" (Irq *ḥiya*).

1254 *ḥawar-/*ḥayar- "breed, multiply"

Sem **ḥayar-* "having many cattle and a big family": Arab *ḥay-ar-*, *ḥiyar-*.
LEC **ḥor-* < **ḥawar-* "multiply (domestic animals)": Gid *hor*.
Cf. Or *horii* "cattle", Kns *hor-eeta* "wealth, livestock".

Consonantal alternation *-*w*- ~ *-*y*-.

1255 *ḥawil- "year"

Sem *ḥawl- "year": Arab ḥawl-.
WCh *ḥawil- "year": Fyer *wel*, Sha *wul*, Klr *ʾawul*, DB *wil*.
ECh *ʾaliy- < *ḥayil- "year": Smr *ʾaliya*, Kwn *oleye*, Tum *əlay*, Ndam *lowa*, Gbr *ille*, Mig *ʾila*.
Metathesis and change *-w- > *-y- before a front vowel.

1256 *ḥayaw- "family, people"

Eg *wḥy* "family" (MK).
Metathesis.
SA *ḥayaw- "people": Saho *ḥeaw*.
Rift *ḥay- "kinsfolk, clan": Irq *ḥay*.
The original biconsonantal root?

Derived from *ḥaw-/*ḥay- "man".

1257 *ḥayaw- "animal"

Sem *ḥay(aw)- "animal": Ug *ḥwt*, Hbr *ḥayyā*, Aram (Syr) *ḥayūtō*, Arab *ḥayaw-ān-*.
CCh *χiw- < *χVyVw- "animal": Mnd *χiwa*.
Contraction in Mnd.
ECh *ʾayVw- "animal": Jegu *ʾaiwo*, Bid *ʾawyo*.
Metathesis in Bid.

1258 *ḥaǯar- "beast of prey"

Sem *ḥaḏar- "swamp lynx": Akk *azaru*.
Irregular Akk *a* of the first syllable.
Eg *ḥḏr* "hyaena" (OK).

1259 *ḥeʾ- "seek, find"

Eg *ḥꜣ* "seek" (pyr).
WCh *ḥyaʾ- "find": Paa *ḥya*.
ECh *ʾyaw- "find": Smr *ʾyo*.
Reflects *ḥew-, a morphonological variant of the original root.

1260 *ḥed- "fly" (v.)

Eg *ḥdy* "fly" (v.) (n).
Infinitive in *-y*.
WCh **ḥyad-* "fly" (v.): Gwn *gede*.

1261 *ḥedVʾ- "bird"

Sem **ḥidʾ-* "kite": Arab *ḥidʾ-at-*.
ECh **hyad-hyad-* "ostrich": Kera *heḍheḍi*.
Irregular **h-*. Reduplication. Emphatic *ḍ* < **d* under the influence of the laryngeal.

1262 *ḥenin- "penis, testicles"

Eg *ḥnn* "penis" (pyr).
LEC **ḥenin-* "testicles": Som *ḥeeniin*.

1263 *ḥenVʿ- "fill"

Eg *ḥnʿ* "fill" (gr).
WCh **ḥyan-H-* "fill": Wrj *yan*, Paa *ḥyaŋgu*.
CCh **χyan-* "fill": Lame *yen*, Misme *hen*.
ECh **ʾwan-* < **ʾinwa-* "fill": Smr *ʾon*, Ndam *ʾəna*, Tum *an*, Kbl *wənə*, Mig *ʾunaw*, Brg *ʾuni*, Bid *ween*, Mkk *ʾuune*.

1264 *ḥer- "star"

Eg *ḥry.w* "stars" (pyr).
Vocalic *-y*.
ECh **hyar-* "star": Tum *heru*.
Irregular **h-*. Tum *h-* may also go back to **s-*.
LEC **ḥir-* "light of sun or moon": Arb *hiiro*.

1265 *ḥer- "be dry"

Sem **ḥVr-* "be dried up": Gz *ḥrr*.
ECh **ʾyar-* "dry" (v.): Tum *yə:r*.

1266 *ḥerač-/*ḥeruč- "sow"

Sem **ḥVruṯ-* "sow, till": Akk *erēšu*, Ug *ḥrṯ*, Hbr *ḥrš*, Arab *ḥrṯ* [-*u*-], Gz *ḥrs*.
WCh **rač-* "sow": DB *ras*.
Loss of the anlaut laryngeal or contraction of **ryaHač-*.
ECh **ryaHVs-* "sow": Dng *rēse*.
Metathesis.

An alternative reconstruction is **reḥač-*.

1267 *ḥibVr- "harvest"

Sem **ḥibūr-* "harvest": Akk *ebūru*.
Derived from **ḥVbVr-* "gather".
WCh **ḥirVb-* "harvest, reap": Hs *girbā*.
Metathesis.

1268 *ḥical- "lizard"

Sem **ḥisl-* "small lizard": Arab *ḥisl-*.
CCh **cal-* "lizard": Hwn *ta-sala*, Gis *me-selesele*.
Various prefixes in individual languages. Assimilation of vowels in Gis.

Any connection with Berb **ʔasVl-* "snake, viper" (Ayr *aššel*, Ahg *âššel*, Twl *aššol*) or Berb **ḥaǯVr-* "lizard" (Izy *ḥaǯǯēλ*)?

1269 *ḥidab- "bend"

Sem **ḥVdab-* "be curved": Arab *ḥdb* [-*a*-].
Cf. also Hss *ḥedeb* "hunch-backed", Mhr *ḥedēb* id., Shh *ḥidɛb* id.
CCh **diHVb-* "bend": Daba *dīḅ*.
Metathesis.

An alternative reconstruction is **diḥab-*.

1270 *ḥig- "plant"

Sem **ḥig-* "thorny plant": Akk *egu*, *igu*.
LEC **ḥig-* "kind of aloe": Som *ḥig-*.

1271 *ḥin- "grow"

Berb *ḥVn- "be inflated": Kby *eḥnenni*.
Eg *ḥn* "grow" (gr).
ECh *hin- "increase": Lele *hin*.
Irregular *h-.

1272 *ḥinṭ- "cereal"

Sem *ḥinṭ- "barley, grain": Akk *uṭṭutu*, Ug *ḥṭṭ*, Hbr *ḥiṭṭā*, Aram *ḥinṭ-ət-*, Arab *ḥinṭ-at-*, Soq *ḥinteh*.
HEC *hinṭ-/*hanṭ- "grass": Had *hiṭe*, Kmb *hiṭe*, Bmb *hanṭe*.
*-nṭ- > -ṭ- in Had and Kmb.

Cf. *ḫund- "cereal".

1273 *ḥir- "snake"

Eg *ḥrr.t* "kind of snake, worm" (reg).
ECh *hir- "snake": Tum *hirə*.
Irregular ECh *h-.

1274 *ḥirbaʔ- "chameleon"

Sem *ḥirbāʔ- "chameleon": Arab *ḥirbāʔ-*.
ECh *hir(V)b- "chameleon": Mubi *hirbe*.
Irregular ECh *h-. Sem loanword?

Derived from *ḥir- "snake". An ancient composite?

1275 *ḥis- "faeces"

Eg *ḥs* "faeces" (pyr).
WCh *ḥisa- "faeces": Sura *ʔyɛs*, Chip *ɛɛs*, Ank *ʔyɛs*, Geji *iši*, Say *nyis*, Buli *ʔiš*.
ECh *ʔis- "faeces": Smr *ʔiši-ny*, Ndam *ʔisi-n*, Jegu *ʔis*, Sok *issī*.

1276 *ḥogil- "go, cross"

Sem *ḥVgil-/*ḥVgul- "skip along": Arab *ḥgl* [-i-, -u-].
ECh *ʔwagil- "cross" [1], "jump" [2]: Mobu *ogole* [1], Mkk *ʔiigila* [2].

1277 *ḥoˁ- "medicine, poison"

Eg *wḥˁ.t* "poison" (n).
Vocalic *w*-.
CCh *χwaH- > *χway- "medicine": HNk *wiye*, FKi *wɛy*, Kap *γwe*, FGl *γwoˀyi*.

Cf. Asa *hoˁ*- "cure" (v.).

1278 *ḥok- "scratch"

Sem *ḥuk- "scratch, rub, scrape": Akk *ekēku*, MHbr *ḥkk*, Aram (Syr) *ḥkk*, Arab *ḥkk* [-*u*-], Gz *ḥkk*, Hss *ḥek*.
SA *ḥakuk- "scratch": Saho *ḥakuk*, Afar *ḥakuk*.
Partial reduplication.
LEC *ḥeḳ-/*ḥoḳ- "scratch": Som *ḥoq*-, Or *hooq*- , Rnd *oχ*-, Gid *heq*-, Arb *heeq*-.

Any connection with *ḥak- "stone" ("stone" as a scraping tool)?

1279 *ḥol- "jump"

Sem *ḥūl- "jump (on horse back)": Arab *ḥwl* [-*u*-].
ECh *ˀwal- "jump": Tum *wal*.

1280 *ḥonbal- "bean"

Sem *ḥunbul- "haricot": Arab *ḥunbul*-.
Assimilation of vowels.
WCh *mVbwaHal- "beans": Sura *mbwaalaa*.
Metathesis. Assimilation of *-nb- > -mb-.

*ḥon- may be a prefix. Cf. CCh *ḇul- < *HVbul- "corn, grain": Mnd *ḇula*, Gvo *ḇula*.

1281 *ḥos- "cold" (n.)

Eg *ḥsy* "cold" (NK).
Vocalic *-y* reflecting one of HS front vowels.
CCh *χVs- "cold": Gaa *həs*, Gbn *χəs*.
ECh *ˀwas- "wind": Mig *ˀussu*, Jegu *ˀos*, Sok *oso*.

1282 *ḥoy- "break, strike"

Eg *ḥwy* "strike" (pyr).
Vocalic *-w-*.
WCh **ḥway-* "break": Fyer *hoyo*.

1283 *ḥul- "bird"

Eg *ḥn* "kind of bird" (pyr).
Note Eg *-n* < HS **-l-*.
CCh **χuli-* "dove": HNk *χwuli*, HGh *χwuli*, Kap *χwuli*.

Cf. Dhl *hille* "owl".

1284 *ḥul- "untie"

Sem **ḥul-* "untie": Arab *ḥll* [-*u*-].
WCh **ḥal-* < **ḥula-* "loosen": Bol *ʾall-*.
CCh **ʾul-* "untie": Lame *ʾulee-*, LPe *ʾolai*.
Irregular **ʾ-* < **ḥ-*.
ECh **wul-* < **ʾul-* "loosen": Ndam *wule*.

1285 *ḥum- "be hot"

Sem **ḥum-* "be hot" [1], "warm" [2]: Akk *emēmu* [1], Hbr *ḥām* [2], Aram (Syr) *ḥam* [1], Arab *ḥmm* [-*u*-] [1].
Eg *hm* "be inflamed" (XVIII).
Secondary modification of the laryngeal?
Rift **ham-* "heat (v.)": Irq *ham-esa*.
Cf. Irq *hame* "sweat".

1286 *ḥum- "drive, move"

Eg *ḥmy* "move away" (pyr).
-y is a suffix.
CCh **χum-* "drive": FG *əχam-ti*, Gudu *umsa*, Bch *omo*.

1287 *ḥun- "son, child"

Eg *ḥwn* "boy" (pyr).
WCh **wun-* < **ḥun-* "son": Dwot *wun*, Buli *uni*, Bade *wun*.

Related to **ḥenin-* "penis, testicles"?

1288 *ḥunaḥ- "be afraid"

Eg *ḥnḥ* "fright" (l).
Deverbative noun.
CCh **χunaχ-* "be afraid": Msg *χunaγ*.

Partial reduplication?

1289 *ḥupet- "go"

Eg *ḥpt* "go" (XVIII).
WCh **Hupyat-/*puHyat-* "go out": Ank *ṗet*, Sura *put*, Ang *put*, Mpn *pūt*, Bol *pete*.
CCh **put-* "enter": Gudu *pət*, Bch *puřo*, Mwl *uputo*, Mus *put*.
Cf. Mofu *pat*, *pet* "go out". From **puHVt-*, cf. WCh.

Cf. also Akk *ḫabātu* "wander".

1290 *ḥusam- "weapon"

Sem **ḥušām-* "sabre": Arab *ḥusām-*.
Related to Arab *ḥsm* [-*i*-]"cut".
ECh **sVm-* "axe": Smr *suma*, Sok *som*.
Loss of the anlaut laryngeal.

**ḥu-* may be a prefix.

1291 *ḥusem- "mouse"

Sem **[ḥ]ušum-* "reed-mouse": Akk *ušummu*.
Assimilation of vowels.
CCh **χusyam-* "rat": Log *uχsemī*.
Initial Log *u-* reflects the vowel of the first syllable.

1292 *ḥVbüs- "bind, sew"

Sem **ḥVbiš-* "bind" [1], "envelop" [2]: Hbr *ḥbš* [1], Arab *ḥbs* [-*i*-] [2].
ECh **bVHus-* "sew": Smr *busə*.
Metathesis.

1293 *ḥVčuk- "knife"

Eg *ḥsk.t* "knife" (BD).
WCh **čuk-* "knife": Ang *čuk*, Mpn *čuka*.
Loss of the anlaut laryngeal.

**ḥV-* may be a prefix.

1294 *ḥVdog- "arrow"

Sem **ḥVdig-* "shoot (of an arrow)": Arab *ḥdg* [*-i-*].
Denominative verb with a modified vocalism.
WCh **dVg-* "arrow": Ngz *dəga*.
HEC **dog-* "arrow": Sid *doga*.

**ḥV-* may be a prefix.

1295 *ḥVkay- "call"

Sem **ḥVkVy-* "tell, inform": Arab *ḥky* [*-i-*, *-u-*].
ECh **ʾVwak-/*ʾVyak-* "call": Sbn *ʾwag-a*, Tum *wəg*, Ndam *wuga*, Kwn *e:ke:*, Mkk *wiike*.
Metathesis.

1296 *ḥVmaĉ- "be sour"

Sem **ḥVmaŝ-* "be sour": Akk *emēṣu*, Hbr *ḥmṣ*, Arab *ḥmḍ* [*-a-*, *-u-*], Hss *ḥāmeẓ*.
Secondary **-u-* after a labial.
Eg *ḥmḏ* "vinegar" (n).

Derived from **ḥam-* "salt". For this type of semantic evolution cf. OEng *sūr*, Eng *sour* ~ Lith *sūrus* "salt" (adj.).

1297 *ḥVmus- "roast"

Sem **ḥVmuš-* "roast": Arab *ḥms* [*-u-*].
CCh **mVs-* "roast": Daba *məsa*.
Loss of **HV-*.

**ḥV-* may be a prefix. On the other hand, cf. HS **ḥam-* "be hot".

1298 *ḥVmVr- "be red"

Sem **ḥVmVr-* "be red": Akk *emēru*, Arab *ḥmr*.
Eg *ỉmꜣw* "red color" (NK).
Irregular laryngeal. Sem loanword?

1299 *ḥVrabib- "cold, wind"

Eg *ḥnbb* "wind" (gr).
Note *-n-* < HS **-r-*.
WCh **raḅiḅ-* < **HVrabib-* "coldness": Wrj *raḅiḅya*.
Emphatic *-ḅ-* < **-b-* under the influence of **ḥ-*.

1300 *ḥVsaw-/*ḥVsay- "drink"

Sem **ḥVšVw-* "drink": Arab *ḥsw* [*-u-*].
WCh **swaH-/*say-/*saH-* "drink": Hs *šā*, Sura *šwā*, Ang *šwē*, Chip *šuu*, Ank *sua*, Grk *ta*, Bol *s*, *sa*, Krk *s*, *sa*, Pero *ǯe*, Ngm *sowoo*, Bele *hee*, Krf *see*, Gera *še*, Glm *še-*, Grm *šee-*, Wrj *sa*, Kry *sa*, Diri *čā*, Miya *sa*, Paa *sa*, Cagu *šā*, Siri *sa*, Mbu *sa*, *si*, Jmb *sa*, *si*, Fyer *šo*, DB *šoh* Ngz *sau*.
**swaH-* goes back to **sVwaH-* (metathesis of the original HS **ḥVsaw-*) or to **saw-*. The original initial cluster **ḥsV-* may be reflected in secondary laterals of Geji *ŝawi*, Pol *ŝiyu*.
CCh **sa-/*si-* "drink": Gbn *ši*, Hwn *sa*, Klb *še*, Mrg *sᵓ*, FKi *sa*, Mofu *-s-*, Bld *si*, Muk *sa*, Daba *sa*, Gudu *sa*, FJ *se*, FMb *si*, Mwu *usa*, Log *se*, Bud *hi*, Msg *sa*, Gid *sa*.
The original form of the root **saw-/*say-* was modified in CCh.
ECh **saw-/*say-* "drink": Smr *ša*, Tum *he*, Kbl *suwə*, Kera *se*, Dng *sεε*, Brg *saya*, Sok *sa*.

**ḥV-* may be a prefix. Consonantal alternation **-w-* ~ **-y-*.

1301 *ḥVsub- "count"

Sem **ḥVšub-* "count, think": Hbr *ḥšb*, Aram (Syr) *ḥšb*, Arab *ḥsb* [*-u-*], Gz *ḥsb*, Hss *ḥesōb*.
ECh **ᵓVsVb-* "count": Sbn *ᵓasba*.

1302 *ḥVṭVr- "pay"

Sem **ḥVṭVr-* "pay": Akk *eṭēru.*
Eg *ḥtr* "pay" (n).

1303 *ḥVw- "rain" (v.)

Eg *ḥwy* "rain, flow" (MK).
ECh **ʔVw-* "rain" (v.): Sbn *ʔwā.*
Note ECh *ʔ-.

1304 *ḥVʒ- "vessel"

Eg *ḥz.t* "bottle" (OK).
CCh **χVʒ-* "pot": Tera *həža.*

1305 *ḥVʒim- "sharp object, cut"

Sem **ḥVḏim-* "cut": Arab *ḥḏm* [-*i*-].
CCh **ǯam-* < **ǯyam-* "spear": Msm *dǯam.*
Semantic connection is dubious.

*ḫ̮

1306 *ḫ̮a- "be young"

Eg *ḫ̮* "young" (med).
CCh **γa-γa-* "new" [1], "young" [2]: Mba *haha* [1], Msg *ḥaḥai* [2].
Reduplication.

Note the rare structure of the root **CV-*, cf. also **ḫ̮a-* "speak".

1307 *ḫ̮a- "speak"

CCh **γa-* "speak": Chb *γa.*
Dhl *-χa* "answer" (v.).
Unexpected reflex of **ḫ̮-*.

1308 *ḫaɔ-/*ḫaw- "altar, throne"

Sem *ḫaɔ- "throne canopy": Akk *ḫaɔu*.
Eg *ḫȝw.t* "altar" (pyr).
-*ȝ* stands for a vowel.

Consonantal alternation *-ɔ- ~ *-*w*-.

1309 *ḫaɔ-/*ḫaw- "grind, beat"

CCh *γaɔ- "grind": Gis *heɔe*, Log *χa*.
Assimilation of vowels in Gis.
LEC *ḥaw- "beat": Som *ḥaawi*.
Rift *ḫaɔ- "grind corn": Kwz *ḫaɔ-it-*.

Consonantal alternation *-ɔ- ~ *-*w*-.

1310 *ḫaɔ-/*ḫuɔ- "fire"

CCh *γuɔ- "fire": Mba *hū*, HNk *γwi*, Kap *γwi*, FG *γo*, FKi *uγu*.
Rift *ḫaɔ- "fire": Kwz *ḫaɔo*.

Alternation *a ~ *u. Cf. Eg *ḫȝ* "roast" (n) if only it is not related to HS *q̇ar-/*q̇awar- "burn".

1311 *ḫab- "charcoal"

CCh *γVbu-n- "charcoal": Lam *uγəvii-ni*, Zgh *uvu-re*, Glv *ɔoγvu-ra*, Nak *oγvə-ra*.
Rhotacism in individual CCh languages is regular.
Rift *ḫab- "charcoal": Irq *ḫawo*, Alg *ḫabi*, Bur *ḫabo*.
Note *-*b*- > Irq -*w*-.

1312 *ḫab- "water flow"

Sem *ḫVb- "scoop, draw water": Akk *ḫabû*.
Denominative verb.
WCh *ḫyab- < *ḫabya- "stream": Hs *gēbe*.
CCh *γab(ya)- "water": Bch *γaḅyiy*.
Emphatization of -*ḅ*- under the influence of the laryngeal.

1313 *ḫab-/*ḫabiᵓ- "vessel"

Sem *ḫābiᵓ-/*ḫābiy- "jug, bowl": Arab ḫābiᵓ-at-, ḫābiy-at-, Gz ḫəbay.
Berb *ḫVb- "big wooden plate": Izy *iḥebbi*.
Eg *ḫbb* "vessel" (MK).
Partial reduplication.
WCh *ḫabi(ᵓ)- "pot" [1], "gourd" [2]: Bol *gewi* [1], Krk *gaabi* [1], Ngm *gabi* [1], Krf *giḅi* [1], Ngz *gaḅiya* [2].
LEC *ḥabub- "large gourd": Or *habubbii*.
Partial reduplication.

Eg and LEC may reflect HS *ḫabub-.

1314 *ḫabal- "weakness"

Sem *ḫabal- "lawlessness, oppression" [1], "ache, pain, sickness" [2]: Akk *ḫabâlu* [1], Hbr *ḥēbel* [2], Arab *ḫabal-*, *ḫabāl-* [2].
CCh *bVl- "weakness": Mofu *bəle*.
The initial syllable is lost.
ECh *γVbal- "weaken": Sbn *həbal*.
Denominative verb.

1315 *ḫabal- "tie, plait"

Sem *ḫVbul- "tie (with a rope)": Akk *ḫabālu*, Arab *ḥbl* [-*u*-].
Irregular Akk *ḫ*- ~ Arab *ḥ*-.
WCh *baHal- "tie": Hs *ḅalla*, Sura *ḅal*, Geji *ḅāliwi*.
Metathesis. Emphatic *ḅ*- reflects the inlaut laryngeal.
CCh *baHal- "plait": Bch *bālə*.
Metathesis. Bch long -*ā*- results from a contraction of *-*aHa*-.

An alternative reconstruction is *baḫal-.

1316 *ḫabay- "dance" (v.)

Eg *ḫby* "dance" (v.).
Bed *hawaay-* "dance".
From *ḫabay-. Note the development of intervocalic *-*b*- .

1317 *ḫabur- "wine"

Sem *ḫabur-"kind of wine": Akk *ḫabburu*.

Secondary *-*u*-?
Eg *ḥbꜣ* "stage in beer fermentation" (med).
Irregular *ḥ*-. -*ꜣ* reflects *-*r*-.

A cultural loanword?

1318 *ḫaç- "axe"

Sem **ḫaṣṣ-* "axe": Akk *ḫaṣṣ-innu*.
HEC **haç-* "chopping tool": Bmb *haacce*.
Bmb -*c*- < *-*ç*-?

Connected with **ḫoç-* "break".

1319 *ḫaç- "leaf, plant"

Sem **ḫūṣ-* "leaf": Aram *ḥūṣ*-, Arab *ḫūṣ*-, Soq *ḥēṣ*- .
Contraction of **ḫVwVṣ-*.
Eg *ḥḏ.t* "kind of plant" (n).
Irregular reflex of **ḫ*.
Agaw **χaç-* "leaf": Xmr *ḫaṣaa*, *ḫača*, Kwr *ašaa*, Aun *γači*.

1320 *ḫaĉ- "become dark"

Sem **ḫaŝVw-* "become dark": Akk *ḫašû*.
WCh **ḫaĉ-* "night": Geji *gasi*, Buli *ŋgasi*, Tule *gaŝə*.
Prefix **nV-* in Buli.
LEC **ᶜas-* "evening": Som *ᶜašo*.
Irregular ᶜ-.
HEC **haš̌-* "come (of evening)": Dar *haš̌-*, Sid *haš̌-*.

1321 *ḫaĉaᶜ- "be silent"

Sem **ḫVŝaᶜ-* "be humble" [1], "be calm" [2]: Arab *ḫšᶜ* [-*a*-] [1], Gz *ḫšᶜ* [2].
SA **ʾasaᶜ-* "keep silence": Saho *asaaᶜ*-.
Unexpected reflex of **ḫ*.
Rift **ḫaĉ-* "be silent": Irq *ḫaĉ*-.

1322 *ḫad- "cheek"

Sem **ḫadd-* "cheek": Arab *ḫadd-*, Jib *ḫad*, Hss *ḥadd*.
ECh **γaḍ-* "cheek": Jegu *gede*, Brg *gaḍ-ago*.
Emphatization in Brg caused by HS **ḫ-*.

1323 *ḫadar- "darkness"

Sem **ḫadar-* "be dark" 1, "darkness" 2: Akk *ḫadāru* 1, Arab *ḫadar-* 2.
Cf. Hss *ḥedōr* "put up a sunshade", Mhr *ḥedōr* id., Shh *ḫodor* id.
WCh **dar-* "night": Hs *darē*.
Loss of the anlaut laryngeal.

**ḫa-* may be a prefix. Cf. also CCh **ʔadur-* "evening" (Msg *adura*).

1324 *ḫadir-/*ḫadur- "sleep, be benumbed"

Sem **ḫVdVr-* "remain and keep to a place, be benumbed": Arab *ḫdr*.
SA **ḥVdir-* "sleep": Afar *-iḥdir-*.
LEC **hudur-* "sleep": Som *hurd-*, Rnd *udur-*, Bay *hudur-* .
Assimilation of vowels. Metathesis in Som. Note the reflex of HS **ḫ-*.
Dhl *haḏḏura* "sleep".

1325 *ḫaduĉ- "fly" (n.)

Sem **ḫadūŝ-* "fly": Arab *ḫadūš-*.
WCh **HVdiĉ- < *HVduĉi-* "fly": Sura *ⁿdiši*.

1326 *ḫaʕay- "house"

Eg *ḫʕy.t* "house" (gr).
CCh **γaʔ-/*γay- < *γaʔay-* "house" 1, "compound" 2: Zgh *γaya* 1, Log *γaʔa* 1, Mnd *χa* 2, FKi *γəy* 2, FGl *γyi* 2, HK *γe* 2.

1327 *ḫalaḳ- "clothes"

WCh **ḫal(V)k-* "leather covering loin": Hs *galko*.

Irregular *-*k*-.
Bed *halak* "cloth, kerchief".
Irregular *-*k*-.
SA **ḥalag*- "rag, clothes": Saho *ḥalaga*, Afar *halago*.
Note HS **ḳ* > SA **g*.

Any connection with Sem **ḫulāḳ*-/**ḫālūḳ*- "old or torn clothes" (Akk *ḫulāqu*, Hbr *ḥālūq*, Aram *ḥalūqā*, Arab *ḫālūq*, Soq *ḥalaq*)? The Sem word may be derived from Sem **ḫVlVḳ*- "be torn". In any case the correspondence of velars is irregular.

1328 *ḫalaḳ-/*ḫaluḳ- "give birth, create"

Sem **ḫVluḳ*- "create": Arab *ḫlq* [-*u*-].
WCh **laHaḳ*- "give birth": Sura *laak*.
Metathesis and contarction.

An alternative reconstruction is **laḫaḳ*-/**laḫuḳ*-.

1329 *ḫalaṭ-/*ḫaliṭ- "mix"

Sem **ḫVliṭ*- "mix": Arab *ḫlṭ* [-*i*-], Hss *ḫelōṭ*, Mhr *ḫelōṭ*, Shh *ḫoloṭ*.
WCh **lawaṭ*- < **laHaṭ*-"mix": Bks *lawat*.
Metathesis.
CCh **layaṭ*- "mix": Mofu *lahaḍ*.
Metathesis.

An alternative reconstruction is **laḫaṭ*-/**laḫiṭ*-.

1330 *ḫam- "male relative"

Sem **ḫam*- "father-in-law": Akk *emu*, Hbr *ḥām*, Aram (Syr) *ḥ*[e]-*mō*, Arab *ḫam(w)*-.
CCh **γam*- "chief": Bata *home*, Bch *höme*, *hamɛy*.
Dhl *ḥame* "uncle".

1331 *ḫamaʾ- "rebellion"

Sem **ḫamāʾ*- "rebellion": Akk *ḫammāʾu*.
Eg *iḫm.w* "enemies" (XVIII).
Metathesis.

An alternative reconstruction is *ʾaḫam-. A cultural *Wanderwort*?

1332 *ḫa(n)ĉob- "tree, wood"

Sem *ḫaŝab- "timber": Arab ḫašab-.
Delabialized vowel of the second syllable.
WCh *ĉaHwab- "tree": Bol šōwi, Dera šooḇi.
LEC *ḥançab- "kind of tree": Or hançabii.
Inlaut -ç- may be a result of secondary emphatization caused by the laryngeal. -nç- may go back to a HS prenasalized cluster.

1333 *ḫansab- "vessel"

Sem *ḫanzab- "kind of pot": Akk ḫanzabu.
Is Sem *-nz- a regular reflex of the HS cluster *-ns-?
Eg ḥnbꜣs "vessel" (MK).
Metathesis. Note ḥ- < *ḫ-. The vowel of the second syllable is marked with -ꜣ-.

An alternative reconstruction is *ḫanbas-. An ancient cultural word.

1334 *ḫar- "excrements"

Sem *ḫarʾ-/*ḫary- "excrements": Hbr ḥarāʾīm, Aram (Syr) ḥerāy-, Arab ḫary-.
SA *har- "excrements": Saho haraa, Afar haraa.
LEC *ḥar- "excrements": Som ḥaar.
HEC *har- "mud": Had hara, Kmb haro.

Related to *ḫar- "defecate".

1335 *ḫar- "river"

Sem *ḫarr- "watercourse": Akk ḫarru.
LEC *har- "lake" [1], "river" [2]: Som haro [1], Arb haru [2], Or haroo [1].

1336 *ḫar- "defecate"

Eg wḫꜣ "defecate" (OK).

Initial *w*- reflects a prefix.
LEC **ḥar-* "defecate": Som *ḥaar-*.

1337 *ḫas- "grass"

WCh **ḫasu-* "grass": Zar *gwas*.
ECh **ʔwas-* "grass": Bid *ʔawso*.
Secondary **-wa-*?
LEC **haš-* "leaf": Kns *haša*.

1338 *ḫasay- "grass"

Sem **ḫašVy-* "thymian": Akk *ḫašû*.
Eg *ḫꜣsy.t* "medicinal herb" (med).
-ꜣ- is a vocalic sign.
WCh **ḫasay-* "grass": Hs *gāsayā*.

Derived from **ḫas-* "grass".

1339 *ḫas-/*ḫus- "rub, pound"

Sem **ḫVš-* "crush, pound": Akk *ḫašû*.
CCh **γus-* "crush, rub": Mafa *hus-*.
Bed *-hasi-* "rub".
SA **ḥes-* "rub, pound": Saho *ḥesi-*.
e < **a* after a laryngeal?
HEC **has-* "rub": Bmb *haas-iy-*.

Alternation **a* ~ **u*.

1340 *ḫatVm- "face, nose"

Sem **ḫatm-/*ḫaṭm-* "nose, beak": Hbr *ḥoṭem*, Arab *ḫatm-*.
Secondary emphatic in Hbr.
Eg *ḫnt* "face" (pyr).
Metathesis and regressive assimilation of **-mt-* > *-nt-*.

1341 *ḫaṭ- "dig"

ECh **γat-* "dig": Brg *gatt-*.
LEC **haḍ-* "dig": Or *haaḍa*.
HEC **haḍ-* "dig": Kmb *haaḍ-*.

1342 *ḫawVy- "evening"

Eg *ḫꜣwy* "evening" (pyr).
Vocalic *-ꜣ-*.
CCh **γawVy-* "yesterday": Mnd *ʾawəya*.
A regular reflex of **γ-* in Mnd, cf. s.v. **ḫay-* "voice".

1343 *ḫay- "voice"

CCh **γay-* "voice": Gava *γaya*, Mnd *ʾiye*.
Secondary *-i-* in Mnd before *-y-*.
Dhl *hwayu* "voice, sound, noise".
Sources of Dhl *-wa-* are unknown.

Related to **ḫa-* "speak".

1344 *ḫaʒod- "rot, be rotten"

Eg *ḫzd* "rot" (n.) (l).
ECh **ʒaHwad-* "rotten": Dng *zōḍe*, Bid *zooḍ*.
Metathesis. Note emphatic *-ḍ-* reflecting the lost laryngeal.

An alternative reconstruction is **ʒaḫod-*.

1345 *ḫef- "be light"

Sem **ḫip-* "be light": Arab *ḫff* [*-i-*], Hss *ḫef*, Mhr *ḫef*, Shh *ḫef*.
WCh **fifya-* "light" (adj.): Fyer *fifyo*.
From reduplicated **HVfif-*?
ECh **γyaf-* "light" (adj.): Sok *effi*.
LEC **ḥa[f]-* "thin, light": Or *haṗṗii*.
Secondary Or *-ṗ-* may go back to **-f-* in contact with a laryngeal. The vocalism is irregular.

1346 *ḫek- "wait"

Sem **ḫVkVy-* "wait": Hbr *ḥky*.
Based on biconsonantal **ḫVk-*.
WCh **ḫyak-* "wait": DB *gyok*, Fyer *kwek*.

1347 *ḫil- "pierce"

Sem *ḫVlVy- "cut": Arab ḫly [-i-].
Based on biconsonantal *ḫVl-.
ECh *γil- "pierce": Sok *gile*.

Alternation *i ~ *u.

1348 *ḫilVp- "field"

Sem *ḫilVp- "meadow": Akk *ḫilēpu*.
Eg *ḫnp.t* "field" (XVIII).
Note -n- < HS *-l-.

1349 *ḫiŝ- "peel"

Sem *nVḫaś- "peel off (bark)": Arab *nḫš* [-a-].
Prefix *nV- with modified vocalism.
Dhl *hitl-* "scrape scales off fish".
Rift *ḫiŝ- "peel": Irq *ḫiŝ-it-*.

1350 *ḫiyal- "be clever"

Sem *ḫīl- "imagine" [1], "think" [2]: Arab *ḫyl* [-a-] [1], Gz *ḫly* [2].
LEC *hil- "clever": Or *hilluu*, Boni *hilluu*.
Contraction of *ḫiyVl-.

1351 *ḫoç- "break"

Sem *ḫVṣ- "break off": Akk *ḫaṣāṣu*.
CCh *γwac- "break": Mafa *hwac-*.

1352 *ḫol- "cut"

Sem *ḫul- "pierce": Hbr *ḥll*, Arab *ḫll* [-u-].
ECh *γwal- "cut (animal) into pieces": Kera *hole*.

1353 *ḫom- "be sick, be ill"

Sem *ḫVmVy- "be paralysed": Akk *ḫamû*.
Based on biconsonantal *ḫVm-.

Eg *ḫm* "illness (of stomach)" (med).
ECh **γwam-* "be sick, be ill": Lele *homya*, Kbl *hum-ŋa*.

1354 *ḫon- "sack"

Eg *ḫn* "sack" (XXII).
ECh **γwan-H-* "sack": Kera *hoŋ*.
Secondary **-H-* in the auslaut.

1355 *ḫon- "do, make"

Eg *ḫn* "do, make" (n).
CCh **γwan-* "do, make": Log *γən*, Bud *wan*.

1356 *ḫor- "dry up"

Sem **nVḫVr-* "dry" (adj.): Akk *naḫru*.
Prefix **nV-*.
CCh **γwar-* "dry up": Tera *γwari*, Hwn *χwar*, Boka *χweri*, FG *γwoli*, HF *γwelo*, FJ *χweru*, FMch *χuri*, Nza *hore*, Mafa *gwar*.

1357 *ḫor- "snore"

Sem **ḫir-/*ḫur-* "snore": Arab *ḫrr* [*-i-*, *-u-*].
WCh **ḫa-ḫwar-* "snore": Fyer *gogor*, Bks *hagor*, Sha *ʔahagar*, DB *hagar*.
Partial reduplication. Assimilation of vowels in individual languages.
CCh **γur-* "snore" (n.): Mafa *ghur-ghur*.
Reduplication.

1358 *ḫoras- "mountain"

Sem **ḫurš-* "rock, mountain": Akk *ḫuršu*, Hbr *ḥōreš*.
Eg *ḫꜣs.t* "mountainous region, desert" (pyr).
-ꜣ- < **-r-*.
WCh **rwaHas-* "mountain": Tala *ro:si*.
Metathesis.

1359 *ḫorug- "move"

Sem **ḫVrug-* "go out, drive out": Hbr *ḥrg*, Arab *ḫrg* [*-u-*], Hss *ḥerōg*.
WCh **Hwarug-* "drive away" [1], "enter" [2], "migrate" [3]: Hs *rūga* [1], Jim *orogo* [2], Buli *wərgu* [2], Tala *rəga* [2], Ngz *rəgu* [3].
CCh **rug-* "run": Gude *rug-*.
The initial laryngeal is lost.

1360 *ḫorVç- "receptacle"

Sem **ḫirṣ-* "basket" [1], "water-jar" [2]: Arab *ḫirṣ-* [1], Hss *ḫarṣ*, *ḫerōṣ* [2].
Irregular vocalism.
CCh **γwarVc-* "small pot": HF *γwɔrče*.
LEC **ḥoroç-* "pot": Or *horoçoo*.
Assimilation of vowels.

1361 *ḫotam- "bird"

Sem **ḫutm-* "bird": Akk *ḫutmu*.
ECh **γatVm-* < **γwatam-* "vulture": Kera *atəəme*.
Assimilation of vowels.

1362 *ḫoṭ- "go"

Sem **ḫVṭVw-* "march, go": Arab *ḫṭw* [*-u-*].
Based on biconsonantal **ḫVṭ-*.
CCh **γwaṭ-* "return": Masa *hɔta*.

1363 *ḫub- "hole, pit"

Sem **ḫabb-* "pit": Akk *ḫabbu*.
With secondary *-*a*- before a labial.
Berb **ḫVb-* "hole": Izy *aḫβu*.
CCh **γub-* "hole": Lmn *oghuḇu*.
Emphatization of *-ḇ-* under the influence of the laryngeal.

1364 *ḫubuʒ- "cereal"

Sem **ḫubz-* "bread": Arab *ḫubz-*, Gz *ḫəbəst*, Hss *ḫabz*, Mhr *ḫabz*, Shh *ḫobz*.

CCh *buʒ- "millet": Daba *vuǯi*.
Loss of the initial laryngeal.
ECh *bus- "seed": Mkk *buzu*.
Loss of the initial laryngeal.

*ḫu- may be a prefix.

1365 *ḫubVʔ- "hoe, till" (v.)

Sem *ḫabVʔ- "hoe": Akk *ḫabūtu*.
*-a- < *-u- before the labial.
Eg *ḫbꜣ* "dig, till" (pyr).
Denominative formation.
WCh *ḫubVʔ- "hoe, hoe-handle": Krf *gufe*, Gera *guḅa*, Glm *giḅa*, Bks *huḅ-eŋ*.
-ḅ- reflects the lost auslaut *-ʔ-.

1366 *ḫubVs- "vessel"

Sem *ḫubš- "clay vessel": Akk *ḫubšašû*.
The root is preserved only in a form of a derivative.
Eg *ḫbs* "vessel for myrrha" (gr).

Cf. *ḫansab- "vessel".

1367 *ḫucig- "stone"

Sem *ḫusīg- "stone": Akk *ḫusīgu*.
Eg *ḥsg* "stone" (XVIII).
Irregular *ḥ*- < *ḫ-.

1368 *ḫud- "cut"

Sem *ḫud- "cut" [1], "dig, till" [2]: Akk *ḫadādu* [1], Arab *ḫdd* [-u-] [2].
CCh *γud- "cut": Glv *γud-*, Nak *wiγḍa*.
Prefix *wi- in Nak.

Cf. ECh *γad- < *γwada- "split": Tum *gād*, Ndm *gəda*.

1369 *ḫuᶜ- "put"

Eg *ḫꜣᶜ* "put, lay" (MK).

Traces of the *a*-grade?

CCh **χuy-* < **γuʾi-* "put, throw": HNk *χuyɛ*, Log *hi*.

Irregular development of the initial laryngeal under the influence of the inlaut laryngeal.

1370 *ḫun- "voice, speech"

Eg *ḫn* "speech" (MK).

WCh **ḫun-* "sound or murmur of voices": Hs *gūnī*.

CCh **γun-* "voice": HGh *χuna*.

1371 *ḫun- "tomb, grave"

Eg *ḫnw* "tomb, burial place" (XVIII).

Vocalic *-w*.

ECh **gun-* "grave": Tum *mu-gən*, Ndm *mu-gun*, Dng *ma-gine*, Kbl *čato-gun*.

Prefix **ma-* in most forms. Connected with **gwan-* "bury": Jegu *gon-t-*.

1372 *ḫund- "cereal"

Eg *ḫnd* "kind of cereals".

WCh **ḫund-* "Pennisetum typhoidaeum": Hs *gunḍu*.

Note emphatic *-ḍ-* influenced by the anlaut laryngeal.

1373 *ḫund- "go"

Eg *ḫnd* "go" (gr).

WCh **wunḍ-* < **Hund-* "enter": Zar *wunḍi*.

The reconstruction of **ḫ-* follows from the emphatic reflecting a lost anlaut laryngeal. On the other hand, **ḫ* normally yields to Zar *g-*.

1374 *ḫunʒ-/*ḫunʒ-ir- "pig"

Sem **ḫunzir-* "pig": Akk *ḫuzīru*, Ug *ḫnzr*, Hbr *ḥᵃzīr*, Aram (Syr) *ḥᵉzira*, Arab *ḫinzīr-*.

Note the development of HS cluster **-nʒ-* preserved only in Ug and Arab.

WCh *ḫunʒ- "wild boar": Hs *gunzū*.
CCh *γinʒir- "pig": Ktk *hinzir*.
 Assimilation of vowels. Sem loan-word?
ECh *γunʒir- "pig" [1], "porcupine" [2]: Dng *kinzir* [1], Kbl *kunǯu* [2].
 The reflex of HS *ḫ in Dng is irregular. Assimilation of vowels in Dng.

Note LEC *gol(V)ǯ- "boar" (Or *golǯaa*), HEC *gol(V)ǯ- "boar" (Sid *golja*), Omot *gudin- "boar" (Ome *gudunça*, Kaf *gudino*), a *Wanderwort* of considerable resemblance to *ḫunʒ(ir)-. *-nʒ- seems to be a HS cluster. *ḫunʒ-ir- is a HS derivative. The original root is preserved only in the archaic WCh *ḫunʒ-.

1375 *ḫur- "dig"

Sem *ḫVr- "dig": Akk *ḫeru*, Ug *ḫr*, Gz *ḫrw*.
WCh *ḫur- "enlarge (hole, well)" [1], "dig" [2]: Hs *gūre* [1], Bol *gur* [2].
LEC *hur- "make hole": Or *hura*.

1376 *ḫur- "hole, pit"

Sem *ḫurr- "hole" [1], "grave" [2]: Akk *ḫurru* [1], Ug *ḫr* [2], Hbr *ḥōr* [1], Arab *ḫurr-* [1], Hss *ḫerrayt* [1].
Eg *ḫr* "tomb" (n).
WCh *ḫir- "pit, hole": Wrj *gir-na*, Kry *gir*, Miya *agir*, Paa *ngir*, Siri *γəri*, Jmb *γira*, Brm *čir*, Say *gir*, Buli *γir*, Pol *gir*.
 From *ḫuri-?
LEC *hur- "hole": Or *huraa*.

Derived from *ḫur- "dig".

1377 *ḫuray- "palm tree"

Sem *ḫarVy- "palm sprout": Akk *ḫarû*.
 Assimilation of vowels.
CCh *γuray- "Deleb palm": Msg *ḥurai*, *ḥorai*.
Rift *ḫuray- "Borassus palm": Irq *ḫuray*.

1378 *ḫuruᶜ- "steal"

Eg *ḥwrᶜ* "steal" (n).
 Irregular laryngeal in late Eg. Vocalic *-w-*.

CCh *ɣur- "steal": Chb *χul-*, Bura *χula*, HBaza *ɣuli*, HNk *ɣuli-*, FGl *ɣuli*, HGh *χuri*, FKi *ɣuři*, Gude *χuř-n*, FJ *χuř*, Mwu *uhuro*, Lame *huřa*.
The second syllable is lost in CCH.

1379 *ḫurVb- "bend"

Eg *ḫ3b* "crooked" (med).
CCh *ɣurVb- "bend (down)": Mafa *hurv-*.

1380 *ḫuṭ- "dig, scratch"

Sem *ḫuṭ- "dig" [1], "make signs on the ground" [2]: Akk *ḫaṭātu* [1] [-*u*-], Hss *ḫṭāṭ* [2], Mhr *ḫeṭ* [2], Shh *ḫeṭ* [2].
Dhl *ḥuḍ-* "dig".

Connected with *ḫaṭ- "dig".

1381 *ḫüdad- "stream, river"

Sem *ḫidVd- "narrow river-bed": Jib *ḫided*.
Based on *ḫad(d)- "rivulet" (Arab *ḫadd-*)?
WCh *ḫudad- "stream, flow": Hs *gudāda*.

1382 *ḫVbuč- "be angry"

Sem *ḫVbuṯ- "be angry, be malicious": Arab *ḫbṯ* [-*u*-].
WCh *HVbuči- "angry, bad": Sura *biš*, Ang *bis*.
Voiced *b*- in Sura and Ang point out to a preceding syllable.

1383 *ḫVĉun- "be hard"

Sem *ḫVŝun- "be hard": Arab *ḫšn* [-*u*-].
Assimilation of vowels in *ḫaŝan-.
CCh *ŝVn-H- "hardness": Masa *ŝɛŋɛ*.
Metathesis of the laryngeal. Note the development of *-*n*-*H*- into -*ŋ*-.

1384 *ḫVĉ̣ar- "be green"

Sem *ḫVṣ̂ar- "be green": Arab *ḫḍr* [-*a*-].

WCh **çVr-* "green, unripe": Ngz *ŝər-ət*.
Complete loss of the anlaut laryngeal.

*ḫ*V*- may be a prefix. Any connection with **ḫVçeb-* "be green"?

1385 *ḫVçeb- "be green"

Sem **ḫVṣ̂ib-* "be green" [1], "paint" (v.) [2]: Akk *ḫaṣābu* [1], Arab *ḫḍb* [-*i*-] [2].
CCh *(HV)ẑyab-* "green": Log *ẑebā*.
Auslaut -*ā* in Log may reflect metathesis of the laryngeal and further lengthening of the vowel.

1386 *ḫVf- "break"

Sem **ḫVpVy-* "break": Akk *ḫepû*.
Based on biconsonantal **ḫVp-*.
Eg *ḫfḫf* "break (a statue)" (sait).
Reduplication.

1387 *ḫVl- "close, lock"

Sem **ḫVl-* "lock" (v.): Akk *ḫalālu*.
Eg *ḥn* "close" (XXII).
Irregular *ḥ*- resulting from **ḫ*- in late Eg.

1388 *ḫVlVy- "shine"

Sem **ḫVlVy-* "be light": Akk *ḫelû*.
Eg *ḥ3y* "shine" (XVIII).
Irregular *ḥ*-.

1389 *ḫVn- "preserve, keep"

Sem **ḫan-* "storage place": Jib *ḫan*.
Deverbative?
CCh **γVn-* "preserve, keep, store": Mafa *hən*.

1390 *ḫVpaĉ- "calf" (anat.)

Eg *ḫpš* "calf" (pyr).

WCh *pVḫaĉ- "calf": Mnt *pəγas*.
Metathesis.

An alternative reconstruction is *pVḫaĉ-.

1391 *ḫVsiḳ- "cut, pierce"

Sem *ḫVšiḳ- "pierce": Arab *ḫsq* [-*i*-].
ECh *sik- "cut": Brg *sikki*.
Rift *siḳ- "cut": Irq *siq*-.

Loss of the anlaut laryngeal in ECh and Rift.

1392 *ḫVtik- "cut, divide"

Sem *ḫVtVk- "cut off": Akk *ḫatāku*, Hbr *ḥtk*.
WCh *tik- "divide": Bol *tikk*-.
Cf. *tik- "half" (Bol *tika*, Dera *tik*, Tng *tik-t*).
CCh *tik- "divide": FM *tik*, Mrg *tikiya*.
The anlaut laryngeal is lost.

*ḫV- may be a prefix.

1393 *ḫVṭVm- "close"

Sem *ḫVṭVm- "stop up": Akk *ḫaṭāmu*.
Eg *ḫtm* "close" (pyr).

Cf. a metathesized deverbative in CCh *tVγum- "dam": Log *tχum*.

1394 *ḫVwar-/*ḫVyar- "be good"

Sem *ḫīr- "be favorable": Arab *ḫyr* [-*i*-].
CCh *χwar- < *γVwar- "good": Gava *χwara*.
Irregular laryngeal.

Consonantal alternation *-w- ~ *-y-.

1395 *ḫVwiṭ-/*ḫVyiṭ- "sew, tie"

Sem *ḫūṭ-/*ḫīṭ- "sew": Aram *ḫwṭ*, Arab *ḫyṭ* [-*i*-], Hss *ḫeyōt*, Mhr *ḫeṭō*, Shh *ḫaṭe*.

WCh *ḫVwiṭ- "untie": Bks *hwet*.
SA *ḥiḍ- "attach camels in Indian file": Afar *ḥiḍ-* .
Contraction.
LEC *ḥiṭ- "tie": Som *ḥeḍ-*, *ḥiḍ-*, Or *hiḍ-* , Rnd *ḥiḍ-*, Kon *hiḍ-*, Gid *hiḍ-*, Arb *hiḍ-*.
HEC *hiṭ- "tie": Bmb *hiḍ-*.
Rift *ḫed- "tie": Alg *ḫeed-*.
Irregular *-d-.
Dhl *hud̲-* "sew".
Contraction. Irregular *-d̲-*.

Consonantal alternation *-w- ~ *-y-. Irregular auslaut stops in Rift and Dhl may be indications of their being loanwords from other Cush branches.

1396 *ḫVwVḳ-/*ḫVyVḳ- "go"

Sem *ḫūḳ- "go": Akk *ḫûqu*.
HEC *hiḳ- < *hVyVḳ- "approach": Bmb *hiiḳ-*.
Contraction.

Consonantal alternation *-w- ~ *-y-.

1397 *ḫVyVṭ- "see, watch"

Sem *ḫiṭ- "observe": Akk *ḫâṭu*.
Eg *ḫty* "see" (BD).
Metathesis. *-t-* < *-ṭ- is regular.

An alternative reconstruction is *ḫVṭVy-.

*k

1398 *ka'- "game"

Eg *ṯ'.w* "game" (sait).
Note the palatalization of *k-.
WCh *ka'aw- "game": Ngz *kāwa*.
Suffix *-aw-.

1399 *kaʾ-/*kaw- "bull"

Eg *kꜣ* "bull" (pyr), Copt **ko* id.: OCopt *ko*.
CCh **kaw-* "bull": Glv *kawa*, Gava *kawa*, Mnd *kawa*.

Consonantal alternation **-ʾ-* ~ **-w-*.

1400 *kaʾ- "say, shout"

Eg *kꜣ* "say" (NK).
CCh **kaʾ-* "say, call": Log *ka*, Bud *ka ǯu*, HNk *ka-* , HF *ka-*, Tera *ga*.
ECh **kaʾ-/*kaw-* "say": Tum *kā*, Dng *kāwe*, Mubi *kā*.
Dhl *kaaʿ-* "shout".
-ʿ- reflecting **-ʾ-*?
Rift **kaw-* "tell": Bur *kaw-*.

1401 *kaʾoc- "vessel"

Sem **kaʾs-* "vessel for beer" [1], "bowl" [2]: Akk *kāsu* [1], Arab *kaʾs-* [2], Hbr *kōs* [2].
Eg *kꜣs* "vessel" (l).
WCh **kwac-* "kind of a drum": Hs *kōçō*.
Contraction from **kaʾwac-*.
CCh **kwac-* "quiver": Hwn *kwasa-ra*, Gbn *kwiči-te*, Boka *kwes-tə*, Wmd *kwaʒa*, Chb *kwaʒa*, Mrg *kwaʒa*, Gude *kwaʒa*, Mwl *koso-ro*, Bch *kwoso-to*, FJ *kwəʒa*, Gudu *kwāʒa*.
Contraction from **kaʾwac-*?

1402 *kaʾup- "cover, close"

Eg *skꜣp* "cover" (caus.), Dem *kp* "cover", Copt **kōp* "hide": Boh *kʾōp*, Shd *kōp*.
Cf. reduplicated *kꜣpꜣp* "cover (with butter, oil)" (sarc).
WCh **kVʾup-* "cover, thatch" [1], "wrap" [2]: Sura *kup* [1], Ang *kūp* [1], Mpn *kūp* [2].
CCh **kap-* "cover (with cloth)": Mafa *kap*.
Contraction fro **kaHup-*.
Wrz **kup-* "close": Gaw *kup*.
Dhl *kupi-* "cover".
Rift **kuf-* "close, shut": Kwz *kuf-um-*.

Semantic syncretism of "close", "shut" and "cover" as in Slav **kryti*.

1403 *ka'Vn- "be true"

Sem **kV'Vn-* "be true": Akk *kânu*.
CCh **kan-* "true" [1], "truth" [2]: Bch *kana* [1], Bud *kani* [2].
From **kaHVn-*.

1404 *kab- "burn, roast"

Sem **kVb-* "burn" [1], "smoulder" [2]: Akk *kabābu* [1], Hbr *kby* [2], Arab *kbw* [2].
Various formations based on biconsonantal **kVb-*.
CCh **kab-* "roast": Bud *kabē*.

Cf. Eg *ḳb* "warm up" (gr) with an unexpected emphatic in the anlaut.

1405 *kab- "go, follow"

WCh **kwab-* < **kab-* "go": Mnt *kop*, Bol *koḅ-*.
**a* > **wa* under the influence of the following labial.
Mgg *khabi* "follow".

1406 *kab- "shoe, sandal"

Eg *ṯb.t*, *ṯbw* "sandal" (pyr).
Note the palatalization of **k-*.
WCh **kab-* "shoes": Ang *kāp*.
LEC **kab-/*kob-* "shoe, sandal": Som *kab*, Or *kobe'*, Boni *kob*, Rnd *kob*, Arb *kobo*, Kon *χop-to*.
Secondary *-o-* before a labial.
Wrz **χop-* "shoe, sandal": Gaw *χope*.
Borrowed from LEC?

An old *Wanderwort*. Any relation to **kab-* "go, follow"?

1407 *kab-/*kib- "(gourd) vessel"

Eg *kb* "vessel" (n).

WCh **kab-* "small calabash": Hs *kābō*.
Dhl *kiβo* "gourd".

Alternation **a* ~ **i*.

1408 *kabel-/*kaber- "shoe, sandal"

ECh **kVb-Vr-* "shoes": Gbr *kob-oro*, Kbl *kob-ro*.
SA **kab-el-* "shoe, sandal": Afar *kabel*.

Derived from **kab-* "shoe, sandal".

1409 *kaber- "bull, buffalo"

CCh **kabyar-* "bull": Bud *kāber*.
HEC **kobir-* "buffalo": Had *kobira*.
Secondary **o* < **a* before a labial.

1410 *kabVr- "be thick"

Sem **kVbur-* "be big, be thick": Akk *kabāru*, Arab *kbr* [*-u-*].
Secondary **-u-*?
WCh **kabVr-* "thickness": Hs *kabrī*.

1411 *kac- "cut, tear"

Sem **kVsVḥ-* "cut": Hbr *ksḥ*, Arab *ksḥ*.
Based on the original biconsonantal **kVs-*?
WCh **kac-* "snap (thread, rope)": Hs *kaça*.
Rift **kaʔas-* "split": Bur *kaʔas-*.
Typical development of the inner vowel into a cluster with a middle laryngeal in Rift .

1412 *kacaf- "metal"

Sem **kasp-* "silver": Akk *kaspu*, Hbr *kesep*.
CCh **kVcaf-* "iron" [1], "sand containing iron" [2]: Log *χsāf* [1], Gis *mu-ksaf* [2].
Prefix **mu-* in Gis.

Names of metals are subject to semantic changes motivated by the history of the material culture, cf., e.g., Hitt *ḫarašu-*

"bronze" borrowed from Akk *ḫurāṣu* "gold" or Finn *vaski* "copper" borrowed from one of IE words for gold (cf. Arm *oski*, Tokh A *wäs*). Such fluctuations may be observed even within one language, cf. Skt *loha-* "copper" and "iron".

1413 *kaf- "descendants, clan"

WCh **kwaf-* < **kafwa-* "inheritance": Mpn *kōp*.
Wrz **kaf-* "clan": Gaw *kaf-ko*.

Cf. Ir *sliocht* "descendants, race, family" ~ MIr *slicht* "trace, track" and, on the other hand, Russ *nasledstvo* "inheritance, heritage" < *sled* "trace".

1414 *kahVp- "hole"

Sem **kahp-* "cavern": Arab *kahf-*.
Copt **kēpi* "vault, cave": Boh *k'ēpi*, Shd *kēpe*.
Not attested in Eg.
WCh **kap-* < **kaHVp-* "hole": Hs *kafā*.
Contraction.
Wrz **kap-* "irrigation ditch": Gaw *kap-ko*.
A loanword?

Cf. Eg *ṯpḥ.t* "hole" (pyr) with a different laryngeal and palatalized *ṯ* < **k*. Metathesis of the original **kahep-* or **kahop-*?

1415 *kaḫ- "house"

Sem **kaḫ-/*kuḫ-* "hut": Arab *kaḫ-*, *kuḫ-*.
Secondary variant in *kuḫ-*.
WCh **kaḫ-* "house (with clay walls)": Hs *kago*, Gwn *kago*.
SA **keH-* "place": Afar *kee*.
From **kaHe-*.

1416 *kakar- "circle, ring"

Sem **kakkar-/*kikkar-* "round bread, disk": Akk *kakkaru*, Hbr *kikkār*.
ECh **kakVr-* "arm-ring, bracelet": Kera *kaakəray*.

Partial reduplication.

1417 *ka-kul- "basket"

Sem **kul-kul-* "basket": Akk *kukkullu*.
Assimilation of vowels.
CCh **kVkVl-/*kulVk-* "basket": Dgh *kwulge*, Nak *klogo*, Gava *kwulekha*, Mus *kekele*.
Some forms underwent metathesis.
Rift **kakul-* "half-calabash": Kwz *kakul-eto*.

Derived from **kol-* "gourd, calabash".

1418 *kal- "go"

Berb **kVl-* "go, march": Siwa *u-kel*, Ntf *ā-kəl*, Mns *χel*.
CCh **kal-* "run, go (quickly)": Mba *kal*, Mafa *kəl*, Gis *kal*.
ECh **kVl-* "enter": Kera *kele*.

Cf. Dhl *kihl-* "run"?

1419 *kal- "female in-law"

Sem **kall-* "daughter-in-law" [1], "bride" [2]; Akk *kallātu* [1], Ug *kl-t* [2], Hbr *kallā* [1], Aram (Syr) *kallətō* [1].
WCh **kalya-* "woman": Zem *kal*, Zar *kəl*, Zak *kyel*, Buu *kəli*, Dok *kəli*.
Cf. Hs *kōlō* "daughters".

Rift **kwalaʾ-* "widow" (Irq *kwalaʾo*, Alg *kwaʾal- itoʾo*, Bur *kwaʾal-itoʾo*, Asa *kalaʾayi*) may also belong to this root and reflect **kol-* together with Hs.

1420 *kalah- "go"

CCh **ka-kVlVh-* "return, retire, go slowly": Mofu *kakəlh*.
Partial reduplication.
SA **kalah-* "travel": Saho *kalaah*, *kalaaḥ*.

Derived from **kal-* "go".

1421 *kalem-/*kulem- "charcoal"

CCh **kimyal-* "charcoal": Bnn *kimela*, BM *kimil-na*.
Metathesis.

ECh *kulim-* "charcoal": Dng *kulmo*, Mig *kolmo*, Bid *kilmo*, Brg *kilmo*, Mubi *kilim*.
Rift *kalem-* "charcoal": Kwz *kalem-uko*.

Alternation *a ~ *u.

1422 *kalim- "insect"

Sem *kalm-* "insect" [1], "louse" [2]: Akk *kalmatu* [1], Aram *kalmətā* [2].
SA *kilim-* "tick": Saho *kilim*, Afar *kilim*.
Assimilation of vowels.

1423 *kalVy- "vessel"

Sem *kalVy-* "vessel": Akk *kalû*, Hbr *kᵉlī*.
WCh *kyal-* < *kayal-* "pot": Dera *kile*, Ngm *kyelle*, Kr *kəli*.
Metathesis.
CCh *kalway-* "pot": Bud *kaloē*.
LEC *kill-* "small bowl": Or *killa*.
Contraction of a metathetic form.

An alternative reconstruction may be *kaVyl-*. Any relation to *kol-* "gourd, calabash"?

1424 *kamaʾ-/*kamay- "food"

Eg *kmy* "food" (gr).
WCh *kamam-* "snack": Hs *kāmāmā*.
Partial reduplication of metathetic *kām-* < *kaHam-*.
ECh *kaʾam-* "mush": Tum *kām*.
Metathesis. Cf. *kwam-* "eat": Smr *kwam*, Mkk *koome*.

An alternative reconstruction is *kaʾam-/*kayam-*.

1425 *kan- "dog"

ECh *kanya-* "dog": Dng *kanya*, Jegu *kany-*.
Omot *kan-* "dog": Ome *kana*, *kanaa*, Mao *kano*.

A morphonological variant of *kun-* id., *küHen-* id.

1426 *kanap- "wing"

Sem *kanap-* "wing": Akk *kappu*, Ug *knp*, Hbr *kānāp*, Aram (Syr) *ken^e^pō*, Arab *kanaf-*, Gz *kənf*.
Agaw *kan(V)p-/*kin(V)p-* "wing": Bil *kanfi*, Xmt *kenfaa*, Kwr *kamb*, Kem *kämbii*, Aun *kenfii*.
Traces of *i*-grade in Xmt and Aun.

1427 *kanpar-/*kanpur- "lip, muzzle"

Berb *kVnfur-* "lip, muzzle": Ntf *a-kenfur*, Snus *a- kenfur*.
WCh *kapur-* "mouth": Mnt *kapur*.
Agaw *kanpar-* "lip": Bil *kanfər*, Kwr *kanpər*, Kem *kəmbər*, Aun *kanfar*.
SA *kamfer-* "muzzle": Saho *kamfer*.
Assimilation of *-np- > *-mf-.
LEC *gafur-* "muzzle": Som *gafuur*.
Irregular *g- < *k- and loss of inlaut *-n-. An expressive form with irregular phonetic changes or a loanword?

1428 *kap- "hand"

Sem *kapp-* "hand": Akk *kappu*, Ug *kp*, Hbr *kap*, Aram (Syr) *kappō*, Arab *kaff-*, Hss *kef*, Mhr *kef*.
Eg *kp* "enemy's hands separated from his arms; cut off hand" (n).

1429 *kap- "earth"

WCh *kapu-* "red sorrel": Mpn *kupu*.
Wrz *kap-* "earth": Gaw *kappe*.

1430 *kap- "house"

Sem *kupp-* "building": Akk *kuppātu*.
Note *u.
Eg *kȝp* "house" (MK).
Vocalic -ȝ-.
WCh *kap-* "hut": Hs *kafē*.
CCh *kVp-* "house": Tera *kipi*.

Connected with *kaʾup-* "cover, close"?

1431 *kapaʾ- "move, go"

Sem *kVpaʾ- "go away": Arab *kfʾ* [-*a*-].
WCh *kap- "come": Mnt *kop*.
Loss of the auslaut laryngeal.

1432 *kar- "lamb"

Sem *karr- "lamb" [1], "fattened lamb, ram" [2]: Akk *karru* [1], Ug *kr* [1], Hbr *kar* [2].
Berb *kVrVw-/*kVrVy- "lamb" [1], "young ram" [2]: Ayr *a-kərwa* [1], Twl *a-kərwa* [1], Sml *i-kru* [2], Kby *i-kərri* [1].
Derivative in *-w-/*-y-. Cf. WCh?
WCh *karwa- "sheep" [1], "lamb, bull" [2]: Wnd *karo* [1], Tng *karwa* [2].
LEC *kar- "heifer goats" (coll.): Arb *kaariy*.

1433 *kar- "sun"

Sem *karar- "day heat": Akk *kararû*.
Partial reduplication.
WCh *kar- "sun": Bele *kaara*.

1434 *kar-/*kayar- "dog"

WCh *kar-/*kayar- "dog": Hs *karē*, Brw *kəra*, Say *kara*, Bks *kyara*, Klr *gyara*, DB *čira*.
CCh *kīr- < *kVyVr- "dog": Lmn *kīrrɛ*, Mnd *kəre*, Suk *kīrra*, Gid *kəre*.
SA *kar- "dog": Saho *kare*.
LEC *ka[y]ir- "dog": Arb *kair*, *ker*.
Secondary *-i- after *-y-.
Wrz *χa[y]ar- "dog": War *χɛro*, Gaw *haaro*, Gob *hɛɛro*, Cam *karo*.

*kayar- seems to be a secondary formation based on *kar- preserved in SA and, to some extent, in WCh.

1435 *kariĉ- "belly"

Sem *kariŝ- "belly": Akk *karšu*, Hbr *kārēŝ*, Aram (Syr) *karsō*, Arab *kariš*-, Gz *karš*, Hss *kēreś*, Mhr *kēreś*, Shh *šurś*.

Wrz **korVs-* "meat": Gaw *korse*.
Vocalism is not clear.

Semantically, the connection between "meat" and various words for inner organs may be corroborated by such IE correspondences as ON *kjǫt* "meat" ~ Skt *guda-* "intestines".

1436 *kas- "fall"

Sem **nVkuš-* "turn over" [1], "fall" [2]: Arab *nks* [*-u-*] [1], Jib *nkos* [2].
Prefix **nV-* with modified root vocalism.
CCh **kas-* "fall": Msg *kasa*.

1437 *kat- "back"

ECh **kat-* "back": Bid *kate*.
Rift **kat-* "cow's hump": Alg *kata*, Bur *kata-ŋ*.

1438 *kat- "be small"

Sem **kVt-* "weak": Akk *katû*.
Eg *kt* "small" (MK).
WCh **kat-* "small": Sura *kat*, Mpn *kat*.

Cf. WCh **kwati-* "small, narrow" (Ang *kwīt*) and CCh **kwati-* "small" (Mafa *kwiteʾe*) reflecting a different root vowel.

1439 *kat- "move, go"

Eg *ktkt* "move" (Amar).
Reduplication.
ECh **kat-* "go, go out" [1], "follow" [2]: Mubi *kāt* [1], Brg *kaati* [1], Bid *kaat* [1], Kwn *kote* [2].
LEC **kat-* "run": Or *kaat-*.
Omot **kat-* "hurry, hasten": Kaf *kaat-*, Mch *kaata-*, Bwo *kat-*.

ECh, LEC and Omot may reflect a prototype with an inlaut laryngeal **kaHat-/*kawat-*. Cf. also in WCh: Hs *katākatā* "first efforts of a child to walk".

1440 *katum- "metal"

Sem **kVtm-* "gold": Hbr *ketem*.
WCh **katum-* "pig of iron": Hs *katūmā*.

See our notes to **kacaf-* "metal".

1441 *kaw- "set fire"

Sem **kūy-* "burn" [1], "kindle fire" [2]: Akk *kawû* [1], Hbr *kwy* [1], Arab *kwy* [-*i*-] [2].
Based on **kVw-*.
WCh **kaw-/*kawVy-* "roast": Tng *kawe*, Wrj *kaw*, Jmb *kaw*, Miya *kaw*, Kry *kaw*, Paa *ku*, Cagu *kuwa*, Siri *ku*, Ngz *kauyu*.
Cf. a similar structure with final **-y-* in Sem.
CCh **ku[w]-* "be hot": Log *kku*.
Cf. **kuw-* "fire, hotness" (LPe *k^{w}u*, Suk *khu*, Bnn *kuwa*, Zime *ku*).
ECh **kVwiy-* "set fire, fry, burn": Lele *kūy*, Mubi *kɛwī*, Tbn *kūyē*, Kera *ki*.
Cf. Sem and WCh forms in **-y-*.

There are indications of a parallel variant that may be reconstructed as **kawVy-*.

1442 *ke^{c}Vc- "be angry"

Sem **kV^{c}Vs-* "be ill-tempered": Hbr *k^{c}s*.
Eg *khs* "anger" (XVIII).
Irregular laryngeal.
ECh **kyas-* < **kyaHVs-* "angry": Sok *kesi kesi*.

1443 *ken- "cereal"

Sem **kin-* "cereal": Akk *kinītu*.
WCh **kyan-* "seed": Ang *kēn*.

1444 *ken- "know, learn"

Eg *ṯny* "learn" (MK).
Palatalized **k-* before a middle vowel.
ECh **kwan-* < **kyanu-* "knowledge": Mkk *konya*.

Bed *kan-* "know".
Unclear *-a-*.
Agaw **kan-t-/*kin-t-* "learn" [1], "see" [2]: Bil *kən-t-* [1], Xmr *kin-t-* [1], Kwr *kin-t-* [1], Aun *kan-t-* [2].
HEC **ken-* "know": Had *ken-*.

Cf. Sem **kVhan-/*kVhun-* "foretell, predict": Arab *khn* [*-a-*, *-u-*].

1445 *kenaḥ- "darkness"

Eg *knḥ.w* "darkness" (BD).
No traces of palatalization!
ECh **kyanaH-* "night": Nch *kenā*.

1446 *kenum- "darkness"

Eg *knm.t* "darkness" (BD).
No traces of palatalization!
CCh **kyanum-* "night": Bud *kenum*.
ECh **kyalVm-* "shadow": Mig *kelmo*, Mkk *kelēmo*, Sok *kilmio*.
**-l-* < HS **-n-* dissimilated before **-m-*.

Related to **kenaḥ-* "darkness".

1447 *ket- "tie"

Eg *ṯt* "untie, disengage" (n).
Palatalization of **k-*.
ECh **kyat-* "tie": Mkk *kette*, *gitte*.

1448 *kew-/*key- "wind"

Eg *ṯ3w* "wind, air" (pyr), Copt **t'ēw* "wind, air": Boh *t'ēou*, Shd *tēu*.
Vocalic *-3-*.
WCh **kyay-* "wind": Paa *key*.

Consonantal alternation **-w-* ~ **-y-*.

1449 *ki- "leg"

Eg *ṯyṯy* "leg" (BD).
Reduplication. Palatalization of **k-*.
WCh **ki-* "hip, thigh": Sura *čī*, Ang *či*, Chip *ši*.
Palatalization of **k-* before **-i-*.

1450 *kiʔ- "man, child"

Eg *ṯȝy* "man" (pyr).
Vocalic *-y*. Note the palatalization of **k-*.
ECh **kiʔ-* "child": Gbr *kīe*.

1451 *kiʔ- "put on (clothes)"

Eg *ṯȝy* "put on (clothes)" (NK).
Note the palatalization of **k-*.
CCh **kaʔ-/*kiʔ-* "put on (clothes)": Gis *ki*, Gudu *kā*, Nza *kaʔa*, Bch *kā*.
**kaʔ-* goes back to **kiʔa-*.

Cf. LEC **kaʔ-/*kaw-* "place, put, lay" (Or *kaaya*, Arb *kaw-*).

1452 *kiʔVd- "earth, ground"

Sem **kīd-* "outside region": Akk *kīdu*.
ECh **kiḍ- < *kiHVd-* "earth, ground": Mig *kida*, Brg *kiḍo*, Mubi *kiḍi*, Dng *kiḍa*.
Emphatization of **-d-* under the influence of the laryngeal.

1453 *kič- "bite"

Sem **nVkVṯ-* "bite": Aram (Syr) *nkt*, Gz *nks*.
Prefix **nV-*.
Berb **kVs-* "bite": Ahg *əkš*.
HEC **kis-* "bite": Sid *kis-*.
Irregular *-s-*.

1454 *kič- "basket, container"

WCh **kuč-* "basket": Fyer *kučči*, Ank *ta-kuči*, Mpn *kəči*.

-*u*- from HS **ü*?
Agaw **kič-* "basket": Xmr *kizaa*, Kem *kišaa*.
LEC **kiš-* "sack": Som *kiiš*, Or *keešaa*.

1455 *kil- "fence"

WCh **kil-* "fence": Hs *killā*.
Cf. Brm *kwal* "house", Bks *kyel* "place", DB *kil* id., Buli *kila* id.
LEC **kel-* "compound, fence": Or *kellaa*.

Cf. also ECh **kul-* "hut, town" (Lele *kul*, Kera *kuli*, Smr *kūlū*, Kwn *kulū*).

1456 *kilam- "ivory"

Sem **kilām-* "ivory": Akk *kilāmu, gilāmu*.
Eg *kmry* "ivory" (n).
Metathesis.

Ancient *Wanderwort*? The alternative reconstruction is **kimal-*.

1457 *kilbab-/*kirbab- "insect"

Sem **kulbāb-* "ant": Akk *kulbābu*.
**u* < **i* under the influence of **b*.
CCh **kirbab-* "flea": Bud *kirbābo*.

Irregular alternation of liquids. Partial reduplication?

1458 *kin- "egg"

Sem **mV-kan-* "lay eggs": Arab *mkn* [-*a*-].
Derivative with a prefix **mV-* and modified vocalism.
WCh **kin-* "egg": Diri *akin*.
LEC **ʾu-kun-* "egg": Som (dial.) *ʾukun*, *ukkun*, Rnd *ukun*.
Prefix **ʾu-*. Assimilation from **ʾu-kin-*. This word was obviously influenced by another LEC word for "egg" (cf. Som *ugaḥ* and the like).

Relation to Rift **ḳan-* "egg" (Irq *qanhi*, Alg *qanaʾi*, Bur *qanaya*) doubtful in view of the initial **ḳ-*.

1459 *kin- "count"

Eg *t̲nw* "count" (pyr).
Suffix *-w*?
WCh **ḳinu-* "count": Mnt *kūn*, Wrj *ḳin-*, Kry *kin-*, Miya *ḳən-*, Paa *ḳən-*, Cagu *kən-*, Siri *ḳənu*, Mbu *ḳən*, Jmb *ḳən*.
Secondary emphatic?

Irregular alternation **k* ~ **ḳ*.

1460 *kir- "steal"

WCh **kir-* "steal": Wrj *kir-ai*, Kry *kir*, Mbu *kir*, Paa *kəra*, Jmb *kəra*, Miya *akir*, Siri *kəri*, Ngz *kəru*, Bade *kəlu*.
Wrz **kereᶜ-* "steal": Gaw *kereᶜ-*.
Secondary *-eᶜ-*?

1461 *kirim- "genitals"

Sem **kirim-* "womb": Akk *kirimu*.
Eg *t̲ꜣm* "foreskin" (MK).
Note *-ꜣ-* < **-r-*.

Semantic development may be problematic.

1462 *kir-kar- "camel"

Sem **kir-kār-* "she-camel": Hbr *kirkārā*.
Berb **kVr-kar-* "camels" (pl.): Ayr *i-kərkar*, Twl *i- kərkar*.

Reduplication. Related to Dhl *kiri* "giraffe"?

1463 *kiʒ- "container"

Eg *t̲z.t* "box" (OK).
Palatalization of **k-*.
Agaw **kiʒ-* "basket": Xmr *kizaa*, *kižaa*.

1464 *ko-ko- "vessel"

Eg *t̲t̲* "vessel" (n).
Palatalization of **k-*.

WCh **kwak-* "pot": Gera *kwaka*.
From **kwakwa-*?
CCh **kwakway-* "calabash": Mtk *kokway*.
Stem **kwakwa-* with a suffix *-*ay*-.

Reduplication. The original root may be preserved in ECh **kay-* "pot": Mkk *keyye*.

1465 *koʾaf- "door, gate"

WCh **kwaʾaf-* "doorway, gateway": Hs *ḳōfa*.
Rift **kaʾaf-* "door, gate": Bur *kaʾafu*, Kwz *kaʾaf-uko*.
Assimilation of vowels.

Derived from *ʾ*af-* "mouth" with a prefix **ko-*?

1466 *kob- "bend"

Sem **nVkub-* "incline, bend": Arab *nkb* [-*u*-].
Prefix **nV-*. Cf. Arab *kbb* [-*u*-] "upturn".
CCh **kwab-ay-* "bend": Bud *kobei-hi*.

1467 *koč- "be big"

Sem **kVṯ-* "be massive": Akk *kašāšu*.
WCh **kwač-* "high, long": Fyer *koos*.
CCh **kwač-* "many, much": Mba *kočo*.

1468 *koĉaʾ- "peel, tear"

Sem **kVŝaʾ-* "peel": Arab *kŝʾ* [-*a*-].
WCh **kwaĉ-* "tear": Bul *kwəŝu*.
Loss of the auslaut laryngeal.

1469 *kod- "work, be tired"

Sem **kud-* "work (hard), be tired": Arab *kdd* [-*u*-].
ECh **kad-* "be tired" [1], "be tired (of feet)" [2]: Sok *kadi* [1], Mkk *giḍḍe*.
Secondary emphatization in Mkk (reflecting **kadyaH-*?). Vocalism *-*a*- of a stative.

Wrz *kod- "work": Gaw *koδaδ-*.
Partial reduplication.

1470 *koᶜar- "drive away"

Sem *kVᶜar- "drive, push": Arab *kᶜr* [-*a*-].
WCh *kwaHar- "drive away": Hs *kōrā*, Buli *karu*.

Cf. CCh *kar-uw- "hunt" (FKi *karuwa*).

1471 *koh- "egg"

WCh *ḳwah- < *kwah- "egg": Hs *ḳwai*, Grk *nkie*.
Shift of the emphatization. Prefix in Grk.
Bed *kʷahi* "egg".
Wrz *ʔu-kah- "egg": Gaw *ukāhe*.
Probably, Wrz does not belong here if it is related to Som *ugaḥ* id. and the like.

1472 *koḥan- "shine; light"

Eg *ṯḥn* "shine" (pyr).
Palatalization of *k-.
WCh *kwan-H- "light, day": Tng *kəŋ*, DB *ma-kon*.
Metathesis. Prefix *ma- in DB.
Wrz *ḳan- < *kVHan- "day": Gaw *ḳane*.

1473 *kol- "gourd, calabash"

Eg *ṯꜣ.t* "vessel" (OK).
Palatalization of *k-. Note -ꜣ- < *-l-.
WCh *kwal- "calabash": Hs *kullu*, Bol *kula*, Tng *kwali*, Pero *kwali*.
Cf. Hs *kwala* "metal water-bottle" and, with partial reduplication *kōlōlō* "kind of bottle-gourd".
CCh *kwal- "calabash, pot: Gvo *kwəla*, HGh *kuli*.
ECh *kwal- "jug" [1], "pot" [2]: Bid *kolle* [1], Mubi *kōli* [2], Sok *kō-kolo* [2].
Reduplication in Sok. Cf. Mig *kolo-ngane* "clay mug".
LEC *ʔV-kol- "skin bucket": Or *okolee*.
Prefix *ʔV-.

1474 *kol- "return, go around"

WCh **kwal-* "return": Bele *kolu-*.
LEC **koll-* "go around, run here and there": Or *kolla-ʾa*.

Related to **kal-* "go"?

1475 *kolab- "container"

Sem **kVlūb-* "basket": Hbr *kᵉlūb*.
Secondary vocalism?
Eg *ṯrb* "vessel" (n), *ṯꜣb* (XVIII).
Loanword from Sem?
WCh **kwalab-* "glass bottle": Hs *kwalabā*.
CCh **kwalab-* "bottle": Mafa *kwalaba*.
Hs loanword?

Derived from **kol-* "gourd, calabash".

1476 *kom- "vessel"

Eg *km.ty* "vessel" (XVIII).
No traces of palatalization.
WCh **kwam-* "kind of calabash or gourd": Hs *kōmō*.
CCh **kwam-* "calabash": Bud *kɔmo*.

1477 *kom- "cereal"

Eg *kꜣm.wt.t* "barley" (BD).
No traces of palatalization.
WCh **kwam-* "peanut" [1], "maize" [2]: Sura *kɔm* [1], Pero *koomo* [2].
CCh **kwam-* "guinea corn": Nza *kʷəmə*.

Cf. WCh **kima-* "grain": Mnt *šiεm*, Brm *kim*?

1478 *kom- "fowl"

Sem **kumVy-* "waterfowl": Akk *kumû*.
WCh **kwam-* "old hen or guinea-fowl" [1], "hen" [2]: Hs *kwammā* [1], Tng *kom* [2], Bol *kom* [2].

1479 *kom- "cattle"

WCh *kwam- "cow" [1], "bull" [2]: Bol *kwəm* [1], Krk *kwam* [1], Ngm *kwəm* [1], Ngz *kwam* [2], Bade *kwam* [2].
CCh *kum- < *kwamu- "meat": Brm *kum*, Chb *kum*, Mrg *kum*, Klb *kum*, Wmd *kumu*.
ECh *kwama- "buffalo" [1], "meat" [2]: Sok *kām* [1], Dng *kuma* [2], Mubi *kome* [2].
Agaw *kim- "cattle, cow": Bil *kim*, Xmr *kim*, Kwr *kim*, Dmb *kim*, Kem *kemaa*, Aun *kemii*.
Innovative *-i-?

1480 *kor- "ass, donkey"

Sem *kurr- "young of an ass, foal": Arab *kurr-*.
WCh *kwar- "ass, donkey": Bol *koro*, Krk *kwaro*, Ngm *kɔro*, Ngz *kwara*, Bade *kōro-n*.
CCh *kwar- "ass, donkey": Tera *koro*, Gaa *kwari*, Gbn *kwari*, Hwn *kwara*, Klb *kwara*, Gude *kwara*, Gudu *kwara*, Bch *kwarɛy-to*, Bud *koro*, Msg *kurɛk*, Gid *koro*, Lame *karo*, LPe *koro*, Masa *kɔrɔ-ta*, Bnn *kwəra*.
Cf. also Nza *kərə* "horse".
ECh *kwar- "ass, donkey": Smr *kora*, Tum *kora*, Ndm *kurō*, Nch *kora*, Kbl *kura*, Dor *kura*, Kwn *kurā*.
Omot *kur- "ass, donkey": Ome *kuraa*, Kaf *kuuroo*, Mch *kuro*, Gim *kur*.

1481 *kor- "(be) round"

Sem *kur- "ball": Arab *kur-at-*.
Cf. Arab *krw* [-*u*-] "give spherical form to smth.".
Note the anomalous morphological structure of the noun.
WCh *kwar-kwar- "round": Maha *korkor*.
Reduplication.

Cf. Dhl *kiir-ooδ-* "make in a ball".

1482 *kor- "be angry"

Sem *kVrVh- "be unhappy, be disgusted" [1], "hate" [2]: Arab *krh*, Hss *kerōh*, Mhr *kerōh*, Shh *kereh*.

Based on biconsonantal **kVr-*?

WCh **kwar-* "hate, disgust": Sura *kwar*.

Any relation to **kar-* "punish": Ang *kār*, Sura *kar*, Fyer *kar*?

Agaw **kwar-* "be angry": Xmr k^w*ar-*, Kwr k^w*ar-*, Dmb k^w*ar-*, Aun k^w*al-*.

SA **kur-* "anger, wrath": Saho *kuraa*.

Omot **kar-* "be angry": Kaf *kaar*.

The source of **-a-* is not clear.

Dhl *kor-* "be in trouble".

1483 *koraᶜ- "field"

Eg *ṯrᶜ* "field" (gr).

Palatalization of **k-*.

WCh **kwaHar-* "farm": Bol *koori*, Ngm *kori*, Pero *kuuri*.

Metathesis.

The alternative reconstruction is **koᶜar-*.

1484 *kos- "tooth"

Eg *ṯs* "tooth" (MK).

Palatalization of **k-*.

Bed *koos* "tooth".

Rift **koʔos-* "molar": Kwz *koʔos-iko*.

Cf. Irq *goso* "incisor"? Note the inlaut laryngeal in *- *oʔo-* developed from **-o-*.

Connected with **kos-* "pierce, cut"?

1485 *kos- "pierce, cut"

WCh **kVs-* "cut (with a knife)": Paa *kəs*.

ECh **kyas-* < **kwasi-* "pierce": Kwn *kesi*.

Omot **koš-* "pierce": Mch *kossi*, Bwo *koš-*.

1486 *koʒ- "knot, unite"

Sem **kūz-* "unite, collect": Arab *kwz* [*-a-*].

Based on **kVz-*.

Eg *ṯz* "knot (v.)" (a), "unite" (n).

Palatalization of *k- > ṯ- may be caused by a rounded vowel.

1487 *koʒ- "be dry"

Sem *kuz- "be dry": Arab kzz [-u-].
CCh *kaʒ- "dry up": Bud kaǯu.
Unexpected *-a-.
ECh *kVʒ- "dry up": Mkk koḍḍe, guḍḍe.

1488 *kub- "house"

Sem *kūb- "building": Akk kūbu.
ECh *kub- "straw hut": Smr kubī.

1489 *kuc- "clothes"

Sem *kus- "kind of clothes": Akk kusītu, Ug ks-t.
Eg kɜs "kind of clothes" (1).
-ɜ- may reflect a vowel.

Cf. WCh *kic- "plait" (Hs kiçē), ECh *kwas- "spin" (Tum koǯ).

1490 *kučer- "fat, grease"

Sem *kuṯr- "suet": Arab kuẓr-.
WCh *kuč̣yar- "fat, grease": Hs kiçe, Bol šidor, Dera šuḍot, Ngm šiḍar.

1491 *kuf- "river"

Sem *kupp- "water spring": Akk kuppu.
CCh *kuf- "river" [1], "lake" [2]: Gaa kufa [1], Gbn kufa [2], Chb kufa [2], Hwn kufa-rā [1].

1492 *kuhaᵓ- "speak, shout"

Eg khɜ "utter a cry" (MK).
Vocalic -ɜ.
WCh *kuh- "shout": Dera kui, kuhi.
CCh *kVᵓah- "speak": Log kāha.
Metathesis.

1493 *kul- "kidney"

Sem **kuly-* "kidney": Akk *kalītu*, Ug *klyt*, Hbr *kᵉlāyōt* (pl.), *kilyā*, Aram (Syr) *kulitō*, Arab *kuly-at-*, Gz *kʷəlīt*, Hss *kelīt*, Mhr *kelyīt*.
CCh **kul-kul-* "kidney": Gaa *kulkul-ara*.
Reduplication.
LEC **kal-/*kulal-* "kidney": Som *kalli*, Or *kalee*, *kulali-ti* (pl.), Kon *χalla*.
Cf. Arb *kal-ano* id.
Dhl *kalle* "kidney".
From **kulal-*?

In Cush there exists a parallel formation **kel-*, cf. LEC **kel-* (Som *kellii*) and Omot **kel-* (Ome *kellawa*).

1494 *kulum- "fish"

WCh **kulVm-* "large fish": Hs *kulmā*.
SA **kullum-* "fish": Afar *kullum*, *kulluum*.
LEC **kullum-* "fish": Som *kalluumo* (pl.), Bay *kunnumi*.
Som *-a-* is secondary. Assimilation of sonants in Bay.

Any connection with Sem **kall-* "fish, whale" (Shh *kāl*, Mhr *kell*)?

1495 *kulup- "worm, crocodile"

Sem **kulup-* "worm": Akk *kuluppu*.
Eg *kꜣp.w* "crocodile" (MK).
-ꜣ- goes back to **-l-*.

Related to **kulum-* "fish"?

1496 *kum- "be black"

Eg *km* "black" (pyr), Copt **kame* "black": Boh *k'ame*, Shd *kame*.
Wrz **kum-* "black": Gaw *kumma*.

Cf. Agaw **kVm-* "be evening": Aun *kəm-əŋ*.

1497 *kum- "take, get"

Sem **ḥVkum-* "take": Akk *ekēmu*, Arab *ḥkm* [*-u-*].

Prefix **ḥV-*.

CCh **kum-* "obtain": FK *kum-anuʾ*, FG *kum-ʾvwi*.

Rift **kom-* "have" [1], "grip" [2]: Irq *kom-* [1], Bur *kom-* [1], Asa *kom-* [1], Kwz *kom-os-* [2].

Dhl *kam-* "hold".

Unexpected vocalism.

1498 *kun- "dog"

Berb **kun-* "dog": Gua *cuna*.

Omot **kunan-* "dog": Kaf *kunano*, Mch *kunano*.

Partial reduplication.

Related to **kan-*, **küHen-* id.

1499 *kunač- "cereal"

Sem **kunaṯ-* "emmer": Akk *kunāsu*, Aram (Syr) *kunnātā*.

CCh **kanVč̣-* "sorghum": Log *kansē*.

Assimilation of vowels from **kanas-* < **kunas-*?

Derived from **ken-* "cereal"?

1500 *kunak- "tree"

Sem **kanak-* "kind of tree": Akk *kanaktu*.

Assimilation of vowels.

WCh **kunak-* "sheanut tree": Kry *kunnaku*.

1501 *kur- "boat"

Eg *kr* "boat" (n).

ECh **kur-ay-* "boat": Smr *kuroi*.

1502 *kur- "river, lake"

WCh **kur-* "pond": Ang *kur*.

ECh **kur-* "river" [1], "pond" [2], "lake" [3]: Smr *kuri* [1], Sok *korō* [2], Jegu *kūrāye* [3].

Agaw **kur-* "river": Bil *kuraa*, Dmb *kuraa*, Kwr *kuraa*, Kem *kuraa*.

LEC **kur-* "rivulet": Or *kuree*.

1503 *kur- ''knife''

Eg *krkr* ''knife'' (gr).
Reduplication.
ECh **kur-* ''knife'': Smr *kura*.
Rift **kirar-* ''axe'': Bur *kirara*.
Partial reduplication with modified vocalism.

1504 *kur- ''mountain''

WCh **kir-* < **kuri-* ''hill'': Grk *kir*.
CCh **kur-* ''mountain'': Ksr *kuř*, Log *kurr*.
LEC **kur-* ''mountain'': Som *kur*.

1505 *kurak- ''bird''

Sem **kurk-* ''crane'': Akk *kurku*, Aram (Syr) *kurkəyī*, Arab *kurk-īy-*, Gz *k*^{w}*ärāki*.
CCh **kurak-* ''dove, francolin'': Mba *kūrakay*, Gudu *kurku-to*, Nza *kurkute*, Lame *kuruk*, LPe *koroku*.
Secondary *-u-/-o-* of the second syllable in Lame and LPe.

Descriptive stem.

1506 *kus- ''be small''

Sem **wVkVš-/*yVkVš-* ''become small'': Arab *wks*, *yks*.
Prefix **wV-/*yV-*.
WCh **kus-* ''short'': Ank *kuss*.
CCh **kus-* ''small'': Chb *ŋkusu*, Klb *kušu*, Mrg *kwušu*.
Prefix **nV-* in Chb.

1507 *kus- ''rub, pound''

Sem **kuš-* ''pound'': Arab *kss* [-*u*-].
WCh **kus-* ''rub'': Mpn *kus*.
CCh **kwas-* ''rub'': Tera *kwəš-ara*, Zgh *kas-duwe*.

Related to **kos-* ''tooth''? Any connection with **kus-* ''be small'' (cf. ON *smār* ''little'' < IE **smē-* ''rub'')?

1508 *kus- "meat, bull"

Berb **kus-* "meat": Lib *kusu.*
WCh **kus-* "bull": Sura *kus*, Ang *kus*, Mnt *kūs.*

Cf. ECh **kas-* "bull": Bid *kas-kō*. Semantically, cf. an exact parallel in Av *gav-* "ox, cow" and also "meat".

1509 *kuw- "be dark"

Eg *kkw* "dark" (pyr).
Partial reduplication.
WCh **kuw-* "dark": Ang *pi-kwi*, Chip *pe-kowo*, Sura *koo*, Mpn *kūo.*
Prefix **pi-* in Ang and Chip.

1510 *kuw-/*kuy- "shout"

WCh **kuw-* "shout" (n.): Hs *kūwa.*
Agaw **kuy-* "emit sounds": Aun *koy-ŋ.*

Consonantal alternation **-w-* ~ **-y-.*

1511 *küHen- "dog"

WCh **kuHen-* "dog": Fyer *k^{w}eeŋ.*
Fyer *-ŋ* goes back to **-n-H-.*
Mgg *kwehen* "dog".
Omot **keHen-* "dog": Dime *keenu.*

Related to **kan-*, **kun-* id.

1512 *kün- "rise, raise"

Eg *ṯny* "raise high" (pyr).
Note the palatalization of **k-.*
WCh **kunwa-* "rise" [1], "lift" [2]: Bol *kon* [1 2], Dwot *kun* [2].

1513 *kün- "woman, co-wife"

Sem **kann-/*kinn-* "co-wife" [1], "female in-law" [2]: Akk *kinītu* [1], Arab *kann-at-* [2].
Secondary variant with **-a*?

Berb *kVn- "co-wife": Izy *iken*, Snus *ta-kna*, Kby *ṭa-kna*.
WCh *kin- "co-wife" [1], "sister" [2]: Tng *kin* [2], Wrj *kinai* [1], Kry *kin* [1], Miya *kin* [1], Cagu *kine* [1], Mbu *kina* [1], Jmb *kina* [1], Sha *čin* [2], Klr *kin* [2].
Irregular development of *-ü-.
Agaw *kwin- "woman": Bil *ɔγiinaa*, Xmr *iuunaa*, Xmt *eqʷen*, Kwr *iewiina*, Dmb *kiuunaa*, Kem *yiwiinaa*, Aun *χuonaa*.

Cf. numerous Cush forms with a voiced stop in the anlaut: Agaw *gan- "mother" (Bil *ganaa*, Kwr *ganaa*, Kem *gänaa*), Omot *gen- "woman, lady" (Ome *gennee*, Kaf *gennee*, Mch *gänne*), Dhl *gaana* "woman".

1514 *küsan- "beans"

Sem *kišan- "bean": Akk *kiššānu*.
CCh *gusan-H- "kind of beans": Mofu *gusaŋ*.
Irregular voiced *g < *k.

1515 *küʒ- "slave"

Sem *kizVy- "servant": Akk *kizû*.
CCh *kuʒ- "slave": Bch *küsa*, Gudu *kuza*.

1516 *kVcVm- "beat, break"

Sem *kVsim- "beat, break into pieces": Akk *kasāmu*, Hbr *ksm*, Arab *ksm* [-*i*-].
Eg *ksm* "strike" (MK).

1517 *kVĉ- "dig"

Sem *nVkiŝ-/*nVkuŝ- "empty, dig": Arab *nkš* [-*i*-, -*u*-].
Prefix *nV-.
ECh *kaĉ- "dig, bury": Kwn *kasi*, *kesi*.

Cf. CCh *kVč- "dig": Mofu *kəč*-?

1518 *kVmVʾ- "bind"

Sem *kVmVʾ- "bind": Akk *kamû*.

Eg *ṯ3m* "binding" (XVIII).

Metathesis. Note the palatalization of **k-*.

The alternative reconstruction is **kVᵓVm-*.

1519 *kVnVy- "call"

Sem **kVnVy-* "call (by name)": Hbr *kny*, Arab *kny* [-*i*-].
Eg *kny* "call" (reg).

1520 *kVrVb- "ask"

Sem **kVrVb-* "ask, request": Akk *karābu*.
Eg *i3kb* "complain" (pyr).

Metathesis. Initial *i*- may reflect a prefix or a front vowel of the first syllable.

The alternative reconstruction is **rVkVb-*.

1521 *kVwVl-/*kVyVl- "dog, wolf"

Berb **kVwVl-* "wolf, jackal": Tua *akūlen*.
CCh **kyal-* < **kVyal-* "dog": Ksr *kele*, Log *kəle*, Bud *kelī*.

Sem **kalb-* "dog" may also belong here as a reflex of **kal-* with the suffix of harmful animals **-b-*. Note the consonantal alternation **-w-* ~ **-y-*.

*ḳ

1522 *ḳaᵓ- "see"

Eg *ḳ3ḳ3* "look" (n).

Reduplication.

WCh **ḳa-* "see": Maha *kai*, Bgh *kwa*, Kir *kwē*, Ngz *ika*.

Bgh and Kir go back to **ḳwaᵓ-* < **ḳaw-*.

ECh **kaᵓ-* "see": Tum *ka*.

1523 *ḳa'-/*ḳaw-/*ḳay- "move upwards, fly"

Eg *ḳꜣ* "be high" (pyr).
WCh **ḳa'-* "rise": Sura *kaa*, Chip *kaa*.
CCh **kwa'-* "raise, lift": Gudu *k^w^o:*.
From **ḳaw-*?
ECh **kaw-/*kay-* "fly" 1, "rise" 2: Mobu *kaye* 1, Bid *kaaw* 2.

Consonantal alternation **-'-* ~ **-w-* ~ **-y-*.

1524 *ḳa'-/*ḳay- "spit"

Sem **ḳī'-* "spit": Hbr *qy'*.
Transformation of the original biliteral root into a **CVyVC-* structure. Cf. Akk *gâ'u*, *kâ'u* id.?
Eg *ḳꜣꜥ* "spit out" (MK).
Based on the original **ḳꜣ*?
ECh **ka'ak-* "spit": Dng *kaake*.
Reduplication.

1525 *ḳa'-/*ḳay- "egg"

WCh **ḳwa'-/*ḳway-* "egg": Hs *ḳwai*, Grk *nkie*.
Prefix in Grk.
Omot **ḳew-* "egg": Yam *keewa*.

1526 *ḳab- "vessel"

Sem **ḳab-* "goblet": Akk *qabūtu*.
Eg *ḳby* "mug" (MK).
Suffix *-y*?
WCh **kaḅ-* < **ḳab-* "basket": Sha *kaḅa*, DB *kaḅa*.
Shift of emphatization.

1527 *ḳab- "cold"

Eg *ḳb*, *ḳbb* "cold".
LEC **ḳab-* "cold": Som *qabow*, Rnd *χobo*, Arb *ḳab-*.
Som and Rnd go back to **ḳab-aw-*.

1528 *ḳab- "speak, shout"

Sem **ḳVb-* "say": Akk *qabû*.
WCh **ḳab-* "name" (v.): Tng *kɛb-*.
ECh **kVb-* "talk": Ndm *kəba*.
LEC **ḳab-ḳab-* "shout" (n.): Som *qabqab-*.
Reduplication.

1529 *ḳabul- "heart, stomach"

Sem **ḳalb-* "heart, soul, middle": Arab *qalb-*.
Metathesis.
WCh **ḳabul-* "stomach": Siri *bokule*, Mbu *ḳubulo*.
Assimilation of vowels. Metathesis in Siri.
CCh **kuɓar-* < **ḳubal-* "heart": Hwn *kuɓar-fara*.
Metathesis.

Alternative reconstructions are **ḳalub-* and **baḳul-* . Any relation to Afar *qabul* "fat" (n.)?

1530 *ḳaç- "bone"

Sem **ḳaṣṣ-* "breast, sternum": Arab *qaṣṣ-*.
Agaw **nV-[ḳ]ac-* "bone": Bil *naaš*, Xmr *ŋac*, Kwr *naaš*, Dmb *naaš*, Kem *ŋaš*, Aun *ŋac*, Dmt *ŋaaç*.
Prefix **nV-*.
Wrz **mi-ḳeč-* "bone": War *mi-ḳeče*.
Prefix **mV-*. The vowel is not regular.

Cf. **ḳas-* "bone".

1531 *ḳaç-/*ḳuç- "cut"

Sem **ḳuṣ-* "cut": Akk *qaṣāṣu*, Hbr *qṣṣ*, *qṣy*, Aram *qṣṣ*, Arab *qṣṣ* [-*u*-], Shh *qeṣ*, Soq *qeṣ*.
WCh **kaç-* < **ḳaç-* "scrape, plane (wood)": Hs *kāçā*.
Dissimilation of emphatics.
Dhl *k'ats-* "circumcise".
Omot **ḳuç-* "circumcise": Maji *ḳuç-*.

Alternation **a* ~ **u*. Cf. **ḳuĉ-* "cut, pierce".

1532 *ḳač- ''divide''

ECh *kač- ''part, divorce'': Bid kač-.
Rift *ḳas- ''divide'': Irq qasis-.

Cf. WCh *kač- ''place in portions'': Hs kasa (with deglottalization).

1533 *ḳad- ''skin''

Sem *ḳadd- ''lamb skin'': Arab qadd-.
WCh *kaḍ- < *ḳad- ''skin'': Krf kaḍa.
Shift of emphatization.

1534 *ḳad- ''vessel''

Sem *ḳadaḥ- ''pot, bowl'': Akk qadû, Arab qadaḥ-.
Based on the original *ḳad-?
LEC *ḳadad- ''vessel, gourd'': Or qadaada.
Partial reduplication.

Cf. another morphonological variant in *ḳod- ''vessel''.

1535 *ḳad-/*ḳawad- ''strike''

CCh *kaḍ- < *ḳad- ''strike'': Gis kaḍ, Mofu kəḍ- , Mafa kaḍ-.
ECh *kawaḍ- < *ḳawad- ''strike'': Mig kooḍo.
Shift of emphatization.
Bed kaḍaw ''strike''.
Metathesis. Note the shift of emphatization similar to Chadic.

The original morphological structure is preserved in CCh.

1536 *ḳaduḥ- ''fly'' (n.)

Sem *ḳadūḥ- ''fly'' (n.): Arab qadūḥ-.
WCh *ḳud- < *ḳudaH- ''fly'' (n.): Hs ḳudā.
Metathesis of vowels.

1537 *ḳaḥ- ''earth, sand''

Eg ḳɜḥ ''earth'' (MK).

Vocalic -*ǝ*-.

CCh **kay-kay-* "sand": Muk *kaykay*, Msg *kaikai*.

Reduplication.

1538 *ḳaḥaḥ- "cough" (v.)

CCh **kaχag-* "cough": Bud *kahagɛ*.

Dissimilation from **kaχaχ-*?

ECh **kaHak-* "cough": Bid *kaak*.

Dissimilation from **kahah-*?

LEC **ḳak(V)k-* "severe cough": Or *qakkee*.

Descriptive root. An alternative reconstruction may be **ḳaḥaḳ-* or **ḳaḥak-*.

1539 *ḳaḳ-/*ḳuḳ- "cuckoo, hen"

Sem **ḳaḳVy-* "bird": Akk *qaqû*.

Eg *ḳḳ* "cuckoo" (NK).

WCh **kukway-* "rooster": Fyer *kukwe*.

CCh **kwak-* "hen": Gul *kwaku*.

ECh **kVkay-* "bird": Bid *keeke*.

Descriptive root. Alternation **a* ~ **u*.

1540 *ḳal- "fall"

Sem **ḳīl-* "fall": Akk *qiālu*, Ug *ql*.

Based on **ḳVl-*.

CCh **kal-* "fall": Mafa *kal-*.

ECh **kal-* "drop": Bid *ʾakal*.

1541 *ḳal-/*ḳawal- "speak"

Sem **ḳūl-* "speak": Arab *qwl* [-*u*-].

Related to **ḳāl-* "voice" (Hbr *qōl*, Aram *qāl*, Gz *qāl*).

ECh **kawal-* "cry, shout" [1], "speak, call" [2]: Lele *ya-kolo* [1], Kbl *ye-kuwǝlǝ* , Dng *kole* [2], Jegu *kol* [2], Brg *kole* [2], Bid *kol* [2].

Prefix **ya-* in Lele and Kbl.

SA **ḳal-* "say, think": Afar *-ḳal-*.

The original biconsonantal root structure is preserved in SA.

1542 *ḳal-/*ḳil- ''be small''

Sem **ḳil-* ''be small, be light'': Akk *qallu*, Hbr *qll*, Arab *qll* [-*i*-], Hss *qel*, Soq *qel*.
WCh **ḳal-* ''small'': Dera *kalla*.
ECh **kal-* ''small'': Kbl *kāle*.
LEC **ḳal-* ''thin, slender'': Or *qalʔaa*, *qallaa*, Kon *quallaʾ-*.

Alternation **a* ~ **i*. Cf. CCh **kul-* ''short'': Gudu *kul*.

1543 *ḳam- ''rise, lift''

Sem **ḳūm-* ''stand up, get up'': Hbr *qwm*, Arab *qwm* [-*u*-], SAr *qwm*, Gz *qwm*.
Secondary transformation of a biconsonantal root into a **CVwVC-* structure.
WCh **ḳam-* ''lift'': Geji *kami*, Buli *kəmu*.

1544 *ḳamVḥ- ''stick''

Eg *ḳmḥ* ''twig'' (n).
WCh **ḳam-* ''stick'': Sura *kam*, Ang *kam*, Mpn *kam*.
Loss of the auslaut laryngeal.

1545 *ḳamVḥ- ''flour''

Sem **ḳamḥ-* ''flour'': Akk *qēmu*, Hbr *qemaḥ*, Aram (Syr) *qemḥō*, Arab *qamḥ-*, Gz *qamḥ*.
HEC **ḳam(ay)-* ''flour'': Bmb *ḳamay*, Had *ḳama*, Kmb *ḳama*.

1546 *ḳan- ''plait''

Berb **ḳVn-* ''tie'': Kby *əqqən*.
Eg *ḳn* ''weave'' (gr).
Cf. *ḳny* ''weaver'' (MK).
WCh **ḳanu-* ''tie'': Cagu *ḳun-*, Bgh *kan*, Buli *kənnu*.
CCh **kanwa-* ''plait'': Lame *kənwa*, Msm *kan*.
ECh **kwan-* < **kanwa-* ''twist'' [1], ''plait'' [2]: Tum *koŋ* [1], Mkk *kini* [2].
Secondary -*i*- in Mkk.

1547 *ḳan- "say, shout"

WCh **ḳwan-* < **ḳanu-* "say": Say *kwan*, *kwani*.
Omot **ḳan-* "shout": Ome *ḳan-*.

1548 *ḳap- "head, occiput"

Sem **ḳapa[y]-* "occiput": Aram (Syr) *qōpyō*, Arab *qafā-*.
Berb **ḳaf-* "head": Ghd *iγaf*, Kby *ēγaf*.
ECh **kwap-* < **kapwa-* "occiput": Dng *kopo*, Mig *kupo*, Jegu *kofo*.

1549 *ḳar- "horn"

Sem **ḳarn-* "horn": Akk *qarnu*, Ug *qrn*, Hbr *qeren*, Aram (Syr) *qarnō*, Arab *qarn-*, Gz *qarn*, Hss *qōn*, Mhr *qōn*, Shh *qun*, Soq *qan*.
Derivative in **-n-*.
Eg *ḳr.ty* "horns" (dual) (NK).
Omot **[ḳ]ar-* "horn": Kaf *karoo*, Mch *karo*.

1550 *ḳar- "cloud"

Eg *ḳr* "cloud" (pyr).
WCh **ḳar-* "cloud": Bol *kɔriya*.

1551 *ḳar- "finish"

Eg *ḳr* "end (of a book)" (n).
WCh **ḳarya-* "finish": Hs *ḳāre*, Tng *ker*, Buli *kyeru*.
ECh **kar-* "finish": Kwn *kar*, Mobu *kəre*.

1552 *ḳar- "mountain"

Sem **ḳār-* "single mountain, hill": Arab *qār-at-*.
Berb **ḳar-* "hill": Shl *iγar*.
Eg *ḳȝȝ* "hill".
-ȝȝ < **-r-*?
LEC **ḳar-* "high mountain, summit": Som *qar*, Or *qara*.

1553 *ḳar- "burn; fire"

Eg *ḳrr* "fire, glaze (pots)" (pyr).

Partial reduplication.
WCh **ḳar-* "burn": Kr *karu*, Krf *kaʔu*, *kaaru*.
CCh **kar-* "fire": Mnd *kara*, Glv *kara*, Zgh *kara*.
Cf. Mofu *kakər* "burn" with partial reduplication.

1554 *ḳar- "(be) cold"

Sem **ḳarr-* "(be) cold": Hbr *qar*, Arab *qarr-*, Gz *qʷrr*.
WCh **ḳarar-* "cold (of water, weather)": Hs *kararā*.
Partial reduplication.

A morphonological variant of **ḳor-* "cold" (n.).

1555 *ḳar- "call, shout"

Sem **ḳVrVʔ-* "call, shout" [1], "read" [2]: Akk *qerû* [1], Ug *qrʔ* [1], Hbr *qrʔ* [1 2], Aram *qrʔ* [1], Arab *qrʔ* [-*a*-, -*u*-] [2].
Based on biconsonantal **ḳVr-*.
Berb **ḳVrVy-* "call" (n.): Tua *ta-γeri-t*.
Based on biconsonantal **ḳVr-*.
WCh **ḳar-* "cry out": Hs *ḳārā*.

1556 *ḳaraʕ- "cut"

Sem **ḳVʕar-* "cut (trees)": Arab *qʕr* [-*a*-].
Metathesis.
WCh **ḳar(aH)-/*ḳir-* "cut": Hs *ḳira*, Bol *kar*, Krk *karaa*, Dera *kara-*, Ngm *kara-*.
ECh **kVr-* "carve": Ndm *kəra*.
Agaw **ḳaraʕ-* "cut": Bil *ḳaraaʕ y-*.
LEC **ḳar-* "sharp, point" (v.): Or *qara*.
Cf. also LEC **ḳor-* "cut, carve" (Som *qor-*, Or *qor-* , Arb *qor-*), **ḳar-* "shave oneself" (Arb *qar-*).
Wrz **ḳar-* "sharp": Gaw *qaru*.
HEC **ḳar-* "be sharp": Sid *ḳar-aaʔm-*.
Dhl *k'eer-* "cut".
Metathesis and contraction.

1557 *ḳas- "bone"

Berb **ḳVs-* "bone": Ahg *eγes*, Tua *eγēs*, Snus *īγes*, Kby *īγes*, Siwa *aγes*.

Eg *ḳs* "bone" (pyr), Copt **kas* id.: Boh *kas*, Shd *kas*.
WCh **ḫa-ḳas-* "bone": Hs *ḳašī*, Wrj *ḳāsū-na*, Kry *ḳāsu*, Miya *kusi*, Paa *ḳəsi-ki*, Cagu *ḳeḳesəna*, Mbu *ḳaḳasə*, Jmb *ḳəḳasi*, Bks *kyas*, Sha *gyiš-aw*, Klr *gyiš-aw*, DB *kyas*.
Prefix **ḳa-*.
ECh **kas-* "bone": Kwn *kisi-gi*, Dng *kāso*, Bid *kas-ko*.
Assimilation of vowels in Kwn.
LEC **ḳas-* "bone, leg": Gel *ḳas*.
Omot **ḳas-/*ḳus-* "bone": Nao *ḳus*, Dime *ḳas*, *ḳus*.
Unexpected **-u-*.

1558 *ḳaṭ-/*ḳuṭ- "cut"

Sem **ḳuṭ-* "cut": Arab *qṭṭ* [*-u-*], Gz *q^wṭṭ*, Amh *q^wṭṭ*.
The vocalism **u* may be reflected in labialized velars of Gz and Amh.
LEC **ḳat-* < **ḳaṭ-* "circumcise": Bay *ḳat-*.
Dissimilation of emphatics.
Omot **ḳuṭ-* "cut": Kaf *ḳuṭ-*.
Rift **ḳat-* "circumcise": Kwz *ḳat-*.
Dissimilation of emphatics.
Dhl *k'aat'-aaδ-* "divide".

Alternation **a* ~ **u*.

1559 *ḳaw- "nail, claw"

WCh **ḳaw-* "finger-nail": Wrj *ḳəwi-na*, Mbu *ḳawi*, Jmb *ḳuya*.
ECh **kawak-* "finger-nail": Mkk *kooka*.
Partial reduplication.
Wrz **ḳoy-* < **ḳaway-* "claw": Gaw *qoy-akko*.

1560 *ḳawas-/*ḳayas- "bow, arrow"

Sem **ḳawš-* "bow": Akk *qaštu*, Hbr *qešet*, Arab *qaws-*, Gz *qast*.
CCh **kyas-* < **k[a]yas-* "arrow" [1], "bow" [2]: Mba *kese* [1], Msg *kise* [2].
ECh **kyas-* < **k[a]yas-* "bow": Tum *kēse*, Bid *kēse*, Mig *kese*, Sok *kɛsɛ* (< Arab?).

Cf. also Rift **ḳas-* "arrow" in Kwz *ḳasa-mato*. Note the consonantal alternation **-w-* ~ **-y-*.

1561 *ḳawat- "food"

Sem *ḳawt- "food": Hss *qūt*, Mhr *qawt*, Shh *qit*.
WCh *ḳwatu- < *ḳVwatu- "food, bread": Tng *kutu*, *kwete*.
CCh *kwat- < *kVwat- "food": Lame *kwati*.

1562 *ḳayaç- "end, finish"

Sem *ḳīṣ- "end, finish" (n. and v.): Hbr *qēṣ*, Jib *ḳeṣi*.
WCh *ḳayac- < *ḳayaç- "end, finish": Sura *kyes*, Mpn *kes*.
Dissimilation of emphatics.

1563 *ḳayiç̌- "summer"

Sem *ḳayṯ̣- "summer": Hbr *qayiṣ*, Aram (Syr) *qaytō*, Jib *qoẓ*, Hss *qayẓ*, Mhr *qayẓ*, Shh *qoẓ*, Soq *qiyaṭ*.
WCh *ḳiç̌- "summer": Buli *kis*, Zul *gisi*.
Contraction of *-ayi- > *-i-.
Omot *ḳeç- "heat" (n.): Mch *ḳeç̌ç̌i*.
Related to *ḳeç- "be hot, be warm": Ome *ḳič̌u*, Mch *ḳeç̌ç̌i*.

1564 *ḳeʔ- "house"

CCh *kyay- "house": Pad *keya*.
From *kyaH-.
LEC *ḳeʔ- "enclosure, compound": Or *qeeʔee*.
Omot *ḳeʔ- "house": Gim *keeʔoo*.

Any connection with Hs *ḳauye* "village"?

1565 *ḳeĉ̣- "break"

Sem *ḳīṣ̂- "break, split": Arab *qyḍ* [-*i*-].
Based on biconsonantal *ḳVṣ̂-.
ECh *kyaĉ̣- "break, skin": Bid *keḍy*.

1566 *ḳen- "kill"

Sem *ḳVnaʔ- "kill": Arab *qnʔ* [-*a*-].
Based on biliteral *ḳVn-.
Eg *ḳn* "kill" (reg).

CCh *kyan- "kill, break in pieces": Mnd *kyɛn-*.

1567 *ḳenin- "vessel"

Sem *ḳinīn- "bottle": Arab *qinnīn-at-*.
CCh *ḳyanin-H- "small pot": Gudu *kēniŋ*.

Partial reduplication?

1568 *ḳer- "dwelling"

Sem *ḳary- "town, village": Ug *qr-t*, *qry-t*, Hbr *qiryā*, Aram (Syr) *qerī-t-*, Arab *qary-at-*, SAr *qr*, Jib *sirɛ-t*.
Secondary vocalism.
ECh *kyar- "house": Smr *kerī*.
Omot *ḳer- "house, dwelling": Ome *ḳera*.

A morphonological variant of *ḳor- "house, place".

1569 *ḳeran- "monkey"

WCh *ḳyaran-H- "monkey": Bks *kyeraŋ*.
Suffix *-H-.
LEC *ḳaran- "vervet monkey": Arb *ḳaarran*.
Assimilation of vowels.

Cf. WCh *ḳar- "monkey" (Sura *kar*, Ang *ker*) as a possible reflection of the original HS *ḳar- id. See *ḳerVd- "monkey".

1570 *ḳerVd- "monkey"

Sem *ḳird- "monkey": Arab *qird-*.
ECh *mV-kyar(V)ḍ- "green monkey": Mig *mekerḍa*.
Prefix *ma-. Phonetically, *ḳyar(V)d- > *kyar(V)ḍ-.

Related to *ḳeran- id. Apparently, there existed HS *ḳer- "monkey".

1571 *ḳiḥ- "moon"

Eg *ḳḥy* "moon" (BD).
Vocalic *-y*.

CCh *kiy- < *kiH- "moon": Gis *kiya*, Bld *kiya*, Mtk *kiya*.
ECh *kway- < *kwaHi- "moon": Dng *kɔyɛ*, Mig *koyo*, Bid *koya*.
Unexpected vocalism.

1572 *ḳiHVd- "set on fire"

Sem *ḳVHVd- "set on fire": Akk *qâdu*.
WCh *kiḍ- < *ḳid- "burn": Gera *kiḍ*.

Cf. CCh *kwa-kwad- "hotness": Klb *kwakwadu*.

1573 *ḳilVb- "knee"

Eg *ḳꜣb.t* "knee" (LM).
Note -ꜣ- < *-l-.
LEC *[ḳ]ilVb- "knee": Kon *kilba*, Bus *kilba*, Gat *kilba*, Gdl *kilba*.
Omot *kelVḅ- < *ḳelVb-: Gll *keelḅa*.
Shift of emphatization.

1574 *ḳir- "frog"

Sem *ḳVrr- "frog": Arab *qarr-at-*, *qirr-at-*, *qurr-at-*.
Eg *ḳrr* "frog" (n), Copt *krur id.: Boh *k'rour*, Shd *krour*.
Partial reduplication.
CCh *kir- "frog": Daba *kərrəŋ*, Mofu *kakəraŋ*, Gava *kiře*, FBw *kuř-min*.
Partial reduplication in Mofu.
ECh *kir-yan- "frog": Mubi *kirēni*, Sok *koriŋgē*.

1575 *ḳiraḥ- "wound" (v.)

Sem *ḳVraḥ- "wound" (v.): Arab *qrḥ* [-a-].
ECh *kiHVr- "wound" (v.): Mkk *giira*.
Metathesis.

Connected with *ḳuraʿ- "strike, break".

1576 *ḳirop-/*ḳorip- "bark" (n.)

Sem *ḳirp- "bark": Arab *qirf-*.
Cf. Arab *qrf* "peel (bark)", Gz *qrf* id.

WCh *ḳwarip- "bark": Cagu ḳorōpe, Brw kworəp, Wnd kworip.

Metathesis of vowels in Sem or WCh. Cf. *ḳolif- id. Any connection with *ḳur- "skin, bark"? In Cush, there are several similar forms with a voiced auslaut: Bed kurbe "skin", Agaw *ḳwarab- "skin" (Kem k^wɔrɛvɛ), Omot *ḳurub- "skin" (Ome ḳurubi).

1577 *ḳirVb- "breast, belly"

Sem *ḳirb- "intestines" [1], "belly" [2], "side" [3]: Akk qirbu [1], Hbr qereb [2], Arab qurb-, qurub- [3].

Eg ḳɜb "gut" (med).

HS *-r- > Eg -ɜ-.

Wrz *ker(V)p- "breast": Gaw kerpe.

Irregular anlaut?

Cf. SA *gar(V)b- "belly" (Saho garbaa, Afar garbaa).

1578 *ḳobaḥ- "cloud, sky"

Eg ḳbḥ.w "sky" (pyr).

WCh *ḳwaḅay- < *ḳwabaH- "cloud": Bol kebe, Krk kwabo, Ngm keḅe.

1579 *ḳod- "vessel"

Eg ḳd "pot" (med).

Cf. Copt *kot "basket" (Fym kat, Boh kot and the like)?

WCh *kwaḍ- < *ḳwad- "calabash": Krf kwaḍo, Gera kwaḍa.

CCh *nV-ḳwad- "bottle": Log ŋkōda.

Prefix *nV-.

ECh *kwaḍ- < *ḳwad- "pot": Dng kɔḍa.

LEC *ḳod- "receptacle": Or qodaa.

Dhl k'oo̱do "kind of calabash".

Cf. *ḳad- "vessel".

1580 *ḳol- "egg"

CCh *kwal- "egg": Bata kwalɔ.

Agaw *ʾVn-ḳwalal- ''egg'': Kem *ənḳulal*, Aun *ənkʷlal*.
Prefix *ʾVn-. Partial reduplication.

1581 *ḳol- ''look, see''

Sem *mVḳul- ''look'': Arab *mql* [-u-].
Prefix *mV-.
Berb *ḳVl- ''look'': Izy *smuqeḷ*.
ECh *kwal- ''see'': Ndm *kə:la*, Jegu *ʾakal-*.
Agaw *ḳwal- ''look, see'': Bil *ḳʷal*, Xmr *ḳʷal*, Xmt *ḳaal-*, Kwr *ψʷaal*, Dmb *ḳʷaal*, Kem *χal*.
LEC *ḳolal- ''see'': Som *qollaali-*.
Partial reduplication.

1582 *ḳol- ''earthenware''

Sem *ḳull- ''clay mug'' [1], ''jug'' [2]: Akk *qulliu* [1], Arab *qull-at-* [2].
HEC *ḳol- ''jar'': Bmb *ḳole*.

1583 *ḳol- ''head, nape''

Berb *ḳVl-ḳul- ''occiput'': Izy *aqeḷquḷ*.
Reduplication.
WCh *ḳwa-ḳwal- ''brain'': Hs *ḳwaḳwalwā*.
Partial reduplication.
ECh *kwa-kVl- ''brain'': Kwan *kokəl*.
Partial reduplication.
LEC *ḳol- ''nape'': Or *qolee*.
HEC *ḳoʾ(V)l- ''nape, back of neck'': Had *ḳoʾlo*, Kmb *ḳoʾlu*.
Secondary *-ʾ-.

Quite probably, related to *ḳol- ''earthenware''. Cf. Lat *testa* ''potsherd'' > Rom **testa* ''head''.

1584 *ḳol- ''be hot, burn''

Sem *ḳVlVw- ''roast'': Akk *qalû*, Arab *qlw* [-i-, -u-].
Based on *ḳVl-.
CCh *kwalu- ''hotness'': Bch *kwul-*.

1585 *ḳolif- "bark" (n.)

Sem *ḳulip- "bark": Akk *quliptu*, Hbr *qᵉlippā*, Arab *qulāf-at-*, Hss *qelfēt*, Mhr *qelēfōt*, Soq *qalifoh*.
Cf. Arab *qlf* "peel" (v.), Gz *qʷlf* id. Secondary vocalism in Arab.
SA *kolof- "bark": Saho *kolofo*.
Irregular *k-. Assimilation of vowels.
LEC *ḳolof- "bark" 1, "foreskin" 2: Som *qolof* 1, Or *qolofa* 2, Kon *qolfa* 1.
Assimilation of vowels.
Wrz *ḳofol- "bark": Gaw *qoffol*.
Assimilation of vowels. Metathesis.

1586 *ḳom- "house, enclosure"

WCh *ḳwama- "hut": Ang *kwam*, Kry *ḳam*, Miya *ḳam*, Siri *ḳami*, Mbu *ḳam*.
Rift *ḳwam- "enclosure": Bur *qwama*, Kwz *kw'ama*.

1587 *ḳomal- "insect"

Sem *ḳaml- "flea" 1, "louse" 2: Arab *qaml-* 1, SAr *qmlt* 2, Gz *qʷemāl* 2, Tgy *qʷemāl* 2.
Ethio-Sem forms may reflect an earlier rounded vowel of the root.
CCh *kwamal- "ant": Bud *komāli*.

1588 *ḳop- "container"

Sem *ḳupp- "box" 1, "basket" 2: Akk *quppu* 1, Arab *quff-at-* 2, Shh *qefet* 2, Mhr *qeffēt* 2, Soq *q̇efɛt* 2.
Cf. Akk *qappatu* "basket", Gz *qafo* id.
CCh *kVp- "calabash": Bch *kpa*.
ECh *kwap- "box": Mkk *koop*.
LEC *ḳuf- "basket": Som *quffo*.

1589 *ḳor- "house, place"

Sem *ḳur-an- "villages" (pl.): Arab *qur-an-*.
Suffix *-an-*.

WCh *ḳwar- ''hut'': Krk *kwaro*.
Cf. partial reduplication in DB *kukor* ''stone wall'', see CCh.
CCh *kwa-kwar- ''town'': Mtk *kwokwař*.
Partial reduplication (cf. WCh).
ECh *kwaru- ''place'': Lele *kūr*, Kbl *kɔrr*.
LEC *ḳor- ''block'': Or *qoroo*.
Rift *ḳor- ''brick house'': Irq *qoori*.

A morphonological variant of *ḳer- ''dwelling''.

1590 *ḳor- ''speak, ask''

CCh *kwar- ''speak'': Zgh *kwaraya*, Gava *kwər-*.
LEC *ḳor- ''examine, question'': Or *qora*.
Reduplication in Or *qorqoro* ''ask''.
HEC *ḳor- ''ask (in investigation)'': Gel *ḳor-*.

Related to *ḳar-/*ḳir- ''call, shout''?

1591 *ḳor- ''cold'' (n.)

Sem *ḳurr- ''cold'': Akk *qirru*, Hbr *qor*, Aram (Syr) *qurō*, Arab *qurr-*, *qirr-*, Gz *qʷər*.
LEC *ḳor(r)- ''intense cold'': Or *qorra*.
HEC *ḳor(r)- ''cold'': Sid *qorre*.

Derived from *ḳar- ''(be) cold''.

1592 *ḳoreŝ- ''cut''

Sem *ḳVriś- ''cut into parts'': Akk *qarāšu*, Arab *qrš* [-*i*-, -*u*-].
HEC *ḳores- ''break (bread)'': Had *ḳoreš-*, Kmb *ḳoros-*.

Note the unusual vocalic pattern. Cf. *ḳaraʕ- ''cut''?

1593 *ḳoriʔ- ''bird''

Sem *ḳariʔ- ''kind of bird'': Hbr *qorēʔ*, Arab *qāriyy-at-*.
Irregular vocalism.
WCh *ḳyar- < *ḳwari- ''hen'': Mnt *kier*.
CCh *kwar(i)- ''duck'': Mofu *kwerekwere*.
Reduplication.

ECh *kwar- "duck" [1], "chicken, rooster" [2]: Kera *akorkoro* [1], Dng *kokira* [2], Jegu *kokore* [2], Mubi *kurī* [2], Mig *kukkira, kokiro* [2].
Various types of reduplication.
LEC *ḳor- "kite": Arb *qore*.

1594 *ḳorVᶜ- "shield"

Eg *ḳrᶜ.w* "shield" (XIX).
ECh *kwar- "shield": Mkk *korko*, Sok *kokēre*.
Partial reduplications. Loss of the auslaut laryngeal.

1595 *ḳos- "strike"

WCh *ḳwas- "strike": Hs *dan-ḳwasa*, Ang *kwas*.
ECh *kVs- "break, strike": Mkk *koss-, gusse*.
LEC *ḳos- "knock, peck": Or *qossaˀa*.
HEC *ḳas- "strike, pierce": Sid *ḳas-*, Had *kaass-*, Bmb *kas-*, Kmb *kas-*.
The root vowel is irregular.

1596 *ḳotir-/*ḳotur- "be small"

Sem *ḳVtir-/*ḳVtur- "live modestly, make meager": Arab *qtr* [-*i*-, -*u*-].
CCh *kwatVr- "small": Mtk *kwotř*.

1597 *ḳoṭiᶜ- "end, finish" (v.)

Sem *ḳVṭVᶜ- "finish, be finished" [1], "be spent" [2]: Akk *qatû* [1], Arab *qṭᶜ* [2].
WCh *kwaṭi- < *ḳwaṭi- "end, finish": Ang *küt*, Siri *kwata*, Fyer *ḳit*, Tng *kwaḍe*, Siri *kwata*.
Dissimilation of emphatics.
CCh *kaṭ- < *kwaṭa- "end, finish": Msg *kata*.

1598 *ḳoy- "bird"

Eg *ḳy* "bird" (XVIII).
WCh *ḳway- "hen": Sura *kwɛɛ, kyɛ*, Ang *ki*, Mnt *kiyɛ*.
CCh *kuy- "hawk": Mnd *kuye*.

ECh *kway- ''bird'': Kwn *koyō*.
Cf. Mkk *kaawa* ''dove''.

1599 *ḳub- ''roof, house''

Sem *ḳubb- ''cupola'': Arab *qubb-at-*.
CCh *kub- ''hut'': Tera *kəba*, Gude *kuva*, FM *kuvu*.

1600 *ḳuĉ̣- ''cut, pierce''

Sem *ḳVṣ̂- ''pierce'': Arab *qḍḍ*.
WCh *ḳVĉ̣- ''cut, split'': Jmb *kəṣ̂*.
CCh *kVŝ- ''cut'': Zgh *kŝu-naya*.
Rift *ḳuĉ- ''cut'': Bur *quuĉ-*.

Cf. *ḳaç- ''cut''.

1601 *ḳud- ''cut, tear''

Sem *ḳud- ''cut'' [1], ''tear'' [2]: Hbr *qdd* [1], Aram *qdd* [1], Arab *qdd* [-*u*-] [1 2], Gz *qdd* [1], Tgr *qdd* [2], Amh *qdd* [2], Arg *qdd* [2], Hrr *qdd* [2], Gur *qdd* [2].
CCh *kuḍi- ''tear, pluck'': Mafa *kwiḍ-*, *ŋgwiḍ-*.
Agaw *ḳidid- ''tear'': Aun *qeded-əŋ*.
Partial reduplication.
LEC *ḳod- ''divide'': Or *qood-*.
Omot *ḳad-/*ḳod- ''divide'': Kaf *ḳodi*, Mch *ḳoodi*.

1602 *ḳudaḥ- ''dig''

Sem *ḳVdVḥ- ''make holes'': Arab *qdḥ*.
ECh *kudaH- ''dig'': Ndm *kudā*.
Wrz *ḳod- ''dig'': Gaw *qoδ-*.

1603 *ḳuḳ- ''bark'' (n.)

Eg *ḳḳ.ty* ''bark'' (gr).
WCh *ʾa-ḳuḳwaḳ- ''bark'' [1], ''skin'' [2]: Klr *ak'uk'wɛg* [1], Ang *kuk* [2].
Partial reduplication in Klr.

1604 *ḳul- "lift, rise"

Sem *ḳVl- "raise": Arab *qll*.
Berb *ḳVwVl- "rise": Sml *γuli*, *γli*, Sgh *eγlīy*.
Inlaut *-w- continuing HS *u?
CCh *kul- "lift": HNk *kulu*, Kap *kəl-te*, HF *kəli-*, FKi *kəltuʾ*.

1605 *ḳum- "sweep"

Sem *ḳVm- "sweep": Arab *qmm*.
WCh *ḳum- "sweep": Chip *kum*, Ank *kum*, Grk *kokum*.
Partial reduplication in Grk.

1606 *ḳum- "be hot, burn"

Sem *ḳVm- "burn": Akk *qamû*.
WCh *ḳum- "become hot": Bol *kum*.

1607 *ḳur- "go around, follow"

WCh *ḳur- "go around": Bol *kur*.
CCh *kur- "accompany": FMch *kuri*.
ECh *kwar- "go away" [1], "follow, turn" [2]: Kera *koore* [1], Mkk *guzze* [2].
LEC *ḳor- "run back and forth": Or *qoraʾa*.

1608 *ḳur- "skin, bark"

WCh *ḳur- "skin, bark": Bgh *kwar*, Wnd *kur*, Tala *kuur*, Zul *kuuri*, Bot *koore*, Kir *kwār*, Pol *kūri*, Geji *kūr*, Brw *kūru*.
Omot *ḳur- "skin, bark": Ome *ḳuuro*, *kurra*.

1609 *ḳurab- "insect"

Sem *ʿaḳrab- "scorpion": Hbr *ʿaqrāb*, Aram (Syr) *ʿeqarbō*, Arab *ʿaqrab-*.
Prefix *ʿa-.
WCh *ḳurVb- "ant": Glm *kurba*.

1610 *ḳuraˁ- "strike, break"

Sem *ḳVraˁ- "strike (with a stick)": Arab *qrˁ* [-*a*-].
Based on *ḳVr-?
WCh *ḳir- "grind" [1], "blow" [2]: Glm *kir* [1], Ang *kīr* [2].
Loss of the auslaut laryngeal. Secondary *i.
CCh *kur- "forge": FJ *kura*.
Loss of the auslaut laryngeal.
LEC *ḳuraʔ- "hit, bat": Or *quraʔa*.

1611 *ḳurom- "cut, bite"

Sem *ḳVrum- "cut with teeth": Arab *qrm* [-*u*-].
WCh *ḳurwam- "cut or bite head off" [1], "cut" [2]: Hs *ḳurmē* [1], Ang *karm* [2].

1612 *ḳuruc- "rope"

Sem *ḳurus- "belt": Akk *kurussu*.
Irregular reflection of *ḳ.
Eg *ḳꜣs* "cord" (pyr).
-*ꜣ*- continues HS *-*r*-.

A cultural loanword?

1613 *ḳut- "beat, break"

Sem *wVḳVt-/*yVḳVt- "beat (smb.)": Arab *wqt*, *yqt*.
Prefix *wV-/*yV-.
ECh *kut- "break, pound": Kwn *kutē*.

Cf. also Rift *ḳet- "break in pieces": Irq *qet-is-*, Bur *qet-is-*.

1614 *ḳut- "feed, cook"

Sem *ḳūt- "feed": Arab *qwt* [-*u*-].
Derivative based on *ḳVt-.
WCh *ḳut- "prepare food, cook": Tng *kute*.

Related to *ḳawat- "food".

1615 *ḳuṭun- "be small"

Sem **ḳVṭVn-* "be small, be thin": Hbr *qṭn*, Gz *qṭn*, Hss *qayṭen*, Mhr *qayṭen*, Shh *qeṭen*.
CCh **kuṭun-* "short, small": Tera *kutun*.

Related to **ḳotir-/*ḳotur-* "be small"?

1616 *ḳüč- "insect"

ECh **guč-*"termite": Lele *gusi*.
Agaw **ḳič-* "worm": Bil *ḳešaa*, Xmr *ḥesaa*, Kwr *χešii*, Dmb *χesee*, Kem *χəšaa*.
Dhl *k'utsi* "bee larva".

1617 *ḳüd- "genitals"

CCh **kuḍ-* < **ḳud-* "testicles": Mnd *kuḍa*, Pad *kuda-ma*, Mtk *kuḍe-eč*.

Shift of emphatization.

Agaw **ḳwid-* "anus, vulva": Xmr *χʷedaa*.
LEC **ḳod-* "penis": Som *qoodo*, *qooḍo*.

1618 *ḳüdur- "vessel"

Sem **ḳidr-* "earthenware": Hbr *qᵉdērā*, Aram *qidrā*, Arab *qidr-*, Hss *qeder*, Mhr *qāder*.
ECh **gudur-* "pot": Kera *gədərya*, Mubi *gudur*.

1619 *ḳün- "(be) white, (be) yellow"

Eg *ḳny.t* "yellow color" (NK).

Vocalic *-y*.

CCh **kun-H-* "white": Bch *kuŋ*, Bata *kuŋe*.

1620 *ḳür- "snake"

Eg *iḳr.w* "kind of snake" (pyr).

i- may be a prefix lost in Chadic or a vocalic sign for a front vowel.

WCh **ḳur-* "snake": Tng *kurot*, Bol *kureeḍi*.

CCh *kur- ''snake'': Bnn *kuriya*.

Cf. a denominative formation in Sem *ḳur- ''hiss (of a snake)'': Arab *qrr* [-*u*-].

1621 *ḳVĉeb- ''cut''

Sem *ḳVṣ̂Vb- ''cut'': Arab *qḍb*.
ECh *kVĉyap- < *kVĉyab- ''cut'': Bid *keḍep*.
Note the unvoiced anlaut.

Derived from *ḳuĉ- ''cut, pierce''.

1622 *ḳVᶜoḥ- ''shoulder''

Eg *ḳᶜḥ* ''shoulder, arm'' (MK).
Rift *kwaḥ- < *ḳwaḥ- ''shoulder'': Irq *kwaḥa*, Alg *kwaḥu*, Bur *kwaḥa*.
Dissimilation of emphatics. The inlaut *-ᶜ- is not preserved.

1623 *ḳVḳ- ''eat, bite''

Eg *ḳḳ* ''eat'' (XVIII).
WCh *ḳVḳ- ''bite'': Kry *kəki*.

A nominal reflex of *ḳVḳ- may be preserved in Dhl *k'ok'o* ''throat''.

1624 *ḳVl- ''spin''

Sem *ḳVl-ḳVl- ''brandish, agitate'': Gz *qʷlqʷl*.
Reduplication.
Berb *ḳVl- ''spin'': Tua *eɣli*.

1625 *ḳVlVc- ''spit''

Sem *ḳVlVs- ''spit'': Arab *qls*.
Eg *ḳȝs* ''spit''.
-ȝ- continues HS *-l-.

1626 *ḳVr- "dry" (v.)

Sem *ḳVr- "drying": Akk *qarūru*.
Berb *ḳVr- "be dry": Tua *iɣar*.

1627 *ḳVrVs- "freeze"

Sem *ḳVrVš- "freeze"; Aram (Syr) *qrš*, Arab *qrs*.
Berb *ḳVrVs- "freeze": Tua *ɣeres*.

Derived from *ḳar- "(be) cold", *ḳor- "cold" (n.).

1628 *ḳVw-/*ḳVy- "remain, wait"

Sem *ḳVw- "remain" [1], "wait" [2]: Akk *qū'u* [2], Hbr *qwy* [2], Aram (Syr) *qw'* [1 2].
CCh *ki- < *ḳVy- "remain": Log *ki*.
Omot *ḳVwVy- "remain, wait": Kaf *ḳee-*, *ḳeey-*, *ḳway-*.

Consonantal alternation *-w- ~ *-y-.

1629 *ḳVyVn- "forge"

Sem *ḳīn- "forge": Arab *qyn* [-*i*-].
WCh *ḳyan-un- < *ḳVyan-un- "forge": Hs *ḳyanuna*.
Partial reduplication.

1630 *ḳVǯor- "dirt, be dirty"

Sem *ḳVḏar-/*ḳVḏur- "be dirty": Arab *qḏr* [-*a*- , -*u*-].
Cf. Hbr *qdr* "be dark".
ECh *gVǯwar- "faeces, silt": Kera *goder*.

*l

1631 *la'- "be tired, be sick"

Sem *lV'ay- "be tired" [1], "be slow" [2]: Hbr *l'y* [1], Arab *l'y* [-*a*-] [2].
Cf. also Akk *la'û* "weak (?)" (in context with *šerru* "baby").
Sem verb is based on biconsonantal *lV'-.

WCh **laʾ-* "sickness, pain": Sura *laa*, Ang *le*.
Nominal derivative.

Cf. ECh **law-* "to become weak for lack of water (of plants)": Bid *law*.

1632 *laʾ-/*law- "cattle"

Sem **laʾ-/*liʾ-* "cow" [1], "heifer" [2], "wild bull" [3]: Akk *lû* [1], Hbr *lēʾā* [2], Arab *laʾ-* [3], Jib *leʾ* [3], Soq *ʾəlha* [1].
Forms reflecting **-i-* may belong to a different ablaut grade.
WCh **laʾ-* "cow": Dera *la*.
WCh **laʾu-* "meat" may belong to the same root.
Agaw **law-/*luw-* "cattle, cow": Bil *laaw*, Xmr *luwaa*, Aun *luwaa*.
Secondary **-u-* before a labial.
SA **laʾ-/*law-* "cattle, herd": Saho *laa*, Afar *laa*, *low*.
LEC **loʾ-/*low-* "cattle": Som *looʾ*, Or *loo-n*, Kon *lowaa*, Gdl *loha*.
Secondary **-o-*.
Wrz **loʾ-* "cow": Gaw *loʾo*, Cam *looʾoo*, Hrs *loʾo*, Dob *loʾo*, Grr *loʾo*.
Secondary **-o-*.

1633 *laʾad- "field"

Eg *ỉꜣd.t* "field" (MK).
Initial *ỉ-* goes back to **l-*.
ECh **lawad-* < **laHad-* "field": Jegu *lood*.
LEC **lad-* "land": Or *laddaa*.
Contraction.

1634 *lab- "cereal"

Sem **lāb-* "roasted corn": Akk *lābtu*.
Eg *nb* "cereal" (gr).
Note *n-* < HS **l-*.

1635 *lab- "cow, bull"

Eg *nb.t* "cow" (gr).
n- < HS **l-*.
ECh **labi-* "cattle" [1], "bull" [2]: Smr *labei* [1], Ndam *lībe* [2], Lele *ku-lba*.

1636 *labiʾ-/*libaʾ- "lion"

Sem **labiʾ-* "lion" [1], "lioness" [2]: Akk *labʾu* [1], Ug *lbu* [1], Hbr *lābīʾ* [2], Arab *labuʾ-* [2].
WCh **lVbVʾ-Vr-* "wild cat": Sura *rəḅəl*.
Suffix **-r-*. Note *-ḅ-* < **-bʾ-*.
CCh **ʾa-lib-ar-* "lion" [1], "hyaena" [2]: Hwn *lifāri* [1], Mrg *ha-livari* [1], Klb *lēvari* [1], Chb *ʾalvari* [1], Hld *luvari* [1], HF *luveri* [1], HB *livəru* [1], HNk *livəri* [1], Lam *ərvare* [1], Mnd *ʾuruvwəri* [1], Glv *ʾarvara* [1], FMch *luvari* [1], Gude *livara* [1], Mtk *laval* [2].
Note that Mtk reflects the original structure with **-ʾar-* > *-al*.
SA **lub-ak-* "lion": Saho *lubaak*, Afar *lubaak*.
Suffix **-ak-*. **i* > *u* before a labial.
LEC **lib-aḥ-* "lion": Som *libaḥ*.
Suffix **-ḥ-* or an irregular continuation of the auslaut laryngeal of the original HS form?

Metathesis of root vowels.

1637 *lag- "river"

CCh **lagwa-* "river": Zgh *gu-lagwa*, Bnn *loka*.
Prefix **gu-* in Zgh. Unvoiced Bnn *-k-* seems to be not quite regular.
LEC **lag-* "river": Or *laga*.
HEC **lag-* "river": Sid *laga*.
Borrowed from LEC?

1638 *laġ- "speak"

Sem **laġ-/*luġ-* "speak, chat": Hbr *lʿʿ*, Arab *lġw* [*-a-*, *-u-*].
WCh **laġ-* "speak": Fyer *lak*, Bks *lak*, DB *lak*.

1639 *laġ-/*luġ- "neck, throat"

Sem **luġ-* "throat": Hbr *loaʿ*, Arab *luġ-at-*.
Dhl *lak'a* "area under chin".

Alternation **a* ~ **u*. Cf. WCh **laʿ-* "neck" (Sha *laha*, DB *la*, Bks *la*) and CCh **lay-* id. (Mba *le*).

1640 *lahas- "lick"

Sem **lVhaš-* "lick": Arab *lhs* [-*a*-].
Cf. also *lḥs* id. [-*a*-].
WCh **laHVs-* "lick": Hs *lāsā*.

If the inlaut laryngeal is of secondary origin, the root may be related to **les-* "tongue".

1641 *laḥak̇-/*laḥik̇- "clay"

Sem **laḥak̇-* "clay": Arab *laḥaq-*.
Berb **lak̇-* "clay": Ahg *ta-laq*.
Bed *likʷ* "clay".
Contraction from **lVHik̇-*?

1642 *laḥam- "meat, food"

Sem **laḥm-* "bread, food" [1], "meat" [2]: Hbr *leḥem* [1], Aram (Syr) *laḥmā* [1], Arab *laḥm-*, *laḥam-* [2].
Cf. Akk *laḫāmu* "to eat", Arab *lḥm* [-*a*-]"feed with meat".
WCh **laHam-* "meat": Brm *laamu*, Grn *laam*.
Note Hs *lamai* "tuwo".

1643 *laḫ- "sheep, goat"

Berb **laH-* "ram": Ayr *tele*, Ahg *e-lah-əy*, Sus *tili*, Fgg *tili*.
Eg *ʿnḫ* "goat" (XIX).
Prefix **ʿV-*. Note *-n-* < **l*.
Bed *naaʾ* "sheep".
Note *n-* < **l-*.
SA **laḥ-* "she-goat": Saho *laḥ*, Afar *laaḥ*.
LEC **laḥ-* "fat-tailed sheep": Som *laḥ*.
Cf. also Arb *leh* "ewe".
HEC **lah-* "she-goat": Sid *laah*.
Rift **leʾ-* "goat": Irq *leʾi*.
Irregular **-ʾ-*.

1644 *laḫ- "knife, axe"

Eg *nḫꜣ* "knife" (TS).

Vocalic *-ꜣ*.
CCh **laγ-* "spear" [1], "axe" [2]: Log *laγa* [1], Bud *lai* [1], Gude *raχa* [2], FBw *rəχ-an* [2], FMch *raχa* [2], FJ *laχa* [2].

1645 *lak- "think"

Eg *nkꜣ* "think" (MK).
Vocalic *-ꜣ*.
CCh **lak-* "think": Gis *lak*.

Cf. Or *lakkaaʷa* "count" (v.), Sid *lakkaʔ-* "measure" (v.)?

1646 *laḳ- "kite"

Sem **laḳ(w)-* "she-kite, female eagle": Ug *lqh*, Arab *laqw-at-*.
WCh **lVwVḳ-* "vulture": Mpn *look*.
Secondary development of **laḳ-*.
CCh **la-lak-* "kite": Msm *lolokoi*, Bnn *laraka*.
Partial reduplication. Dissimilation of *liquida* in Bnn.

1647 *lal- "goat, cattle"

Sem **laliʔ-* "goat": Akk *lalû*, *laliʔu*, Soq *luloh*.
LEC **lal-* "she-goat" [1], "cattle" [2]: Or *lal-eesa* [1], Rnd *lolyo* [2].
HEC **lal-* "cattle": Sid *laalo*, Dar *laalo*, Ala *laalo*, Kmb *laalu*.

Reduplication of **laʔ-/*law-* "cattle" or **laḫ-* "sheep, goat"?

1648 *lam- "speak, shout"

Eg *nmy* "shout, cry" (MK).
Suffix *-y*.
WCh **lam-* "say": Ank *lem*.
CCh **lam-* "cry" [1], "speak" [2]: Lame *lam* [1], Mwu *u-lamo* [2].
ECh **lVm-* "speak": Mwu *ləme*.

1649 *lam- "lie" (v.)

ECh **lam-* "lie": Sbn *lama*.
Rift **lam-* "lie": Irq *lama*, Bur *lama*.

1650 *lam- "be soft"

WCh **lwam-* < **lam-* "be soft": Ang *lōm*.
Vowel change before a labial.
Agaw **lim-* "be tender": Xmr *lilem*, Xmt *ləmlim*, Kwr *lələm*, Kem *ləməy*.
Secondary vocalism in a reduplicated stem.

1651 *lap- "spleen"

WCh **lap-* "spleen" [1], "liver" [2]: Sura *llap* [1], Ang *lap* [1], Klr *ma-laf* [2].
Prefix **ma-* in Klr.
SA **ʔa-lef-* "spleen": Afar *aleefu*.
Prefix **ʔa-*. Secondary **-e-*.
LEC **lap-* "heart, chest": Or *lap̣p̣ee*.
Secondary emphatic in Or?
Dhl *λafi* "lungs".
Note *λ-* and irregular *-f-*.

1652 *lap- "beans, corn"

Sem **lupp-* "beans": Akk *luppu*.
Vowel labialized before **-p-*.
Eg *npy* "seed, grain" (n).
Suffix *-y*, cf. ECh.
ECh **lap-* "millet": Sok *lap-iya*.

1653 *lap-/*lawap- "be wet"

Eg *npꜣ* "wet" (sarc).
-ꜣ is a vocalic sign.
ECh **lawap-* "wet": Ndam *lwap*, Smr *lawe*.
Secondary estension of **lap-*.

1654 *larVy- "stick"

Sem **larVy-* "twig": Akk *larû*.
Eg *ꜣry.t* "stick" (MK).
Eg *ꜣ-* < HS **l-*.

Another possibility for Eg is to compare it with ECh *ʾ*war-* "stick": Jegu *ʾorra*.

1655 *lat- "skin"

Eg *ntnt* "skin" (med).
Reduplication. Eg *n-* < **l-*.
WCh **lat-* "skin": Zar *laat*.
Cf. deverbative **lut-* "skin" (v.): Fyer *lut*.

1656 *lat- "man"

Eg *nty.w* "people, men" (OK).
-y may be a suffix or a reflex of a front vowel.
WCh **lat-* "person": Maha *latu*.

1657 *lat- "destroy, split, grind"

Sem **lVtaʾ-* "split" [1], "strike" [2]: Akk *letû* [1], Arab *ltʾ* [*-a-*] [2].
Based on biconsonantal **lVt-*.
Eg *nt* "slaughter" (gr).
WCh **latu-* "grind": Klr *lot*.
ECh **lVt-* "destroy": Mkk *litt-*.

1658 *lawVy- "twist, bend"

Sem **lūy-* "twist, bend" [1], "turn" [2]: Arab *lwy* [*-i-*] [1], Jib *lwy* [2], Hss *lewō* [2], Mhr *lewō* [2], Shh *le* [2].
WCh **lawya-* < **lawVy-* "bend": Hs *lauya*.
CCh **lay-* "fold": Lame *lei*.
Contraction of **lawVy-*.

1659 *lay- "water; pour"

WCh **lay-* "pour": Ang *le*.
ECh **law-/*lay-* "pour out" [1], "wet" (v.) [2]: Sok *ileo* [1], Tum *lāw* [2].
Secondary variant in **-w-*.
SA **lay-* "water": Saho *laye*, Afar *lay*, *le*.

1660 *leʾ- "shine"

Sem **lVʾ-lVʾ-* "shine (of a star)": Arab *lʾlʾ*.
Reduplication.
WCh **lyaʾ-* "begin (of the day)": DB *leʾ*.
SA **lelaᶜ-* "day": Saho *läläᶜ*, Afar *läläᶜ*.
Reduplication. Note the development of hS **-ʾ-*.

Any relation to Irq *loʾa* "sun, God", Bur *letu* "sun", Alg *leleʾa* id. in Rift?

1661 *leʾ-/*lew- "put on (clothes)"

Eg *nw* "put on (clothes)" (l).
WCh **lyaʾ-* "dress" (v.): Sura *lee*.
ECh **lVw-* "put on (clothes)": Tum *ləw*.

Consonantal alternation **-ʾ-* ~ **-w-*.

1662 *leb- "elephant"

Eg *ꜣbw* "elephant" (OK).
ꜣ- < HS **l-*.
WCh **lab-* < **lyaba-* "elephant": Tng *laba-ta*.
Suffix *-ta*?
CCh **nyab-* "elephant": Log *nevi*.
Irregular **n-* < **l-*.
ECh **lyab-* "elephant": Mkk *ʾelbi*.
With a typical Mkk metathesis in the first syllable.
Any relation to Or *arba* "elephant"?

1663 *leĉum- "fish"

Berb **licVm-* "fish": Ghd *u-lisma*, Ghat *a-ləmšay*.
Metathesis in Ghat.
Eg *nšmw.t* "fish" (NK).
Final *-w* indicates **u* of the second syllable.
WCh **l(y)amVĉ-* "fish": Hs *lamsa*.

1664 *len- "be soft"

Sem **līn-* "be soft, become soft" [1], "soften" [2]: Arab *lyn* [*-i-*] [1],

Mhr *liyōn* [1], Jib *lɛ:n* [1], Hss *alyin* [2], Mhr *alyin* [2], Shh *ɛlyīn* [2].
Based on **lVn-*.

Eg *nny* ''be tired, be lazy''.
Metathesis. For the meaning, cf. MHG *weich* ''soft'' and ''weak''.

WCh **lyan-* < **lVyan-* ''soft'': Ang *len*.
Cf. reduplication in Chip *lenlen*. The same root may be also reflected in Sura *non* id. with assimilation.

1665 *ler- ''time''

Eg *nry* ''time, moment'' (NK).
Vocalic *-y*.

CCh **lyar-/*lwar-* ''time'': Mtk *lɛř*, Bnn *lora*.

1666 *les- ''tongue''

Sem **lišān-* ''tongue'': Akk *lišānu*, Ug *lšn*, Hbr *lāšōn*, Aram (Syr) *leššōnō*, Arab *lisān-*, Gz *lesān*, Jib *elsen*, Hss *lẽšen*, Mhr *lẽšen*, Shh *lišɛn*, Soq *lešin*.
Suffix **-ān-*.

Berb **lVs-* ''tongue'': Siwa *elles*, Kby *iləs*.

Eg *ns* ''tongue'' (pyr), Copt **les* ''tongue'': Fym *les*, Akh *les*, Boh *las*, Shd *las*.
Copt attests the character of the sonant orthographically denoted as *n-* in Eg.

WCh **ḥa-lis-um-* ''tongue'': Hs *halše*, *harše*, Sura *liis*, Ang *leus*, Chip *liis*, Mnt *liis*, Grk *lis*, Bol *lisi-m*, Krk *lusu*, Ngm *linsa*, Maha *ḍi-lis*, Krf *ilmiši*, Gera *ḍe-linsa*, Glm *lim*, Grm *limši*, Fyer *lis*, Bks *ʾalis*, Sha *ʾaləs*, DB *lis*.
Prefix **ḥa-* and a suffix of body parts.

CCh **ʾV-lyas-* ''tongue'': Gis *eles*, Msg *ɛlɛsi*.
Prefix **ʾV-*.

ECh **lyas-* ''tongue'': Mig *li-t*, Mubi *lesi*, Mkk *ʾilze*, Dng *lɛ:s-ɛn*, *leese*.
Metathesis in Mkk, see s.v. **leb-* ''elephant''.

Omot **mi-las-* ''tongue'': Kaf *mi-laso*.
Prefix **mi-*.

See **lahas-* ''lick''.

1667 *liʾaf- "fingernail, claw"

Eg *ἰȝf.t* "claw (of the vulture)".
CCh **li-lif-* "fingernail": Masa *lilifa*.
Partial reduplication.
Bed *neʾaaf* "fingernail, claw".
Note initial **n-* < **l-*.
SA **lifiʿ-* "fingernail, claw": Saho *lifiʿ*.
Metathesis. Note the development of HS **ʾ-*.

1668 *lib-/*lub- "heart"

Sem **libab-* "heart": Akk *libbu*, Ug *lb*, Hbr *lēb*, Aram (Syr) *lebbō*, Arab *lubb-*, Gz *ləbb*, Hss *ḥelbēb*, Mhr *ḥewbēb*, Shh *ūb*, Soq *elbeb*.
Eg *ἰb* "heart" (pyr).
**l-* > *ἰ-* before a front vowel.
WCh **lVb-* "lungs": Chip *ləp*.
CCh **(HV-)lib-* "belly, stomach" [1], "heart" [2]: Daba *liḇī* [1], Mus *lib(i)* [1], Mnd *ʾurvə-ŋude* [2], Glv *rivi-ḍiya* [2], Zgh *arve* [2].
ECh **lub-* "heart": Mkk *ʾulbo*.
Metathesis in Mkk, cf. **leb-* "elephant".
Agaw **lVb-ak-* "heart": Bil *läbbäka*, Kwr *läbakaa*, Dmb *läbakaa*, Kem *ləbäkaa*.
Suffix **-ak-*.
SA **lub(b)-* "heart": Afar *lubbi*.
LEC **lab-/*lub-* "heart": Som *laab*, Or *lubbu*, *labbe*.
Secondary **-a-*.
Omot **lib-* "heart" [1], "belly" [2]: Anf *yiboo* [1], Gll *libʾa* [2].
Rift **lib-* "chest": Asa *liba*.

Alternation **i* ~ **u*.

1669 *lič- "be weak, be soft"

Sem **lVṯ-lVṯ-* "linger, tarry": Arab *lṯlṯ*.
Reduplication. On the semantic development see s.v. **layan-* "be soft".
Agaw **lič-* "be soft": Xmr *lis-*.
SA **lis-lis-* "soft": Saho *lislis*.
Reduplication. Not quite regular **-s-* < HS **-č-*.

1670 *lihab- "burn"

Sem **lVhab-* "burn, be bright": Hbr *lhb*, Arab *lhb* [*-a-*], Gz *lhb*.
Eg *rhb* "glow".
Note *r-*.
Agaw **lib- < *liHVb-* "heat, cook" (v.): Kem *läb-*, *ləb-*.

Cf. also Bed *liw-* "burn" as a possible continuation of **lib-*.

1671 *liḥap- "cover"

Sem **lVḥap-* "envelop, cover": Arab *lḥf* [*-a-*], Jib *elḥef*.
WCh **lip̣- < *liHVp-* "cover": Hs *lulluḅa*, Bol *liḅḅ-*, Dera *lipe*.
Reduplication in Hs. Secondary emphatic **p̣* goes back to **p* in contact with a laryngeal.

1672 *liḥum- "kill, fight"

Sem **lVḥum-* "kill, fight": Hbr *lḥm*, Arab *lḥm* [*-u-*].
CCh **lim- < *liHVm-* "war": Lmn *ləmo*, Daba *lim*.

1673 *liḳam-/*liḳim- "eat, swallow"

Sem **lVḳam-* "swallow, eat, gobble (a mouthful)": Arab *lqm* [*-a-*].
ECh **ligam-* "eat": Tum *lagəm*, Kbl *liyəm*.
LEC **liḳim-* "swallow": Or *liqim-s-*.
Assimilation of vowels.

Derived from **lVḳ-* "lick". On the other hand, cf. Sem **lVḥam-* "eat, feed" (see s.v. **laḥam-* "meat").

1674 *lil- "water; be wet"

Berb **lil-* "sea, river": Nfs *iləl*, Zng *ell*, Sus *ill*.
Cf. Lib **lil-* "water" (apud Hdt.: λιλυ) and Fgg *ill* "weep".
Cf. also Kby derivative *s-lil* "wash".
Bed *lil-* "be wet".

Reduplication of **lay-* "water; pour".

1675 *liw- "cloud, sky"

Eg *nw.t* "sky" (pyr).
*Eg n- < HS *l-.*
WCh **liw-ay-* "cloud": Sura *lluu*, Chip *liwu*, Bgh *lway*, Mnt *luo*.

1676 *liwVč- "mix"

Sem **lūṯ-* "knead, mix": Akk *lâšu*, Hbr *lwš*, Arab *lwṯ* [-*u*-].
ECh **liwVč-* "mix": Mobu *luse*, Ngam *lise*, Dng *lewsi*.

1677 *loʾ- "breath, soul"

Eg *nȝw* "breath" (XVIII).
Vocalic -*w*.
WCh **lwaʾ-* "soul": DB *lwaʾ*.

1678 *loḳum- "camel"

Berb **lVḳum-* "camel": Siwa *a-lɣom*, Ntf *a-lɣum*, Tlt *a-lɣum*, Izy *alɣem*, Kby *a-lɣʷəm*, Rif *aλɣəm*, Wrg *aḷəm*.
WCh **raḳum-* < **rwaḳum-* "camel": Hs *rāḳumi*.
Irregular **r* < **l*.
CCh **lukVm-* "camel, horse": Mba *lukma*.
Cf. Log *kurguma* "camel".
ECh **lwaḳum-* "camel": Tum *lɔgma*, *loguma*, Dng *lokumo*, Ndam *lugumo*, Brg *lokomo*, Jegu *logom*.
Cf. Kbl *lak'ma* "horse".

A cultural term that may be a *Wanderwort* (of Berber origin?).

1679 *lo-lüm- "insect"

ECh **lwa-lVm-* "ant": Jegu *lolmo*.
LEC **lu-lum-* "larvae of mosquitoes": Som *lulumo* (pl.).

Reduplication of **lüm-* "termite".

1680 *lom- "bird"

Eg *nm* "kind of bird" (l).
CCh **lwam-* "dove": Ngw *loma*.

1681 *lub- "be thirsty"

Sem **lūb-* "be thirsty": Arab *lwb*.
Based on HS **lub-*.
Eg *ỉby* "be thirsty".
Reflects **lVbVy-*.
Dhl *λuuβ-* "sip".
Note *λ-*.

1682 *lubaḫ- "strike"

Sem **lVbaḫ-* "strike": Arab *lbḫ* [*-a-*].
ECh **lVb-* "strike": Tum *ləbə*.
Loss of the auslaut laryngeal.
Dhl *luβ-* "beat".

1683 *luġab- "be tired"

Sem **lVġab-/*lVġub-* "be exhausted": Arab *lġb* [*-a-* , *-u-*].
WCh **lub-* "be tired": Dera *luba*.
Contraction from **lVHub-*.
CCh **luHVb-* "tiredness": Kap *luḅwɛ*, HF *liḅi*, Bnn *lobuwa*, FMch *ruḅu*.
Nominal derivative with a different vocalism.

1684 *luḥur- "cloth"

Eg *nḥr.w* "kind of dress" (gr).
WCh **luHur-* "striped cloth": Hs *nūrū*, *lūrū*.

1685 *luk- "bird"

ECh **lukuk-* "kind of bird": Bid *lukuku*.
Partial reduplication.
LEC **luk(k)-* "hen": Som *luki*, Or *lukku*, Bay *luk- ale*, Arb *lukku*.
HEC **lukk-* "hen": Bmb *lukk-ančo*.

1686 *luk- "road"

CCh **lak-* "road": Klb *laku*, Bura *laku*, Mrg *lagu*.

Intervocalic **-k-* > Mrg *-g-*.
LEC **luk-* "crossroads of forest paths": Or *lookoo*, *luukoo*.

1687 *lum- "eat"

Sem **lum-* "chew": Akk *lamāmu* [*-u-*].
CCh **lum-* "bite, eat": Mba *lum*, Msg *lama*, *luma*.

Cf. Sem **lVḥam-* "eat, feed" (see s.v. **laḥam-* "meat").

1688 *lum- "gather"

Sem **lum-* "gather": Arab *lmm* [*-u-*].
ECh **lam-/*lum-* "gather": Mubi *lamma*, Bid *lum*, Mig *lumme*.

1689 *lübaḥ- "be wet"

Eg *ỉbḥ* "wet" (MK).
Palatalization of **l-* > *ỉ-*.
CCh **luḅa-* < **lubaH-* "wet" (v.): Bura *liḅ-enta*, Hld *lüḅ-uri*, Chb *luṗ-ti*, Wmd *luṗ-ta*, HF *ləḅ-əši*, FG *luḅwi-ti*, Kap *luḅi-ke*, Gava *luḅ-*, Daba *lub*, Msg *laḅ*, Zime *laḅ*.
ECh **lub-* "wet": Kera *lubi*.

1690 *lüf- "cloud, fog"

Eg *nfy* "fog" (gr).
Vocalic *-y*.
WCh **lVfVf-* "cloud": Kry *ləfəfə*.
Partial reduplication.
CCh **luf-* "cloud": Daba *luv*.

1691 *lüm- "boat"

Eg *ỉmw* "kind of ship" (OK).
Palatalization of **l-* > *ỉ-*.
CCh **lum-* "boat": Zime *lum*.

1692 *lüm- "big, many"

Sem **liʔVm-* "thousand" < *"many": Akk *lim*, Ug *lʔm*.

Based on **lim-*.

WCh **lumum-* "in quantity": Hs *lumumu*.

Partial reduplication. Cf. also Hs *lamama* "in great quantity".

HEC **lum-* "big": Dar *lumo*.

1693 *lüm- "termite"

Sem **nimm-* "termite": Arab *nimm-at-*.

Assimilation of consonants.

CCh **lum-* "termite": Bura *luma*, Chb *ləma*, Kap *luma*, HK *luma*.

1694 *lünaḳ- "net"

Eg *i͗nḳ* "net" (LM).

Palatalization of **l-* > *i͗-*.

WCh **lunaḳ-* "net": Mnt *lung*, Ank *lang*.

1695 *l[ü]w- "house, dwelling"

Berb **liw-* "room": Ghd *ta-līw-in*.

Eg *nw.t* "village, town" (pyr).

WCh **lu[w]-* "house, hut": Sura *lu*, Ang *lū*, Chip *lə*.

CCh **luw-* "town": Zgh *luwa*.

ECh **ʾa-luw-* "interior dwelling space": Kera *aluwa*.

Dhl *lawa* "village".

Unexpected vowel.

1696 *lVk-/*lVḳ- "leg"

Sem **ʾilk-* "heel": Akk *ilku*.

Prefix **ʾi-*.

Berb **lVḳ-* "leg, calf": Twl *eləγ*, Ahg *ēləγ*, Izy *ileγ*.

Agaw **lik(u)-* "leg, hip": Bil *likʷ*, Xmr *likʷ*, Xmt *lukʷ*, Kwr *likʷ*, Dmb *likʷ*, Kem *läkʷə*, Aun *ləkʷ*.

SA **lak-* "hip, thigh, leg": Saho *lak*, Afar *lak*.

LEC **luk-/*luḳ-* "leg, hip": Som *lug*, Or *luka*, *lukaa*, Rnd *lux*, Bay *lukka*, Arb *lukk*, Kon *log-da*, Gdl *lukkɛ-to*.

HEC **lek-/*lok-* "leg, hip": Sid *lekkee*, Dar *lekka*, Had *lokko*, Ala *lokka-ti*, Bmb *luka*, *lukka*, Kmb *lokka-ta*.

Wrz *luχ- "leg": War *luχ-te*, Gaw *luχ-te*, Gob *luh-*, Cam *luʾge*. Dhl *luka* "thigh".

Irregular *k ~ *ḳ in various branches of HS.

1697 *lVḳ- "lick"

Sem *luḳ- "lick, lap": Hbr *lqq*, Arab *lqq* [-u-].
Cf. Akk *leku* "lick" (< *lVhVḳ-).
Berb *lVḳ- "lick": Twl *əlləγ*, Ahg *əlləγ*, Mzab *əlləγ*.
WCh *laḳ- "eat greedily" [1], "lick" [2]: Hs *laḳe* [1], Bks *lok* [2], DB *loḳ* [2].
ECh *lya-lik- "lick": Mig *lelliko*.
Partial reduplication.
Bed *lak-* "lick".
LEC *liḳ-/*loḳ- "swallow, lap": Som *liq-*, Kon *loq-*, Gid *loq-*, Had *liq-iç̌-*.
Vocalism *o may be secondary.

*m

1698 *ma-/*mi- "mouth"

Berb *mV- "mouth": Ghd *a-mi*, Awj *am*, Ahg *i-mi*, Zng *i-mmi*.
CCh *ma-/*mi- "mouth": Bata *mee*, Daba *ma*, Nza *ma*, Msg *maa*, *mii*, Gid *mo*.

One of the cases representing a rare root pattern *CV-*.

1699 *maʾ- "water"

Sem *maʾ-/*may- "water": Akk *mû*, Ug *my*, Hbr *mayim* (pl.), Aram (Syr) *mayyō* (pl.), Arab *māʾ-*, Gz *māy*.
Berb *mV- "water" (pl.): Izy *aman*, Kby *aman*.
Eg *mw* "water" (pyr).
WCh *maʾ- "water": Geji *maa*, Grn *maa*.
CCh *maʾ-/*maw- "river" [1], "water" [2], "dew" [3]: FKi *məwa* [1], Gude *maʾin* [2], FBw *maʾyin* [2], Log *mū* [3].
If Log is not from *maʾu- it may go back to an apophonic variant *muʾ-, cf. Bed.

Bed *muʾ-* "liquid".
A reflex of *u*-grade?
Dhl *maʾa* "water".
Rift **maʾ-ay-* "water": Irq *maʾay*, Asa *maʾa*, Kwz *maʾaya*.

Note parallel forms with sonants **may-* and **maw-* in Sem, Eg and CCh. Sem, Berb and CCh may reflect an archaic HS plural **maʾ-in-*!

1700 *maʾin- "woman, wife"

WCh **maʾin-* "wife, woman": Ngm *mīno*, Krk *men*.
CCh **min-* "woman": Gude *munii*, Msg *minne*.
Gude *-u-* is irregular.
ECh **maʾan-* "co-wife": Kera *maanə*.
Assimilation of vowels.
LEC **min-/*ʾamin-* "woman": Bay *amine*, Gel *minne*.
HEC **men-/*ʾamen-* "woman": Sid *meen-to* (pl.), Ala *mɛɛn-*, Bmb *aamɛɛn-*.
Omot **maʾin-* "wife": Shn *maan* (pl.), Gim *main*.
Rift **ʾamen-* "wife": Irq *ameni*, Bur *ameni*.
Dhl *maani* "barren woman".
Contraction.

In Cush, several branches reflect **ʾamin-*.

1701 *mabar- "mouth"

WCh **mabar-* "mouth": Hs *mabāri*.
Bed *ambar* "mouth".

WCh **ma-* and Bed *am-* reflect the HS correspondence that may be also traced between Cush prefix **ʾam-* and Chadic prefix **ma-*.

1702 *mač- "be drunk"

WCh **miwač-* "beer": Ang *mos*, Sura *mwos*, Ank *mwess*, Mpn *mwes*, Grk *mut-*, Mnt *mus*.
Derived from **mač-*?
LEC **mač-* "be drunk": Or *mačaw-*.

Note *-č-* preserved in Or in contrast to the expected reflex of HS **č* > LEC **s*, **š*. Derived from the original noun?
Omot **mač-* "be drunk": Ome *matto-*, Kaf *maš-*, Mch *maša*.
Denominative form?

1703 *maç- "press, cut"

WCh **maç-* "press, squeeze": Hs *māṣa*.
Omot **maçç-* "cut": Kaf *maç̌ç̌-*.

As to semantics, cf. W *trychu* "cut" ~ OEng *thrycean* "press".

1704 *mag- "be numerous, be big"

CCh **magwa-* "big, long, high": Mus *mogwa*.
ECh **mag-* "much, many": Tum *māg*.
SA **mag-/*mang-* "be strong" [1], "be numerous" [2], "fill" [3], "plenty" [4]: Saho *meng-* [1], *meg-* [2], Afar *mag-* [2], *mangoo* [4].
Nasal infix in certain forms.

1705 *mag- "be bad"

WCh **mug-* "bad": Hs *mūgu*.
Secondary formation with modified vocalism.
Bed *maag* "be bad".
LEC **mag-* "be bad": Or *magu*.

1706 *maˁ- "grain, cereal"

Sem **māˁ-* "corn, seed": Hbr *māˁā*.
ECh **may-* "millet": Smr *may*, Ndam *may*.
ECh **may-* may reflect earlier **maH(i)-*.

1707 *maˁaw-/*maˁay- "wind"

Eg *mȝˁw* "wind" (MK).
-ȝ- stands for a vowel of the first syllable.
ECh **maHay-* "wind": Mkk *maaye*.

Consonantal alternation **-w-* ~ **-y-*.

1708 *maᶜid- "stomach"

Sem *maᶜVd- "stomach": Arab *maᶜid-at-*.
Cf. also Arab *maᶜad-* "side"?
CCh *mVHid- "liver": Chb *midɛ*, Ngw *miḍa*, Mrg *miḍa*.
ECh *myad- "belly": Jegu *med-et*.
*-ya- results from a contraction of *-aHi-.

1709 *mahar- "suck"

Eg *mhr* "suck, milk" (gr).
WCh *maHar- "suck": Ang *mōr*.
A regular contraction.

1710 *mahor- "slave, soldier"

Sem *mVhVr- "service man, soldier": Ug *mhr*.
Cf. the semantic development of OIr *ōc* "young" (adj.) → "young man" → "warrior".
WCh *maHwar- "slave": Klr *mahor*, DB *moor*.
CCh *mVhwar- "immigrant": Lame *muhor*.
Secondary *-u-* after a labial.

1711 *mahaw-/*mahay- "forget"

Eg *mhy* "be forgetful (of heart)" (MK).
CCh *maw- < *maHaw- "forget": Bnn *mawa*.
Contraction.
Agaw *may- "forget": Xmr *mii-t-*, Kwr *mey*, Dmb *mey*, Kem *maay*.
Narrow vowels in Xmr, Kwr and Dmb continue *-a- before *-y-.

Consonantal alternation *-w- ~ *-y-.

1712 *maḫ- "tie"

Eg *mḫꜣ* "tie" (MK).
Vocalic *-ꜣ*.
ECh *maH- "tie": Smr *mā*.

1713 *maḫal- "box, basket"

Sem *maḫal- "box, basket": Akk *maḫḫalu*.
Eg *mhn* "box" (n).
Irregular reflection of the laryngeal in late Eg.

Sem loanword in Eg?

1714 *maḫVy- "wind"

Sem *maḫVy- "storm": Akk *meḫû*.
Eg *imꜣḫ* "turbulence" (sarc).
Metathesis. Vocalic *-ꜣ-*.

The alternative reconstruction is *yVmaḫ-.

1715 *makay- "stick"

Sem *makVy- "stick": Akk *makūtu*.
CCh *makay- "stick": Bud *makai*.

1716 *makil- "boat"

Sem *magīl- "barque, boat": Akk *magīlu*.
Akk *-g-* substitutes *k?
Eg *mkr* "ship" (XXII).
Sem loanword? Note *-r* < *-l.

1717 *makVr- "(be) red"

Sem *makr- "red": Akk *makrû*.
Eg *mkrr* "unknown color" (gr).
-rr may continue *-r- or reflect a partial reduplication.

1718 *maḳV'- "vessel"

Sem *maḳV'- "vessel for offerings": Akk *maqqû*.
Eg *mḏꜣ* "measure (for dates)" (n).
Palatalization of *-ḳ-.
HEC *maHaḳ- "jar for milking": Sid *maaḳḳe*.
Metathesis.

1719 *malaw- "desert"

Sem **malaw-* "desert": Arab *malā(ʾ)-*.
-ʾ- is of orthographic value only.
Eg *mrw* "desert".
Note *-r-* < HS **-l-*.

1720 *mam- "forget, doubt"

WCh **mam-* "forget": Siri *mama*, Mbu *mamw-*, Jmb *mama*.
LEC **mam-* "doubt": Or *mama*.

Semantically, *tertium comparationis* may be formulated as * "not know". Hence, "not know exactly" → "doubt".

1721 *man- "know, test"

Sem **mVnVw-* "count" [1], "test, try" [2]: Akk *manū* [1], Hbr *mny* [1], Arab *mnw* [-*u*-] [2].
Based on biliteral **mVn-*. The meaning "test, try" may be the most archaic in this group of words, serving as a source of other meanings connected with intellectual activities as such.
WCh **man-* "know": Mnt *man*, Ank *man*, Mpn *mān*, Bol *mon*, Ngm *man*.
CCh **man-/*mun-* "understand, analyze": Lame *man*, *mun*.
Secondary **-u-*.
LEC **man-* "mind": Som *maan*.

Cf. also Eg *mn.t* "manner, way" (MK)?

1722 *man-/*mayan- "man"

Berb **mīn-* < **mVyVn-* "man": Zng *mīn*.
WCh **man-/*min-* "man": Krk *mun* (pl.), Pol *məni*, Dwot *mani*, Buli *mən*, Bar *mani*, Kir *mīni* (pl.), Bol *menni*, Geji *māni*, Say *mwan*.
The variant **min-* may go back to **mVyVn-*.
CCh **mayan-* "man": Log *meeni*.
LEC **mun-* "male": Som *mun*.
Secondary **-u-*, cf. Omot.
HEC **man-* "people": Sid *maana*, Dar *maana*, Had *maana*, Kmb *maana*, Tmb *mana*.

Omot **mon-* < **man-* "people": Yam *monoo.*

Note a morphonological co-variant of the root with an inlaut sonant. Cf. also Dhl *manaᶜe* "child".

1723 *man-/*min- "house"

Eg *mn* "room" (MK), Copt **monē* "dwelling, inn": Boh *monē*, Shd *monē.*

Copt may be borrowed from Gk *μονή.*

WCh **man-/*min-* "house" [1], "place" [2]: Tng *man* [1], Dera *məna* [1], Pero *mina* [1], Sha *mun* [2].

Secondary *-u-* in Sha.

CCh **min-* "door": Msg *min*, *mŋ*.

ECh **man-* "place": Smr *mana*, Ndam *mān*, Tum *man*.

LEC **man-/*min-* "house": Som *miin*, Or *mana*, *manaa*, Boni *miŋ*, Arb *min*.

Wrz **man-* "house": Gaw *mano*.

HEC **min-* "house": Sid *mine*, Dar *mine*, Had *mine*, Kmb *mine*.

Dhl *mini* "house".

Alternation **a* ~ **i*.

1724 *mang- "millet, lentils"

Sem **mang-/*magg-* "beans, lentils": Akk *mangu*, Arab *magg-*.

HEC **manḳ-* "millet": Bmb *manḳo*.

Secondary emphatic **ḳ* < **g*?

One of the cases in which HS stops display irregularities when appearing after nasals, in HS clusters.

1725 *manVᶜ- "hold, take"

Sem **mVnVᶜ-* "hold, take hold of": Jib *minaᶜ*, Hss *mōna*, Mhr *mōna*, Shh *minaᶜ*.

WCh **man-H-* "take": Sura *maŋ*, Grk *maŋ*, Mpn *maŋ*.

1726 *maq- "pour"

Sem **mVḫ-* "pour": Akk *maḫāḫu*.

Berb **mVγ-* "be wet": Izy *emmeγ*.

Eg *mḥy* "pour" (gr).
-ḥ- from *-ẖ-* in late Eg.
WCh **maHay-* "pour, wet": Dera *māy-*.
The development of **-q-* in this case is irregular. Cf. **muq-* "be wet".

1727 *mar- "slave"

Eg *mr.t* "serf" (OK).
WCh **mar-* "slave": Siri *marə-čək*, Mbu *mar*, Jmb *mar-ǯu*.
CCh **mVr-* "slave": FKi *məra*.

1728 *mar- "cow, bull"

Eg *mr.t* "cow" (gr).
CCh **mar-* "sacrificial bull": Mafa *maray*.
LEC **mar-* "calf": Arb *maar*.

1729 *mar- "sheep, goat"

Sem **ʾimmar-* "sheep, lamb": Akk *immeru*, Ug *ʾimr*, Phn *ʾmr*, Pun *ʾmr*, Aram (Bibl) *ʾimmar*, (Palest) *ʾimmerā*, (Syr) *ʾemmerā*, Arab *ʾimmar-*.
WCh **mar-* "goat" 1, "ram" 2: Tng *mara* 1, Pol *mar* 1, Geji *mal* 1, Buli *mar* 1, Bks *maray* 2.
SA **mar-* "sheep": Saho *maruu*, *maaruu*, Afar *maruu*, *maaruu*.

Apparently, this root has no etymological connection with **mar-* "cow, bull".

1730 *mar- "bind, roll up"

Eg *mr* "bind, tie" (med).
WCh **mar-* "twist, wring": Tng *mari*.
LEC **mar-* "roll up, turn": Or *mar-*, *maar-*.
Rift **mar-* "twist": Irq *marra*.

1731 *mar- "walk"

Sem **mur-* "go away": Arab *mrr* [*-u-*].
**-u-* may be secondary.

Berb *mVr- ''pass by'': Ayr *əmmər*.
WCh *mir-/*mur- ''run'': Miya *mir-*, Mbu *mur-*.
Secondary vocalism?
HEC *mar- ''go'': Bmb *mar-*, Had *mar-*, Kmb *mar-*, Sid *mar-*.
Dhl *mar-* ''go round''.

1732 *mar- ''house''

Eg *mr* ''pyramid'' (OK).
Note the semantic development.
Agaw *mar- ''yard'': Bil *maraa*.
Rift *mar- ''house'': Irq *maray* (pl.), Bur *mara*, Asa *mor-ok*.

1733 *mar- ''drop, rain''

Sem *mar- ''drop'': Hbr *mār*.
ECh *mar- ''rain'': Smr *ma:ri*

Cf. Berb *mVr- ''pour'' (Kby *əmmir*) as a continuation of the corresponding HS verb.

1734 *mar- ''be sour''

Sem *mar- ''(be) bitter'': Akk *marāru*, Hbr *mar*, Arab *mrr* [-*a*-, -*u*-], Soq *mrr*, Hss *mer*, Mhr *mer*, Shh *mur*.
For a similar semantic evolution see s.v. *ḥamaĉ- ''be sour''.
Eg *ʿmꜣ* ''become sour'' (pyr).
Prefix ʿ-.
WCh *mar- ''sour'': Ang *mer*.

1735 *mar- ''field''

Eg *mr* ''pasture'' (OK).
WCh *mar- ''field, farm'': Chip *mar*, Mnt *mai*, Sura *mār*, Ang *mār*.
Development of *-r in Mnt is regular.
ECh *mar- ''earth'': Sok *māro*.

1736 *mar- ''be ill, be weak''

Sem *mVrah- ''be weak, suffer'': Arab *mrh* [-*a*-].
Derivative based on *mar-.

Eg *mr* "be ill" (pyr).
ECh **maHyar-* "become weak": Bid *meer*.
Based on **mar-*?
Rift **maʾar-* "weak": Asa *maʾara*.

Cf. also LEC **mar-* "kind of smallpox" (Or *maaree*)? Note a morphological variant **maHar-/*maHer-* in ECh and Rift that may correspond to Sem **marah-*. If so, Eg remains isolated.

1737 *mar- "recover, be healthy"

Sem **mar-* "healthy, strong": Akk *marmaru*, Arab *marīr-* .
Reduplications based on **mar-*. Cf. Hss *merret* "strength".
WCh **mar-* "recover": Hs *māre*.

1738 *mar- "hoe" (n.)

Sem **marr-* "hoe, spade" [1], "iron spade" [2]: Akk *marru* [1], Aram (Syr) *marr-*, *maʾr-* [1], Arab *marr-* [2].
Eg *mr* "hoe" (a).
ECh **mar-/*mir-* "hoe": Smr *mara*, Sbn *miri*.
HEC **morar-* < **marar-* "hook of the plough": Had *moraara*.
Partial reduplication.

Related to **mar-* "dig".

1739 *mar- "dig"

Sem **mur-* "dig": Akk *marāru* [*-u-*].
Secondary **-u-*.
WCh **mari-* "hoe, farm" (v.): Ang *mār*, Bol *mar*, Dera *na mira*.

1740 *mar-/*maraʾ- "man"

Sem **marʾ-* "son" [1], "master" [2], "man, husband" [3]: Akk *māru* [1], Aram (Bibl) *mārē* [2],Arab *marʾ-*, *murʾ-* [3], SAr *mrʾ* [3].
Eg *mr.w*"people" (OK).
WCh **maʾar-* "boy" [1], "masculine" [2]: DB *maar* [1], Fyer *mara* [2].
Metathesis.
ECh **maʾar-* "uncle": Mig *maar*.
Metathesis.

The alternative reconstruction is **maʔar-*. There are no traces of *-ʔ- in Eg.

1741 *marVg- "field"

Sem **marg-* "meadow": Arab *marg-*.
ECh **mVrVg-* < **marug-* "field": Dng *morgo*.

Cf. LEC **marVg-* "grass" (Or *marga*)? Derived from **mar-* "field".

1742 *marVʕ- "be right, be true"

Eg *mȝʕ* "be true" (a).
Note *-ȝ-* < **-r-*.
CCh **mar-* "right" (adj.): Zgh *maraⁿ*.

1743 *ma-rVḳ- "stair, staircase"

Sem **marḳ-* "stair": Arab *marq-at-*.
Eg *mȝḳ* "staircase" (pyr), Dem *mḳy*, Copt **muki*: Boh *mouki*.
Sem loanword?

Derived from **reḳ(ay)-* "climb".

1744 *masak- "skin"

Sem **mašk-* "skin" [1], "skin bag" [2]: Akk *mašku* [1], Hbr *mešek* [2], Aram (Syr) *meškō* [1], Arab *mask-* [1].
Eg *mskȝ* "skin, hide" (pyr).
Final *-ȝ* may indicate **a* of the second syllable.

Ancient Sem loanword in Eg?

1745 *masiʔ- "take, steal"

Sem **mVšVʔ-* "rob": Akk *mašāʔu*.
WCh **mus-* "take (away)": Hs *amše*, Sha *mus*, Klr *mus*.
Secondary formation with a prefix in Hs. Unexpected vocalism.
ECh **maʔis-* "steal" [1], "catch" [2]: Mig *māso* [1], Bid *miis* [1], Mobu *maše* [2].

Metathesis. Cf. also Tum *muǯ* "steal", Ndam *muǯ-ən* id.
HEC **mas-* "take": Sid *mass-*, Had *mass-*.

The alternative reconstruction is **maʾis-*.

1746 *mat- "go, walk"

Eg *nmt* "march" (pyr).
Prefix **nV-*.
WCh **mat-* "come": Ang *mēt*, Fyer *moot*.
SA **mat-* "come": Saho *-amat-*, *-emet-*, Afar *-mat-*.

1747 *maṭar- "water"

Sem **maṭar-* "streaming water" [1], "rain" [2]: Akk *miṭirtu* [1], Ug *mṭr* [2], Hbr *māṭār* [2], Aram (Syr) *meṭrō* [2], Arab *maṭar-* [2].
Eg *mtr* "water" (Amarna).

1748 *mawaç-/*mayaç- "wash"

Sem **mūṣ-* "wash": Arab *mwṣ* [*-u-*].
Cf. Arab *mṣmṣ* "rinse".
CCh **mac-/*muc-* "wash": Msg *masa*, Masa *musu-mo*.
LEC **mVyVç-* "wash": Som *mayḍ-*, Or *miiç-*.
HEC **mVyVç-* "wash": Sid *maço*, Kmb *meççeʾ*, Kab *meççi-*, Ala *meççi-*.
Omot **mayaç-* "wash": Ome *meç̌-*, Kaf *maač-*.

Consonantal alternation **-w-* ~ **-y-*.

1749 *mawar- "roof, house"

WCh **mawar-* "roof": Sha *mawar*, DB *mawar*.
LEC **mōr-* < **mawar-* "manger" [1], "home" [2]: Or *moora* [1], Boni *moor* [2].

Related to **mar-* "house".

1750 *mawaṭ-/*mayaṭ- "tree"

CCh **mVṭ-* "baobab": HNk *mətɛ*, HGh *mate*, HF *məd-* .
Cf. also HNk *mudɛ* id.

ECh **mawat-* "kind of tree": Mkk *moote*.
LEC **mēṭ-* < **mayaṭ-* "palm tree": Or *meeṭii*.

Consonantal alternation **-w-* ~ **-y-*. Probably, related to **muṭ-* "stick".

1751 *mawut- "die"

Sem **mūt-* "die": Akk *mâtu*, Hbr *mwt*, Aram *mwt*, Arab *mwt* [*-u-*], Gz *mōta*, Hss *mōt*, Mhr *mōt*.
Berb **mVt-* "die": Ayr *ammat*, Izy *emmeт*, Kby *emmet*, *əmməт*.
Eg *mt*, *mwt* "die" (pyr).
WCh **mawut-* "die": Hs *mutu*, Sura *muut*, Ang *muut*, Chip *muut*, Grk *mud*, Bol *mot*, Krk *mēt-*, Tng *mud-*, Ngm *mato*, Maha *muto*, Bele *motu-*, Krf *muk-ko*, Gera *mudu-*, Glm *məz-*, Grm *mut-*, Wrj *miy-*, Kry *miya*, Diri *matu*, Miya *miy-*, Paa *miy-*, Cagu *mōs-en*, Pol *misi*, Geji *musu*, Brm *mise*, Say *mišī*, Dwot *mus*, Buli *mušī*, Fyer *mot*, Bks *mot*, Sha *mot*, Klr *mot*.
CCh **mat-/*matVw-* "die": Bura *mta*, Chb *mti*, Mrg *mtu*, HF *mto*, HNk *mtɛ*, HGh *mtɛ*, FG *mti*, Kap *mti*, Mnd *mat*, Bld *muč*, Nza *mute*, Log *mti*, Bud *matte*, Lame *mata*, Masa *mita*, Bnn *matua*.
Metathesis in **matVw-* > Bnn *matua*.
ECh **mawut-* "die": Smr *made*, Tum *māde*, Dng *muutu*, Mubi *māt*, Sok *mūta*, *mīta*.
LEC **mūt-* < **mVwVt-* "die" [1], "deadly ill" [2]: Rnd *amut* (1st sg.) [1], Gid *muut* [2].

1752 *may- "go, come"

Eg *nmy* "go" (pyr).
Prefix **nV-*.
WCh **may-* "return": Bol *maa*, Dera *mai*.
CCh **may-* "go" [1], "come" [2]: Gis *me* [1], Masa *mai* [2].
ECh **maw-/*may-* "outrun" [1], "enter" [2]: Mobu *maye* [1], Sbn *mwə* [2].
SA **maH-* "come": Saho *ma*, Afar *ma*.
LEC **may-* "come": Arb *maye*.

ECh and SA seem to reflect co-variants of the main root with consonantal alternations.

1753 *mayas- "know, hear"

WCh **mayas-* "know": Tuli *mēsī*.
Bed *maasu(w)-* "hear".
From **mayas-* with **-y-* > **-H-*?

1754 *maǯiʔ- "vessel"

Sem **maḏiʔ-* "bronze vessel": Akk *maziû*.
Eg *mḏꜣy* "vessel" (n).

Sem loanword in Eg?

1755 *meciṭ-/*mecuṭ- "squeeze"

Sem **mVsuṭ-* "squeeze": Arab *msṭ* [*-u-*].
WCh **nyacuṭ-* "squeeze": Krk *nǯaḍu*, Tng *sond-*, Glm *čuuz*, Geji *četi*, Dwot *nzət*.
CCh **nVciṭ-* "press": Tera *nǯeḍi*, Ngw *nsitə*.

In WCh and CCh **n-* reflects the assimilation of **m-*.

1756 *meḥ- "swim"

Eg *mḥy* "swim, navigate" (a).
Vocalic *-y*.
WCh **myaH-* "swim": Bgh *myau*.

1757 *meḥas- "big snake, crocodile"

Eg *mzḥ* "crocodile" (OK).
Metathesis.
WCh **myaHas-* "python": Hs *mēsā*.
LEC **mas-* "snake": Som *mas-*.
Contraction.
HEC **hamas-* "snake": Sid *hamaso*, Had *hamas-iččo*, Bmb *hamasi*.
Metathesis. Assimilation of vowels.

1758 *mek- "stone"

Sem **mikk-* "stone": Akk *mikku*, *mekku*.
Eg *mꜣṯ* "granite" (OK).

Together, Eg *-ȝ-* and Sem **i* may reflect only HS **e*.

1759 *mer- "be near"

Eg *mr* "nearness" (t).
ECh **myar-* "near, close": Nch *mera*, Kbl *mra*.

1760 *mer- "beast of prey"

CCh **myar-* "serval, wild cat": Lame *mĕr*, *mereo*, LPe *meri-an*.
Rift **mer-* "lion": Asa *mer-ok*.
Cf. Alg *mariyamo* "wild cat".

1761 *meriʾ- "see, watch"

Sem **ʾVmVr-* "see": Akk *amāru*, Ug *ʾamr*.
Metathesis.
Eg *mȝȝ* "see" (westc).
The alternative comparison for *mȝȝ* is CCh **myaʾ-* "see" (Bud *me*).
ECh **myar-* "look, peer": Bid *mer*.
Agaw **mirriʿ-* "look, watch": Bil *miliʿ y-*.

1762 *met-met- "speak, shout"

Eg *mtmt* "speak" (XVIII).
ECh **myat-myat-* "shout": Sok *metemeteŋ*.

Reduplication.

1763 *metiʾ- "spear"

Eg *mtȝy.t* "spear" (BD).
ECh **myat-* "spear": Bid *meta*.
Loss of the auslaut laryngeal.

1764 *mi(ʾ)- "child"

Eg *my* "sperm, son" (XIX).
Wrz **miʾay-* "baby, boy": Gaw *miʾay*.

1765 *miʔ- "antelope"

Eg *mꜣ* "antelope" (pyr).
CCh **miyaw- < *miʔ-aw-* "antelope": Lame *miyeo*, LPe *miyeo*, Zime *miyeo*.
Agaw **miHiw-* "kind of gazelle": Kem *meewaa*.

1766 *miʔes- "tree"

Sem **mVHVš-* "kind of tree": Akk *mēšu*.
WCh **myas- < *mVHyas-* "mahogany" [1], "locust-bean" [2]: Chip *mɛs* [1], Mpn *mes* [2].
CCh **myas- < *mVHyas-* "tamarind": Log *mesā*.
HEC **miʔes-* "cedar": Bmb *miʔeesaa*.

1767 *migir- "grass"

Berb **mVgVr-* "cut (grass)": Kby *emger*.
Denominative verb.
LEC **migir-* "kind of tough grass": Or *migira*.
HEC **migir-* "grass": Had *migira*.
Rift **magir-/*migir-* "firewood": Irq *migir-*, Alg *magiru*.

1768 *mi-ʕVbal- "arrow, spear"

Sem **mi-ʕ(V)bal-* "arrow": Arab *miʕbal-at-*.
Eg *mʕbꜣ* "harpune" (pyr).
Sem loanword?
WCh **ʔumbul- < *mubul-* "throw (a spear)": Bol *ʔumbul*.
Denominative verb.

1769 *mič- "son, child"

Sem **mVṯ-* "son": Ug *mṯ*.
Eg *ms* "child" (pyr), Copt **mes*: Akh *mes*, Boh *mas*, Shd *mas*.
ECh **mič-* "son, child": Bid *mičo*, *miča*, Mig *mīča*.

1770 *min- "water, river"

Eg *myn.t* "waters" (pyr).
Vocalic *-y-*.

CCh *min- ''river'' [1], ''dew'' [2]: FG *mini* [1], Kap *minε* [2], Mwu *minu* [1].

1771 *min- ''worm''

Sem *mūn-* ''caterpillar'': Akk *mūnu*.
From *min-?
Berb *mVn-* ''flea's eggs'': Twl *imniwan*.
Meaning?
LEC *min(n)-* ''tapeworm'': Or *minni*, Arb *miinne*.
HEC *min(n)-* ''tapeworm'': Dar *minne*.
Rift *menan-* ''tapeworm'': Asa *menana*.

1772 *min- ''want''

Sem *mVnVy-* ''want'': Arab *mny*, Soq *mny*, Gz *mny*, Tgy *mny*.
CCh *min-* ''want'': Masa *min*.

1773 *minVᶜ- ''cow''

Eg *mnᶜ.t* ''cow'' (pyr).
Agaw *miHVn-* ''young cow'': Kem *miyän*.
Metathesis.

1774 *mir- ''river''

Eg *mr* ''channel, pond''.
CCh *mir-* ''river'' [1], ''pool'' [2]: FM *mirə* [1], Mus *amrai* [2].
Prefix *a-* in Mus.

1775 *miṭ- ''insect''

CCh *mVd-* ''mosquito'': Tera *mədə*.
Irregular Tera *-d-* < HS *-ṭ-.
LEC *miṭ-* ''worm'' [1], ''black ant'' [2]: Som *miḍ* [1], Or *miṭii* [2].
HEC *miṭ-* ''ant'': Sid *miṭa*.
Dhl *mu̱ta* ''small ant''.
-u- < *-i- after *m-.

1776 *miṭ- "pull"

Sem **muṭ-* "pull, stretch": Arab *mṭṭ* [-*u*-], Hss *meṭ*, Mhr *meṭ*, Shh *miṭ*.
Secondary vowel.
CCh **miṭ-* "pull": Mtk *mit*.

1777 *moʔ- "stick"

Eg *mꜣw* "stick" (pyr).
CCh **ʔu-mwaʔ-* "twig": Msg *umo*.
Prefix **ʔu-*.

1778 *moʔ- "be new"

Eg *mꜣ* "new" (OK).
WCh **mwaʔ-* "new": Fyer *mu*, Klr *mōhwɛ*, DB *mwa*.
CCh **mway-* "new": Tera *mewa*, Mofu *mɔuya*.

1779 *modaṭ- "tear"

CCh **mwaḍ-* < **mwadVH-* "tear": Gis *moḍ*.
LEC **mudaḥ-* "tear off": Som *muḍaḥ-*.
Som *ḍ* < **d* has been influenced by the laryngeal.

1780 *mog- "head"

CCh **mog-* "head": Mnj *mok*, Msg *mok*.
HEC **mug-* "head": Bmb *muga*.

1781 *moʕuḥ- "bury"

Eg *mʕḥʕ.t* "tomb" (MK).
Unexpected final -ʕ.
CCh **mwaHu-* "bury": Lame *muʔu*, Msg *mou*.
Wrz **may-* "bury": Gaw *may-*.

1782 *mon- "move, go"

Berb **mun-* "accompany": Izy *mun*.
Eg *mnmn* "move (away)" (OK).

Reduplication.

WCh **mwan-* "go" [1], "ride" [2], "come" [3]: Ang *mwen*, Sura *mwān* [2], Say *man* [3].

Related to WCh **man-* "return" (Ngm *man*) and CCh **min-/*mun-* id. (FJ *mun*, FM *min*, Mwu *umina*, Bch *muna*) if the above forms are not analyzed as **ma-n-* and **mi-n-/*mu-n-* correspondingly.

1783 *monVḥ- "slave"

Eg *mnḥ* "slave" (n).

WCh **mwan-* "slave": Bgh *mwan*.

Loss of the auslaut laryngeal.

1784 *moriʔ-/*moriḥ- "fat, oil"

Sem **mariʔ-* "fat" [1], "fat cattle" [2]: Akk *marû* [1], Ug *mru* [2], Hbr *meriʔ* [2].

Cf. Arab *mrḫ* [-*a*-]"oil" (v.).

Eg *mrḥ.t* "fat, grease" (OK).

WCh **mwaHir-* "fat, oil": Hs *mai*, Sura *mwɔɔr*, Ang *mūr*, *mwūr*, Mpn *muur*, *mwoor*, *myar*, Bol *mor*, Krk *meru*, Ngm *mor*, Maha *mor*, Bele *muru*, Krf *muru*, Gera *moori*, Glm *mər*, Grm *moori*, Pol *mīri*, Geji *mili*, Brw *miyir*, Say *mīr*, *māyi*, Kir *mār*, Tala *mīr*, Sha *maḥ*, Ngz *mərək*.

Metathesis.

CCh **mar-* "fat, grease": Tera *mər̆*, Gude *mara*, Gudu *mar̆*, Bch *marəy*, Nza *mare*.

From **mwara-*.

LEC **mor-* "fat": Or *moora*.

Irregular correspondences of laryngeals.

1785 *mos- "weapon"

Sem **mūšay-* "razor" [1], "knife" [2]: Arab *mūsay-* [1], Soq *mos* [2], Shr *mus* [2], Mhr *maus* [2].

Secondary **-u-* after a labial.

WCh **mas-* "spear": Hs *māši*.

From **mwas-*.

CCh *mwasa- "spear" 1, "iron" 2: Chb mwaši 1, Klb masu 1, Ngm mwasu 1, Wmd masu 1, Hil masu 1, Daba məsa 2, Mus masa 2.
ECh *mwasa- "iron": Mubi masiyo.
Rift *muš- "spear": Asa muš-uk.

1786 *mos- "give birth"

Eg *msy* "give birth" (pyr).
Suffix *-y*.
CCh **mwas-* "give birth": Bata *mwaza*, Bch *mwasa*, Mwu *kumwaša*.
Prefix **ku-* in Mwu.

1787 *muʾ- "man"

WCh **muʾ-* "man": Dera *mu*, Tng *muu*, pl. *mi*.
CCh **miʾ-* "people": Log *mi*.
*From *muʾi-?*
LEC **moH-* "man": Arb *mo*, *moh*.
Omot **maʾ-/*moʾ-* "man": Hozo *mo*, Sezo *mao*.
Rift **muʾ-* "people": Irq *mu*, Kwz *meʾ-iko*.

1788 *mud- "speak"

Berb **mVwVd-* "ask, pray": Twl *mud*.
Based on **mVd-*.
Eg *mdw* "speak" (pyr), Copt **mute*: Boh *mout*, Shd *moute*.
Vocalic *-w*.
WCh **muḍ-* "answer": Hs *muḍa*.
Unexpected **ḍ*.
CCh **mud-* "speak": Msg *muda*.
ECh **mad-* "ask" 1, "call" 2: Jegu *mād* 1, Ndam *madidī* 2.
Partial reduplication in Ndam. Secondary vocalism?

Cf. LEC **mod-* "think" (< HS **mVwVd-* or **mVd-*): Som *mood-*?

1789 *muk- "press"

Sem **muk-* "be pressed": Hbr *mkk* [*-u-*].
WCh **muk-* "press": Ang *muk*.

1790 *muk- "suck, drink"

Sem *muk-* "suck": Arab *mkk* [-*u*-].
WCh *muk-* "sip" [1], "chew" [2]: Ang *muk* [1], Mpn *muk* [1], Bol *mukk* [2].

1791 *mulak-/*mulik- "stranger, chief"

Sem *malik-* "king": Akk *malku*, *maliku*, Hbr *melek*, Arab *malk-*, *malik-*.
-u- > *-a-* after a labial.
WCh *mulVk-* "stranger": Wrj *məlki-zəhə-*, Diri *murkyu*.
CCh *mulak-* "stranger": Suk *malak*, Gis *mulak*.

The semantic connection of "stranger" and "ruler" reflects a certain historical reality of a "king" or "chief" belonging to or coming from an outside socio-ethnic group. At the same time, note CCh *mul-* "king" (Bnn *mula*, Masa *mula*), ECh *mul-* id. (Kwn *mulā-te*).

1792 *muluᶜ- "lizard"

WCh *muluH-* "gray lizard": Bks *mulu-sus*.
Cf. Hs *mulwa* "short thick snake".
SA *muluᶜ-* "lizard": Afar *mulluᶜ-it*.
LEC *muluᶜ-* "lizard": Som *muluᶜa*.

1793 *mun- "bird"

Eg *mnw.t* "dove, turtle" (OK).
WCh *mun-* "bird": Kry *mūnu*.

Cf. a partial reduplication in ECh *minin-* "kind of bird": Bid *mininiyo*.

1794 *mun- "heart, liver"

CCh *mun-* "liver": Hwn *məna-ra*, Gbn *mənaʾəta*, Gaa *mənə-tla*, HNk *mne*, Kap *mune*, FG *mini*, Mtk *məna-ḍ*, Tera *mənamәna*.
Dhl *muna* "heart".
Cf. *mani* "large intestine"?
Rift *mun-* "heart": Irq *muna*, Bur *muna*, Kwz *mun- ako*, Asa *mon-ok*.

1795 *mun- ''be, remain''

Eg *mn* ''remain'' (pyr).
WCh **mun-* ''remain'': DB *mun*.
CCh **min-* < **muni-* ''be'': Msg *mine*.

1796 *muneʾ- ''love'' (v.)

Sem **mun-* ''love'' [1], ''be favorable'' [2], ''desire'' [3]: Akk *menû* [1], Arab *mnn* [-*u*-] [2], Soq *mny* [3], Jib *mutni* [3].
WCh **munya-* ''love, like'': Fyer *muni*, Sha *mun*, Pero *meno*.
CCh **mun-* ''preferred'': Lame *mun*.

1797 *mun-/*muyun- ''ash, coal''

Eg *mn.w* ''ash, coal'' (gr).
WCh **muyun-* ''ash'': Bgh *muyun*.

Note the root pattern with ''optional'' C^2 = *-y-*.

1798 *munaḥ-/*muniḥ- ''give''

Sem **mVnaḥ-/*mVniḥ-* ''give'' [1], ''offer'' [2]: Arab *mnḥ* [-*a*-, -*i*-] [1], Soq *mnḥ* [1 2].
WCh **mun-* ''give'': Pero *munu*.

1799 *muq- ''be wet''

Sem **muḫ-* ''soak, dissolve'': Akk *maḫāḫu* [-*u*-].
Berb **mVγ-* ''be damp'': Ahg *əmməγ*, Twl *əmməγ*.
ECh **muk-* ''rinse out'': Mkk *muk-*.

1800 *muqeq- ''marrow, brain''

Sem **muḫḫ-* ''marrow'' [1], ''brain'' [2],: Akk *muḫḫu* [1 3], Ug *mḫ* [1 2], Hbr *mōᵃḥ* [2], Aram (Syr) *muḥḥō* [1 2], Arab *muḫḫ-* [2].
CCh **mVqyaq-* ''brain'': Mnd *məkχyekχe*.

Derived from **muq-* ''be wet''? Cf. Skt *majjan-* ''brain'', Av *mazga* id., Slav **mozgъ* id. ~ IE **mezg-* ''dip, sink''.

1801 *muġaʾ-/*muġaw- ‘‘male relative’’

Sem *maḫāʾ- ‘‘uncle’’: Akk *maḫāʾu*.
Usual development of *u after a labial.
Eg *mhw.t* ‘‘relative; subordinate; family’’ (MK).
Irregular reflex of HS *-q̇-.
WCh *muq̇aʾ- ‘‘king’’: Jim *mugaʾa*.
CCh *mVq̇- ‘‘king’’: Kap *məγɛ*, Log *mγai*, Bud *mei*.

Consonantal alternation *-ʾ- ~ *-w-. Note the semantic shift in Chadic.

1802 *muq̇Vʾ- ‘‘strike, pierce’’

Sem *mVḫVʾ- ‘‘beat, flog’’: Aram (Syr) *mḥʾ*.
Eg *mḫꜣ* ‘‘pierce (with a spear)’’.
WCh *muHVq- ‘‘strike’’: Hs *mūḳa*.
Metathesis.
ECh *muk- ‘‘beat’’: Mig *mukkiyo*.
Rift *muχ- ‘‘fight’’: Irq *muχ-*.

Cf. Dhl *mukk-eeδ-* ‘‘take by force, plunder’’?

1803 *mur- ‘‘man’’

WCh *mur- ‘‘servant’’: Hs *murī-ma*.
CCh *mur- ‘‘man’’: Gudu *mər̆*, Nza *murɛ*, Bch *murɛy*, Bata *mur̆ən*.
HEC *mur- ‘‘infant’’: Sid *mure*.

1804 *murVḥ- ‘‘feed’’

Sem *mVrVḥ- ‘‘feed’’: Akk *marû*.
ECh *muHVr- ‘‘food’’: Ndam *mūr*, Bid *muro*.
Metathesis.

Related to *moriʾ-/*moriḥ- ‘‘fat, oil’’.

1805 *murVṭ- ‘‘beard, chin’’

Eg *mrt* ‘‘chin’’ (l).
From Berb (Nfs *tu-mar-t* ‘‘beard’’)?
WCh *murVṭ- ‘‘beard’’: Diri *mulḍu*.

The word seems to be derived from a root preserved also in Chadic, cf. WCh **mar-/*mur-* "beard": Wrj *mara*, Kry *mar*, Siri *muri*, Ngz *mari*.

1806 *mut- "man"

Sem **mut-* "man" [1], "nobleman" [2]: Akk *mutu* [1 2], Ug *mt* [1], Hbr *mᵉtīm* [1] (pl.).

Secondary vocalism influenced by the initial labial.

WCh **mut-* "man": Hs *mut-um*.

ECh **muti-* "man": Dng *miti-ko*, Sok *mati*, *muti*.

This root describes "man" as "mortal", cf. **mawut-* "die". The same semantic development is well-known in IE, cf. Skt *mrta-* "dead" ~ Av *mašya-*, OPers *martiya-* "man".

1807 *muṭ- "stick"

Sem **maṭ-* "stick, branch": Hbr *maṭe*.

Eg *mdw* "stick" (OK).

1808 *m[u]yir- "snake"

WCh **mVyir-* "python": Sura *miyir*, Ang *myirm*, Chip *mir*, Mpn *mer*, *mīr*.

Agaw **mir-/*mur-* "snake": Bil *mər-aawaa*, Kem *mεr-εwa*, *mär-äwaa*, Dmb *merwaa*, Dmt *murii*, Aun *muri*.

1809 *muǯ- "cattle"

Eg *mḏ.t* "cattle" (OK).

ECh **muǯ-* "ox": Brg *mūzo*.

1810 *müʾ- "lion"

Eg *mꜣy* "lion" (pyr).

Vocalic *-y*.

ECh **muʾi-* "lion": Smr *mi*, *mui*, Tum *mui*, *mūy*, Ndam *mui*.

1811 *mVʾad- "be large"

Sem **mVʾād-* "many, much" [1], "very" [2]: Akk *mādu* [1], Hbr *meʾōd* [2].
CCh **mVd-* "large": Daba *mədde*.
Contraction.

1812 *mVd- "knife, axe"

Sem **mVdy-* "knife": Arab *mady-at-*, *midy-at-*, *mudy-at-* .
WCh **ʾi-mVd-* "small axe": Grk *imda*.
CCh **mVd-* "axe": Gudu *mədö-čü*.

1813 *mVdun- "vessel"

Berb **mVdun-* "kind of pan" [1], "kind of basin" [2]: Izn *mädun* [1], Kby *amdun* [2].
WCh **nVdun-H-* "pot" [1], "drum" [2]: Sha *nduŋ* [1], Klr *nduŋ* [2].
Assimilation of the initial **m-*.

1814 *mVl- "speak, call"

Sem **mVl-* "speak": Aram *mll*.
Berb **mVl-* "say, indicate" [1], "shout, call" [2]: Twl *əməl* [1], Kby *mmel* [2].

1815 *mVlog- "bosom; suck"

Sem **mVlag-/*mVlug-* "suck": Arab *mlg* [-*a*-, -*u*-].
Eg *mnḏ* "bosom, udder" (pyr), Copt **mnot*: Boh *mnot*.
Note the progressive palatalization of **-g-*.

1816 *mVlVḥ-/*mVlVḫ- "be good"

Sem **mVlVḥ-* "be good": Arab *mlḥ*.
Eg *mnḫ* "be fitting, fit".

Irregular correspondence of laryngeals.

1817 *mVsaw-/*mVsay- "cereal"

Eg *msy* "kind of corn" (n).

CCh *mVsaw- "millet": Log *msoā*.

Consonantal alternation *-w- ~ *-y-.

1818 *mVtaḳ- "be sweet"

Sem *mVtVḳ- "be sweet": Akk *matāqu*, Hbr *mtq*, Hss *maṭq*, Mhr *maṭq*, Shh *maṭq*, Soq *maṭaq*.
CCh *mVtak- "sweet": Mtk *mtake*.

1819 *mVṭur- "run"

Sem *mVṭur- "go fast (of horses)": Arab *mṭr* [-u-].
CCh *mVṭVr- "run": Glv *mdər-*.

*n

1820 *naʔ-/*naw-/*nay- "see"

Berb *nVn- "see": Izy *anni*.
Reduplication.
Eg *nw* "see" (XVIII).
WCh *naʔ-/*nay- "see": Sura *naa*, Ang *ne*, Chip *naa*, Bol *innaa-*, Krk *naa*, Krf *nee*, Gera *nee*, Glm *ny*, Grm *nee*, Wrj *nah*, Kry *nahə*, Miya *nay*, Mbu *naγ*.
CCh *naʔ-/*niʔ- "see": Tera *na*, Gbn *ni*, Mnd *nə-* .
*niʔ- goes back to *nVy-.
LEC *nay- "learn": Arb *nay-*.
The semantic shift is similar to the development of Goth *witan* "know" < IE *weid- "see".

Consonantal alternation *-ʔ- ~ *-w- ~ *-y-.

1821 *naʔib- "left"

Eg *iʒby* "left" (pyr).
Note *i-* < HS *n-. Vocalic *-y*.
WCh *naḅ- < *naʔVb- "left": Zar *naḅi*.

While WCh reflects initial *n-, Eg may well indicate *l- > *i-*.

If *l- was originally in the anlaut, the reconstruction *laʾVb- is to be connected with HS *lib-/*lub- "heart". If *n- is reconstructed in HS, cf. *nib- "heart".

1822 *nab- "speak; name"

Sem *nVb- "call" 1, "speak" 2, "nominate" 3: Akk *nabû* 1, Hbr *nbʾ* 2, SAr *nbʾ* 2, Gz *nbb* 2, Soq *nbʾ* 3, Jib *enbe* 3.
WCh *nab- "read, count": Tng *nabi*.
Omot *nab- "name": Hmr *nabi*, *naabi*.
Deverbative formation.

1823 *nabal- "arrow, spear"

Sem *nabl- "arrow": Arab *nabl-*.
Rift *labal- "spear": Irq *lawala*, Alg *labala*, Bur *labala*.
Assimilation of the initial *n- > *l-.

1824 *nacin- "(be) sharp"

Sem *nasin- "sharp point, nail": Akk *nasinu*.
Eg *nšny* "sharp" (NK).
š < *s before *i.

1825 *naç- "speak, call"

Sem *nVṣ- "dictate (a letter)": Arab *nṣṣ*.
Eg *nḏ* "call" (OK).
ECh *nas- "chat": Tum *naǯ*.
Voicing of auslaut *-s- > -ǯ.

1826 *nad-/*nid- "go, walk"

Sem *nid- "go fast" 1, "run (away)" 2: Ug *ndd* 1, Hbr *ndd* 2, Aram (Bibl) *ndd* 2, Arab *ndd* [-i-] 2.
Cf. also Hbr *ndʾ*, *ndy* "move away".
Berb *nVyVd- "walk": Izy *nyuddu*.
Based on *nVd-.
Eg *nwd* "move" (med).
Based on *nVd-.

WCh *nVd- ''go (away)'' [1], ''come'' [2]: Bol *ndi-* [1], Krk *nde-*, *ndayi* [1], Krf *ndo* [2], Pol *nduwu* [1].
CCh *nad- ''come'': Wmd *and-əw*.

Alternation *a ~ *i.

1827 *nadaᶜ- ''swallow''

CCh *nVda- ''swallow'': HNk *nda-re*, FK *nda-*, HF *ndaχo*, Glv *ndu*, Mofu *nd-*, Gude *nday-*.
SA *nadaᶜ- ''swallow'': Saho *nadaᶜ-*, Afar *nadaᶜ-*.

1828 *naf- ''breath''

Eg *nf* ''breath'' (NK).
SA *naf- ''breath, soul'' [1], ''face'' [2]: Saho *naf* [1], Afar *neef* [2].
LEC *naf- ''breath, soul'' [1], ''body'' [2]: Som *naf*, *neef* [1], Or *nafa* [2], Arb *nafa* [2].

Related to *nif- ''smell, breathe''.

1829 *nafar- ''man''

Sem *napr- ''man, group of men'': Arab *nafr-*.
WCh *nafar- ''man'': DB *naafara*.

Derived from *naf- ''man, person'' preserved only in WCh: DB *nāf*, Gul *nāfu*. Cf. also Pero *neepe* ''first born child''.

1830 *nafus- ''breath''

Sem *napš- ''breath, soul'': Akk *napištu*, Ug *npš*, Hbr *nepeš*, Aram (Syr) *napšā*, Arab *nafs-*, Gz *nafs*, Hss *nefeset*, Mhr *nefesēt*, Shh *nefsɛt*.
Berb *nVfas- ''breath'': Ahg *u-nfas*.
Metathesis of vowels.
WCh *nufas- ''breath'': Hs *numfāšī*, *lumfāšī*, Sha *lafwos*, *lufwos*.
Secondary nasal infix in Hs and dissimilation of *n- in Sha. Metathesis of vowels.
CCh *na[f]us- ''soul'': Log *nawusə*.
A widely attested semantic pattern, cf. Lat *anima* ''breath'' → ''soul''.
SA *nafVs- ''breathing'': Saho *nafse*.

Metathesis of vowels explained by the influence of verbal forms. Derived from **naf-* "breath". Related to **nufas-* "blow, breathe". Cf. also Sem **nVšVp-* "blow" (Akk *našāpu*, Hbr *nšp*, Aram *nšp*) and Eg *nšp* "breathe" (gr) if these are not derived from **sip-* "blow".

1831 *nagaĉ-/*naguĉ- "ruler, man"

Sem **nVguŝ-* "ruler": Arab *nigāš-*, Gz *nəguŝ*.
Cf. also SAr *ngŝwn* "king's title". Arab may be a Gz loanword or a deverbative.
CCh **ma-nVgaŝ-* "bridegroom": Gis *mangaŝ*.
Prefix **ma-*.
LEC **ʾangaš-* "tribal chief" 1, "eldest son" 2: Som *ugaas* 1, Or *angafu* 2.
Metathesis in the anlaut. Assimilation of vowels in Or. Note **-ng-* > *-g-* in Som.
Omot **ʾangus-* "first-born son": Ome *angussaa*.
As in LEC, initial **ʾVn-* corresponds to Chadic and Sem **nV-*. **-s-* < HS **-ĉ-* is not quite regular.

1832 *nag[i]H- "cattle"

Sem **naᶜg-* "sheep": Arab *naᶜg-at-*.
Metathesis.
Eg *ngȝ* "bull" (OK).
WCh **nungi-* "cow": Sura *niŋ*, Ang *nüng*, Mnt *nung*.
WCh, presumably, represents a partial reduplication **nu-nVgi-* from **nu-nVgiH-*. On the other hand, WCh could be borrowed from Fulbe.

Note contradictory evidence of Sem and Eg as far as the laryngeal is concerned.

1833 *naᶜVw- "snake, worm"

Eg *nᶜw* "kind of snake" (BD).
WCh **nVHVw-* "snake": Sura *ŋwɔɔ*, Chip *nwɔ*, Mpn *nwo*.
Omot **naHu-* "worm": Kaf *nau-ttoo*.

1834 *nahaḳ- “cry”

Sem *nVhaḳ-/*nVhuḳ- “cry, shout” [1], “bray” [2]: Akk *nâqu* [1], Hbr *nhq* [1], Arab *nhq* [-*a*-, -*u*-] [1], Gz *nhq* [1], Hss *nekāq* [2], Mhr *nehēq* [2], Shh *nhεq* [2].
ECh *nak- < *naHak- “cry”: Kera *nak-te*.
Contraction.

Cf. CCh *nyaχ- “ask”: Daba *neχu*.

1835 *naḥ- “want”

Eg *nḥy* “want” (MK).
-*y* is a suffix.
CCh *naH- “want, love”: Glv *nā*.

1836 *naḫ- “oil, fat”

Sem *nāḫ- “fat, grease”: Akk *nāḫu*.
Eg *nḥḥ* “oil” (n).
Partial reduplication. -*ḥ*- is a late Eg reflex of -*ḫ*-.

Irregular correspondence of laryngeals. A cultural word?

1837 *naḫ- “bend” (intr.)

Sem *nVḫ- “bend”: Arab *nḫḫ*.
Agaw *naH- “bend”: Bil *naʾy*-.

Cf. Bed *nuʾ*- “lower, put”.

1838 *naḫas- “pierce”

Sem *nVḫaš-/*nVḫuš- “prick”: Arab *nḫs* [-*a*-, -*u*-].
WCh *nas- “pierce (with spear)”: Hs *naše*.
ECh *nas- < *naHas- “pierce”: Mobu *nase*, Ngam *nesi*.

1839 *naḫür- “nose”

Sem *naḫīr- “nostrils” [1], “nose” [2]: Akk *naḫīru* [1], Hbr *n^{e}ḥīrayim* [1], Aram (Syr) *nəḥīrē* [1], Arab *manḫir*- [1], Jib *naḥer* [2], Soq *naḥrir* [2].
Prefix *ma- in Arab.
Berb *nVḫur- “nose”: Ghat *a-nǯur*, Ahg *a-nġur*.

1840 *nakar-/*nakir- "refuse, deny"

Sem **nVkar-* "ignore, disapprove": Arab *nkr* [*-a-*], Jib *nkɔr*.
ECh **nakir-* "refuse": Tob *naar*, Dng *nakir*.

Derivative from **kor-* preserved only in Chadic: WCh **kwar-* "refuse" (Sura *kwar*) and CCh **kyar-/*kwar-* "refuse" (Hwn *kar*, Gaa *kər-fa*, Gbn *ker-fa*, Mwu *ukoro*, FMch *kara*).

1841 *nam- "man"

ECh **nam-* "people": Tum *nemi-nam*.
Old collective. Cf. Kwn *nom-tō* "woman", Sib (pl.) *nam-de* id.
SA **num-* "man": Afar *nuum*, *nuumuu*.
Probably, **u* < **a* before **-m-*.
LEC **nam-/*nim-* "man": Som *nin*, Or *nama*, Kon *nama*, Bus *nama*, Gdl *nama*.
Regular Som *-n* < **-m*. Vocalism of Som has no support in other forms.
Omot **nam-* "man" [1], "son" [2]: Kaf *anaamoo* [1], Mch *naamo* [2].

1842 *nan- "god"

Eg *nn* "primeval god [Urgott]" (gr).
WCh **nan-* "god": Sura *nān*, Ang *nen*, Mnt *nān*, Ank *nān*, Mpn *nān*.

1843 *nan- "go, walk"

Berb **nVn-* "go across": Izy *ennu*.
Eg *nny* "go" (pyr).
-y is a suffix.
CCh **nan-* "go": Masa *nana*.
LEC **nan-* "go round" [1], "walk" [2]: Or *naanna*^{w}*a* [1], Arb *nanni-ete* [2].
Reduplication?

1844 *nani[ḳ]- "plant"

Sem **naniḳ-* "plant": Akk *naniqu*.
Eg *ỉnnk* "medicinal herb" (med).
Prefix *ỉ-*?

Irregular correspondence of Sem **ḳ* ~ Eg *k*. A loanword?

1845 *nap- "intestine"

Eg *npȝ* "guts" (sarc).
Vocalic *-ȝ*.
CCh **ni-nap-* "liver": Daba *ninap*.
Partial reduplication. Cf. also FKi *nəffo* "heart", Log *nəfu* id.

1846 *napil- "snake, worm"

Sem **napil-* "caterpillar": Akk *nappillu*.
Eg *npn* "snake" (reg).
-n < HS **-l-*.

1847 *naw- "be tired"

Eg *nw* "weak" (MK).
WCh **naʾ-/*naw-/*nay-* "be tired": Ank *ne*, Geji *naʾ- wi*, Wrj *nuw-*, Kry *nuwa*.
Secondary *-ʾ-* in Geji? Cf. also Kry *nuwa* "tiredness".

Any connection with **naw-/*nay-* "be bad"?

1848 *naw-/*nay- "be bad"

Eg *ny.t* "evil" (BD).
WCh **niʾaw-* "be bad": Ank *niau*.
Modification of the original stem.
ECh **naw-* "evil, terrible": Mkk *nāwa*.

Consonantal alternation **-w-* ~ **-y-*.

1849 *nawaĉ- "wine, beer"

Sem **na[w]aŝ-* "kind of beer": Akk *nāšu*.
Eg *wnš.t* "wine" (XIX).
Metathesis.

An alternative reconstruction is **wanaĉ-*.

1850 *nayaw- "vessel"

Eg *nyw* "pot" (med), *nw* (n).

ECh *nayaw-* "mug": Jegu *naayo*.

1851 *neʾul- "moisten"

Sem *nVʾVl-* "moisten": Akk *naʾālu*.
CCh *nVHul-* "moisten": Masa *ŋul-*.
Masa *ŋ-* < *nH-*.
ECh *nyaHul-* "rain" (v.): Sbn *nwə:lə:*, Mig *nyālo*.

1852 *neb- "swim"

Eg *nby* "swim" (pyr).
Vocalic *-y*.
CCh *nyabi-* "swim": Gul *nebia*.

1853 *neĉaʿ- "inhale through the nose"

Sem *nVŝaʿ-* "introduce a medicine through the nose" [1], "sniff, snuffle" [2]: Arab *nšʿ* [*-a-*] [1], Hss *še-nśā* [2], Mhr *še-nśē* [3], Jib *niśa* [4].
Berb *nV[c]-* "sneeze": Nfs *ə-nzu*, Siwa *ə-nzu*, Mzab *ə-nzu*, Sml *t-inzi*.
WCh *nyaHVĉ-* "breathe": Klr *nos*, Bol *nēs-*.
ECh *nyaHas-* "breathe": Mig *naaso*, Bid *nēs*.
Metathesis.

Cf. *nVĉaġ-* "inhale through the nose".

1854 *neg- "ask, shout"

Eg *nḏ* "ask (advice)" (pyr).
Palatalization of *g* after *e*.
CCh *nVg-* "answer": Glv *nggw*.
ECh *nyag-* "shout": Sok *negi*.

1855 *neḫ- "spit"

Eg *nẖ* "spit" (pyr).
CCh *nyah-* "spit": Mnd *nyahə*, Bata *naewi*, Mwl *nayi*.

1856 *neḫ- "saliva"

Eg *nḫ* "saliva" (pyr).
CCh **nyah-* "saliva": Mnd *nyɛhɛ*, Lame *neʾe*.

Derived from **neḫ-* "spit". Reduplicated in ECh **naHan-* "saliva": Brg *naani*.

1857 *nek- "punish"

Eg *nyk* "punish" (pyr).
Vocalic *-y*.
CCh **nyak-* "punish": Bch *nyaka*.

Cf. ECh **nik-* "disobey": Mkk *nīke*.

1858 *nes- "sand"

Eg *nš* "sand" (1).
Irregular *-š* < **-s-*.
WCh **ni-nyas-* "sand": Kir *nineyesi*, Tala *nyenyes*.
Partial reduplication.

1859 *nes- "red"

Eg *ỉns* "red" (pyr).
ỉ- may be a prefix.
CCh **nyas-* "red": Hwn *nyis*.

1860 *ni- "water"

Eg *nwy.t*, *n.t* "water" (MK).
CCh **ni-* "water": Msm *nī*.

1861 *niʾan-/*niwan "finger, fingernail"

WCh **niwan-* "nail": Bgh *nyoon*, *nywoon*, Kir *nyoon*.
Agaw **naʾan-* "hand" [1], "finger" [2]: Bil *naŋ* [1], Xmr *nän* [1], Xmt *naan* [1], Kwr *naan*, *naana* [1 2], Kem *naan* [2].
Assimilation of vowels.

Reduplication of HS **ʿVn-* in Eg *ʿn* "fingernail" (pyr)? Consonantal alternation **-ʾ-* ~ **-w-*.

1862 *nib- "heart"

CCh **nib-* "heart": Daba *niv*, Mus *nəv*.
Omot **nib-* "heart": Yam *nibaa*, Kaf *nibboo*, Mch *nibbo*, Bwo *niiba*.

Cf. **lib-/*lub-* id.

1863 *nib- "pour"

Sem **nVbVᶜ-* "sprinkle, flow": Hbr *nbᶜ*, Aram (Syr) *nᵉbaᶜ*, Arab *nbᶜ* [*-a-*, *-i-*, *-u-*].
Based on biconsonantal **nVb-*.
Eg *nby* "cast metal" (v.) (pyr).
Infinitive in *-y*.

1864 *nibuč- "dig"

Sem **nVbuṯ-* "dig out": Arab *nbṯ* [*-u-*], Jib *nbṯ*, Hss *nebōt*.
WCh **bičVn-* "bury": Hs *bisne*.
Metathesis.

The alternative reconstruction is **bičun-*.

1865 *nif- "smell, breathe"

Sem **nVpaḥ-* "smell" (intr.): Arab *nfḥ* [*-a-*], Jib *nifχ*, Soq *nafaḥ*.
Secondary formation based on **nap-*?
Eg *nfy* "breathe" (n).
CCh **nif-* "breathe, smell": Daba *nip*, Mus *nəp*.

For the semantic development, cf. Bret *c'houez* "smell" and "breath".

1866 *nig- "break"

Eg *ngy* "break" (NK).
Infinitive in *-y*.
CCh **lig-* < **nig-* "break": Mba *ligi*.

1867 *nigal- "sickle, sword"

Sem **ni(m)gal-* "sickle": Akk *ningallu*, *nimgallu*, Arab *mingal-*, Hbr *maggal*.

Note a nasal infix and various assimilations.
WCh **kasa-nVgal-* "sword": Wrj *kasagāla*, Kry *kamsagal*, Cagu *kasaŋgalen*, Jmb *kasəngali*.
Compound consisting of **kas-* "war" and **nVgal-* "sickle".
CCh **nVgil-* < **nigal-* "knife": Gude *ngila*, Nza *ngəla*.
ECh **ʾangul-* "sickle": Bid *ʾangul*.
Irregular vocalism.

Related to **nVgil-* "cut".

1868 *niʿar- "prick, be sharp"

Sem **nVʿar-* "prick, knock": Arab *nʿr* [-*a*-].
WCh **nar-* "spear": Tng *nar*.
Deverbative. Contraction from **niHar-*.
ECh **nyar-* < **niHar-* "sharp": Mkk *nyerere*, Ndam *nyar*.
Partial reduplication in Mkk.

1869 *nihar- "flow"

Sem **nVhar-* "flow": Arab *nhr* [-*a*-].
Related to **nahar-* "river": Akk *nāru*, Ug *nhr*, Hbr *nāhār*, Aram *nahrā*, Arab *nahr-*.
ECh **nyar-* < **niHar-* "flow slowly": Mkk *nyernyire*.
Reduplication.

1870 *niḥas- "snake"

Sem **naḥas-* "snake": Ug *nḥš*, Hbr *nāḥāš*.
Assimilation of vowels. Cf. Arab *ḥanaš-* "reptile, snake"?
WCh **nyas-* < **niHas-* "python": Bks *nyeš*, DB *nis*.

1871 *niḳ- "grind"

Eg *nḏ* "grind" (OK).
Progressive palatalization of **-ḳ-*.
WCh **niḳu-* "grind": Hs *niḳa*, Fyer *niḳ*, Bks *nuk*.
Cf. partial reduplication in **ni-nuḳ-* id.: Sura *nuŋ*, Sha *nuŋ*, Klr *nyiŋ*.

1872 *niḳ-/*nuḳ- "lick"

Sem **yVnVḳ-* "lick": Akk *enēqu*, Hbr *ynq*.
Prefix **yV-*.
Eg *snḳ* "suck" (pyr).
Causative in *s-*.
WCh **nVḳ-* "lick": Wrj *nəḳə*, Kry *nəkə*.
CCh **niḳ-* "lick": Mba *nik*.
Dhl *nuuḳ-* "suck beer through a straw".

Cf. LEC **nug-* "suck": Arb *nuug-*. Alternation **i* ~ **u*.

1873 *niḳif- "tree, bush"

Sem **niḳip-* "bush": Akk *niqiptu*.
Eg *nḏf.t* "tree" (OK).
Palatalization of **ḳ*.

1874 *niḳud- "bird"

Sem **niḳūd-* "swamp bird": Akk *niqūdu*.
CCh **nVguḍ-* < **nVḳud-* "dove" [1], "bird" [2]: Gbn *ŋgudiya* [1], Gaa *guḍiya* [1], Bud *ŋgudo* [2].

1875 *nim- "vessel"

Sem **ʾinim-* "goblet": Akk *inimmû*.
**ʾi-* may be a prefix.
Eg *nm* "vessel" (NK).

1876 *nin- "be tired"

Eg *nny* "be tired" (MK).
Vocalic *-y*.
WCh **nin-* "be tired": Ang *nyin*.
ECh **linVy-* "become tired": Tum *lən̄*, Ndm *linya*.
With dissimilation of **n-* > **l-*.

Reduplication of **naw-* "be tired".

1877 *nin-/*nun- "water"

Eg *nnw* "water" (pyr).
CCh **nin-* "water, dew": Msm *nina*, Msg *eneni*, Mba *nini-ḍ*.

Alternation **i* ~ **u*. Any relation to Sem **nun-* "fish"?

1878 *ninay- "man"

Eg *wnny.w* "people, men" (XVIII).
w- is a prefix.
WCh **ninVy-* "man": Pero *ninya*.
Omot **nVna[y]-* "relative, nephew": Ome *nainaa*, Gim *niania*.

Cf. ECh **nun-* "(dead) body": Mkk *nuune*?

1879 *niwiw- "plant"

Eg *nywyw* "kind of plant" (med).
CCh **nVwVw-* "grass": Gudu *nwu:wa*.

Partial reduplication?

1880 *noḥ- "tie"

Eg *nwḥ* "tie" (BD).
Vocalic *-w-*.
WCh **nwaH-* "tie": Bks *noʾ*, Sha *noʾ*.

1881 *noḳ- "water"

Sem **nVḳ-* "pour out": Akk *naqû*.
Denominative verb?
Eg *nḳw.t* "liquid" (med).
Vocalic *-w*.
Ome **noḳ-* "water": Ari *noḳa*, *noka*, Dime *naayo*, Banna *nooqo*, Karo *nuḳo*.

1882 *nufas- "blow. breathe"

Sem **nVpVš-* "blow, breathe": Akk *napāšu*, Soq *nefoš*.

WCh **nufas-* "breathe": Hs *numfāsa*, *lumfasā*, DB *nafos*, Kul *nos*, Sha *lufwos*.
Agaw **nVfVs-* "blow": Aun *nefes-əŋ*.

1883 *nug- "cry" (v. and n.)

Sem **nug-* "cry": Akk *nagāgu* [*-u-*].
Eg *ngg* "cry (of a goose)" (pyr).

1884 *num- "lie" (v.)

Sem **nim-/*num-* "lie, gossip": Arab *nmm* [*-i-*, *-u-*].
WCh **num-* "lie"; Ang *nüm*.

1885 *nutaʾ- "go, run"

Sem **nVtaʾ-* "go out": Arab *ntʾ* [*-a-*].
Eg *ntꜣ* "run" (pyr).
WCh **nuHVt-* "pass (by)": Ngz *nūtu*.

1886 *numur- "leopard, hyaena"

Sem **namir-* "leopard" < * "spotted": Akk *nimru*, Hbr *nāmēr*, Aram (Syr) *nemrō*, Arab *nimr-*, *namir-*, Gz *namr*, Hss *nemr*.
WCh **murum-* "hyaena": Bks *murum*, Sha *murum*, DB *murum*.
Assimilation of nasals. Metathesis.

An alternative reconstruction is **nurum-*.

1887 *nüs- "woman"

Sem **nišw-* "woman": Hbr *nāšīm* (pl.), Aram *neššē*, Arab *nisw-at-*.
WCh **nus-* "woman" [1], "female" (adj.) [2]: Fyer *nusi* [1], Sha *nisi* [2].
CCh **nus-* "woman": Tera *nušu*, Glv *nusa*, Gvo *nusa*.
LEC **ʾa-nVs-* "sister": Gel *anso*.
**ʾa-* is a prefix.

Connected with **nüs-* "man".

1888 *nüs- "man"

Sem **niš-* "man": Akk *nisū*, (pl.) *nišī*, Ug *nš-m*, Aram (Syr) *nōšō*, Arab *nās-* (coll.).
Eg *nswy.w* "servants" (MK).
WCh **nusi-* "brother": Bks *nus*, DB *nis*.
Agaw **nVs-* "male": Kem *näsiyä*.
Omot **nuš-* "husband": Nao *nuuše*.

1889 *nVbir- "increase"

Sem **nVbir-* "increase, grow": Arab *nbr* [-*i*-].
CCh **mVbVr-* < **nVbVr-* "increase": Glv *mbər-*, Nak *mbər-*.
Assimilation of the initial nasal.

1890 *nVcaᶜ- "tear out"

Sem **nVsaᶜ-* "tear out": Ug *nsᶜ*, Hbr *nsᶜ*, Aram *nsᶜ*, Arab *nsᶜ* [-*a*-].
WCh **nVcaᶜ-* "tear out, pull": Krk *nza*, Paa *ca*.

1891 *nVčuw- "wolf, jackal"

Eg *wnš* "wolf" (OK).
Metathesis.
WCh **nVčuw-* "wild dog": Sura *nčuwɛ*, Ang *čewe*.
Secondary development of the root vowel before **w*. Assimilation of vowels in Ang.

Cf. Rift **ʾinça(n)w-* < **niçaw-* "jackal" (Irq *inçaŋw*), Sem **layṯ-* "lion" (Akk *nēšu*, Hbr *layiš*, Arab *layṯ-*) and Dhl *naᶜeeṯe* "dog".

1892 *nVĉaġ- "inhale through the nose"

Sem **nVŝaġ-* "introduce a medicine through the nose": Arab *nšġ* [-*a*-], Tgy *nsᶜ*.
Berb **nVγVʒ-* "swallow mucus from the nose": Ghat *zu-nγəz*, Ayr *zə-nγəz*, Ahg *zu-nγəh*, Twl *zə-nγəz*.
Metathesis.

An alternative reconstruction is **nVġaĉ-*. Cf. also **noĉaᶜ-* id.

1893 *nVdaw- "speak, call"

Sem **nVdaw-* "call": Arab *ndw* [-*a*-].
WCh **nVd-* "speak, say": Diri *nda*, Miya *and-*, Mbu *nd-*.
Loss of the auslaut laryngeal.
CCh **nVdVy-* "ask": Zgh *ndiyʾa*.

1894 *nVfVᶜ- "go"

Sem **nVpVᶜ-* "go": Akk *nepû*.
Eg *nfᶜ* "go (from)" (MK).

1895 *nVg- "shine; light"

Sem **nVgVh-* "shine": Ug *ngh*, Hbr *ngh*, Aram *ngh*, Arab *ngh*, Gz *ngh*.
Based on biliteral **nVg-*.
CCh **nVgya-* < **nVgVy-* "light" (n.): Mnd *ŋγya*, Mnd *eŋγa*.

Cf. ECh **nVg-* "tomorrow": Sok *nogo*.

1896 *nVgil- "cut"

Sem **nVgil-* "mow, reap": Arab *ngl* [-*i*-].
CCh **nVgVl-* "cut": Mafa *ngəl-*.

1897 *nVgol- "throw"

Sem **nVgil-* "throw": Arab *ngl* [-*i*-].
WCh **nVgwal-* "throw": Glm *ŋgwal*, Gera *ŋwal*.

1898 *nVguf- "cut, break"

Sem **nVgup-* "hew, cut": Arab *ngf* [-*u*-].
CCh **nVguf-* "break (pottery)": Mofu *nguf*.

Derived from **gif-* "strike, pierce"?

1899 *nVgVᶜ- "break, strike"

Sem **nVgVᶜ-* "strike, crack": Hbr *ngᶜ*, Gz *nagwaᶜ*.

CCh **nVg-* "break": Daba *nga*, Log *ggē*, Bud *gai*.

Derived from **nig-* "break".

1900 *nVḫaʒ- "pierce"

Sem **nVḫaz-* "pierce (with a weapon)": Arab *nḫz* [*-a-*].
CCh **nVγVʒ-* "throw (a spear)": Mafa *ngəz-*.

Cf. **naḫas-* id.

1901 *nVḫor- "snore"

Sem **nVḫir-/*nVḫur-* "snore": Arab *nḫr* [*-i-*, *-u-*], Jib *ənḫerer*, *naḫar*, Hss *enḫērōr*, Mhr *enḫērōr*, Shh *enḫerer*.
WCh **nVḫwar-* "snore": Krk *ngor*, Kry *ngər-ən*, Cagu *ngwar*, Mbu *ngur-tə*.
ECh **nVγwar-* "snore": Sbn *ŋwərə*, Mobu *ongore*, Ngm *oŋgore*.

Derived from **naḫür-* "nose".

1902 *nVkVl- "be evil"

Sem **nVkVl-* "have ill intentions, be perfidious" [1], "teach a lesson" [2]: Akk *nakālu* [1], Hbr *nkl* [1], Aram *nkl* [1], Arab *nkl* [2].
Eg *nkn* "cause evil, harm, damage" (MK).

1903 *nVmVs- "move"

Sem **nVmVš-* "move, start": Akk *namāšu*.
Eg *nms* "come" (XIX).

1904 *nVsoġ- "pull"

Sem **nVšVġ-* "pull, pull out hair": Jib *nisəġ*.
CCh **nVsVγ-* "pull": Kap *nsχu-mte*, HF *nsəχu-so*, *sχu-nto*.
ECh **swag-* "pull": Tob *soge*.

ECh probably continues a root without prefix **nV-*.

1905 *nVtVf- ''spit, sprinkle''

Sem *nVtVp- ''spit out'': Arg *ntf*.
Eg *ntf* ''sprinkle'' (OK).

Derived from *tuf- ''spit''.

1906 *nVwur- ''light'' (n.)

Sem *nīr-/*nūr- ''light'' (n.): Akk *nūru*, Ug *nr*, *nyr*, Hbr *nīr*.
Contraction.
CCh *nVwur- ''light'' (n.): Log *nūr*.

1907 *nVwVq- ''rest'' (v.)

Sem *nūḫ- ''rest, be still'': Akk *nâḫu*, Ug *nwḫ*, Hbr *nwḥ*.
Cf. Arab *nwḫ* ''put a camel on its knees''.
WCh *nVwVq- ''rest'' (v.): Sura *nook*, Mpn *nook*.
Cf. Ang *nyok* ''life, rest''.

1908 *nVyVᶜ- ''turn''

Sem *nīᶜ- ''turn'' [1], ''be bent'' [2]: Akk *nêʾu* [1], Arab *nyᶜ* [-*i*-] [2].
Eg *nᶜy* ''turn'' (OK).
Metathesis.

An alternative reconstruction is *nVᶜVy-.

1909 *nVʒal- ''flow, pour''

Sem *nVzVl- ''flow'': Hbr *nzl*.
WCh *nVʒal- ''pour'': Bol *nzolu-*, Krk *nzalu*, Ngm *nzal*, Kry *zal*.

*p

1910 *paʾ- ''dig, bury''

CCh *paH- ''bury'': Mus *pa*, Mba *pā*, Log *fā*, Tera *pa-ra*, Hwn *pa-ŋ*.

Cf. reduplication in Mofu *pāpa* "till land with a spade".
Rift *poʾ-* "dig (hole)": Kwz *poʾ-otis*.
Assimilation of vowels.

Cf. Dhl *p'u*ᶜᶜ*-uδ-* "drill hole"?

1911 *paʾ-/*paw- "fly, jump"

Eg *pꜣ* "fly" *(pyr)*.
WCh **paH-* "fly": Klr *phaχ*.
CCh **paw-* "jump quickly": Mofu *paw*.

Consonantal alternation *-ʾ- ~ *-*w*-.

1912 *paʾ-/*paw-/*pay- "split, tear"

Sem **pVʾay-* "split" [1], "pierce" [2]: Hbr *pʾy* [1], Arab *fʾy* [-*a*-] [1 2].
Based on biconsonantal **pVʾ-*.
WCh **pay-* "break in pieces": Bol *poyy-*.
Cf. Tng *pawa* "act of slaughtering"
CCh **puw-* < **pawu-* "split, tear into pieces": Mofu *puw-* .
Secondary **u* before a labial.

Consonantal alternation *-ʾ- ~ *-*w*- ~ *-*y*-.

1913 *paʾir- "mouse, rat"

Sem **paʾr* "rat": Arab *faʾr-*.
Cf. also reduplicated Akk *perūrūtu*.
WCh **p̣yar-* < **paʾir-* "mouse, rat": Hs *ɓerā*.
Emphatic **p̣*- continues **p*- in contact with a laryngeal.

1914 *paʾuḳ-/*payuḳ- "be thin"

Sem **pīḳ-* "be thin, be narrow": Akk *piāqu*.
Eg *pꜣḳ* "thin" (NK).
WCh **pak-* "broad and thin": Hs *fakā*.
Contraction of **paʾVk-*.
CCh **fuk-* "thin": Msg *fuki*.
Contraction?

1915 *paʾus- "axe"

Sem *paʾš- "axe": Akk *pāšu*, Arab *faʾs-*, Soq *foʾs*, Shh *fuʾs*, Mhr *fos*.
ECh *paʾas- "axe": Jegu *fas*, Sok *pas*, Smr *bas*.
Borrowed from Sem?
HEC *faʾas- "axe": Sid *faase*.
Borrowed from Sem?
Dhl *fat'so* "axe".
Phonological details are not quite clear.

1916 *pac- "destroy, break"

Sem *pVs- "destroy, break": Akk *pasāsu*, Aram (Mand) *pss*.
ECh *pac- "break": Tum *paǯ*.
Voicing of the auslaut affricate in Tum.

1917 *paç̌-/*piç̌- "scrape, scrub"

WCh *pVç̌- "pare": Dera *peḍe*.
CCh *pač- "sweep": Mafa *pac-*.
LEC *fa[ç]- "scrape away": Som *faḍ-*.
HEC *fiç- "comb" (v.): Kab *fiç̌ç̌o*.
Omot *piç- "scrub": Mch *p̣iç̌ç̌a*.
Secondary emphatic *p̣-* in Mch.

Alternation *a ~ *i.

1918 *paĉ- "card, comb" (v.)

Sem *nVpuŝ- "separate wool with fingers, card": Arab *nfŝ* [-*u*-].
Secondary *u. Prefix *nV-.
Berb *fVs- "separate, card": Kby *əfsi*.
WCh *paĉ- "comb hair": Mpn *paas*.

Related to *pVĉ- "distribute, divide"?

1919 *paĉ- "straddle, spread"

Eg *pšš* "straddle, spread" *(pyr)*.
ECh *paĉ- "bifurcate" (v.): Bid *paačo*.

1920 *pag- "split, chop"

Sem *pag- "strike" [1], "split, furrow" [2]: Hbr pgᶜ [1], Arab fgg [-a-] [2].
-ᶜ- in Hbr seems to be an extension of a biconsonantal stem.
Eg pgꜣ "kill (enemies)" (XVIII).
ECh *pag- "chop": Tum pog.

1921 *pag- "open"

Sem *pVg- "open": Arab fgw [-u-].
Cf. Hss feggēt "broad spacing of the teeth".
Eg pgꜣ "open" (MK).
Vocalic -ꜣ.

1922 *pagal- "vessel"

Sem *pagal- "vessel (for libations)": Akk pagalu.
Eg pgꜣ "bowl" (MK).
-ꜣ < HS *-l-.

1923 *paᶜur- "dove"

Eg pᶜr.t "dove" (NK).
WCh *ṗar- < *paHVr- "quail": Hs ɓarwā.
*ṗ- < *p- in contact with a laryngeal.
CCh *puruw- < *paruw- "turtle dove": Mwl puruwo, Nza puruwe.

1924 *paḥar- "dig"

Sem *pVḥVr- "dig (earth)": Arab fḥr, Gz fḥr, Amh farä.
WCh *paHar- "making holes for seeds": Ngz paaru.

Cf. SA *faraᶜ- "dig" (Saho faraᶜ) with a different laryngeal.

1925 *paḥoç- "scrape, cut"

Sem *pVḥaṣ- "scratch earth, dig'''': Arab fḥṣ [-a-].
WCh *pVwaç- < *paHwaç- "scrape, rub": Ang pos, Mpn pwās, pwēs.

1926 *paḫ- "close, lock"

Sem *pVḫVʔ- "close, lock": Akk *peḫû*.
Based on *pVḫ-.
WCh *paH- "close": Sura *pā*, Ang *pō*, Bol *fa*, Krk *f-*, Fyer *pa*, Bks *vo*, Sha *vu*, Klr *fu*, DB *voh*.

1927 *paḫ- "field"

Eg *pḫꜣ.t* "field" (n).
Vocalic *-ꜣ*.
WCh *paḫ- "cleared open space, farm": Hs *fagē*.

1928 *paḫal- "leg, thigh"

Sem *paḫal- "thigh": Akk *paḫallu*.
WCh *pyal- < *paHal- "thigh": Ang *pyāl*.
CCh *paχVl- "leg, thigh": Daba *poχol*, Tera *boli*, Mus *bul*.
Related to *paḫud- "leg, thigh".

1929 *paḫal- "break through, split"

Sem *pVlaḫ- "split": Hbr *plḥ*, Arab *flḫ* [-a-].
Metathesis.
Eg *pḫꜣ* "split, break through" (MK).
-ꜣ < HS *-l-.
WCh *paHal- "break through" [1], "strike" [2]: Hs *ɓalle* [1], Tng *pāle* [2], Pero *pāl* [2].
CCh *pal- "break": Mafa *pal-*.
ECh *palVw- "break": Kera *palwe*.
From *palVH-, metathesis from *paHVl-.

1930 *paḫid- "fall, throw"

Eg *pḫd* "throw down" (NK).
WCh *paHid- "fall": Hs *fāḍi*, Chip *pit-*, Ank *petta*.

1931 *paḫud- "leg, thigh"

Sem *paḫud- "thigh": Hbr *paḥᵃdayim* (dual.), Aram (Syr) *pūḥd-*, Mhr *faḫed*, Shh *fuḫud*.

Cf. Arab *faḫd-* id., Hss *efḫād* id.

Eg *ḫpd* "thigh" (pyr).

Metathesis.

CCh **fVHuḍ-* "thigh": Gaa *fuḍ-ata*, Gbn *fəḍ-ətə*, Boka *fuḍ-ətə*.

Irregular **f-* instead of **p-*.

ECh **paHud-* "hip, thigh": Jegu *paado*, Mubi *fūdi*, Brg *faadi*.

LEC **baʾud-* "hip": Som *baʾudo*.

Note initial voiced **b-*.

Omot **paHad-al-* "inside of the thigh": Ome *paadaallaa*.

Assimilation of vowels. Suffix **-al-*.

Any connection with WCh **pund-* "thigh" (Bol *pundo*, Krk *fəntau*, Dera *pundo*, Ngm *hundo*, Krf *fonḍo*, Gera *pindi*, Glm *pənda*)?

1932 *pak- "jaw, cheek"

Sem **pakk-* "jaw": Arab *fakk-*.

WCh **ka-pak-* "cheek": DB *ka-pak*.

Prefix **ka-*.

CCh **pVk-* "cheek": HB *pəku*, HNk *pəki*.

1933 *pakuḥ- "hand, arm"

Sem **pakḥ-* "palm": Arab *fakḥ-at-*.

WCh **paku-* "wing, arm": Tng *paka*, Wrj *pak-ai*, Kry *pak*, Miya *pak*, Paa *puka*.

Cf. partial reduplication in Hs *fuffuke*, *fiffike* "wing".

1934 *paḳ- "go (out)"

Sem **pūḳ-* "let out": Hbr *pwq*.

Based on the earlier **pVḳ-*. Cf. **nVpVḳ-* "go out": Ug *nfq*, Aram *npq*, Arab *nfq* [*-a-*, *-u-*]

WCh **paḳ-* "follow": Sha *pak*.

CCh **pVk-* "walk": Mofu *pək-*.

1935 *paḳVʾ- "bark, skin"

Sem **paḳʾ-* "placenta": Arab *faqʾ-*.

CCh **paku-* "husk": Mofa *to-pokw*.

Dhl *pak'o* "tree bark, half beehive".

Cf. Kwz *paʔuko* "bark" with *-k-* < **-ḳ-*?

1936 *pal- "fall"

Sem **nVpVl-* "fall": Akk *napālu*, Ug *npl*, Hbr *npl*, Aram (Syr) *nfl*.
Prefix **nV-*.
WCh **pal-*"fall": Sura *pal*, Chip *pal*, Dera *yupele*.
Prefix **yu-* in Dera.

1937 *pal- "break"

Sem **pVl-* "break, crush": Aram (Syr) *pll*.
CCh **pal-* "break (stone)": Mafa *pal*.

Connected with **pal-* "cut, divide"?

1938 *pal- "cut, divide"

Sem **pVl-* "strike with a sword, behead, wean" [1], "divide, separate" [2], "cut, split" [3]: Arab *fly*, *flw* [1], Gz *fly* [2], Amh *fälläl* [3].
WCh **pal-* "cut off": Hs *falle*.
CCh **pal-* "cut": Zime *fal*.
ECh **pal-* "carve, cut, peel": Tum *pāl*, Sok *fal*.
SA **fVl-* "separate": Saho *-ifli-*.
LEC **fil-* "separate, comb": Arb *fil-*.
Vocalism is not clear.
Agaw **fal-* "divide": Bil *fäl-*, Kwr *fäl-*, Dmb *fäl-*.

1939 *palah- "earth, land"

CCh **palah-* "plain": Mofu *palah*, Gis *pala*.
Dhl *paλλaʔ-amo* "glade"

Cf. Sem **palaḥ-* "land" (Arab *falaḥ-at-*) if the latter is not derived from Arab *flḥ* "till" [*-a-*].

1940 *palay- "cloth"

Eg *pȝy* "cloth" (BD).
WCh **pāl-* < **payal-* "cloth": Wrj *pāla*.

Metathesis.

May be connected with a verb registered in Rift **pal-* "twist fibers into cord": Kwz *pal-*.

1941 *pan- "drive away"

Sem **pun-* "drive (camels)" [1], "let go" [2]: Arab *fnn* [-*u*-] [1], Gz *fnw* [2].

Secondary *-*u*-.

WCh **pan-* "drive away": Ang *pan*.

1942 *pan- "side, distance"

Sem **pVnVʔ-* "side, direction": Aram (Jud) *pənī-t-*.
Berb **fVn-* "opposite side": Sml *a-fna*.
SA **fan-* "interval": Saho *faan*, Afar *faan*.

Related to **pon-/*ponVʕ-* "turn, return".

1943 *pan-/*pin- "face"

Sem **pan-* "face": Akk *pānu* (pl.), Ug *pn*, Phn *pn*, Hbr *pānīm* (pl.).
ECh **pVn-* "temple": Kera *pən-ay*.

Suffix -*ay* in Kera.

Agaw **fin-* "forehead, face": Aun *fen*, *feni*.

Rift **pand-* "lump on the head" [1], "forehead,brow" [2] (Irq *panda* [1], Alg *paanda* [2], Bur *paanda* [2]) may be also connected with this root if *-*d*- is treated as a suffix. Note alternation **a* ~ **i*.

1944 *paHand- "bow"

WCh **pand-* < **paHand-* "bow": Krk *panda*, Krf *fanda*, Glm *panda*.
Wrz **paHant-* "bow": Dul *pahante*.

1945 *paneḳ- "container"

Sem **panīḳ-* "big sack" (for earth)": Arab *fanīq-at-*.
Eg *pnḳ* "bucket" (OK).
WCh **paḳyan-* "pot": Klr *fakyen*.

Metathesis. Klr *f-* < **p-* is not regular.

Any connection with WCh **pan-* "preserve, keep" (Ang *pan*)?

1946 *paq- "tear"

CCh **pVqya-* "tear": HNk *pkya-χumte*, HF *pχya-χuntu*.
Agaw **paχ-* "tear, split": Aun *paγ-s-*, Dmt *paγ-s-*.

1947 *paq̇- "assemble, gather"

Berb **fVḳ-* "pick together, assemble": Ahg *nə-fəḳḳi*.
WCh **paq̇-* "put one thing on the top of another": Ang *pak*.

1948 *par- "fetters"

Berb **far-* "fetters": Ahg *te-ffar-t*, Twl *te-ffār-t*.
Eg *prw.t* "fetters" (pyr).
Suffix *-w*.

1949 *par- "house, enclosure"

Berb **far(r)-* "enclosure": Ahg *a-farra*, Twl *a-farra*.
Eg *pr* "house" (OK).
ECh **par-* "hangar": Mig *para*.

1950 *par- "cattle"

Sem **parr-* "(young) bull": Ug *pr-m*, Hbr *par*, Arab *farr-*.
Eg *pry* "bull-fight" (MK).
CCh **par-* "cattle": Mba *far-ay*.
Suffix *-ay* in Mba.

1951 *par- "break, thresh"

Sem **pVr-* "break": Akk *parāru*, Hbr *prr*, *pwr*, Aram (Jud) *prr*, Arab *fry* [*-i-*].
Reduplication in Amh *färäfärä*, Hrr *firäfära* "crumble".
Berb **fVr-* "thresh, be threshed": Snus *frurī*, Sml *fruri*.
WCh **par-* "smash" [1], "break into pieces" [2]: Ang *par-p* [1], Tng *puure* [2].

1952 *par- "jump"

CCh **par(ya)-* "jump": Bud *fer*, Msg *pər*, *bara*.
Bed *far* "jump".
Agaw **pVr-* "jump": Aun *pərr-iŋ*.
SA **pVr-* "jump": Saho *pərr*, Afar *pərr*.

1953 *par- "finger"

WCh **par-* "finger, nail": Hs *far-če*, Gwn *apir-ači*.
ECh **pyar-* < **pari-* "finger": Dng *pεεr-me*, Mubi *fēri*.
SA **fer-* "finger": Saho *fera*, Afar *fera*, *feera*.
Secondary vocalism?
LEC **par-/*per-* "finger": Som *far*, Rnd *farro*, Bay *pεr*, Arb *farro* (pl.).
HEC **far-* "finger": Kmb *far*.
Omot **par-* "finger": Ome *par-taa*, *har-çaa*.

1954 *par- "look, seek"

WCh **par-* "look for, find": Bol *par-*, Tng *pari*.
CCh **pVr-* "look, watch": Gis *pir*, *pur*, *pr*.
Agaw **par-* "be open (of eyes)": Aun *parr-*.

Cf. Sem **pVHVr-* "seek" (Akk *pâru*) and Berb **fVrVy-* "feel": Ahg *a-fri*?

1955 *par-/*pir- "go out"

Eg *pry* "go out" (MK).
Infinitive in *-y*.
Bed *fira* "go out".
SA **far-* "go out": Saho *far*.
HEC **fir-* "go out": Had *fir*.

Alternation **a* ~ **i*.

1956 *para^{c}- "knife, axe"

Sem **parā^{c}-* "axe": Arab *farrā^{c}-at-*.
Secondary formation.

Berb **fVr-* "dagger, sharp tool, sword": Zng *te-feri*, Fgg *ta-fəru-t*, Izy *τa-fλu-t*.
ECh **paHar-* "knife": Mig *pēru*.
Metathesis.

An alternative reconstruction is **paᶜar-*.

1957 *parVm- "cut, split"

Sem **pVrim-* "cut": Arab *frm* [-*i*-].
ECh **param-* "sickle": Kera *pāram*.
Deverbative noun.
Rift **param-* "split (wood)": Asa *param-es-*.

1958 *paroḳ- "tear, rip"

Sem **pVrVḳ-* "tear off" [1], "divide" [2]: Hbr *prq* [1], Mhr *ferōq* [2].
WCh **park-* < **parVḳ-* "rip and remove": Hs *farkā*.
ECh **parwak-* "tear, pluck feathers": Kera *parge*, Bid *porok*.

Cf. Dhl *poroḥ-* "pull apart".

1959 *paruç- "cut, break through"

Sem **pVruṣ-* "make a hole" [1], "break through (a wall)" [2], "cut, pierce" [3]: Akk *parāṣu* [1], Hbr *prṣ* [2], Aram (Jud) *prṣ* [2], Arab *frṣ* [-*u*-] [3].
CCh **pVrVç-* "cut": Mofu *pərč-*.

1960 *parüĉ̣- "tear"

CCh **purŝ-* < **paruŝ-* "tear off": Mafa *purŝ-*.
Omot **parič̣-* "be torn out": Mch *ṗarič̣a*.
Mch *ṗ-* < **p-* under the influence of the following emphatic.

1961 *parVd- "equid"

Sem **pVrd-* "donkey" [1], "mule" [2]: Akk *perdu* [1], Hbr *pered* [2].
Agaw **par(V)d-* "horse": Bil *farda*.
LEC **par(V)d-* "horse": Or *farda*.

LEC loanword in Agaw or Agaw loanword in LEC?

1962 *pasuq- "arrow"

Sem *pašḫ- "spear": Akk *pašḫu*.
WCh *pasuq- "arrow": Kr *fasku*, Pero *puʒuk*, Dera *pek*.

1963 *pasVk- "piece of wood"

Sem *pašk- "log, splinter": Akk *pašku*.
Berb *fVsVk- "stick (in bull's nostrils)" 1, "furniture" 2: Twl *i-fəšk-ən* 1, Sml *i-fəšk-ən* 2.

1964 *pat- "skin"

WCh *pat- "skin": Hs *fatā*, Gwn *patā*, Wrj *patai*.
CCh *pVt- "skin": HF *pta*, HGh *pta*, *wpta*.
Omot *fat- "skin" 1, "snake skin" 2: Ome *faata* 1, Nao *fatu* 1, Gll *footi* 2.

1965 *pay- "go"

Eg *ᶜpy* "go" (pyr).
Prefix *ᶜV-.
WCh *pay-/*piy- "return" 1, "go" 2: Wrj *pəyi* 1, Kry *piy* 1, Diri *piy* 1, Sha *fay* 2, Klr *pa* 2.
CCh *p[a]y- "cross" 1, "go out" 2: Log *piya* 1, Lame *-pa-* 2.
ECh *paHaw- "outrun": Tum *paaaw*.
Agaw *fVy- "go away, go out": Kwr *fee-*, Dmb *fee-*, *fii-* , Kem *fee-*, Aun *fi-*.

1966 *pay- "flea"

Eg *py* "flea" (med).
ECh *pay- "flying termite": Mkk *peyyo*.

Cf. reduplication in WCh *pi-pi- "flea": Pero *pībi*.

1967 *paʒ- "metal"

Sem *paz- "pure gold": Hbr *paz*.
ECh *paʒ- "iron": Tum *paaǯ*.

One more example of semantic syncretism in the early vocabulary of metallurgy.

1968 *pec- "mosquito"

ECh **pyas-* "mosquito": Mkk *pesso*.
But cf. other ECh forms reflecting **bis-*: Jegu *bīso*, Mig *bīse*.
LEC **pac-* "mosquito": Or *faaca*.
Assimilation of vowels in LEC.

Cf. also reduplicated Sem **pas-pas-* "bug" (Arab *fas-fas-*).

1969 *ped- "call"

Sem **pid-* "shout, call": Arab *fdd* [-*i*-].
WCh **pyad-* "call, speak": Hs *faḍā*, Sura *pɛt*, *pit*, Mpn *pet*, Ang *pit*.

Cf. Dhl *puδ-uδ-* "tell"?

1970 *peḥas- "wet, sprinkle"

Sem **pVḥaš-* "wet, moisten": Arab *fḥs* [-*a*-].
WCh **pyaHVs-* "spurt water from one's mouth": Hs *fēsa*.
ECh **pyas-* "ḅe) wet": Sok *peso*.

1971 *per- "bird"

Sem **pirr-* "quail": Arab *firr-at-*.
Reduplication in Gz *fərfər-t* id.
WCh **pyar-* "small bird": Hs *fērū*.

1972 *per- "refuse"

Sem **pVr-* "forbid, refuse": Hbr *prr*.
CCh **pyar-* "refuse": Hil *pyɛri*.

1973 *piʾaʿ- "rain"

Eg *pꜣʿ.t* "sky waters" (pyr).
CCh **piʾaʿ-* "rainy season": Msg *pīaʿ*, Mofu *piya*, Mba *piya*.

1974 *pic- "hand"

Sem **pas-/*pis-* "palm": Aram (Bibl) *pas-*, (Jud) *pis-t-*.

Berb *fus- "hand": Ahg *a-fus*, Ghat *a-fus*, Ghd *u-fəs*, Siwa *fuus*, Sml *a-fus*, Rif *a-fus*, Kby *a-fus*.

Irregular *s < HS *c. Secondary *-u- < *-i- after a labial.

ECh *pis- "hand, arm": Dng *pise*, Mig *pesse*, Bid *pese*, Mubi *foso*.

1975 *pič- "cloth"

Sem *pVṯ- "cloth": Hbr *pešet*.
Eg *psš.t* "mat" (MK).

-*sš* is an orthographic representation of *-č-.

WCh *pič- "shroud": DB *pis*.
ECh *pVč- "apron": Kera *pəsi*.

1976 *pič- "spit"

Sem *nVpiṯ- "spit": Ug *nfṯ*, Arab *nfṯ* [-*i*-, -*u*-].

Prefix *nV-.

Berb *fVs- "spit": Ntf *s-ufs*, Izy *fs*, Snus *s-ufəs*.
WCh *pič/s- "spit": Krf *fiš-*, Gera *fiisii-*, Glm *pəs*, Kry *pəcə*, Diri *pəǯa*, Paa *pəsu*, Cagu *pəč*, Jmb *fəs*.
CCh *pič- "spew": Tera *pəšə*, Bch *fisə*.
ECh *pič- "spit": Mig *pisaw*.

1977 *pig- "stretch"

Sem *pVg- "draw (the bow)": Arab *fgg*.
Eg *pḏ* "draw (the string").

Progressive palatalization of *-g-.

WCh *pig- "pluck out, draw out (sword)": Hs *figā*.

1978 *pil- "insect"

CCh *pilu- "mosquito": Mba *fulay*, Mus *afili*.
Agaw *pil- "flea": Kwr *peliya*, Kem *fäle*.
Omot *pil- "flea": Kaf *pillo*.

Cf. Rift *paʾal- "flying termite": Kwz *paʾal-iko*.

1979 *pilaḳ- "knife"

Sem *pilaḳ- "dagger" [1], "axe, hoe" [2]: Akk *pilaqqu* [1], Aram (Syr) *pelq-* [2].

Berb **bVlVḳ-* "blade": Ahg *ta-bləq*.
Irregular **b-* < HS **p-*.

1980 *piliç- "divide"

Sem **pVlVṣ-* "divide, split": Gz *flṣ*, Tgr *flṣ*, Tgy *flṣ*, Amh *flṣ*.
Agaw **filiç-* "divide": Aun *felec-*.

1981 *pir- "fly, soar"

Sem **pVr-* "fly" [1], "flee" [2]: Ug *pr* [1], Aram *prr* [1], Arab *frr* [2], Hss *fer* [1], Mhr *farr* [1], Soq *fer* [1], Tgy *frr* [1].
Berb **fVr-* "fly": Ahg *fərə-t*, Sml *firri*.
Eg *pry* "soar, rise" (pyr).
Related to *pry* "go out".
WCh **pir-* "soar" [1], "stretch the wings" [2]: Hs *fīra* [1], Ang *pīr* [2].
CCh **pVr-* "bird's flight": Mafa *parr*, *perr*.
Bed *fir* "fly".
Agaw **fir-* "fly": Bil *fir y-*.

1982 *pir- "lock" (n.)

Berb **fir-* "lock" [1], "iron horse-lock" [2]: Zng *ti-fer-an* [1], Izy *tay-ffər-t* [2].
Eg *pꜣy* "part of the doorlock".
-ꜣ- < HS **-r-*.

1983 *pir- "fruit, corn"

Sem **pir-* "fruit": Phn *pr*, Ug *pr*, Hbr *pə rī*, Aram (Syr) *pērā*, Gz *fəre*.
Cf. Hss *ferrāt* "unripe fruit", Mhr *ferrāt* id., Shh *ferrot* id.
Berb **far-* "corn": Gua *a-faro*.
The vocalism may reflect a different alternation grade.
Eg *pr.t* "fruit, crop, seed" (OK).
Agaw **fir-* "fruit" [1], "corn" [2]: Bil *fir* [1], Xmr *fira* [1], Kwr *fira* [1], Dmb *fira* [1], Kem *fir* [2].
SA **fir-* "flowers, fruit": Saho *fire*.
LEC **fir-* "fruit": Or *firi*.

1984 *piraḫ- "sprout, flower"

Sem **piraḫ-* "sprout" [1], "flower" [2]: Akk *perʾu* [1], Ug *prḫ*, Hbr *peraḫ*, Aram (Syr) *parḥō* [2], Arab *farḫ-* [1], Gz *farḫa* [1].
Eg *prḫ* "flower" (n).

Derived from **pir-* "fruit, corn".

1985 *piraṭ- "break, split"

Sem **pVrVṭ-* "break": Amh *färräṭä*
WCh **pirVṭ-* "split (firewood)": Hs *firḍe*.
Cf. irregular *-rḍ-* < **-rṭ-*. Cf. also Hs *farḍā*, *farḍo*, *furḍa* "crack (nuts)".
ECh **pyarVt-* < **pirat-* "break, crack": Kera *perte*.
HEC **fir(V)ṭ-* "cut, prune": Bmb *firṭ-*.

1986 *piric- "break, grind"

Sem **pVris-* "break" [1], "tear" [2]: Aram (Syr) *prs* [1], Arab *frs* [*-i-*] [1 2].
CCh **pVrVc-* "grind": Mofu *pîrs-*.
ECh **pirVs-* "crush (grain)": Mkk *pirza*.
Agaw **firis-* "be destroyed": Aun *feres-əŋ*.

1987 *pirig- "separate"

Sem **pVrig-* "open, enlarge, separate": Arab *frg* [*-i-*].
ECh **pirVg-* "separate": Bid *pirgay*.

1988 *pirVq- "scratch"

Eg *pꜣḫ* "scratch (eyes)".
-ꜣ- < HS **-r-*.
ECh **pirVk-* "scratch": Kera *pirki*.

1989 *pitaḥ- "open"

Sem **pVtaḥ-* "open": Akk *petû*, Ug *ptḥ*, Hbr *ptḥ*, Aram (Syr) *ptḥ*, Arab *ftḥ* [*-a-*], Gz *ftḥ*, Hss *fetōḥ*, Mhr *fōteḥ*, Shh *fetaḥ*.
CCh **pVtVH-* "open (of eyes or anus)": Mofu *pəth-*.

ECh **pit-* "open": Bid *pit*, Sok *fitifiti*.
Reduplication in Sok.

1990 *piṭ- "bark" (n.)

CCh **piṭ-* "bark": Mofu *papət*, Mafa *pit-*.
Partial reduplication in Mofu.
ECh **pyat-* "bark": Kera *pete*.
Wrz **feṭ-* "bark": Hrs *feeṭe*.

1991 *poʾad- "close, cover"

Sem **pVʾVd-* "close": Akk *pâdu*.
CCh **pwaʾad-* "wrap up": Mofu *paḍ-*, Nza *paḍi*, Gis *foḍ*.
ECh **pwad-* "cover": Mobu *podde*.

1992 *poĉ- "smear, scatter"

Sem **pVŝ-* "spread" [1], "smear" [2], "scatter" [3]: Akk *pašāšu* [1 2], Hbr *pŝy* [1], Aram (Jud) *psy* [1], Arab *fšw* [*-u-*] [1 3], Soq *piŝi* [1], Tgy *fss* [1], Tgr *fss* [1], Amh *fss* [1].
WCh **pwaĉi-* "anoint" [1], "scatter" [2]: Ang *pwis* [1], Tng *peḍa* [2].

Etymologically identical with **pVĉ-* "distribute, divide"?

1993 *poʿ- "give birth"

Eg *pʿpʿ* "give birth" (gr).
Reduplication.
CCh **pway-/*pwaH-* "give birth": Gude *pwɛy-ik*, FM *pɔyi*, FB *pwe*.

1994 *poḥaĉ̣- "separate, split"

Sem **pVḥaṣ̂-* "separate, split": Arab *fḥḍ* [*-a-*].
Eg *pḥḏ* "separate, split open".
LEC **foHoç-* "separate": Arb *fooḍ-*.
Assimilation of vowels.
HEC **faʾaç-* "cut maize": Kmb *faaç-*.
Assimilation of vowels.

1995 *pok- "mug, bowl"

Sem **pak-* "bottle, mug": Hbr *pak*.
**u* > **a* after a labial.
CCh **pwak-* "water pot": Gaa *pokə-ta*, Gbn *pokə-tə*.
ECh **pVk-* "bowl": Kera *pəka*.

1996 *poḳ- "peel, skin" (v.)

Sem **pVḳVʾ-* "peel, shell" (v.): Aram (Syr) *pqʾ*.
WCh **pwaḳ-* "skin, peel": Ang *pok*.
ECh **pwag-/*pwak-* "skin" (v.) [1], "shell, pluck feathers" [2]: Tum *pəg* [1], Ndam *pə:gə* [1], Kera *poke* [2].

Connected with **paḳVʾ-* "bark, skin".

1997 *poḳaᶜ- "beer, sauce"

Sem **puḳāᶜ-* "beer, juice": Arab *fuqqāᶜ-*.
WCh **pwaḳ-* "sauce": Sura *pok*, Ang *pwuk*, Mpn *puk*.

1998 *poḳVᶜ- "cut, split":

Sem **pVḳVᶜ-* "split, break, wound": Gz *fqᶜ*.
CCh **pok-* "chop": Msm *pok*.

1999 *poliḳ- "split"

Sem **pVliḳ-* "kill, slaughter" [1], "cut" [2]: Akk *palāqu* [1], Arab *flq* [-*i*-] [2].
LEC **folVḳ-* "break off": Or *folloqa*.

Derived from **pal-* "cut, divide".

2000 *pon-/*ponVᶜ- "turn, return"

Sem **pVn-* "turn": Ug *pnn*, Hbr *pny*, Aram (Syr) *pnʾ*, *pny*.
Eg *pnᶜ* "turn" (pyr).
CCh **fwan-H-* "return": Lame *fɔŋ*, LPe *faŋ*.

2001 *puc- "burn"

Eg *wps* "burn" (NK).
w- stands for a rounded root vowel.
CCh **pVc-* "roast": FKi *wča*, HK *psa-*, HB *pceyo*, HGh *wsaže*, Mnd *pšapša*.
Reduplication in Mnd.

2002 *puc- "tear into pieces"

Sem **pVsaʾ-* "tear into pieces": Arab *fsʾ* [-*a*-].
Based on **pVs-*.
CCh **puc-* "tear into pieces, pluck": Mafa *puc-*.

2003 *puč̣- "urine"

Sem **paṯ̣ṯ̣-* "horse urine": Arab *faẓẓ-*.
Berb **fVç̣-* "urine": Ahg *ta-fəẓẓ-a*.
Borrowed from Arab?
WCh **puč̣i-ar-*"urine": Hs *fiçārī*, Wrj *cəpr-ai*, Kry *cipir*, Diri *axəbəla*, Miya *cəpur*, Paa *cipura*, Siri *č̣ipəri*, Pol *bəs*, Geji *ḅasi*, Brm *ḅas*, Say *ḅes*, Dwot *ḅuzari*, Buli *ḅəs*.
ECh **puč̣i-* "urine": Tum *bə:ʒər*, Ndam *buǯ*, Dng *piḍye*, Mig *piǯi*, Brg *pidye*.

2004 *puĉ̣- "break, crush"

Sem **puṣ̂-* "break, crush": Hbr *pṣpṣ*, Arab *fḍḍ* [-*u*-].
Reduplication in Hbr.
CCh **puŝ-* "break": Kap *puŝe*, HNk *pŝe*, HF *pŝo*.

2005 *pudaġ-/*pudiġ- "break, split"

Sem **pVdaġ-* "break": Arab *fdġ* [-*a*-].
CCh **puḍik-* "split": Mofu *pədḳ-*, Gis *puḍik*.
From **pudiḳ-* < **pudiġ-*.

2006 *puḥ- "strike"

Sem **nVpaḥ-* "strike with a sabre": Arab *nfḥ* [-*a*-]
Prefix **nV-*.

Dhl *puḥ-*"hit, strike (with sharp instrument)".
Cf. also *paḥ-*"hit, shoot".
Rift **puḥ-*"hit": Kwz *puχ-umis*.

2007 *puḥar- "jump"

Eg *pḥrr* "run" (pyr).
Note double *-rr*.
WCh **p̂ura-* < **puHar-* "jump": Hs *ƥurā*, Ang *pyar*, Ank *p̂ār*, Mpn *paar*.
Emphatization of **p-*.
ECh **paHar-* "jump": Smr *pâr*.

2008 *puk- "winnow"

Berb **fVk-* "winnow, peel (corn)": Ahg *fukk-ət-*.
WCh **puk-* "winnow": Tng *puk*.

2009 *pur- "cut"

Sem **pVrVy-* "cut": Akk *parû*, Arab *fry* [*-i-*].
Reduplication in Arab *frfr* "cut, split".
Berb **fVr-* "shave, cut hair": Ahg *əfr-ən*.
WCh **pur-* "prepare field by cutting trees": Tng *pure*.

2010 *pur- "container"

Sem **parr-* "kind of vessel" [1], "pot" [2]: Akk *parūtu* [1], Hbr *pārur* [2].
Derivatives of **parr-* in Akk and Hbr.
Eg *pr* "box" (MK).
WCh **pur-* "large beer-pot": Tng *puuri*.

2011 *pur- "tear"

Berb **fVrVy-* "tear": Kby *fri*.
Based on **fVr-*.
CCh **pur-* "tear": Daba *pur*.
Rift **puruᶜ-* "strip off": Irq *puruᶜ-us-*, Alg *puruᶜ-*.
Secondary laryngeal.

2012 *pur- "flower, grass"

Berb **fVr-* "kind of grass": Sml *a-fər*, Rif *friw*.
WCh **pur-* "tobacco flower" [1], "flower" [2], "grass" [3]: Hs *furē* [1], Paa *pure* [2], Cagu *pəre* [2], Pero *pure* [3].
CCh **fwar-* "flower": Dgh *fəra*, Bud *phōrio*.
Bed *far* "flower" (pl.)
Note the modified vocalism of pl.
LEC **fur-* "kind of grass": Or *fura*.
Omot **pur-* "flower": Yam *furaa*.

Connected with **pir-* "fruit, corn".

2013 *pur- "untie"

Berb **fVr-* "untie": Kby *ə-fru*.
CCh **pir-/*pur-* "untie": Tera *pərə*, Wmd *piri*, Mtk *pər*, FBw *pir*, Bch *para*, Mwu *upuran*, Gude *pur-gič*.
ECh **puwir-* < **puʾir-* "untie": Smr *ʾawər*, Nch *pure*, Lele *poor*, Kbl *puwər*, Kera *fere*, Kwan *apre*, Dng *i- pire*, Mig *ʾi-piro*, Mkk *ʾeppire*.
Secondary laryngeal in the inlaut.
LEC **pur-* "untie, disengage": Som *furayya*, Or *furra*.
**u* may reflect a different alternation grade.

2014 *purVs- "cut, separate"

Sem **pVrVš-* "separate": Aram (Syr) *prš*.
Berb **fVrVs-* "separate" [1], "cut" [2]: Sml *fərs* [1 2], Twl *əfrəs* [2], Ahg *əfrəs* [2].
ECh **purVs-* "split": Sok *purse*.

2015 *putir- "mat"

Sem **putr-* "mat": Arab *futr-*.
Secondary **u*?
WCh **ka-pVtir-* "mat": Wnd *kaptir*, Dwot *kaptur*.
Prefix **ka-*.

2016 *puwad- "heart"

Sem **pawād-/*puʾād-* "heart": Arab *fawād-*, *fuʾād-* .

WCh **pūd-* "heart": Sura *puut*, Ang *put*.
Contraction from **puwad-*.
ECh **pwad-pwad-* "lungs": Smr *pədəpədə*, Tum *podpod*, Ndam *pət-pət*.
Reduplication.

2017 *pVˀin- "break, grind"

Sem **pVˀVn-* "grind": Akk *pênu*.
WCh **pVHin-* "break": Ang *pīn*, Mpn *pīn*.

2018 *pVˀud- "knee"

Berb **fud-* "knee": Nfs *u-fed*, Siwa *fūd*, Ghat *a-fud*, Ahg *a-fud*, Zng *o-ffud*, Sml *a-fūd*, Ntf *a-fud*, Izy *a- fuδ*, Rif *fud*, Mzb *fud*.
Eg *pꜣḏ*, *pꜣd* "knee" (med), *pd* (XVIII).

The ancient form of Eg seems to be preserved as *pꜣḏ*. If so, the unusual correspondence Eg *ḏ* ~ Berb **d* needs further analysis.

2019 *pVĉ- "distribute, divide"

Sem **pVŝ-* "distribute": Aram (Syr) *pss*, Arab *fšš*.
Eg *psš*, *pšs*, *pš* "divide" (MK).
Note *sš* and *šs* as graphic representations of a lateral.

2020 *pVd- "move"

Sem **pid-* "march, go (of cattle)": Arab *fdd* [*-i-*].
ECh **pad-/*pud-* "pass by": Tum *pəd*, Ndm *pada*, Lele *pudu*.

The root vocalism of Sem and ECh is contradictory. Cf. also Berb **fVd-* "let in" (Sha *s-ifəd*) and Eg *ꜣpd* "run, hurry" (XVIII).

2021 *pVg- "take"

Sem **pūg-* "take away": Akk *puāgu*.
Based on biconsonantal **pVg-*.
ECh **pVg-* "take": Tum *pəg*.

2022 *pVˁal- ''work, make''

Sem **pVˁal-* ''work, do, make'': Phn *pˁl*, Hbr *pˁl*, Aram (Syr) *pˁl*, Arab *fˁl* [-*a*-], SAr *pˁl*.
LEC **pal-* ''make'': Som *fal-*, Boni *fal-*.
Ome **pal-* ''create, make'': Kaf *hal*, Mch *p̣alli*.
Dhl *fal-* ''do''.

Contraction in all Cush forms.

2023 *pVḫ- ''exchange, sell''

Sem **pVḫ-* ''exchange'': Akk *puḫḫu*.
CCh **pVχwa-* ''sell'': HNk *pəχwi*, Kap *pəχwi*.
WCh **pay-* < **paH(ī)-* ''commerce'': Tng *paya*.
Deverbative with modified vocalism.

2024 *pVḫVr- ''gather''

Sem **pVḫVr-* ''assemble'': Akk *paḫāru*.
Cf. a nominal derivative **puḫ(V)r-* ''assembly, gathering'': Akk *puḫru*, Ug *pḫr*.
ECh **pVr-* ''gather'': Kbl *pərrə*.

2025 *pVlaḥ- ''split, cut''

Sem **pVlaḥ-* ''split'' [1], ''till, cultivate'' [2]: Hbr *plḥ* [1], Aram *plḥ* [2], Arab *flḥ* [-*a*-] [1 2].
Berb **fVlVh-* ''cut, split'': Ahg *ə-fləh*.
Irregular laryngeal.

Derived from **pal-* ''cut''.

2026 *pVlVs- ''split, pierce''

Sem **pVlVš-* ''pierce'': Akk *palāšu*.
Eg *pns* ''cut'' (pyr).
-n- < HS **-l-*.

The alternative reconstruction is **pVsVl-*.

2027 *pVriʒ- "cut, separate"

Sem **pVriz-* "separate": Arab *frz* [-*i*-], Mhr *ferōz*.
Berb **fVrVʒ-* "cut": Snus *əfrəz*.

2028 *pVt- "scorpion"

Eg *ptt* "scorpion" (l).
Partial reduplication.
CCh **pVt-* "scorpion": HF *ptu*, HB *wto*, FKi *ti*.

2029 *pVṭtis- "flatten"

Sem **pVṭiš-* "flatten, forge": Arab *fṭs* [-*i*-].
Cf. **paṭiš-* "hammer": Hbr *paṭṭīš*, Aram (Jud) *paṭṭīs-*.
Eg *pds* "make flat, trample down".
Regular *-d-* < **-ṭ-*.

2030 *pVtoḳ- "split, cut"

Sem **pVtuḳ-* "break, split, separate": Arab *ftq* [-*u*-].
Berb **fVtVk-* "open" 1, "cut" 2: Siwa *əftək* 1, Ahg *əftək* 1 2, Izy *frek* 2, Izy *frek* 1, Kby *eftek* 1.
Unexpected **k* < HS **ḳ*.
CCh **pVtwak-* "split": Mofu *pətkw-*.
-kw < **-ḳ-* under the influence of **-wa-*.
LEC **fotoḳ-* "chip" (v.): Or *fottoqa*.
Assimilation of vowels.

*q

2031 *qab- "kill"

Eg *ḫb* "kill" (gr).
WCh **qab-* "kill": Tng *kabi*.

2032 *qafV^c- "hold"

Sem **ḫVp-* "pack": Akk *ḫapû*.

Eg *ḫf*ᶜ "catch, grasp, pack" (pyr).

Cf. also *ḫf*ᶜ "fist" (pyr).

WCh **qaf-* "security of hold" [1], "grasp, seize" [2]: Hs *kaf* [1], Say *ngəp* [1], Ngz *gafau* [2], Bade *gaf* [2].

Cf. Dhl *ḥap-* "snatch quickly".

2033 *qam- "possess"

Eg *ḫ3m* "possess, hold" (MK).

Vocalic *-3-*.

WCh **qam-* "grasp": Hs *kāma*.

Dhl *kam-* "hold".

Rift **kom-* "hold, have": Irq *kom-*, Bur *kom-*, Asa *kom-* , Kwz *komos-*.

Secondary **-o-* before a labial.

2034 *qapuĉ- "arm, shoulder"

Eg *ḫpš* "arm" (MK).

WCh **qapuĉ-* "shoulder": Bul *gapuŝa*.

2035 *qatam- "ring, seal"

Sem **ḫatm-* "ring" [1], seal (on a ring)" [2]: Hbr *ḥotēm* [1 2], Arab *ḫatm-* [1 2], Jib *ḫotem* [1], Hss *ḫōtem* [1], Shh *ḫotem* [1].

Eg *ḫtm* "stamp, seal" (OK).

WCh **qatam-* "ring": Miya *katam*.

2036 *qaway- "be empty"

Sem **ḫūy-* "be empty": Arab *ḫwy* [*-i-*].

WCh **qāy-* < **qaway-* "empty": Tng *kaayi*, *gaye*.

2037 *qet- "tear"

Eg *ḫtt* "tear off" (MK).

WCh **qyat-* "tear, rend": Hs *kēta*.

2038 *qiᵓ- "plaiting"

Sem **ḫiᵓ-* "kind of clothes": Akk *ḫiᵓu*.

Eg *ḫꜣ.t* "kind of plaiting" (NK).

2039 *qirim- "separate, divide"

Sem **ḫVrim-* "separate, isolate" [1], "pierce" [2]: Akk *ḫarāmu* [1], Arab *ḫrm* [-*i*-] [2].
WCh **qirVm-* "stub with a knife, cut or bite head off": Hs *kirma, kirme*.

2040 *qiŝ- "grind, rub"

WCh **qiŝ-* "thrash": Hs *kilā*.
CCh **qiẑ-* "thrash, beat": Mafa *kəẑ-*.
Rift **ḫiŝ-* "rub": Alg *ḫiŝ-*.

2041 *qoᵓ- "mix"

Eg *ḫꜣw* "mix" (med).
Vocalic *-ꜣ*.
WCh **qwaᵓ-* "mix": Fyer *goo*.

2042 *qoĉ- "pierce"

Sem **ḫūŝ-* "pierce" [1], "penetrate, pierce camel's nose with a stick" [2]: Arab *ḫwš* [-*u*-] [1], Jib *ḫeŝŝ* [2].
Inlaut **-w-* reflects the original structure with **-o-*.
Omot **koč-* "pierce": Kaf *kočč-*.
Irregular **-č-*.

2043 *qom- "gather, join"

Sem **ḫVm-* "gather": Akk *ḫamāmu*.
WCh **qwam-* "join": Grk *kwom*.

2044 *qor- "shout, say"

Sem **ḫūr-* "bellow": Arab *ḫwr* [-*u*-].
Based ob biconsonantal **ḫVr-*.
Berb **kur-* "call": Ahg *kur-ət*.
Eg *ḫr* "say" (OK).

WCh **qwar-* "groan" [1], "shout, cry, call" [2]: Ang *gwar* [1], Kry *kwar* [2], Miya *kwar* [2], Jmb *gwar-al* [2].

2045 *qot- "take (by force)"

Sem **ẖVt-* "take somebody's share": Arab *ẖtt*.
WCh **qwat-* "take thing by force": Hs *kwātā*, *kwāče*.

2046 *qot- "elbow"

Eg *ẖt* "elbow" (MK).
WCh **qu-qwat-* "elbow": Sha *kukwat*.
Partial reduplication.

2047 *quʾab- "knife, sickle"

Eg *ẖꜣb* "chisel" (BD).
WCh **quʾab-* "sword, knife": Hs *takōbī*, Sura *kəp*, Ang *küp*.
Prefix *ta-* in Hs.

2048 *qudam- "pot"

Sem **ẖadām-* "night pot": Arab *ẖaddām-at-*.
Assimilation of vowels.
WCh **qudam-* "pot": Bol *kudam*.

2049 *qul- "hoe" (n.)

Eg *ḥnn* "hoe" (pyr).
Irregular laryngeal.
CCh **qul-* "hoe": Wmd *kul*, Hld *kwulu*.

Cf. Rift **ẖwal-* "dig up, till": Alg *ẖwal-*, Kwz *ẖoẖwal-*.

2050 *qur- "voice, noise"

Eg *ẖrw* "voice, noise" (pyr).
Vocalic *-w*.
WCh **qur-* "scream, cry" (n.): Hs *kurūruwa*.
Rift **ẖur-* "rumble, roar": Irq *ẖur-ay*.

Related to **qor-* "shout, say".

2051 *qurap- "beat"

Sem *ḫVrVp- "strike back": Akk *ḫarāpu*.
WCh *qurVp- "whipping": Hs *kurfō*.
ECh *karap- "kick, trample": Bid *ʾarap*, Dng *karpe*.

2052 *qüʒ- "be angry"

Eg *ḫzy* "angry" (MK).
-y stands for a front vowel.
WCh *quz- "be angry": Tng *kuz-*.

2053 *qVbVʾ- "break, destroy"

Eg *ḫbꜣ* "destroy" (pyr).
WCh *qVHVb- "break": Tng *keeb*.
Metathesis.

Cf. *qab- "kill".

*q̇

2054 *q̇ac- "valley, river bed"

Berb *γVʒ- "river bed, wadi": Ahg *ta-γəzz-it*.
Rift *ḫas- "valley or ravine without running water": Irq *ḫasa*.

2055 *q̇aç-/*q̇VwVç- "sand"

Sem *ḫūṣ-/*ḫīṣ- "sand, gravel": Akk *ḫiṣṣu*, Gz *ḫoṣā*.
Secondary formation with inlaut *-w-/*-y-. Cf. Agaw.
WCh *q̇as- < *q̇aç- "earth, sand": Hs *ḳasā*.
Agaw *ḳūš- < *ḳVwVš- "sand": Bil *ḳūšā*.
Omot *ḳaç- "sand": Kaf *ḳāčo*, Nao *ḳaṣa*, Gim *ḳačay*, *ḳač*.

Cf., with a different anlaut laryngeal: Rift *haç- "sand" (Irq *has-aŋ*, Kwz *has-inko*, Asa *haj-at*).

2056 *q̇aĉ- "be friable"

Sem **ḫVṣ̂-* "be friable": Arab *ḫḏw*.
ECh **kVĉ̣-* "crumble": Bid *koḍyoḍy*.
Partial reduplication.
LEC **ḳaç-* "walk on grain and spoil it": Or *qaçaʾa*.

2057 *q̇alüm- "boat"

Sem **ḫalim-* "raft": Akk *ḫallimu*.
Eg *ḫmn.ty* "ship" (OK).
Metathesis.
CCh **q̇walum-* < **q̇alum-* "boat": Msg *ḫɔlum*, Log *γ'oam*.
Log *γ'oam* < **γ'walam*.

2058 *q̇am-/*q̇ayam- "tent, house"

Sem **ḫaym-* "tent" [1], "hut, cabin" [2]: Ug *ḫm-t* [1], Arab *ḫaym- at* [1 2], SAr *ḫym* [2], Gz *ḫaymat* [1], Tgr *ḫaymät* [2], Amh *haym- ät* [2], Jib *ḫom* (pl.) [1], Hss *ḫīm-ēt-* [1 2].
Berb **γ(V)yam-* "tent" [1], "village" [2]: Ayr *ta-γyam-t* [1], Ahg *ta-ḫyam-t* [1], Twl *ta-γyam-t* [1], Ntf *ta-ḫyam-t* [2], Kby *a-ḫḫam* [1].
Eg *ḫm* "temple" (pyr).
ECh **kam-kam-* "camp": Mig *kankama*, Bid *kamkama*.
Reduplication. Dissimilation of nasals in Mig.

2059 *q̇an- "tent, house"

Eg *ḫn* "tent" (pyr).
WCh **q̇an-* "hut": Wrj ḳ*an-na*, Cagu ḳ*an*, Jmb *gan*.

Cf. **q̇am-/*q̇ayam-* id.

2060 *q̇aniç-/*q̇uniç- "leg"

Sem **ḫanṣ-* "hip": Akk *ḫanṣātu*, Hbr *ḫ^{a}lāṣāyim* (dual.), Aram *ḥarᵊ ṣīm*.
Irregular sonants.
Eg *ḫnḏ* "part of the leg" (pyr).
CCh **q̇uniç-* "hip, knee": Gis *mit-kinǯa*, Glv *γunǯa*, Zgh *gwuǯe*, Gava *gwiʒa*.

Alternation **a* ~ **u*.

2061 *q̇ar- "fish"

Eg *ḫꜣ.t* "kind of fish" (a).
 -ꜣ < HS *-r-.
WCh **q̇ar-* "fish with sharp fins": Hs *ḳarāyā*.
LEC **ḳar-* "fish": Gel *kaara*.
Wrz **χar-* "fish": Gaw *χaare*, Cam *ḫaar-ite*, Hrs *haar-icce*, Dob *haar-icce*, Gll *haare*.
Ome **ḳar-* "fish": Hmr *kara*, *kaara*.

2062 *q̇ar-/*q̇awar- "burn"

Eg *ḫr.t* "flame" (reg).
 Cf. also *ḫꜣ* "roast" (n).
WCh **q̇awVr-* "roast (without oil)": Hs *ḳaurarā*.
 Secondary *-w-?
Rift **ḫwar-* "fry" [1], "hot" [2]: Bur *χweraʾes-* [1], Alg *χwereʾes-* [1], Asa *hareta* [2].

2063 *q̇araw- "war, fight"

Eg *ḫrwyw* "war".
 Partial reduplication.
WCh **q̇ar[a]w-* "fight": Hs *ḳārō*.
ECh **kVraw-* "war": Tum *kəraw*.
 Cf. Kera *kuuri* "fight" (v.).

2064 *q̇ayul- "equid"

Sem **ḫayl-* "horse" [1], "mare" [2]: Arab *ḫayl-* (pl.) [1], Soq *ḫayl-* [2], Hss *ḫeyōl* (pl.) [1].
Berb **γayul-* "horse" [1], "mare" [2], "donkey" [3], "mule" [4]: Jrb *tə-γalli-t* [4], Nfs *tə-γəll-ət* [2], Skn *t-γall-ən* [1], Sml *a-γγul* [3], Sgr *a-γγul* [3], Mzab *t-γalli-t* [1], Wrg *a-γγul* [3], Snd *a-γγul* [3].
LEC **ḳay(V)l-* "foal": Som *qayl*.

2065 *q̇en- "go, walk"

Eg *ḫny* "walk" (l).
WCh **q̇yana-* "enter, go": Tng *kɛn*, Fyer *gan*.
ECh **gin-* "go out": Sok *gine*.

2066 *q̇of- "hoof"

Sem **ḫupp-* "hoof": Arab *ḫuff-*, Hss *ḫef*, Mhr *ḫef*, Shh *ḫaf*.
WCh **q̇waf-* "hoof": Hs *ḳwāfa*, Ang *kwēp*.

2067 *q̇ol- "testicles"

WCh **q̇wal-* "testicles": Hs *ḳwālātai*, Ang *gwal*.
CCh **q̇wal-* "penis" [1], "testicles" [2]: Bura *kwal* [1], Klb *kwal* [1], Mrg *kwal* [1], FGH *kwəlaku* [1], Bch *kwaley* [2].
ECh **kwal-* "testicles" [1], "penis" [2]: Kera *kələŋ* [1], Kwan *kalasa* [1], Mkk *kole* [2].
Agaw **ḳwil-* "testicles": Bil *ḳʷelaa*.
Omot **ḳull-* "testicles": Kaf *ḳuroo*.

Cf. Dhl *kʷ'all-iδ-* "have an erection".

2068 *q̇on- "river"

Eg *ḫnw* "rivulet" (XVIII).
Vocalic *-w*.
ECh **kwan-* "river": Ndam *kwan*.

2069 *q̇oq̇- "throat"

Eg *ḫḫ* "throat" (MK).
WCh **q̇waq̇-* "throat": Hs *māḳōḳo*, Grk *γγa*, Bgh *gway*.
Prefix in Hs.
CCh **q̇[w]ay-* "throat": Log *γ'ayī*, Bud *wui*, Gul *uē*, Kus *uā*.
Dhl *k'ok'o* "throat".

Reduplication?

2070 *q̇or- "tooth"

WCh **ḫa-q̇war-* "tooth": Hs *haḳōrī*, Fyer *hagor*, Bks *ʾagur*, Sha *ʾagaḥa*, Klr *ʾagwer*, DB *gur*.
Prefix **ḫa-*.
Bed *kwir* "tooth".

2071 *q̇or- "shell"

WCh **q̇war-* "shell of tortoise": Hs *ḳwarya.*
Rift **ḫoror-* "cowry shell": Irq *χoror-ami.*
Partial reduplication.

2072 *q̇or- "bird"

Eg *ḫꜣr* "goose" (BD).
-ꜣ- stand for a vowel.
HEC **ḳur-* "crow": Ala *qura*, Tmb *qura.*

Descriptive root.

2073 *q̇ul- "vessel"

Berb **γVlal-* "wooden vase": Ghd *a-γlal.*
Partial reduplication.
Eg *ḫꜣw* "vessel" (pyr).
-w stand for HS **u* in the root.
WCh **ḳulul-* "big pot": Hs *ḳūlūlu.*
Assimilation of vowels. Partial reduplication.

Partial reduplication in Berb and WCh.

2074 *q̇VyVb- "deceive"

Sem **ḫīb-* "deceive"; Arab *ḫyb.*
CCh **q̇VyVb-* "deceive": Daba *kīḅ.*
Contraction. Emphatization is caused by **q̇.*

*r

2075 *raʾ- "sing"

ECh **raʾ-aw-/*raʾ-ay-* "sing": Mubi *rewa*, Brg *raaya*, Bid *raa-.*
Rift **raʾ-* "sing": Irq *daʾ-*, Alg *raʾ-*, Bur *raʾ-am-*, Asa *raʾ-at-.*
Cf. a reduplication in WCh: Hs *raira* "sing", *rēra* id.

2076 *raʾ- "water level"

Berb **Ha-ray-* "water level (in a vessel)": Ahg *t-ăray- t.*
Prefix **Ha-.*
Eg *rꜣ* "water-line" (MK).

2077 *raʾ-/*raw-/*ray- "be, become, make"

Eg *iry* "be, do, make" (OK), Copt **ʾiri*: Fym *ili*, Akh *eire*, Boh *iri*, Shd *eire.*
WCh **raʾ-/*raw-* "become" [1], "work" [2]: Gwn *ra* [1], Bks *ro* [2].
CCh **ray-* "become, build": Lame *re*, *rey*.
ECh **riy-* "become" [1], "work, make" [2]: Dng *orriye* [1], *riyo* [2], Bid *riy* [2].
Secondary **i* before **y*.
Rift **raʾ-* "stay, remain": Asa *raʾ-*.
Dhl *raw-* "stay, remain".

Consonantal alternation **-ʾ-* ~ **-w-* ~ **-y-*.

2078 *raʾib- "dirt"

Sem **rāʾib-* "dirty": Arab *rāʾib-*.
WCh **rāḅ-* < **raʾib-* "diarrhoetic excrement": Hs *rāḅo*.
Contraction.

2079 *raʾob- "rain"

WCh **raʾVb-* "dew": Hs *rāḅā*.
SA **rVHob-* "rain": Saho *rob*, Afar *roob*.
LEC **rVHob-* "rain": Som *roob*, Or *rooba*, Boni *roob*, Kon *roopa*, Gid *roop*.

Cf. Sem **rVbīb-* "rain" (pl.): Hbr *rᵉbībīm*.

2080 *raʾup- "finish" (v.)

CCh **ruf-* < **rafu-* "finish, end": Mafa *ruf-*.
Irregular **f*.
HEC **rap̣-* < **raʾVp-* "be finished": Sid *raap̣-*.
Emphatic *-p̣-* in contact with a laryngeal.

2081 *raç- "go, run"

Sem *rVwVṣ- "run": Akk râṣu, Hbr rwṣ, Aram rhṣ, Gz rwṣ.
Secondary formation in *-w-.
WCh *raç-/*riç- "go": Hs rāçe, Dwot ris.
ECh *ʾa-ras- "walk in large steps": Bid ʾaras.
Prefix *ʾa-.
Dhl raṯ- "go, walk".

2082 *racaḥ- "pour, soak"

Sem *rVŝaḥ- "leak": Arab ršḥ [-a-].
WCh *rVĉ- "moisten": Ngz rəẑu.
ECh *raĉ- "wet, soak": Mobu rase, Ngm rasī.

Cf. *riĉ- "sprinkle".

2083 *rad- "foot, trace"

Eg rd "foot" (pyr), Copt *rat "foot, trace": Akh ret, reet, Boh rat-, Shd rat-.
LEC *rad- "footprint": Som raad.

Cf. also SA *radd- "descendant" (Afar raddi) and, probably, Omot *rot- "foot" (Hmr roti, rroti).

2084 *rad-/*rid- "go, run"

Sem *rVdVw-/*rVdVy- "go" [1], "walk, tread" [2], "beat the ground in running" [3]: Akk redû [1], Hbr rdy, rdw [2], Aram (Syr) rdy, rdw [2], Arab rdy [3].
Cf. Arab rwd "run to and fro".
SA *rad- "run": Afar rad-, -erd-.
LEC *rid- "run": Som ord-, Boni -irid-, Rnd -irid-.

Connected with *rad- "foot". Alternation *a ~ *i.

2085 *radoʾ- "be bad, be rotten"

Sem *rVduʾ- "be spoiled, be bad": Arab rdʾ, rdw [-u-].
WCh *raḍ- < *radVH- "rot": Wrj raḍə, Kry raḍ-, Siri raḍa, Mbu raḍ-.
CCh *rwad- < *radwa(H)- "bad": Nak $r^{w}ad$.

2086 *raf- ''dwelling''

Berb **rVf-* ''kind of room'': Ghd *ə-rref*.
CCh **raf-* ''hut'': Tera *rafa*.

2087 *rag-/*rug- ''tremble''

Sem **rug-* ''tremble'': Arab *rgg* [-*u*-].
ECh **rag-* ''tremble'': Kwan *rake*, Mobu *lage*.
Irregular Kwan *-k-* < **-g-*.

Alternation **a* ~ **u*.

2088 *raᶜ- ''sun, god''

Eg *rᶜ* ''sun, Sun-god'' (pyr), Copt **rē*: Akh *ri*, Boh *rē*, Shd *rē*.
WCh **rayi-* < **raHi-* ''sun'': Geji *ri*, Sha *are*.
ECh **raH-* ''sun, god'': Mkk *ra*, Bid *rāya*.

Any relation to Sem **rayᶜ-* ''daylight'' (Arab *rayᶜ-*) and Eg *ᶜry* ''sky'' (gr)?

2089 *raᶜad- ''thunder''

Sem **raᶜd-* ''storm, thunder'': Akk *rādu*, Arab *raᶜd-* , Gz *raᶜād*.
Cf. also Hbr *rᶜd* ''tremble'', Arab *rᶜd* [-*a*-, - *u*-] ''thunder'' (v.).
WCh **ᶜarad-* ''thunder'': Pol *haradu*, Miya *araduwa*.
Metathesis.
CCh **raHad-* ''thunder'': Mnd *řade*, Log *rāde*.

2090 *rahaw-/*rahay- ''bird''

Sem **rahw-* ''crane'': Arab *rahw-*.
WCh **raHaw-/*raHay-* ''bird'': Bol *rayo*, Krk *rāyi*, Ngm *rāyi*, Bele *raawi*.
ECh **rāy-* < **raHay-* ''vulture'': Mig *rāya*.
LEC **raHaw-* ''large bird'': Arb *raaw*.

2091 *raḥ- ''hand, arm''

Sem **rāḥ-/*rīḥ-* ''hand, palm'': Akk *rittu*, Ug *rḥt*, Aram (Syr) *laḥᵊ tō*, Arab *rāḥ-at-*, Tgr *räḥat*.

WCh *raH-/*riH- "arm": Klr *riyaw*, Sha *riyaw*, Bks *ra*, DB *ra*.
CCh *raH- "arm": Mtk *ř̌ay*.

2092 *raḫ-/*riḫ- "mix"

Sem *riḫ- "mix": Akk *raḫāḫu*, Arab *rḫḫ* [-*i*-].
WCh *rVy- < *raHi- "mix up": Bks *royi*.
ECh *raHwa- "mix": Mig *rawwo*.

Alternation *a ~ *i.

2093 *raḫil- "sheep"

Sem *raḫil- "sheep" [1], "lamb" [2]: Akk *laḫru* [1], Hbr *rāḥēl* [1], Aram (Jud) *raḥl-* [1], Arab *riḫl-*, *raḫil-* [1], Soq *reḥl-oh* [2].
Metathesis of liquids in Akk. In Hbr the word is attested as a proper name. Arab -*i*- may be a result of the assimilation of vowels.
Eg *rhny* "Amon's lamb" (NK).
Secondary *h* < *ḫ in Late Eg. Vocalic -*y*.

Probably, connected with SA *reH- "she-goat" (Afar *ree-ta*) and LEC *reH- id. (Som *rih*, Or *ree*, Rnd *riyyo*).

2094 *rak-/*rik- "be thin"

Sem *rik- "be thin, be weak": Hbr *rak*, Arab *rkk* [-*i*-].
WCh *rak- "be thin": Hs *rāke*, Dera *rago*.
ECh *rVk- "become meager": Mkk *ˀerk-iyo*.

Alternation *a ~ *i.

2095 *raḳ- "bank, coast"

Sem *raḳḳ- "bank, coast": Akk *raqqatu*.
Eg *rwḏ* "bank, coast" (n).
Palatalization and inlaut -*w*- reflect a secondary formation *rVwVḳ-.

2096 *ram- "land, field"

Eg *rmrm.t* "kind of field" (pyr).

Reduplication.
WCh *ram-* "land, place": DB *ram.*

2097 *ram- "throw"

Sem **rVmVy-* "throw, shoot": Akk *ramû*, Hbr *rmy*, Arab *rmy* [-*i*-]. Based on **rVm-*.
ECh **ram-* "throw" [1], "shoot" [2]: Ngam *ram* [1], Mobu *rame* [1], Smr *ram* [2].

2098 *ram- "roar, speak"

Sem **rVm-* "roar": Akk *ramāmu*, Arab *rmm* [-*u*-].
WCh **ram-* "tell": Ngz *ramu.*

2099 *ramVk- "(free) man"

Sem **ramk-* "priest": Akk *ramku.*
Eg *rmṯ* "man" (pyr).
Progressive palatalization of **k.*

2100 *rasVw- "death, sleep"

Eg *rsw.t* "dream, sleep" (n.) (MK).
WCh **ras-* "death": Hs *rasūwa.*

2101 *raw- "sky"

Eg *rw* "sky" (pyr).
WCh **rVw-* "sky": Krk *rəwi*, Fyer *ruruwe.*
Partial reduplication in Fyer. Cf. **riʾ-* "cloud": Bks *riʾ*, DB *riʾ*.
Rift **raw-* "sky": Bur *raw.*

2102 *rawad- "descend"

Sem **wVrVd-* "descend" [1], "come" [2]: Akk *warādu* [1], Hbr *yrd* [1], Arab *wrd* [2], Gz *wrd* [1].
Metathesis.
SA **ra[w]ad-* "descend": Saho *raad-*, Afar *raad-*.

2103 *rawaḥ- "move, walk"

Sem **rūḥ-* "go away": Arab *rwḥ* [*-u-*].
Berb **rVwVH-* "come": Izy *τuλud*.
WCh **raw-/*ray-* "enter" [1], "run" [2]: Ank *ru* [1], Grk *ru* [1], Bol *rii-* [1], Krk *raa* [1], Bele *rii-* [1], Krf *rii-* [1], Gera *rii-* [1], Glm *ry-* [1], Grm *rii-* [1], Dira *riya* [2], Cagu *rey* [2], Ngz *rəwə* [2].
Loss of the auslaut laryngeal.
LEC **ra[w]aḥ-* "follow": Rnd *raaḥ-*.

2104 *reʔ- "see"

Sem **rVʔVy-* "see": Hbr *rʔy*, Arab *rʔy*, SAr *rʔy*, Gz *rʔy*.
Bed *reh-*, *erh-* "see".

2105 *reb- "all"

Eg *nb* "all, every" (pyr), Copt **nib*: Fym *nibi*, Boh *nib-*, Shd *nim*.
Irregular *n-* < **r-*. Assimilation of consonants in Shd.
WCh **ryab-* "all": Sha *ryap*.

2106 *reẖ- "man"

Eg *rẖy.t* "men" (pyr).
Vocalic *-y*.
WCh **ryaH-* "male" (adj.): Bks *re*.

Cf. CCh **raH-* "man": LPe *raʔ* (in a phrase *sum raʔ* "person" ← *"man's name")

2107 *reḳ- "pour, soak"

Sem **rVḳ-* "pour out" [1], "sprinkle" [2]: Hbr *rwq*, *ryq* [1], Gz *rqy* [2].
WCh **ryaḳ-* "moisten": Dera *reke*.

2108 *reḳ-/*reḳay- "climb"

Sem **rVḳay-* "climb, rise": Arab *rqy* [*-a-*].
WCh **ryaḳVy-* "rise": Klr *regy-*.
LEC **riḳ-* "climb": Or *riqa*.

2109 *reḳid- "jump"

Sem **rVḳVd-* "jump": Akk *raqādu*, Hbr *rqd*, Aram (Jud) *rqd*.
Cf. also Arab *raqad-ān-* "jump, leap".
ECh **ryaḍik-* < **ryadiḳ-* "jump": Dng *rɛḍikɛ*.
Metathesis.

Derived from **reḳ-/*reḳay-* "climb"?

2110 *rib- "vessel"

Sem **rīb-* "vessel": Akk *rību*.
Eg *rb.t* "copper pot".
CCh **rVb-* "pot": Mrg *r̃r̃ba*.

2111 *riĉ- "sprinkle"

Sem **rVŝ-* "sprinkle": Arab *ršš*, Hss *reś*.
Agaw **ʔa-rič-* "sprinkle": Aun *areč-əŋ*.
Prefix **ʔa-*.

2112 *ridaġ- "dirt"

Sem **radaġ-* "dirt": Arab *radaġ-at-*.
Assimilation of vowels.
CCh **ridaH-* "dirt": FG *r̃r̃ḍa*, Kap *rrḍa*, HF *ʔurḍa*, Gudu *ridē*.
Gudu reflects **riday-* < **ridaH-*.

2113 *rigad- "foot, leg"

WCh **gVrVd-* "leg": Wrj *gərdai*, Cagu *gərde*.
Metathesis.
Bed *ragad* "foot, leg".
Assimilation of vowels.
SA **rigid-* "foot, leg": Saho *rigid*.
Assimilation of vowels.
Rift **digir-* "foot trace": Irq *digir*.
Metathesis.

2114 *ri^{c}- "break"

Sem *rVc- "break": Hbr *r^{cc}*.
CCh *riy- < *riH- "destroy": Gis *riye*.

2115 *ri^{c}- "drive, chase"

Sem *rVcay- "graze" [1], "herd" (v.) [2]: Akk *re'ū* [2], Ug *r^{c}y* [2], Hbr *r^{c}y* [1], Arab *r^{c}y* [-a-] [2], SAr *r^{c}y* [1], Gz *r^{c}y* [2], Hss *rō* [2], Mhr *rō* [2], Soq *re^{c}e* [2].
Based on *rVc-.
LEC *'a-ri'- "chase": Or *ari'a*.

2116 *ri^{c}- "friend"

Sem *rī^{c}- "friend": Akk *rū'u*, Hbr *rē^{ac}*.
ECh *rVHi- "friend" [1], "husband" [2]: Dng *roya*, Mubi *ro*.
Secondary vocalism?

2117 *rih- "evening"

Eg *rwhꜣ* "evening" (n).
Reflects *riwah- based on *rih-.
CCh *riH- "evening": Lame *riya*, Zime *ria*.
Lame *-y-* < *-H-.

2118 *riḥim- "uterus, pregnancy"

Sem *raḥm-/*riḥm- "uterus": Akk *rēmu*, Hbr *reḥem*, Aram (Jud) *raḥam-*, Arab *riḥm-*, *raḥim-*.
LEC *riHim- "pregnant": Or *riimaa*.

2119 *rim- "insect"

Sem *rimm- "ant, larva": Akk *rimmatu*, Arab *rimm-at-*.
ECh *'i-ri-rim- "insect": Bid *'irīrimo*.
Partial reduplication.
SA *rimm- "worm": Saho *rimme*.
LEC *rimm- "ant, termite": Or *rimma*.
Cf. also Or *raammoo* "worm, parasite".

Cf. WCh *ma-ryam- "scorpion" (Hs *maryamu*)?

2120 *rim- "rise"

Sem **rūm-* "be high": Hbr *rwm*.
Based on **rVm-*.
WCh **rim-* "stand (on hind legs)": Hs *rīmī*.

2121 *rim- "earth, clay"

Sem **rimm-* "wet earth": Arab *rimm-*.
Eg *ỉm* "clay" (MK).
Note *ỉ-* < **r-*, cf. **rüwun-* "wind".

2122 *riman- "fruit"

Sem **rimān-* "granate": Akk *lurmu*, Hbr *rimmōn*, Arab *rummān-*.
Assimilation of sonants and metathesis in Akk.
Eg *rrm.t* "fruit" (NK).
Assimilation of *liquida* and metathesis.

2123 *ripan- "hair"

Eg *nꜣp* "hairlock" (pyr).
Metathesis **nirap-* from **ripan-*?
LEC **rifan-* "hair": Or *rifen-sa*, Arb *riyfan*, Gdl *riyfan-ta*, Arb *ruufan*.
Wrz **rifan-* "hair": War *rrifo-ko*, Hrs *rifan-ko*, Dob *rifak-ko*.

2124 *riw-/*riy- "play"

Eg *rwy.t* "kind of game" (MK).
WCh **ri-riy-* "children's game": Hs *rīriya*.
Partial reduplication.
CCh **riw-* "play": Zime *riu*.

Consonantal alternation **-w-* ~ **-y-*.

2125 *riw-/*riy- "fire; burn"

Eg *rwy* "flame" (n).
Vocalic *-y*.
CCh **ray-/*riy-* "burn": Daba *ri*, Masa *raia-*.

Consonantal alternation **-w-* ~ **-y-*.

2126 *riyVᶜ- "grow"

Sem **riᶜ-* "grow": Arab *ryᶜ* [*-i-*].
WCh **riy-* "multiply": Tng *riy*.

2127 *roʾ- "snake"

Eg *rꜣ* "snake" (NK).
WCh **rwaʾ-* "cobra": DB *rwa*.

2128 *rob- "rhinoceros, hyppopotamus"

Eg *irbꜣ* "kind of animal, rhinoceros (?)" (OK).
Prefix *i-*.
LEC **rob-* "hyppopotamus": Or *roobi*.
HEC **rob-* "hyppopotamus": Sid *robee*, Had *lobe*.
Irregular *l-* in Had.

2129 *rog- "cereal"

Eg *rḏrḏ* "cereals" (gr).
Reduplication. Progressive palatalization of **g*.
WCh **rwag-* "cassawa": Hs *rōgo*.

2130 *roq- "bird"

Sem **ruḫḫ-* "fabulous bird": Arab *ruḫḫ-*.
Eg *rḫy.t* "kind of bird" (OK).
Suffix *-y*.
CCh **ruq-* "ostrich": Lame *ruko*.
ECh **rwak-* "heron": Mkk *rooke*.

2131 *rubud- "ashes"

Sem **rubd-* "colour of ash, ashen": Arab *rubd-at-*.
WCh **rubuḍ-* "hot fine ash": Hs *rubuḍī*.
Secondary emphatic. Another variant is Hs *ribiḍī*.

2132 *ruḥ- "breath, soul"

Sem **rūḥ-* "blow, breath" 1, "spirit" 2: Hbr *rūᵃḥ* 1, Aram (Syr) *rūḥ-* 2, Arab *rūḥ-* 2.

SA **roḥ-* "breath, soul": Saho *roḥe*.
LEC **ruḥ-* "breath, soul": Som *ruuḥ*.

2133 *rukub- "knee, thigh"

Sem **rukb-* "knee": Arab *rukb-at-*.
Cf. also Aram *ʾarkūbā* id.
CCh **rukub-* "thigh": Zgh *rukufe*.
Zgh *-f-* < **-b-*?

2134 *rum- "lion"

Eg *ꜣm* "lion" (gr).
WCh **ʾirum-* "leopard": Diri *ʾirum*, Pol *yərum*.
CCh **lum-* < **HV-rum-* "lion": Lame *lumu*, LPe *lumu*.

2135 *rusup- "ash"

Sem **rVšp-* "ashes, flame": Hbr *rešep*.
WCh **rup̣us-* "hot ashes": Hs *ruḅušī*.
Metathesis. Note emphatic **p̣*.

2136 *ruy- "tree"

Eg *wry.t* "trees" (XXII).
Vocalic *w-*.
WCh **ruy-* "tree, forest": Krk *riya*, Ngm *royi*, Tng *riya*, Bele *ru*, Krf *ru*, Gera *ry*.

2137 *rüʾ- "intestine"

Sem **riʾ-* "lungs": Hbr *rēʾā*, Arab *riʾ-at-*, *riyy-at-*, Hss *reyī*, Mhr *ḥe-ryī*, Shh *rōt*.
Berb **rV-* "lung(s)": Izy *τuλin* (pl.), Kby *τurəṭ*.
WCh **ruy-* < **ruH-* "intestine": Siri *ruya*.
Cf. **raw-* id.: Jmb *rawi*, Mbu *rawwi*, Cagu *roh-on*.

2138 *rüḳ- "be thin"

Sem **riḳ-* "be thin" [1], "be shallow" [2]: Akk *raqāqu* [1], Arab *rqq*

[-*i*-] [1], Gz *rqq* [1], Jib *reḳḳ* [2], Hss *req* [2], Mhr *req* [2], Shh *rεq* [2].
WCh **ruḳ-* "become meager": Bol *rukk-*.

2139 *rüm- "be bad, be rotten"

Sem **rim-* "be rotten (of bones)" [1], "be worn, be frayed" [2]: Hbr *rmm* [1], Arab *rmm* [-*i*-] [1], Hss *rem* [2], Mhr *rem* [2], Shh *rim* [2].
WCh **rVm-* "bad": Bol *romo*.
ECh **rum-* "rot": Mkk *ruume*.

2140 *rüw- "water"

Sem **riw-/*riy-* "moistening" [1], "abundant water" [2]: Hbr *rī* [1], Arab *riway-* [2].
Eg *wrw* "pond" (pyr).
Orthographic representation of **rVw-*.
WCh **ruw-* "water, rain": Hs *ruwā*.

Cf. Rift **raʾ-* "dew": Alg *raʾu*, Bur *raʾu*. Eg *wrrw* "pit filled with water, basin" (MK) may be a derivative.

2141 *rüwun- "wind"

Eg *i͗wn* "wind" (pyr).
Note *i͗-* < **r-*.
WCh **ruwun-* "wind": Kry *ruwun*, Miya *ruwun*, Mbu *ruwən*.

2142 *rVʾ-/*rVw- "speak"

Sem **rūy-* "render other person's words": Arab *rwy* [-*i*-].
Eg *rꜣ* "sentence, speech, language" (pyr).

Consonantal alternation **-ʾ-* ~ **-w-*.

2143 *rVhob- "be hot"

Eg *rhb* "hot ashes" (BD), Copt **ʾelhōb*: Akh *lhōb*, Boh *elhōb*, Shd *elhōb*.
ECh **rVHwab-* "hot ashes": Bid *roob*.

2144 *rVhVn- "leave"

Eg *rhn* "leave, lean" (MK).
CCh **lVn-* < **rVHVn-*"leave": Gid *lən*.

2145 *rVsVᶜ- "evil; be evil"

Sem **rVšVᶜ-* "treat severely" [1], "be evil, behave badly" [2], "be slack" [3], "forget, neglect" [4]: Akk *ruššû* [1], Hbr *ršᶜ* [2], Arab *rsᶜ* [3], Gz *rsᶜ* [4].
Eg *ᶜrš* "evil" (XVIII).
Metathesis. Irregular *-š* < **-s-*.

An alternative reconstruction is **ᶜVrVs-*.

*s

2146 *sa- "house"

Eg *s.t* "dwelling, place" (pyr), Copt **se* "house": Boh *se-*, Shd *se-*.
WCh **sV-saw-* "hut": Ngz *səsau*.
Reduplication.

2147 *saʾ- "climb, stand up"

Sem **šVʾVw-* "climb": Arab *sʾw* [*-u-*].
Based on **šVʾ-*.
CCh **saʾ-* "stand up": Log *sa*.
ECh **saw-/*say-* "stand up": Smr *so*, Sbn *swā*, Tob *say*.
From **saʾ-*.
Dhl *saa-ḍ-* "stand".

2148 *saʾ-/*saw- "tree"

Sem **šaʾ-* "tree": Akk *šāʾu*.
WCh **saw-/*say-* "tree with thorns": Tng *saawe, saaye*.
CCh **syaʾ-* < **say-* "wood": Gaa *šeʾa*.
ECh **sVw-* < **sVʾ-* "tree": Sok *səwi*.

Consonantal alternation **-ʾ-* ~ **-w-*.

2149 *saˀaf- "snare"

Berb **saf-* "snare": Shn *a-saf.*
Contraction.
WCh **saˀaf-* "snare": Hs *safū, sahū.*

2150 *saˀap- "hair"

Sem **šaˀap-* "horse mane": Arab *saˀaf-.*
LEC **sap-* "pubic hair": Or *sap̣ii.*
Or *-p̣-* reflects the influence of a lost inlaut laryngeal.

2151 *sab- "bird"

Sem **šab-šab-* "small bird": Tgr *säbsab.*
Reduplication.
Berb **sVbib-* "small bird": Ahg *šəbibi.*
Partial reduplication.
ECh **syab- < *sabi-* "dove": Kbl *te-seba.*
Prefix *te-* in Kbl.

2152 *sab- "be hot, burn"

Eg *ȝsb* "burn" (BD).
Initial *ȝ-* may reflect a prefix or indicate the root vowel **a.*
ECh **sab-* "burn": Tum *hab.*

2153 *sab- "go, walk"

Sem **šVb-* "walk slowly" 1, "come" 2: Arab *sbsb* 1, Tgr *šbb* 2.
Reduplication in Arab.
WCh **sabVH-* "return" 1, "go out" 2: Hs *saḅō* 1, Diri *səbo* 2.
Suffix **-VH-.*
CCh **sVb-* "go out" 1, "drive" 2: Daba *subu* 1, FBw *səbi* 2.
ECh **sab-* "walk" (n.): Sbn *saba.*

2154 *sab- "wall"

Eg *sb.t.y* "wall" (XVIII).
SA **sab-sab-* "wall": Afar *sabsab.*
Reduplication.

2155 *sabV³-/*sabVy- "sin, lie"

Eg *sby* "rebellion" (MK).
WCh **saḇ-* < **sabV³-* "sin" [1], "evil" [2], "lie" [3]: Hs *sāḇō* [1], Tng *saḇyo* [2], Pero *čaba* [3].
Suffix *-*VH*-?
LEC **sob-* "lie" (v.): Or *soba*.
Secondary **-o-* before a labial.

Consonantal alternation *-³- ~ *-*y*-.

2156 *sab-sib- "hairlock"

Sem **šab-šib-* "dishevelled hair": Arab (dial.) *sabāsib-* (pl.).
Berb **sVb-sub-* "hairlock": Kby *a-šəbšub*.
Secondary **u*?

Reduplication of the original **sab-* "hair", cf. **sabib-* id.

2157 *sabaḥ- "bird"

Eg *sbḥ* "kind of bird" (OK).
WCh **saHab-* "guinea fowl": Cagu *sāḇ-un*.
Metathesis.

2158 *sabib- "hair"

Sem **šabīb-* "mane, hair of the tail": Arab *sabīb-*.
Berb **sVbVb-* "eyebrow" [1], "hair" [2]: Izd *a-šβaβ* [1], Kby *a-səbbub* [2].
Partial reduplication. Related to **sab-sib-* "hairlock".

2159 *sabil-/*sabul- "iron, weapon"

Sem **šabal-* "bunch of spears": Arab *sabal-*.
Berb **sVbul-* "long knife, dagger" [1], "long needle" [2]: Ghd *a-ssəbul-ət* [1], Sml *a-sbūl* [2], Ahg *tə-subl-a* [2], Snus *ti-ssubl-a* [2], Nfs *tə-ssubl-a* [2].
LEC **sibil-* "iron": Or *sibillaa*.
Assimilation of vowels from **sabil-*.
HEC **sibil-* "iron": Sid *sibillaa*.
Assimilation of vowels, cf. LEC. A LEC loanword?

2160 *sad- "rope"

Sem **ma-šad-* "bast rope": Arab *masad-*.
Prefix **ma-*. Cf. denominative Arab *msd* [-*u*-]"plait".
ECh **sad-* "rope": Smr *sādi*.

2161 *saduf-/*siduf- "container"

Sem **šadup-* "box for tablets": Akk *šaduppu*.
Eg *sdf* "measure (for figs)" (n).
CCh **sidVf-* "pot": Mtk *šidɛf*.
Secondary vowel of the second syllable.

Alternation **a* ~ **i*.

2162 *saf- "bird"

Sem **sVpVᶜ-* "falcon": Arab *ʾasfaᶜ-*.
Derivative in **ʾa-*.
Berb **saf-* "kind of bird": Ayr *t-əssaf*.
Eg *sf.t* "kind of bird" (gr).
WCh **saHaf-* "falcon, hawk": Hs *šāfo*, *šāho*.
Metathesis.

Any relation to HS **saf-/*suf-* "soar, jump"? Note that Sem and WCh reflect a derivative: **safaᶜ-* "bird".

2163 *saf- "morning"

WCh **saf-* "early morning": Hs *sāfē*.
LEC **saf-* "mid-morning": Or *saafaa*.

2164 *saf-/*suf- "soar, jump"

Sem **šup-* "soar": Arab *sff* [-*u*-].
CCh **saf-* "jump": Mofu *safə*, Log *safə*.

Alternation **a* ~ **u*.

2165 *safih- "fool"

Sem **šafih-* "fool": Arab *safīh-*.

WCh **saf-* "fool": Hs *sāfā*.
Loss of the auslaut laryngeal.

2166 *sag- "bring"

Eg *sḏꜣ* "bring" (pyr).
Progressive palatalization of **g*.
ECh **sag-* "bring": Smr *sagə*, Mubi *sagu*.

2167 *saᶜ- "do, make"

Sem **šVᶜay-* "do, act": Arab *sᶜy* [-*a*-].
Based on an earlier **sVᶜ-*.
CCh **saH-* "do, make": Msg *sa*.

2168 *saᶜab- "cut"

Eg *sᶜb* "cut, castrate" (MK).
WCh **saHVb-* "cut (hair)": Hs *saḅe*.
ECh **saHab-* "carve": Kwn *sābe*.

Cf. ECh **samb-* "cut": Mobu *sāmbe*, Ngm *sambe*. Derived from **sib-* "cut".

2169 *saḥ- "wind"

Sem **šaḥāḥ-* "wind" [1], "air, atmosphere" [2]: Akk *šēḫu*, Arab *saḥāḥ-*.
Partial reduplication.
Eg *swḥ* "wind" (XXII).
Secondary formation with C^2 = -*w*- based on **sVḥ-*.

2170 *saḥan- "break, cut"

Sem **šVḥan-* "break": Arab *sḥn* [-*a*-].
WCh **saHan-* "grind": DB *šon*.
CCh **san-H-* "cut": Msg *saŋ*.
Metathesis.

2171 *saḫ- "bile, urine"

Eg *sḫ* "bile" (med).
Rift **saḫ-* "gall bladder" [1], "urine" [2]: Irq *saḫi* [1], Kwz *saha* [2].
Dhl *saaḥaw-* "urinate".
Verbal derivative.

2172 *saḫan- "burn, be warm"

Sem **šVḫan-* "be warm, be hot" [1], "be inflamed" [2], "warm" (v.) [3]: Akk *šaḫānu* [1], Ug *šḫn* [2], Arab *sḫn* [*-a-*, *-u-*] [1], Gz *sḫn* [1], Tgy *sähanä* [1], Jib *šχan* [3].
WCh **saHan-* "warm (v.); be hot": Bks *san*, DB *san*, Peo *čeno*.

2173 *saḫim- "bat"

Eg *sꜣḫm.w* "bat" (MK).
-ꜣ- may reflect **a*.
CCh **sim-* "bat": Msg *šimašim-et*.
Reduplication in Msg. **sim-* may reflect an earlier **sVHim-* .

2174 *sak- "row"

Sem **šakk-* "row": Arab *sakk-*.
WCh **sak-* "row": Sura *saak*.
If not borrowed from Arab.

2175 *sak- "ass"

Eg *sk* "young of an ass" (n), Copt **sēh* id.: Boh *sēh*, Shd *sēh*.
WCh **sak-* "ass": Pol *šaki*.

2176 *sak- "pour, flow"

Eg *sṯꜣ* "flow" (XVIII).
Palatalization of **k*.
WCh **sak-* "filter" (v.) [1], "pour" [2]: Ang *šak* [1], Diri *səka* [2], Miya *səka* [2], Jmb *səka* [2].
CCh **sVk-* "pour": HNk *ška-la*, FG *ška-mti*.

2177 *sak-/*suk- "hoe" (v.)

Sem **šuk-* "harrow" (v.): Akk *šakāku* [-*u*-].
Berb **sVk-* "plough, till": Mzab *skka*.
Eg *skȝ* "hoe" (v.) (pyr), Copt **sk'ay*: Boh *sk'ai*, Shd *skai*.
Vocalic -*ȝ*.
WCh **sak-/*suk-* "plough" (v.): Sura *sak*, Tng *suk*.

Alternation **a* ~ **u*.

2178 *saḳ- "weave, plait"

WCh **saḳ-* "plait": Hs *sāḳa*, Gwn *saka*, *šaka*, Ang *sak*, Brm *sake*.
CCh **sa-sak-* "weave": Msg *sasaka*.
Partial reduplication.
Agaw **saḳ-* "plait, sew" [1], "weave" [2]: Bil *saḳw-* [1], Xmr *saḳ-* [1], Kwr *saγ-* [1], Dmb *šaγ-* [1], Kem *saaχ-* [2], Aun *saχ-*, *saγ-* [1].
Dhl *sook'-* "twist".
Cf. also *sakaʔ-* "plait, twist".

2179 *saḳ- "leg"

Sem **šāḳ-* "leg": Akk *sāqu*, Hbr *šōq*, Aram (Syr) *šōqō*, Arab *sāq-*.
WCh **saḳu-* "leg": Bks *saku-r*, Sha *səkaʔu*, Bol *šeke*, Ngm *seke*.
CCh **sak-* "leg": Mtk *sak*, Gude *səke*, Kus *msake*, Sok *saka-dum*.

2180 *saḳ- "cut"

Eg *sḳḳ* "cut" (NK).
WCh **saḳ-* "cut (down)" [1], "carpenter" [2]: Hs *sassaḳā* [2], Gwn *šešeke* [1 2], Ang *sak* [1], Sha *šak* [1], Ngz *sasku* [1 2].

2181 *salaᶜ- "tear, break"

Sem **šVlaᶜ-* "pierce, split": Arab *slᶜ* [-*a*-].
Together with Hbr *slᶜ* may go back to **sVlaᶜ-*.
WCh **sal-* "cut": Gera *šallə-*.

2182 *salam- "tree"

Sem **šalām-* "kind of tree": Arab *salām-*.
ECh **sVlVm-* "kind of tree": Mig *solmo*.

2183 *salap- "plant"

Sem **šalap-* "marsh plant": Akk *šalapānu*.
Derivative in *-ān-*.
Eg *srp.t* "plant" (gr).

2184 *salaq- "skin" (v.)

Sem **šVlaḫ-/*šVluḫ-* "tear out" [1], "skin" (v.) [2], "change skin (of serpents)" [3]: Akk *šalāḫu* [1], Hbr *šlḥ* [2], Arab *slḫ* [*-a-*, *-u-*] [3].
ECh **salak-* "skin" (v.): Mubi *sallaka*.

2185 *sam- "poison"

Sem **šamm-* "poison": Akk *šammu*, Arab *samm-*, *simm-*, *summ-*, Tgy *səmi*, Har *summi*, Soq *sam*, Hss *sem*, Mhr *sem*, Shh *sεm*.
CCh **sam-* "poison": Mba *sam*.

2186 *sam- "be high"

Sem **šVmVw-* "be high, rise": Arab *smw* [*-u-*].
Based on biconsonantal **šVm-*.
WCh **sam-* "lift (with both hands)": Tng *sami*.

2187 *sam-sam- "insect"

Sem **šum-šum-* "red ant": Arab *sumsum-*.
Secondary vocalism.
ECh **sam-sam-* "flea": Lele *samasama*.

Reduplication. Cf. a non-reduplicated form attested in Hs *šam* "kind of insect".

2188 *samaʾ- "sky"

Sem **šamāʾ-/*šamāy-* "sky": Akk *šamû*, Ug *šmm*, Hbr *šāmayim*, Aram (Syr) *šemayyō*, Arab *samāʾ-*, Gz *samāy*, Hss *semē*, Mhr *semēʿ*.
WCh **sam-* "sky": Hs *sama*.
From Arab?

2189 *saman- "be still, sit"

Eg *smn* "remain still" (XVIII).
CCh **saman-* "sit": Msg *samana*.

2190 *sa(m)bir- "bird"

Berb **sṾbibir-* "butterfly; small bird": Kby *i-mə- šbibir*.
Reduplication.
WCh **sabir-* "kind of bird": Hs *šābiri*.
Note the loss of the nasal element in the WCh reflex of *-*mb*-.
ECh **sabir-* "guinea fowl": Smr *sibir*, Sok *sōir*.
Bed *šambar* "pelican".
Assimilation of vowels.
LEC **šimbir-* "kind of bird": Som *šimbir*, Or *šimbira*, *simbira*.
Assimilation of vowels.

2191 *samf- "basket"

WCh **samf-* "basket made of grass": Hs *samfo*.
LEC **sumf-* "basket": Or *suumfa*.
Secondary **u* before a labial.
HEC **samf-* "basket made of grass": Had *samfo*.

Cf. also CCh "basket" **ʒamf-* (Masa *zamfa*) with an unexpected **ʒ*-.

2192 *san- "year"

Sem **šan-* "year": Akk *šattu*, Ug *šnt*, Hbr *šānā*, Aram (Syr) *šattō*, Arab *san-at-*, Hss *senet*, Mhr *senēt*, Soq *sanah*.
WCh **sVn-* "rainy season": Tng *sene*.
Cf. also a derivative **wa-sVn-* "year, rainy season" (Wrj *wasən-na*, Kry *wasən*, Diri *ašen*, Miya *wasəsen*, Siri *wasənuwa*, Mbu *wasən*, Jmb *wasun*, Pol *waŝin*, Geji *waŝin*, Say *waŝun*). Bol *soni* "year", Ngm *sani* id. may be Arab loanwords.

2193 *san-/*sin- "brother"

Eg *sn* "brother" (pyr), Copt **son*: Fym *san*, Akh *san*, Boh *son*, Shd *son*.

WCh **sVn-* "brother": Cagu *šən*.
Cf. Mpn *son* "relatives, clan".
ECh **sin-* "(elder) brother": Tum *həna*, Kwan *sēni*, Bid *sin-te*, Sbn *syan*, Kera *seenə*, Dng *sin*, Jegu *šin*, Mubi *sin*, Sok *šin-tu*.
Bed *saan* "brother".
Agaw **šan-* "brothers" (pl.): Bil *šan-*, Kem *šän*.
Wrz **ʔa-šin-* "nephew": Gaw *ašin-ko*.

Alternation **a* ~ **i* in which **a* seems to be connected with pl., as in Agaw.

2194 *san-/*sin- "nose"

Agaw **ʔa-san-/*ʔa-sin-* "nose": Xmr *esiŋ*, Xmt *asən*, Kem *əssan*.
SA **san-* "nose": Saho *san*, Afar *san*.
LEC **san-/*sin-* "nose": Som *san*, Boni *saŋa*, Rnd *sän*, Gel *sɔɔnɔ*, Kon *soona*, Bus *sino*, Gdl *sina*, Arb *soono*.
HEC **san-* "nose": Sid *sano*, Dar *sano*, Had *sane*, Ala *sano*, Bmb *sanna*, Kmb *sane*, Tmb *sana*.
Dhl *sina* "nose".
Omot **sin-* "nose": Ome *siŋan*, Gim *sən*, Nao *sin-us*, Maji *sinu*.

Alternation **a* ~ **i*. Some forms reflect a laryngeal in the auslaut (HS **san-H-/*sin-H-*). The stem is present only in Cush but its derivatives in other families prove its HS status. Cf. also Wrz **sind-* id. (War *sindi-*, Gaw *sinde*, Gob *sənde*, Cam *sindi-*) and Omot **sinṭ-/*sind-* id. (Ome *sinḍaa*, Mch *šiiṭo*, Anf *šinto*, Bwo *šinṭa*). Related to HS **sin-* "smell" (v.).

2195 *san-/*sun- "be satisfied"

Sem **šVnVy-* "be satisfied": Arab *sny*.
WCh **san-H-* "be glad": Sura *šaŋ*.
CCh **sVn-* "wish": Lame *səna*.
Omot **šun-* "love": Yam *šun-*, Kaf *šun-*, Anf *šun-*, Bwo *šun-*, Mch *šunn-*, Gim *šun-*.

Alternation **a* ~ **u*.

2196 *sanb- "lungs, breath"

Eg *snb* "breath" (gr).

Bed *samb-ut* ''lungs''.
Agaw **sanb-* ''lungs'': Bil *sänbii*, Xmr *sebbaa*, Kwr *sambaa*, Kem *sambii*, Aun *saambii*.
LEC **samb-* ''lungs'': Som *sambab*, Or *somba*, Arb *soñbot*.
HEC **šamb-* ''lungs'': Sid *šamboo*, Dar *šoombu*, Kab *šombo*.
Omot **šomb-* ''lungs'': Kaf *šomboo*, Mch *šombo*.

Assimilation **-nb-* > **-mb-* in most Cush languages.

2197 *saniʔ- ''go, run''

Sem **šVnVʔ-* ''trot'' (v.): Akk *šanû*.
WCh **san-H-* ''go out'': Fyer *saŋ*.
LEC **seHen-* < **saHin-* ''enter'': Or *seena*.
Metathesis and contraction.

2198 *saniH-/*siniH- ''know, remember''

Berb **sin-* ''know'': Izy *isin*.
WCh **saniH-/*siniH-* ''know'': Hs *sani*, *šina*, Wrj *sən*, Kry *sən*, Diri *čən*, Miya *sən*, Paa *sinə*, Cagu *sən*, Siri *səniwi*, Mbu *sin*, Jmb *sən*, Say *yisəŋ*, Fyer *šaŋ*, Bks *šaŋi*, Sha *syen*, Klr *syen*.
CCh **san-H-/*sin-H-* ''know'' [1], ''remember'' [2]: Hwn *sən* [1], Mrg *sini* [2], Hil *sini* [1], Gis *san*, *sin* [1], Bld *šiŋ* [1], Log *sən* [1], Bud *hin* [1].
ECh **sin-* ''know'': Ndam *asine*, Mobu *asəne*.
LEC **seHen-* ''memory'': Or *seenaa*.
Metathesis. LEC goes back to **saHin-* with assimilation of vowels.
Alternation **a* ~ **i*. Related to **sun-* ''know''.

2199 *san-sun- ''smell'' (v.)

Eg *snsn* ''breathe, smell'' (MK).
WCh **san-sun-* ''smell'': Hs *sunsunā*, *sansanā*, Paa *sasun*.

Reduplication of **sin-* ''smell''.

2200 *saq- ''house''

Sem **ʔašaḫ-* ''barn'': Akk *ašaḫḫu*.
Prefix **ʔa-*.

WCh **sVq-* "house": Krf *šoko*.

Cf. Berb **sVk-* "build": Ghd *u-sək*.

2201 *saqam- "knife"

Eg *sḫm* "sword" (gr).
WCh **saqam-* "knife": Tng *sakam*.

2202 *sar- "wind"

Sem **šār-* "wind": Akk *šāru*.
WCh **sarar-* "cold wind": Hs *sarāra*.
Partial reduplication.

2203 *sar-/*sayar- "go"

Sem **šīr-* "go": Arab *syr* [-*i*-], Hss *seyōr*, Mhr *seyōr*.
Based on the original **šVr-*. Cf. Arab *sry* "travel at night" [-*i*-].
WCh **sayar-* "go": Sura *sor*.
CCh **sar-* "return": Hil *šař*.
ECh **sar-* "arrive": Mig *saraw*.

2204 *sasog- "tree"

Sem **šašūg-* "fruit tree": Akk *šaššūgu*, *šaššūqu*.
Eg *ssḏ* "wood" (pyr).
Progressive assimilation of **-g-*.

Partial reduplication of **sog-* "tree, wood".

2205 *sataw-/*satay- "drink"

Sem **šVtVy-* "drink": Akk *šatû*, Ug *šty*, Hbr *šty*, Aram *šty*, Gz *satya*, Tgr *sätäyä*, Har *säče*.
CCh **sawat-* "be thirsty": Mafa *sawat-*.
Metathesis.

Consonantal alternation **-w-* ~ **-y-*.

2206 *saṭüᶜ- "morning"

Sem *šaṭīᶜ- "dawn": Arab *saṭīᶜ-*.
WCh *saHuṭ- "morning": Bol *sato*, Buli *swidi*, Say *suta*, Dwot *soḍo*.
Metathesis.

2207 *saw-/*suᵓ- "go, run"

Sem *šVᵓVw- "run": Akk *šaᵓu*.
Based on *šVw-?
Berb *sV- "come": Kby *as*.
WCh *suᵓ- "run" [1], "enter" [2], "go out" [3]: Sura *su* [1], Ang *su* [1], Ank *su* [1], Grk *tu* [1], Pero *čü* [1], Pol *sā* [2], Fyer *sa* [3].
CCh *saw-/*suᵓ- "come" [1], "return" [2], "enter, go out" [3]: HF *šo* [2], Dgh *sawa* [1], Zgh *sawa* [1], Mofu *sawa* [2], Gis *sawa* [1], Bld *sawa* [1], Log *sa-*, *so-* [3].
SA *saH- "enter": Saho *sau*, Afar *sau*.
LEC *seᵓ- "go": Arb *seᵓ-aḍ-*.
Secondary *e.

2208 *sawaḥ- "bowl, basin"

Sem *šāḥ- < *ša[w]aḥ- "washing basin": Akk *šāḫu*.
Eg *swḥ.t* "bowl" (MK).

2209 *sawis- "snake, worm"

Sem *šūš- < *šVwVš- "worm": Arab *sūs-*.
Contraction.
LEC *šawis- "snake": Or *šaawwisa*.

Cf. CCh *sis- "snake": HNk *šiši*, FKi *šiši*, FG *šiši*, Kap *šiši*, Zgh *šiši*.

2210 *sawVḥ- "egg"

Eg *swḥ.t* "egg" (pyr).
WCh *saHVw- "egg": Wrj *cu-na*, Kry *ṣū*, Paa *asi*, Cagu *sohoyi*, Siri *ṣaw*, Mbu *çū*, Jmb *ašu*.
Metathesis.

Etymologically connected with *sawaḥ- "bowl, basin", cf. Skt *kośa-* "container, cup" → "egg".

2211 *sayab- "hair"

Sem **šayb-* "horse hair": Arab *sayb-*.
Berb **sVbV[y]-* "tail": Ayr *ta-sba-t*.
Metathesis.
ECh **syab- < *sVyab-* "hair": Kbl *ke-sebo*.
Prefix *ke-* in Kbl.

Cf. **sabib-* "hair".

2212 *sayaf- "knife, axe"

Sem **šayp-* "sword": Arab *sayf-*, Hss *sēf*.
WCh **sayaf-* "axe": Sura *sεp*, Ang *sap*, *sep*, *Mpn səhəp*, Ank *s'ap*, Chip *sεp*, Mnt *sεp*, Ank *sap*.
Omot **šVyVf-* "sword": Kaf *seefoo*.
Arab loanword?

Cf. Eg *zf* "knife" (MK) with unexpected *z-*.

2213 *sayal- "water flow"

Sem **šayl-* "current": Arab *sayl-*.
Cf. also Arab *syl* "flow" [*-i-*].
ECh **sēl- < *sayal-* "basin": Mkk *seelo*.

2214 *seb- "flow, pour"

Sem **šVb-* "flow" 1, "draw (water)" 2, "be poured" 3: Hbr *šʔb* 2, Aram *šʔb* 2, Arab *syb* [*-i-*] 1, Gz *sbb* 2.
Various formations based on **šVb-*.
ECh **sVb-* "pour": Mok *zibbe*.

2215 *sebit- "cut"

Sem **šVbit-/*šVbut-* "cut, shave": Arab *sbt* [*-i-*, *- u-*].
Secondary variant with **-u-* after a labial.
WCh **syabVt-* "strike with a knife": Hs *šabta*.
Note Hs *ša- < *sya-*.

Derived from **sib-* "cut, strike".

2216 *sef- "snake"

Sem *šipp- "winged snake" [1], "centipede" [2]: Arab siff-, suff- [1], Tgr səf [2].
Eg sfy "snake" (reg).
Vocalic -y.
ECh *syap- "snake": Kwan sēpi.
Omot *šef- "snake, lizard": Kaf šef-ittoo.

2217 *seḥ-/*seḥeḥ- "insect"

Eg sḥyḥ.t "kind of insect" (med).
Partial reduplication?
Bed see, sʾee "louse".

Cf. ECh *swaw- (< *swaH- ?)"termite": Mkk soowo.

2218 *sek- "pull"

Eg sṯȝ "pull" (pyr).
Progressive reduplication of *-k-.
Bed seku, soku "pull".
Assimilation of vowels in soku < seku.

2219 *seḳ- "walk, run"

WCh *syaḳ- "run away": Hs šēḳa.
CCh *suḳ- "come": HF sko, HNk skəy, HGh sugəy, FKi sku, FG suki, Zgh suɣaya.
From *syaḳu-?
HEC *šiḳ- "approach": Sid šiḳḳi i-, Had šiikaʾ-.

Related to *saḳ- "leg".

2220 *seḳ- "drink, give a drink"

Sem *šVḳ- "drink" [1], "give a drink" [2]: Akk šaqû [2], Ug šqy [1], Jib šeḳe [2].
WCh *syaḳu- "pour into vessel" [1], "give water (to a baby)" [2]: Hs šeḳa [1], Tng soke [2].
CCh *syaχwa- "drink" : HNk seχwi, FG sɛgwi, Kap seχwu.
Irregular *-χ-.

2221 *sen- "mug, pot"

Eg *sn.w* "mug" (MK).
CCh **syan-* "pot": Gul *seni*.

2222 *ser- "grind"

Eg *sȝy* "grind".
-*ȝ*- < HS *-*r*-.
CCh **syar-* "grind": Mba *ser*, Msg *sərə*.

2223 *ser- "cough" (n.)

Eg *sry.t* "cough" (med).
-*y* stand for a front vowel.
CCh **syar-* "cough": Daba *šeři*.

Cf. Arab *saʕr-* id.

2224 *sew-/*ŝew- "be dry"

Eg *šw* "dry" (med), *sšwy* "dry up" (pyr).
š- reflects an anlaut lateral.
WCh **syaH(a)-* "become dry": Bol *saa*, Krk *saa*, Dera *sēe*, Ngm *sa*.
CCh **sway-* "become dry": ZBt *soia*.
ECh **sVw-* "dry up": Mobu *səwe*.

Irregular correspondence of sibilants. WCh and CCh display considerable morphonological changes of the original stem: WCh **syaH-* < **syaw-* and CCh **sway-* < **swaʔi-*.

2225 *si- "go, come"

Eg *sysy* "hurry, hasten" (sarc).
No traces of the laryngeal. Reduplication.
WCh **siy-* "return": Tng *siy*.
CCh **si-* "come": Chb *si*, Bura *si*, Klb *ši-*, Wmd *ša*, Gude *ši*, Nza *ši*, FJ *si*, FMch *ši*, Bch *ši*, Bata *si*, *sa*.

Cf. Sem **šVʕay-* "go" (Arab *sʕy* [-*a*-], Soq *šeʕe*, Jib *šaʕe*) that may be a derivation based on **šVy-*.

2226 *siʾon-/*siwan- "sleep"

Sem **wVšVn-* "sleep": Hbr *yšn*, Arab *wsn*.
Metathesis. Cf. also **šin-* "sleep" (n.): Akk *šittu*, Ug *šnt*, Hbr *šēnā*, Aram (Syr) *šenᵉtō*, Arab *sin-at-*.
WCh **sVn-* "sleep": Bol *sunu*, Tng *sine*, Ngm *sun*, Krf *šan-*, Gera *sin*, Glm *san*, Wrj *sən*, Kry *sənasan*, Miya *sən*, Paa *asin*, Siri *sun-suni*, Mbu *sən*, Bks *sun-at*, DB *sunan*.
CCh **siʾwan-* "dream": Gbn *sənaʾ-ata*, Boka *sin-ata*, Bura *suni*, Chb *sini*, Klb *šəʾūnyi*, Mba *saŋ*, Mnd *šine*, Zgh *suwana*, Gvo *suwana*, Daba *šini*, Gude *sənin*, Gudu *syon-cii*, Nza *soʾoni*, Log *san*, Lame *syɛne*, Bnn *siyena*.
ECh **suwan-* "sleep, dream": Lele *sōn*, Kera *soone*, Kwan *suwən*, Mig *suniyi*, Jegu *suun-*, Mubi *suno*, Brg *soona*, Mkk *suun-*, Sok *sonisoni*.
SA **son-* "sleep" (n.): Saho *sonoo*, Afar *sonoo*.
Contraction.

2227 *siʾub- "worm"

Eg *sȝb.t* "motley snake" (pyr).
ECh **sub-* < **sVHub-* "worm": Lele *subo*.
LEC **siHib-* "worm": Or *siiba*.
Assimilation of vowels.

There exists a possibility of comparing the above forms with Sem **ṯuʿb-* "big snake" (Arab *ṯuʿb-ān-* (note, however, an irregular *-ʿ-). If this comparison is valid, one should reconstruct HS **č-* in the anlaut.

2228 *sib- "rope"

Sem **šibb-* "belt" [1], "rope, thin cloth" [2]: Akk *šibbu* [1], Arab *sibb-* [2].
ECh **sib-* "string, rope": Mkk *sibe*.
LEC **seb-* "belt, leather strap": Som *seeb*, Gel *seeb*.
HEC **sib-* "string, rope": Sid *sibo*.

Cf. Cush words for "sandal": Bed *šib*, Rift **ʾišib-* (Asa *išiba*)?

2229 *sib- "tree"

WCh **sib-* "tree": Chip *šip*, Mnt *šip*.

ECh **sub-* < **sibu-* "tamarind": Sbn *subu.*
LEC **sib(b)-* "kind of tree": Or *sibbee.*
HEC **sib(b)-* "kind of tree": Kmb *sibbe-ta.*

2230 *sib- "cut"

Sem **šVb-* "cut": Hbr *šbb*, Arab *sbb.*
Eg *sby* "cut, castrate" (OK).
Infinitive in *-y.*
Agaw **sab-/*sib-* "pierce, stab": Bil *sab*, Xmr *sib*, Dmt *siäb*, Kwr *sab*, Dmb *sab*, Kem *säb.*

2231 *sib- "be angry"

Sem **šub-* "insult" (v.): Arab *sbb* [-*u*-], Mhr *seb*, Jib *sebb.*
Secondary labialized vowel.
WCh **sib-* "be angry": Wrj *šib-*, Diri *šubu.*
Assimilation in Diri.
Bed *sebib* "punish, reprimand".
Partial reduplication.

2232 *sibin- "oil, butter"

WCh **sibVn-* "oil": Wrj *šivəna.*
LEC **sibin-* "butter": Arb *siibin.*

Derived from a root preserved in WCh **sib-* "oil": Kry *šiv*, Miya *šu*, Diri *subu.* Cf. **siman-* "oil, fat".

2233 *sigaʿ- "speak, moan"

Sem **šVgaʿ-*"moan" (v.): Arab *sgʿ* [-*a*-].
WCh **siHVg-* "talk": Ang *šeuk.*
Metathesis.

2234 *sigul- "stamp, seal"

Sem **šigil-* "roll, scroll, register": Arab *sigill-.*
If not from Lat *sigillum.*
Eg *sḏꜣw.t* "stamp, seal" (OK).

Palatalization of **-g-*.

A cultural term, probably, a Sem loanword in Eg.

2235 *siᶜüm- "cereal"

Eg *šmᶜy* "barley" (OK).
Metathesis. Vocalic *-y*.
CCh **siHum-* "seed" [1], "millet" [2], "corn" [3]: Mba *siyom* [1], Bata *sūme* [2], Bud *šimo* [3].
Mba *-y-* < **-H-*.
ECh **siHVm-* "sorghum": Bid *sīma*.
Contraction.

2236 *siḥaf- "shave"

Sem **šVḥap-* "shave (head)": Arab *sḥf* [*-a-*].
WCh **syaf-* < **siHaf-* "take off a thin shaving": Hs *šēfe*.
Contraction.

2237 *siḥaṭ- "cut, slaughter"

Sem **šVḥaṭ-* "slaughter": Hbr *šḥṭ*, Aram *šḥṭ*, Arab *sḥṭ* [*-a-*], Soq *sḥaṭ*, Hss *seḥāṭ*, Mhr *seḥāṭ*.
CCh **syat-* < **siHat-* "cut": Mafa *šet*.
ECh **sēt-* < **siHat-* "cut": Bid *seet*.

Cf. WCh **siṭaṭ-* "cut, sharpen": Hs *šittā*, Bol *sott*, Ngz *sətu*.

2238 *siḫ- "milk"

Eg *sḫ.w* "milk" (gr).
ECh **siH-* "milk": Dor *sī*.

2239 *sik- "boat, ship"

Eg *sk.ty* "kind of ship" (n).
WCh **sik-* "boat": Ank *šik*.

2240 *sikun- "dwell, sit"

Sem **šVkun-* "place, impose" [1], "stay, dwell" [2]: Akk *šakā-nu* [1], Hbr *škn* [2], Arab *skn* [-*u*-] [2], Jib *skun* [1], Hss *sekōn* [2].
WCh **sikun-* "sit" [1], "rest" [2]: Jmb *šinkə* [1], Pol *šəγən* [1], Bgh *səgəne* [2].
Rift **sukunun-* "squat": Irq *sukununu-ʾat-*.
Partial reduplication and assimilation of vowels.

Cf. Dhl *sukk-eem-* "remain still".

2241 *silaḥ- "sharp weapon"

Sem **šilāḥ-* "weapon" [1], "javelin" [2]: Ug *šlḥ* [2], Hbr *šelaḥ* [2], Aram *šilḥā* [1], Arab *silāḥ-* [1].
Eg *sȝẖ.t* "knife" (gr).
Irregular laryngeal in a late Eg form.
WCh **sil-* "axe": Paa *šila*.
Loss of the auslaut laryngeal.
CCh **sil-* < **siHVl-* "arrow": Gul *sīl*.
Agaw **sil-* "knife": Xmr *sil*.

2242 *sim- "meet"

WCh **sim-* "meet": Tng *sim-*, *simb-*.
Secondary *-mb-*.
LEC **sim-* "meet": Or *sima*.

2243 *sim- "suck"

Berb **sVm-* "suck": Kby *summ*.
ECh **sim-* "suck": Smr *šišom*, Sbn *sisəm*, Sok *ʾəsime*.
Rift **seʾem-* "suck in air": Kwz *seʾem-*.
Based on **sem-*.

2244 *sim- "call, speak"

Sem **šVmVw-/*šVmVy-* "call, give name": Arab *smw*, *smy* [-*u*-], Hss *hēm*, Mhr *hmō*, Shh *šmi*.
Based on **šVm-*.
Berb **sVm-* "call, name" (v.): Kby *səmmi*.

Eg *smy* "tell" (n).
Infinitive in *-y*.
CCh **syam-sim-* "whisper": Bid *sēsem*, Mig *semsimo*.
An onomatopeia?
LEC **sim-* "welcome" (v.): Or *sima*.

2245 *sim-/*simaᶜ- "hear; ear"

Sem **šVmaᶜ-* "hear": Akk *šemû*, Ug *šmᶜ*, Hbr *šmᶜ*, Aram (Syr) *šmᶜ*, Arab *smᶜ* [*-a-*], SAr *śmᶜ*, Mand *šma*, Gz *smᶜ*, Tgr *sämᶜa*, Tgy *sämᶜe*, Har *sämaʾa*, Amh *sämma*, Arg *sämma*, Gaf *sämmä*, Gur *säma*, Hss *hōma*, Mhr *hēma*, Shh *šiᶜ*, Soq *hyemaᶜ*.
Eg *sm.t* "ears" (n).
CCh **ŝim-* "ear": Tera *ẑim*, Bura *ŝim*, Chb *ŝəma*, Klb *himi*, Hil *χimi*, Mba *ŝumo*, HB *ŝəmə*, Hwn *ŝəmɛ*, FKi *ŝimu*, FG *ŝimwu*, Kap *ŝiməy*, Mnd *χ̂ima*, Zgh *ŝime*, Glv *χimiye*, Gdf *χ̂ima*, Nak *ŝimiya*, Mofu *ŝumay*, Bld *ŝəmay*, Muk *ŝum*, Mnj *ŝimay*, Daba *ẑimi*, Gudu *ŝim*, Log *ŝim*, Kus *ŝmē*, Msg *χ̂imē*.
Irregular **ŝ-*, hypothetically, continuing **H-s-*. Several forms may reflect **ŝimay-* < **ŝimaH-*.
ECh **sim-/*sum-* "ear": Smr *sumi*, Tum *hīm*, Ndam *ham*, Nch *semang*, Lele *suma*, Gbr *suma-in*, Kbl *sami*, Dor *sumami*, Mubi *somāmu*.
Partial reduplication in Dor and Mubi. Forms with *-u-* are secondary. The ECh word is contaminated with **sVm-* "name" < HS **süm-*, cf. full neutralization of these meanings in Ndam *ham* "name, ear" and the like.

2246 *simaḫ- "tree, bush"

Sem **šimāḫ-* "thorny bush": Akk *šimāḫu*, *šemāḫu*.
HEC **sim-* "young ensete tree": Sid *sima*, Gel *sima*, Kab *sima*.
Loss of the auslaut laryngeal.

2247 *siman- "oil, fat"

Sem **šamn-* "oil" [1], "fat, grease" [2], "fatness" [3], "melting butter" [4]: Akk *šamanu*, *šamnu* [1], Hbr *šemen* [2], Aram (Syr) *šumnō* [3], Arab *samn-* [4], Jib *šəmnun* [2].
Assimilation of vowels.
WCh **sinam-* "oil": Diri *sinama*.

Metathesis.

CCh **sVmVn-* "thick, fat": Log *s'əmən*.

ECh **siwan-* "oil": Smr *swānē*, Ndam *swān*, Kwan *suwāne*, Bid *seweŋ*, Mig *sewen*, Brg *sewen*, Sok *sunnē*.

Note transformation of intervocalic **-m-* > **-w-*.

Presumably, derived from **sim-* id. preserved in Berb **sVm-* "fat" (Kby *τassəmτ*).

2248 *sin- "tongue"

Eg *sn.w* "tongue" (gr).

WCh **sin-* "tongue": Diri *šin-ḍu*.

CCh **sin-* "tongue": Hwn *šɛne-wura*, Masa *sinano*, Bnn *sin-da*.

Partial reduplication in Masa.

2249 *sin- "earth, clay"

Eg *syn* "clay" (OK).

Vocalic *-y*.

WCh **sin-* "field": Wrj *sənan*, Kry *sin*, Diri *səna*, Siri *sinawi*, Paa *sina*, Cagu *sinan*.

*CCh *sin-* "field": Lame *šini*, LPe *šine*, Masa *senena*.

ECh **sinya-* "earth" [1], "sand" [2]: Smr *sinya* [1], Ndam *həny* [1], Tum *həŋ* [1], Jegu *šeny-* [2], Mubi *sin-ok* [2], Brg *sanyo* [2], Sok *sinē* [2].

2250 *sin- "tooth"

Sem **šinn-* "tooth": Akk *šinnu*, Ug *šn*, Hbr *šēn*, Aram (Syr) *šennō*, Arab *sinn-*, Gz *sənn*, Tgy *sənni*, Arg *sən*, Har *sən*, Gur *sən*, Gaf *sənä*.

Berb **sin-* "tooth": Ahg *esin*.

WCh **sin-* "tooth": Pol *šin*, Geji *šiŋ*, Zem *šan*, *šin*, Brw *šen*, Say *šin*, Dwot *šin*, Bol *šin*.

CCh **ŝin-* < **ḥa-sin-* "tooth": Gaa *ŝena*, Gbn *ŝene*, Hwn *ŝana*, Mba *šɛŋ*, HNk *ŝine*, FG *ŝəini*, Kap *ŝənɛ*, Gis *ŝeŋ*, Bld *sliŋ*, Mtk *ŝɛnnɛ*, Bnn *sina*.

Note the secondary lateralization of **-s-* preceded by a laryngeal.

ECh **siHan-* < **Ha-sin-* "tooth": Smr *san-dē*, Tum *hiin*, Ndam *han*,

Gbr *k-song*, Dor *ga-sena*, Dng *saaŋo*, Mig *sa:nu*, Jegu *saŋo*, Bid *seenō*, Mubi *siŋaŋu*, Brg *saŋo*, Sok *sən*.
Rift **siḥin-* "tooth": Irq *siḥino*, Alg *siḥino*, Bur *siḥino*.
Metathesis from **ḥV-sin-*.

2251 *sin- "smell" (v.)

Eg *sn* "smell" (pyr).
ECh **sunVn-* "smell": Tum *hunən*.
Partial reduplication with modified vocalism.
SA **sin-* "smell": Saho *siin-*.

Related to **san-/*sin-* "nose".

2252 *sinak-/*sinaḳ- "tongue"

Eg *snk* "tongue" (XVIII).
WCh **sinaḳ-* "tongue": Wrj *šinḳə-*, Kry *sinakə*, Miya *šinaki*, Paa *šinḳi*, Cagu *šinḳ-an*, Siri *šənaḳi*, Mbu *šinaḳo*, Jmb *sənakə-lan*.

Irregular correspondence Eg *k* ~ WCh **ḳ*. Derived from **sin-* "tongue".

2253 *sip- "river, river-bed"

Sem **šīp-* "bank, coast": Arab *sīf-*, Jib *sif-t*.
Berb **sif-/*suf-* "valley" [1], "river, rivulet" [2]: Ahg *a-suf* [1], Sml *a-sif* [2], Mzab *suf* [2], Snd *suf* [2], Shau *suf* [2], Kby *ta-sif-t*, *a-sif* [2].
-u- < **-i-* before a labial.
WCh **sip-* "river": Ank *šip*.

2254 *sip- "blow"

Sem **šVpVy-* "raise dust (of the wind)": Arab *sfy* [*-i-*].
Based on **šVp-*.
CCh **sip-* "blow": Gaa *šipənči*, Gbn *sipenči*, Boka *šipa-ḍa*.
Cf. Dgh *safa* "breathe", Mafa *saf-* id.?

Any connection with Sem **nVšVp-* "blow" (Akk *našāpu*, Hbr *nšp*, Aram *nšp*) and Eg *nšp* "breathe" (gr)?

2255 *sip- "rope"

Eg *sp* "ropes for ship building" (OK).
ECh **sip-* "string, rope": Mig *sippu*, Sok *sipo*, *šifi*.
LEC **šep-* "leather strap": Som *šeep-ako*, Or *seep̣-ani*.

2256 *siq- "knife"

Sem **šīẖ-* "big knife": Arab *sīẖ-*.
WCh **siq-* "knife": Mnt *šik*, Ank *šik*.

2257 *sir- "kite"

Eg *syꜣ.w* "kite" (gr).
-y- stands for a front vowel.
WCh **sirwa-* "kite": Hs *širwā*.

has *sir-/*sur- "sing"

Sem **šīr-* "sing": Ug *šyr*, Hbr *šyr*, Aram *šyr*.
Based on biconsonantal **šVr-* < **sir-*.
ECh **sir-* "sing": Kwan *sire*.
Omot **sur-* "sing": Yam *sur*.

Alternation **i* ~ **u*.

2259 *sirVf- "warm"

Eg *srf* "warm" (pyr).
CCh **sirVf-* "covered with sweat": Mafa *širf-eʔe*.

For the semantic development, cf. HS **daf-* "heat, sweat".

2260 *sireḥ- "river"

Eg *šrḥ* "rivulet" (gr).
WCh **sirya-* "river, spring": Siri *sərə-ngi*, Jmb *sirya*.

2261 *sisaʔ- "night, darkness"

Eg *ššꜣ.t* "night" (pyr).
š- < **s-* before a front vowel.

WCh **sis-* "shadow": Zaar *šis*.
CCh **sisaʾ-* "evening" [1], "shadow" [2]: Gul *saassa* [1], Msg *šešē* [2], Nza *furi-šišiʾi* [2].
Metathesis and assimilation of vowels in Gul.

2262 *sisim- "cloth"

Eg *ssmy* "cloth" (gr).
Vocalic *-y*.
CCh **sisVm-* "woman's bodycloth": Hwn *šisəm-ař*.

2263 *sitay- "vessel"

Eg *styy* "bottle" (n).
ECh **ʾa-sVtay-* "pot": Kwan *aste*.

2264 *siṭ- "go, come"

Sem **šVṭVw-* "make large steps": Arab *sṭw* [-*u*-].
Based on biconsonantal **šVṭ-*.
WCh **siṭ-* "enter": Ang *sīt*.
CCh **sVt-* "pass by": Log *sto*.

2265 *soʾ- "back"

Eg *sꜣ* "back" (pyr).
CCh **swaʾ-* "back": Gdf *so*.
Cf. also **suχwa-* id. (Glv *suχa*, Nak *suχwa*).

2266 *soʾ- "barn"

Eg *sꜣ* "barn" (gr).
WCh **sway-* < **swaH-* "house, barn": DB *swey*, Glm *soo*, Grm *soo*.
CCh **syaʾ-/*swaʾ-* "compound" [1], "house" [2]: FMb *seʾi* [1], Lame *syo* [2], LPe *syo*, *so* [2], Zime *sō*, *uso* [2].

2267 *soʾit- "dirt, be dirty"

Eg *sꜣt* "dirt" (NK).
CCh **swat-* "dirt": Bnn *sɔtɔ*, BM *sotiya*.

Metathesis.
ECh *sit- "be dirty": Sok *šita*.
Contraction.

2268 *sof- "cut wood"

Eg *sfsf* "cut with a knife" (XVIII).
Reduplication.
LEC **sof-* "plane wood": Or *sof-*.
HEC **sof-* "plane wood": Sid *sof-*.

2269 *sog- "tree, wood"

CCh **swag-* "firewood": Mafa *soegwe*.
LEC **sog-sog-* "kind of acacia": Som *sogsog*.
Reduplication.

2270 *soʿ- "cereal"

Sem **šuʿʿ-* "cereal" [1], "corn" [2], "wild wheat" [3]: Akk *šuʾu* [1], Ug *sʿ-t* [2], Arab *suʿʿ-* [3].
HEC **soʾ-* "barley": Had *soʾo*, Gel *soʾa*, Kab *soʾa*.
Note HS *-ʿ- > HEC *-ʾ- in the intervocalic position.

2271 *soʿar- "set fire, burn"

Sem **šVʿar-* "set fire": Arab *sʿr* [-*a*-].
WCh **sawar-* < **swaHar-* "roast" [1], "burn" [2]: Hs *sōya* [1], Ang *sūr* [1], Bol *surru* [1], Krk *surū* [1], Ngm *sur* [1], Krf *šuru* [1], *Pero čuuro* [1], Dera *wuri* [1], Gera *sur-* [1], Glm *sər-* [1], Brm *sure* [2].
CCh **sawar-* < **swaHar-* "roast": Tera *zurr*, Hwn *sər-aŋ*, Boka *sura-ḍa*, Kap *sur̆-kɛ*, Mafa *sawar*, Gudu *sərā*, FMb *šir*, Bch *sərā*.
Unexpected -*i*- in FMb. Note voiced anlaut in Tera.
ECh **sur-* "roast": Mkk *zuriye*.

Cf. Eg *wsr* "fire" going back to **sor-*.

2272 *soḥ- "pit, hole"

Sem **šūḥ-* "pit, hole": Ug *šḥ*, Hbr *šūḥā*.
WCh **sway-* < **swaH-* "hole, spring": Bks *swey*, DB *swey*.

2273 *sol- "be quiet"

Sem **šVl-* "be quiet" [1], "be careless" [2]: Hbr *šly* [1], Aram *šlh* [2].
ECh **swal-* "keep silence": Sok *sōlē*.

2274 *sol- "pull"

Sem **šul-* "pull, draw" [1], "drag away" [2]: Hbr *šly* [1], Arab *sll* [*-u-*] [1], Jib *sell* [2].
WCh **sol-* "pull": Ang *šwal*, Tng *sol*, Krf *šollu*.
CCh **sVl-* "pull": Mofu *səl-*.
Partial reduplication in Mba *sisal* id.

2275 *so(m)b- "pubic hair"

Sem **ʾišb-* "pubic hair": Arab *ʾisb-*.
Derived from **šVb-*.
HEC **šomb-* "pubic hair": Sid *šoobba*, Had *šoomba*, Kab *šäbbä*, Kmb *šobba-ta*.

One of the cases in which prenasalized clusters appear as voiced stops in Sem.

2276 *son- "river"

Eg *swn.w* "waters" (BD).
Vocalic *-w-*.
Dhl *sooni* "river".
Rift **soʾon-* "river": Asa *soʾon-k*.
Secondary inlaut *-ʾ-*.

Cf. CCh **sin-* "river": Mrg *sina*.

2277 *sop- "speak, ask"

Sem **šVpVH-* "ask": Akk *šepû*.
Based on **šVp-*.
WCh **swap-* "speak": Tng *sɔp*.

2278 *soq- "pull"

Sem **šVḫVw-* "pull": Jib *šχe*.
Derived from biconsonantal **šVḫ-*.

CCh **sVq-* ''pull'': HNk *askəy*, Kap *nsχu-mte*, HF *sχu-nto*.
ECh **swag-* ''pull'': Tob *soge*.
Note *-g- < *-q-.

2279 *soyam- ''grass''

ECh **swawam-* < **swayam-* ''grass'': Bid *sooma*.
LEC **soyam-* ''kind of plant'': Or *sooyama*.

2280 *suʾim- ''hair''

Eg *smȝ* ''hair'' (pyr), Copt **smaw* ''temple'': OCopt *smau*, Boh *smau*, Shd *smau*, *smaau*.
Metathesis.
WCh **suHim-* ''growth of hair'' 1, ''hair'' 2, ''pubic hair'' 3: Hs *sūmā* 1, Ngm *som* 2, Tng *simī-ne* 3.
Omot **som(m)-* ''hair'': Yam *somme*.
Contraction.
Rift **sVʾVm-* ''hair'' 1, ''hairdress'' 2: Irq *sεʾεεmi* 1, Asa *sem-ug* 2.

2281 *suʾum- ''sell, buy''

Sem **šVʾVm-* ''buy'' 1, ''sell'' 2: Akk *šâmu* 1, Jib *śε:m* 2, Soq *sʾm* 2.
CCh **sum-* ''buy'': Mafa *sum*.
Contraction.
ECh **suʾum-* ''sell'': Dng *suumiye*, Brg *suumi*.

2282 *suf- ''smell'' (v.)

Sem **šūp-* ''smell, sniff (around)'' (v.): Arab *swf* [-*u*-].
Based on **šup-*.
LEC **suf-* ''smell'' (v.): Or *suf-*.

2283 *suᶜVr- ''tree, forest''

Eg *sᶜr* ''forest'' (n).
WCh **sur-* ''kind of tree'': Ang *sur*, Mpn *sur*.

2284 *suh-/*suhay- "shout"

Eg *swhy* "shout" (XVIII).
CCh **suw-* < **suH-* "shout, cry" [1], "answer" [2]: Log *suwe* [1], Hld *šuwa* [2].
ECh **sway-* < **suHay-* "shout": Smr *swōy*, Jegu *soy*.

2285 *suḥ- "flow"

Sem **šuḥ-* "flow, pour": Arab *sḥḥ* [-*u*-].
Cf. *syḥ* [-*i*-] "flow, spread upon the surface".
WCh **suHi-* "pour": Bks *šu*, DB *šun*, Fyer *ši*.
ECh **saHay-* "wet": Kera *saaye*.

2286 *suk- "spear"

Eg *sk* "spear" (MK).
CCh **suk-* "spear": Gaa *šuk-ta*, Gbn *suk-te*.

Connected with **suk-* "slaughter"?

2287 *suk- "slaughter"

Sem **šuk-* "cut (ears)": Arab *skk* [-*u*-].
WCh **suk-* "slaughtering (a camel)": Hs *suka*.
Agaw **suk-* "slaughter cattle (after funeral)": Bil *suuk-*.

2288 *suḳ- "push, pull"

Sem **šūḳ-* "push": Arab *swq* [-*u*-].
Based on **šVḳ-*.
WCh **sa-suḳ-* "drive away": Hs *sāsuḳa*.
Partial reduplication.
ECh **swak-* "push": Kera *soke*.
Dhl *šuuk'-* "pull, draw".

2289 *suḳaᶜ- "beat"

Sem **šVḳaᶜ-* "knock": Arab *sqᶜ* [-*a*-].
HEC **suḳ(ḳ)-* "beat, hit": Had *suḳḳ-*.

Wrz **šoḳ-* "hit": Gaw *šoq*.

Related to **suḳ-* "push, pull"? The auslaut laryngeal is lost in Cush.

2290 *suḳul- "foot, leg"

ECh **sugul-* "thigh": Sok *sugul*.
Omot **sukul-* "foot": Ome *sukule*.

Assimilation of vowels. No traces of the emphatic.

Derived from **saḳ-* "leg".

2291 *sulak- "bird"

Sem **šulak-* "chicken (of a partridge)": Arab *sulak-*.
ECh **sulVk-* "guinea fowl": Kera *sulku*, Kwan *sulkō*.

2292 *sulVḥ- "wall"

Sem **šalḥ-/*šulḥ-* "wall": Akk *šalḫu*, *šulḫu*.
Eg *swɜḥ.t* "fortified site" (MK).

-w- stands for a rounded vowels.

2293 *su(m)bVl- "band, plait"

Sem **šubl-* "hem": Hbr *šōbel*.
Eg *sbn* "band, bandage" (l).
ECh **sVmbVl-* "plait": Mobu *səmbəle*.

HS cluster **-mb-*?

2294 *sun- "know"

Eg *swn* "know" (l), Copt **sow(u)n*: Boh *sōoun*, Shd *sooun*.
Berb **sVn-* "know": Tua *essen*, Sgh *-ssən*, Kby *issin*.
CCh **sun-* "know": Daba *sun-*.

2295 *sunaḥ- "know, imagine"

Sem **šVnaḥ-* "appear in somebody's mind": Arab *snḥ* [-*a*-].
ECh **suHan-* "know": Tum *han*, Mkk *suun-*.

Metathesis.

Derived from **sun-* "know".

2296 *sunb- "cloud, sky"

Eg *sbn.t* "sky" (gr).
Metathesis.
CCh **χa-sumb-* "cloud": Gbn *χusəmba*, Hwn *hašumbē*.
Prefix **χa-*.

2297 *supay- "spear"

Sem **šVpāy-* "sharp driving stick": Aram (Syr) *šəpāi-*.
WCh **suyap-* "spear": Mnt *šuyɛp*.
Metathesis.

Cf. CCh **sap-* "spear": Bnn *sappa*.

2298 *sur- "rope"

Sem **šurr-* "umbilical cord": Hbr *šor*, Arab *surr-*.
Eg *wsr.t* "rope" (XX).
Vocalic *w-*.
Wrz **sur-* "rope": Gaw *surre*.

An alternative parallel for Eg *wsr.t* is Sem **waṯal-* id. (Arab *waṯal-*) from **wačal-*.

2299 *surVʔ- "eye"

Sem **šurʔ-* "eyelid": Akk *šurʔu*.
Eg *wsr.t* "eye" (gr).
Vocalic *w-*. Loss of the laryngeal in late Eg.

2300 *susan- "grass, lotus"

Sem **šūšān-* "grass" [1], "lotus, lily" [2]: Akk *šišnu* [1], Hbr *šōšān* [2], Arab *sūsān-* [2].
Borrowed from Eg?
Eg *sššn* "lotus" (pyr), *ššn* id. (MK).
Dissimilation.

2301 *suwak- "go, come"

Sem **šūk-* "march and stumble": Arab *swk* [*-u-*].
WCh **suk-* "galloping": Hs *suka*.
Contraction.
ECh **suk-* "come": Mubi *suk*.
LEC **sok(k)-* "go away": Or *sokka*.
Cf. also reduplication in Or *suksuka* "run, trot".

Cf. **seḳ-* "walk, run". Cf. also Bed *sak-* "go"; Agaw **sVk-* "approach" (Bil *səkʷ-r-*), LEC **sok(k)-* "leave" (Or *sokka*), Omot **šak-/*šik-* "approach, come" (Ome *šik-*, Kaf *šakk-*).

2302 *süf- "wool, cotton"

Sem **šip-* "wool": Akk *šipātu*.
WCh **suf-* "wool cloth": Hs *sūfī*.
Bed *suf* "cotton".

2303 *sük- "sow"

Eg *sṯy* "sow" (pyr).
From **sik-*, with palatalization of **-k-*.
WCh **suk-* "sow": Hs *šūka*.
Omot **šok-* "sow": Kaf *šok*, Bwo *šok*.

2304 *süm- "name"

Sem **šim-* "name": Akk *šumu*, Ug *šm*, Hbr *šēm*, Aram (Syr) *šᵉmō*, Arab (dial.) *sim-*, SAr *s¹m*, Shr *šum*, Gz *səm*, Tgr *səm*, Tgy *səm*, Amh *səm*, Arg *səm*, Gur *səm*, Gaf *səmʷä*.
WCh **sumi-* "name": Hs *sūnā*, Sura *sum*, Ang *süm*, Mnt *sum*, Ank *sum*, Grk *təm*, Bol *sun*, Krk *səm*, Tng *svmə*, Ngm *sun*, Maha *sum*, Bele *hin-ti*, Krf *šimi*, Gera *səma*, Glm *šim*, Grm *šimi*, Diri *šin*, Paa *sim*, *sun*, Cagu *siman*, Mbu *šin*, Pol *sum*, *səm*, Geji *šin*, Brw *šim*, *šin*, Bgh *isum*, Kir *wusum*, *wusəm*, Tala *sum*, *səm*, Klr *sim*, DB *sum*.
CCh **ŝim(ya)-* "name": Tera *lim*, Gaa *ŝima*, Gbn *ŝima*, Hwn *ŝimə*, Chb *ŝima*, Mig *ŝim*, Mba *ŝim*, FKi *ŝəm*, Daba *ẑimi*, Gude *ləma*, Gudu *lim*, FJ *ẑimu*, Log *ŝemi*, Bud *hɛmi*, LPe *šem-ḍe*, Masa *šema*, Msm *sem*.
Irregular lateral resulting from the contamination with the word for "ear".

ECh *sVm- "name": Smr *sumi*, Tum *hīm*, Ndam *ham*, Mig *seme*, Mubi *same*, Mkk *suma*.

Connected with *sim- "call, speak".

2305 *süp- "pole, beam"

Sem *šīp- "beam": Akk *šīpu*.
WCh *sup- "pole, support": Mpn *sup*, Tng *suup*.

2306 *süt- "woman"

Sem *šitt- "lady": Ug *št*, Arab *sitt-*.
Berb *sut- "women": Kby *suṭ*.
WCh *sut- "sister": Tng *sut*.
CCh *sut- "girl": Mwu *suti*.

2307 *sVf- "break"

Sem *šūp- "grind": Hbr *šwf*, Aram *šwf*.
Based on *šVp-.
Ef *sfsf* "break" (XVIII).
Reduplication.

2308 *sVfif- "snake"

Sem *šVpīp- "kind of snake": Hbr *šᵉ pīp-ōn*.
Berb *sVfuf- "snake": Zng *te-sfuf-əh*.
*-u- < *-i- between labials.

Partial reduplication of *sef- "snake".

2309 *sVḥal- "weave"

Sem *šVḥal- "make a cloth (of separate threads)": Arab *sḥl* [-*a*-].
WCh *sVHVl- "mat": *Ang sö:l*.

2310 *sVk- "smell" (v.)

Sem *šVhVk- "blow": Arab *shk* [-*a*-].
Based on *šVk-.

Eg *sṯy* "smell" (n.) (pyr).
Suffix *-y*.
CCh **sVk-* "smell": Gbn *sək-tə*.

2311 *sVḳVr- "strike, pierce"

Sem **šVḳVr-* "pierce": Akk *šaqāru*, Gz *sq*^{w}*r*, Tgy *säq*^{w}*ärä*.
Eg *sḳr* "strike" (pyr).

2312 *sVp- "plait, sew"

Sem **šup-* "tie" [1], "plait" [1], "sew" [3]: Akk *sepû* [1], Arab *sff* [*-u-*] [2], Gz *sfy* [2], Hrr *säfa* [3], Gur *sefä* [3].
Eg *spy* "bind up (a ship)" (pyr).
Suffix *-y*.
ECh **sVp-* "spin, twist": Mig *sipiyo*.
LEC **sup(p)-* "darn": Or *suppa*.
Wrz **šap-* "tie, sew": Gaw *šap-*, *šapp-*.
Omot **šip(p)-* "plait, sew": Kaf *šipp-*, Mch *šippi-*, Gim *sif-*.

Chaotic correspondences of vowels. Derived from **sip-* "rope".

2313 *sVtVp- "cut, slaughter"

Sem **šVtVp-* "cut out": Akk *šatāpu*.
Eg *stp* "slaughter" (pyr).

*ŝ

2314 *ŝa³-/*ŝaw- "wish, like"

Sem **śī³-* "wish": Arab *šy³* [*-a-*].
Based on **śV³-*.
Dhl *hlaw-* "love, like".
Rift **ŝa³-* "like": Irq *ŝaa³-*, Alg *ŝaa³-*, Bur *ŝa³-*.

For the semantic development, cf. Sp *querer* "wish" → "love".
Note a consonantal alternation **-³-* ~ **-w-*.

2315 *ŝab- "mix, knead"

Sem *śūb- "mix": Arab šwb [-u-].
Based on *śVb-.
Eg šbb "mix, knead" (OK).
Partial reduplication.
WCh *ŝaḅ-/*ŝamḅ- "mix, knead": Bol lomb-, Tng lamb-, Wrj laḅə, Kry laḅə, Miya laḅ, Paa ẑaḅu, Siri ŝaḅa.
Secondary emphatization. Note a nasal infix in Bol and Tng.
Bed šaawi "mix, collect".
-w- < *-b- in the intervocalic position.

2316 *ŝab- "rib"

ECh *ŝVb- "rib": Kbl ka-səba.
Prefix *ka-.
Rift *ŝab- "diaphragm" [1], "rib" [2]: Irq ŝawi [1], Bur ŝabi [2].

Cf. Som laab id. with l- as a reflex of the lateral?

2317 *ŝab- "axe, sword"

Sem *śabaw- "blade (of a sword)": Arab šabā-t-.
Derived from *śab-.
WCh *ŝab- "sword" [1], "axe" [2]: Hs zābō [1], zābi [2].

Cf. CCh *ẑamb-/*ẑimb- "axe": HNk ẑimbwe, Mofu ẑamba, Gis ẑimbe.

2318 *ŝab- "plant"

Eg šȝb "kind of plant" (pyr).
Vocalic -ȝ-.
WCh *ŝab- "grass": Tng laba.
Dhl hlaaβ-une "leaf".
Irq *ŝab- "bush": Ala ŝaba.

2319 *ŝabab- "reed flute"

Sem *śabab- "reed flute": Arab šabbab-at-.
Cf. Akk šabî-t- "musical instrument".
Berb *sab(V)b- "flute": Mns ta-sabbuṯ.

Eg *šbb* "reed, reed tube" (med).

Partial reduplication of **ŝab-* "plant"?

2320 *ŝabaḥ- "cut"

Sem **śVbaḥ-* "split": Arab *šbḥ* [-*a*-].
WCh **ŝabVḥ-* "wound, stab (with a knife)": Hs *zabga*.

Connected with **ŝab-* "axe, sword".

2321 *ŝabVb- "tie, weave"

Sem **śVbVb-* "bind, tie": Arab *šbb*.
WCh **ŝabVb-* "weave": Bol *loḇḇ-*.
Secondary emphatization.

Partial reduplication of unattested **ŝab-*.

2322 *ŝadoʾ-/*ŝadoy- "pull out"

Eg *šdy* "pull out" (med).
WCh **ŝa-ŝadwaʾ-* "draw out": Hs *zazzaḍō*.
Partial reduplication.

Consonantal alternation **-ʾ-* ~ **-y-*.

2323 *ŝaᶜ- "cow, bull"

WCh **ŝaH-* "bull" [1], "cow" [2]: Dera *la* [2], Pol *ŝa* [1 2], Geji *ŝa* [2], Dwot *ŝa* [2], Ngz *ŝa* [2].
CCh **ẑa-* "cow, bull, cattle": Tera *ẑa*, HG *ŝa*, Glv *ŝa*, Gis *ŝa*, Msg *χ̃e*, Gul *χ̃a*, FJ *ẑa-ŋ*, Mtk *ẑe*, Mrg *ŝa*, Gbn *ŝa-ta*, Boka *lə-tə*, Ksr *sā*, Bud *hā*.
Bed *šaʾ* "cow".
SA **saᶜ-* "cattle": Saho *saᶜa*, Afar *saaᶜ*.
LEC **saᶜ-* "cow": Som *saᶜ*, Or *saaʾaa*, Arb *seʾ*.
HEC **saʾ-* "cow": Sid *saʾaa*, Had *saayya*, Kmb *sayaa*.
Rift **ŝeH-/*ŝaHe-* "cow": Irq *ŝee*, Alg *ŝee*, Bur *ŝee*, Asa *ŝe-ok*, Kwz *ŝae-ko*.

Cf. an isolated form in Berb: Kby *τišτan* "kine".

2324 *ŝak- "feather, wing"

Sem **śūk-* "become fully fledged": Arab *šwk*.
Derived from a noun. Secondary inlaut **-w-*.
CCh **ẑakwa-* "feather": Glv *ẑākwa*, Gdf *ẑakwa*.

2325 *ŝam- "plant, flower"

Sem **śamm-* "plant": Akk *šammu*.
Eg *šmʒw* "flower" (med).
Vocalic *-ʒ-* and suffix *-w*.

2326 *ŝam- "bird"

Eg *šm* "kind of bird" (XXII).
CCh **ʾa-ẑam-* "falcon": Gis *ʾaẑam*.
Prefix **ʾa-*.

2327 *ŝam- "be possible, be able"

WCh **ŝam-* "do, make, be possible": Ngz *ẑamu*.
CCh **ẑam-* "can": Log *ẑəm*.
Rift **ŝam-* "allow": Asa *ŝam-*.
Semantically, "allow" ← "make possible".

2328 *ŝam- "burn; lightning"

Eg *šm*, *šmm* "be hot, be burning" (OK).
Berb **sam-* "lightning": Ahg *e-ssam*, Ndir *i-ssim*, Fgg *u-səm*.
Secondary *-i-* in Ndir.

2329 *ŝam- "sun"

Sem **śamš-* "sun" [1], "sun-heat" [2]: Akk *šamšu* [1], Hbr *šemeš* [1], Aram (Syr) *šemš-* [1], Arab *šams-* [1], SAr *śmš* [1], Tgr *šämš* [1], Soq *šam* [1], Jib *s̱um* [2].
Partial reduplication and dissimilation from **śamś-*.
Eg *sšm.t* "moon-disc" (gr).
sš- reflects **ŝ-*.
WCh **ŝam-* "sun": Ang *lem*.

Related to **ŝam-* "burn; lightning".

2330 *ŝap- "receive"

Eg *šzp* "receive" (pyr).
šz- may reflect a lateral.
WCh **ŝap-* "receive": Sura *lap*, Ank *lāp*, Grk *lāp*, Mpn *lap*.

Cf. Rift **ŝa[p]-* "get": Irq *ŝaw-*, Bur *ŝaw-*?

2331 *ŝar- "clothes"

Eg *šr.t* "clothes" (gr).
WCh **ŝarar-* "rags": Hs *zarāra*.
Partial reduplication.
SA **sar-* "clothes": Saho *sara*, Afar *sara*.

2332 *ŝat- "tie, weave"

Sem **śVt-* "tie, weave": Akk *šatû*, Jib *seṭṭ*.
WCh **ŝat-* "spin": Bks *lat*.

2333 *ŝeb- "wind"

Sem **śib-* "wind": Akk *šub-tu*, Soq *šiboh*.
CCh **ẑVb-* "storm": FKi *ẑəva*.
ECh **ŝyab-* "wind": Kera *ke-seba*.
Prefix **kya-*.

2334 *ŝiḥar- "open"

Sem **śVḥar-* "be open, open (mouth)": Arab *šḥr* [*-a-*].
Cf. Arab *šrḥ* "open", *šrʿ* id.
WCh **ŝiHar-* "open": Cagu *ẑar*, Mbu *ẑir*.

2335 *ŝimar- "green plant"

Sem **śimār-* "dill": Akk *šimru*, Arab *šamār-*.
Assimilation in Arab.
HEC **simar-* "cabbage": Had *simmaroʾo*, Kab *simmara*.

2336 *ŝip- "light, day"

Eg *ssp̌* "light" (MK).
Note *sš-* < **ŝ-*.
Berb **sVf-* "day": Ghd *a-sef*, Ahg *essef*.
WCh **ŝip-* "light": Ang *mege-ləp*, Pero *lip*.

Related to **ŝVp-* "shine, be light".

2337 *ŝob- "set fire"

Sem **śub-* "burn, be hot" [1], "set fire" [2], "warm" (v.) [3]: Akk *šabābu* [1], Arab *šbb* [-*u*-] [2], Soq *šbb* [3].
WCh **ŝa(m)b-* "take fire" [1], "set fire" [2]: Ang *lap lap* [1], Tng *lamb-* [2].
Secondary **-a-* < **-wa-*.
ECh **ŝwab-* "flame" (v.): Bid *ʾolob*.

2338 *ŝuf- "heat, boil"

WCh **ŝafaf-* "heat up, make hot": Hs *zāfafā*.
Partial reduplication with modified vocalism.
Rift **ŝuf-* "boil": Asa *ŝuf-*.

2339 *ŝur- "pour"

Sem **śur-* "pour": Arab *šrr* [-*u*-].
WCh **ŝur-* "pour": Paa *ẑur*.
CCh **ẑVr-* "pour out": Mofu *ẑər*.

2340 *ŝVp- "shine, be light"

Eg *ssp̌* "be light" (pyr).
sš- reflects **ŝ-*.
WCh **ŝVp-* "shine": Sura *ləp*.

2341 *ŝVw- "light, lightning"

Eg *šw* "light, sun" (NK).
CCh **ʾa-ẑVw-* "lightning": Daba *aẑəw*.
Prefix **ʾa-*.

*t

2342 *taˀ- "gate, house"

Eg *tꜣ* "gate" (XIX).
CCh *ˀ*i-taˀ-* "hut": Daba *ita*.
Prefix *ˀ*i-*.
ECh *ˀ*a-taˀ-ay-* "kitchen": Kera *ataaya*.
Prefix *ˀ*a-* < *ˀ*i-*, cf. CCh.

2343 *taˀ- "eat"

Sem *tVˀ-/*tVw-* "eat": Akk *taˀu*, Jib *te*, Sok *teˀ* (imp.), Hss *tewō*, Mhr *tewō*, Shh *teˀ*.
WCh *taˀ-/*tiˀ-* "eat": Hs *čī*, Gera *tii*, Bol *tii-* , Maha *ti*, Krf *tii-*, Glm *č-*, Dera *twi*, Krk *tu*, Ngm *ta*, Wrj *ta*, *tau*, Diri *ču*, Mbu *tī*, Jim *tī*, *tā*, Siri *tū*, Cagu *čū*, DB *čuh*, Sha *ci*, Klr *ci*, Ngz *ta*.
CCh *ti-* < *taˀi-* "eat": Lame *ti*, LPe *ti*, Msm *ti*.
ECh *ta(y)-/*ti(y)-* "eat": Jegu *t-*, Mig *tiyaw*, Bid *taa*, Mubi *tuwa*, *tiya*, Dng *tē*, Brg *taya*.

2344 *taˀ-/*taw- "ash"

Eg *tꜣ.w* "ash" (med).
Cf. *tꜣ* "be hot" (OK).
WCh *taw-taw-* "ash": Klr *atoto*.
Reduplication.

Consonantal alternation *-ˀ- ~ *-w-.

2345 *taˀ-/*taw-/*tay- "go, run"

Sem *ˀ*VtVw-/*ˀ*VtVy-* "arrive, come" [1], "return" [2]: Ug *ˀtw* [1], Aram *ˀty* [1], Arab *ˀty* [-*i*-] [1], SAr *ˀtw* [1], Gz *ˀtw* [2].
Prefix *ˀ*V-*.
WCh *ta-/*taw-* "enter" [1], "go" [2]: Ang *te* [1], Geji *tewi* [1], Dwot *təχ* [1], Dera *tawi* [2].
CCh *taˀ-/*tay-* "follow" [1], "go" [2]: Bud *tea* [1], Zime *ta* [2], Msm *ta* [2].
ECh *taˀ-/*tay-* "drive" [1], "go" [2]: Lele *tee* [1], Kbl *tayi* [1], Mkk *taaˀe* [2].

Agaw **tuʾ-* "enter": Aun *tu-ŋ*.
LEC **tiʾ-* "run": Bay *ti-*.
A different alternation grade or a case of phonetic development from **tVy-*.

Consonantal alternation **-ʾ-* ~ **-w-* ~ **-y-*.

2346 *taʾay-/*taway- "cloth"

Eg *tȝy.t.t* "cloth" (pyr).
ECh **taway-* "kerchief": Jegu *tawaaye*.

Consonantal alternation **-ʾ-* ~ **-w-*.

2347 *tab-/*tib- "foot, heel"

WCh **tab-* "palm or sole": Bks *taba*.
ECh **tab-* "foot": Kbl *taba*, Mobu *taba*.
SA **tibiʿ-* "foot, heel": Afar *tibiʿ*.
Unexpected *-ʿ-.
LEC **teb-* "foot": Arb *teb*.

Alternation **a* ~ **i*.

2348 *tabaʿ- "follow"

Sem **tVbaʿ-* "follow": Hbr *tbʿ*, Arab *tbʿ* [*-a-*], Jib *teʿ*, Hss *tōba*, Mhr *tōba*, Shh *tẽʿ*.
ECh **taHab-* "follow": Lele *tāb*, Kbl *ta:bi ka:si*.
Metathesis.

2349 *taf- "hand"

WCh **taf-* "hand, palm": Hs *tāfī*, Bol *tafi*, DB *taf*.
CCh **tufi-* "hand": Nza *tivi*, Bch *tufa*, *tufɛy*.
Contamination with **tuf-* "five".
ECh **taf-* "hand": Sok *tafa*.
Agaw **taf-* "hand": Aun *taf-*.

2350 *taf- "clap"

WCh **taf-* "clap (the hands)" [1], "take a handful" [2]: Hs *tāfa* [1], *tafē* [2].

Omot *taf- ‘‘clap’’: Kaf tap.

Derived from *taf- ‘‘hand, arm’’.

2351 *taf- ‘‘go’’

Eg tfy ‘‘move away’’ (n).
Suffix -y.
WCh *taf- ‘‘go, go out’’ [1], ‘‘follow’’ [2]: Hs tafi [1], Gwn tafi [1], Bol taf- [1], Krk taf- [1], Dera tai [1], Wrj taw- [2], Paa taf- [2], Siri taf- [2], Ngz təfu [1].

Alternation *a ~ *i. Cf. Dhl ṯipp-eem- ‘‘come from’’?

2352 *taf-taf- ‘‘henna’’

Eg tftf ‘‘henna’’.
WCh *taf-taf- ‘‘henna’’ [1], ‘‘Cochlospermum tinctorium’’ [2]: Hs taftaf [1], Ngz taftaf [2].

Reduplication.

2353 *tag- ‘‘go, run’’

WCh *tag- ‘‘run away’’: Glm tāg-.
LEC *tag- ‘‘go’’: Som tag.
Omot *teg- ‘‘go’’: Nao tɛg, Shk təg.
Secondary *-e-?

2354 *taˁ- ‘‘flow’’

Sem *tīˁ- ‘‘flow’’ [1], ‘‘pour (of rain)’’ [2]: Arab tyˁ [-i-] [1], Tgr ʾä-twa [2].
Based on *taˁ-.
WCh *ta-/*ti- ‘‘ooze’’ [1], ‘‘rain’’ (v.) [2]: Ang ta [1], Tng ti [2].
LEC *toʾ- ‘‘draw water’’: Or toʾa.
The source of *o is not clear.
Dhl t’a-δ- ‘‘wet’’ (v.).
Is t’- a regular reflex of *t-?

2355 *ta^cab- "be tired, be ill"

Sem *tV^cab- "be tired": Arab t^cb [-a-].
WCh *taHab- "be ill": Hs taḅu.
ECh *ta'ab- "become tired": Mubi ta'aba.

Cf. SA *tib- "be still": Saho tib, Afar tib?

2356 *taḫ-/*tuḫ- "belly"

Sem *tāḫ- "inside, intestines": Akk tāḫu.
WCh *tuH-/*tuH-ki- "belly, inside" [1], "body" [2]: Hs čiki [1], Cagu cuke [2], Kir tuwok [1], Geji tuki [1], Pol tu [1], Zem tuko [1], Brw tu [1], Say tu [1], Brm tuk [1], Dwot tu [1], Ngz təka [2].
*-ki is a morpheme of parts of the body.

Alternation *a ~ *u.

2357 *tak- "fly, moth"

Sem *takk- "moth": Aram (Jud) takk-.
Eg tkk.t "ichneumon fly".
Dhl ṯakkwa'e "dung beatle".

2358 *takoc- "trample, pound"

Sem *tVkVs- "trample": Aram (Jud) tks.
WCh *takwac- "pound": Ngz takwsu.

Derived from *tuk- "beat, press".

2359 *takon- "suck blood"

WCh *takwan- "bleed (smb.)": Mbu takwana, Diri takwan, Miya takwam, Siri takwana.
Agaw *tVkwan- "bugs": Bil təχ^wan, Xmr təχ^wan, Kwr tuukaan, Kem tuχaanaa.
SA *tVkwan- "bugs": Saho tək^wan, Afar tək^wan.
LEC *tukan- "bug": Or tukana.
Metathesis of vowels. An Agaw loanword?

Note nominal forms in Cush. Derived from *tak- "fly, moth"?

2360 *taḳ- "lizard, chameleon"

Berb **tVḳ-tVḳ-* "lizard": Ahg *e-mə-təɣtəɣ*.
Reduplication.
WCh **taḳ-* "chameleon": Siri *tāḳi*, Jmb *ataɣa*.
Prefix *a-* in Jmb.

2361 *taḳar- "stick, pole"

Sem **taḳr-* "stick, sceptre": Aram (Syr) *taqr-*.
WCh **taḳar-* "long bamboo pole": Ngz *takarwa*.

2362 *tal-/*tul- "speak"

Sem **tul-* "pronounce distinctly" [1], "recite" [2]: Akk *tēlu* [1], Arab *tlw* [*-u-*] [2].
WCh **tal-* "ask": Sura *tal*, Ank *tal-*.

Alternation **a* ~ **u*. Cf. also ECh **tulul-* "cry" (n.): Kera *tulul*.

2363 *talim- "brother"

Sem **talīm-* "privileged brother": Akk *talīmu*.
CCh **twalim-* < **talim-* "brother": Msg *tollimma*.

2364 *tam-tam- "strike, press"

Sem **tVm-tVm-* "strike, knock": Tgy *tämtäma*.
Eg *tmtm* "press, grind".
CCh **tam-tam-* "slap": Mafa *tamtam*.

Reduplication of **tum-* "break, beat".

2365 *tamuʾ- "speak, shout"

Sem **tVmVʾ-* "swear": Akk *tamû*.
WCh **tamu(H)-* "tell": Ank *tum*, Krk *tam*.
Rift **taʾam-* "shout": Kwz *taʾam-*.
Metathesis and assimilation of **tamuʾ-* or secondary development of **tam-*.

2366 *tamVs- "pound, squeeze"

Sem *tVmVš- "squeeze": Tgr tämsā.
WCh *tamVs- "pound": Hs tamsa.
LEC *tamVs- "spread out, scatter": Or tamsa-ʾa.

Derived from *tum-.

2367 *tan- "snake, worm"

Sem *tannīn- "big serpent, crocodile": Hbr tannīn, Arab tinnīn-.
Partial reduplication.
WCh *tan- "earth worm": Hs tānā.

2368 *tan- "container"

Sem *tann- "wooden bowl": Akk tannu.
Eg tn.w "basket" (gr).

2369 *tanhal-/*tanhil- "container"

Eg tnhr "box" (sarc).
Note -r < *-l-.
WCh *tanHal- "pot": Bgh taŋal.
CCh *tinHil- < *tanHil- "pot": Gis tiŋgile.
Assimilation of vowels.

An old compound? Cf. a similar morphonological structure in *dawḫal- "vessel" and *tuḫal- "container".

2370 *taq̇-/*tiq̇- "strike"

Sem *tīḫ- "strike (with a stick)": Arab tyḫ [-i-].
Based on *tVḫ-.
WCh *taq̇-/*tiq̇- "strike, kick": Hs tīḳa, Ngz təku.

2371 *tar- "collect, mix"

WCh *tar- "collect": Hs tāra, Krk taru, Say tarə.
Dhl ṯar- "mix".

2372 *tar- "tear, cut"

Sem **mVtur-* "cut": Arab *mtr* [-*u*-].
Prefix **mV-*. Modified vocalism.
WCh **tar-/*tur-* "tear" [1], "break" [2]: Glm *tar-* [1], Klr *tur* [2], DB *tar* [2].
LEC **tarar-* "cut, scratch": Or *tarara*.
Partial reduplication.

2373 *tar- "pull, draw"

Sem **mVtur-* "pull": Arab *mtr* [-*u*-].
Prefix **mV-* in Arab. Modified vocalism. Cf. Jib *terr* "drag, lead away".
CCh **tyar-* < **tarí-* "draw": Bud *terí*.
ECh **tar-* "be stretched": Tob *tārē*.

2374 *taraẖ- "hole, pit"

Sem **taraẖ-* "slope of a mine": Akk *taraẖẖu*.
CCh **taraɣ-* "hole": Bud *taragā*.

2375 *taruw- "kind of tree"

Berb **tVrVw-* "kind of pole": Aks *a-tru*.
WCh **taru-* "kind of tree": Hs *taruwā*.

2376 *tarVc- "break, tear"

Sem **tVrVs-* "break": Gz *täräsä*, Gur *tärräsä*.
WCh **tarVc-* "break into pieces": Hs *tarçe*.
LEC **tarVs-* "be torn": Or *tarsaʾa*.

Derived from **tar-* "tear, cut".

2377 *tat- "sow, plant"

CCh **tVt-* "sow": Tera *təta*.
Rift **tat-* "plant" (v.): Kwz *tat-*.

Reduplication.

2378 *taw- "hip, thigh"

Eg *twꜣ.t* "hip, thigh" (gr).
Vocalic *-ꜣ*.
ECh **taw-* "hip, thigh": Kera *tawa*.

2379 *taw- "forget"

Berb **tVw-* "forget": Izy *ettu*, *əttu*.
WCh **taw-* "forget": Wrj *taw*, Diri *tawa*, Ngz *tuwaye*.

Cf. Eg *thy* "be forgetful (of heart)" (MK).

2380 *taw-/*tay- "hoe"

Berb **taw-* "spade, hoe": Ghat *ta-taw-t*, Ahg *tattawt*.
WCh **tVy-* "hoe": Miya *tiyi*.

Consonantal alternation **-w-* ~ **-y-*.

2381 *taw-/*tay- "hunger"

Sem **tawan-* "hunger": Arab *tawan-*.
Derivative in *-an-*?
ECh **tay-* "hunger": Kera *tay*.

Consonantal alternation **-w-* ~ **-y-*.

2382 *taw-/*tay- "speak, shout, call"

Eg *tyꜣ* "shout (of pain)" (med).
Vocalic *-ꜣ*.
WCh **tay-* "greet": Tng *tay*.
CCh **taʾ-/*taw-* "speak" [1], "shout" [2]: Heba *atau* [1], Glv *ta-* [1], Kus *to* [2].
ECh **tay-* "call": Lele *tey*, Tob *te*.
Omot **taw-* "tell, speak": Kaf *taw-*, Bwo *tau* (imper.).

Consonantal alternation **-w-* ~ **-y-*.

2383 *tawar-/*tayar- "pole, stick"

Sem **tVwVr-* "crossbeam": Tgr *tor*.

Eg *twr* "reed" (med).
WCh **tayar-* "stick": Gera *teera*.

Consonantal alternation **-w-* ~ **-y-*.

2384 *tayaʒ- "pierce, break"

Sem **tīz-* "pierce and tremble (of arrow)": Arab *tyz* [-*i*-].
Berb **tVyVʒ-* "notch": Izd *tizi*.
WCh **taʒ-* "split": Hs *tazge*.
Suffix *-ge*?
ECh **ta[y]aʒ-* "break": Tum *tāǯ*.
Agaw **tayVz-* "strike, hit": Xmr *tays-*, Xmt *taz*, Aun *tas-*, Dmt *taš-*.

2385 *tayVs- "goat"

Sem **tayaš-* "goat": Hbr *tayiš*, Aram (Syr) *tayšā*, Arab *tays-*, Soq *teš*, Jib *tuš*, *teš*, Hss *tāyeh*, Mhr *tāyeh*, Shh *tuš*.
Cf. Akk *daššu* id.
ECh **tVyVs-* "goat": Mubi *tēs*.
If not an Arab loanword.

2386 *teʔ- "earth"

Eg *tꜣ* "earth" (pyr), Copt **to*: Boh *t'o*, Shd *to*.
CCh **tyaʔ-/*tyay-* "sand": Mwu *teo*, Bch *tiyey*.
ECh **tyaw-/*tyay-* "earth" [1], "clay" [2]: Lele *tēy* [1], Kera *tiiwə* [2].
LEC **taʔ-* "fertile soil": Or *taaʔoo*.
From **teʔ-*?

2387 *teḥal- "spleen, liver"

Sem **ṭiḥāl-* "spleen": Hbr *ṭᵉḥōl*, Arab *ṭiḥāl-*.
Emphatization of HS **t-* or an old emphatic.
ECh **tyaHal-* "liver": Tum *telu*, Ndam *ta:lū*.

2388 *tek- "take"

Eg *tkk* "grasp, seize" (MK).
Partial reduplication.
WCh **tyak-* "take": Sha *tək*, DB *tyek*.
CCh **tyak-* "take": Msg *taka*, *tega*.

2389 *ter- "weapon"

Sem **tir-* "stick with a hook": Tgr *tir*.
Eg *ỉtꜣ* "kind of weapon" (NK).
Graphic representation of **tir-*.
ECh **tVr-* "knife": Kera *tər-tə*.
LEC **ter-* "spear": Som *teeri*.

Cf. a corresponding verb in Dhl *ṯaar-* "pierce".

2390 *ti-/*tiw- "bread, flour"

Eg *t* "bread" (pyr).
WCh **tuw-* < **tiw-* "food made of flour, tuwo": Hs *tuwō*.
ECh **ti-* "flour": Tob *ti*.

2391 *tiˀ-/*tVy- "dominate"

Berb **tVy-* "excel": Sml *äti*.
WCh **tiˀ-* "dominate, possess": Tng *ti*.
Rift **tiˀ-* "be prominent, emerge": Ir *tiˀ-it-* , Alg *tiˀ-itis-*.
Connected with **tVy-* "father, chief"? Note the consonantal alternation **-ˀ-* ~ **-y-*.

2392 *tiˀin- "tree"

Sem **tiˀn-* "fig tree": Akk *tittu*, Hbr *tᵉˀēnā*, Aram (Syr) *tēttā*.
CCh **tiyin-* < **tiˀin-* "mahogany": Hwn *tinə*, Gaa *tin-da*, Gbr *tiyin-da*.

2393 *tibin- "brain, marrow"

Eg *tbn* "marrow" (med).
CCh **tiḅin-* "brain": Gbn *tiḅin-de*.
Secondary emphatic.

2394 *tič- "break"

Eg *tyšs* "grind" (OK).
Note *-šs* < **-č-*.
WCh **tič-* "thresh" [1], "squeeze" [2]: Hs *tisa* [1], Bks *tis* [2].

Omot **tič-* ‘‘break’’: Kaf *tičč-*, *tiš-*, Mch *tiiččii*, Bwo *tic*.

2395 *tihim- ‘‘strike’’

Sem **hVtim-* ‘‘strike’’: Arab *htm* [-*i*-].
Metathesis.
Eg *thm* ‘‘push, pierce’’ (med).
WCh **tiHim-* ‘‘strike’’: Hs *tīmā*.

2396 *tihir- ‘‘warrior, courtier’’

Sem **ti[h]ir-* ‘‘courtier’’: Akk *tīru*.
Eg *thr* ‘‘Asiatic warrior’’ (XVIII).

A cultural loanword?

2397 *tihur- ‘‘tear’’

Sem **hVtur-* ‘‘tear, rip’’: Arab *htr* [-*u*-].
Metathesis.
WCh **tiHur-* ‘‘tear, pluck’’: Ang *tīr*, Gera *tûr*.

2398 *tik-/*tiyak- ‘‘neck, occiput’’

Sem **tikk-* ‘‘neck, occiput’’: Akk *tikku*, *tīku*.
WCh **tiyak-* ‘‘occiput’’ [1], ‘‘neck’’ [2]: Sura *tɔ:k* [1], Ang *tok* [2], Chip *tɔk* [2], Mnt *tok* [2], Ank *tiyək* [2].

2399 *tuḳ- ‘‘strike, break’’

Berb **tVḳ-tVḳ-* ‘‘break, be broken’’: Ahg *təγtəγ*.
Reduplication.
LEC **tuḳ-* ‘‘strike’’: Or *tuq-*.

2400 *ti(m)b- ‘‘navel’’

WCh **timb-* ‘‘navel’’: Bol *tumb-*, Krk *timbi*, Ngm *timbo*.
Agaw **ʾi-tib-* ‘‘navel’’: Bil *itibaa*.

Cf. Bed *teefa* ‘‘navel’’ and ECh **dif-* (Sok *diff-in*)?

2401 *tin- "tendon, muscle"

Sem **watīn-* "aorta": Arab *watīn-*.
Prefix **wa-*.
Agaw **tin-* "kind of muscle": Kem *tinaa*.

2402 *tinuq- "stay, dwell"

Sem **tVnuḫ-* "stay, dwell": Arab *tnḫ* [-*u*-].
WCh **tinuq-* "stay, dwell" [1], "sit" [2]: Sura *tɔn* [1], Ang *tong* [1 2], Ank *tong* [2], Grk *tung* [2], Krk *tiŋg-* [2], Krf *tingu* [2], Glm *tungw-* [2].
Agaw **tinu[χ]-* "dwell": Kwr *tänkw*, Dmb *tenku*, Kem *tänkə*.

2403 *tir- "liver, vein"

WCh **tir-* "liver" [1], "kidney" [2], "vein" [3]: Pol *wa-teraʔe* [1], Paa *tir-ḳwasa* [2], Miya *tir* [3].
SA **tiraw-* "liver": Saho *tiraw*, Afar *tiroo*.
Suffix **-aw-*.
LEC **tir(aw)-* "liver": Som *tiro*, *traw*, Or *tiruu*, Gel *čira*, Kon *tira*, Gat *tira*, Gdl *šira*, Arb *tira*.
Suffix **-aw-*.
Wrz **tir-* "liver": War *čira*, *čire*, Gaw *tire*, *cire*, Gob *čir-*, Hrs *ciire*, Dob *ciire*.
Omot **tir-/*tur-* "liver": Ome *tire*, Gll *tuʔri*, Ari *twri*.
Cf. a derivative in **tiro[w]-* "liver": Hmr *tiirooboo*.

2404 *tir- "building"

Sem **tīr-* "part of the building" [1], "wall, fence" [2]: Akk *tēru* [1], Hbr *tīrā* [2].
Eg *ỉtr.t* "temple" (OK).
ỉ- is a prefix or a sign for a root vowel.
ECh **tir-* "house": Smr *čire*, Kwn *tər*.

2405 *tir- "run"

Sem **tir-/*tur-* "run fast" [1], "hurry, hasten" [2]: Arab *trr* [-*i*-, -*u*-] [1], Tgy *trr* [2].
Secondary **-u-*.
Berb **tVr-tVr-* "drive, make run": Ahg *tərtər*.

Reduplication.
ECh *tVr- "run": Kera *təra*, Kwan *tara*.

2406 *tir- "sew, plait"

WCh *tir- "sew": Kry *tər*, Miya *tir*, Fyer *tōr*.
Fyer may go back to *taru- or *tiwar-.
CCh *tir- "plait": Daba *tir*, Mofu *tər-ḍ-*.
SA *tar-tar- "sew": Saho *tartar-*, Afar *tartar-*.
Reduplication with modified vocalism.

2407 *tis- "sit"

Eg *tys* "sit" (l).
Vocalic *-y-*.
WCh *tVs- "sit": Tala *təsu*.
Cf. Sha *təs* "put down".

2408 *tiyaʾ-/*tiyaw- "be true, be right"

Eg *tyw* "true" (MK).
WCh *tVyVʾ- "right" (adj.): Kry *atey*, Miya *teʾe*, Mbu *tehu*.
ECh *tiyaw- "right" (adj.): Mig *tiyawa*.

Consonantal alternation *-ʾ- ~ *-w-.

2409 *tof- "tie"

Eg *ntf* "untie" (n).
Prefix *nV-.
WCh *twaf- "tie up": Sha *tof*, Klr *tof*.
Cf. Sura *te:p* "plait", Chip *tɛp-ka* id.
CCh *twaf- "sew" [1], "tie" [2]: Gis *tof* [1], Mofu *təf-* [1 2].

2410 *tok- "speak, ask"

Berb *tVk- "inquire": Ayr *sə-təkk-ət*, Twl *sə-təkk-ət*.
WCh *twak- "talk" [1], "ask" [2]: Ang *tok* [1], Paa *taku* [2].

2411 *tor- "clean (v.)

Eg *twr* "clean" (MK).
Vocalic *-w-*.
CCh **twar-* "sweep": Masa *tɔr-amo*, Msm *tor*.

2412 *tuĉ- "spit"

Berb **tuc-* "cough": Sml *ttusu*.
Eg *ntš* "sprinkle" (med).
Prefix **nV-*.
WCh **tuĉi-* "spit": Sura *tus*, Ang *tis*.

2413 *tuf- "spit"

Sem **tup-* "spit" [1], "spit blood" [2]: Aram (Jud) *tpp* [1], Arab *tff* [*-u-*] [2], Gz *tfʾ* [1], Tgy *tfʾ* [1], Amh *tff* [1], Gaf *tff* [1], Hrr *tf* [1], Gur *tf* [1].
Eg *tf* "spit" (pyr).
WCh **tuf-* "spit": Hs *tōfā*, Bol *tuf*, Dera *tuvi*, Ngm *tup*, Fyer *tuf*, Sha *tuf*, DB *tuf*, Ngz *təpku*.
CCh **tuf-* "spit": Mba *tuf*, Zgh *tfa*, Glv *taf-*, Mofu *-təf-*, Daba *tif*, Bch *tufə*, Log *tufi*, Zime *tufo*, Masa *tuf- nā*.
ECh **tuf-* "spit": Kera *tufi*, Kwan *atəpē*, Mubi *tuffa*, Brg *čifi*.
Brg *čifi* < **tufi-*.
Agaw **tif-* "spit": Bil *ṭif*, Xmr *tif y-*, Kem *təff y-* .
Secondary *-i-*? Unexpected *ṭ-* in Bil.
Bed *tuf* "spit".
LEC **tuf-* "spit": Som *tuf*, Or *tufe*, Arb *tuf-*.
HEC **tuf-* "spit": Sid *tufi*.

2414 *tug- "strike"

WCh **tug-* "pound, thresh": Tng *tuge*.
CCh **twagVy-* "strike": BM *togiya*, Masa *toia*.
ECh **twaga-* "strike": Nch *tagi*, Gbr *togoi*.
Omot **tug-* "strike": Kaf *tuug*, *tuuge*.

2415 *tuḫal- "container"

Sem **tuḫal-* "basket": Akk *tuḫallu*.

WCh *tuHal- "pot": Sura *tugul*, Ang *tūl*, Mpn *tūl*, Kry *n-dul*, Miya *duwal*, Siri *n-duli*.
ECh *tVHVl- "pot": Mkk *toolo*.
Agaw *tul- "kind of earthenware": Kem *tolaa*.

2416 *tuk- "beat, press"

Sem *tuk- "press" [1], "destroy, cut" [2]: Akk *takāku* [1], Arab *tkk* [-*u*-] [2].
Berb *tVk- "knock": Ahg *tək-ət*.
WCh *tak-/*tuk- "trample, step on" [1], "beat" [2], "push" [3]: Hs *tāka* [1], Ngm *tako* [2], Bks *tuk* [3], DB *tuk* [3], Ngz *tak-du* [1].
CCh *tukwa- "clap" [1], "strike" [2]: Gis *tukwa-* [1], Log *tku* [2].
SA *tak-/*tok- "strike": Afar *tak-*, *-ootok-*.
Omot *tuk- "hit, strike": Kaf *tuk-*.

2417 *tukaʾ- "burn; ash"

Eg *tkꜣ* "burn" (reg), Copt *tōk: Boh *t'ōk*, Shd *tōk*.
WCh *tuʾak- "ash": Hs *tōkā*.
Metathesis.

2418 *tuḳ- "go, run"

Sem *tVḳ-tVḳ- "advance quickly": Arab *tqtq*.
Reduplication.
Berb *tVḳVy- "mend one's pace": Ahg *təɣiy-ət*.
WCh *tuḳwa- "go away" [1], "run" [2]: Hs *tūḳa* [1], Dera *tako* [1], DB *tok* [2].
CCh *tVḳwa- "follow": Hwn *təkwa*.
HEC *ṭoḳ- "run away": Sid *ṭoḳ-*.
Initial *ṭ- < *t- under the influence of *-ḳ-.

2419 *tul- "pierce"

Eg *wtn* "pierce" (n).
Vocalic *w*-.
CCh *tul- "pierce": Chb *ntəli*, Nza *təl-*, FJ *tula-*, Mwu *utulo*.
Rift *tul- "split into two": Kwz *tul-as-*.

2420 *tul- ''hang''

Sem **tVlVy-* ''hang'': Akk *tullû*, Hbr *tly*.
Based on **tVl-*.
ECh **tul-* ''hang'': Ndam *tula*, Lele *tuul*.

2421 *tum- ''break, beat''

WCh **tumi-* ''destroy'' 1, ''break'' 2: Mnt *tam*, *tum* 1, Wrj *təm* 2, Kry *tum* 2, Cagu *tam* 2, Mbu *tim* 2, Jmb *tuma* 2.
CCh **tum-* ''hit'': Msm *tum*, Mafa *tʋm*.
LEC **tum-* ''beat, pound'': Som *tum-*, Or *tuma*, Rnd *tum*, Arb *tum-*.

2422 *tupaḥ- ''apple''

Sem **tupāḥ-* ''apple'': Hbr *tappūaḥ*, Arab *tuffāḥ-*.
Berb **tVfaḥ-* ''apples'': Izy *etteffaḥ*.
From Arab?

2423 *tuq- ''pour''

Sem **tuḫ-* ''pour, pour too much'': Akk *taḫāḫu* [-*u*-].
WCh **taq-* < **tuqa-* ''pour'': Sura *tak*.
CCh **tuqa-* ''pour out'': Bud *tuka-*.

2424 *tur- ''push''

Sem **tVr-* ''push gently'': Soq *ter*.
Cf. **tar-* ''blow'' (n.): Arab *tār-*.
WCh **turi-* ''push'': Hs *tūra*, Gwn *tūraa*, Grk *tir*, Krf *tuuru-*, Gera *tuurə-*, Say *turi*.
ECh **tur-* ''push'': Dng *ture*.

2425 *tur- ''lift''

Sem **tVrVʔ-* ''lift'': Akk *tarû*.
Based on biliteral **tVr-*.
Eg *twꜣ* ''lift'' (pyr).
Vocalic *-w-*.
CCh **turi-* ''lift'': Gaa *itiri*, Gab *tiri*, Boka *tiri*, Hwo *turaŋ*.
Cf. also Tera dial. *dira* id.

2426 *turVb- "earth, sand"

Sem **turb-* "earth, dust": Akk *tarbuʾtu*, Arab *turb-*, *turb-at-*, *turāb-*.
Cf. Hss *terōb* "do the ritual ablutions with sand".
WCh **turVb-* "sandy soil": Hs *turḅāyā*.
Secondary emphatic.

2427 *tuwur- "turn"

Sem **tūr-* "turn": Akk *târu*, Arab *twr* [*-u-*].
CCh **tuwur-* "turn": Daba *tuwur*.

2428 *tüʾal- "tree, bush"

Sem **tiʾal-* "white cedar": Akk *tiʾalu*.
CCh **tuwal-* < **tuʾal-* "sheanut tree": Hwn *tūwala*.
ECh **twal-* < **tuʾal-* "bush": Kwan *tolā*.

2429 *tül- "hill"

Sem **tall-/*till-* "hill": Akk *tīlu*, Ug *tl*, Hbr *tēl*, Aram (Syr) *tellō*, Arab *tall-*.
WCh **tul-* "hill-top": Hs *tull-uwā*.
LEC **tul-* "hill": Or *tuluu*.
HEC **tul-* "hill": Sid *tullo*.

2430 *t[ü]m- "fish"

Eg *tm.t* "kind of fish" (med).
CCh **tum-* "fish": Msg *tum*.
**ü* is reconstructed on the basis of forms appearing in HS compound **tüm-meḥas-*. This root serves as a second component of a Cush composite for "fish": LEC **ḳur-tum-* (Or *qurtummi*, Gdl *kurtum-ɛt*) and HEC **ḳir-tum-/*ḳur-tum-* (Sid *ḳiltiʾmi*, Dar *ḳultuʾme*, Had *ḳurṭume*, Ala *ḳurčum-et*, Bmb *ḳur-ṭume*, Kmb *ḳurtum*).

2431 *tüm-meḥas- "crocodile, snake"

Sem **timšāḥ-* "crocodile": Arab *timsāḥ-*.
Haplology and metathesis.

Eg *tšmm* ''crocodile'' (gr).
Metathesis and loss of the laryngeal in Late Eg. Note irregular *-š-* < **-s-*.
CCh **timyas-* < **tumyaHas-* ''horned viper'': Mofu *timeš*.
ECh **tumVs-* ''crocodile'': Mubi *tumsa*, Mkk *tumsa*.
Borrowed from Arab?

Compound with the original meaning''snake-fish'' of **t[ü]m-* ''fish'' and **meḥas-* ''big snake, crocodile''.

2432 *tVb- ''move upwards''

Sem **tVb-* ''rise'': Akk *tebû*.
Berb **tVb-* ''lay off, raise'': Ahg *a-təb*.
Eg *tbtb* ''pull up, raise''.
Reduplication.

Cf. **tab(b)-* ''uphill, slope'': Or *tabba*.

2433 *tVfal-/*tVfil- ''spit''

Sem **tVpil-/*tVpul-* ''spit'': Arab *tfl* [*-i-*, *-u-*], Jib *tfol*, Hss *tefōl*, Mhr *tefōl*, Shh *tfol*.
CCh **tVfal-* ''spit'': Muk *tfala*.

Derived from **tuf-* ''spit''.

2434 *tVk-tVk- ''trample, knock''

Sem **tVk-tVk-* ''trample'': Arab *tktk*.
Berb **tVk-tVk-* ''knock slightly'': Ahg *təktək*.
Eg *tktk* ''trample (enemies)''.

Reduplication of **tuk-* ''beat, press''.

2435 *tVm-tVm- ''speak indistinctly''

Sem **tVm-tVm-* ''stammer'' [1], ''grumble'' [2]: Arab *tmtm* [1], Jib *ettəmtim* [2].
Berb **tVm-tVm-* ''whisper'' (n.): Izd *a-təmtəm*.

Reduplication.

2436 *tVrVk- "beat, strike"

Sem **tVrVk-* "beat": Akk *tarāku*.
Berb **tVrVk-* "strike": Ahg *ə-trək*.

2437 *tVwVr- "flow"

Sem **tūr-* "flow": Arab *twr* [-*u*-].
Berb **tVwVr-* "be full (of liquid)": Ahg *ə-twər*.
Eg *twr* "waters" (BD).
Deverbative?

2438 *tVy- "father, chief"

Berb **tVy-* "stepfather": Ahg *tey*.
Eg *ỉty* "father, monarch, prince" (OK).

*ṭ

2439 *ṭaʔ-/*ṭaw- "fold, spin"

Sem **ṭūy-* "spin" [1], "fold, wrap" [2], "turn" [3], "plait, twist" [4]: Akk *ṭawû* [1], Hbr *ṭwy* [1], Aram *ṭwy* [1], Arab *ṭwy* [-*i*-] [2], Gz *ṭwy* [3], Tgr *ṭäwa* [3 4], Hrr *ṭewō* [2], Gur *aṭwayyä* [4].
Based on biconsonantal **ṭVw-*.
WCh **ṭaṭ-* "spin": Ang *tat*.
Reduplication.
Berb **ṭVw-/*ṭVy-* "be folded" [1], "fold, bend" [2]: Ahg *a-ḍə* [1], Twl *a-ḍu* [2], Sgr *a-ḍi* [2].
Bed *ḍaʔ* "plait, weave".
LEC **ḍaw-* "spin": Or *ḍaw-*.
Consonantal alternation **-ʔ-* ~ **-w-*.

2440 *ṭaʔ-/*ṭaw- "go, come"

Sem **ṭūʔ-* "go and come" [1], "come" [2]: Arab *ṭwʔ* [-*u*-] [1], Hss *ṭewō* [2].
Based on **ṭVw-*.
WCh **ṭaʔ-* "go": Wrj *ṭa-n*, Siri *ṭa*, Jmb *da*.

CCh *ṭuw- < *ṭVw- ‘‘go’’: Bnn *tuwwa*.
ECh *tawi- ‘‘go, walk’’: Tum *tiw*, Sok *teui*.
Agaw *ṭaw- ‘‘enter’’: Bil *tuw*, Xmt *ṭaw*, Kwr *tuw*, Dmb *tuw*, Kem *tuw*, Aun *ṭuu*, Dmt *ṭow*.

Consonantal alternation *-ʾ- ~ *-w-.

2441 *ṭaʾ-/*ṭaw-/*ṭay- ‘‘cloth’’

WCh *ṭay- ‘‘mat’’: Hs *taitai*, *taitayī*.
Reduplication.
Bed *ḍaʾ* ‘‘cloth’’.
LEC *ḍaw- ‘‘cloth’’: Or *ḍaw-*.
Omot *[ṭ]aH- ‘‘clothes’’: Anf *ta-ho*.

Consonantal alternation *-ʾ- ~ *-w- ~ *-y-.

2442 *ṭaʾum- ‘‘speak’’

WCh *ṭaʾum- ‘‘sing’’: Mnt *tam*, Wrj *ṭəm*, Mbu *ṭəm*, Kry *tuma*, Paa *təma*, Miya *ṭām*, Jim *duma*.
HEC *ṭaʾVm- ‘‘ask’’: Sid *ṭaʾm-*, Kab *ṭaʾm-*, Had *ṭam-*.

2443 *ṭaʾür- ‘‘bird’’

Sem *ṭaʾir- ‘‘bird, fly’’: Arab *ṭaʾir-*.
CCh *ṭūr- < *ṭVʾur- ‘‘partridge’’: Gis *tūro*.
ECh *tur- ‘‘hen’’: Nch *turo-ba*, Kbl *turo*.
Contraction.
Bed *an-ḍiro* ‘‘hen’’.
Prefix *an-*.
Cf. Berb *ṭir- ‘‘falcon’’: Izy *eṭṭiλ*, Izd *ə-ṭṭir*.

2444 *ṭab- ‘‘tribe’’

Sem *ṭVb- ‘‘tribe’’: Gur *ṭəb*.
Berb *ṭab- ‘‘crowd, meeting’’: Ahg *ə-ṭṭabu*.

2445 *ṭab- ‘‘plug, bolt’’

Sem *ṭabb- ‘‘plug’’: Arab *ṭabb-at-*.

Berb *ṭab- "lock, bolt": Siwa *ə-ṭṭāb-ət*.

Cf. WCh *ṭVḅ- < *ṭVb- "close, cover": Kry *ṭəḅə*, Jmb *dəḅa*.

2446 *ṭab- "cut, tear"

Sem *ṭVb- "skin" (v.): Gog *ṭäbba* 2, Gur *ṭäbba* 2, Slt *ṭäbä* 2.
Eg *dbdb* "pierce, tear" (l).
Reduplication.
WCh *taḅ- < *ṭab- "rip (garment)": Hs *tāḅe*.
Shift of emphatization.

2447 *ṭab- "catch, seize"

Eg *dbdb* "catch, seize".
Reduplication.
WCh *taḅ- < *ṭab- "catch, seize": Hs *taḅē*, Glm *tab*, Gera *taw*, Geji *doḅi*.
CCh *tVḅ- < *ṭVb- "take": Mofu *təḅ-*.
ECh *tiḅ- < *ṭib- "plunder": Mkk *tiḅa*.

2448 *ṭab- "container"

Eg *tb.t* "box" (gr).
WCh *taḅ < *ṭab- "sack, bag, quiver": Bol *taba*, Ngz *taḅa*.
Cf. Ang *tip* "sack".
CCh *ṭiḅ- < *ṭib- "calabash": Gaa *tiḅa*, Gbn *tiḅe*.
Cf. also *ṭimb- id.: Lame *tɛmbi*, LPe *timbi*, ZBt *timbī*. Secondary *-i-?
HEC *ṭab- "clay plate": Had *ṭaabaʔu*, Kmb *ṭaba-ta*.

2449 *ṭabaḳ- "container"

Sem *ṭabaḳ- "tray, pan": Aram *ṭabāq-*, Arab *ṭabaq-*.
CCh *taḅak- < *ṭabaḳ- "bag": Gis *taḅak-*.
If not an Arab loanword.

Derived from *ṭab- "container".

2450 *ṭabVl- "drum"

Sem *ṭabl- "drum": Akk ṭabalu, Aram (Syr) ṭabl-, Arab ṭabl-, Gur ṭabl-, Hss ṭabl, Mhr ṭābel, Shh ṭɛl.
Berb *ṭVbVl- "drum": Ahg e-ṭṭebel, Twl e- ṭṭebel, Kby ə-ṭṭbol.
Sem loanword?
Eg tbn "drum" (gr).

Derived from *ṭab- "container".

2451 *ṭaĉ- "fly" (v.)

Sem *ṭūŝ- "fly" [1], "jump up" [2]: Hbr ṭwŝ [1], Jib ṭeŝŝ [2].
Based on *ṭVŝ-.
WCh *ṭaĉ- "fly": Hs tāšì.

2452 *ṭag-/*ṭug- "ear"

ECh *tug- "ear": Kwan tuga.
SA *ḍag- "eardrum": Afar ḍaaga.
LEC *ḍeg-/*ḍog- "ear": Som ḍeg, Rnd dogo.
Vocalism is not clear.
HEC *ṭag- "ear": Bmb ḍaga.

Alternation *a ~ *u.

2453 *ṭaˁ-ṭaˁ- "trample"

Sem *ṭVˁ-ṭVˁ- "trample": Arab ṭˁṭˁ.
WCh *ṭaṭ- "kick": Ang tat.
LEC *ḍaˁ-ḍaˁ- march, trample": Som ḍaˁḍaˁ.

Reduplication.

2454 *ṭaˁam- "taste, eat"

Sem *ṭVˁam- "taste, eat": Hbr ṭˁm, Aram ṭˁm, Arab ṭˁm [-a-], Gz ṭˁm, Jib ṭaˁam, Soq ṭaˁam, Hss ṭām, Mhr ṭām, Shh ṭˁam.
SA *ḍaˁam- "taste" (v.): Saho ḍaˁam-.
Assimilation of vowels.
LEC *ḍaˁam- "taste" (n.): Som ḍaˁan.
Assimilation of vowels.

Dhl *ṯem-* "try, look at".

-e- results from a contraction.

2455 *ṭaḥan- "grind, forge"

Sem **ṭVḥan-* "grind corn, pound": Hbr *ṭḥn*, Arab *ṭḥn* [*-a-*], Jib *ṭaḥan*, Soq *ṭaḥan*, Hss *ṭeḥān*, Mhr *ṭeḥān*, Shh *ṭḥān*.
WCh **ṭaHan-* "press down" [1], "forge" [2]: Ang *ten* [1], Tng *toni* [2].

Contraction.

2456 *ṭaḥin- "tooth"

Sem **ṭāḥin-* "molar": Arab *ṭāḥin-at-*.
WCh **ṭVḥin-* "tooth": Wrj *təyn-*, Kry *tin*, Miya *tiyim*, Paa *udini*, Cagu *dīne*, Mbu *ṭīno*, Jmb *dīna*.

Connected with **ṭaḥan-* "grind, forge" (cf. a similar motivation of IE **g'ombhos* "tooth" ← **g'em-* "grind").

2457 *ṭal- "give birth"

SA **ḍal-* "give birth": Saho *ḍal*, Afar *ḍal*.
LEC **ḍal-* "give birth": Som *ḍal*, Or *ḍal*.

Isolated verbal stem on which more widespread derivatives are based, cf. **ṭal-* "young animal".

2458 *ṭal- "young animal"

Berb **ṭVl-* "calf": Twl *ă-ḍēl*.
WCh **ṭal-* "young animal following its mother": Hs *ṭāl-iyō*.

Derived from **ṭal-* "give birth". Cf. Sem **ṭalay-* "boy" (Aram *ṭalay-*), "she-goat" (Gz *ṭāli*).

2459 *ṭal- "dew, drop"

Sem **ṭall-* "dew, drizzle": Hbr *ṭal*, Aram (Syr) *ṭall-*, Arab *ṭall-*, Gz *ṭal*, Hss *ṭel*, Mhr *ṭel*, Shh *ṭɛhl*.
CCh **ṭVl-* "drop" (n.): Bud *tolo*.

Cf. a derivative in LEC **ḍol-* "big white cloud": Som *ḍol*?

2460 *ṭal-/*ṭul- "flow, pour"

Sem *ṭul- "sprinkle" [1], "moisten" [2]: Hbr *ṭlˀ* [1], Arab *ṭll* [-*u*-] [2], Gz *ṭll* [2].
WCh **ṭal-* "flow": Bks *tal*.

Alternation **a* ~ **u*.

2461 *ṭanaˀ- "weave, sew"

Sem **ṭVnVˀ-* "weave" [1], "tie, plait" [2]: Akk *ṭenu* [1], Hbr *ṭnˀ* [2].
WCh **ṭaˀan-* "sew": Sura *taan*, Mpn *taan*, Ang *ten*, Mnt *tan*, Ank *tan*.
Metathesis. Cf .WCh **ṭyan-H-* "rope": Sura *tɛŋ*, Ang *tang*, Mnt *teng*, Ank *tieng*, Mpn *teŋ*.

2462 *ṭaraḳ- "snare"

Sem **ṭarḳ-* "trap, net": Arab *ṭaraq-*, *ṭarq-*.
WCh **ṭarVḳ-* "snare, trap": Hs *tarko*.
A Sem loanword?

2463 *ṭarer- "drip"

Berb **ṭVrVr-* "sprinkle": Ahg *e-ḍrer*.
ECh **tarVr-* "water flow": Mig *tarro*.
LEC **ḍarer-* "dripping": Som *ḍarer*.

2464 *ṭarip- "tree"

Sem **ṭarpaˀ-* "tamarind": Akk *ṭarpaˀu*.
ECh **tirip-* "kind of tree": Bid *tirip*.
Assimilation of vowels.

2465 *ṭas- "dish"

Sem **ṭass-* "dish": Arab *ṭass-*, *ṭās-*.
Berb **ṭas-* "dish": Izd *a-ṭṭas*, Kby *a-ṭṭas*.
WCh **ṭas-* "dish": Hs *ṭāsā*.

Berb and WCh forms may be Arab loanwords.

2466 *ṭaw- "roof"

Eg *twꜣ.t* "temple roof" (gr).
Vocalic *-ꜣ*.
WCh **ṭaw-* "roof": Fyer *taw*, Wrj *ṭuwai*.

2467 *ṭem- "hide, close"

Sem **ṭVm-* "close (ears)": Akk *ṭummumu*.
D stirpes.
Eg *tmm* "close" (pyr).
CCh **ṭyam-* "hide": Bud *tema-hi*.

2468 *ṭiʔuḥ-/*ṭiwuḥ- "kill, destroy"

Sem **ṭūḥ-* "perish": Arab *ṭwḥ*.
Eg *tꜣḥ* "kill" (gr).
WCh **ṭiʔuḥ-* "kill": Sura *tu*, Ang *tu*, Chip *to*, Wrj *təγ*, Kry *tə:γ-*, Diri *tu*, Miya *təy*, Cagu *tiyu*, Siri *təγ*, Mbu *təγ*, Jmb *tiy-*, Brm *tuge*.

Consonantal alternation *-ʔ- ~ *-w-.

2469 *ṭibaʕ- "push"

Sem **ṭVbaʕ-* "put a seal": Arab *ṭbʕ* [-a-].
LEC **ḍīb-* < **ḍiHab-* "push": Or *ḍiiba*.
Metathesis.

2470 *ṭif- "drop, rain"

Sem **ṭipp-* "drop": Hbr *ṭippā*, Aram (Bibl) *ṭipp-*.
WCh **ṭaf-* < **ṭifa-* "rainy season": Bks *tafu*.
CCh **ṭa-ṭVf-* "drizzle": Mofu *tatəf*.
Partial reduplication.

2471 *ṭif-ṭif- "drizzle, drops"

Sem **ṭip-ṭip-* "drizzle" (n.): Tgr *ṭifṭif*, Tgy *ṭifṭif*.
Eg *dfdf.t* "drops" (XX).

Reduplication of **ṭif-* "drop, rain".

2472 *ṭin- "earth, dirt"

Sem **ṭīn-* "clay, earth, dirt": Aram (Syr) *ṭīnō*, Arab *ṭīn-*, Jib *ṭun*, Hss *ṭayn*, Mhr *ṭayn*, Shh *ṭin*.
Eg *ỉtn*, *ỉwtn* "earth" (a).
CCh **ṭVn-* "earth": Log *tən*.

2473 *ṭir- "mug, pot"

WCh **ṭyarVr-* "small basket": Hs *tērērē*.
Partial reduplication.
ECh **tir-* "mug": Kera *tirə*.
LEC **ḍer-* "pot": Som *ḍeri*.

2474 *ṭob- "leather strap"

WCh **ṭwab-* "loin cloth": Hs *tōbī*.
CCh **tVḅ-* < **ṭVb-* "rope": Mafa *təḅa*.
Shift of emphatization.
Omot **ṭub-* "hide used as a shroud": Kaf *ṭubboo*.

2475 *ṭub- "young person"

CCh **ṭub-* "younger sibling": Gis *tuba*.
LEC **ḍob-* "young person": Or *ṭobbee*.
Note Or *ṭ-*.

2476 *ṭub- "drip, be wet"

Sem **ṭVb-* "drip": Tgr *ṭab bäla*, Gur *ṭab balä*.
Cf. also Gz *nṭb* id.
Berb **ṭVb-* "drip": Ahg *əṭṭəb*.
ECh **tubi-* "humid": Smr *tuba*, Nch *tibi*.
LEC **ḍub-* "soak": Or *ḍuuba*.

2477 *ṭub- "cover"

Berb **ṭVb-* "cover": Ayr *ə-ḍəb*, Twl *ə-ḍəb*.
WCh **tuḅ-* < **ṭub-* "cover": Kry *təḅə*, Jmb *duḅa*.

2478 *ṭuč- "cacare, pedere"

Sem **ṭVṯVʔ-* "cacare": Arab *ṭṯʔ*.
From biconsonantal **ṭVṯ-*.
WCh **ṭuči-* "pedere" [1], "cacare" [2]: Hs *tūsa* [1], Bgh *ti:s* [2].
LEC **ḍuš-* "pedere": Som *ḍus*, Or *ḍuufa*.

2479 *ṭuĉar- "container"

Sem **ṭuŝar-* "bag": Akk *tušaru*.
Eg *dšr.t* "vessel" (pyr).

2480 *ṭuʕan-/*ṭuʕun- "pierce, pinch"

Sem **ṭVʕan-* "pierce with a spear" [1], "thrust at" [2]: Arab *ṭʕn* [-*a*-] [1], Hss *ṭōn* [2], Mhr *ṭān* [2], Shh *ṭʕan* [2].
WCh **tuHun-* "pinch": Mpn *tuun*.

2481 *ṭu(m)f- "fill, be full"

Sem **ṭVp-* "be full": Akk *ṭapāpu*.
WCh **ṭumf-* "fill up": Hs *tumfaye*.
Secondary nasal infix?

2482 *ṭup- "jump"

Sem **ṭVp-* "jump": Hbr *ṭpp*.
HEC **ṭop(p)-* "jump": Had *ṭopp-*.
Omot **ṭup(p)-* "run away" [1], "jump" [2]: Kaf *ṭup-* [1], Mch *ṭuṗṗi-* [2].

2483 *ṭup- "clap, grasp, take"

Sem **ṭVp-* "take, grasp" [1], "clap" [2], "give" [3], "stretch hand" [4]: Arab *ṭff* [-*u*-] [1], Gur *ṭf*, *ṭff* [2], Soq *ṭef* [3], *ṭayif* [4].
Berb **ṭVf-* "grasp, seize": Nfs *əṭṭəf*, Siwa *əṭṭəf*, Ghat *əṭṭəf*, Ahg *əṭṭəf*, Zng *yo-ḍof*, Rif *əṭṭəf*, Kby *əṭṭəf*.
HEC **ṭep-* "stretch hand": Sid *ṭeep*.
Secondary **-e-*?

2484 *ṭuraḥ- "throw, fall"

Sem **ṭVraḥ-* "throw": Arab *ṭrḥ* [-*a*-].
CCh **ṭurVH-* "fall": Ngw *tiri*, HF *turi*, HNk *tərɛ*, HGh *təre*, FKi *təřuʾ*, FG *tərəyə*.

2485 *ṭVn- "call, speak"

Sem **ṭin-* "buzz, tinkle" [1], "call" [2]: Arab *ṭnn* [-*i*-] [1], Gur *ṭäna*, *ṭänna* [2].
WCh **ṭwan-* "speak": Grk *ke-ton*, Sha *ton*.

Irregular correspondence of vowels.

2486 *ṭVr- "take away"

Sem **ʾVṭVr-* "take away": Akk *eṭēru*.
Other laryngeals may be postulated in the anlaut.
The initial **HV-* appears to be a prefix.
Eg *dr* "take away" (pyr).
Eg *d* < HS **ṭ* is regular.

*W

2487 *wa- "burn, roast"

CCh **wa-* "roast": Mwu *u-wo*.
Cf. reduplicated **wa-wa-* "fire, heat; burn" (Mofu *waw*, *awaw*, Mnd *wawa*).
ECh **wa-* "roast" [1], "be hot" [2]: Smr *wa* [1], Tum *woi* [2].
Agaw **wa-* "burn, be hot": Kwr *waa*.

2488 *waʾ-/*way- "be glad"

Eg *ỉwꜣ* "be glad, rejoice" (n).
Prefix *ỉ*-. The meaning is not quite definite.
WCh **way-* "be glad": Tng *way*.

Consonantal alternation *-ʾ- ~ *-*y*-.

2489 *waʾ-/*way- "go, come"

Eg *wꜣy* "come" (MK).
Vocalic *-ꜣ-*.
WCh **waʾ-* "return" [1], "go (away)" [2], "come" [3]: Ang *wē* [1], Mnt *wa* [2], Dera *wa-* [3], Tng *wa-* [3], Fyer *wu* [2], Bks *wa* [2].
CCh **waʾi-* "go" [1], "come" [2]: Hwn *wi*, Mba *wo* [2].
ECh **waʾ-* "run": Smr *wa*, Sbn *wa*.
Omot **waH-* "come": Kaf *waa*, Anf *waa*, Bwo *waa*, Gim *wo*.

Consonantal alternation **-ʾ-* ~ **-y-*.

2490 *waʾar- "dance" (v.)

Eg *wꜣr* "dance" (v.) (gr).
The meaning is not quite definite.
ECh **waHar-* "dance" (v.): Bid *waar*, Mig *waaro*.

2491 *waʾaŝ- "be happy"

Eg *wꜣš* "be happy" (a).
ECh **waHaŝ-* "be happy": Kera *waale*.

2492 *waçVʿ- "bird"

Sem **waṣʿ-* "little bird": Arab *waṣʿ-*.
Eg *wḏʿ* "grey crane" (OK).

2493 *waĉ- "man"

Eg *wꜣš.t* "description of men" (pyr).
Vocalic *-ꜣ-*.
WCh **waĉ-* "father-in-law": Bks *was*, DB *waš*.

2494 *waĉ-/*ʾoĉ- "hen"

Eg *wšꜣ.t* "poultry" (MK).
Vocalic *-ꜣ-*.
ECh **ʾwas-* "hen": Mkk *ʾosso*.

Consonantal alternation in the anlaut.

2495 *waĉaˁ- "stand up"

Sem *wVŝVˁ- "climb, mount": Arab *wŝˁ*.
ECh *waĉ- "stand up": Mig *wačaw*, Sok *wəsə*.

2496 *wad- "love, want"

Sem *wad- "love, want": Ug *ydd*, Hbr *ydd*, Arab *wdd* [-*a*-], Gz *wdd*.
CCh *waḍ- "want": Mofu -*wuḍ*-, Gis *waḍ*, *wuḍ*.
Secondary emphatic.

2497 *wad- "cook, roast"

Eg *wdd* "be cooked" (med).
Partial reduplication.
WCh *waḍ- "cook": Grk *uat*, Krk *waḍu*, Dera *wuri*, Ngm *woḍ*-, Gera *waḍ*-, Glm *wary*-.
Secondary emphatic.
LEC *wad- "roast": Or *waada*, Kon *waat*-, Arb *wad*-, *waad*-.
Wrz *wat- "roast": Gaw *waat*-.

2498 *wadak- "fat, grease"

Sem *wadak- "fat, grease": Arab *wadak*-.
WCh *duk- "fat, grease": Pol *duku*.
From *dVwVk-.
CCh *dwak- < *dVwak- "fatness": Gbn *ndoku-ri*, Hwo *ndəw-rara*, Glv *ndəyu-ga*, Zgh *ndəya*, Gava *ndəya*, Gaa *daku-raba*.
Metathesis in WCh and CCh.

2499 *wagal- "fright, fear"

Sem *wVgal- "be frightened": Arab *wgl* [-*a*-].
ECh *walVg- "fright, fear": Kera *walga*.
Metathesis.

Cf. *wagar- "be afraid" and *wahal- "be afraid".

2500 *wagar- "be afraid"

Sem *wVgar- "be afraid": Hbr *ygr*, Arab *wgr* [-*a*-].

ECh *ʾurVg- "fear": Mkk ʾurg-.
Metathesis.

2501 *waᶜ- "beast of prey"

Sem *waᶜ-waᶜ- "jackal, fox": Arab waᶜwaᶜ-.
Reduplication.
Eg wᶜ.ty "lion" (gr).

2502 *waᶜab-/*yaᶜab- "wash"

Eg wᶜb "wash" (pyr), Copt *wop id.: Shd ouop.
CCh *yaHab- "wash": Kus ubau, HNk yəḅu-, Kap yaḅu- , FGl ʾyeḅa-, HGh yaḅa-, Bch yəḅʷə.

Consonantal alternation *w- ~ *y- in the anlaut.

2503 *waᶜan- "conifer"

Eg wᶜn "conifer" (XVIII).
CCh *waHan- "wood, firewood": Log wahan, Gul wān.

2504 *waᶜar- "go, run"

Sem *wVᶜVr- "walk, go": Akk âru, wâru.
Eg wᶜr "run away" (MK).
CCh *wVraw- < *wVraH- "return": Zgh wrawa.
Metathesis.
HEC *waHar- "come": Had waar-.

Etymologically connected with *waᶜVr- "leg".

2505 *waᶜül- "antelope"

Sem *waᶜil- "antelope" [1], "ibex" [2]: Ug yᶜl [1], Hbr yāᶜēl [1], Aram yaᶜlā [1], Arab waᶜil-, waᶜul- [2], SAr wᶜl [1], Gz wəᶜla [1], Mhr wēl [1], Hss wāl [1].
WCh *wul- < *wVʾul- "antelope": Geji wulli, ulli.
ECh *wayil- < *waʾil- "antelope": Lele ol, Kbl yilə.
LEC *ʾaw(V)l- "gazelle": Som ʾawl-kii.
Metathesis.

2506 *waʿVr- "leg"

Eg *wʿr.t* "leg" (MK).
WCh **war-* < **waHVr-* "leg": Ank *warr*.
CCh **wVr-* "leg": Msg *werē*.

Cf. Sem **warr-* "hip-bone" (Arab *warr-*)?

2507 *wahig-/*yahig- "burn"

Sem **wVhig-/*yVhig-* "burn and shine (of fire)": Arab *whg*, *yhg* [-*i*-].
ECh **Hig-* < **wVHig-* "burn": Mig *ʾiggo*, Bid *ʾegey*.
Rift **yog-* "fire": Asa *yogo*.
Note initial **y-*.

Consonantal alternation **w-* ~ **y-*.

2508 *wahal- "be afraid"

Sem **wVhal-* "be afraid": Arab *whl* [-*a*-].
WCh **wawal-* < *waHal-* "be afraid": Paa *wowal*.
ECh **yal-* "be afraid": Sok *yele*.

2509 *waḥ- "break"

Eg *wḥꜣ* "break stones" (OK).
Vocalic -*ꜣ*.
CCh **wa[χ]-* "break": Gis *wah*.
Cf. Mofu -*uh*- id.

2510 *waḥ- "die; death"

Eg *wḥꜣ* "deadly illness" (med).
Deverbative. -*ꜣ* stand for the root vowel **a*.
WCh **waḥ-* "perish": DB *wah*.
CCh **waH-/*way-* "death": Gude *wa*, Nza *wo*, Bch *wɛy*.

2511 *waḥ- "put"

Eg *wꜣḥ* "put" (pyr), Copt **wōh*: Fym *ouōh*, Akh *ouōh*, Boh *ouoh*, Shd *ouōh*.
WCh **wuH-* "put": Dera *wui*.

Secondary **u*.
ECh **waH-* "lay down": Jegu *ʾoo*.

2512 *waḥiʿ- "fish, catch"

Eg *wḥʿ* "fish" (v.) (n).
WCh **waHi-* "fish, catch" (v.): Tng *oi*.

2513 *waḥVʿ- "loosen, uncover"

Eg *wḥʿ* "loosen" (pyr).
WCh **waH-* "loosen, uncover, open": Sura *wɔɔ*, Ank *wau*.

2514 *waḫ- "want"

Sem **wVḫVy-* "tend, plan, suggest": Arab *wḫy* [*-i-*].
Eg *wḫȝ* "want, look for" (MK), Copt **wōḫe*: Fym *ouōš*, Akh *ouōḫe*, Boh *ouōš*, Shd *ouōš*.
CCh **way-* < **waH-* "want, look for": Mnd *waya*, Zime *wa*.
ECh **wVH-* "look for": Mkk *wiʾe*.

2515 *waḫ- "be dark, be black"

Eg *wḫ*, *wḫȝ* "dark" (MK).
Vocalic *-ȝ*.
WCh **wuH-* < **waHu-* "black": Grk *wuu*.

2516 *wakib- "go"

Sem **wVkVb-* "go slowly" [1], "enter" [2]: Arab *wkb* [*-i-*], Hss *wekōb* [2], Mhr *wekōb* [2], Shh *ekob* [2].
WCh **kwab-* < **kawVb-* "come, pass by": Mnt *kop*, Bol *koḅ-*, Tng *koobe*.
Metathesis. Secondary emphatic in Bol.

Derived from **kab-* "go, follow".

2517 *waḳ- "be afraid"

Sem **wVḳVy-* "be afraid": Ug *wqy*, Arab (VIII) *wqy*.

Based on **wVḳ-*.
WCh **waḳ-* "frighten": Sura *wuk*, Ang *wok*.

2518 *waḳaᶜ- "fall"

Sem **wVḳaᶜ-* "fall": Arab *wqᶜ* [-*a*-].
WCh **wuḳ-* "fall": Dera *wukot*, Tng *wuge*, *uk*.
Secondary **-u-*?
CCh **wak-* "fall": Mofu *wak*.
Cf. Kus *akai* id. < **wakaH-*?

2519 *wal- "lamentation; weep"

Sem **wal-wāl-* "lamentations": Arab *walwāl-at-*.
Reduplication.
WCh **wal-/*wil-* "cry, sob": Ang *wāl*, Chip *wil*.
ECh **wal-* "funeral song": Sok *olu*.

2520 *walad- "boy, child"

Sem **walad-* "boy, child": Akk *ildu*, Ug *yld*, Hbr *yeled*, Arab *walad-*, Gz *wald*.
Cf. Akk *līdu* id.
LEC **wadal-* "brother" [1], "young man" [2]: Rnd *walal* [1], Bay *wɔdala* [2].
Metathesis. Assimilation of consonants in Rnd.

Derived from **wiled-* "give birth".

2521 *walaᶜ- "love" (v.)

Sem **wVlaᶜ-* "be infatuated": Arab *wlᶜ* [-*a*-].
WCh **waHal-* "love": Sura *wal*, Mpn *wāl*.
Metathesis.

2522 *walem- "right (side)"

Eg *wnmy* "to the right" (pyr), Copt **winam*: Fym *iōnam*, Boh *ouinam*, Shd *ounam*.
Vocalic *-y*.

ECh **walyam-* "right" (adj.): Kbl *uolema*.
Cf. Smr *oama* id. < **olama*?

2523 *wamaʔ- "swear, call"

Sem **wVmaʔ-* "swear, make a sign": Akk *wamāʔu*, Aram *ʔimō*, Arab *wmʔ* [*-a-*].
LEC **waHam-* "call, invite": Or *waama*.
Metathesis.

2524 *wan- "open"

Eg *wn* "open" (pyr).
WCh **wan-H-* "open": Sura *waŋ*, Mpn *waŋ*, Fyer *waŋ*.
Note a laryngeal suffix.
ECh **wVn-* "open": Mubi *wen*.

2525 *wan- "light" (n.)

Eg *wny* "light" (gr), Copt **wōyini*: Boh *ouōini*, Shd *ouoein*.
Suffix *-y*.
WCh **wun-* "day": Hs *wuni*, Ngz *wəni*.
Secondary **-u-*?
CCh **wan-* "day": Daba *wan*, Mus *waŋ*.
Secondary laryngeal in Mus.

2526 *war- "throw"

Sem **wur-* "throw": Ug *yry*, Hbr *yry*, Arab *wrr* [*-u-*], Gz *wrw*.
Secondary vocalism after a labial.
ECh **war-* "throw, cast": Kbl *wəri*, *weri*, Dng *ore*.
Agaw **wa-wVr-* "throw": Aun *wowər-əŋ*.
Partial reduplication.

2527 *war- "bull, cow"

Eg *wr-* "kind of cattle" (OK), *wr.t* "sacred cow" (MK).
WCh **warar-* "vicious bull": Hs *wārārī*.
Partial reduplication.

2528 *war- ‘‘burn; flame’’

Sem **wVrVy-* ‘‘be lit up (of fire)’’: Arab *wry*.
Based on **wVr-*.
Eg *wr.t* ‘‘definition of the flame’’ (gr).
Cf. Eg *wꜣwꜣ.t* ‘‘fire’’ (XVIII).
CCh **war-* ‘‘roast’’: Zime *wor*.

2529 *war-/*ʔur- ‘‘be big, be strong’’

Sem **wVrVy-* ‘‘be fat’’: Arab *wry*.
Based on biconsonantal **wVr-*.
Eg *wr* ‘‘big; strength’’ (pyr).
WCh **war-* ‘‘strength’’ ^{1}, ‘‘surpass’’ ^{2}: Ank *warr* ^{1}, Glm *war-* ^{2}, Gera *wur-* ^{2}.
Cf. Ang *war-ŋ* ‘‘big’’.
Rift **ʔur-* ‘‘big, large’’: Irq *ur*.

Consonantal alternation *ʔ- ~ *w-.

2530 *was- ‘‘cut’’

Eg *wsy* ‘‘saw (wood)’’ (OK).
Suffix *-y*.
WCh **was-* ‘‘cut’’: Bol *wasš-*.

2531 *wasaʕ- ‘‘be big’’

Sem **wVsaʕ-* ‘‘be spatious, big’’: Arab *wsʕ*, *ysʕ* [*-a-*].
WCh **was-* ‘‘swell’’: Paa *wasu*.
ECh **waHas-* ‘‘swell, become bigger’’: Mig *waase*, Bid *waas*.
Metathesis.

2532 *wat- ‘‘roll up’’

Eg *wt*, *wyt* ‘‘roll up’’ (pyr).
WCh **wat-* ‘‘unfold’’: Sura *wat*.

2533 *wat- ‘‘walk’’

Eg *swtwt* ‘‘walk’’ (XVIII).

Reduplication with causative *s*-.
WCh **wat*- ''come'': Pero *wat*, Tng *wato*, Say *wət*.

2534 *wat- ''call, speak''

WCh **wat*- ''call'': Pero *wat*.
CCh **wat*- ''call'': Tera *wat*.
Omot **wat-/*yat*- ''say, speak'': Ome *ot*, *yot*, *iwet*-, Yam *it*-, Gim *ayṭ*-.

2535 *way- ''say''

CCh **way*- ''answer'': HF *wɛ*, Kap *wɛy*, FJ *wəy*.
ECh **way*- ''say'': Smr *way*-.
Omot **way*- ''say'': Sezo *wɛ*.

2536 *way- ''be far''

Eg *wꜣy* ''be far away'' (pyr), Copt **wey*: Fym *ouēi*, Akh *oue*, Boh *ouei*.
WCh **yi-way*- ''far'': Wrj *yiwei*.
Prefix **yi*-.

2537 *wayal- ''decline, forget''

Eg *wyn* ''decline'' (MK), *wyꜣ* (NK).
Note *-*l*- > -*n* and, later, -*ꜣ*.
ECh **wayal*- ''forget'': Mubi *wayal*, *wayil*.
LEC **walal*- ''not know'': Or *walʔaala*.
Assimilated from **wayal*-?

2538 *waǯam- ''intestines''

Sem **wa*ḏ*am*- ''belly with intestines'': Arab *wa*ḏ*am-at*-.
Eg *wzmw* ''unidentified body-part'' (pyr).
Anomalous *z* < **ǯ*.

Related or identical to **waǯan-/*waǯin*- ''heart, intestines''.

2539 *waǯan-/*waǯin- "heart, intestines"

Berb **waʒan-* "intestines": Sus *wadan*.
CCh **wyanǯi-* < **waǯin-* "intestines": Daba *wenǯi*.
Metathesis.
Agaw **waʒan-* "belly, heart": Bil *wɔdän*.
SA **waʒan-* "belly": Saho *waʒano*, *wadano*, Afar *wadanaa*.
LEC **waʒin-* "heart": Som *wadna*, Gel *wɔdimi*.
HEC **waʒan-* "heart": Sid *wadana*, *wodana*, Had *wodano*, Ala *wozana*, Bmb *wɔɔdɛna*, Kmb *wozäna*, Tmb *wazano*.
Omot **waʒen-* "heart": Ome *wazɛna*.

Cf. WCh **haǯin-* < **ha-[wa]ǯin-* "intestines" (Hs *hanǯi*, Krk *azi*, Bol *azin*, Ngm *hazî*, Krf *aǯǯo*, Glm *aši*, Gera *haza*, Sha *ʾaⁿǯi*) and Dhl *ⁿdzone* "spleen", the latter, probably, reflecting a metathesis of **waǯan-* > **ǯawan-*.

2540 *wiled- "give birth"

Sem **wVlVd-* "give birth": Akk *walādu*, *alādu*, Ug *yld*, Hbr *yld*, Aram (Syr) *ʾīled*, Arab *wld* [-*i*-], Gz *wld*.
ECh **yidyal-* < **widyal-* "give birth": Smr *yidele*.
Metathesis.

2541 *wisan- "sleep"

Sem **wVšan-* "sleep": Hbr *yšn*, Arab *wsn* [-*a*-].
CCh **wisan-H-* "sleep": Log *wisan*, Msg *huiseŋ*.
Suffix **-H-*. Log may be an Arab loanword.

2542 *wiy- "tree"

Eg *ỉwy* "kind of tree" (gr).
CCh **wiy-* "bush": Nza *wiye*.
ECh **wuy-* < **wiy-* "acacia": Sok *wui*.

2543 *wuĉ- "urine"

Eg *wzš.t*, *wšš.t* "urine" (pyr).
-zš and *-šš* are graphic symbols for the Eg reflex of **- ĉ-*.
ECh **wuĉ-* "urine": Smr *ʾuǯo*, Ngam *wūǯo*, Tum *wuǯ*, Mobu *uǯe*, Ndam *wuǯo*.

2544 *wug- "move quickly"

Sem **wug-* "be fast, be quick": Arab *wgg* [-*u*-].
ECh **wug-* "run": Ndam *wuga*.

2545 *wul- "rope"

Eg *wn.t* "rope" (pyr).
WCh **wul-* "rope": Glm *wula*, Gera *wula*.

2546 *wuleḫ- "be green"

Eg *wꜣḫy* "be green" (pyr).
WCh **wVl-* "green": Dera *wəli-wəli*.
Reduplication.
CCh **wulyaH-* "green": Boka *weχa*, Hwo *wuleɣ-ən*.
Contraction in Boka.

2547 *wulig- "enter, pass"

Sem **wVlig-* "enter": Arab *wlg* [-*i*-].
WCh **wulVg-* "pass by": Hs *wulga*.

2548 *wur- "pit, hole"

Sem **warr-* "pit": Arab *warr-at-*.
**u* > *a* after a labial.
WCh **wur-* "pit, furrow": Ngz *wuriya*.
Cf. Tng *wure* "dig (a hole)".
CCh **wur-* "hole": HNk *wure*.

2549 *wur- "water"

Eg *wrw* "pond" (pyr).
WCh **wur-* "stream" [1], "lake" [2]: Hs *wuriya* [1], Miya *wər* [2].
Contraction.

2550 *wurVm- "roof"

Eg *wrm* "pavilion" (pyr), "roof" (n).
WCh **wurVm-* "cover, thatch": Tng *wurme*.
Denominative verb?

2551 *wül- "vessel"

Eg *wnw* "beer-mug" (gr).
CCh **wul-* "bowl, calabash": Msg *ulai*, Mnj *wula*.
LEC **wil-* "gourd": Or *willee*.

2552 *wüç- "send, order"

Sem **wVṣVy-* "order" (v.): Arab *wṣy*.
Based on **wVṣ-*.
Eg *wḏy* "send" (XVIII), *wḏ* "order" (BD).
WCh **wuç-* "send": Tng *wude*.

2553 *wüp- "open"

Eg *wpy* "open" (pyr).
Vocalic *-y*. Cf. *wp* "door" (OK).
WCh **wup-* "open": Dwot *wup*.

2554 *wVĉar- "be hostile"

Sem **ṣ̂ūr-* "be hostile, persecute": Hbr *ṣwr*.
Metathesis.
Berb **wVẓar-* "torture" (v.): Ayr *uẓar*, Twl *uẓar*.

Derived from **ĉ̣ir-* id.

2555 *wVgab- "cut, pierce"

Sem **gūb-* "cut, pierce": Arab *gwb* [*-u-*].
Metathesis.
WCh **[w]Vgab-* "cut": Ang *gap*, Chip *gəp*, Mnt *gap*, Ank *gup*, Bol *guw*, Tng *kab-*.

2556 *wVgVm- "strike, grind"

Sem **wVgVm-* "strike (with fist)": Arab *wgm*.
Eg *wgm* "grind" (OK).

2557 *wVgVr- "dig; cavern"

Sem **wagr-* "cavern, hole": Arab *wagr-*.
Apparently, a deverbative. Cf. *wigār-* id.
WCh **wugVr-* "hollow out, groove": Tng *wugre*.

2558 *wVhup- "grass, flower"

Sem **wVhip-* "be covered with leaves": Arab *whf* [-*i*-].
Derived from a nominal stem.
WCh **wVp-* "grass": Wnd *wəp*.
ECh **hVwuf-* "flower": Kera *huufi*.
Metathesis.

2559 *wVlVm- "eat; food"

Sem **wVlVm-* "give a meal, feed" [1], "prepare a meal" [2]: Arab *wlm* [1], Hss *awlōm* [2], Mhr *awōlem* [2], Shh *ulm* [2].
Eg *wnm* "eat" (pyr).
ECh **wVlVm-* "food": Kbl *wəlmə*.

Derived from **lam-/*lum-* "eat".

2560 *wVriḳ- "be green"

Sem **wVriḳ-* "be greenish": Akk *warāqu*, *arāqu*, Hbr *yrq*, Arab *wrq* [-*i*-].
Eg *wȝḏ* "green color" (BD).
Palatalization of **ḳ* > ḏ.

2561 *wVŝVm- "slaughter" (v.)

Sem **wVśVm-/*yVśVm-* "tattoo" (v.): Arab *wšm*, *yšm*.
Eg *wšm* "slaughter" (v.) (gr).

2562 *wVṭen- "dwell, stay"

Sem **wVṭin-* "dwell, stay": Arab *wṭn* [-*i*-].
WCh **ṭyan-* "sit": Tala *ten*.
Loss of initial **wV-*.

**wV-* may be a prefix.

2563 *wVṭVf- "rain, pour"

Sem *wVṭVp-* "rain" (v.): Arab *wṭf*.
Berb *wVṭVf-* "ritual ablution": Ahg *ūḍūf*.

Derived from *ṭif-* "drop, rain".

*y

2564 *ya- "call, speak"

Eg *iy* "saying" (BD).
WCh *ya-* "call": Pero *yo*.
CCh *ya-* "call": Gudu *'ya*, Bnn *ya-mu*.
Cf. *yiw-* "ask" (FKi *yiwa-*, HNk *yuwe*, Chb *yuwe*).
ECh *ya(y)-* "call": Gbr *ye*.
Agaw *yV-* "say": Xmr *yi-*, *y-*, Xmt *y-*, Kwr *y-*, Dmb *y-*, Kem *y-*.
SA *ya-/*yi-* "say": Saho *ya-*, *ii-*, Afar *ii-*, *iiy-*.
LEC *ya-* "say" [1], "shout" [2]: Som *ii-* [1], Or *iyya* [2], Gel *y-* [1].
HEC *yV-* "say": Sid *i-*, *y-*, Had *yi-*, *y-*, Ala *i-*, *yii-*, Bmb *i-*, *y-*, Kmb *yi-*, *y-*.
Omot *yV-* "say": Ome *y-*, Kaf *y-*.

2565 *ya'- "place, house"

Eg *i3.t* "place" (pyr).
CCh *yay-* < *yaH-* "building": Muk *yay*.
Cf. Gude *ya* "door".
ECh *ya'-* "house": Gbr *iā*, Kbl *ya*.

2566 *ya'- "go, come, run"

Berb *yaH-* "come": Izy *iya*, Kby *əyya* (imper.).
WCh *ya'-/*yaw-* "go" [1], "run" [2], "come" [3]: Grk *ya* [1], Dera *ya* [1], Krf *yow-* [1], Bgh *yuway* [2], DB *yo* [1], Ngz *ya* [3].
CCh *ya'-* "come": Daba *ya*.
ECh *ya'-* "go": Tum *ye*, Gbr *yə*, Tob *yə*.
LEC *ya'-* "run away": Som *yaa'-*.
Cf. Or *yaa'a* "flow".

Omot **yaʾ-* "come" [1], "run away" [2]: Ome *ya-* [1], Hozo *yɛi* [2], Sezo *yɛ* [2].

2567 *yaʾ-/*yaw- "water, river"

CCh **yawi-* "water": Mnd *yewe*, Zgh *yiwe*, Glv *iywa*.
**-i-* is secondary. Cf. also a partial reduplication in Mafa *yayaw-* "water used for diluting beer".
Rift **yaʾ-* "river" (Irq *yaʾe*).

Connected with **yaw-* "pour, flow". Consonantal alternation **-ʾ-* ~ **-w-*.

2568 *yaʾ-/*yaw- "foot, leg"

WCh **yaw-* "foot": Dera *yo*, Tng *yo*.
Rift **yaʾ-* "foot, leg": Irq *yaʾe*, Alg *yaʾe*, Bur *yaʾe*, Kwz *yaʾo*.

Connected with **yaʾ-/*yaw-* "go, come, run". Consonantal alternation **-ʾ-* ~ **-w-*.

2569 *yab-/*ʾib- "thirst"

WCh **yab-/*yib-* "thirst": Bgh *yip*, Kir *yap*.
ECh **ʾib-in-* "thirst": Jegu *ʾibin-*.
Derivative in **-in-*.
Bed *yawa* "thirst", *yiwai* "thirst".
Intervocalic **-b-* > *-w-*.

Consonantal alternation **ʾ-* ~ **y-* in the anlaut.

2570 *yabil- "bull, ram"

Sem **yabil-* "ram": Hbr *yōbēl*.
Eg *ibȝ.w* "ovis tragelaphus" (OK).
-ȝ < HS **-l-*.
CCh **bVl-* "kind of ram": Mafa *bəlaw*.
ECh **bilVy-* "buffalo": Mkk *bilyo*.
Metathesis.

2571 *yaĉ-/*wa-yaĉ- "dog"

Eg *iš* pl. "dogs pulling the ship of the Sun-god" (n).
Bed *yaas* "dog".
HEC **wis-* "dog": Had *wiša*.
Contraction from **wVyVs-*.
Omot **wayVs-* "dogs": Ome *wayše*.

A derivative from this root is found in Berb **wVs[i]n* "jackal": Ghd *weššin*, Sml *uššən*, Nfs *uššen*, Qbl *uššen*. Note prefix **wa-* in HEC and Omot.

2572 *yad- "bird"

Eg *idw* "kind of bird" (med).
Suffix *-w*.
WCh **yadi-* "bird": Grk *yad*, Dera *yidəyo*, Tng *ʾidi*, Maha *widi*, Fyer *yadu*, Klr *yidi*.

2573 *yadaᶜ- "know, think"

Sem **wVdVᶜ-* "know": Akk *edû*, Ug *ydᶜ*, Hbr *ydᶜ*, Aram *ydᶜ*, Hss *yōda*, Mhr *wēda*, Shh *edaᶜ*, Soq *edaᶜ*.
Eg *idᶜ* "clever" (n).
Borrowed from Sem?
LEC **yaHad-* "think": Or *yaada*.

2574 *yal- "stick, branch"

Eg *iȝȝ.t* "branch, scepter" (MK).
WCh **yal-* "stick": Tng *ala*, Bks *yal*.

2575 *yam- "water, sea"

Sem **yamm-* "sea": Hbr *yām*, Ug *ym*, Arab *yamm-*.
CCh **yami-* "water": Gbn *yeme*, Chb *yimi*, HNk *yɛmi*, FKi *yamu*, FG *yimu*, Gis *ʾiyam*, Daba *yim*, Msg *yem*, Bld *yam*, Mofu *yam*.

Eg *ym* "sea" (XVIII) is a Sem loanword.

2576 *yam- "day"

Sem **yawm-* "day": Akk *ūmu*, Ug *ym*, Hbr *yōm*, Aram (Syr) *yawmō*, Arab *yawm-*, Soq *yom*.
Cf. Jib *yum* "sun, light", Gz *yom* "today". Based on biconsonantal **yam-*?
ECh **yam-* "day": Jegu *yom*.

Note LEC **yawan-* "(this) time" (Or *yoowana*)?

2577 *yamaʾ- "wood, tree"

Eg *imꜣ* "fruit-tree; wood" (pyr).
WCh **yaHam-* "wood, firewood": Ang *yōm*, Sura *yoɣom*.

2578 *yamin- "right (side)"

Sem **yamīn-* "right (hand)": Akk *imnu*, Ug *ymn*, Hbr *yāmīn*, Aram (Syr) *yāmināy*, Arab *yamīn-*, Gz *yammān*.
Berb **(yV)mVn-* "direct": Izy *mni*, *imna*.
Eg *imn* "right (side)" (pyr).

2579 *yar- "fire; burn"

Eg *ir.t* "flame" (gr).
The meaning is not quite definite.
WCh **yar-* "burn": Bgh *yar*.
CCh **yVr-* "heat": Bud *yir-ow*.
ECh **yar-* "burn": Dng *yere*.

2580 *yar-/*yaraḫ- "cereal"

Sem **yaraḫ-* "kind of barley": Akk *yaraḫḫu*.
Eg *iry.t* "corn (as donation)" (XVIII).
ECh **yar-* "corn": Sok *yɛre*.

2581 *yaraʾ-/*yaraw- "reed"

Sem **yaraʾ-* "reed not used for writing": Arab *yaraʾ-*.
Eg *iꜣrw* "reed, rush" (pyr), *iꜣr* "kind of plant" (med).
WCh **yVraw-* "reed": Tng *yiro*.

Consonantal alternation *-ʾ- ~ *-*w*-.

2582 *yasar- "straight"

Sem **yašar-* "straight": Akk *išaru*, Hbr *yāšār*, Aram *yašrā*.
Cf. also Arab *yasar-* "easy, tractable".
LEC **sir-* < **sVyVr-* "straight": Or *sirri*.
Metathesis.
HEC **sayar-* "straight": Sid *sēra*.

2583 *yatin- "day, sun"

Eg *itn* "sun" (MK).
ECh **yatin-H-* "day": Jegu *yetiŋ*, *ʾetiŋ*.

2584 *yaw- "pour, flow"

Eg *iwy* "pour out" (MK).
WCh **yaw-* "leak, drip": Ngz *yau*.

2585 *yawan-/*yawin- "silt, clay"

Sem **yawīn-* "silt, dirt": Hbr *yāwēn*.
WCh **wan-* < **yawan-* "clay": Ang *uan*, *wan*, Ank *uan*, Sura *wan*.

2586 *yawin- "water"

Eg *iwny* "waters" (gr).
Vocalic *-y*.
CCh **yawin-* "water": Bnn *yowino*.

Derived from **yaʾ-/*yaw-* "water, river".

2587 *yawir- "neck, throat"

Eg *iwȝy.t* "throat" (gr).
WCh **ḥa-yawir-* "neck, throat": Grk *arreu*, Dera *wura*, Wrj *ɣyir-na*, Kry *ɣwir*, *wir*, Mbu *ɣwiro*, *wiro*, Miya *wir*, Cagu *wire*, Siri *yiri*, Brm *wiyer*, Dwot *ʾyar*, Say *yər*, Pol *yuar*, Klr *wir*.
Prefix **ḥa-*.

CCh **wur-* ''neck'': FG *wuri*, FMch *wura*, FBw *uura*, Gude *wuro*, FK *wura*.

Secondary **-u-*.

ECh **wVr-* ''neck'': Jegu *were*.

2588 *yayVḥ- ''grass, plant''

Eg *iyḥ* ''water plant'' (XVIII).
WCh **yay- < *yayVH-* ''grass'': Hs *yāyē*.

2589 *yiʾ- ''back''

Eg *iꜣ.t* ''back'' (OK).
CCh **yaʾ-/*yiʾ-* ''back'': Mrg *yi*, Log *ya-hə*, Mnd *yi-ga*.
Agaw **yiw-* ''small of the back, waist'': Kwr *yewi*.

2590 *yiʾ-/*yiw- ''house''

Eg *iwy.t* ''house, town block'' (MK).
WCh **yiʾ-* ''place'': Kry *iyu*, Cagu *yī*, Mbu *yī*.

Consonantal alternation **-ʾ- ~ *-w-*.

2591 *yil- ''earth, field''

Eg *iyr* ''field'' (1).
WCh **yila-* ''earth'': Sura *yil*, Ang *yil*, Mnt *ka-iil*, Ank *yil*, Grk *ril*, Krk *yali*, Tng *yelli*, Pero *illiy*, Ngm *ʾɛli*, Glm *yil*, Grn *yil*.

2592 *yipaʿ- ''shine''

Sem **yVpVʿ-* ''shine'': Hbr *ypʿ*.
CCh **pay- < *paH-* ''dawn'' [1], ''sun'' [2]: Daba *pay* [1], Gid *pāya* [2].
LEC **[y]if-* ''shine'': Or *ifa*.

2593 *yubil- ''flow''

Sem **wVbil-* ''rain abundantly (of the sky)'': Arab *wbl* [- *i*-].
WCh **yubVl-* ''dip, dive'': Yng *yuble*.

Related to **bol-* ''flow, be wet''.

2594 *yubVs- "be dry"

Sem **yVbVš-* "be dry": Hbr *ybš*, Arab *ybs*, SAr *ybs*, Gz *ybs*.
WCh **bu[y]Vs-* "dry up": Hs *būše*.
Metathesis.

2595 *yuw- "cow, bull"

Eg *iwȝ* "bull" (pyr).
Bed *yuwe* "cow".

*ʒ

2596 *ʒa- "man"

Eg *z* "man" (OK).
WCh **ʒa-f-/*ʒi-f-* "man": Cagu *zafu*, *ǯufu*, Wrj *ǯifa*.
Suffix *-f-*. Other forms have an additional prefix: Diri *nǯəvu*, Paa *nǯuu*.
CCh **ʒa-/*ʒu-* "man": Kap *za*, HNk *za*, HF *zu*, HBt *zu*.
ECh **nV-ǯa(w)-* < **nV-ʒa(w)* "man": Jegu *ǯa*, Mubi *nǯō*, Brg *ǯa*.
**-ǯ-* < **-ʒ-* in contact with the prefix. In Jegu and Brg the initial sonant is lost.

Some of the forms are contaminated with **ʒa-/*ʒi-* "body, meat".

2597 *ʒa-/*ʒi- "body, meat"

Eg *ḏ.t* "body" (pyr).
ḏ- < **ʒ-* before a front vowel?
WCh **ʒi-/*ʒu-* "body": Bol *zuwo*, Krk *zu*, Krf *ǯi*, Gera *zuwi*, Glm *ǯi*, Grm *ǯii*.
CCh **ʒa-* "body": Bura *ʒa*, Chb *ʒa*, Ngw *ʒa*, Klb *ʒa*, Hld *ʒaw*, Wmd *iʒəw*, Mrg *uʒu*, Mrg *wuʒu*.
ECh **ʒi-* "body": Dng *zi-r*, Mig *zi*, Jegu *zii-to*, Mubi *jo-c*, Bid *zii-te*, Brg *zi*.
Agaw **ʒiy-* "body, meat": Xmr *ziyaa*, Xmt *siya*, Kwr *zeyaa*, Dmb *zeyaa*, Kem *siyaa*.

Contaminated with *ʒa- ''man''. Alternation *a ~ *i.

2598 *ʒaʾ-/*ʒaw- ''go, come''

Eg *zȝw* ''go slowly, crawl'' (OK).
WCh *ʒaʾ- ''come'' [1], ''enter'' [2]: Hs *zō* [1], Wrj *zau* [2], Kry *zau* [2], Paa *za* [2], Mbu *za-* [2], Jmb *za-* [2].
CCh *ʒaw-/*ʒay- ''walk'' [1], ''enter'' [2]: Log *zuwa* [1], LPe *ze* [2].
ECh *nV-ǯaw- < *nV-ʒaw- ''go'': Jegu *ǯawo*, Mubi *nǯaa*, *nǯau*.
*-ǯ- < *-ʒ- in contact with the prefix.

Consonantal alternation *-ʾ- ~ *-w-.

2599 *ʒaʾ- ''son''

Eg *zȝ* ''son'' (pyr).
CCh *ʒaʾ-/*ʒay- ''son'': FG *ža*, Gis *za*, Gude *nzu*, Gudu *nǯi*, Nza *nzəy*, Bch *nze*.

2600 *ʒaʾar- ''plant''

Eg *zȝr.t* ''garden plant'' (sarc).
WCh *mu-ʒaHar- ''grass'': Bks *muzaar*.
Prefix *mu-.
ECh *ʾa-ʒVHVr- ''flower'': Bid *ʾozooro*.
Prefix *ʾa-.

2601 *ʒab- ''insect''

Eg *zb.t* ''kind of insect, parasite'' (MK).
Cf. *ḏdb.t* ''scorpion'' (1).
CCh *ʒab- ''termite'': Tera *zaḅa*.
Secondary emphatic.

2602 *ʒab- ''hair, wool''

Sem *zabab- ''wool, down, thick hair'': Arab *zabab-*.
Partial reduplication.
Berb *ʒVb- ''hair, wool'': Zng *aʾ-zbi*.
Eg *zb.t* ''hairlock'' (RGr).
LEC *ʒab- ''hair'': Or *daabee*, *dɛbb-ɛsa*.

2603 *ʒagül- "monkey"

ECh **ʒugul-* "monkey": Brg *zuguli*.
Assimilation of vowels from **ʒagul-*.
Agaw **ʒagill-* "monkey": Bil *ǯäggira*, Xmt *ziägeraa*, Kwr *ǯägiraa*, Kem *ǯegəraa*, Aun *zagree*, Dmt *zagree*.

2604 *ʒaʕab-/*ʒaʕib- "cut; axe"

Sem **zVʕab-* "cut, chop": Arab *zʕb* [-*a*-].
WCh **ʒaHib-* "axe": Hs *zāḃī*, Pero *ǯibi*.

2605 *ʒaḥaf- "drag oneself, crawl"

Sem **zVḥVp-* "drag oneself, creep, crawl": Arab *zḥf*, Hss *zeḥāf*, Mhr *zeḥāf*, Shh *zḥaf*.
LEC **ʒaHaf-* "drag oneself, crawl": Kon *taaf-*, Glb *zaaf-*.

2606 *ʒak-/*ʒik- "go, come"

Sem **zik-* "march (in small steps)": Arab *zkk* [-*i*-].
WCh **ʒVk-* "come": Tum *ǯek*.

Alternation **a* ~ **i*.

2607 *ʒam- "think, remember"

Sem **zVm-* "think": Hbr *zmm*.
WCh **ʒum-* < **ʒamu-* "remember": Pol *zum*.
CCh **ʒam-* "think": Glv *dzam*.

2608 *ʒamVn- "dwell, stay"

Eg *zmn* "stay, dwell" (pyr).
WCh **ʒamVn-* "stay": Hs *zamna*, *zauna*.

An original root may be represented in Dhl *jem-* "stay in a place".

2609 *ʒan- "pour, flow"

Sem **zVn-* "rain" (v.): Akk *zanānu*.

WCh **ʒan-* "pour out": Diri *zan*.
ECh **ʒyan-* "flow, ooze": Bid *zenyzeny*.
Reduplication.

2610 *ʒariḳ-/*ʒaruḳ- "throw, push"

Sem **zVrVḳ-* "throw" [1], "dart" (v.) [2]: Hbr *zrq* [1], Aram *zrq* [1], Arab *zrq* [1], Hss *zerōq* [2], Mhr *zerōq* [2], Shh *zoroq* [2].
SA **ʒVrig-* "stir": Saho *-izrig-*, *-idrig-*.
LEC **ʒarug-/*ʒaruk-* "shift, push": Som *durk-*, *durug-*, Arb *zarug-*, Arb *zurg-*, *zurug-*.

**-g-/*-k-* in SA and LEC seem to continue emphatic **-ḳ-* .

2611 *ʒaw- "stick"

Eg *zꜣw* "twig" (BD).
WCh **ʒaw-* "stick": Ngz *zawa*.
CCh **ʒaw-* "stick": Log *zawa*.
Cf. Chb *zuwa*, Mrg *əzuwa* that may also go back to **ʒuwal-*.

2612 *ʒaw-/*ʒay- "rope"

Eg *ỉzy* "rope" (NK).
WCh **ʒaw-/*ʒay-* "rope": Miya *žowu*, Ngz *zayi*, Bade *zayi*.
CCh **ʒaw-/*ʒaʔu-* "rope": Tera *zo*, HGh *zuwi*, HB *zuwo*, Kap *zuwɛ*, Mnd *zāwa*, Gude *zuʔwa*, Nza *zoʔo*, FMch *zuʔu*, Lame *zeo*, Mafa *zaya*.
ECh **ʒa-* "rope": Tum *hā*, Ndam *ha*.

Consonantal alternation **-w-* ~ **-y-*.

2613 *ʒaw-/*ʒay- "fly" (v.)

ECh **ʒaw-/*ʒay-* "fly" (v.): Kwn *sayi*, Tob *say*, Lele *se*, Bid *zew*, Mkk *zaawo*.
Rift **ǯVʔ-* "fly, jump": Asa *jiʔ-it-*.
Cf. Alg *coʔ-ot-* id. Rift **ǯ-* may be a regular reflex of HS **ʒ-*.
Consonantal alternation **-w-* ~ **-y-*.

2614 *ʒaw-/*ʒuw- "rain"

Eg *zwzw* "kind of pool" (pyr).
WCh **ʒaw-/*ʒaʾ-* "water, rain": Cagu *zāw*, Geji *ziye*, Say *ža*, Dwot *ža*.
Geji reflects **ʒay-/*ʒiy-*.
ECh **ʒVw-* "rain" (v.): Tum *həw*.
Agaw **ʒuw-* "rain": Bil *zuwaa*, Xmr *zoowaa*, Xmt *suwaa*, Kwr *suwaa*, Dmb *suwaa*, Kem *suwaa*.
From **ʒaw-*.

2615 *ʒiʾVp- "cut"

Sem **zVʾVp-* "be cut off": Arab *zʾf*.
Berb **ʒVf-* "plane, shave": Ayr *zaf-at*.
Eg *ỉzp* "chop with axe" (OK).
Metathesis. Initial *ỉ-* continues *ʾ- before a HS front vowel.

2616 *ʒib- "go, walk"

Eg *zby* "walk, pass" (pyr).
Infinitive in *-y*.
WCh **ʒib-* "follow": Diri *žibu*.
CCh **ʒib-* "go out" [1], "follow" [2]: WMrg *zuba* [1], Mrg *ziḅu* [2], Log *zbi* [2].

Cf. ECh **ǯwab-* < **ǯab-* "follow": Bid *ǯob*.

2617 *ʒib- "plaiting"

Berb **ʒib-* "net (for hairdressing)": Ghd *ta-zība*.
WCh **ʒib-/*ʒub-* "basket" [1], "mat" [2]: Hs *zūbā* [1], Glm *ǯiba* [2].

2618 *ʒiban- "plaiting"

Sem **zibn-* "reed mat": Akk *zibnu*.
Berb **ʒVban-* "palm bast": Ghd *a-zbān*.

Derived from **ʒib-* id.

2619 *ʒid- "increase"

Sem *zayad-* "increase": Arab *zyd* [-*i*-], Hss *zōd*, Mhr *zeyōd*, Shh *zɛd*, Soq *zed*.

Based on the original **zid-*.

ECh *ʒid-* "increase": Kbl *ǯidə*, Dng *ziddiye*, Mok *ziid-* (< Arab?).

2620 *ʒif- "goat, sheep"

Sem *zīp-* "sheep": Akk *zīpu*.

CCh *ʒif-/*ʒuf-* "he-goat": HF *žifa*, Kap *žufa*.

2621 *ʒik- "shoulder"

ECh *ʒik-* "arm, shoulder": Ndam *ǯik-am*, Kwn *ǯigi-d*.

Agaw *ʒikk-* "shoulder" [1], "back" [2]: Bil *zeeg*, *zäg* [1], Xmr *ziig* [1], Xmt *siig* [2].

Omot *zikk-* "back": Ome *zikkoo*.

2622 *ʒik- "body, meat"

WCh *ʒik-* "body": Hs *ǯiki*, Sura *šik*, Ang *šeuk*, Grk *tək*, Dera *yik*, Tng *ʾik*, Pero *šik*, Ngm *zugo*, Bele *hiko*, Bgh *šok*, Sha *šok*, Klr *zigy*.

ECh *ʒi[k]-* "body": Tum *hig*, Ndam *həgʾ*, Mubi *jič*.

Agaw *ǯik-* "meat": Bil *zegaa*, (pl.) *zik*.

Derived from **ʒa-/*ʒi-* id.

2623 *ʒil- "go, come"

Sem *zil-* "walk fast": Arab *zll* [-*i*-].

Berb *zVl-* "run": Kby *azzəl*.

Eg *zny* "come" (MK).

CCh *ʒul-* "follow": HNk *zulu*.

2624 *ʒimol- "darkness"

Eg *zmȝw* "darkness" (XVIII).

ECh *zimwal-* "darkness": Mig *zimolo*.

2625 *ʒin- "hide, leather"

WCh *ʒin-* "hide": Bol *zino*.
Cf. Siri *zənu* "skin" (v.).
Omot *ʒen-* "hide": Gll *zeena*.

2626 *ʒin- "blood"

Eg *znf* "blood" (pyr).
Suffix *-f*?
WCh *ʒin-* "blood": Hs *ǯinī*.

2627 *ʒinaʔ- "urine"

Sem *zVnaʔ-* "keep from urinating": Arab *znʔ* [*-a-*].
Denominative formation.
WCh *kV-ʒin-H-* "urine": Sura *kə-ʒiŋ*, Ang *ngəzəŋ*, Chip *kəzəŋ*, Ank *kəsəŋ*.
Prefix *kV-*.

2628 *ʒinb- "gourd vessel"

Eg *znb.t* "bottle" (gr).
WCh *ʒimb-* "gourd": Glm *žimbu*.
Assimilation *-nb-* > *-mb-*.

2629 *ʒir- "vessel"

Sem *zīr-* "big vessel": Arab *zīr-*.
Eg *i̓d̠r.t* "kind of vessel" (n).
d̠- < *ʒ-* before a front vowel?
CCh *ʒir-* "pot": Tera *žira*.

2630 *ʒor- "bird"

Eg *zwrw.t* "kind of bird" (MK).
Suffix *-w*.
WCh *ʒar-* "crow": Kry *zarazar*.
Reduplication.
CCh *ʒwar-* "vulture": Gis *ʒoroʒoro*.
Reduplication.

ECh *ʒar- "kind of bird": Bid zarzari.
Reduplication.

Cf. Sem *zur-zur-, *zar-zir- "kind of bird" and HS *ʒuray(V)ḳ- "raven". Secondary *-a- in WCh and ECh.

2631 *ʒub- "pour"

Sem *zub- "fill (wine skin)": Arab zbb [-u-].
Cf. Sem *zūb- "flow": Akk zâbu, Hbr zwb, Aram zwb, Arab zwb.
WCh *ʒub- "pour": Hs zuba.

2632 *ʒum- "rob"

Sem *zVm- "be robbed": Akk zummû.
D stirpes in Akk.
CCh *ʒum- "rob": Log zum.

2633 *ʒunaḫ- "smell, stink"

Sem *zVnaḫ- "be rotten": Arab znḫ [-a-].
CCh *ʒunaH- "smell" (n.) [1], "smell" (v.) [2]: Kam zuŋwi [1], FG zunayi [1], Nza zən [2], FM zunu-ft [2].

2634 *ʒur- "ram"

Eg zr "ram" (pyr).
CCh *ʒur- "ram": FKi žūrā.

2635 *ʒuray(V)ḳ- "raven"

Sem *zurayḳ- "raven": Arab zurayq-.
WCh *nV-ʒaraḳ- "raven": Krk nzaraku, Miya žarakə.
Assimilation of vowels. Prefix n- in Krk.

Connected with *ʒor- "bird"?

2636 *ʒuwVᶜ- "be afraid"

Sem *zūᶜ- "tremble of fear": Hbr zwᶜ.

WCh *ʒuw- "be afraid": Bol *zuw*.

2637 *ʒük- "dig"

Sem *ᶜVziḳ- "dig": Hbr *ᶜzḳ*, Arab *ᶜzḳ* [-*i*-].
Prefix *ᶜV-. Irregular *-ḳ-.
Eg *zk* "dig (a pond)" (pyr).
WCh *ʒuk- "dig, scratch": Bol *zuk-*, Tng *suke*.

2638 *ʒVb- "carry, bring"

Sem *zVbVy- "carry (load)": Arab *zby* [-*i*-].
Based on *zVb-.
Eg *zby* "bring" (pyr).
CCh *ʒVḅ- "take, lift": Gis *zeḅ*, *zuḅ*, *zoḅ*.
Secondary emphatic.

2639 *ʒVg- "marry, join"

Sem *zūg- "marry, join": Hbr *zwg*, Arab *zwg*.
Generally believed to be a Gk loanword.
Berb *ʒVg- "copulate": Izy *zeġ*.

2640 *ʒVrab- "flow"

Sem *zVrab- "flow": Arab *zrb* [-*a*-].
Eg *zꜣb* "flow" (pyr).

*ǯ

2641 *ǯaʾar- "insect"

Eg *ḏꜣr.t* "scorpion" (OK).
WCh *nV-ǯar- "termite": Sura *nǯar*.
Prefix *nV-.
CCh *ǯaray-/*ǯayar- < *ǯaHar- "locust": Gis *ʒaray*, Msm *dʒēr*.
ECh *ǯaHar- "locust": Bid *ǯaariyo*.

2642 *ǯaʾar- ‟cook, boil"

Eg *ḏꜣr* ‟cook" (gr).
CCh **ǯar-* ‟boil": Msm *ʒar*.
ECh **ʾaǯVr-* ‟boil": Tum *ʾaǯər*.
Metathesis.

2643 *ǯaʾir- ‟feline, viverra"

WCh **ǯar-* ‟lion": Wrj *ǯara-waŝ*.
CCh **ǯar-* ‟lion": Bch *žara*.
LEC **ʾaǯur-* ‟viverra": Or *adurree*.
Metathesis.
Wrz **ʾatur-* ‟wild cat": Dob *aturre*, Gll *aturre*.
Metathesis.
Omot **ǯaHer-* ‟viverra": Kaf *yeeroo*, *ǯäro*.
Rift **ǯeʾir-* ‟viverra": Alg *ǯeʾira*, Bur *ǯiʾerare*.

An alternative reconstruction is **ʾaǯir-*.

2644 *ǯab- ‟breast"

WCh **ǯab-* ‟breast": Krk *ǯaba*.
Bed *daba*, *daaba* ‟forehead, breast".
Agaw **ǯab-* ‟front": Bil *ǯaab*, Kwr *ǯaab*, Dmb *ǯaab*, Kem *ǯaab*.
SA **ǯabVˁ-* ‟armpit": Afar *dabˁe*.
Secondary laryngeal.
Rift **daʾab-* ‟breast": Irq *daʾawe*, Alg *daʾawi*, Bur *daʾeo*.
Laryngeal infix.

2645 *ǯab- ‟gather"

Eg *ḏdb* ‟gather" (MK).
ḏd- stands for **ǯ-*.
CCh **nV-ǯVb-* ‟gather, collect": Mofu *nǯəb*.
Prefix **nV-*.
ECh **ǯab-* ‟gather": Tum *ǯaab*.

2646 *ǯabaḥ-/*ǯibiḥ- ‟make sacrifice"

Sem **ḏVbVḥ-* ‟make sacrifice": Ug *dbḥ*, Phn *zbḥ*, Hbr *zbḥ*, Aram (Bibl) *dbḥ*, Arab *ḏbḥ*, Gz *zbḥ*.

ECh *ǯiHib- "make sacrifice": Bid *ziib*.
Metathesis.
LEC *ǯabaḥ- "slaughter": Som *dabaaḥ-*.

Alternation *a ~ *i.

2647 *ǯabiʾ- "clothes"

Eg *ḏbꜣ* "kind of clothes" (NK), *ḏbꜣy* (sarc).
CCh *ǯabiH- "loin-cloth": Bura *žaḅi*, Chb *zaḅi*, Mrg *žɛḅi*.

2648 *ǯafor-/*ǯifor- "temple"

Sem *ḏip̣r- "temple": Arab *ḏifra(y)-*.
Derivative in *-ay-*.
LEC *[ǯ]afor- "temple": Som *ḍafoor*, Or *ḍaffora*.

Alternation *a ~ *i.

2649 *ǯaḥ- "back"

Eg *ḏd* "backbone" (gr).
WCh *ǯaḥ- "lower back": Bks *ǯaha*.
CCh *ʒaχ- "back": Suk *dzhaχ*.
Omot *zaH- "back": Ome *zahi*.

2650 *ǯaḳun-/*ǯiḳun- "beard, chin"

Sem *ḏaḳn-/*ḏiḳn- "beard" [1], "bearded chin" [2]: Akk *ziqnu* [1], Ug *dqn* [1], Hbr *zāqān* [1 2], Aram *diqn-* [1], Arab *ḏaq(a)n-* [1], Soq *diqehon* [1].
WCh *ǯaḳVn-/*ǯiḳVn- "chin": Grm *ǯang-umu*, Ngz *ǯigəna*.
ECh *ǯiḳum- "chin, jaw": Tum *ǯigəm*, Mkk *zukimo*, Mig *zukumo*, *sukumo*.
*-m- < *-n- after a velar?

Alternation *a ~ *i.

2651 *ǯam- "ask"

Eg *sḏm* "interrogate" (OK).
Causative in *s-*.
CCh *ǯam- "ask": Log *zāma*, Tera *zəmi*.

2652 *ǯa(m)b- "fly" (n.)

Sem *ḏumb- "fly": Akk *zumbu*, Tgr *zəmbi*, Amh *zəmb*, Arg *zəmb*, Gaf *zəmbä*, Hrr *zəmbi*, Gur *zəmb*, Mhr *ḏebb-et*, Hrs *ḏebb-et*, Jib *ḏəbb-ət*.

Secondary *-*u*- before a labial.

Berb *ʒVb- "fly": Ghat *a-zəb*, Ayr *e-zəb*, Ahg *a-həb*, Twl *i-zəbb*, Tsl *i-zəbb*, Izy *i-zəβ*.

WCh *ǯamb- "fly": Tng *šombo*.

CCh *ǯabiʔ- "fly": FG *žiḅi*, FBw *ǯebi*.

Suffix *-*iʔ*-.

2653 *ǯa(m)bib- "fly" (n.)

Sem *ḏVbVb- "fly": Hbr *zəbūb*, Aram *dəbbōb*, Arab *ḏubāb-*, *ḏibbāb-at-*, Soq *dbib-oh*.

Berb *ʒVbib- "species of coleoptera": Ahg *a-zəbibibər*.

HEC *ǯVmbib- "gnat, mosquito": Kmb *zəmbib-uite*.

Derived from *ǯa(m)b- id.

2654 *ǯan-/*ǯin- "child"

Eg *ḏꜣn.w* "young people" (pyr).

Vocalic -*ꜣ*-.

WCh *ǯin- "son, child": Hs *ǯinǯirī*, Wrj *ǯina*, Kry *ǯin*, Mbu *ǯin*.

Hs reflects a reduplication with dissimilation of sonants.

Agaw *ǯan-/*ǯin- "brother": Bil *dan*, Xmr *zin*, Xmt *izzän*, Kwr *zän*, Dmb *zän*, Kem *zän*.

Alternation *a ~ *i.

2655 *ǯar-/*ǯur- "throw"

Sem *ḏur- "scatter": Arab *ḏrr* [-*u*-].

ECh *ǯar- "throw": Smr *ǯar*, Dng *zɛɛrɛ*.

Irregular correspondence of vowels.

2656 *ǯeʔ-/*ǯew- "shout, ask"

Eg *ḏwy* "call" (pyr).

CCh *ǯyaw- "ask": Mrg *ǯo*, Wmd *ǯewe*.
Rift *ǯeʾ- "shout, ask": Irq *tseʾ-*, Asa *jeʾ-em-it*, Kwz *tsaʾ-am-*.
Consonantal alternation *-ʾ- ~ *-w-.

2657 *ǯef- "throw"

Sem *ḫVḏip- "throw": Arab *ḫḏf* [-*i*-].
Prefix *ḫV-.
Eg *ḏfy* "sink" (med).
Infinitive in *-y*.
WCh *ǯyaf- "throw": Hs *ǯēfa*.

2658 *ǯeHun- "elephant"

WCh *ǯun-H- "rhinoceros": Paa *ǯuŋgwa*, Diri *ǯuŋgwa*, Siri *ǯəŋwa*.
Metathesis.
CCh *čuHwan- "elephant": Tera *ojuwan*, Gbn *čuwene*, Hwn *čūwāna*, FJ *ǯuʾwuni*, Gude *čona*, FK *čuwuna*.
Irregular *č-.
ECh *ǯun- "elephant": Gbr *ǯenu*, Kbl *ǯuno*, Dor *ǯunu*, Ndam *čun*.
Irregular anlaut in Ndam.
Agaw *ǯiHun- "elephant": Bil *ǯaanaa*, Xmr *zehon*, Kwr *ǯaanaa*, Dmb *ǯaanaa*, Aun *ziġoni*.

Cf. WCh *yaHun- "elephant": Bol *yauno*, Krk *uwan*, Nga *yawan*, Krf *yuuni*, Glm *yuwun*, Gera *üwuni*, Mbu *yawən*, Miya *yəwun*, Siri *yiwani*, Jmb *yawan*. Maybe, *yaHun- < *ǯyaHun-. Apparently, this is a cultural word with a complicated history of borrowings from one group to another.

2659 *ǯiʾ-/*ǯuw- "insect"

Berb *ʒVy- "fly": Kby *izi*.
Eg *ḏw.t* "kind of insect" (n).
CCh *ǯiʾ-/*ǯuw- "fly": FKi *žu*, FJ *wʒiʾyu*, Gude *ǯiʾ-in*, Log *zū*, HF *žuwi*, FMch *jiʾi*, Nak *juya*, Mafa *ʒuway*, Gava *njuwa*, Glv *njuya*, Zgh *nzuwe*.
Rift *ǯuʾ- "gnat": Irq *tsuʾa*.

Consonantal alternation *-ʾ- ~ *-w-. In WCh the root appears in a reduplicated form, cf. Klr *ʾajijuwaw* "fly".

2660 *ǯiʾib- "beast of prey"

Sem *ḏiʾb- "jackal" [1], "wolf" [2], "hyaena" [3]: Akk *zību* [1], Hbr *zəʾēb* [2], Aram (Syr) *diʾb-* [2], Arab *ḏiʾb-* [2], Gz *zəʾb* [3].
Berb *dib- "jackal": Izy *βenδibbun*.
Initial *d- reflects a HS alternation of *ǯ- ~ *d-?
Eg *zꜣb* "jackal" (pyr).
Irregular *z-*.
WCh *ǯib- "viverra": Ngz *ǯib-da*.
ECh *ǯabiy- "hyaena": Mig *ǯabiya*, Bid *ǯebey-gi*.
Bed *diib* "wolf".

2661 *ǯibaʿ- "bull"

Eg *ḏbʿ* "bull" (math).
CCh *ǯibay- < *ʒibaH- "cattle tax": Log *ǯibaya*.
LEC *ǯib- "young bull": Or *dib-icca*.

2662 *ǯibar- "bee, fly"

Sem *ḏVbār- "bee": Hbr *dᵉbōrā*, Mhr *ḏebēr*, Shh *εḏbōr*, Hss *ḏebēr*, Soq *edbehir*.
Note irregular Hbr *d-*.
WCh *ma-ǯibar- "kind of fly": Hs *māǯiḅāri*.
Secondary emphatic. Prefix *ma-.

Derived from *ǯa(m)b- "fly"?

2663 *ǯigal- "bird"

WCh *ǯigal- "griffon-vulture": Hs *ǯigal*.
Agaw *ǯigal- "bird": Bil *ǯagalaa*, Kwr *ǯäkel* (pl.), Dmb *ǯeelaa*, Kem *ǯeelaa*.
Assimilation of vowels in Bil.

2664 *ǯiḳan- "old man"

Sem *ḏiḳn- "old man": Arab *ḏiqn-*.
A different pattern in Hbr *zāqēn* id.
WCh *ma-ǯiḳan- "old": Krk *mačigan*.
Prefix *ma-.

Agaw *ǯVḳVn- "old man": Bil *dəχna*.

Related to *ǯaḳun-/*ǯiḳun- "beard, chin"?

2665 *ǯinab- "tail"

Sem **ḏanab-/*ḏinab-* "tail": Akk *zibbatu*, Ug *ḏnbt*, Hbr *zānāb*, Aram (Syr) *dunbō*, Arab *ḏanab-*, Gz *zanab*, Hss *ḏenēb*, Mhr *ḏenōb*, Shh *ḏunub*, Soq *denob*.
Omot **ǯiban-/*ǯuban-* "tail": Baa *doobanna*, Hmr *dubaana*, Kar *dibini*.
Metathesis.

2666 *ǯo- "penis"

Eg *ḏ.t* "penis" (BD).
ECh **ǯwa-* "penis": Ndam *ǯo*.

2667 *ǯor- "sand, dust"

Sem **ḏurw-* "dust": Arab *ḏurw-*.
Based on biconsonantal **ḏur-*.
WCh **ǯwar-* "sand": DB *ǯoor*.

2668 *ǯuʔ- "go"

Eg *wḏȝ* "go" (MK).
w- reflects a rounded root vowel. Cf. also causitive *sḏȝ* (pyr), *swḏȝ* (BD).
WCh **ǯuʔ-* "go": Ngz *ǯu*.

2669 *ǯub- "flow, pour"

Sem **ḏūb-* "flow" [1], "pour" [2], "melt" [3]: Akk *zâbu* [1], Hbr *zwb* [2], Aram *dwb* [2], Arab *ḏwb* [-*u*-] [3], Hss *ḏeyōb* [3], Mhr *ḏeyōb* [3], Shh *ḏɛb* [3].
Based on **ḏVb-*. Cf. also Arab *ḏʕb* id.
Eg *ḏbb* "waters" (n).
Partial reduplication.
WCh **ǯub-* "pour": Bol *ǯubb-*.
CCh **ǯub-* "be wet": Mofu *ǯəb*, Daba *ǯup*.

2670 *ǯug- "drink, swallow"

Sem **ḏV'ag-* "drink": Arab *ḏ'g* [-*a*-].
Based on **ḏug-*.
LEC **ǯug-* "swallowing": Som *ǯug-*.

2671 *ǯVHVǯ- "divide"

Sem **ḏVHVḏ-* "divide": Akk *zâzu*.
ECh **ǯVǯ-* "divide": Tum *ǯəǯ*.

2672 *ǯVhab- "go, trot"

Sem **ḏVhab-* "go away": Arab *ḏhb* [-*a*-].
WCh **ǯVHVb-* "trot": Ang *ǯōp*.
Regular Ang unvoicing in the auslaut.

INDEX OF MEANINGS

The present index includes English translations of Hamito-Semitic forms adduced in the Dictionary. Numbers refer to Hamito-Semitic reconstructions.

braid 579
brain 1583 1800 2393
branch 371 1807 2574
bread 224 265 271 559 1111 1364 1561 1642 2390
break 235 373 408 536 605 635 642 756 794 795 799 804 812 1186 1193 1282 1351 1386 1516 1565 1566 1592 1595 1610 1613 1866 1898 1899 1912 1916 1929 1937 1951 1959 1985 1986 1998 1999 2004 2005 2016 2030 2053 2114 2170 2181 2307 2372 2376 2384 2394 2399 2421 2509
break off 170 240 1351 1999
break through 830 1929
breast 144 251 360 462 826 1071 1072 1094 1251 1530 1577 2644
breath 151 1677 1828 1830 2132 2196
breathe 151 814 821 1853 1865 1882 2199
breech 332
breed 1254
bride 1419
bridegroom 659 1831
bright 231 515 1670
bring 99 157 937 2166 2638
broken 2399
bronze vessel 1754
brother 23 145 288 613 1182 1888 2193 2363 2520 2654
brother-in-law 437
brow 858
brown 307 686
bubble 449
bucket 668 1945
buffalo 883 905 1409 1479 2570
bug 88 197 2357
build 252 261 342 703 912 929 1137 building 264 359 1166 1430 1488 2404 2565
bulge 1123
bulky 1005
bull 67 183 227 310 477 896 905 1077 1399 1409 1432 1479 1508 1632 1635 1728 1832 1950 2323 2527 2570 2595 2661
bull-fight 1950
burn 62 72 129 137 189 282 353 459 818 819 931 971 1078 1118 1184 1404 1441 1553 1572 1584 1606 1670 2001 2062 2125 2152 2172 2271 2328 2337 2417 2487 2507 2528 2579
burning 2328
bury 159 365 739 875 1517 1781 1864 1910
bush 31 155 1052 1873 2246 2318 2428 2542
butcher (v.) 1248
butter 2232
butterfly 286 2190
buttock 636 691 731
buy 254 543 2281
buzz 745 2485

cabbage 395 722 2335
cabin 2058
cacare 2478
calabash 156 349 404 663 670 734 853 878 989 1121 1407 1417 1464 1473 1476 1579 1588 2448 2551
calf 57 173 227 340 896 1100 1728 2458
calf (anat.) 11 396 1390 1696
call 417 427 696 724 800 911 998 1107 1295 1400 1519 1541 1555 1788 1814 1822 1825 1893 1969 2044 2244 2382 2485 2523 2534 2564 2656
calm 1321
camel 90 183 310 1462 1678
camp 1214 2058
can 184 530 2327 cane 228
canopy 1308
capture 1147
card 1918
care 1120
carry 787 937 1153 2638
carpenter 2180
carve 799 981 1248 1556 1938 2168
cassawa 2129
cast 1863 2526
castrate 2168 2230
cat 751 1171
catarrh 690
catch 35 96 181 463 473 496 957 1147 1744 2032 2447 2512
caterpillar 316 1771 1846
cattle 57 227 310 1098 1479 1632 1635 1647 1809 1832 1950 2323 2527
cattle-pen 973
cauldron 734
cave 1414
cavern 1414 2557
caviar 113
cavity 987 1239
cedar 1766 2428
centipede 2216
cereal 224 559 720 1167 1210 1247 1272

enraged 897
ensete tree 2246
enter 41 65 157 237 550 669 676 697 700 701 707 879 910 1178 1189 1207 1228 1289 1359 1373 1418 1752 2065 2103 2197 2207 2264 2345 2440 2516 2547 2598
entrance 854
envelop 1292 1671
equid 641 667 780 1961 2064
erase 822
escape 230 619
estimate 767
evening 38 64 552 1008 1145 1320 1342 2117 2261
evident 498
evil 270 355 1848 1902 2145 2155
examine 201 1590
excel 2391
exchange 2023
excrement 1175 1334
exhausted 149 861 1683
exhaustion 149
exist 238 932 1069 1148
expectorate 169
explain 483
extinguish 87
extract oil 499
eye 93 110 112 204 851 1084 1101 2299
eyebrow 2158
eyelash 204
eyelid 204 2299

face 817 851 863 914 1340 1943
faeces 390 486 546 1116 1175 1275 1630
falcon 356 2162 2326
fall 4 456 562 625 655 793 1152 1163 1436 1540 1930 1936 2484 2518
family 2 647 906 1038 1256 1801
family member 49 97
famine 885
fang 1235
far 2536
farm (n.) 5 1483 1735
farm (v.) 1739
farmer 70 860
fast 2544
fat (adj.) 1005 2529
fat (n.) 27 726 1099 1490 1784 1836 2247 2498
fat tail 27
fatigue 174
father 2 154 165 2438
father-in-law 182 1330 2493
favorable 1394
fear 178 833 2499 2500
feather 205 2324
feed 472 565 1614 1804 2559
feline 751 1171 2643
female 141
female in-law 1419 1513
female relative 20
fence 22 100 608 671 852 1188 1214 1455 2404
ferocious animal 56
fertile land 48
fertile soil 871 975 2386
fertilize 871
fester 308
fetish 571
fetters 1948
fever 14
feverous 575
field 16 48 210 337 385 421 522 857 890 1054 1222 1348 1483 1633 1735 1741 1927 2096 2249 2591
fierce animal 186
fig tree 1126 2392
fight 578 753 1672 1802 2063
figure 863
fill 161 888 1263 1704 2481 2631
fill up 161
filter (v.) 2176
find 926 974 1259 1954
fine 704
finger 211 292 434 513 1861 1953
fingernail 292 513 972 1559 1667 1861
finish 1551 1562 1597 2080
finished 2080
fire 24 82 819 928 930 1055 1187 1310 1553 2125 2507 2579
firewood 1767 2269 2503
first-born 1831
fish 138 317 963 968 1044 1085 1117 1211 1494 1663 2061 2430
fish (v.) 463 473 2512
fish roe 113
fit 1815
flame 282 2125 2135 2337 2528 2579
flat 2029
flatten 2029
flea 345 1457 1587 1771 1966 1978 2187
flee 202 1981
flesh 13 128 825
flight 1981

injure 940
in-law 108 437
inquire 2410
insatiable 1157
insect 88 197 316 345 606 609 679 708 776 807 978 1034 1124 1422 1457 1587 1609 1616 1679 1775 1978 2119 2187 2217 2601 2641 2659
insert 673
inside 2356
instruct 387
insufficient 1013
insult 121 2231
intention 466
interior 909
interrogate 2651
interval 1942
intestine 346 991 995 1170 1243 1251 1577 1845 2137 2356 2538 2539
invite 2523
iron 55 60 290 419 1412 1440 1785 1967 2159
iron weapon 1785
irrigation ditch 158
isolate 2039
ivory 1456

jackal 119 464 1521 1891 2501 2660
jar 94 349 705 1582 1718
javeline 2241
jaw 866 990 1932 2650
jerboa 507
join 12 422 471 586 2043 2639
joint 859
jubba 969
jug 663 894 979 1313 1473 1582
juice 1997
jump 130 142 219 284 291 296 411 810 1060 1276 1279 1911 1952 2007 2109 2164 2451 2482 2613
jump at 411
juniper 654
just 1045

keep 1011 1389
kerchief 1327 2346
kick 2051 2370 2453
kid 196
kidney 44 870 1493 2403
kill 194 1004 1024 1566 1672 1920 2031 2468
king 250 311 386 1791 1801
kinsfolk 1256
kitchen 2342
kite 52 410 439 443 736 1108 1261 1593 1646 2257
knead 642 1676 2315
knee 396 828 962 983 993 1573 2018 2060 2133
knife 259 457 514 535 567 570 610 644 665 1041 1293 1503 1644 1785 1812 1867 1956 1979 2047 2159 2201 2212 2241 2256 2389
knock 1595 1868 2364 2434
knot 1058 1486
know 37 75 201 222 275 378 387 504 505 618 622 1056 1074 1089 1103 1444 1721 1753 2198 2294 2295 2573
knowledge 1444

lacerate 786
lady 20 2306
lake 243 305 329 523 869 884 1335 1491 1502 2549
lamb 173 196 341 381 1432 1729 2093
lame 1125
lame person 1125
lamentation 2519
land 53 321 421 522 871 975 1633 1939 2096
language 79 2142
lap 396 1697
large 919 1811 2529
larva 2119
larva of mosquito 1679
larynx 1234
last 643
lawlessness 1314
lay 1369
lay down 2511
lay eggs 881 1458
lay off 929 2432
lazy 1664
lead 313 593
leaf 540 958 1030 1049 1059 1319 1337 2318
leak 2082 2584
learn 222 378 618 718 1056 1444 1820
leather 699 1327 2625
leather sack 71 249
leather shield 661
leather strap 2255 2474
leave 230 593
leech 1110
left 1821
leg 11 190 396 470 773 778 828 891 1031

HANDBUCH DER ORIENTALISTIK

Abt. I: DER NAHE UND MITTLERE OSTEN

ISSN 0169-9423

Band 1. Ägyptologie

1. *Ägyptische Schrift und Sprache.* Mit Beiträgen von H. Brunner, H. Kees, S. Morenz, E. Otto, S. Schott. Mit Zusätzen von H. Brunner. Nachdruck der Erstausgabe (1959). 1973.
   ISBN 90 04 03777 2
2. *Literatur.* Mit Beiträgen von H. Altenmüller, H. Brunner, G. Fecht, H. Grapow, H. Kees, S. Morenz, E. Otto, S. Schott, J. Spiegel, W. Westendorf. 2. verbesserte und erweiterte Auflage. 1970. ISBN 90 04 00849 7
3. HELCK, W. *Geschichte des alten Ägypten.* Nachdruck mit Berichtigungen und Ergänzungen. 1981. ISBN 90 04 06497 4

Band 2. Keilschriftforschung und alte Geschichte Vorderasiens

1-2/2. *Altkleinasiatische Sprachen [und Elamitisch].* Mit Beiträgen von J. Friedrich, E. Reiner, A. Kammenhuber, G. Neumann, A. Heubeck. 1969. ISBN 90 04 00852 7

3. SCHMÖKEL, H. *Geschichte des alten Vorderasien.* Reprint. 1979. ISBN 90 04 00853 5

4/2. *Orientalische Geschichte von Kyros bis Mohammed.* Mit Beiträgen von A. Dietrich, G. Widengren, F. M. Heichelheim. 1966. ISBN 90 04 00854 3

Band 3. Semitistik

Semitistik. Mit Beiträgen von A. Baumstark, C. Brockelmann, E. L. Dietrich, J. Fück, M. Höfner, E. Littmann, A. Rücker, B. Spuler. Nachdruck der Erstausgabe (1953-1954). 1964. ISBN 90 04 00855 1

Band 4. Iranistik

1. *Linguistik.* Mit Beiträgen von K. Hoffmann, W. B. Henning, H. W. Bailey, G. Morgenstierne, W. Lentz. Nachdruck der Erstausgabe (1958). 1967. ISBN 90 04 03017 4

2/1. *Literatur.* Mit Beiträgen von I. Gershevitch, M. Boyce, O. Hansen, B. Spuler, M. J. Dresden. 1968. ISBN 90 04 00857 8

2/2. *History of Persian Literature from the Beginning of the Islamic Period to the Present Day.* With Contributions by G. Morrison, J. Baldick and Sh. Kadkanī. 1981. ISBN 90 04 06481 8

3. KRAUSE, W. *Tocharisch.* Nachdruck der Erstausgabe (1955) mit Zusätzen und Berichtigungen. 1971. ISBN 90 04 03194 4

Band 5. Altaistik

1. *Turkologie.* Mit Beiträgen von A. von Gabain, O. Pritsak, J. Benzing, K. H. Menges, A. Temir, Z. V. Togan, F. Taeschner, O. Spies, A. Caferoglu, A. Battal-Tamays. Reprint with additions of the 1st (1963) ed. 1982. ISBN 90 04 06555 5
2. *Mongolistik.* Mit Beiträgen von N. Poppe, U. Posch, G. Doerfer, P. Aalto, D. Schröder, O. Pritsak, W. Heissig. 1964. ISBN 90 04 00859 4
3. *Tungusologie.* Mit Beiträgen von W. Fuchs, I. A. Lopatin, K. H. Menges, D. Sinor. 1968. ISBN 90 04 00860 8

Band 6. Geschichte der islamischen Länder

5/1. *Regierung und Verwaltung des Vorderen Orients in islamischer Zeit.* Mit Beiträgen von H. R. Idris und K. Röhrborn. 1979. ISBN 90 04 05915 6

5/2. *Regierung und Verwaltung des Vorderen Orients in islamischer Zeit.* 2. Mit Beiträgen von D. Sourdel und J. Bosch Vilá. 1988. ISBN 90 04 08550 5

6/1. *Wirtschaftsgeschichte des Vorderen Orients in islamischer Zeit.* Mit Beiträgen von B. Lewis, M. Rodinson, G. Baer, H. Müller, A. S. Ehrenkreutz, E. Ashtor, B. Spuler, A. K. S. Lambton, R. C. Cooper, B. Rosenberger, R. Arié, L. Bolens, T. Fahd. 1977.
ISBN 90 04 04802 2

Band 7.

Armenisch und Kaukasische Sprachen. Mit Beiträgen von G. Deeters, G. R. Solta, V. Inglisian. 1963. ISBN 90 04 00862 4

Band 8. Religion

1/1. *Religionsgeschichte des alten Orients.* Mit Beiträgen von E. Otto, O. Eissfeldt, H. Otten, J. Hempel. 1964. ISBN 90 04 00863 2

1/2/2/1. BOYCE, M. *A History of Zoroastrianism. The Early Period.* Rev. ed. 1989. ISBN 90 04 08847 4

1/2/2/2. BOYCE, M. *A History of Zoroastrianism. Under the Achaemenians.* 1982. ISBN 90 04 06506 7

1/2/2/3. BOYCE, M. and GRENET, F. *A History of Zoroastrianism. Zoroastrianism under Macedonian and Roman Rule.* With F. Grenet. Contribution by R. Beck. 1991. ISBN 90 04 09271 4

2. *Religionsgeschichte des Orients in der Zeit der Weltreligionen.* Mit Beiträgen von A. Adam, A. J. Arberry, E. L. Dietrich, J. W. Fück, A. von Gabain, J. Leipoldt, B. Spuler, R. Strothman, G. Widengren. 1961. ISBN 90 04 00864 0

Ergänzungsband 1

1. HINZ, W. *Islamische Maße und Gewichte umgerechnet ins metrische System.* Nachdruck der Erstausgabe (1955) mit Zusätzen und Berichtigungen. 1970. ISBN 90 04 00865 9

Ergänzungsband 2

1. GROHMANN, A. *Arabische Chronologie und Arabische Papyruskunde.* Mit Beiträgen von J. Mayr und W. C. Til. 1966. ISBN 90 04 00866 7
2. KHOURY, R. G. *Chrestomathie de papyrologie arabe.* Documents relatifs à la vie priveé, sociale et administrative dans les premiers siècles islamiques. 1992. ISBN 90 04 09551 9

Ergänzungsband 3

Orientalisches Recht. Mit Beiträgen von E. Seidl, V. Korošc, E. Pritsch, O. Spies, E. Tyan, J. Baz, Ch. Chehata, Ch. Samaran, J. Roussier, J. Lapanne-Joinville, S. Ş. Ansay. 1964. ISBN 90 04 00867 5

Ergänzungsband 5

1/1. BORGER, R. *Das zweite Jahrtausend vor Chr.* Mit Verbesserungen und Zusätzen. Nachdruck der Erstausgabe (1961). 1964. ISBN 90 04 00869 1

1/2. SCHRAMM, W. *[Einleitung in die assyrischen Königsinschriften, 2:] 934-722 v. Chr.* 1973. ISBN 90 04 03783 7

Ergänzungsband 6

1. ULLMANN, M. *Die Medizin im Islam.* 1970. ISBN 90 04 00870 5
2. ULLMANN, M. *Die Natur- und Geheimwissenschaften im Islam.* 1972. ISBN 90 04 03423 4

Ergänzungsband 7

GOMAA, I. *A Historical Chart of the Muslim World.* 1972. ISBN 90 04 03333 5

Ergänzungsband 8

KORNRUMPF, H.-J. *Osmanische Bibliographie mit besonderer Berücksichtigung der Türkei in Europa.* Unter Mitarbeit von J. Kornrumpf. 1973. ISBN 90 04 03549 4

Ergänzungsband 9

FIRRO, K. M. *A History of the Druzes.* 1992. ISBN 90 04 09437 7

Band 10

STRIJP, R. *Cultural Anthropology of the Middle East. A Bibliography.* Vol. 1: 1965-1987. 1992. ISBN 90 04 09604 3

Band 11
ENDRESS, G. & GUTAS, D. (eds.). *A Greek and Arabic Lexicon.* (*GALex*) Materials for a Dictionary of the Mediæval Translations from Greek into Arabic.
Fascicle 1. Introduction—Sources—ʾ – ʾ-kh-r. Compiled by G. Endress & D. Gutas, with the assistance of K. Alshut, R. Arnzen, Chr. Hein, St. Pohl, M. Schmeink. 1992. ISBN 90 04 09494 6
Fascicle 2. ʾ-kh-r – ʾ-ṣ-l. Compiled by G. Endress & D. Gutas, with the assistance of K. Alshut, R. Arnzen, Chr. Hein, St. Pohl, M. Schmeink. 1993. ISBN 90 04 09893 3

Band 12
JAYYUSI, S. K. (ed.). *The Legacy of Muslim Spain.* Chief consultant to the editor, M. Marín. 2nd ed. 1994. ISBN 90 04 09599 3

Band 13
HUNWICK, J. O. and O'FAHEY, R. S. (eds.). *Arabic Literature of Africa.*
Volume I. *The Writings of Eastern Sudanic Africa to c. 1900.* Compiled by R. S. O'Fahey, with the assistance of M. I. Abu Salim, A. Hofheinz, Y. M. Ibrahim, B. Radtke and K. S. Vikør. 1994. ISBN 90 04 09450 4

Band 14
DECKER, W. und HERB, M. *Bildatlas zum Sport im alten Ägypten. Corpus der bildlichen Quellen zu Leibesübungen, Spiel, Jagd, Tanz und verwandten Themen.* Bd.1: Text. Bd. 2: Abbildungen. 1994. ISBN 90 04 09974 3 (Set)

Band 15
HAAS, V. *Geschichte der hethitischen Religion.* 1994. ISBN 90 04 09799 6

Band 16
NEUSNER, J. (ed.). *Judaism in Late Antiquity.* Part One: The Literary and Archaeological Sources. 1994. ISBN 90 04 10129 2

Band 17
NEUSNER, J. (ed.). *Judaism in Late Antiquity.* Part Two: Historical Syntheses. 1994. ISBN 90 04 09799 6

Band 18
OREL, V. E. and STOLBOVA, O. V. (eds.). *Hamito-Semitic Etymological Dictionary.* Materials for a Reconstruction. 1994. ISBN 90 04 10051 2

Band 19
AL-ZWAINI, L. and PETERS, R. *A Bibliography of Islamic Law, 1980-1993.* 1994. ISBN 90 04 10009 1